The Christian History of the Constitution of the United States of America

"WHERE THE SPIRIT OF THE LORD IS, THERE IS LIBERTY." II CORINTHIANS 3:17

The Christian History of the Constitution of the United States of America

American Revolution Bicentennial Edition

Christian Self-Government

A compilation by Verna M. Hall

edited by Joseph Allan Montgomery

introduction by Felix Morley

Foundation for American Christian Education

San Francisco, California

FIRST REVISED EDITION

Published by
THE FOUNDATION FOR AMERICAN CHRISTIAN EDUCATION
Box 27035, San Francisco, California 94127

Published by The American Christian Constitution Press

Printed by The Iversen Associates
New York, New York

Charts designed by John Grossman
San Francisco, California

Library of Congress Catalog Card Number: 61-16012

First Printing Revised Edition
November 24, 1966

Second Printing Revised Edition
February, 1972

AMERICAN REVOLUTION BICENTENNIAL EDITION
April 19, 1975

Eagle cast by Paul Revere for General Henry Knox

DEDICATION

THIS volume and those to follow are dedicated to the Christian principle upon which this nation is founded, and to each American of this and succeeding generations, that he may remember his Christian heritage and live so as to raise the standard of his Pilgrim and Puritan fathers into its larger and fuller expression of individual liberty.

Preface to the American Revolution Bicentennial Edition

"The more thoroughly a nation deals with its history, the more decidedly will it recognize and own an over-ruling Providence therein, and the more religious a nation will it become; while the more superficially it deals with its history, seeing only secondary causes and human agencies, the more irreligious will it be."

Rev. A. W. Foljambe, January 5, 1876

As America approaches her two hundredth birthday, and enters into her third century as the world's first Christian Republic, it is appropriate for the American Christian to pause and ask: How did the blessings of liberty which I enjoy today come about? Did Christianity have anything to do with the American Revolution? What can I teach the next generation about the Hand of God in American history?

America's Christian history has not been taught in Christian schools and colleges for over one hundred years. This fact has contributed to the rise of secularism —the "irreligious" spirit—more than any other single educational factor. With few exceptions Christian institutions teach a secular interpretation of history —not the Providential approach referred to by the Reverend Foljambe in the quotation above. As Americans and as Christians have moved away from the teaching of history from its original sources they have accepted the interpretations of those who deal with history "seeing only secondary causes and human agencies." The result has been our separation of history from God as the Author of History. Ignorance, then is our enemy—ignorance of the Hand of God in American history.

Yet God in His infinite patience has given us these years of the Bicentennial of the War for Independence and of the establishment of the Constitution of the United States of America to cause us to remember Him. "In all thy ways acknowledge Him" we are admonished in Scripture. Can we willfully disregard the voices of those historians who credit America with a Christian history? Was our emergence as a "separate and equal" nation just human history or was it the fulfillment of God's purpose as stated by the Pilgrims to "propagate and advance ye gospell of ye kingdom of Christ in those remote parts of ye world?" Can we, or should we, disregard the evidences of our Providential deliverance during the seven long years of the American Revolution? Should we credit the victory to man or to God?

To ignore the centuries of the progress of the Gospel and of Christianity's westward course is to deny the power of Christ in bringing forth liberty for the individual in both civil and religious spheres. Nor should we ignore the one hundred and fifty years of Biblical education in colonial America which produced a new standard of literacy for the world and astounded Europe with the "lucid exposition of constitutional principles" in the American State Papers. Should we continue to separate ourselves from the recognition of the Biblical principles of Christian self-government, Christian property, and voluntary Christian unity which found their ultimate protection in the United States Constitution?

The time has come to strengthen our American Christian homes and to return them to their historic role of building the foundations of America's Christian character. The Biblical education of the homes of the American Revolution provided the prayerful support for our "ragged Continentals" and enabled them to win our independence from the world's greatest military power of that day.

The Ministers of the Gospel played a significant part in the American Revolution. Through the Artillery, Election and Fast Day sermons particularly, they educated the people in the Biblical principles of civil government. They did not separate American Independence in the civil sphere from American Independence in the sphere of religious liberty. The Reverend John Witherspoon, a member of the Continental Congress, in a Fast Day Sermon called for by the Continental Congress, in 1776 stated:

"*It is in the man of piety and inward principle that we may expect to find the uncorrupted patriot, the useful citizen, and the invincible soldier,—God grant that in America true religion and civil liberty may be inseparable, and the unjust attempts to destroy the one, may in the issue tend to the support and establishment of both.*"

But the blessings of liberty in America cannot be perpetuated unless the principles of that liberty are re-identified and re-affirmed in each generation.

This is the role of Christian schools and colleges. America's founding and establishment was the result of a people educated in Christian principles. Only a knowledge of these Biblical principles can ensure the continuance of them in the civil and religious spheres. It is our prayer that during these Bicentennial years, Christian educators will not continue to accept "irreligious" interpretations of American history. It is our prayer that Christian schools and colleges will separate from secularism and construct a truly distinctive curricula that includes America's Christian history.

This year marks the 200th anniversary of April 19, 1775—Lexington and Concord. It was there the first blood of the American Revolution was shed. On the next page is one of the documents evidencing the Christian history of the American Revolution. It is a Massachusetts Proclamation for a day of Prayer, Humiliation and Fasting and was issued by the Provincial Congress four days before the Battles of Lexington and Concord. A similar Proclamation had been issued by Governor Trumbull in the sister colony of Connecticut calling for a day of Prayer, Humiliation and Fasting on April 19, 1775—the actual day of the confrontation. Thus, Massachusetts called for prayer before the historic day and Connecticut actually was in prayer on that eventful day. Is it any wonder the restraining Hand of God held American guns on Lexington Green so that the shots *not fired* were a testimony to the determination of the Colonists not to start an aggressive war against their brethren?

But an equally remarkable testimony of Christian forebearance is in the recognition that for fourteen months after Lexington and Concord—and after Bunker Hill and Ticonderoga—our Provincial statesmen in the Continental Congress continued to wait for His Gracious Majesty, George III, to honor their petition setting forth their colonial grievances. Not until the Americans were convinced there was no means of reconciliation, did they set forth the reasons for their separation into an independent nation in that famous statement known as the American Declaration of Independence in July of 1776.

Verna M. Hall Rosalie J. Slater

April 19, 1975
San Francisco, California

In *Provincial Congrefs,*

Concord, *April* 15, 1775.

WHEREAS it has pleafed the righteous Sovereign of the Univerfe, in juft Indignation againft the Sins of a People long bleffed with ineftimable Privileges, civil and religious, to fuffer the Plots of wicked Men on both Sides of the Atlantcik, who for many Years have inceffantly laboured to fap the Foundation of our public Liberties, fo far to fucceed; that we fee the New-England *Colonies reduced to the ungrateful Alternative of a tame Submiffion to a State of abfolute Vaffalage to the Will of a defpotic Minifter—or of preparing themfelves fpeedily to defend, at the Hazard of Life, the unalienable Rights of themfelves and Pofterity, againft the avowed Hoftilities of their Parent State, who openly threatens to wreft them from their Hands by Fire and Sword.*

In Circumftances dark as thefe, it becomes us, as Men and Chriftians, to reflect that, whilft every prudent Meafure fhould be taken to ward off the impending Judgments, or prepare to act a proper Part under them when they come; at the fame Time, all Confidence muft be with-held from the Means we ufe; and repofed only on that GOD who rules in the Armies of Heaven, and without whofe Bleffing the beft human Counfels are but Foolifhnefs—and all created Power Vanity;

It is the Happinefs of his Church that, when the Powers of Earth and Hell combine againft it, and thofe who fhould be Nurfing Fathers become its Perfecutors—then the Throne of Grace is of the eafieft Accefs—and its Appeal thither is gracioufly invited by the Father of Mercies, who has affured it, that when his Children ask Bread he will not give them a Stone;

THEREFORE, in Compliance with the laudable Practice of the People of GOD in all Ages, with humble Regard to the Steps of Divine Providence towards this oppreffed, threatened and endangered People, and efpecially in Obedience to the Command of Heaven, that binds us *to call on him in the Day of Trouble,*——

RESOLVED, That it be, and hereby is recommended to the good People of this Colony, of all Denominations, That THURSDAY the Eleventh Day of *May* next be fet apart as a Day of Public Humiliation, Fafting and Prayer; that a total Abftinence from fervile Labor and Recreation be obferved, and all their religious Affemblies folemnly convened, to humble themfelves before GOD under the heavy Judgments felt and feared, to confefs the Sins that have deferved them, to implore the Forgivenefs of all our Tranfgreffions, and a Spirit of Repentance and Reformation—and a Bleffing on the Hufbandry, Manufactures, and other lawful Employments of this People; and efpecially that the Union of the American Colonies in Defence of their Rights (for which hitherto we defire to thank Almighty GOD) may be preferved and confirmed,—that the Provincial and efpecially the Continental CONGRESSES, may be directed to fuch Meafures as GOD will countenance.—That the People of *Great-Britain*, and their Rulers, may have their Eyes open'd to difcern the Things that fhall make for the Peace of the Nation and all its Connexions——And that AMERICA may foon behold a gracious Interpofition of Heaven, for the Redrefs of her many Grievances, the Reftoration of all her invaded Liberties, and their Security to the lateft Generations.

By Order of the Provincial Congrefs,

JOHN HANCOCK, Prefident.

PREFACE

THE reader may find it of interest to know a little of how these volumes came to be published, and why they are called "Christian History of the Constitution of the United States of America."

For about twenty years the compiler of these volumes searched for tne fundamental reason why America embarked upon a path of socialism, and why Americans continue to travel this ever-increasing and widening road. About four years ago the answer became an obvious one; a scheduled talk before a small P-TA meeting was cancelled by the Trustees of the school when they learned I was to speak on the religious nature of the Constitution and the Declaration of Independence. It seemed to me that this incident revealed a startling fact; that Americans evidently had forgotten the Christian foundation upon which this nation is reared and the importance of its relation to the form of government established by the Constitution. We as a people, were allowing ourselves to become separated from the keystone of our national structure - our Christian heritage - through such occurrences as had happened at this small school. By omission, America had deflected into socialism. The keystone in the arch of our national structure has been loosened.

In proportion as Americans let go of faith in the absolute power of God, they have accepted the belief in an all powerful State. This is true of peoples or nations, for their idea of God determines the form of their civil, political, religious and social institutions. Communism and socialism are anti-God and anti-Christian; the battle against communism and socialism never was, and is not now, just economic and political; it is religious. Shall Christianity be taken captive?

Today, when thinking and talking in terms of civil government, our ignorance of fundamental Christian history in the founding of our country becomes at once apparent. We invariably reject or misconstrue references to the word Christian - in relation to civil governments - as being doctrinal and sectarian. Our Christian history as a nation does not involve doctrinal or sectarian views, and our failure to understand this, largely contributes to the present disregard of Christianity in relation to civil government. Each religion has a form of government, and Christianity astonished the world by establishing self-government. With the landing of the Pilgrims in 1620, Christian self-government became the foundation stone of the United States of America. "The stone which the builders refused is become the head stone of the corner." (Psalm 118:22; Matt. 21:42).

The history of our Christian heritage as documented in these volumes is but a small portion of the vast amount of evidence left dormant about a hundred years, awaiting the lens of an awakened America to bring it forth. America aware of, and living according to, the Christian principle, participating in Christian worship, is like unto the sun dispelling the darkness. The dark night of collectivism can be dispelled by the sunlight of the Christ.

"Then spake Jesus again unto them, saying, I am the light of the world: he that followeth me shall not walk in darkness, but shall have the light of life" (John 8:12).

"Ye are the light of the world" (Matthew 5:14).

"The night is far spent, the day is at hand: let us therefore cast off the works of darkness, and let us put on the armour of light" (Romans 13:12).

My generation was in the universities when Americans began to alter the original form of their Federal and State governments from those established upon individual and local self-government, to governments paving the way for ever-increasing socialism. Our education afforded us very little pertaining to the true history of our country and its fundamental principles. Like a great many of my contemporaries, I found my work in the newly-created bureaus of the Federal government fascinating and exciting, for new opportunities were opened for government to do things for people and communities.

Thus I experienced the beginnings of socialism; I saw the thoroughness of socialistic organization descend like a pall upon every facet of our economy and culture, altering almost everything. The deep sense of patriotism and love of country instilled in me by my mother, asked this question, Is this alteration really for the good? To answer this question it was necessary to know the real motive and purpose of America. Were we like other nations in our idea of government or were we different? Reading and studying American history revealed the fact that this nation is unique; it had a singular beginning; it has the sacred covenant of individual freedom or local self-government in all spheres entrusted to its care.

After this discovery I left government service and in 1947 began a Constitution study group for individuals interested in economic and constitutional principles. These study groups were patterned after those I was establishing for a national business organization. Although this study of the Constitution was helpful in revealing to each individual member just how far America had strayed from its original course of local self-governing institutions, yet this activity did not disclose the underlying reason for the deflection into socialism, or the way to arrest its growth, or to repair the damage done.

Continual observance of national and world affairs, the cancelled talk incident of four years ago, showed the vital necessity of making available for Americans the Christian History of their Constitution. It became apparent just how necessary it was to set forth the connection between Christianity, individual freedom, and local self-government. The failure to remember this connection, hidden all the while by a gossamer web, is the obvious reason why the American people are deflecting into socialism degree by degree. These volumes are the consequence.

The study meetings now began to lift this gossamer veil which had been hiding the influence of Christianity. It could now be seen that the socialistic problem confronting the nation is the same problem, but with a different name, which has confronted Christianity periodically during its steady march westward. Whenever Christianity declined in a people's heart, "philosophy and vain deceit, after the tradition of men, after the rudiments of the world, and not after Christ" (Col. 2:8), rose in its various forms.

Dr. Jedidiah Morse describes just such a time in our own history in the following excerpt from an Election Sermon delivered in Charlestown, April 25, 1799, from the Bible text, "If the foundations be destroyed, what can the righteous do?" (Psalm 11:3). "Our dangers are of two kinds, those which affect our religion, and those which affect our government. They are, however, so closely allied that they cannot, with propriety, be separated. The foundations which support the interests of Christianity, are also necessary to support a free and equal government like our own. In all those countries where there is little or no religion, or a very gross and corrupt one, as in Mahometan and Pagan countries, there you will find, with scarcely a single exception, arbitrary and tyrannical governments, gross ignorance and wickedness, and deplorable wretchedness among the people.

To the kindly influence of Christianity we owe that degree of civil freedom, and political and social happiness which mankind now enjoy. In proportion as the genuine effects of Christianity are diminished in any nation, either through unbelief, or the corruption of its doctrines, or the neglect of its institutions; in the same proportion will the people of that nation recede from the blessings of genuine freedom, and approximate the miseries of complete despotism. I hold this to be a truth confirmed by experience. If so, it follows, that all efforts made to destroy the foundations of our holy religion, ultimately tend to the subversion also of our political freedom and happiness. Whenever the pillars of Christianity shall be overthrown, our present republican forms of government, and all the blessings which flow from them, must fall with them."

This volume, the first of three, on the "Christian History of the Constitution of the United States" is the result of the enthusiastic reception of a pre-publication edition that was called the "Historic Origin of the Constitution of the United States". That pre-publication edition tested the readiness of the American people to return to their Christian inheritance. To the Directors of American Principle, Inc., who were willing to lend their good name and support to that edition, my grateful appreciation. To those individuals who loyally attended the study meetings, my gratitude. Each individual is important in an activity of this scope, and without the evidence of the loving-kindness of Christian fellowship, it is difficult to found an idea.

Many indeed were the friends who voluntarily devoted long hours of faithful work to help bring about a pre-publication edition. I should particularly like to express my heartfelt appreciation and thanks to the following: Joseph Allan Montgomery for his difficult editing task beautifully done; D'Esta L. Davenport for selecting the article on the Bible, and for her work with Mr. Montgomery in preparing the valuable marginal notes; Mary Elaine Adams for the illuminating biographical sketches of the historians used; and for their assistance in various ways - Kay Bullock, Miriam Cameron, Gertrude L. Haller, and Martha Fenn Nuckols.

Benefiting from the experience of a pre-publication edition, Volume I of "Christian History of the Constitution of the United States", covers the development of Self-Government from its beginnings in the primitive Christian churches, through the American Revolution. Volume II will record the source of the idea of Union and its development in America from 1643 through the Articles of Confederation; this volume will also contrast for the reader the American and French Revolutions, as to origin, character and consequence. Volume III will show how the Christian principle of Self-Government evolved as the Union, how it was wrought out in the Constitutional Convention, and how the Constitution itself, was adopted by the several States.

The majority of my generation now coming into leadership in government, business, and other areas, does not know the Christian history of America. It has been reared in a socialistic environment of government, therefore, this is a critical time because our link in Christianity's chain, weak and pulling apart after thirty years of socialism, either will be broken, or it will be reforged so that the chain of Christianity may go forward unbroken.

"Ye are a chosen generation, a royal priesthood, an holy nation, a peculiar people; that ye should show forth the praises of Him who hath called you out of darkness into His marvellous light" (I Peter 2:9).

"Ye were sometimes darkness, but now are ye light in the Lord: walk as children of light" (Ephesians 5:8).

San Francisco, California
September 17, 1960

Verna M. Hall

CONTENTS

CONTENTS

CONTENTS

CONTENTS

CONTENTS

ILLUSTRATIVE CHARTS

APPENDICES

CONTENTS

INDICES

INTRODUCTION

WHEN the individual is in good health, mental and physical, he generally has some primary purpose, and guides his life accordingly. The nature of his purpose is of the greatest import, since it reveals the basic character of the man. But even an unhallowed purpose is preferable to one of mere vegetation. The shark is not an admirable creature, but rates a good deal higher in the scale of life than does the jellyfish.

Nations, which are rather arbitrary collections of men under a common government, are political mechanisms which have purpose only in the sense that it can be attributed to an automobile. We speak of national purpose, however, because every government necessarily reflects the personality of those in the driving seats. Under a dictatorship the national purpose is clearly discernible as that of the dominant group or individual. Under a representative government, like that of the United States, national purpose will tend to reflect that of the people as a whole. In recent years this refined conception of government has been subjected to increasingly serious challenge, by no means only from the Communists.

We fail to meet this challenge when we ask, as many are asking nowadays, whether our country as a nation any longer has any purpose, and if so what it is. No official commission is needed, and none could be qualified, to answer those questions. Nor can any Gallup Poll reliably determine the animating desires of even a truly representative cross-section of Americans.

The sad fact that some of us have no life purpose worthy of that name is not the only reason for the inadequacy of any sampling or enumerative process. Others, with definite purpose, will not always admit, even to themselves, what it really is. Moreover, the purposes of the resolute, for good or evil, are much more influential than those of waverers, though sometimes only in the long run. No census can by itself separate the real leaders from the mere manipulators of public opinion. Christ is the greatest leader mankind has ever had. Yet, during His life on earth, only a handful of humble people recognized Him as such.

Therefore we cannot speak of current national purpose with any certainty, even assuming that it would be desirable, in time of crisis, to compress all individual opinion in a single mould. What we can easily rediscover, and usefully reflect upon, however, is the original design of this Republic. Its architects knew very well not only what they were doing, but also why. So a comparison of present unsure attitudes with the well-defined ideas of our forefathers will at least show whether the American tradition still lives; whether the Star-Spangled Banner still waves - or merely flaps fitfully against a towering and over-decorated staff.

Something of these original plans can of course be learned from close study of our existing institutions. Even as transformed, most of these bear traces of their first construction. The Supreme Court, for instance, is still organized and staffed along the lines anticipated in 1787. But those who planned it as a necessary instrument of federalism would be horrified by the aggressively centralizing character of many of its recent opinions.

The mere examination of political institutions, however, gives no more than a clue to their fundamental purpose. That which they had has been largely discarded; that which they seem to be acquiring is not fully established. So, if it is the hallmark of our national significance that is sought, it is to the record that we must look. That record has long been available to the few who are trained in research and library techniques. This book will bring it into every home where there are ears attuned to something of more significance than the "singing commercial".

The history of the United States, as an independent nation, can properly be said to start with those two documents of which almost all Americans know something - the Declaration of Independence and the Constitution. But both of these great landmarks in the long struggle for human freedom owe most of their efficacy to the already well tested ideas which they incorporated. Jefferson, who drafted the Declaration, freely admitted his great indebtedness to Locke. And both Hamilton and Madison, throughout the Federalist essays, proclaimed the influence on the Constitution of Montesquieu and other political philosophers.

Whence, then, did the ideas basic to American government originally emanate, and to what source must we look for a simple clarification of its original purpose? To ask these questions should be to answer them. The New Testament is the wellspring from which our political thought derives and the idealistic goal of that thinking was a political and social system actively conductive to Christian practise. As the contemporary historian of Plymouth Plantation wrote, the motive of those who sailed on the "Mayflower" was their "great hope and inward zeal...for propagating and advancing the Gospel of the Kingdom of Christ in those remote parts of the world".

Substantial excerpts from Governor Bradford's account of the New England origin are found in this volume, together with the sharply contrasting story of the Virginia settlements. Here also is Locke's famous treatise Of Civil-Government and those parts of Montesquieu's Spirit of Laws which prompted the Founding Fathers to separate and balance political powers. But, as shown by the Table of Contents, these are only illustrations. Other documentation gives the historic background of every major principle embodied in the American form of government. No captive of the Red Chinese who had read this book could ever have been brainwashed, for he would have realized to the marrow of his being the superiority of the principles for which America stood.

Unfortunately, one must use the past tense. With the decline of both religious conviction and observance a grave decay has spread, both wide and deep. And while there are now symptoms of recovery, of which this book is one, they appear after the termites of disbelief have jeopardized the very foundations of our civilization. In one of the many memorable passages quoted in the following pages, Alexis de Tocqueville notes that the Americans of his day held religion "to be indispensable to the maintenance of Republican institutions". One should recall that this shrewd observer did not expect the institutions to outlast the faith on which they were grounded.

The essence of our now weakened Christianity is self-discipline, as preached and practised by Christ Jesus. Those who can thus govern themselves have little need of managerial government. So, when Americans gloried in being a Christian people, it was possible to replace the domination of the British monarchy by a system in which the greater part of all governmental activities were localized. The "determination", in Madison's memorable words, was "to rest all our political experiments on the capacity of mankind for self-government". That capacity, among the early Americans, the independent churches had done more than any other single agency to develop.

So important were these churches, in the conduct of education and in behalf of the general welfare, that the Bill of Rights specifically prohibits Congress from passing any law "respecting an establishment of religion, or prohibiting the free exercise thereof". No one church was to be preferred to another and government should keep its hands off all of them. Yet, by supremely ironic interpretation, the provision protecting the churches against the State has come to be used to subordinate them to the State. The separation is today outrageously interpreted to mean that Christianity shall not be taught in the public schools of a Christian nation.

With such a complete corruption of original purpose it would be strange indeed if there were not widespread confusion as to what America stands for in the world today. Clearly the best way to confront that confusion is to recall what our collective purpose used to be, in the thought of those leaders in many lines who made it a beacon for the oppressed of all mankind. And that thought, of course, should be read as it was composed. To have it summarized, and often consciously distorted, by teachers with a Marxist axe to grind, is worse than useless.

Authentic reanimation of the national heritage is the achievement of the American Christian Constitution Press, in making this unique book available at this critical time. It is not primarily a work of reference, even though invaluable as such. It is, rather, a book for browsing in the quiet of the home, and next for utilization in those neighborhood discussion groups which happily are beginning to compete with Bingo parties as antidotes for boredom.

A word of caution: The way to read the pages that follow with most enjoyment is not to plod from cover to cover. If you have only a few minutes to spare, select from the Table of Contents one of the briefer bits of documentation and examine it in the well-edited setting. Then, with an evening free, sit down with John Locke or stout old Governor Bradford. Learn from the latter how, three centuries before the New Deal, Massachusetts tried and discarded Planned Economy, and how Free Enterprise then brought the colonists through hardship that most of us today would deem intolerable. Before long you will find yourself familiar with every chapter and verse of this American Epic, in much the same eclectic yet thorough manner by which our forebears absorbed the family Bible.

This volume tells how and why Americans learned self-government. Its concern is clarification of the origin and purpose of our institutions. Their development will be documented by later volumes in the series. Well begun, however, is half done. The following pages are vital in themselves and will continue to be essential to understand the still unfolding tale. It may be that we have passed the summit of achievement and, like others before us, are on the downgrade now. As to that, none can speak with assurance. The outcome depends on whether the ideas and ideals so ably presented in this compact book are meaningless or vital, to you and to your friends.

Gibson Island, Md.
July 4, 1960

Felix Morley

"WHERE THE SPIRIT OF THE LORD IS, THERE IS LIBERTY".

II Corinthians 3:17

"The summer after the blazing Starre (whose motion in the Heavens was from East to West, poynting out to the sons of men the progress of the glorious Gospell of Christ, the glorious King of his Churches) even about the yeare 1618." (Edward Johnson, "Wonder-working Providence".)

"Is it not that, in the chain of human events, the birthday of the nation is indissolubly linked with the birth-day of the Saviour?"

John Quincy Adams, 1837

CHRISTIAN SELF-GOVERNMENT

Part One

THE CHRISTIAN IDEA Of Man and Government

"For the law was given by Moses, but grace and truth came by Jesus Christ."

- John 1:17

"Ye shall know the truth, and the truth shall make you free."

- John 8:32

"As Men we have God for our King, and are under the Law of Reason: as Christians, we have Jesus the Messiah for our King, and are under the Law reveal'd by him in the Gospel."

- John Locke, "The Reasonableness of Christianity", 1695

"...And Reason, which is that Law, teaches all Mankind, who will but consult it, that being all equal and independent, no one ought to harm another in his Life, Health, Liberty, or Possessions..."

- John Locke, "Of Civil-Government", 1689

"...The right to freedom being the gift of God Almighty...'The Rights of the Colonists as Christians'...may be best understood by reading and carefully studying the institutes of the great Law Giver...which are to be found clearly written and promulgated in the New Testament."

- Samuel Adams, "Rights of the Colonists", 1772

"The dread and redoubtable sovereign, when traced to his ultimate and genuine source, has been found, as he ought to have been found, in the free and independent man...This truth, so simple and natural, and yet so neglected or despised, may be appreciated as the first and fundamental principle in the science of government."

- James Wilson, "Study of Law in the United States", 1790-91

SAMUEL ADAMS

"There were very few whose minds could comprehend the important distinctions which were then agitated, or whose reasoning could discern the approaching events of that controversy. Mr. Adams, buoyed up by a sense of the justice and righteousness of the colonists' demands, stood forth first in their defence, and heroically won his title - THE FATHER OF THE REVOLUTION. In 1764, he was elected to prepare the instructions of the town of Boston to their representatives in the General Assembly. The document is now in existence, and contains the first public denial of the right of the British Parliament to tax the colonies..."

- "American Eloquence", 1857

"Let divines and philosophers, statesmen and patriots, unite their endeavors to renovate the age, by impressing the minds of men with the importance of educating their little boys and girls, of inculcating in the minds of youth the fear and love of the Deity and universal philanthropy, and, in subordination to these great principles, the love of their country; of instructing them in the art of self-government, without which they never can act a wise part in the government of societies, great or small; in short, of leading them in the study and practice of the exalted virtues of the Christian system..."

- Samuel Adams, Boston, October 4, 1790

"Where the Spirit of the Lord is, there is liberty."

THE CHRISTIAN IDEA OF MAN

THIS nation has in its keeping 'the last word in human political institutions,' - the Republican form of Government.

Spirit of a New Civilization

"The vast region which the flag of the United States protects was, two centuries and a half ago, the roaming ground of tribes of Indians...It was virtually a waste awaiting, in the order of Providence, the magic influence of an incoming race, imbued with the spirit of a new civilization. The period referred to was an epoch in which there had been a providential preparation for great events in the Old World. It was an era of wonderful discovery in the heavens and the earth. It was also the period of the Reformation. This, in its essence, was the assertion of the principle of individuality, or of true spiritual freedom; and in the beginning, not by Protestants alone, of whom Luther was the great exponent, but by Catholics also, represented in the polished and profound Reuchlin.

Assertion of principle of individuality

Though first occupied with subjects not connected with political speculation, yet it was natural and inevitable, that inquiry should widen out from the realm of the Church into that of the State. Then a fresh impetus was given to that transformation of society, which began when Christianity - the basis of the good, permanent, and progressive in modern civilization - first appeared in the world. At that time, social order rested on the assumed natural inequality of men. The individual was regarded as of value only as he formed a part of the political fabric, and was able to contribute to its uses, as though it were the end of his being to aggrandize the State. This was the pagan idea of man. The wisest philosophers of antiquity could not rise above it. Its influence imbued the pagan world. The State regarded as of paramount importance, not the man, but the citizen whose physical and intellectual forces it absorbed. If this tended to foster lofty civic virtues and splendid individual culture in the classes whom the State selected as the

Pagan Idea of Man

The above excerpts are from Richard Frothingham's "The Rise of the Republic of the United States" - 1890

Man superior to the State:

THE CHRISTIAN IDEA OF MAN

recipients of its favors, it bore hard on those whom the State virtually ignored, - on laboring men, mechanics, the poor, captives in war, slaves, and woman. This low view of man was exerting its full influence when Rome was at the height of its power and glory. Christianity then appeared with its central doctrine, that man was created in the Divine image, and destined for immortality; pronouncing, that, in the eye of God, all men are equal. This asserted for the individual an independent value. It occasioned the great inference, that man is superior to the State, which ought to be fashioned for his use. This was the advent of a new spirit and a new power in the world. The struggle between the pagan and Christian elements was severe. In four centuries, civil society was transformed from the pagan basis to that of Christianity. But, long after Rome had crumbled, the influence of Paganism, under various forms, continued to operate; and especially the idea, that man was made for the State, the office of which, or of a divine right vested in one, or in a privileged few, was to fashion the thought and control the action of the many. Its embodiment in arbitrary power, both in ecclesiastical and political affairs, continued to oppress and benumb the intellect, until the Reformation roused a spirit of activity in the bosom of the Church. The new life thus started in the domain of religion soon communicated itself to other provinces... There then rose, above the low level of a corrupt political world, a class of thinkers who grasped the idea that the State ought to exist for man; that justice, protection, and the common good, ought to be the aim of government... Among them were John Milton, imbued with the very spirit of the Reformation, who defended the noble thesis, that freedom is the native right of man, and gave the world a mighty and still unsurpassed plea for liberty of utterance; John Locke... was so successful in catching and expressing the liberal spirit of his age, in his work on Civil Government, that it became the platform of a great political party, and gradually widened out into an influence that operated far beyond the thought or the theory of its adherents; so that, Hallam says, 'while silently spreading its fibres from its roots over Europe and America, it prepared the way for theories hardly bolder in their announcement, but expressed with more passionate ardor, from which the last and present age have sprung.' This historical judgment is applicable to a line of illustrious characters, who grasped the Christian idea of man; and, because of the brilliancy of their service in behalf of human rights, they deserve a place among the morning stars of the American constellation."

John Milton

Locke's Civil Government

The above excerpts are from Richard Frothingham's "The Rise of the Republic of the United States" - 1890

Chain of Christianity Moves Westward

THE ROLE OF GEOGRAPHY

ASIA

"Characteristics and function"

ASIA is the largest of the continents, the most central, the only one with which all the others are closely connected; and the one whose different physical regions show the greatest contrasts, and are separated by the greatest barriers. This great and strongly marked continent is the continent of origins. The human family, its races and civilizations, and the systems of religion which rule the most enlightened nations, all had their beginning here. By the great diversity of its physical features and climate, and the strong barriers isolating them one from another, Asia was admirably fitted to promote the formation of a diversity of races; while its close connection with the other continents facilitated their dispersion throughout the earth.

EUROPE

"Characteristics and function"

EUROPE shows a diversity of structure even greater than that of Asia; but with smaller areas, more moderate forms of relief, less extreme contrasts of climate, a more generally fertile soil, and everywhere an abundance of the most useful minerals; while the relative extent of its coast line - its maritime zone - is greater than that of any other continent. This continent is especially fitted, by its diversity, to foster the formation of distinct nationalities, each developing in an especial direction. Moreover, the proximity of these nations one to another, the greater facility of communication between them, and, above all, the common highway to the sea, nowhere very distant, facilitates mutual intercourse, the lack of which arrested the progress of the civilization of Asia. Though not the continent of origins, Europe is emphatically the continent of development. The Indo-European race - the people of progress - find their fullest expansion and activity, not in their original seat in Iran, but in Europe, whence they are spreading over all the quarters of the

The above excerpts are from Arnold Guyot's "Physical Geography" - 1873 (Emphasis by Guyot)

globe. The arts and learning of antiquity attained their highest development, not in western Asia and Egypt, the places of their origin, but in Greece and Rome. Christianity, also, only germinated in western Asia. Transplanted to Europe, it gradually attained its full development, and became the foundation on which is reared the vast and noble edifice of modern civilization.

AMERICA

"Characteristics and function"

AMERICA, different in position, structure, and climatic conditions, from both the other northern continents, seems destined to play a part in the history of mankind unlike that of Europe and Asia, though not less noble than either. The structure of this continent is characterized by a unity and simplicity as striking as is the diversity of Europe. In its climate, those contrasts in temperature which are so violent in Asia, and still prevail in Europe, are obliterated. Nowhere do we find in America those local centres, each having a strongly marked individuality, which fostered the progress of the race in its infancy and its youth; but everywhere provision is made for mutual intercourse, a common life, and the blending of the entire population into one. Evidently this continent was not designed to give birth and development to a new civilization; but to receive one ready-made, and to furnish to the cultivated race of the Old World the scene most worthy of their activity. Its vast plains, overflowing with natural wealth, are turned towards Europe, and its largest rivers discharge into the Atlantic; while its lofty mountains, and less fertile lands, are removed far towards its western shores. Thus it seems to invite the Indo-European race, the people of progress, to new fields of action; to encourage their expansion throughout its entire territory, and their fusion into one nation; while it opens for them a pathway to all the nations of the earth. America, therefore, with her cultured and progressive people, and her social organization, founded upon the principle of the equality and brotherhood of all mankind, seems destined to furnish the most complete expression of the Christian civilization; and to become the fountain of a new and higher life for all the races of men.

CONCLUSION. Each continent has, therefore, a well-defined individuality, which fits it for an especial function. The fullness of nature's life is typified by Africa, with its superabundant wealth and power of animal life; South America, with its exuberance of vegetation; and Australia, with its antiquated forms of plants and animals.

The above excerpts are from Arnold Guyot's "Physical Geography" - 1873 (Emphasis by Guyot)

"In the grand drama of man's life and development, Asia, Europe, and America play distinct parts, for which each seems to have been admirably prepared. Truly no blind force gave our Earth the forms so well adapted to perform these functions. The conclusion is irresistible -- that the entire globe is a grand organism, every feature of which is the outgrowth of a definite plan of the all-wise Creator for the education of the human family, and the manifestation of his own glory."

The above excerpts are from Arnold Guyot's "Physical Geography" - 1873 (Emphasis by Guyot)

AMERICA

DEVELOPMENT OF THE INDIVIDUAL MAN

IT is plain that we have entered on a New Era, the most extraordinary and momentous the world has ever seen. The old and imperfect is being cleared away and everything thoroughly reconstructed. The explanation is that we are now setting us the grand Temple of Civilization, the separate stone and pillars of which each nation and age was commissioned to hew and carve, and, so to speak, left in the quarry to await the time when, all the materials being ready, the Master Builder should collect all the scattered parts and raise the whole edifice at once, to the astonishment and joy of mankind. All the institutions and civilizations of the past may be considered temporary, erected in haste from the materials nearest at hand, not for permanence, but to serve the present turn while the special task of the nation or age was being performed. The races and ages nearer the birth of mankind worked on rougher parts of the edifice, that entered into the foundations; those grand races, the Greek and the Roman, furnished the noble outline which the nations of modern Europe perfected while they supplied what was still lacking for use and adornment. America was reserved, designedly, for so many ages, to furnish a suitable and unencumbered location for the central halls and mightiest pillars of the completed structure. Our fathers cleared the ground and laid the foundation deep down on the living rock, that is to say, on Human Rights. That they seldom failed to place stone, pillar and column in just position the work, as we find it, proves, and we have little to do but to clear away the rubbish, beautify the

Temple of Civilization

Nature of past civilizations

America and Human Rights

The above excerpts are from Charles Bancroft's "The Footprints of Time" - 1879

grounds, and put the whole to its proper use. We begin to see that Time, Thought, and Experience have not wrought in vain, that Progress is not a phantom of the imagination, that the human race is essentially a Unit, that it has been growing through all the centuries and is now approaching the prime of its manhood, just ready to enter on its special career with its grandest work still to do. The energies of all the races are preparing for unheard of achievements. The world has never been so completely and so wisely busy as now, and America stands between modern Europe and ancient Asia, receiving from, and giving to both. Her institutions are founded on principles so just and so humane that, when administered with due wisdom and skill, they will embarrass and restrain the proper activities of man at no point.

America the model

"America stands a model which other nations will carefully copy, in due time, as they can adapt themselves and change their institutions. There may be no literal copy or close formal imitation; but there is little doubt that the spirit and true sense of our Declaration of Independence will finally mould the structure and control the workings of all governments...

Individual benefit

"Our people are busy using their liberties and energies, each for his individual benefit, as is quite right and proper; since the welfare of individuals makes the prosperity of the community. But a government left to take care of itself is prone to do that work only too well. We have done well and wisely in important crises; but a more intelligent and constant watchfulness over the ordinary course of public affairs would have been still better...

Minimum of governmental interference

'"Knowledge is power,' when wisely applied; and a more accurate acquaintance with their government and its history will enable American Citizens to mould it more wisely still, to correct all defects of administration, and to speedily reach that minimum of governmental interference with the efforts and interests of the citizens which shall give them the fullest liberty consistent with security and surrender the whole round of human life, as completely as possible to the beneficient action of natural law.

Westward movement

CONCLUSION. We see here again the operation of that constant law that impelled men, or moved the 'Star of Empire', westward. The form of the continents, the character of the surface and the

The above excerpts are from Charles Bancroft's "The Footprints of Time" - 1879

"RELIGION STANDS ON TIP-TOE IN OUR LAND, READIE TO PASS TO THE AMERICAN STRAND."
—George Herbert

HENRY HELWYS 1612
JOHN MILTON 1608
RICHARD MATHER 1596
WILLIAM BRADFORD 1590
JOHN WINTHROP 1588
THOMAS HOOKER 1586
HUGO GROTIUS 1583
JOHN ROBINSON 1575
WILLIAM BREWSTER 1563
GENEVA BIBLE 1557

PRELUDE TO AMERICA

RICHARD HOOKER 1554?
GASPARD DE COLIGNY 1519
JOHN FOX 1516
JOHN CALVIN 1509
JOHN KNOX 1505?
WILLIAM TYNDALE 1494
MILES COVERDALE 1488
HUGH LATIMER 1485
ULRICH ZWINGLI 1484
MARTIN LUTHER 1483
JOHANN GUTENBERG 1396
JOHN HUSS 1369
WYCLIFFE 1324?

MORNING STARS OF REFORMATION

MAGNA CHARTA 1215

IRELAND—PATRICK 389
AUGUSTINE 354
JEROME 340

FOURTH CENTURY

GERMANY
BRITAIN
SPAIN
FRANCE—FRANKS (GAUL)

SECOND CENTURY

ROME
GREECE
EUROPE—LYDIA (ACTS 16)

FIRST WESTWARD PLANTING OF SEEDS OF CHRISTIANITY

FIRST CENTURY

AMERICA'S PLANTING

JAMESTOWN 1607
KING JAMES BIBLE 1611
MAYFLOWER COMPACT 1620

PILGRIMS LAND AT PLYMOUTH 1620
PETITION OF RIGHT 1628
JOHN BUNYAN 1628

WILLIAM PENN 1644
BILL OF RIGHTS 1689
LOCKE'S TREATISE ON GOVERNMENT 1689

CHRISTOPHER DOCK 1698
JONATHAN EDWARDS 1703
JOHN AND CHARLES WESLEY 1703, 1707

GEORGE WHITEFIELD 1714
MONTESQUIEU 'THE SPIRIT OF LAWS' 1748
BLACKSTONE'S "COMMENTARIES" 1765

THE DECLARATION OF INDEPENDENCE 1776

A NEW NATION

THE CONSTITUTION OF THE UNITED STATES OF AMERICA 1787

NINETEENTH CENTURY

THE MONROE DOCTRINE 1823

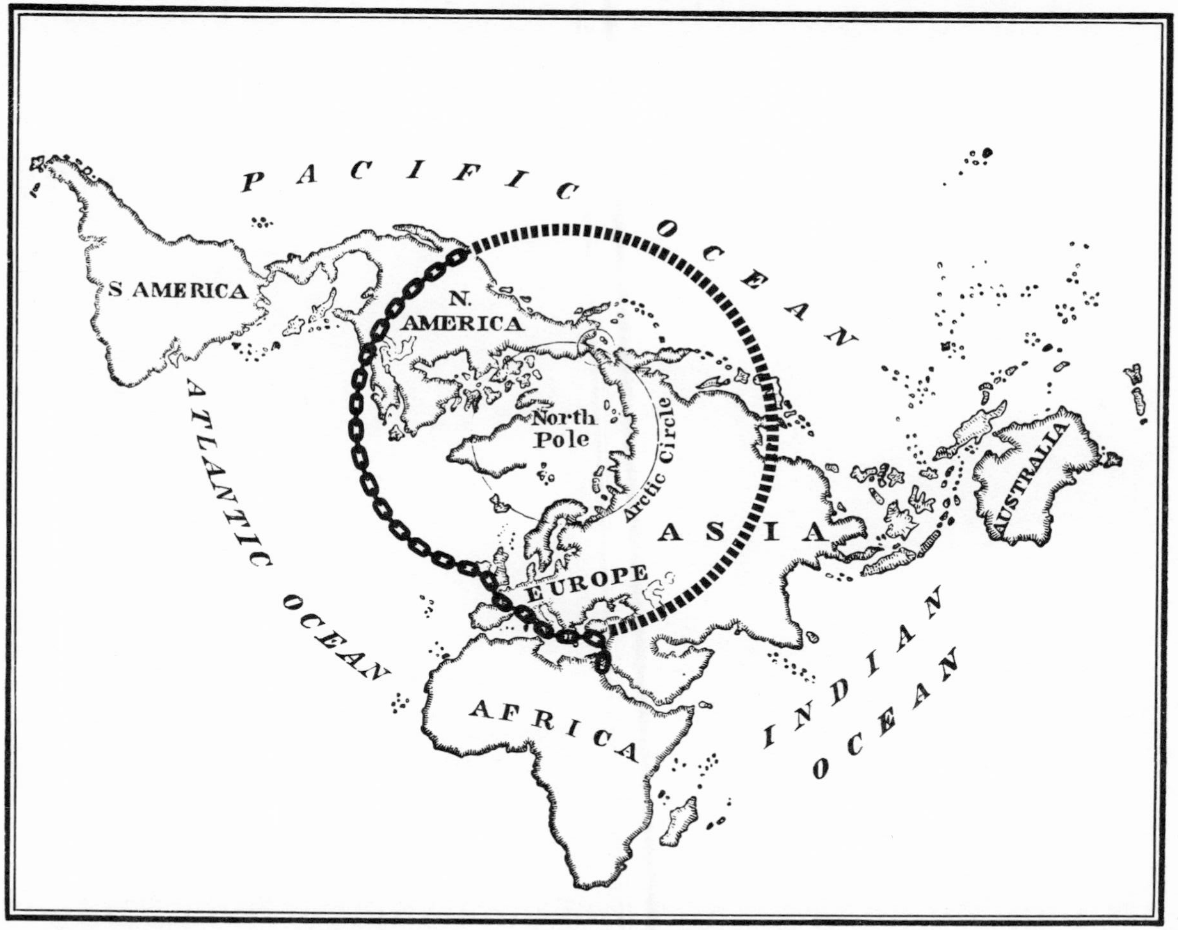

"ITS WESTERN COURSE THROUGH CHINA AND JAPAN IS IMPEDED . . . BY MODERNISM."
—Abraham Kuyper, 1898, Princeton

WESTWARD THE COURSE OF EMPIRE

"WESTWARD THE COURSE OF EMPIRE TAKES ITS WAY,
THE FIRST FOUR ACTS ALREADY PAST,
A FIFTH SHALL CLOSE THE DRAMA WITH THE DAY;
TIME'S NOBLEST OFFSPRING IS THE LAST."
—Berkeley

PACIFIC OCEAN
S AMERICA
N. AMERICA
North Pole
Arctic Circle
ATLANTIC OCEAN
EUROPE
ASIA
AFRICA
INDIAN OCEAN
AUSTRALIA

APOSTLES AND DISCIPLES
PAUL'S MISSIONARY JOURNEYS

JESUS CHRIST AND GOSPEL—GRACE
MOSES AND TEN COMMANDMENTS—LAW

CHAIN OF CHRISTIANITY MOVES WESTWARD

WITH "SIGNS FOLLOWING"

Note: This list of names, events, and nations is not intended to be exhaustive, but rather indicative of the fact that God used men and nations through Christ to bring forth America and her form of government, for His glory and for all the nations of the earth.

climate, provided a natural and desirable opening only in that direction. The overplus of population, the discontent of some part of the people with existing government, the restlessness of adventurers, or the requirements of trade and commerce produced a migration. The colony, instructed by the experience of the parent state, was free to improve on its institutions. Colonies have almost always prospered more than the mother country.

"Transplanting seems to improve both the stock and the institutions. Greece was colonized from Asia, as was Rome; Miletus, Syracuse, and other Greek colonies excelled the mother cities in wealth, and though the free structure of Grecian government allowed a natural development at home and made Athens the metropolis, yet its marvelous genius was nourished and stimulated by the colonies. Carthage was greater and stronger than Tyre, and contended with Rome for the control of the world; the most western nations of Europe were colonized from Rome and Germany, and have taken the lead in later progress, while America has always displayed the lusty, fertile vigor of a young life.

Progress of individual man

"Thus the conformation of the surface of the earth, and the peculiarly fruitful character of a transplanted civilization, have always furnished an escape from the embarrassing fixity of an old state, in the same western direction, and the old and the new unite to establish frequent stages of progress. In this way a continuous growth has been secured that impresses on advancing culture the same unity, from first to last, that we see in the growth and mental development of the individual man.

Two thousand years' development

"We have seen the aggregation and primary discipline of mankind in the simple but extensive despotisms of western Asia, varied in Palestine by a theocratic system which has produced the world's great religion, and in Egypt by the predominance of a learned priestly caste. We saw an improvement made in Greece to meet the demands of intellectual development. Their intelligence, however, was a spontaneous outburst, of necessity immature. Two thousand years of training, and the addition of many new elements were required before mind could rule the world; but Greece, by the attractiveness of her art and culture, set man at work on the great problem of politics and life.

"Rome followed to organize government and consolidate the civilizations, to ripen their fruit and transmit the seed to a

The above excerpts are from Charles Bancroft's "The Footprints of Time" - 1879

more favorable time, and to new and better races. A complete civilization was impossible without well digested science, which had its remote roots in Greece; and law, which was gradually produced by the grand Roman republic; and a clear understanding of the profound yet simple precepts of Jesus Christ.

Law and Science - Precepts of Jesus Christ

"Western Europe received all the wisdom and experience of the ancient world, and labored well at the grand problem though she did not completely solve it. She, however, made an immense advance toward it, and her children, rich in her experience, instructed at once by her success and her mistakes, and aided always by her wisdom, found (let us hope) in America the goal of their noblest aspirations.

Western Europe

"Thus we find the spirit of progress traversing the whole course of human history, constantly advancing through all the confusion of rising and falling states, of battle, seige and slaughter, of victory and defeat; through the varying fortunes and ultimate extinction of monarchy, republic, and empire; through barbaric irruption and desolation, feudal isolation, spiritual supremacy, the heroic rush and conflict of the Cross and the Cresent; amid the busy hum of industry, through the marts of trade and behind the gliding keels of commerce; through the bloody conflicts of commons, nobles, kings and kaisers to New and Free America. There the Englishman, the German, the Frenchman, the Italian, the Scandinavian, the Asiatic, and the African all meet as equals. There they are free to speak, to think, and to act. They bring the common contributions of character, energy and activity to the support and enlargement of a common country, and the spread of its influence and enlightenment through all the lands of their origin.

"As America is the common ground on which all the currents, hastening by lightning and by steam, seek again every quarter of the earth with kindly greeting, to renew the relations broken in the original separation of the races, and to cement, by exchanges mutually profitable, a new and better unity of mankind. As the heart in the human body receives the current of blood from all parts of the system, and, having revitalized it, returns it with fresh elements of strength, so America adopts the children of all lands only to return a manhood ennobled by a sense of its own dignity through the practice of a system of self-government which improves the condition and promotes the interest of each while it produces harm to none.

Manhood ennobled in America

The above excerpts are from Charles Bancroft's "The Footprints of Time" - 1879

America colonizer of Ideas

"America, then, will colonize Ideas, extensively, when her institutions are thoroughly matured. The process, indeed, commenced with her birth, and her Spirit sails with her ships in every sea and visits all lands. All the past has contributed to the excellence of her foundation, and modern Europe has supplied her with the most desirable building material both of ideas and of men. Without Asia, Greece, and Rome, there would have been a very imperfect modern Europe; and without modern Europe, America must have begun at the beginning, with all the lessons, discoveries and discipline of thousands of years to learn. Happily, we seem authorized to believe that, as she concludes the possible great migrations of humanity, she has so well learned the lessons of experience as to have given due flexibility and capacity of improvement to all her institutions, and, when necessary can reconstruct herself within herself. If this is true, she will reach the goal of all progress by furnishing to each individual among her citizens such aid as a state can give to make the most of himself, to reach the fullest expression of his value."

The above excerpts are from Charles Bancroft's "The Footprints of Time" - 1879

NATION MAKING

THE METHODS AND THEIR RESULTS

WITH great political systems, as with typical forms of organic life, the processes of development and of extinction are exceedingly slow, and it is seldom that the stages can be sharply marked by dates... But to understand them, one must do much more than merely catalogue the facts of political history; one must acquire a knowledge of the drifts and tendencies of human thought and feeling and action from the earliest ages to the times in which we live. In covering so wide a field we cannot of course expect to obtain anything like complete results. In order to make a statement simple enough to be generally intelligible, it is necessary to pass over many circumstances and many considerations that might in one way and another qualify what we have to say. Nevertheless it is quite possible for us to discern, in their bold general outlines, some historic truths of supreme importance...

Development and extinction exceedingly slow

"For in order to understand this slow but mighty change, we must look a little into that process of nation-making which has been going on since prehistoric ages and is going on here among us today, and from the recorded experience of men in times long past we may gather lessons of infinite value for ourselves and for our children's children. As in all the achievements of mankind, it is only after much weary experiment and many a heart-sickening failure that success is attained, so has it been especially with nation-making. Skill in the political art is the fruit of ages of intellectual and moral discipline; and just as picture-writing had to come before printing and canoes before steamboats, so the cruder political methods had to be tried and found wanting, amid the tears and groans of unnumbered generations, before methods less crude could be put into operation...

"If we look back for a moment to the primitive stages of society, we may picture to ourselves the surface of the earth sparsely and scantily covered with wandering tribes of savages, rude in morals and manners, narrow and monotonous in experience, sustaining life very much as lower animals sustain it, by gathering wild fruits or slaying wild game, and waging chronic warfare alike with powerful beasts and with rival tribes of men. In the

The above excerpts are from John Fiske's "The Beginnings of New England" - 1889

Political History is the History of Nation Making

widest sense the subject of political history is the description of the processes by which under favourable circumstances, innumerable such primitive tribes have become welded together into mighty nations, with elevated standards of morals and manners, with wide and varied experience, sustaining life and ministering to human happiness by elaborate arts and sciences, and putting a curb upon warfare by limiting its scope, diminishing its cruelty, and interrupting it by intervals of peace.... The story, as laid before us in the records of three thousand years, is fascinating and absorbing in its human interest for those who content themselves with the study of its countless personal incidents, and neglect its profound philosophical lessons. But for those who study it in the scientific spirit, the human interest of its details becomes still more intensely fascinating and absorbing .... By such meditation upon men's thoughts and deeds is the understanding purified, till we become better able to comprehend our relations to the world and the duty that lies upon each of us to shape his conduct rightly.

The Oriental Method of Nation Making

"In welding together of primitive shifting tribes into stable and powerful nations, we can seem to discern three different methods that have been followed at different times and places, with widely different results. In all cases the fusion has been effected by war, but it has gone on in three broadly contrasting ways. The first of these methods, which has been followed from time immemorial in the Oriental world, may be roughly described as conquest without incorporation. A tribe grows to national dimensions by conquering and annexing its neighbors, without admitting them to a share in its political life. Probably there is always at first some incorporation, or even perhaps some crude germ of federative alliance; but this goes very little way, - only far enough to fuse together a few closely related tribes, agreeing in speech and habits, into a single great tribe that can overwhelm its neighbors. In early society this sort of incorporation cannot go far without being stopped by some impassable barrier of language or religion. After reaching this point, the conquering tribe simply annexes its neighbors and makes them its slaves. It becomes a superior caste, ruling over vanquished peoples, whom it oppresses with frightful cruelty, while living on the fruits of their toil in what has been aptly termed Oriental luxury....

"In this first method of nation-making then, which we may call the Oriental method, one now sees but little to commend. It was better than savagery, and for a long time no more efficient method was possible, but the leading peoples of the world have long since outgrown it; and although the resulting form of political government

The above excerpts are from John Fiske's "The Beginnings of New England" - 1889

is the oldest we know and is not yet extinct, it nevertheless has not the elements of permanence. Sooner or later it will disappear, as savagery is disappearing, as the rudest types of inchoate human society have disappeared.

The Roman Method of Nation Making

"The second method by which nations have been made may be called the Roman method; and we may briefly describe it as conquest with incorporation, but without representation. The secret of Rome's wonderful strength lay in the fact that she incorporated the vanquished peoples into her own body politic.... Never before had so many people been brought under one government without making slaves of most of them. Liberty had existed before, whether in barbaric tribes or in Greek cities. Union had existed before, in Assyrian or Persian despotisms. Now liberty and union were for the first time joined together, with consequences enduring and stupendous. The whole Mediterranean world was brought under one government; ancient barriers of religion, speech, and custom were overthrown in every direction; and innumerable barbarian tribes, from the Alps to the wilds of northern Britain, from the Bay of Biscay to the Carpathian Mountains, were more or less completely transformed into Roman citizens, protected by Roman law, and sharing in the material and spiritual benefits of Roman civilization. Gradually the whole vast structure became permeated by Hellenic and Jewish thought, and thus were laid the lasting foundations of modern society, of a common Christendom, furnished with a common stock of ideas concerning man's relation to God and the world, and acknowledging a common standard of right and wrong. This was a prodigious work, which raised human life to a much higher plane than that which it had formerly occupied, and endless gratitude is due to the thousands of steadfast men who in one way or another devoted their lives to its accomplishment.

Its Essential Defect

"This Roman method of nation-making had nevertheless its fatal shortcomings, and it was only very slowly, moreover, that it wrought out its own best results.... The essential vice of the Roman system was that it had been unable to avoid weakening the spirit of personal independence and crushing out local self-government among the peoples to whom it had been applied. It owed its wonderful success to joining Liberty with Union, but as it went on it found itself compelled gradually to sacrifice Liberty to Union, strengthening the hands of the central government and enlarging its functions more and more, until by and by the political life of the several parts had so far died away that, under the pressure of attack from without, the Union fell to pieces and the whole political system had to be slowly and painfully reconstructed.

The above excerpts are from John Fiske's "The Beginnings of New England" - 1889

"Now if we ask why the Roman government found itself thus obliged to sacrifice personal liberty and local independence to the paramount necessity of holding the empire together, the answer will point us to the essential and fundamental vice of the Roman method of nation-making. It lacked the principle of representation. The old Roman world knew nothing of representative assemblies. Its senates were assemblies of notables, constituting in the main an aristocracy of men who had held high office; its popular assemblies were primary assemblies, - town meetings. There was no notion of such a thing as political power delegated by the people to representatives who were to wield it away from home and out of sight of their constituents. The Roman's only notion of delegated power was that of authority delegated by the government to its generals and prefects who discharged at a distance its military and civil functions. When, therefore, the Roman popular government, originally adapted to a single city, had come to extend itself over a large part of the world, it lacked the one institution by means of which government could be carried on over so vast an area without degenerating into despotism....

It Knew Nothing of Representation

"The third method of nation-making may be called the Teutonic or preeminently the English method. It differs from the Oriental and Roman methods which we have been considering in a feature of most profound significance; it contains the principle of representation. For this reason, though like all nation-making it was in its early stages attended with war and conquest, it nevertheless does not necessarily require war and conquest in order to be put into operation. Of the other two methods war was an essential part.... We have seen, that for want of representation the Roman method failed when applied to an immense territory, and the government tended to become more and more despotic, to revert toward the Oriental type. Now of the English or Teutonic method, I say, war is not an essential part; for where representative government is once established, it is possible for a great nation to be formed by the peaceful coalescence of neighbouring states, or by their union into a federal body.... Now federalism, though its rise and establishment may be incidentally accompanied by warfare, is nevertheless in spirit pacific. Conquest in the Oriental sense is quite incompatible with it; conquest in the Roman sense is hardly less so....

The English Method of Nation Making

"But federalism, with its pacific implications, was not an invention of the Teutonic mind. The idea was familiar to the city communities of ancient Greece, which, along with their intense love of self-government, felt the need of combined action for warding off

The above excerpts are from John Fiske's "The Beginnings of New England" - 1889

external attack.... Until the idea of power delegated by the people has become familiar to men's minds in its practical bearings, it was impossible to create a great nation without crushing out the political life of some of its parts. Some centre of power was sure to absorb all the political life, and grow at the expense of the outlying parts, until the result was a centralized despotism. Hence it came to be one of the commonplace assumptions of political writers that republics must be small, that free government is practicable only in a confined area, and that the only strong and durable government, capable of maintaining order throughout a vast territory, is some form of absolute monarchy. It was quite natural that people should formerly have held this opinion, and it is indeed not yet quite obsolete, but its fallaciousness will become more and more apparent as American history is better understood. Our experience has now so far widened that we can see that despotism is not the strongest but well nigh the weakest form of government; that centralized administrations, like that of the Roman Empire, have fallen to pieces, not because of too much but because of too little freedom; and that the only perdurable government must be that which succeeds in achieving national unity on a grand scale, without weakening the sense of personal and local independence. For in the body politic this spirit of freedom is as the red corpuscles in the blood; it carries the life with it. It makes the difference between a society of self-respecting men and women and a society of puppets. Your nation may have art, poetry, and science, all the refinements of civilized life, all the comforts and safeguards that human ingenuity can devise; but if it lose this spirit of personal and local independence, it is doomed and deserves its doom.

Fallacy of the Notion that Republics Must be Small

"Wherever we find Teutonic tribes settling down over a wide area, we find them holding their primary assemblies, usually their annual March-meetings. Everywhere, too, we find some attempt at representative assemblies, based on the principle of the three estates, clergy, nobles, and commons. But nowhere save in England does the representative principle become firmly established, at first in county-meetings, afterward in a national parliament limiting the powers of the national monarch as the primary tribal assembly had limited the powers of the tribal chief. It is for this reason that we must call the method of nation-making by means of a representative assembly the English method. While the idea of representation was perhaps the common property of the Teutonic tribes, it was only in England that it was successfully put into practice and became the dominant political idea .... In America the Teutonic idea has been worked out even more completely than in Britain....

The above excerpts are from John Fiske's "The Beginnings of New England" - 1889

"Between the eighth and the eleventh centuries, when the formation of English nationality was approaching completion, it received a fresh and powerful infusion of Teutonism in the swarms of heathen Northmen or Danes who occupied the eastern coasts, struggled long for the supremacy, and gradually becoming christianized, for a moment succeeded in seizing the crown....

"By the thirteenth century the increasing power and pretentions of the crown, as the unification of English nationality went on, brought about a result unlike anything known on the continent of Europe; it brought about a resistless coalition between the great nobles, the rural gentry and yeomanry, and the burghers of the towns, for the purpose of curbing royalty, arresting the progress of centralization, and setting up representative government on a truly national scale....

Eternal Vigilance is the Price of Liberty

"The fundamental principles of political freedom is 'no taxation without representation'; you must not take a farthing of my money without consulting my wishes as to the use that shall be made of it. Only when this principle of justice was first practically recognized, did government begin to divorce itself from the primitive bestial barbaric system of tyranny and plunder, and to ally itself with the forces that in the fulness of time are to bring peace on earth and good will to men. Of all dates in history, therefore, there is none more fit to be commemorated than 1265; for in that year there was first asserted and applied at Westminster, on a national scale, that fundamental principle of 'no taxation without representation', that innermost kernel of the English Idea, which the Stamp Act Congress defended at New York exactly five hundred years afterward. When we think of these dates, by the way, we realize the import of the saying that in the sight of the Lord a thousand years are but as a day, and we feel that the work of the Lord cannot be done by the listless or the slothful. So much time and so much strife by sea and land has it taken to secure beyond peradventure the boon to mankind for which Earl Simon gave up his noble life on the field of Eversham! Nor without unremitting watchfulness can we be sure that the day of peril is yet past. From kings, indeed, we have no more to fear; they have come to be as spooks and bogies of the nursery. But the gravest dangers are those which present themselves in new forms, against which people's minds have not yet been fortified with traditional sentiments and phrases. The inherited predatory tendency of men to seize upon the fruits of other people's labor is still very strong, and while we have nothing more to fear from kings, we may yet have trouble enough from commercial monopolies and favored

The above excerpts are from John Fiske's "The Beginnings of New England" - 1889

industries, marching to the polls their hordes of bribed retainers. Well indeed has it been said that eternal vigilance is the price of liberty. God never meant that in this fair but treacherous world in which He placed us we should earn our salvation without steadfast labor."

The above excerpts are from John Fiske's "The Beginnings of New England" - 1889

Christian Church Polity A.D. 1-1607

CHURCHES OF THE FIRST CENTURY MAINTAINED LOCAL SELF-GOVERNMENT

IN the beginning, Christianity was simply Gospel. Ecclesiastical organization was not the cause, but the effect of life. Churches were constituted by the spontaneous association of believers. Individuals and families, drawn toward each other by their common trust in Jesus the Christ, and their common interest in the good news concerning the kingdom of God, became a community united, not by external bonds, but by the vital force of distinctive ideas and principles. New affections became the bond of a new brotherhood, and the new brotherhood, with its mutual duties and united responsibilities, became an organized society... Their new ideas and new sympathies and hopes were a bond of union; and though not yet separated from the Jewish people, nor anticipating such a separation, they were beginning to be a distinct community with a life of their own -- a community almost unorganized, so far as the record shows, and yet distinct in the midst of the Jewish nation, like that nation in the midst of the Roman Empire. A new and unique commonwealth had begun to live, and must needs grow into some organized form according to its nature... Having seen that the process of organization in the mother church at Jerusalem was essentially democratic while under the immediate guidance of the apostles, we need positive information to convince us that in other places the process by which believers in Christ became an organized body was materially different. But there is no such information. On the contrary, there are indications that in every place the society of believers in Christ was a little republic...

Beginning

Unique Commonwealth

Each church a little Republic

The above excerpts are from Leonard Bacon's "Genesis of the New England Churches" - 1874

New Testament source of polity

"Every reader of the New Testament books may gather up for himself the hints which they gave, incidentally, about the churches of Galatia, or the saints at Philippi 'with the bishops and deacons,' or 'the Churches of the Thessalonians,' or 'the seven churches of Asia,' or the seemingly unorganized fraternity of believers at Rome. He may observe the traces and rudiments of organization among 'the holy and faithful brethren in Christ' at Colosse, or among those whom Peter and James and the author of the Epistle to the Hebrews addressed in their writings. He may scrutinize the pastoral epistles to ascertain how far the development of ecclesiastical institutions had advanced in the latest years of the apostle Paul. For the purposes of this history, it will be enough to give some results of such an inquiry without repeating the process.

Local institution

"The churches instituted by the apostles were local institutions only. Nothing like a national church, distinct and individual among co-ordinate national churches -- nothing like a provincial church, having jurisdiction over many congregations within certain geographical boundaries, natural or political -- appears in the writings or acts of the apostles... But that the organized church, in the primitive age of Christianity, was always a local institution - never national, never provincial or diocesan - is a proposition which few will deny.

Responsible to Christ

"Each local church was complete in itself, and was held responsible to Christ for its own character, and the character of those whom it retained in its fellowship...

"Particular churches, in that age, were related to each other as constituent portions of the Universal Church. Their unity was their one faith and hope. It was the unity of common ideas and principles distinguishing them from all the world besides -- of common interests and efforts, of common trials and perils, and of mutual affection...

Local self-governing bodies compose Universal Church

"Such were the churches at the date of the New Testament Scriptures.

"It is not difficult to understand the process of their origin and organization if we recollect distinctly what Christianity was at the beginning, before it was developed into what is now called doctrine, and what change it wrought in the consciousness and relations of those who received it.

The above excerpts are from Leonard Bacon's "Genesis of the New England Churches" - 1874

A.D. 100 - 400

CENTRALIZATION UNDER EPISCOPAL FORM OF GOVERNMENT SUPPLANTS LOCAL SELF-GOVERNMENTS

Primitive church altered by A.D. 312

WHEN Christianity, by the conversion of Constantine (A.D. 312), became the dominant religion in the Roman Empire, the church polity then existing was in some respects widely different from that of the primitive churches. Less than three hundred years after the beginning at Jerusalem, the government of the churches had become essentially episcopal, though the bishops every where were elected by the Christian people. Often, if not always, the authority of the bishop, instead of being simply parochial, extended over many congregations, the mother church, in which the bishop had his throne, or sedes (see), being surrounded with dependent congregations, all under one government. The bishop had under him a body of presbyters, who were his council and helpers, and to whom he assigned their duties. Not unfrequently the bishops of a district or province were assembled in synods or councils to deliberate on affairs of general interest, such as disputed points of doctrine, and questions about uniformity in worship and discipline. There was a firmly established distinction between clergy and laity, the clergy consisting of three orders or gradations, bishops, presbyters, and deacons. It has been sometimes assumed that what was in the fourth century must have been from the beginning. The fact, so conspicuous in the survey of that age, that the then existing church polity was substantially what is now called episcopal, has been thought to prove that the churches never were organized and governed in any other way; especially as there are no traces of any revolutionary conflict by which one polity was substituted for another, and no exact line can be drawn to mark the beginning of the distinction between presbyters and bishops, or the transfer of power from self-governing Christian assemblies to a hierarchy. Constantine did not institute the episcopal form of government over the churches - he found it already existing, with its roots in the past; and in adopting Christianity as the religion of the empire, he adopted that ecclesiastical polity. What, then, had become of the polity which we find in the New Testament? At what date was it superseded? Who introduced another constitution in the place of it? Such is the outline of an argument which often seems conclusive. The fallacy lies in the assumption that church government, once instituted, will perpetuate itself, and can be changed only by a revolutionary agitation...

Episcopal form of government developed prior to Constantine

The above excerpts are from Leonard Bacon's "Genesis of the New England Churches" - 1874

"Ecclesiastical polity grew, age after age"

"As the New Testament gives us no system of definite and formulated dogmas in theology, so it gives us no completed system of church government. Ecclesiastical polity grew, age after age, just as theology grew. What there was of organization in the primitive churches was more like the organization of a seed than like the organization of the tree in its maturity. The period between the day of Pentecost and the middle of the second century - or the narrower period between the date of the Pastoral Epistles and the beginning of that century - could not but be a period of rapid development in the Christian commonwealth. Nor did the growth of ecclesiastical polity terminate then. It went on, imperceptibly but steadily, to the age of Constantine - as it went on afterward to the age of Luther - as it goes on now, even in communities most abhorrent of progress and most observant of traditions.

The loss of liberty unsuspected

"The circumstances of that early development determined in many respects, its character and tendency. In that age the churches had no experience to guide them or to warn them. They knew nothing of what we know from the history of eighteen centuries. Why should they be jealous for their liberty? How should they be expected to detect and resist the beginning of lordship over God's heritage? We must remember, too, that in those times of inexperience the development of the Christian organization was a development under pressure. Christianity, often persecuted, always 'an illict religion,' was making its way in the presence of powerful enemies. Its natural leaders, the 'bishops and deacons,' freely chosen in every church were of necessity, intrusted with large powers over the endangered flock, and, of course, power was accumulating in their hands. The churches were in cities; for it was in cities that the new doctrine and worship could obtain a foothold. Such churches, as they grew, were naturally distributed, rather than divided, into a plurality of assemblies governed by one venerable company of bishops or elders, and served by one corps of deacons. Equally natural was it for each mother church to become still more extended by spreading itself out into the suburbs and surrounding villages; all believers in the city and its suburbs, or in the country round about, being recognized as constituting one ecclesia with one administration.

"In the growth of such a community, as its affairs become more complicated, one of the elders or overseers must needs become the moderator or chairman of the board; and to him the chief oversight must be intrusted. At first that presiding elder is only a leader, foremost among brethren who are equal in authority;

The above excerpts are from Leonard Bacon's "Genesis of the New England Churches" - 1874

First departure from the primitive polity

but by degrees he becomes a superior officer with distinctive powers. A tendency to monarchy begins to be developed in what was at first a simple republic. The principle of equality and fraternity begins to be superseded by the spirit of authority and subordination. This may be noted as the first departure from the simplicity of the primitive polity...

A. D. 1370 - 1555

TO RECOVER THE PRIMITIVE GOSPEL

Beginning of The Reformation in England

Twofold character of Reformation in England

IN England, the twofold character of the Reformation was more conspicuous than in any other country. Elsewhere,...that great revolution was effected, under the providence of God, by a concurrence of political with religious forces. Princes and statesmen, or the leaders of petty republics, in the one hand, and reforming preachers and writers on the other hand, were fellow-workers. But in England, more than any where else, the Reformation resembled some great river formed by the confluence of two streams which, like the Missouri and the Mississippi, refused to mingle though flowing in the one channel...Considered as a religious movement, the Reformation in England began with Wycliffe, more than a hundred and fifty years before Luther. Fitly has the stout-hearted Englishman been called 'the morning star' of the day which had its sunrise in the sixteenth century...Considered in the other aspect, namely, as a political or national movement, the English Reformation, at its beginning, had no visible connection with the religious movement among the people...

Individual souls

"The great Reformation in the sixteenth century was an attempt to recover the primitive Gospel...What was, at first, the experience of individual souls struggling with the great question, 'How shall man be just with God,' driven back from tradition to the Scriptures, and finding rest in Christ the one mediator between God and men, became, at that juncture, a new announcement of the primitive Gospel...

The above excerpts are from Leonard Bacon's "Genesis of the New England Churches" - 1874

A. D. 1560

PRESBYTERIAN FORM OF GOVERNMENT Modifies EPISCOPAL FORM OF GOVERNMENT.

Conflict of church Protestantism with government Protestantism

Puritans wanted Reformation of the National Church by national authority

THEN began that age-long conflict in the Church of England between the government Protestantism, on the one hand, completed and immovable, and the demand, on the other hand, for a more thorough reformation that should carry the National Church and the national Christianity back to the original purity portrayed in the Scriptures. On one side were the court, and those who were called 'the court clergy'. On the other side were the PURITANS, so named from their demand for purity in the worship of God and in the administration of Christ's ordinances... There were Puritans more or less decided in their opinions, and more or less resolute in word and deed; but, at first, there was no Puritan party acting in concert under acknowledged leaders... Such was the origin of Puritanism in England, and such was its position three hundred years ago, when Elizabeth was queen. It was not, nor did it intend to be, a secession or separation from the National Church. It must not be thought that the Puritans were 'Dissenters' in the modern meaning of that word. They were not Congregationalists in their theory of the church; nor, at first, were they even Presbyterians. Certainly the great body of them, in the earliest stages of the conflict, had not arrived at the conclusion that diocesan episcopacy must be got rid of. At first the most advanced of them were only 'Nonconformists,' deviating from some of the prescribed regulations in the performance of public worship. As Christian Englishmen, they were, according to the theory which I have called nationalism, members of the Church of England; and what they desired was not liberty to withdraw from that National Church and to organize what would now be called a distinct 'denomination;' nor was it merely liberty in the National Church to worship according to their own idea of Christian simplicity and purity - though, doubtless, many of them would have been contented with that. What they desired was reformation of the National Church itself by national authority... While the conflict was in its earliest stage, the episcopal element in the constitution of the ecclesiastical establishment seems not to have been seriously called in question. On the contrary, it was conceded by those who desired more reformation that the king might lawfully appoint officers to superintend and govern the clergy, ... Conscience, in conscientious men, when it has been roused to declare itself, is an obstinate thing...

The above excerpts are from Leonard Bacon's "Genesis of the New England Churches" - 1874

A company of Puritans who ventured to meet for worship in their own way (1567), found that there were penalties for the nonconforming laity as well as for nonconforming clergymen. Their meeting was broken up, and a large number of them were imprisoned to study in their confinement the principles of church order. In all parts of England there were similiar proceedings.

Laity encounter Act of Uniformity

"Not many years passed before the conflict entered on another stage of its progress, and new questions were opened between the Puritans and those who ruled the ecclesiastical establishment. The rigorous enforcement of the Act of Uniformity by bishops on laity as well as clergy, and the forcible suppression of the private assemblies in which nonconformists ventured to meet for social worship, had an effect which a little knowledge of human nature might have anticipated...

Cartwright introduces presbyterian form of government

"Thomas Cartwright, ... Professor of Divinity in the University of Cambridge, a man of great celebrity for learning and eloquence, began (1570) to discuss in his lectures the theory of church government as given in the Scriptures; and he did not hesitate to say in what particulars the actual arrangements for the government of the Church of England were widely divergent from the most ancient examples, and especially from the authoritative precedents and principles of the New Testament. Still holding the vicious theory that an independent Christian nation is an independent Christian church, he aimed at nothing more than a complete reformation by the government; but the system which he would have the queen and Parliament establish in England was essentially that of Geneva and of Scotland... Under Cartwright's influence, English Puritanism became, essentially, in its ideas and aspirations, Presbyterianism like that of Holland or of Scotland.

Conflict in National Church

"To describe the progress of that controversy in the Church of England would be aside from our purpose. It was a long and bitter controversy. On one side there was power, on the other side there was the obstinacy of conscience... On one side were some good men and learned, conservative by nature and by training, who thankfully accepted as much of reformation as the queen would give them, and quietly waited for more, with many other men, not so good nor so learned, whose feeling was that the queen had already done quite enough, and even more than enough, in the way of church reformation. On the other side there was no less of learning, and much more of earnest religious feeling. On one side was the fixed purpose

The above excerpts are from Leonard Bacon's "Genesis of the New England Churches" - 1874

of Elizabeth Tudor, and (after a while) of the prelates who depended on her favor, to extinguish the nonconforming and reforming party by deprivation and silencing, by exorbitant fines, by confinement in loathsome and pestilential prisons. On the other side there was the invisible yet invincible might of those who suffer for conscience sake... Both held a fatal error in assuming that there must be a national church, one and indivisible, and that the reformation of the church could be wrought only by the legislative and executive sovereignty of the nation... What Puritanism demanded was an ecclesiastical reformation to be made by the national authority... No withdrawal from the National Church was to be thought of, for that would be schism...

A.D. 1558 - 1567

DID THE APOSTLES INSTITUTE ANY NATIONAL CHURCH?

"If the Apostle Paul, who was an inspired person, had not dominion over the faith of the churches, how came the Roman emperor, or other Christian princes, by such a jurisdiction -- which has no foundation in the law of nature or in the New Testament?"
-Daniel Neal "History of the Puritans" - 1731

BUT under oppression men sometimes get new light. As the urging of conformity to an obnoxious ritual led Thomas Cartwright and others to investigate the theory of church government, and to demand a warrent from the Scriptures for the system of diocesan episcopacy, so, under the discipline of impoverishing fines and tedious imprisonments, some of the sufferers began to doubt whether the exceptional institution called the Church of England - having Elizabeth Tudor as its supreme ruler on earth, to whom every minister of God's word was responsible for his preaching and for all his spiritual administrations - was really a church of Christ in any legitimate meaning of that phrase. The more they studied the New Testament, the less they could find bearing a resemblance to that or any other National Church. Questions were beginning to emerge which had not yet been fairly considered. Did the apostles institute any national church?... If not, what was his intention when he sent forth his disciples to convert all nations? Nonconformists were holding conventicles in private rooms, with the doors shut for fear of informers and persecutors; but in what capacity or character were they thus assembled? What was the relation of such assemblies, and what the relation of the queen's National Church to the true church of Christ in England?... Such questionings among the Puritans gave origin to another party aiming at a more radical reformation. The men of the new party, instead of remaining in the Church of England to reform it, boldly withdrew themselves from that ecclesiastico-political organization,

The above excerpts are from Leonard Bacon's "Genesis of the New England Churches" - 1874

denouncing that and all other so-called national churches as institutions unknown to the law and mind of Christ. The idea of separation, in some sort, from the State Church, in order to regain the simplicity of Christian institutions, must have occurred to many minds, before any attempt was made to propound a theory of separation and to embody it in organized churches...

Separatist party formed

A. D. 1594 - 1600

REFORM WITHOUT TARRYING FOR ANY

Scrooby

IN that region (Scrooby) the idea of 'reformation without tarrying for any' was beginning to take effect. Men were beginning to learn that there might be individual and personal reformation, voluntary conformity to the rules and principles given in the New Testament, without waiting for a reformation of the National Church by the national government. How this came to pass, and by what stages of progress, may be best told by one who had himself no small part in the story. Tracing the movement from an undefined beginning, he tells us that 'by the travail and diligence of some godly and zealous preachers, as in other places of the land, so in the north parts, many became enlightened by the word of God, and had their ignorance and sins discovered by the word of God's grace, and began to reform their lives and make conscience of their ways.' In other words, they began to be conscientious in all things, and were earnest to know the will of God that they might obey it. This was nothing else than private judgment in religion - the practical recognition of individual responsibility to God - the first stage of 'reformation without tarrying for any'. Individuals, one by one, were beginning to reform themselves under the guidance of the Scriptures. What next? As soon as 'the work of God', moving them to live soberly, righteously, and godly, became manifest in them, 'they were both scoffed and scorned by the profane multitude; and the ministers', among whose hearers such changes were taking place, began to experience the oppressive urgency of the queen's hierarchy. Those ministers must submit to 'the yoke of subscription', or be silenced. Nor was this all. Scoffs and scorn might be endured. The silencing of Nonconformist clergymen - if it had merely debarred them from preaching in the pulpits of the state church - would not have been

Hierarchy demands submission

The above excerpts are from Leonard Bacon's "Genesis of the New England Churches" - 1874

an intolerable hardship, so long as there were private houses in which they could meet quietly those who desired to hear them. But the queen's supremacy gave them no such liberty; and the enginery of ecclesiastical oppression was brought to bear on the hearers as well as the preachers. 'The poor people were so urged with apparitors and pursuivants and the commissary courts, as truly their affliction was not small.'

A. D. 1602 - 1607

THE SEPARATISTS and THE BIBLE

The Idea of Local Self-Governing Congregations

Conclusion:

Re-formation of churches

THEY were brought to the conclusion that, whatever might be the Christian character of some congregations in the parishes of England, and however numerous the true followers of Christ and members of his body might be among the English people, the ecclesiastico-political institution called 'the Church of England' was not at all a church in any New Testament meaning of the word, but was (as their experience had proved) a positively anti-christian institution. Having arrived at this conclusion, they could no longer be Puritans merely, waiting and protesting in the hope of a new reformation to be made by national authority in the National Church. They found incumbent on them a personal duty of reformation - even of church reformation - 'without tarrying for any'. As on the first Christians in Antioch and in Rome, before churches existed there, the duty was incumbent of forming churches according to the mind of Christ; so on them, in England, where Christ's institution had been subverted, and a different institution set up in its place, there was incumbent a duty of re-formation of churches. How long the time was in which they were passing through these successive stages of reformation, and at what date they, or any of them, adopted definitely the principle of separation from the state church, we have no means of knowing exactly... It was at the period of transition from the reign of Elizabeth to that of James I., and from the primacy of Whitgift to that of Bancroft, that those 'brethren in the north countries', assuming their rights 'as the Lord's free people', became, by their covenant with each other and with God, a church of Christ, and determinately 'shook off the yoke of antichristian bondage'. Four years later (1607), the people who were thus intent upon 'the positive and practical part of divine

The above excerpts are from Leonard Bacon's "Genesis of the New England Churches" - 1874

institutions', became 'two distinct bodies or churches' for the sake of convenience in holding their assemblies; inasmuch as their homes were dispersed over a territory too wide for their meeting in one place, especially in those times. After the division, one of the two churches met, ordinarily, in the manor-house of Scrooby. As at Colosse there was a church in the house of Philemon, and at Laodicea a church in the house of Nymphas - as at Corinth there was a church in the house of Aquila and Priscilla, and afterward another in their house at Rome, when they had removed their residence to the imperial city - so this church instituted without asking Caesar's permission, might have been called the church that is in the house of William Brewster. There was the germ of New England... How came there to be, just there, the materials out of which these two congregations of Separatists could be gathered? We can understand more readily the growth of an advanced Protestantism in London, and in other centres of influence and of intercourse; but how came there to be in these rural parishes and scattered villages, among a people so remote from the places where agitation and progress would be natural, so much of thought on religious themes, so much of spiritual quickening, so much of movement toward ecclesiastical liberty? Are not these the people who might be expected either to hold fast the ancient superstitions, or to accept, without a murmur of inquiry, whatever may be determined by the queen? The question is answered when the chronicler tells us of the 'godly and zealous preachers' who had propagated in those parts the doctrines of the religious reformation. It was by the preaching of that ancient Gospel, 'repentance toward God and faith toward our Lord Jesus Christ', that so many of the plain country people, far away from the court and the universities and from the great trading towns, had become thoughtful students of the Bible, earnestly inquiring after God's truth, and resolutely determined on personal reformation at whatever cost... The story of what their undertaking cost them begins with the experience of more violent persecutions... Amsterdam was the rendezvous of the fugitives as they made their escape out of England, one by one, or in families. 'In the end, they all got over, some at one time and some at another, and met together again with no small rejoicing'. Meanwhile, by the troubles they had suffered, 'their cause became famous'. Their Christian behavior under persecution 'left a deep impression on the minds of many'. In many a thoughtful mind the inquiry was raised, 'Who and what are these men? What evil have they done? What is it for which they suffer so meekly, and yet so perseveringly?

New church formed in houses of the Separatists

Puritan Separatist becomes a Pilgrim

The above excerpts are from Leonard Bacon's "Genesis of the New England Churches" - 1874

"Who and what were they? Whatever ecclesiastical or political prejudice against them may linger in some quarters, no intelligent reader of history can think of them as frantic enthusiasts, as dupes of knavish leaders, or as in any way dangerous members of society. Some of them were men trained at the English universities, and skilled in the learning and the controversies of their time. Some were not without experience of life in the great world, and in connection with public affairs; others were plain people of the old English yeomanry, who had lived on their hereditary acres - the type and original of our New England farmers. All had gained the intelligence that comes from the diligent study of the Bible, and all were honest and earnest believers in the Christ of the New Testament. Such were the men and the women who were thus driven out of their native England, yet hunted and intercepted in their flight, as if they were criminals escaping from justice. Why did they suffer the spoiling of their goods, arrest, imprisonment, exile?... They had caught from the Bible the idea of a church independent alike of the pope and the queen, independent of Parliament as well as of prelates, and dependent only on Christ. It was their mission to work out and organize that idea..."

Diligent study of the Bible

The above excerpts are from Leonard Bacon's "Genesis of the New England Churches" - 1874

THE REPUBLICAN FORM OF GOVERNMENT

Christian Principles Produce Local Self-Government

IT is remarkable how men of comprehensive views, and free from sectarian bias, have agreed with regard to THE REPUBLICANISM OF CHRISTIANITY. 'Christianity,' says Montesquieu, 'is a stranger to despotic power.' 'The religion,' says De Tocqueville, 'which declares that all are equal in the sight of God, will not refuse to acknowledge that all citizens are equal in the eye of the law. Religion is the companion of liberty in all its battles and all its conflicts; the cradle of its infancy and the divine source of its claims.' 'The friends of liberty in France are accustomed to speak in enthusiastic commendation of the REPUBLICANISM of the Scriptures.' The Abbe' de la Mennais, acknowledged as one of

"Christianity is a stranger to despotic power"

-Montesquieu

The above excerpts are from Edwin Hall's "The Puritans and their Principles" - 1846

the most powerful minds in Europe, little as he regards Christianity as a revelation from God, familiarly speaks of its Author as 'THE GREAT REPUBLICAN.' Our own De Witt Clinton said, 'Christianity, in its essence, its doctrines, and its forms, is republican.'...

"The tendency of the true Gospel principles is to bring the most absolute despotism under the limits of law; to imbue limited monarchies more and more with the spirit of popular institutions; to prepare the people to govern themselves; and finally to establish everywhere the spirit and the reality, if not the very forms of a republic.

"Let us turn once more to the republican features of the churches organized by the Apostles. These churches had officers, which were to be regarded and observed, in their proper sphere, as much as the officers of any other republic. But the manner of their ruling was not to be as 'Lords over God's heritage'; 'Whosoever will be chief among you', said the Saviour, 'let him be your servant'.

"The Apostles themselves gave several striking illustrations of their regard for popular rights. The first public act of the Church, after our Lord's ascension, was the choice of an Apostle in the place of Judas. Peter stands up in the midst of the disciples - the number of names together was about one hundred and twenty - and proposes the matter. The election is made by the body of the Church...

"The accurate historian Mosheim thus states the conclusions to which his own mind came after a most thorough investigation. 'In these primitive times,...the highest authority was in the people, or the whole body of Christians; for even the Apostles themselves inculcated by their example, that nothing of moment was to be done or determined but with the knowledge and consent of the brotherhood.'...'The people did everything that is proper for those in whom the supreme power of the community is vested.'

"Neander, the most distinguished ecclesiastical historian of the present day, says, 'Each individual Church which had a Bishop or Presbyter of its own, assumed to itself the form and rights of a little distinct republic or commonwealth; and with regard to its internal concerns, was wholly regulated by a code of laws, that, if they did not originate with, had at least received the sanction of the people constituting such Church.'"

The above excerpts are from Edwin Hall's "The Puritans and their Principles" - 1846

THE BIBLE IN ENGLISH

"Wickliffe...published certain conclusions...that the New Testament or Gospel is a perfect rule of life and manners and ought to be read by the people...he was the first that translated the New Testament into English."

- Daniel Neal, "History of the Puritans", 1731

WICKLIFFE, the morning-star of the Reformation...was born at Wickliffe, near Richmond, in Yorkshire, about the year 1324, and was educated in Queen's College, Oxford, where he was divinity professor, and afterward pastor of Lutterworth in Leicestershire. He flourished in the latter end of the reign of King Edward III. and the beginning of Richard II., about one hundred and thirty years before the Reformation of Luther... This Wickliffe was a wonderful man for the times in which he lived, which was overspread with the thickest darkness of anti-Christian idolatry...he wrote near two hundred volumes, all which were called in, condemned, and ordered burned, together with his bones, by the Council of Constance, in the year 1425, forty one years after his death; but his doctrine remained, and the number of his disciples, who were distinguished by the name of Lollards..."

The above excerpt is from Daniel Neal's "History of the Puritans" - 1731

SCRIPTURES OPENED to the INDIVIDUAL MAN

Wycliffe Translation to The King James Bible

WYCLIFFE'S Teutonic love of truth, of freedom, and of independence, . . . moved him to give his countrymen the open Scripture as their best safeguard and protection. . . and it was the development of the English language into a literary medium of expression, ripe for his work of translation as Italian had grown ripe for Dante, and as German was presently to grow ripe for Luther, which first made a people's Bible possible. . .

THE WYCLIFFE BIBLE

"And if Wycliffe represents a new movement in our literature, so too does he represent a new departure in our religious history. For the rise of Lollardy, in so far as it was a religious movement, marks the earliest break in the. . . continuity of Latin Christianity in England. . . The Wycliffe Bible was spoken of. . . as being not merely a book but an event. . . It was Chaucer, no doubt, who by his genius impressed the literary stamp on our language, but it was Wycliffe who, in his own field, and addressing his own audience, made ready and prepared the way.

"The rivalry between Norman-French and English had come at length to an end. Largely owing to the loss of Normandy in the reign of King John, and to the loss of Aquitaine in the reign of Edward III., the continental invader had been gradually turning into an Englishman. In the twelfth century English had been to the dominant race nothing else but a foreign language. As the vernacular of everyday life it had naturally remained the spoken language of the subject population; but no Norman magnate of the twelfth century would have used English except under circumstances where his native tongue promised to be unintelligible to those whom he was addressing. With the fourteenth century there had come a great change. The conquered Saxon had at length completed the assimilation of his conqueror, and the Norman had become finally naturalized. While French still kept up its social position as the language of polite society, it had come to be the general practice for every gentleman to know the native English, inasmuch as the foreign settlers now felt themselves to be no longer Normans but Englishmen. . .

The above excerpts are from H. W. Hoare's "The Evolution of the English Bible" - 1901

TYNDALE is the true father of our present English Bible. He is so notwithstanding the fact that he neither originated the idea of a popular version, nor was the first to make one. In these respects the glory rests with his predecessor, Wycliffe. But the English of the fourteenth century is not our English, and Wycliffe's Bible is not a translation at first hand but only a translation of the Latin Bible.

"For felicity of diction, and for dignity of rhythm, Tyndale never has been and never can be surpassed...He worked, like a sane and sound scholar, on the principles of grammar and philology. He endeavored, in a spirit of unpedantic sincerity and conscientiousness, to find out what it was that each sacred writer had meant to say, and then to say it in plain and vigorous Saxon-English with all the idiomatic simplicity, and grace, and stateliness which characterise the Authorized Version...

THE TYNDALE BIBLE

"It has been estimated that, of Tyndale's work as above specified, our Bibles retain at the present day something like eighty per cent, in the Old Testament, and ninety per cent, in the New. If this estimate may be accepted no grander tribute could be paid to the industry, scholarship, and genius of the pioneer whose indomitable resolution enabled him to persevere in labours prolonged through twelve long years of exile from the land that in his own words he so 'loved and longed for'. with the practical certainty of a violent death staring him all the while in the face.

"About the month of May 1524 he left London for Hamburg. The unanimous evidence of his contemporaries supports the view that he was at Wittenberg with Luther, and that he worked there at his translation. His modern biographers, on the other hand, keep him in Hamburg for the whole interval. It is not known how far the work of translation had advanced before Tyndale left for England, but at any rate the New Testament seems to have been ready for the printers by the early summer of 1525...

"But Tyndale had no intention of resting content with what he had achieved. He was soon busily engaged on the Old Testament. In 1530 there accordingly appeared a new volume containing a translation of the Pentateuch from the original Hebrew. In 1531 was published the Book of Jonah with a lengthy Prologue... Now in 1534 there came out a revised edition both of the Pentateuch

The above excerpts are from H. W. Hoare's "The Evolution of the English Bible" - 1901

of 1530 and of the New Testament of 1525, and this latter has always taken rank as its author's masterpiece...In the spring of the next year, during the month of May, 1535, Tyndale was treacherously betrayed to his ever watchful enemies...Partly to his labours in this (a) foreign dungeon we owe the translation of that portion of the Old Testament (Joshua to II Chronicles inclusive), which he left in the charge of his intimate friend and literary executor, the martyr that was to be, John Rogers...

"Within twelve months of the martyrdom of its author at Vilvorde, the translation which 'either with glosses (marginal notes) or without' had been denounced, abused, and burnt at St. Paul's, was now, under its assumed name (the Matthew Bible), formally approved by the King's grace, and published, together with Coverdale's Bible, under the shelter of a royal proclamation and license... Except for Fulke's statement that Matthew's edition was the first 'authorized' English Bible, there is nothing to indicate that it was any earlier in circulation than the Coverdale Edition of 1537, which was 'set forth with the King's most gracious license'.

THE GREAT BIBLE

"...In April 1539, the first edition of this magnificent specimen of the art of printing was ready for publication...One great feature of this Bible is the frontpiece, which is said to have been designed for it by Hans Holbein...

"By an injunction framed as early as 1536, but not issued until September 1538, in virtue of which all clergy were ordered to provide before a specified day 'one boke of the whole Bible, in the largest volume, in Englishe, sett up in summe convenyent place within the churche that ye have care of, whereat your parishoners may most commodiously resort to the same and rede yt.' This injunction had all the authority of a royal proclamation and thus, within thirteen years of the burning of Tyndale's New Testaments at St. Paul's, the battle of the English Bible had been finally won. First forbidden; then silently tolerated; and next licensed, it was now commanded by the King's Highness to be set up for the benefit of each one of the eleven thousand parishes in the land...

THE GENEVAN BIBLE

"The forerunner of the Genevan Bible was an English New Testament which came out in 1557...It is, in the first place, the earliest translation to adopt that division of the text into verses, which was made, during a ride between Paris and Lyons, by Robert Stephens in his Greek Testament of 1551, and which reappears in the Genevan Bible of 1560...

The above excerpts are from H. W. Hoare's "The Evolution of the English Bible" - 1901

"Knox, Coverdale, and several others among the revisers,... left Geneva before their task was complete; but we learn from Anthony A. Wood that 'Whittingham, with one or two more, being resolved to go through with the work, did tarry a year and a half after Queen Elizabeth came to the Crown.' The 'one or two more' appear to have been Anthony Gilby, of Christ's College Cambridge, and Thomas Sampson, Dean of Chichester, and subsequently Dean of Christ Church in the early years of the reign of Elizabeth.

"Based, as regards the Old Testament, mainly on the Great Bible, and, as regards the New Testament, on Whittingham's version of 1557, which was itself a revision of Tyndale, the Genevan Bible was the result of a careful collation with the Hebrew and Greek originals, and of a free use of the best recent Latin versions, especially Beza's, as well as of the standard French and German translations.

"In many ways this edition formed a new departure and offered new attractions. Especially was this the case with regard to bulk. The Great Bible was a huge, unwieldy folio, suited only for liturgical use. Its rival was for the most part issued as a quarto of comfortable size, and at a moderate price. In place of the heavy black letters to which readers had been accustomed, there appeared the clear Roman type with which our modern press has made us familiar. The division of the chapters into verses, however we may condemn it as a literary device, has undeniable advantages, both for the preacher and for private reference and study, to say nothing of its effect in facilitating the prominence that soon began to attach to particular favourite texts.

"Neither cumbersome nor costly; terse, and vigorous in style; literal, and yet boldly idiomatic; the Genevan version was at once a conspicuous advance on all the Biblical labours that had preceded it, and an edition which could fairly claim to be well abreast of the soundest contemporary scholarship.

"Apart, however, from its intrinsic merits, and from its incidental attractions, the introduction of the Bible into England, from the point of view of its authors, was singularly opportune. Secular literature was at this time all but unknown. Shakespeare was not yet born. Spenser was but six years old, and Bacon in his cradle. With the exception of the Bible, the Prayer Book, Foxe's 'Book of Martyrs', and

The above excerpts are from H.W. Hoare's "The Evolution of the English Bible" - 1901

Calvin's 'Institutes', it is difficult to recall a book which had any considerable circulation. Meanwhile the habit of Bible-reading had been steadily gaining a firm hold upon that large and increasing section of the community to which the Genevan Bible would most forcibly appeal.

THE KING JAMES BIBLE

"Elizabeth died in March 1603, and with the accession of James I., we arrive at length within sight of that monumental work which was destined not merely to eclipse but absolutely to efface all rivals, and to enter upon a reign which has endured unbroken for nearly three hundred years, and in the undimmed lustre of which we yet live. We need waste no words in praise of the Authorised Version.

"The conference of 1604, which met by the royal command on the 14th, 16th, and 18th of January at Hampton Court, and in the very palace which had once belonged to Wolsey, had not been called with any view to the production of a new translation of the Bible. The sole object of the meeting was to consider what is known as the 'Millenary Petition'. This was a petition to the throne by the Puritan section of the national Church.... A useful sidelight is thrown upon the matter by the Preface to the Authorised Version. The translators there write as follows:

> "'The very historical truth is, that upon the importunate petitions of the Puritans, the Conference at Hampton Court having been appointed for hearing their complaints, when by force of reason they were put from all other grounds, they had recourse at the last to this shift, that they could not with good conscience subscribe to the Communion Book (i.e., the Prayer Book), since it maintained the Bible as it was there translated, which was, as they said, a most corrupted translation. And although this was judged to be but a very poor and empty shift, yet even hereupon did his Majesty begin to bethink himself of the good that might ensue by a new translation, and presently after gave orders for this translation which is now presented unto thee.'

"The first practical step had naturally been to select a competent committee of revisers. Most probably the King, whose whole heart was in the matter, consulted both Bancroft and the Universities, but to whom the ultimate decision was entrusted is uncertain. It is evident, from what is known of the names

The above excerpts are from H. W. Hoare's "The Evolution of the English Bible" - 1901

on the list which has come down to us, that all possible pains were taken to secure the services of the best available men. The only qualification which was held to be indispensable was that the revisers should be Biblical students of proved capacity.

"Puritan Churchmen and Anglican Churchmen, linguists and theologians, laymen and divines, worked harmoniously side by side.

"Fifty-four of the most prominent scholars appear to have been originally selected to constitute the committee, but the lists that have come down to us include the names of only forty-seven. Why this was so we have no information, nor has any satisfactory explanation of the discrepancy been hitherto offered. What, however, is of the more importance is that the appointments were in no case lightly made, but that the utmost care and catholicity of mind was exercised in the matter. Hugh Broughton was probably the greatest Hebraist of the time, but he was a man of such ungovernable temper, and one so impossible to work with, that his cooperation was not invited.

"The revisers were organized in six companies. Two of these held their meetings at Oxford, two at Cambridge, two at Westminster. The representative of the Puritans at Hampton Court, Dr. Reynolds, one of the foremost scholars of the day, was on the Oxford committee, and among his colleagues was Dr. Miles Smith, who 'Had Hebrew at his finger ends.' and was moreover one of the final supervisors and the author of the very interesting and instructive preface which, though there is no room for it in our overcrowded Bibles, was prefixed to the completed work in 1611.

"The instructions to which reference has been made appear on the whole to have been admirably conceived, and a copy of them was presented to each of the six companies. They ran as follows:

> '...Every particular man of each company to take the same chapter or chapters: and having translated or amended them severally by himself where he thinketh good, all to meet together, confer what they have done, and agree for their parts what shall stand.
>
> 'As any one company hath dispatched any one book in this manner, they shall send it to the rest to be considered of seriously and judiciously, for his Majesty is very careful in this point.

The above excerpts are from H. W. Hoare's "The Evolution of the English Bible" - 1901

'If any company, upon the review of the book so sent, doubt or differ upon any place, to send them word thereof, note the place, and withal send the reasons: to which if they consent not, the difference to be compounded at the general meeting, which is to be of the chief persons of each company at the end of the work.

'When any place of special obscurity is doubted of, letters to be directed by authority to be sent to any learned man in the land for his judgment.

'Letters to be sent from every bishop to the rest of his clergy, admonishing them of this translation in hand, and to move and charge as many as being skilful in the tongues, and having taken pains in that kind, to send his particular observations to the company either at Westminster, Cambridge, or Oxford...

'These translations to be used when they agree better with the text than the Bishops' Bible: Tindale's, Matthew's, Coverdale's, Whitchurch's, Geneva...'

"It is supposed that some three years were spent in arranging for the payment of expenses, in the individual study of the text, and in labours of an anticipatory character, three more in organised and joint work, and a brief nine months in a final revision in London by the representative committee of six...

"In 1611 the Authorized Version, a folio volume in black-letter type, was issued to the public. It had no notes, and the interpretation of it was therefore left perfectly free...It has already been translated into something like two hundred different languages and dialects, and not less than three million copies of it are now year by year poured out from the English Press. In sober earnest may we say that 'its sound has gone forth into all lands, and its words unto the ends of the world'.

"The description which has been given of the evolution of our Authorized Version may now perhaps best be completed by a consideration of the happy conjunction of circumstances to which its unique greatness is in part, at any rate, to be ascribed. In the first place, then, the King's Bible was indebted for its success to the personal qualifications of the revisers. They were the picked scholars and linguists of their day. They were also men of profound and unaffected piety. Let them speak for themselves.

The above excerpts are from H. W. Hoare's "The Evolution of the English Bible" - 1901

Preface to the Authorized Version

'In what sort did these assemble? In the trust of their own knowledge, or of their sharpness of wit, or deepness of judgment? At no hand. They trusted in Him that hath the key of David, opening and no man shutting; they prayed to the Lord, O let Thy Scriptures be my pure delight; let me not be deceived in them, neither let me deceive by them. In this confidence and with this devotion did they assemble together...Neither did we think (it) much to consult the translators or commentators, Chaldee, Hebrew, Syrian, Greek, or Latin; no, nor the Spanish, French, Italian, or Dutch; neither did we disdain to revise that which we had done, and to bring back to the anvil that which we had hammered...'

"...The predominance of Saxon words in this version is very remarkable. As compared with Latin words they actually constitute some nine-tenths of it. In Shakespeare the proportion is approximately eighty-five per cent., in Swift, ninety, in Johnson seventy-five, in Gibbon seventy. In the Lord's Prayer no less than fifty-nine words out of sixty-five are of Saxon origin...They had ready to hand the rich results of nearly a century of diligent and unintermittent labour in the field of Biblical study. The great lines which were to be followed had long since been marked out by Wycliffe, Tyndale, and Coverdale, while useful side-lights could be derived from the Latin and modern translations above enumerated. It is very essential to bear this consideration in mind if we are to take a just view of the literary style of our Authorized Version...The last decade of the sixteenth century had witnessed an outburst of genius, whether in poetry, in the drama, or in prose, to which it would indeed be difficult to find a parallel. The names of Shakespeare, Marlow, Spenser, Hooker, Chapman, Bacon, Jonson, Sidney,...form a galaxy of greatness before which we can only bow our heads. There had been long years of preparation...A terrible danger, nerving and bracing the whole community into strenuous effort, gave place all at once to an indescribable sense of relief. As it had been in Greece after Marathon, Plataea, and Salamis, so was it in this land of ours when the Spaniard spread his wings and fled away. Suddenly, almost as if by magic, the world of literature was seen bursting into loveliest blossom, and the national language clothing itself in strength, in richness, and in power...It was in some such air as this that the translators of the King's Bible lived and moved and had their being."

The above excerpts are from H. W. Hoare's "The Evolution of the English Bible" - 1901

Part Two

AMERICAN BACKGROUND in England

"The harvest truly is great, but the labourers are few; pray ye therefore the Lord of the harvest, that he would send forth labourers into his harvest."

- Luke 10:2

"The Sidneys, and Miltons, and Lockes of England were teachers in America as well as in their native land, and more effectual, because their instructions fell in a readier... The spirit was kindled in England; it went with Robinson's congregation to Holland; it landed with them at Plymouth; it was the basis of the first constitution..."

- Jared Sparks, "American History"
Professor of Ancient and Modern History, Harvard, 1839.

"This appears so plainly in scripture, that the assertors of liberty want no other patron than God himself; and His word so fully justifies what we contend for..."

"Magna Charta could give nothing to the people, who, in themselves, had all; and only reduced into a small volume, the rights which the nation was resolved to maintain; brought the king to confess, they were perpetually inherent and time out of mind enjoyed, and to swear that he would no way violate them..."

- Algernon Sidney, "Discourses Concerning Government", 1698.

"The study of morality... of this there are books enough writ both by ancient and modern philosophers; but the morality of the Gospel doth so exceed them all, that, to give a man a full knowledge of true morality, I shall send him to no other book, but the New Testament."

- John Locke, "Some Thoughts Concerning Reading and Study", 1689.

MAGNA CHARTA

"Our writer...tells us that formerly the right of taxation was in the King only. I should have been glad if he had pointed us to that time. We know that kings - even English kings - have lost their crowns and their heads for assuming such a right. 'Tis true this strange claim has occasioned much contention, and it always will as long as the people understand the great charter of nature upon which Magna Charta itself is founded, - No man can take another's property from him without his consent. This is the law of nature; and a violation of it is the same thing, whether it be done by one man who is called a king, or by five hundred of another denomination..."

-Samuel Adams
Boston Gazette
Jan. 9, 1769

"The Great Charta was discussed, agreed to, and signed in a single day...The Charter of Henry the First formed the basis of the whole, and the additions to it are for the most part formal recognitions of the judicial and administrative changes introduced by Henry the Second. But the vague expressions of the older charters were now exchanged for precise and elaborate provisions...the Great Charter marks the transition from the age of traditional rights, preserved in the nation's memory... to the age of written legislation..."

- John Richard Green, "History of the English People"

A.D. 1215

JOHN, by the grace of God, King of England, Lord of Ireland, Duke of Normandy, Aquitaine, and Count of Anjou, to his Archbishops, Bishops, Abbots, Earls, Barons, Justiciaries, Foresters...and his faithful subjects, greeting. Know ye, that we, in the presence of God, and for the salvation of our soul, and the souls of all our ancestors and heirs, and unto the honor of God and the advancement of Holy Church, and amendment of our Realm...have, in the first place, granted to God, and by this our present Charter confirmed, for us and our heirs for ever:

"That the Church of England shall be free, and have her whole rights, and her liberties...We also have granted to all the freemen of our kingdom for us and for our heirs for ever, all the underwritten liberties to be had and holden by them and their heirs, of us and our heirs for ever...

The above excerpts are from "Old South Leaflets No. 5"

"No scutage or aid shall be imposed in our kingdom, unless by the general council of our kingdom; except for ransoming our person, making our eldest son a knight, and once for marrying our eldest daughter; and for these there shall be paid no more than a reasonable aid. In like manner it shall be concerning the aids of the City of London.

"And the City of London shall have its ancient liberties and free customs, as well by land as by water: furthermore, we will and grant that all other cities and boroughs, and towns and ports, shall have all their liberties and free customs.

"And for holding the general council of the kingdom concerning the assessment of aids, except in the three cases aforesaid, and for the assessing of scutages we shall cause to be summoned the archbishops, bishops, abbots, earls, and greater barons of the realm, singly by our letters. And furthermore, we shall cause to be summoned generally, by our sheriffs and bailiffs, all others who hold us in chief, for a certain day. that is to say, forty days before their meeting at least, and to a certain place; and in all letters of such summons we will declare the cause of such summons. And summons being thus made, the business shall proceed on the day appointed, according to the advice of such as shall be present, although all that were summoned came not...

"A freeman shall not be amerced for a small offence, but only according to the degree of the offence; and for a great crime according to the heinousness of it, saving to him his contenement; and after the same manner a merchant, saving to him his merchandise. And a villein shall be amerced after the same manner, saving to him his wainage, if he falls under our mercy; and none of the aforesaid amerciaments shall be assessed but by the oath of honest men in the neighborhood.

"Earls and barons shall not be amerced but by their peers, after the degree of the offence...

"No constable or bailiff of ours shall take corn or other chattels of any man unless he presently give him money for it, or hath respite of payment by the good-will of the seller.

"No constable shall distrain any knight to give money for castle-guard, if he himself will do it in his person, or by another able man, in case he cannot do it through any reasonable cause...

The above excerpts are from "Old South Leaflets No. 5"

"No sheriff or bailiff of ours, or any other, shall take horses or carts of any freeman for carriage, without the assent of the said freeman.

"Neither shall we nor our bailiffs take any man's timber for our castles or other uses, unless by the consent of the owner of the timber...

"Nothing from henceforth shall be given or taken for a writ of inquisition of life or limb, but it shall be granted freely, and not denied...

"No freeman shall be taken or imprisoned, or disseised, or outlawed, or banished, or any ways destroyed, nor will we pass upon him, nor will we send upon him, unless by the lawful judgment of his peers, or by the law of the land.

"We will sell to no man, we will not deny to any man, either justice or right...

"If any one has been dispossessed or deprived by us, without the lawful judgment of his peers, of his lands, castles, liberties, or right, we will forthwith restore them to him; and if any dispute arise upon this head, let the matter be decided by the five-and-twenty barons hereafter mentioned, for the preservation of the peace...

"All unjust and illegal fines made by us, and all amerciaments imposed unjustly and contrary to the law of the land, shall be entirely given up, or else be left to the decision of the five-and-twenty barons hereafter mentioned for the preservation of the peace, or of the major part of them, together with the aforesaid Stephen, Archbishop of Canterbury, if he can be present, and others whom he shall think fit to invite...

"All the aforesaid customs and liberties, which we have granted to be holden in our kingdom, as much as it belongs to us, all people in our kingdom, as well clergy as laity, shall observe, as far as they are concerned, towards their dependents.

"And whereas, for the honor of God and the amendment of our kingdom, and for the better quieting the discord that has arisen between us and our barons, we have granted all these things aforesaid; willing to render them firm and lasting, we do give and grant our subjects the underwritten security, namely

The above excerpts are from "Old South Leaflets No. 5"

that the barons may choose five-and-twenty barons of the kingdom whom they think convenient, and cause to be observed, the peace and liberties we have granted them, and by this our present Charter confirmed in this manner... Given under our hand, in the presence of the witnesses above named, and many others, in the meadow called Runingmede, between Windsor and Staines, the 15th day of June, in the 17th year of our reign."

The above excerpts are from "Old South Leaflets No. 5"

ANCIENT RIGHTS OF ENGLISHMEN

The Petition of Right

ON the 5th day of June, 1628, the House of Commons presented the most extraordinary spectacle, perhaps in all its history. The famous Petition of Right had been passed by both Houses, and the royal answer had just been received. Its tone was that of gracious assent, but it omitted the necessary legal formalities, and the Commons well knew what this meant. They were to be tricked with sweet words, and the petition was not to acquire the force of a statute. How was it possible to deal with such a slippery creature? There was but one way of saving the dignity of the throne without sacrificing the liberty of the people, and that was to hold the king's ministers responsible to Parliament, in anticipation of modern methods. It was accordingly proposed to impeach the Duke of Buckingham before the House of Lords. The Speaker now 'brought an imperious message from the king, ...warning them that he would not tolerate any aspersion upon his ministers.' Nothing daunted by this, Sir John Eliot arose to lead the debate, when the Speaker called him to order in view of the king's message. 'Amid a deadly stillness' Eliot sat down and burst into tears. For a moment the House was overcome with despair. Deprived of all constitutional methods of redress, they suddenly saw yawning before them the direful alternative - slavery or civil war. Since the day of Bosworth a hundred and fifty years had passed without fighting worthy of mention on English soil, such an era of peace as had hardly ever before been seen on the earth; now half the Nation was to be pitted against the other half, families were to be divided against themselves, as in the dreadful days of the Roses, and with what consequences no one could foresee.

The above excerpts are from John Fiske's "The Beginnings of New England" - 1889

'Let us sit in silence,' quoth Sir Dudley Digges, 'we are miserable, we know not what to do!' Nay, cried Sir Nathaniel Rich, 'we must now speak, or forever hold our peace.' Then did grim Mr. Prynne and Sir Edward Coke mingle their words with sobs, while there were few dry eyes in the House. Presently they found their voices, and used them in a way that rung from the startled king his formal assent to the Petition of Right."

The above excerpts are from John Fiske's "The Beginnings of New England" - 1889

PETITION OF RIGHT

HUMBLY show unto our Sovereign Lord the King, the Lords, Spiritual and Temporal, and Commons in Parliament assembled, that whereas it is declared and enacted by a statute made in the time of the reign of King Edward the First, commonly called Statutum de tallagio non concedendo, that no tallage or aid shall be laid or levied by the King or his heirs in this realm, without the good will and assent of the Archbishops, Bishops, Earls, Barons, Knights, Burgesses, and other the freemen of the commonalty of this realm: and by authority of Parliament holden in the five and twentieth year of the reign of King Edward the Third, it is declared and enacted, that from thenceforth no person shall be compelled to make any loans to the King against his will, because such loans were against reason and the franchise of the land; and by other laws of this realm it is provided, that none should be charged by any charge or imposition, called a Benevolence, nor by such like charge: by which, the statutes before-mentioned, and other the good laws and statutes of this realm, your subjects have inherited this freedom, that they should not be compelled to contribute to any tax, tallage, aid, or other like charge, not set by common consent in Parliament....

"And where also by the statute called, 'The Great Charter of the Liberties of England,' it is declared and enacted, that no freeman

The above excerpts are from Adams and Stephens' "Select Documents of English Constitutional History" - 1901

Lawful Judgment

may be taken or imprisoned or be disseised of his freehold or liberties, or his free customs, or be outlawed or exiled, or in any manner destroyed, but by the lawful judgment of his peers, or by the law of the land.

Due process of law

"And in the eight and twentieth year of the reign of King Edward the Third, it was declared and enacted by authority of Parliament, that no man of what estate or condition that he be, should be put out of his lands or tenements, nor taken, nor imprisoned, nor disherited, nor put to death, without being brought to answer by due process of law...

No billeting without consent

"And whereas of late great companies of soldiers and mariners have been dispersed into divers counties of the realm, and the inhabitants against their wills have been compelled to receive them into their houses, and there to suffer them to sojourn, against the laws and customs of this realm, and to the great grievance and vexation of the people.

Civil law replaces martial law

"And whereas also by authority of Parliament, in the 25th year of the reign of King Edward the Third, it is declared and enacted, that no man shall be forejudged of life or limb against the form of the Great Charter, and the law of the land; and by the said Great Charter and other the laws and statutes of this your realm, no man ought to be adjudged to death, but by the laws established in this your realm, either by the customs of the same realm or by Acts of Parliament...

Rights of the people

"They do therefore humbly pray your Most Excellent Majesty, that no man hereafter be compelled to make or yield any gift, loan, benevolence, tax, or such like charge, without common consent by Act of Parliament; and that none be called to make answer, or take such oath, or to give attendance, or be confined, or otherwise molested or disquieted concerning the same, or for refusal thereof; and that no freeman, in any such manner as is before-mentioned, be imprisoned or detained; and that your Majesty will be pleased to remove the said soldiers and mariners, and that your people may not be so burdened in time to come; and that the aforesaid commissions for proceeding by martial law, may be revoked and annulled; and that hereafter no commissions of like nature may issue forth to any person or persons whatsoever, to be executed as aforesaid, lest by colour of them any of your Majesty's subjects be destroyed or put to death, contrary to the laws and franchise of the land.

"All which they most humbly pray of your Most Excellent Majesty, as their rights and liberties according to the laws and statutes of

The above excerpts are from Adams and Stephens' "Select Documents of English Constitutional History" - 1901

this realm: and that your Majesty would also vouchsafe to declare, that the awards, doings, and proceedings to the prejudice of your people, in any of the premises, shall not be drawn hereafter into consequence or example: and that your Majesty would be also graciously pleased, for the further comfort and safety of your people, to declare your royal will and pleasure, that in the things aforesaid all your officers and ministers shall serve you, according to the laws and statutes of this realm, as they tender the honour of your Majesty, and the prosperity of this kingdom."

The above excerpts are from Adams and Stephens' "Select Documents of English Constitutional History" - 1901

RIGHTS & LIBERTIES

ENGLISH BILL OF RIGHTS

Westminster, December 16, 1689

WHEREAS the lords spiritual and temporal and commons assembled at Westminster lawfully, fully and freely representing all the estates of the people of this realm, did upon the thirteenth day of February in the year of our Lord one thousand six hundred eighty-eight, present unto Their Majesties, then called and known by the names and style of William and Mary, prince and princess of Orange, being present in their proper persons, a certain declaration in writing made by the said lords and commons in the words following viz.:

"Whereas the late king James the Second by the assistance of divers evil counsellors, judges and ministers employed by him did endeavour to subvert and extirpate the Protestant religion and the laws and liberties of this kingdom.

"By assuming and exercising a power of dispensing with and suspending of laws, and the execution of laws, without consent of parliament.

The above excerpts are from Adams and Stephens' "Select Documents of English Constitutional History" - 1901

"By committing and prosecuting divers worthy prelates for humbly petitioning to be excused from concurring to the said assumed power.

"By issuing and causing to be executed a commission under the great seal for erecting a court, called the court of commissioners for ecclesiastical causes.

"By levying money for and to the use of the crown, by pretence of prerogative, for other time and in other manner than the same was granted by parliament.

"By raising and keeping a standing army within this kingdom in time of peace, without consent of parliament, and quartering of soldiers contrary to law.

"By causing several good subjects being Protestants to be disarmed, at the same time when papists were both armed and employed, contrary to law.

"By violating the freedom of election of members to serve in parliament.

"By prosecutions in the court of King's bench for matters and causes cognizable only in parliament, and by divers other arbitrary and illegal courses.

"And whereas of late years partial, corrupt and unqualified persons have been returned and served on juries in trials, and particularly divers jurors in trials for high treason, which were not freeholders.

"And excessive bail hath been required of persons committed in criminal cases, to elude the benefit of the laws made for the liberty of the subjects.

"And excessive fines have been imposed.

"And illegal and cruel punishments have been inflicted.

"And several grants and promises made of fines and forfeitures before any conviction or judgment against the persons upon whom the same were to be levied.

"All which are utterly and directly contrary to the known laws and statutes and freedom of this realm..."

The above excerpts are from Adams and Stephens' "Select Documents of English Constitutional History" - 1901

"And thereupon the said lords spiritual and temporal and commons pursuant to their respective letters and elections being now assembled in a full and free representative of this nation, taking into their most serious consideration the best means for attaining the ends aforesaid, do in the first place (as their ancestors in like case have usually done) for the vindicating and asserting their ancient rights and liberties, declare:

"That the pretended power of suspending of laws or the execution of laws by regal authority without consent of parliament is illegal.

"That the pretended power of dispensing with laws or the execution of laws by regal authority as it hath been assumed and exercised of late is illegal.

"That the commission for erecting the late court of commissioners for ecclesiastical causes and all other commissions and courts of like nature are illegal and pernicious.

"That the levying money for or to the use of the crown by pretence of prerogative without grant of parliament for a longer time or in other manner than the same is or shall be granted is illegal.

"That it is the right of the subjects to petition the king and all commitments and prosecutions for such petitioning are illegal.

"That the raising or keeping a standing army within the kingdom in time of peace unless it be with consent of parliament is against law.

"That the subjects which are Protestants may have arms for their defence suitable to their conditions and as allowed by law.

"That election of members of parliament ought to be free.

"That the freedom of speech and debates or proceedings in parliament ought not to be impeached or questioned in any court or place out of parliament.

"That excessive bail ought not to be required nor excessive fines imposed nor cruel and unusual punishments inflicted.

"That jurors ought to be duly impanelled and returned and jurors which pass upon men in trials for high treason ought to be freeholders.

The above excerpts are from Adams and Stephens' "Select Documents of English Constitutional History" - 1901

"That all grants and promises of fines and forfeitures of particular persons before conviction are illegal and void. And that for redress of all grievances and for the amending, strengthening and preserving of the laws parliaments ought to be held frequently. And they do claim, demand and insist upon all and singular the premises as their undoubted rights and liberties and that no declarations, judgments, doings or proceedings to the prejudice of the people in any of the said premises ought in any wise to be drawn hereafter into consequence or example."...

The above excerpts are from Adams and Stephens' "Select Documents of English Constitutional History" - 1901

FROM ENGLAND TO NEW ENGLAND

Influence of Wickliffe, Luther and Calvin

Wickliffe

DOMINION', said Wickliffe, 'belongs to grace'; meaning, as I believe, that the feudal government, which rests on the sword, should yield to a government resting on moral principles. And he knew the right method to hasten the coming revolution. 'Truth', he asserted with wisest benevolence, 'truth shines more brightly the more widely it is diffused'; and, catching the plebeian language that lived on the lips of the multitude, her intellectual freedom, she acknowledges the benefactions of Wickliffe. Who will venture to measure the consequences of actions by the apparent humility or the remoteness of their origin? The mysterious influence of that Power which enchains the destinies of states, overruling the decisions of sovereigns and the forethought of statesmen, often deduces the greatest events from the least commanding causes. A Genoese adventurer, discovering America, changed the commerce of the world; an obscure German, inventing the printing-press, rendered possible the universal diffusion of increased intelligence; an Augustine monk, denouncing indulgences, introduced a schism in religion, and changed the foundations of European politics; a young French refugee, skilled alike in theology and civil law, in the duties of magistrates and the dialectics of religion controversy, entering the republic of Geneva, and conforming its ecclesiastical discipline to the principles of republican simplicity, established a party, of which Englishmen became members, and New England the asylum."

Luther and Calvin

The above excerpts are from George Bancroft's "History of the United States" - 1850

PURITAN POLITICS 1600 to 1640

The Puritan a Scripturist

THE Puritan was a Scripturist, - a Scripturist with all his heart, if, as yet, with imperfect intelligence... He cherished the scheme of looking to the word of God as his sole and universal directory.

The Puritan a literal interpreter

"The word had been but lately made the common property by the Reformation. The preparation for interpreting it possessed by the best scholars of the day was inadequate, and the judicious application of such learning as existed was disturbed by the rashness of enthusiasm and novelty. The Puritan searched the Bible, not only for principles and rules, but for mandates, - and, when he could find none of these, for analogies, - to guide him in precise arrangements of public administration, and in the minutest points of individual conduct. By it he settled cases of conscience, and in this casuistry his learning and ingenuity were largely employed. His objections to the government of the Church by bishops were founded, not so much on any bad working of that policy, as on the defect of authority for it in the New Testament; and he preferred his plain hierarchy of pastors, teachers, elders, and deacons, not primarily because it tended more to edification, but because Paul had specified their offices by name. He took the Scriptures as a homogeneous and rounded whole, and scarcely distinguished between the authority of Moses and the authority of Christ. The position of violent antagonism, into which he was brought by passing circumstances, led him to resort for guidance even more readily to the Old Testament than to the New. The Opposing party in the State was associated in his mind with the Philistine and Amorite foes of the ancient chosen people; and he read the doom of the king and his wanton courtiers in the Psalm which put the 'high praises of God' in the mouth of God's people, 'and a two-edged sword in their hand, to bind their kings with chains and their nobles with fetters of iron.' His theory of municipal law aimed at the emendation of the traditional system of his country by an adoption of provisions promulgated to a people of peculiar position and destiny, in a distant age and land; he would have witchcraft, Sabbath-breaking, and filial disobedience weighed in the judicial scales of a Hebrew Sanhedrim. His forms of speech were influenced

Valued Old Testament

The above excerpts are from John Palfrey's "History of New England" - 1859

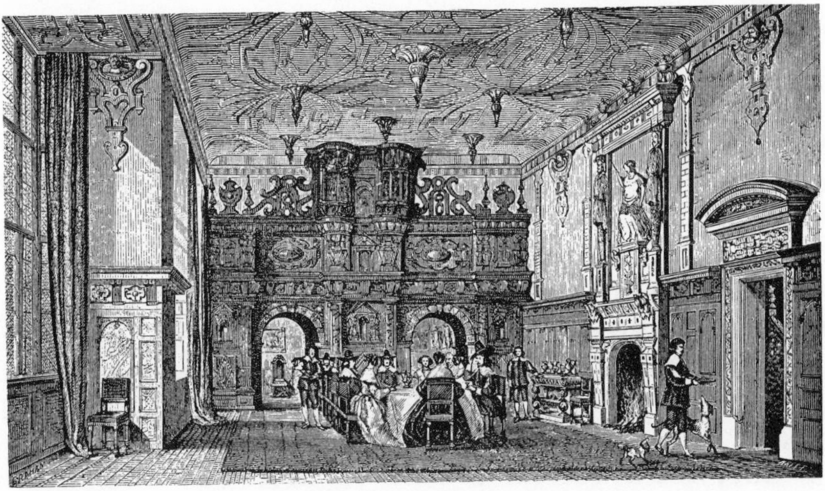

Puritan Manor-House in England

Reverence for the Bible

The Puritan a moralist

Political and social corruption in England

by this fond reverence for the Bible. The history of the Israelitish tribes was his favorite storehouse for topics of argument and eloquence, and he named his children after the Christian graces, still oftener after the worthies of Palastine...The Puritan was a strict Moralist. He might be ridiculed for being over-scrupulous, but never reproached for laxity. Most wisely, by precept, influence, and example, - unwisely by too severe law, when he obtained the power, - he endeavored to repress prevailing vice, and organize a Christian people. When he insisted on a hearing, villainous men and shameless women, whose abominations were a foul offence in the sight of God, and of all who revered God, were flaunting in the royal drawing-rooms. The foundations of public honor and prosperity were sapped...Writers who assailed his religious position, at the same time echoed his complaints of the prevailing immorality. 'The court of this king (James I) was a nursery of lust and intemperance... To keep the people in their deplorable security, till vengeance overtook them, they were entertained with masks, stage-plays, and all sorts of ruder sports. Then began murder, incest, adultery, drunkenness, swearing, fornication, and all sort of ribaldry, to be not concealed, but countenanced vices, because they held such conformity with the court example.' The Puritan's mistake at a later period was, that he undertook by public regulation what public regulation can never achieve, and, by aiming to form a nation of saints, introduced hypocrites among them to defeat their objects and bring scandal on their cause, while the saints were made no more numerous and no better. But, at the time to which the preceding narrative relates, nothing in his course was apparent but the eminently upright and Christian purpose. What there was of a practical indiscretion and error, was to be made manifest in the experiment of a later period.

The above excerpts are from John Palfrey's "History of New England" - 1859

"In politics, the Puritan was the Liberal of his day.

Liberal of his day

"If he construed his duties to God in the spirit of a narrow interpretation, that punctilious sense of religious responsibility impelled him to limit the assumptions of human government. In no stress, in no delirium, of politics, could a Puritan have been brought to teach, that, for either public or private conduct, there is some law of man above the law of God. Penetrated with the opposite conviction, he found himself enforced, at last, to overset the Stuart throne. Service which he believed the authority of God to claim, he saw himself forbidden by human authority to pay. That issue, presented to him, made him in politics a casuist, an innovator, the architect of a new system. From the time when the problem, with which for a while he struggled, was worked out, governments over the British race were to rest on the public consent, and to be administered for the public benefit. Such was the brightness of the light to which he made his way through many scenes of darkness.

Puritan habits and manners

"When, after the restoration of the Stuart line, an unbridled licentiousness of manners had succeeded to his austerity, - when an ornate beastliness was the fashion of the men and women in high places, and such writers as Wycherley and Mrs. Behn expressed and formed the morals of so many clamorers for Lord Clarendon's creed, - the ribald wits of the time so grossly marred the record of the Puritan, that it is difficult even for those who sympathize with his views in religion and politics to recover a just conception of his dignified and manly character, as it existed in the days which must be referred to for a true delineation. Nor has this been wholly the result of injustice on the part of writers depicting what they wanted the moral capacity to estimate with justness. The character had itself degenerated, in reaching the time when it came under their observation.

Popularity brought decline

"Puritanism, from the outbreat of the Great Rebellion, was subjected to the infelicities and abuses which necessarily attend a formidable and successful party. When it clothed itself with the associations of power and grandeur, vulgar men, without being sordid or ambitious, followed its modes, and by their vulgarity exaggerated and degraded them. When it came to have honors and fortunes to bestow, base men attached themselves to it for the promotion of their base ends; and the excesses of the dishonest pretender brought into discredit and ridicule the practices of the sincere devotee."

First 40 years most representative of Puritan in England

The above excerpts are from John Palfrey's "History of New England" - 1859

LOCKE

"OF CIVIL-GOVERNMENT"

SIDNEY

"DISCOURSES CONCERNING GOVERNMENT"

"The mischievous doctrines of Rousseau had found few readers and fewer admirers among the Americans. The Principles upon which their Revolution was conducted were those of Sidney and Locke."

- John Fiske

"THE PERIOD, COUNTRYMEN, IS ALREADY COME... This day we are called upon to give a glorious example of what the wisest and best of men were rejoiced to view, only in speculation... Immortal spirits of Hampden, Locke and Sidney! will it not add to your benevolent joys to behold your posterity rising to the dignity of men, and evincing to the world the reality and expediency of your systems..."

- Samuel Adams, August 1, 1776

"It is certainly very material that the true doctrines of liberty, as exemplified in our political systems, should be inculcated on those who are to sustain and may administer it... Sidney and Locke are admirably calculated to impress on young minds the right of nations to establish their own governments, and to inspire a love of free ones..."

- James Madison to Thomas Jefferson, 1825

THE

WORKS

OF

JOHN LOCKE Esq;

In Three Volumes.

The CONTENTS of which follow in the next Leaf.

With ALPHABETICAL TABLES.

VOL. I.

LONDON,

Printed for JOHN CHURCHILL at the Black Swan in *Pater-noster-Row*, and SAM. MANSHIP at the Ship in *Cornhil.* M.DCC.XIV.

TITLE PAGE of the 1714 edition, from which all the works of Locke reproduced in this volume are taken.

First forty years most representative of Puritan in England

"But, whatever may have taken place later, the Puritanism of the first forty years of the seventeenth century was not tainted with degrading or ungraceful associations of any sort. The rank, the wealth, the chivalry, the genius, the learning, the accomplishments, the social refinements and elegance of the time, were largely represented in its ranks."

The above excerpts are from John Palfrey's "History of New England" - 1859

Reverse of a French Medal of Locke.

"'Where law ends,' says Mr. Locke, 'tyranny begins, if the law be transgressed to another's harm.'"

Samuel Adams,
Boston Gazette - 1768

Locke's Influence

Philosopher of the American Revolution

Locke, in particular, was the authority to whom the Patriots paid greatest deference. He was the most famous of seventeenth century democratic theorists, and his ideas had their due weight with the colonists. Almost every writer seems to have been influenced by him, many quoted his words, and the argument of others shows the unmistakable imprint of his philosophy. The first great speech of Otis was wholly based upon Locke's ideas; Samuel Adams, on the 'Rights of the Colonists as Men and as British Subjects', followed the same model. Many of the phrases of the Declaration of Independence may be found in Locke's Treatise; there is hardly any important writer of this time who does not openly refer to Locke, or tacitly follow the lead he had taken. The argument in regard to the limitations upon Parliament was taken from Locke's reflections on the 'supreme legislature' and the necessary restrictions upon its authority. No one stated more strongly than did he the basis for the doctrine that 'taxation without representation is tyranny'. No better epitome of the Revolutionary theory could be found than in John Locke on civil government."

The above excerpt is from C. Edward Merriam's "A History of American Political Theories" - 1903

"...JOHN LOCKE was the son of John Locke of Pensford in Somersetshire. He was born at Wrington, seven or eight miles from Bristol, and, according to the parish-register, baptized the 29th of August, 1632...Our author began his studies in Westminster school, where he continued till the year 1651; and from thence was sent to Christ-Church college in Oxford. He took the degree of Bachelor of Arts in 1655, and that of Master in 1658. But though he made this progress in the usual course of studies at that time, yet he often said, that what he had learned there was of little use to him, to enlighten and enlarge his mind.

The above excerpts are from "An Essay Concerning Human Understanding", Second American Edition, Brattleboro, Vt., 1806

"While he was at Oxford in 1666, he became acquainted with the Lord Ashley, afterwards Earl of Shaftsbury....He urged him to apply himself to the study of political and religious matters; in which Mr. Locke made so great a progress that Lord Ashley began to consult him upon all occasions....

"In 1668, our author attended the Earl and Countess of Northumberland into France....Mr. Locke, upon his return to his native country, lived, as before, at the Lord Ashley's who was then Chancellor of the Exchequer; but made frequent visits to Oxford, for consulting books in the prosecution of his studies....While he was at the Lord Ashley's, he inspected the education of that Lord's only son, who was then about sixteen years of age....In 1670 and the year following, our author began to form a plan of his 'Essay on Human Understanding,' at the earnest request of Mr. Tyrrell, Dr. Thomas, and some other friends, who met frequently in his chamber to converse together on philosophical subjects; but his employments and avocations prevented him from finishing it then. About this time, it is supposed, he was made a fellow of the Royal Society. In 1672, his great patron, Lord Ashley, was created Earl of Shaftesbury, and Lord High Chancellor of England, who appointed him Secretary of the Presentation of Benefices; which place he held till the end of the year 1673, when his Lordship resigned the Great Seal. Mr. Locke, to whom the Earl had communicated his most secret affairs, was disgraced together with him; and assisted the Earl in publishing some treatises, which were designed to excite the people to watch the conduct....and to oppose the arbitrary designs of the Court.

"In 1675, he travelled into France, on account of his health. At Montpelier he stayed a considerable time; and there his first acquaintance arose with Mr. Herbert, afterwards Earl of Pembroke, to whom he dedicated his Essay on Human Understanding....From Montpelier he went to Paris, where he contracted a friendship with Mr. Justel, whose house was at that time the place of resort for men of letters; and there he saw M. Guenolon, the famous physician of Amsterdam, who read lectures in anatomy with great applause. He became acquainted likewise with Mr. Soignard, who showed him a copy of his 'Harmonia Evangelica,' which gave great pleasure to Mr. Locke, as he had a high value for the scriptures. The Earl of Shaftesbury being restored to favour at Court, and made President at the Council in 1679, thought proper to send for Mr. Locke to London, but that Nobleman did not continue long

Locke held a high value for the Scriptures

The above excerpts are from "An Essay Concerning Human Understanding", Second American Edition, Brattleboro, Vt., 1806

in his post; for refusing to comply with the designs of the Court, ...fresh crimes were laid to his charge, and he was sent to the Tower; when the Earl obtained his discharge from that place, he retired to Holland; and Mr. Locke, not thinking himself safe in England, followed his Noble patron thither, who died soon after. During our author's stay in Holland, he renewed his acquaintance with M. Guenelon, who introduced him to many learned persons of Amsterdam. Here Mr. Locke contracted a friendship with Mr. Limborch, professor of divinity among the remonstrants, and the most learned Mr. Le Clerc, which he cultivated after his return to England, and continued to the end of his life. During his residence in Holland, he was accused at Court of having written certain tracts against the government, which were afterwards discovered to be written by another person; and upon that suspicion he was deprived of his place of student of Christ Church.

William Penn friend of John Locke

"After the death of King Charles II. Mr. William Penn, who had known our author at the University, used his interest with King James to procure a pardon for him; and would have obtained it, if Mr. Locke had not answered that he had no occasion for a pardon, since he had not been guilty of any crime. In the year 1685, when the Duke of Monmouth and his party were making preparations in Holland for his unfortunate enterprise, the English Envoy at the Hague had orders to demand Mr. Locke and eighty-three other persons to be delivered up to the States General, upon which he lay concealed to the year following. During this confinement, our author wrote his letter of Toleration, which was first published in Latin....This letter he afterwards translated into English, and published at London in the year 1690. At Amsterdam he formed a weekly assembly, consisting of Mr. Limborch, Mr. Le Clerc, and others, for conversation upon important subjects; but these conferences were much interrupted, by the frequent changes he was forced to make of the places of his residence. Our author's great work, the 'Essay concerning Human Understanding,' he had been employed about for some years, and he finished it in Holland about the end of the year 1687. He made an abridgment of it himself, which his friend Mr. Le Clerc translated into French, and inserted in one of his 'Bibliothiques.' This abridgment was so highly approved of by all persons of understanding, and sincere lovers of truth, that they expressed the strongest desire to see the whole work.

"Letter of Toleration" published in 1690

"At length the happy Revolution of 1688, by the courage and good conduct of the Prince of Orange, opened a way for Mr. Locke's

The above excerpts are from "An Essay Concerning Human Understanding", Second American Edition, Brattleboro, Vt., 1806

Locke returns from exile

return to his own country, whither he came in the fleet which conveyed the Princess of Orange: and, upon the restoration of public liberty, he thought it proper to assert his own private rights. He endeavoured, therefore, to procure his restoration to his place of student of Christ Church; not that he designed to return thither, but only that it might appear from thence that he had been unjustly deprived of it. But when he found that the College could not be prevailed on to dispossess the person who had been elected in his room, and that they would only admit him as a supernumerary student, he desisted from his claim. He was now at full liberty to pursue his speculations; and accordingly, in the year 1689, he published his 'Essay on Human Understanding.' This work, which has made our Author's name immortal, and which does honour to our country, gave great offence to many people at the first publication. It was proposed, at a meeting of the heads of houses of the University of Oxford, to censure and discourage the reading of it; and after various debates, among themselves, it was concluded that each head of an house should endeavour to prevent its being read in his college. The reason of this is obvious; Mr. Locke had let in more light upon the minds of men than was consistent with the dark designs of some persons. In the same year, Mr. Locke also published his 'Two Treatises on Government,' in which he fully vindicated the principles upon which 'the Revolution' was founded, and entirely overturned all the doctrines of slavery...

"Essay on Human Understanding" published in 1689

Oxford University suppresses Locke's ideas

"Two Treatises on Government" published

"About this time the public coin was very bad, having been so much clipped, and no care used to remedy it, that it wanted about a third of its due value. The effect of this was, that the people thought themselves a great deal richer than indeed they were; for though the coin was yet raised in its value by public authority, it was put off in trade for above a third part more than it weighed. Mr. Locke had observed this disorder ever since his return to England, and he frequently spoke of it, that some measures might be taken to prevent it. He said, 'that the nation was in greater danger from a secret, unobserved abuse, than from all those other evils, of which persons were generally so apprehensive; and that if care was not taken to rectify the coin, that irregularity alone would prove fatal to us, ...' To assist the great men at the head of affairs...to form a right understanding of this matter, and to excite them to rectify this shameful abuse, Mr. Locke published a little treatise, entitled, 'Some Considerations of the Consequences of the lowering of the Interest and raising the Value of Money;' ... He fully showed to the world by these discourses, that he was as able to reason on trade and business as on the most abstract points

Locke observed: "danger from a secret unobserved abuse"

The above excerpts are from "An Essay Concerning Human Understanding", Second American Edition, Brattleboro, Vt., 1806

1698: Thoughts Concerning the Education of Children

of science, and that he was none of those philosophers who spent their lives in search of truths merely speculative, and who, by their ignorance of those things which concern the public good, are incapable of serving their country...In 1693 he published his 'Thoughts concerning the Education of Children;' but he improved it considerably afterwards. In 1695 Mr. Locke published his treatise of 'the Reasonableness of Christianity,' in which he has proved that the Christian Religion, as delivered in the scriptures, and free from all corrupt mixtures, is the most reasonable institution in the world...The last fourteen or fifteen years of his life Mr. Locke spent chiefly at Oates, seldom coming to town; and, during this agreeable retirement, he applied himself to the study of the scriptures...He admired the wisdom and goodness of God in the method found out for the salvation of mankind: and when he thought upon it, he could not forbear crying out, 'O the depth of the riches of the goodness and knowledge of God.' He was persuaded that men would be convinced of this, by reading the scriptures without prejudice; and he frequently exhorted those with whom he conversed to a serious study of these sacred writings. His own application to this study had given him a more noble and elevated idea of the Christian religion...He...expired on October the 28th, 1704, in the 73d year of his age. Thus died this great and most excellent philosopher, who, after he had bestowed many years in matters of science and speculation, happily turned his thoughts to the study of the scriptures, which he carefully examined with the same liberty he had used in his study of the other sciences; and it is needless to say, how much the Christian world is indebted to him for his paraphrase and comments on some of the epistles which were published after his death...He looked on civility not only as a duty of humanity, but of Christianity; and he thought that it ought to be more pressed and urged upon men than it commonly is...

The Reasonableness of Christianity

Locke studied the Scriptures

Held elevated idea of the Christian religion

Locke disliked those who labor only to destroy

"He disliked those authors who labour only to destroy, without establishing any thing themselves. 'A building,' said he, displeases them. They find great fault in it, let them demolish it, and welcome, if they will, but endeavour to raise another in its place.'...

Locke paraphrases St. Paul's Epistles

"He left several manuscripts behind him, besides his paraphrase on some of St. Paul's epistles, which were published at different times, and are all now added to the collection of his works by M. Desmaizeaux, from whence this account of his life, and this edition of his Essay concerning Human Understanding, and his Thoughts on the Conduct of the Understanding are taken."

The above excerpts are from "An Essay Concerning Human Understanding", Second American Edition, Brattleboro, Vt., 1806

TO THE

READER.

THOU *hast here a* Compleat Collection *of the several Works of Mr.* JOHN LOCKE, *which were publish'd in his Life-time, either with or without his Name to them. And that thou may'st be assur'd that the Latter are truly his, I think it proper to transcribe the following* Clause *out of his last Will and Testament:* " *Whereas the Reverend* " *Dr.* Hudson, *Library-Keeper of the* Bodleian *Li-* " *brary in the University of* Oxford, *writ to me some* " *time since, desiring of me, for the said Library, the* " *Books whereof I was the Author; I did, in return* " *to the honour done me therein, present to the said Li-* " *brary all the Books that were publish'd under my* " *Name; which tho accepted with honourable men-* " *tion of me, yet were not understood to answer the Re-* " *quest made me, it being suppos'd that there were other* " *Treatises whereof I was the Author, which have* " *been publish'd without my Name to them. In compli-* " *ance therefore with what was desir'd in the utmost* " *Extent of it, and in acknowledgment of the Honour* " *done me, in thinking my Writings worthy to be pla-* " *ced among the Works of the Learned in that August* " *Repository; I do hereby further give to the Publick*

[a] " *Library*

The above "To The Reader" is a photostat reproduction taken from the "The Works of John Locke", 1714 edition

To the READER.

"*Library of the Univerſity of* Oxford, *theſe follow-*
"*ing Books ; that is to ſay :* Three Letters concern-
" ing Toleration : Two Treatiſes of Government,
" (*whereof Mr.* Churchill *has publiſh'd ſeveral*
" *Editions, but all very incorrect*) The Reaſonable-
" neſs of Chriſtianity, as deliver'd in the Scrip-
" tures. A Vindication of the Reaſonableneſs of
" Chriſtianity from Mr. *Edwards's* Reflections :
" *And*, A Second Vindication of the Reaſonable-
" neſs of Chriſtianity. *Theſe are all the Books,*
" *whereof I am the Author, which have been pub-*
" *liſh'd without my Name to them.*"

To theſe Books publiſh'd by Mr. LOCKE *in his Life-time, are added theſe following, which have been printed ſince his Death,* viz. *his* Paraphraſe on St. *Paul's* Epiſtles to the *Galatians, Corinthians, Romans,* and *Epheſians : To which is prefix'd,* An Eſſay for the Underſtanding of St. *Paul's* Epiſtles, by conſulting St. *Paul* himſelf. *His* Poſthumous Works : *and* Some familiar Letters between him and his Friends.

As to this Edition of all his Works together, I have this to advertiſe the Reader, that moſt of them are printed from Copies corrected and enlarg'd under Mr. LOCKE'*s own Hand ; and in particular, that the* Two Treatiſes of Government *were never till now, publiſh'd from a Copy corrected by himſelf.*

The above "To The Reader" is a photostat reproduction taken from the "The Works of John Locke", 1714 edition

OF CIVIL-GOVERNMENT.

BOOK II.

CHAP. I.

1. IT having been ſhewn in the foregoing Diſcourſe.

1. That *Adam* had not either by natural Right of Fatherhood, or by poſitive Donation from God, any ſuch Authority over his Children, or Dominion over the World as is pretended.

2. That if he had, his Heirs, yet, had no Right to it.

3. That if his Heirs had, there being no Law of Nature nor poſitive Law of God that determins, which is the Right Heir in all Caſes that may ariſe, the Right of Succeſſion, and conſequently of bearing Rule, could not have been certainly determined.

4. That if even that had been determined, yet the knowledge of which is the eldeſt Line of *Adam*'s Poſterity, being ſo long ſince utterly loſt, that in the Races of Mankind and Families of the World, there remains not to one above another, the leaſt pretence to be the eldeſt Houſe, and to have the Right of Inheritance.

All theſe premiſes having, as I think, been clearly made out, it is impoſſible that the Rulers now on Earth, ſhould make any benefit, or derive any the leaſt ſhadow of Authority from that, which is held to be the Fountain of all Power, *Adam*'s *private Dominion and paternal Juriſdiction*; ſo that, he that will not give juſt occaſion, to think, that all Government in the World is the product only of Force and Violence, and that Men live together by no other Rules but that of Beaſts, where the ſtrongeſt carries it; and ſo lay a Foundation for perpetual Diſorder and Miſchief, Tumult, Sedition and Rebellion, (things that the followers of that Hypotheſis ſo loudly cry out againſt) muſt of neceſſity find out another riſe of Government, another original of Political Power, and another way of deſigning and knowing the Perſons that have it, than what Sir *Robert F.* hath taught us.

2. To this purpoſe, I think it may not be amiſs, to ſet down what I take to be political Power. That the Power of a *Magiſtrate* over a Subject, may be diſtinguiſhed from that of a *Father* over his Children, a *Maſter* over his Servant, a *Husband* over his Wife, and a *Lord* over his Slave. All which diſtinct Powers happening ſometimes together in the ſame Man, if he be conſidered under theſe different Relations, it may help us to diſtinguiſh theſe Powers one from another, and ſhew the difference betwixt a Ruler of a Common-wealth, a Father of a Family, and a Captain of a Galley.

3. *Political Power*, then I take to be a *Right* of making Laws with Penalties of Death, and conſequently all leſs Penalties, for the Regulating and Preſerving of Property, and of employing the force of the Community, in the Execution of ſuch Laws, and in the defence of the Common-wealth from foreign Injury, and all this only for the publick Good.

CHAP.

CHAP. X.

Of the State of Nature.

4. TO underſtand political Power, right, and derive it from its Original, we muſt conſider, what State all Men are naturally in, and that is, a *State of perfect Freedom* to order their Actions, and diſpoſe of their Poſſeſſions, and Perſons as they think fit, within the bounds of the Law of Nature, without asking leave, or depending upon the Will of any other Man.

A *State* alſo *of Equality*, wherein all the Power and Juriſdiction is Reciprocal, no one having more than another; there being nothing more evident, than that Creatures of the ſame ſpecies and rank, promiſcuouſly born to all the ſame advantages of Nature, and the uſe of the ſame Faculties, ſhould alſo be equal one amongſt another without Subordination or Subjection, unleſs the Lord and Maſter of them all, ſhould by any manifeſt Declaration of his Will ſet one above another, and confer on him, by an evident and clear Appointment, an undoubted Right to Dominion and Sovereignty.

5. This *equality* of Men by Nature, the Judicious *Hooker* looks upon as ſo evident in it ſelf, and beyond all queſtion, that he makes it the Foundation of that Obligation to mutual Love amongſt Men, on which he builds the duties they owe one another, and from whence he derives the great Maxims *of Juſtice* and *Charity*. His words are.

The like natural inducement, hath brought Men to know that it is no leſs their Duty, to Love others than themſelves, for ſeeing thoſe things which are equal, muſt needs all have one Meaſure; if I cannot but wiſh to receive good, even as much at every Mans hands, as any Man can wiſh unto his own Soul, how ſhould I look to have any part of my deſire herein ſatisfied, unleſs my ſelf be careful to ſatisfie the like deſire, which is undoubtedly in other Men, being of one and the ſame Nature; to have any thing offered them repugnant to this deſire, muſt needs in all reſpects grieve them as much as me, ſo that if I do harm, I muſt look to ſuffer, there being no reaſon that others ſhould ſhew greater meaſure of love to me, than they have by me, ſhewed unto them; my deſire therefore to be lov'd of my equals in Nature, as much as poſſible may be, impoſeth upon me a natural Duty of bearing to them-ward, fully the like Affection; from which relation of equality between our ſelves and them that are as our ſelves, what ſeveral Rules and Canons, natural reaſon hath drawn, for direction of Life, no Man is Ignorant. Eccl. Pol. Li. 1.

6. But though this be *a State of Liberty*, yet *it is not a State of Licence*; though Man in that State have an uncontrolable Liberty, to diſpoſe of his Perſon or Poſſeſſions, yet he has not Liberty to deſtroy himſelf, or ſo much as any Creature in his Poſſeſſion, but where ſome nobler Uſe, than its bare Preſervation calls for it. The *State of Nature* has a Law of Nature to govern it, which obliges every one: And Reaſon, which is that Law, teaches all Mankind, who will but conſult it, that being all *equal and independent*, no one ought to harm another in his Life, Health, Liberty, or Poſſeſſions. For Men being all the Workmanſhip of one Omnipotent, and infinitely wiſe Maker: All the Servants of one Sovereign Maſter, ſent into the World by his Order, and about his Buſineſs, they are his Property, whoſe Workmanſhip they are, made to laſt during his, not one anothers Pleaſure: And being furniſhed with like Faculties, ſharing all in one Community of Nature, there cannot be ſuppoſed any ſuch *Subordination* among us, that may authorize us to deſtroy one another, as if we were made for one another's Uſes, as the inferior ranks of Creatures are for ours. Every one as he is *bound to preſerve himſelf*, and not to quit his Station wilfully, ſo by the like reaſon, when his own Preſervation comes not in Competition, ought he, as much as he can, *to preſerve the reſt of Mankind*, and may not unleſs it be to do Juſtice on an Offender, take away, or impair the Life, or what tends to the Preſervation of the Life, the Liberty, Health, Limb, or Goods of another.

7. And that all Men may be reſtrained from invading others Rights, and from doing hurt to one another, and the Law of Nature be obſerved, which willeth the Peace and *Preſervation of all Mankind*, the *Execution* of the Law of Nature is in that State, put into every Man's Hands, whereby every one has a Right to puniſh the Trangreſſors of that Law to ſuch a Degree, as may hinder its Violation.

tion. For the *Law of Nature* would, as all other Laws, that concern Men in this World, be in vain, if there were no Body that in the State of Nature, had a *Power to execute* that Law, and thereby preſerve the Innocent and reſtrain Offenders. And if any one in the State of Nature may puniſh another, for any evil he has done, every one may do ſo. For in that *State of perfect Equality*, where naturally there is no Superiority or Juriſdiction of one, over another, what any may do in Proſecution of that Law, every one muſt needs have a Right to do.

8. And thus in the State of Nature, *one Man comes by a Power over another*; but yet no abſolute or arbitrary Power, to uſe a Criminal, when he has got him in his Hands, according to the paſſionate Heats, or boundleſs Extravagancy of his own Will; but only to retribute to him, ſo far, as calm Reaſon and Conſcience dictate what is proportionate to his Tranſgreſſion, which is ſo much as may ſerve for *Reparation* and *Reſtraint*. For theſe two are the only Reaſons, why one Man may lawfully do harm to another, which is that we call *Puniſhment*. In tranſgreſſing the Law of Nature, the Offender declares himſelf to live by another Rule, than that of common Reaſon and Equity, which is that meaſure God has ſet to the actions of Men, for their mutual Security; and ſo he becomes dangerous to Mankind, the Tye, which is to ſecure them from Injury and Violence, being ſlighted and broken by him. Which being a treſpaſs againſt the whole Species, and the Peace and Safety of it, provided for by the Law of Nature, every Man upon this Score, by the Right he hath to preſerve Mankind in general, may reſtrain, or where it is neceſſary, deſtroy things noxious to them, and ſo may bring ſuch evil on any one, who hath tranſgreſſed that Law, as may make him repent the doing of it, and thereby deter him, and, by his Example others, from doing the like Miſchief. And in this Caſe, and upon this Ground, *every Man hath a Right to puniſh the Offender, and be Executioner of the Law of Nature.*

9. I doubt not but this will ſeem a very ſtrange Doctrine to ſome Men: But before they condemn it, I deſire them to reſolve me, by what Right any Prince or State can put to death, or *puniſh an Alien*, for any Crime he commits in their Country. 'Tis certain their Laws by virtue of any Sanction, they receive from the promulgated Will of the Legiſlative, reach not a Stranger: They ſpeak not to him, nor, if they did, is he bound to hearken to them. The legiſlative Authority, by which they are in Force over the Subjects of that Common-wealth, hath no Power over him. Thoſe who have the ſupream Power of making Laws in *England*, *France* or *Holland*, are to an *Indian*, but like the reſt of the World, Men without Authority: And therefore, if by the Law of Nature, every Man hath not a Power to puniſh Offences againſt it, as he ſoberly Judges the Caſe to require, I ſee not how the Magiſtrates of any Community, can *puniſh an Alien* of another Country; ſince in Reference to him, they can have no more Power, than what every Man naturally may have over another.

10. Beſides the Crime which conſiſts in violating the Law, and varying from the right Rule of Reaſon, whereby a Man ſo far becomes degenerate, and declares himſelf to quit the Principles of human Nature, and to be a noxious Creature, there is commonly *Injury* done, ſome Perſon or other, ſome other Man receives Damage by his Tranſgreſſion, in which Caſe he who hath received any Damage, has beſides the right of Puniſhment common to him with other Men, a particular Right to ſeek *Reparation* from him that has done it. And any other Perſon who finds it juſt, may alſo joyn with him that is injur'd, and aſſiſt him in recovering from the Offender, ſo much as may make ſatisfaction for the Harm he has ſuffered.

11. From theſe *two diſtinct Rights*, the one of *puniſhing* the Crime *for reſtraint*, and preventing the like Offence, which right of puniſhing is in every Body; the other of taking *Reparation*, which belongs only to the injured Party, comes it to paſs, that the Magiſtrate, who by being Magiſtrate, hath the common Right of puniſhing put into his Hands, can often, where the publick good demands not the Execution of the Law, *remit* the Puniſhment of criminal Offences by his own Authority, but yet cannot *remit* the Satisfaction due to any private Man, for the Damage he has received. That, he who has ſuffered the Damage has a Right to demand in his own Name, and he alone can remit: The damnified Perſon has this Power of appropriating to himſelf, the Goods or Service of the Offender, *by Right of ſelf-Preſervation*, as every Man has a Power to puniſh the Crime, to prevent its being committed again, *by the Right he has of Preſerving all Mankind*,

and doing all reaſonable things, he can, in order to that end: And thus it is, that every Man in the State of Nature, has a Power to kill a Murderer, both *to deter* others from doing the like Injury, which no Reparation can compenſate, by the Example of the Puniſhment that attends it from every body, and alſo to ſecure Men from the attempts of a Criminal, who having renounced Reaſon, the common Rule and Meaſure, God hath given to Mankind, hath by the unjuſt Violence and Slaughter he hath committed upon one, declared War againſt all Mankind, and therefore may be deſtroyed as a *Lyon* or a *Tyger*, one of thoſe wild ſavage Beaſts, with whom Men can have no Society nor Security: And upon this is grounded that great Law of Nature, *whoſo ſheddeth Man's Blood, by Man ſhall his Blood be ſhed.* And *Cain* was ſo fully convinced, that every one had a Right to deſtroy ſuch a Criminal, that after the Murther of his Brother, he cries out, *Every one that findeth me, ſhall ſlay me*; ſo plain was it writ in the Hearts of all Mankind.

12. By the ſame reaſon, may a Man in the State of Nature *puniſh the leſſer Breaches* of that Law. It will perhaps be demanded with Death? I anſwer, each Tranſgreſſion may be *puniſhed* to that *Degree*, and with ſo much *Severity*, as will ſuffice to make it an ill Bargain to the Offender, give him Cauſe to repent, and terrifie others from doing the like. Every Offence that can be committed in the State of Nature, may in the State of Nature be alſo puniſhed equally, and as far forth as it may, in a Commonwealth. For though it would be beſides my preſent Purpoſe, to enter here into the particulars of the Law of Nature, or its *meaſures of Puniſhment*; yet, it is certain there is ſuch a Law, and that too, as intelligible and plain to a rational Creature, and a Studier of that Law, as the poſitive Laws of Commonwealths; nay poſſibly plainer; as much as Reaſon is eaſier to be underſtood, than the Phanſies and intricate Contrivances of Men, following contrary and hidden Intereſts put into Words; for ſo truly are a great part of the *municipal Laws* of Countries, which are only ſo far right, as they are founded on the Law of Nature, by which they are to be regulated and interpreted.

13. To this ſtrange Doctrine, *viz.* That *in the State of Nature, every one has the Executive Power* of the Law of Nature, I doubt not but it will be objected, that it is unreaſonable for Men to be Judges in their own Caſes, that ſelf-love will make Men partial to themſelves and their Friends: And on the other ſide, that ill Nature, Paſſion and Revenge will carry them too far in puniſhing others; and hence nothing but Confuſion and Diſorder will follow, and that therefore God hath certainly apointed Government to reſtrain the partiality and violence of Men. I eaſily grant, that *Civil Government* is the proper Remedy for the Inconveniencies of the ſtate of Nature, which muſt certainly be great, where Men may be Judges in their own Caſe, ſince 'tis eaſie to be imagined, that he who was ſo unjuſt as to do his Brother an Injury, will ſcarce be ſo juſt as to condemn himſelf for it: But I ſhall deſire thoſe who make this Objection, to remember, that *abſolute Monarchs* are but Men, and if Government is to be the Remedy of thoſe Evils, which neceſſarily follow from Mens being Judges in their own Caſes, and the State of Nature is therefore not to be endured, I deſire to know what kind of Government that is, and how much better it is than the State of Nature, where one Man commanding a Multitude, has the Liberty to be Judge in his own Caſe, and may do to all his Subjects whatever he pleaſes, without the leaſt queſtion or controle of thoſe who execute his Pleaſure? And in whatſoever he doth, whether led by Reaſon, Miſtake or Paſſion, muſt be ſubmitted to? Which Men in the State of Nature are not bound to do one to another: And if he that judges, judges amiſs in his own, or any other Caſe, he is anſwerable for it to the reſt of Mankind.

14. 'Tis often asked as a mighty Objection, *where are*, or ever were, there any *Men in ſuch a ſtate of Nature?* To which it may ſuffice as an Anſwer at preſent: That ſince all Princes and Rulers of *Independent* Governments all through the World, are in a ſtate of Nature, 'tis plain the World never was, nor ever will be, without Numbers of Men in that State. I have named all Governors of *Independent Communities*, whether they are, or are not, in League with others. For 'tis not every Compact that puts an end to the ſtate of Nature between Men, but only this one of agreeing together mutually to enter into one Community, and make one Body Politick; other Promiſes, and Compacts, Men may make one

with

with another, and yet ſtill be in the ſtate of Nature. The Promiſes and Bargains for Truck, *&c.* between the two Men in the deſert Iſland, mentioned by *Garcilaſſo de la Vega*, in his Hiſtory of *Peru*; or between a *Swiſs* and an *Indian*, in the Woods of *America*, are binding to them, though they are perfectly in a ſtate of Nature, in reference to one another. For Truth and keeping of Faith belongs to Men, as Men, and not as Members of Society.

15. To thoſe that ſay, There were never any Men in the State of Nature; I will not only oppoſe the Authority of the judicious *Hooker, Eccl. Pol. Lib.* 1. *Sect.* 10. where he ſays, *The Laws which have been hitherto mentioned*, i. e. the Laws of Nature, *do bind Men abſolutely, even as they are Men, although they have never any ſetled Fellowſhip, never any ſolemn Agreement amongſt themſelves what to do or not to do, but for as much as we are not by our ſelves ſufficient to furniſh our ſelves with competent ſtore of things, needful for ſuch a Life, as our Nature doth deſire, a Life fit for the Dignity of Man; therefore to ſupply thoſe Defects and Imperfections which are in us, as living ſingle and ſolely by our ſelves, we are naturally induced to ſeek Communion and Fellowſhip with others, this was the Cauſe of Mens uniting themſelves, at firſt in politick Societies.* But I moreover affirm, That all Men are naturally in that State, and remain ſo, till by their own Conſents they make themſelves Members of ſome politick Society; and I doubt not in the Sequel of this Diſcourſe, to make it very clear.

CHAP. III.

Of the State of War.

16. THE *State of War* is a ſtate of *Enmity* and *Deſtruction*: And therefore declaring by Word or Action, not a paſſionate and haſty, but a ſedate ſetled Deſign, upon another Man's Life, *puts him in a State of War* with him againſt whom he has declared ſuch an Intention, and ſo has expoſed his Life to the others Power to be taken away by him, or any one that joyns with him in his Defence, and eſpouſes his Quarrel; it being reaſonable and juſt I ſhould have a Right to deſtroy that, which threatens me with Deſtruction. For *by the fundamental Law of Nature, Man being to be preſerved*, as much as poſſible, when all cannot be preſerved, the ſafety of the Innocent is to be preferred: And one may deſtroy a Man who makes War upon him, or has diſcovered an Enmity to his being, for the ſame Reaſon, that he may kill a *Woolf* or a *Lion*; becauſe ſuch Men are not under the ties of the Common-Law of Reaſon, have no other Rule, but that of Force and Violence, and ſo may be treated as Beaſts of Prey, thoſe dangerous and noxious Creatures, that will be ſure to deſtroy him, whenever he falls into their Power.

17. And hence it is, that he who attempts to get another Man into his Abſolute Power, does thereby *put himſelf into a State of War* with him; It being to be underſtood as a Declaration of a deſign upon his Life. For I have reaſon to conclude, that he who would get me into his Power without my Conſent, would uſe me as he pleaſed, when he had got me there, and deſtroy me too, when he had a fancy to it; for no body can deſire to *have me in his abſolute Power*, unleſs it be to compel me by force to that, which is againſt the Right of my Freedom, *i. e.* make me a Slave. To be free from ſuch force is the only ſecurity of my Preſervation; and reaſon bids me look on him, as an Enemy to my Preſervation, who would take away that *Freedom*, which is the fence to it; ſo that he who makes an *attempt to enſlave* me, thereby puts himſelf into a State of War with me. He that in the State of Nature, *would take away the Freedom*, that belongs to any one in that State, muſt neceſſarily be ſuppoſed to have a deſign to take away every thing elſe, that *Freedom* being the Foundation of all the reſt: As he that in the State of Society, would take away the *Freedom* belonging to thoſe of that Society or Common-wealth, muſt be ſuppoſed to deſign to take away from them every thing elſe, and ſo be looked on as *in a State of War*.

18. This makes it lawful for a Man to *kill a Thief*, who has not in the leaſt hurt him, nor declared any Deſign upon his Life, any farther, than by the uſe of Force, ſo to get him in his Power, as to take away his Money, or what he pleaſes

Vol. II. X 2 from

from him; because using Force, where he has no Right, to get me into his Power, let his Pretence be what it will, I have no reason to suppose, that he, who would *take away my Liberty* would not, when he had me in his Power, take away every thing else. And therefore it is lawful for me to treat him, as one who has *put himself into a state of War* with me, *i. e.* kill him if I can; for to that Hazard does he justly expose himself, whoever introduces a State of War, and is aggressor in it.

19. And here we have the plain *Difference between the state of Nature, and the state of War*, which however some Men have confounded, are as far distant, as a state of Peace, good Will, mutual Assistance and Preservation; and a state of Enmity, Malice, Violence and mutual Destruction are one from another. Men living together according to Reason, without a common superior on Earth, with Authority to judge between them, is *properly the state of Nature*. But force, or a declared design of Force upon the Person of another, where there is no common Superior on Earth to appeal to for Relief, *is the state of War*: And 'tis the want of such an Appeal gives a Man the right of War even against an *Aggressor*, though he be in Society and a fellow Subject. Thus a *Thief*, whom I cannot harm, but by Appeal to the Law, for having stolen all that I am worth, I may kill, when he sets on me to rob me but of my Horse or Coat; because the Law, which was made for my Preservation where it cannot interpose to secure my Life from present Force, which if lost, is capable of no Reparation, permits me my own Defence, and the right of War, a Liberty to kill the Aggressor, because the Aggressor allows not time to appeal to our common Judge, nor the decision of the Law, for Remedy in a Case, where the Mischief may be irreparable. *Want of a common Judge with Authority, puts all Men in a state of Nature: Force without Right, upon a Man's Person, makes a state of War*, both where there is, and is not, a common Judge.

20. But when the actual Force is over, the *state of War ceases* betwen those that are in Society, and are equally on both Sides subjected to the fair Determination of the Law; because then there lies open the remedy of Appeal for the past Injury, and to prevent future Harm; but where no such Appeal is, as in the state of Nature, for want of positive Laws, and Judges with Authority to appeal to, *the state of War once begun, continues*, with a right to the innocent Party to destroy the other whenever he can, until the Aggressor offers Peace, and desires Reconciliation on such Terms, as may repair any Wrongs he has already done, and secure the Innocent for the future; nay where an Appeal to the Law, and constituted Judges lies open, but the Remedy is deny'd by a manifest perverting of Justice, and a barefac'd wresting of the Laws to protect or indemnifie the violence or injuries of some Men, or party of Men, *there* it *is* hard to imagine any thing but *a state of War*. For where-ever Violence is used, and Injury done, though by hands appointed to administer Justice, it is still Violence and Injury, however colour'd with the Name, Pretences, or forms of Law, the End whereof being to protect and redress the Innocent, by an unbiassed Application of it, to all who are under it; where-ever that is not *bona fide* done, *War is made* upon the Sufferers, who having no Appeal on Earth to right them, they are left to the only Remedy in such Cases, an Appeal to Heaven.

21. To avoid this *state of War* (wherein there is no Appeal but to Heaven, and wherein every the least Difference is apt to end, where there is no Authority to decide between the Contenders) is one great *reason of Mens putting themselves into Society*, and quitting the State of Nature. For where there is an Authority, a Power on Earth, from which Relief can be had by *Appeal*, there the continuance of the *state of War* is excluded, and the Controversie is decided by that Power. Had there been any such Court, any superior Jurisdiction on Earth, to determine the Right between *Jeptha* and the *Ammonites*, they had never come to a *state of War*, but we see he was forced to appeal to Heaven. *The Lord the Judge* (says he) *be Judge this Day between the Children of* Israel, *and the Children of* Ammon, *Judg.* 11. 27. and then Prosecuting, and relying on his *Appeal*, he leads out his Army to Battle: And therefore in such Controversies, where the Question is put, *who shall be Judge?* It cannot be meant, who shall decide the Controversie; every one knows what *Jephtha* here tells us, that *the Lord the Judge*, shall Judge. Where there is no Judge on Earth, the Appeal lies to God in Heaven. That Question then

then cannot mean, who ſhall judge? whether another hath put himſelf in a *ſtate of War* with me, and whether I may as *Jephtha* did, *appeal to Heaven* in it? Of that I my ſelf can only be Judge in my own Conſcience, as I will anſwer it at the great Day, to the ſupream Judge of all Men.

CHAP. IV.

Of SLAVERY.

22. THE *Natural Liberty* of Man is to be free from any ſuperior Power on Earth, and not to be under the Will or legiſlative Authority of Man, but to have only the Law of Nature for his Rule. The *Liberty of Man*, in Society, is to be under no other legiſlative Power, but that eſtabliſhed, by Conſent, in the Commonwealth; nor under the dominion of any Will, or reſtraint of any Law, but what that Legiſlative ſhall enact, according to the Truſt put in it. Freedom then is not what Sir *R. F.* tells us, *O. A.* 55. *A Liberty for every one to do what he liſts, to live as he pleaſes, and not to be tyed by any Laws:* But *Freedom of Men under Government*, is, to have a ſtanding Rule to live by, common to every one of that Society, and made by the legiſlative Power erected in it; a Liberty to follow my own Will in all things, where that Rule preſcribes not; and not to be ſubject to the inconſtant, uncertain, unknown, arbitrary Will of another Man: As *Freedom of Nature* is to be under no other Reſtraint but the Law of Nature.

23. This *Freedom* from abſolute, arbitrary Power, is ſo neceſſary to, and cloſely joyned with a Man's Preſervation, that he cannot part with it, but by what forfeits his Preſervation and Life together. For a Man, not having the Power of his own Life, *cannot*, by Compact, or his own Conſent, *enſlave himſelf* to any one, nor put himſelf under the abſolute, arbitrary Power of another, to take away his Life, when he pleaſes. No body can give more Power than he has himſelf; and he that cannot take away his own Life, cannot give another Power over it. Indeed having by his Fault, forfeited his own Life, by ſome Act that deſerves Death; he, to whom he has forfeited it, may (when he has him in his Power) delay to take it, and make uſe of him to his own Service, and he does him no Injury by it. For, whenever he finds the hardſhip of his Slavery outweigh the value of his Life, 'tis in his Power, by reſiſting the Will of his Maſter, to draw on himſelf the Death he deſires.

24. This is the perfect condition of *Slavery*, which is nothing elſe, but *the ſtate of War continued, between a lawful Conqueror, and a Captive.* For, if once *Compact* enter between them, and make an Agreement for a limited Power on the one Side, and Obedience on the other, the *ſtate of War and Slavery* ceaſes, as long as the Compact endures. For, as has been ſaid, no Man can, by Agreement, paſs over to another that which he hath not in himſelf, a Power over his own Life.

I confeſs, we find among the *Jews*, as well as other Nations, that Men did ſell themſelves; but, 'tis plain, this was only to *Drudgery, not to Slavery*. For, it is evident, the Perſon ſold was not under an abſolute, arbitrary, deſpotical Power. For the Maſter could not have Power to kill him, at any time, whom at a certain time, he was obliged to let go free out of his Service; and the Maſter of ſuch a Servant was ſo far from having an arbitrary Power over his Life, that he could not at Pleaſure, ſo much as maim him, but the loſs of an Eye, or Tooth, ſet him free, *Exod.* XXI.

CHAP. V.

Of PROPERTY.

25. WHether we conſider natural *Reaſon*, which tells us, that Men, being once born, have a right to their Preſervation, and conſequently to Meat and Drink, and ſuch other things, as Nature affords for their Subſiſtence; or *Revelation*, which gives us an account of thoſe Grants God made of the World

World to *Adam*, and to *Noah*, and his Sons, 'tis very clear, that God, as K. *David* says, *Psal.* CXV. xvj. *has given the Earth to the Children of Men*; given it to Mankind in common. But this being supposed, it seems to some a very great Difficulty, how any one should ever come to have a *Property* in any thing: I will not content my self to answer, That if it be difficult to make out *Property*, upon a Supposition, that God gave the World to *Adam*, and his Posterity in common; it is impossible that any Man, but one universal Monarch should have any *Property* upon a Supposition, that God gave the World to *Adam*, and his Heirs in Succession, exclusive of all the rest of his Posterity. But I shall endeavour to shew, how Men might come to have a *Property* in several parts of that which God gave to Mankind in common, and that without any express Compact of all the Commoners.

26. God, who hath given the World to Men in common, hath also given them reason to make use of it to the best Advantage of Life, and Convenience. The Earth, and all that is therein, is given to Men for the Support and Comfort of their Being. And though all the Fruits it naturally produces, and Beasts it feeds, belong to Mankind in common, as they are produced by the spontaneous Hand of Nature; and no body has originally a private Dominion, exclusive of the rest of Mankind, in any of them, as they are thus in their natural State: yet being given for the use of Men, there must of necessity be *a means to appropriate* them some way or other, before they can be of any use, or at all beneficial to any particular Man. The Fruit, or Venison, which nourishes the wild *Indian*, who knows no Inclosure, and is still a Tenant in common, must be his, and so his, *i. e.* a part of him, that another can no longer have any right to it, before it can do him any Good for the Support of his Life.

27. Though the Earth, and all inferior Creatures be common to all Men, yet every Man has a *Property* in his own *Person*: This no Body has any right to but himself. The *Labour* of his Body, and the *Work* of his Hands, we may say, are properly his. Whatsoever then he removes out of the State that Nature hath provided, and left it in, he hath mixed his *Labour* with, and joyned to it something that is his own, and thereby makes it his *Property*. It being by him removed from the common State Nature hath placed it in, it hath by this *Labour* something annexed to it, that excludes the common Right of other Men. For this *Labour* being the unquestionable Property of the Labourer, no Man but he can have a Right to what that is once joyned to, at least where there is enough, and as good left in common for others.

28. He that is nourished by the Acorns he pickt up under an Oak, or the Apples he gathered from the Trees in the Wood, has certainly appropriated them to himself. No body can deny but the Nourishment is his. I ask then, When did they begin to be his? When he digested? Or when he eat? Or when he boiled? Or when he brought them home? Or when he pickt them up? And 'tis plain, if the first gathering made them not his, nothing else could. That *Labour* put a Distinction between them and common: That added something to them more than Nature, the common Mother of all, had done; and so they became his private Right. And will any one say, he had no Right to those Acorns or Apples, he thus appropriated, because he had not the Consent of all Mankind to make them his? Was it a Robbery thus to assume to himself what belonged to all in common? If such a Consent as that was necessary, Man had starved, notwithstanding the Plenty God had given him. We see in *Commons*, which remain so by Compact, that 'tis the taking any part of what is common, and removing it out of the state Nature leaves it in, which *begins the Property*; without which the Common is of no use. And the taking of this or that part, does not depend on the express Consent of all the Commoners. Thus the Grass my Horse has bit; the Turfs my Servant has cut; and the Ore I have digg'd in any Place, where I have a Right to them in common with others, become my *Property*, without the Assignation or Consent of any body. The *Labour* that was mine, removing them out of that common State they were in, hath *fixed* my *Property* in them.

29. By making an explicit Consent of every Commoner, necessary to any ones appropriating to himself any part of what is given in common, Children or Servants could not cut the Meat, which their Father or Master had provided for them in common, without assigning to every one his peculiar Part,

Tho'

Tho' the Water running in the Fountain be every ones, yet who can doubt, but that in the Pitcher is his only who drew it out? His *Labour* hath taken it out of the Hands of Nature, where it was common, and belong'd equally to all her Children, and *hath* thereby *appropriated* it to himſelf.

30. Thus this Law of Reaſon makes the Deer that *Indian*'s who hath killed it; 'tis allowed to be his Goods, who hath beſtowed his Labour upon it, though before it was the common Right of every one. And amongſt thoſe who are counted the civiliz'd part of Mankind, who have made and multiplied poſitive Laws to determine *Property*, this original Law of Nature, for the *beginning of Property*, in what was before common, ſtill takes place; and by vertue thereof, what Fiſh any one catches in the Ocean, that great and ſtill remaining Common of Mankind; or what Ambergreiſe any one takes up here, is *by* the *Labour* that removes it out of that common State Nature left it in, *made* his *Property*, who takes that Pains about it. And even amongſt us, the Hare that any one is hunting, is thought his who purſues her during the Chaſe. For being a Beaſt that is ſtill looked upon as common, and no Man's private Poſſeſſion; whoever has employ'd ſo much *Labour* about any of that kind, as to find and purſue her, has thereby removed her from the State of Nature, wherein ſhe was common, and hath *begun a Property*.

31. It will perhaps be objected to this, That if gathering the Acorns, or other Fruits of the Earth, *&c.* makes a Right to them, then any one may *ingroſs* as much as he will. To which I anſwer, Not ſo. The ſame Law of Nature, that does by this means give us Property, does alſo *bound* that *Property* too. *God has given us all things richly*, 1 Tim. vi. 12. is the Voice of Reaſon confirmed by Inſpiration. But how far has he given it us? *To enjoy*. As much as any one can make uſe of to any Advantage of Life before it ſpoils; ſo much he may by his Labour fix a Property in: Whatever is beyond this, is more than his Share, and belongs to others. Nothing was made by God for Man to ſpoil or deſtroy. And thus conſidering the Plenty of natural Proviſions there was a long time in the World, and the few Spenders; and to how ſmall a Part of that Proviſion the Induſtry of one Man could extend it ſelf, and ingroſs it to the Prejudice of others; eſpecially keeping within the *Bounds*, ſet by Reaſon, *of* what might ſerve for his *Uſe*; there could be then little room for Quarrels or Contentions about Property ſo eſtabliſh'd.

32. But the *chief Matter of Property* being now not the Fruits of the Earth, and the Beaſts that ſubſiſt on it, but *the Earth it ſelf*; as that which takes in and carries with it all the reſt: I think it is plain, that *Property* in that too is acquir'd as the former. *As much Land* as a Man Tills, Plants, Improves, Cultivates, and can uſe the Product of, ſo much is his *Property*. He by his Labour does, as it were, incloſe it from the Common. Nor will it invalidate his Right to ſay, Every body elſe has an equal Title to it; and therefore he cannot appropriate, he cannot incloſe, without the Conſent of all his Fellow-Commoners, all Mankind. God, when he gave the World in common to all Mankind, commanded Man alſo to labour, and the Penury of his Condition required it of him. God and his Reaſon commanded him to ſubdue the Earth, *i. e.* improve it for the Benefit of Life, and therein lay out ſomething upon it that was his own, his Labour. He that in Obedience to this Command of God, ſubdued, tilled and ſowed any part of it, thereby annexed to it ſomething that was his *Property*, which another had no Title to, nor could without Injury take from him.

33. Nor was this *Appropriation* of any parcel of *Land*, by improving it, any Prejudice to any other Man, ſince there was ſtill enough, and as good left; and more than the yet unprovided could uſe. So that in effect, there was never the leſs left for others becauſe of his Incloſure for himſelf. For he that leaves as much as another can make uſe of, does as good as take nothing at all. No Body could think himſelf injur'd by the drinking of another Man though he took a good Draught, who had a whole River of the ſame Water left him to quench his Thirſt: And the Caſe of Land and Water, where there is enough of both, is perfectly the ſame.

34. God gave the World to Men in common; but ſince he gave it them for their Benefit, and the greateſt conveniencies of Life they were capable to draw from it, it cannot be ſuppoſed he meant it ſhould always remain common and uncultivated,

vated. He gave it to the uſe of the induſtrious and rational, (and *Labour* was to be *his Title* to it;) not to the Fancy or Covetouſneſs of the Quarrelſom and Contentious. He that has as good left for his Improvement, as was already taken up, needed not complain, ought not to meddle with what was already improved by another's Labour: If he did, 'tis plain he deſired the benefit of another's Pains, which he had no right to, and not the Ground which God had given him in common with others to labour on, and whereof there was as good left, as that already poſſeſſed, and more than he knew what to do with, or his Induſtry could reach to.

35. 'Tis true, in *Land* that is *common* in *England*, or any other Country, where there is plenty of People under Government, who have Money and Commerce, no one can incloſe or appropriate any part, without the conſent of all his Fellow-Commoners: Becauſe this is left common by Compact, *i. e.* by the law of the Land, which is not to be violated. And tho' it be common, in reſpect of ſome Men, it is not ſo to all Mankind; but is the joint property of this Country, or this Pariſh. Beſides, the remainder, after ſuch Incloſure, would not be as good to the reſt of the Commoners, as the whole was, when they could all make uſe of the whole; whereas in the Beginning and firſt peopling of the great Common of the World, it was quite otherwiſe. The Law Man was under, was rather for appropriating. God commanded, and his Wants forced him to *labour*. That was his *Property* which could not be taken from him where-ever he had fixed it. And hence ſubduing or cultivating the Earth, and having Dominion, we ſee are joined together. The one gave Title to the other. So that God, by commanding to ſubdue, gave Authority ſo far to *appropriate*: And the Conditionof human Life, which requires Labour and Materials to work on, neceſſarily introduce private Poſſeſſions.

36. Nature has well ſet the *meaſure of Property* by the extent of Mens *Labour and the Conveniencies of Life*: No Man's Labour could ſubdue, or appropriate all; nor could his Enjoyment conſume more than a ſmall Part; ſo that it was impoſſible for any Man, this Way, to intrench upon the Right of another, or acquire to himſelf a Property, to the prejudice of his Neighbour, who would ſtill have room for as good, and as large a Poſſeſſion (after the other had taken out his) as before it was appropriated. *Meaſure* did confine every Man's *Poſſeſſion*, to a very moderate Proportion, and ſuch, as he might appropriate to himſelf, without Injury to any Body, in the firſt Ages of the World, when Men were more in Danger to be loſt, by wandring from their Company, in the then vaſt wilderneſs of the Earth, than to be ſtraitned for want of room to plant in. And the ſame *Meaſure* may be allowed ſtill without Prejudice to any Body, as full as the World ſeems. For ſuppoſing a Man, or Family, in the State they were at firſt peopling of the World by the Children of *Adam*, or *Noah*; let him plant in ſome In-land, vacant places of *America*, we ſhall find that the *Poſſeſſions* he could make himſelf, upon the *Meaſures* we have given, would not be very large, nor, even to this day, prejudice the reſt of Mankind, or give them reaſon to complain, or think themſelves injured by this Man's Incroachment, though the race of Men have now ſpread themſelves to all the corners of the World, and do infinitely exceed the ſmall Number was at the Beginning. Nay, the extent of *Ground* is of ſo little Value, *without Labour*, that I have heard it affirmed, that in *Spain* it ſelf, a Man may be permitted to plough, ſow and reap, without being diſturbed upon Land he has no other Title to, but only his making uſe of it. But, on the contrary, the Inhabitants think themſelves beholden to him, who, by his Induſtry on neglected, and conſequently waſte Land, has increaſed the ſtock of Corn, which they wanted. But be this as it will, which I lay no Streſs on; this I dare boldly affirm, that the ſame *rule of Propriety, (viz.)* that every Man ſhould have as much as he could make uſe of, would hold ſtill in the World, without ſtraitning any Body; ſince there is Land enough in the World to ſuffice double the Inhabitants, had not the *Invention of Money*, and the tacit Agreement of Men, to put a Value on it, introduced (by Conſent) larger Poſſeſſions, and a Right to them; which, how it has done, I ſhall by and by ſhew more at large.

37. This is certain, That in the beginning, before the deſire of having more than Man needed, had altered the intrinſick value of things, which depends only on their uſefulneſs to the Life of Man; or had *agreed, that a little piece of yellow Metal,*

Metal, which would keep without wasting or decay, should be worth a great piece of Flesh, or a whole heap of Corn, though Men had a right to appropriate, by their Labour, each one to himself, as much of the things of Nature, as he could use; yet this could not be much, nor to the Prejudice of others, where the same plenty was still left, to those who would use the same Industry. To which let me add, that he who appropriates Land to himself by his Labour, does not lessen but increase the common stock of Mankind. For the Provisions serving to the support of human Life; produced by one Acre of Inclosed and Cultivated Land are (to speak much within compass) ten times more than those which are yielded by an Acre of Land of an equal richness lying waste in Common. And therefore he that incloses Land, and has a greater plenty of the Conveniencies of Life from ten Acres, than he could have from an hundred left to Nature, may truly be said to give ninety Acres to Mankind. For his Labour now supplies him with Provisions out of ten Acres, which were but the Product of an hundred lying in Common. I have here rated the improv'd Land very low in making its Product but as ten to one, when it is much nearer an hundred to one. For I ask whether in the wild Woods and uncultivated waste of *America* left to Nature without any Improvement, Tillage or Husbandry, a thousand Acres yield the needy and wretched Inhabitants as many Conveniencies of Life, as ten Acres of equally fertile Land do in *Devonshire*, where they are well Cultivated?

Before the appropriation of Land, he who gathered as much of the wild Fruit, killed, caught, or tamed, as many of the Beasts, as he could; he that so imployed his Pains about any of the spontaneous Products of Nature, as any way to alter them, from the state which Nature put them in, *by* placing any of his *Labour* on them, did thereby *acquire a Propriety in them:* But if they perished, in his Possession, without their due Use; if the Fruits rotted, or the Venison putrified, before he could spend it, he offended against the common Law of Nature, and was liable to be punished; he invaded his Neighbour's share, for he had *no Right, farther than his Use* called for any of them, and they might serve to afford him Conveniencies of Life.

38. The same *Measures* governed the *Possession of Land* too: Whatsoever he tilled and reaped, laid up and made use of, before it spoiled, that was his peculiar Right; whatsoever he enclosed, and could feed, and make use of, the Cattle and Product was also his. But if either the Grass of his Inclosure rotted on the Ground, or the Fruit of his planting perished without gathering, and laying up, this part of the Earth, notwithstanding his Inclosure, was still to be looked on as waste, and might be the Possession of any other. Thus, at the beginning, *Cain* might take as much Ground as he could Till, and make it his own Land, and yet leave enough to *Abel*'s Sheep to feed on; a few Acres would serve for both their Possessions. But as Families increased, and industry inlarged their Stocks, their *Possessions inlarged* with the need of them; but yet it was commonly *without any fixed property in the ground* they made use of, till they incorporated, settled themselves together, and built Cities, and then, by consent, they came in time, to set out the *bounds of their distinct Territories*, and agree on limits between them and their Neighbours; and by Laws within themselves, settled the *Properties* of those of the same Society. For we see, that in that part of the World which was first inhabited, and therefore like to be best peopled, even as low down as *Abraham*'s Time, they wandred with their Flocks, and their Herds, which was their substance, freely up and down; and this *Abraham* did, in a Country where he was a Stranger. Whence it is plain, that at least, a great part of the *Land lay in common*; that the Inhabitants valued it not, nor claimed Property in any more than they made use of. But when there was not room enough in the same Place, for their Herds to feed together, they by consent, as *Abraham* and *Lot* did, *Gen.* xiii. 5. separated and inlarged their Pasture, where it best liked them. And for the same Reason *Esau* went from his Father, and his Brother, and planted in *Mount Seir*, *Gen.* xxxvi. 6.

39. And thus, without supposing any private Dominion, and Property in *Adam*, over all the World, exclusive of all other Men, which can no way be proved, nor any ones Property be made out from it; but supposing the *World* given as it was to the Children of Men *in common*, we see how *labour* could make Men distin &

Titles to ſeveral parcels of it, for their private Uſes; wherein there could be no doubt of Right, no room for quarrel.

40 Nor is it ſo ſtrange, as perhaps before conſideration it may appear, that the *Property of Labour* ſhould be able to over-balance the Community of Land. For 'tis *labour* indeed that *puts the difference of value* on every thing; and let any one conſider what the difference is between an Acre of Land planted with Tabacco or Sugar, ſown with Wheat or Barley; and an Acre of the ſame Land lying in common, without any Husbandry upon it, and he will find, that the improvement of *labour makes* the far greater part of the Value. I think it will be but a very modeſt Computation to ſay, that of the *Products* of the Earth uſeful to the Life of Man $\frac{9}{10}$ are the *effects of labour:* Nay, if we will rightly eſtimate things as they come to our Uſe, and caſt up the ſeveral expences about them, what in them is purely owing to *Nature*, and what to *Labour*, we ſhall find, that in moſt of them $\frac{99}{100}$ are wholly to be put on the account of *Labour*.

41. There cannot be a clearer demonſtration of any thing, than ſeveral Nations of the *Americans* are of this, who are rich in Land, and poor in all the Comforts of Life; whom Nature having furniſhed as liberally as any other People, with the materials of Plenty, *i. e.* a fruitful Soil, apt to produce in abundance, what might ſerve for Food, Rayment, and Delight; yet for *want of improving it by Labour*, have not one hundredth part of the Conveniencies we enjoy: And a King of a large and fruitful Territory there Feeds, Lodges, and is clad worſe than a day Labourer in *England*.

42. To make this a little clearer, let us but trace ſome of the ordinary proviſions of Life, through their ſeveral Progreſſes, before they come to our Uſe, and ſee how much they receive of their *value from human Induſtry*. Bread, Wine and Cloath, are things of daily Uſe, and great Plenty, yet notwithſtanding, Acorns, Water and Leaves, or Skins, muſt be our Bread, Drink and Cloathing, did not *labour* furniſh us with theſe more uſeful Commodities. For whatever *Bread* is more worth than Acorns, Wine than Water, and *Cloath* or *Silk*, than Leaves, Skins or Moſs, that is wholly *owing to Labour* and *Induſtry*. The one of theſe being the Food and Rayment which unaſſiſted Nature furniſhes us with; the other Proviſions which our Induſtry and Pains prepare for Us, which how much they exceed the other in Value, when any one hath Computed, he will then ſee, how much *labour makes the far greateſt part of the value* of things we enjoy in this World: And the ground which produces the Materials, is ſcarce to be reckon'd in, as any, or at moſt, but a very ſmall part of it; ſo little, that even amongſt us, Land that is left wholly to Nature, that hath no improvement of Paſturage, Tillage, or Planting, is called, as indeed it is, *Waſte*; and we ſhall find the benefit of it amount to little more than nothing.

This ſhews how much numbers of Men are to be preferred to largeneſs of Dominions; and that the increaſe of Lands, and the right employing of them is the great Art of Government: And that Prince, who ſhall be ſo Wiſe and God-like, as by eſtabliſhed Laws of Liberty to ſecure Protection and Encouragement to the honeſt induſtry of Mankind, againſt the Oppreſſion of Power and Narrowneſs of Party, will quickly be too hard for his Neighbours; But this by the by: To return to the Argument in Hand.

43. An Acre of Land, that bears here twenty Buſhels of Wheat, and another in *America*, which, with the ſame Husbandry, would do the like, are, without doubt, of the ſame natural intrinſick Value: But yet the Benefit Mankind receives from the one in a Year, is worth 5 *l.* and from the other poſſibly not worth a Penny, if all the Profit an *Indian* received from it were to be valued, and ſold here; at leaſt, I may truly ſay, not $\frac{1}{1000}$. 'Tis *Labour* then, which *puts the greateſt part of Value upon Land*, whout which it would ſcarcely be worth any thing: 'Tis to that we owe the greateſt part of all its uſeful Products; for all that the Straw, Bran, Bread, of that Acre of Wheat, is more worth than the Product of an Acre of as good Land, which lies waſte, is all the effect of Labour. For 'tis not barely the Plough-man's Pains, the Reaper's and Threſher's Toil, and the Baker's Sweat, is to be counted into the *Bread* we Eat; the Labour of thoſe who broke the Oxen, who digged and wrought the Iron and Stones, who felled and framed the Timber imployed about the Plough, Mill, Oven, or any other Utenſils, which are a vaſt Number, requiſite to this Corn, from its being Seed to be ſown to its being made

made Bread, muſt all be *charged on* the account of *Labour,* and received as an effect of that: Nature and the Earth furniſhed only the almoſt worthleſs Materials, as in themſelves. 'Twould be a ſtrange *Catalogue of things, that Induſtry provided and made uſe of, about every Loaf of Bread,* before it came to our Uſe, if we could trace them; Iron, Wood, Leather, Bark, Timber, Stone, Bricks, Coals, Lime, Cloth, Dying Drugs, Pitch, Tar, Maſts, Ropes, and all the Materials made uſe of in the Ship, that brought any of the Commodities made uſe of by any of the Workmen, to any part of the Work, all which, 'twould be almoſt impoſſible, at leaſt too long, to reckon up.

44. From all which it is evident, that though the things of Nature are given in common, yet Man by being Maſter of himſelf, and *Proprietor of his own Perſon, and the Actions or Labour of it, had ſtill in himſelf the great Foundation of Property;* and that, which made up the great part of what he applyed to the Support or Comfort of his Being, when Invention and Arts had improved the conveniencies of Life; was perfectly his own, and did not belong in common to others.

45. Thus *Labour,* in the beginning *gave a Right of Property,* wherever any one was pleaſed to imploy it, upon what was common, which remained a long while, the far greater part, and is yet more than Mankind makes uſe of. Men, at firſt, for the moſt part, contented themſelves with what un-aſſiſted Nature offered to their Neceſſities: And though afterwards, in ſome parts of the World, (where the Increaſe of People and Stock, with the *Uſe of Money,* had made Land ſcarce, and ſo of ſome Value) the ſeveral *Communities* ſettled the Bounds of their diſtinct Territories; and by Laws within themſelves, regulated the Properties of the private Men of their Society; and ſo, *by Compact* and Agreement, *ſettled the Property* which Labour and Induſtry began; and the Leagues that have been made between ſeveral States and Kingdoms, either expreſly or tacitly diſowning all Claim and Right to the Land in the others Poſſeſſion, have, by common Conſent, given up their Pretences to their natural common Right, which originally they had to thoſe Countries, and ſo have, by *poſitive Agreement, ſettled a Property* amongſt themſelves, in diſtinct Parts and Parcel of the Earth; yet there are ſtill *great Tracts of Ground* to be found, which, (the Inhabitants thereof not having joyned with the reſt of Mankind, in the conſent of the Uſe of their common Money) *lie waſte,* and are more, than the People, who dwell on it, do, or can make uſe of, and ſo ſtill lie in common. Tho' this can ſcarce happen amongſt that part of Mankind, that have conſented to the Uſe of Money.

46. The greateſt part of *things really uſeful* to the life of Man, and ſuch as the neceſſity of ſubſiſting made the firſt Commoners of the World look after, as it doth the *Americans* now, *are* generally things of *ſhort Duration;* ſuch as, if they are not conſumed by uſe, will decay and periſh of themſelves: Gold, Silver and Diamonds, are things, that Fancy or Agreement hath put the Value on, more than real Uſe, and the neceſſary ſupport of Life. Now of thoſe good things which Nature hath provided in (common, every one had a Right as hath been ſaid) to as much as he could uſe, and *Property* in all he could affect with his Labour; all that his *Induſtry* could extend to, to alter from the ſtate Nature had put it in, was his. He that *gathered* a hundred Buſhels of Acorns or Apples, had thereby a *Property* in them, they were his Goods as ſoon as gathered. He was only to look, that he uſed them before they ſpoiled, elſe he took more than his ſhare, and robb'd others. And indeed it was a fooliſh thing, as well as diſhoneſt, to hoard up more, than he could make uſe of. If he gave away a part to any body elſe, ſo that it periſhed not uſeleſly in his Poſſeſſion, theſe he alſo made uſe of. And if he alſo bartred away Plumbs, that would have rotted in a Week, for Nuts that would laſt good for his eating a whole Year he did no injury; he waſted not the common Stock; deſtroyed no part of the portion of Goods that belonged to others, ſo long as nothing periſhed uſeleſly in his hands. Again, If he would give his Nuts for a piece of Metal, pleaſed with its Colour; or exchange his Sheep for Shells, or Wooll for a ſparkling Peble or a Diamond, and keep thoſe by him all his Life, he invaded not the Right of others, he might heap up as much of theſe durable things as he pleaſed, the *exceeding of the bounds of* his *juſt Property* not lying in the largeneſs of his Poſſeſſion, but the periſhing of any thing uſeleſly in it.

47. And thus *came in the use of Money*, some lasting thing that Men might keep without spoiling, and that by mutual Consent Men would take in exchange for the truly useful, but perishable supports of Life.

48. And as different degrees of Industry were apt to give Men Possessions in different Proportions, so this *Invention of Money* gave them the Opportunity to continue and enlarge them. For supposing an Island, separate from all possible Commerce with the rest of the World, wherein there were but an hundred Families, but there were Sheep, Horses and Cows, with other useful Animals, wholsome Fruits, and Land enough for Corn for a hundred thousand Times as many, but nothing in the Island, either because of its Commonness, or perishableness, fit to supply the place of *Money*: What reason could any one have there to enlarge his Possessions beyond the use of his Family, and a plentiful supply to its *Consumption*, either in what their own Industry produced, or they could barter for like perishable, useful Commodities, with others? Where there is not something, both lasting and scarce, and so valuable, to be hoarded up, there Men will be apt to enlarge their *Possessions of Land*, were it never so rich, never so free for them to take. For I ask, what would a Man value Ten thousand, or an Hundred thousand Acres of excellent *Land*, ready cultivated, and well stocked too with Cattle in the middle of the In-land Parts of *America*, where he had no hopes of Commerce with other parts of the World, to draw *Money* to him by the sale of the Product? It would not be worth the inclosing, and we should see him give up again to the wild Common of Nature, whatever was more than would supply the conveniencies of Life to be had there for him and his Family.

49. Thus in the Beginning all the World was *America*, and more so than that is now; for no such thing as *Money* was any where known. Find out something that hath the *Use and Value of Money* amongst his Neighbours, you shall see the same Man will begin presently to *enlarge* his Possessions.

50. But since Gold and Silver, being little useful to the Life of Man in proportion to Food, Rayment, and Carriage, has its *Value* only from the consent of Men, whereof *Labour* yet *makes*, in great part, *the Measure*, it is plain, that Men have agreed to a disproportionate and unequal *Possession of the Earth*, they having by a tacit and voluntary Consent, found out a Way how a Man may fairly possess more Land, than he himself can use the Product of, by receiving in Exchange for the overplus Gold and Silver, which may be hoarded up without Injury to any one; these Metals not spoiling or decaying in the hands of the Possessor. This Partage of things in an inequality of private Possessions, Men have made practicable out of the bounds of Society, and without Compact only by putting a Value on Gold and Silver, and tacitly agreeing in the use of Money. For in Governments, the Laws regulate the right of Property, and the possession of Land is determined by positive Constitutions.

51. And thus, I think, it is very easie to conceive without any Difficulty, *how Labour could at first begin a title of Property* in the common things of Nature, and how the spending it upon our uses bounded it. So that there could then be no reason of quarreling about Title, nor any doubt about the largeness of Possession it gave. Right and Conveniency went together; for as a Man had a Right to all he could imploy his Labour upon, so he had no Temptation to labour for more than he could make use of. This left no room for Controversie about the Title, nor for Incroachment on the right of others; what Portion a Man carved to himself, was easily seen; and it was useless as well as dishonest to carve himself too much, or take more than he needed.

CHAP. III.

Of Paternal Power.

52. IT may perhaps be censured as an impertinent Criticism in a discourse of this Nature to find fault with Words and Names, that have obtained in the World: And yet possibly it may not be amiss to offer new ones, when the old are apt to lead Men into Mistakes as this of *paternal Power* probably has done, which

which seems so to place the power of Parents over their Children wholly in the *Father*, as if the *Mother* had no share in it, whereas, if we consult Reason or Revelation, we shall find, she hath an equal Title. This may give one reason to ask, whether this might not be more properly called *parental Power*. For whatever obligation Nature and the right of Generation lays on Children, it must certainly bind them equal to both the concurrent Causes of it. And accordingly we see the positive Law of God every where joyns them together, without Distinction when it commands the Obedience of Children, *Honour thy Father and thy Mother*, Exod. 20. 12. *Whosoever curseth his Father or his Mother*, Lev. 20. 9. *Ye shall fear every Man his Mother and his Father*, Lev. 19. 3. *Children obey your Parents*, &c. Eph. 6. 1. is the stile of the Old and New Testament.

53. Had but this one thing been well consider'd, without looking any deeper into the Matter, it might perhaps have kept Men from running into those gross Mistakes, they have made, about this power of Parents; which however it might, without any great Harshness, bear the name of absolute Dominion, and regal Authority, when under the Title of *paternal Power* it seem'd appropriated to the Father, would yet have sounded but odly, and in the very Name shewn the Absurdity, if this supposed absolute Power over Children had been called *Parental*; and thereby have discover'd, that it belong'd to the *Mother* too; for it will but very ill serve the turn of those Men, who contend so much for the absolute power and authority of the *Fatherhood*, as they call it, that the Mother should have any Share in it. And it would have but ill supported the *Monarchy* they contend for, when by the very Name it appeared, that that fundamental Authority, from whence they would derive their Government of a single Person only, was not plac'd in one, but two Persons joyntly. But to let this of Names pass.

54. Though I have said above *Chap. 2. That all Men by Nature are equal*, I cannot be supposed to understand all sorts of *Equality*: *Age* or *Virtue* may give Men a just Precedency: *Excellency of Parts* and *Merit* may place others above the common Level: *Birth* may subject some, and *Alliance* or *Benefits* others to pay an Observance to those to whom Nature, Gratitude, or other Respects may have made it due; and yet all this consists with the *Equality*, which all Men are in, in respect of Jurisdiction or Dominion, one over another; which was the *Equality* I there spoke of, as proper to the Business in hand, being that *equal Right*, that every Man hath, *to his natural Freedom*, without being subjected to the Will or Authority of any other Man.

55. *Children*, I confess, are not born in this full state of *Equality*, though they are born to it. Their Parents have a sort of Rule and Jurisdiction over them, when they come into the World, and for some time after, but 'tis but a temporary one. The Bonds of this Subjection are like the swadling Cloths they are wrapt up in, and supported by in the weakness of their Infancy: Age and Reason as they grow up, loosen them, till at length they drop quite off, and leave a Man at his own free Disposal.

56. *Adam* was created a perfect Man, his Body and Mind in full possession of their Strength and Reason, and so was capable, from the first Instant of his Being to provide for his own Support and Preservation, and govern his Actions according to the Dictates of the Law of Reason which God had implanted in him. From him the World is peopled with his Descendants, who are all born Infants, weak and helpless, without Knowledge or Understanding: But to supply the defects of this imperfect State, till the improvement of Growth and Age had removed them, *Adam* and *Eve*, and after them all *Parents* were, by the Law of Nature, *under an Obligation to preserve, nourish, and educate the Children*, they had begotten; not as their own Workmanship, but the Workmanship of their own Maker, the Almighty, to whom they were to be accountable for them.

57. The Law, that was to govern *Adam*, was the same, that was to govern all his Posterity, the *Law of Reason*. But his Off-spring having another way of entrance into the World, different from him, by a natural Birth, that produced them ignorant and without the use of *Reason*, they were not presently *under that Law*; for no body can be under a Law, which is not promulgated to him; and this Law being promulgated or made known by *Reason* only, he that is not come to the Use of his *Reason*, cannot be said to be *under this Law*; and *Adam*'s Children, being not presently as soon as born *under this Law of Reason*, were not presently

ſently *free*. For *Law*, in its true Notion, *is* not ſo much the Limitation as *the direction of a free and intelligent Agent* to his proper Intereſt, and preſcribes no farther than is for the general Good of thoſe under that Law: Could they be happier without it, the *Law*, as an uſeleſs thing, would of itſelf vaniſh; and that ill deſerves the Name of Confinement which hedges us in only from Bogs and Precipices. So that, however it may be miſtaken, *the end of Law is* not to aboliſh or reſtrain, but *to preſerve and enlarge Freedom* For in all the ſtates of created Beings capable of Laws, *where there is no Law, there is no Freedom*. For *Liberty* is to be free from Reſtraint and Violence from others; which cannot be, where there is no Law: But Freedom is not, as we are told, *A Liberty for every Man to do what he liſts:* (For who could be Free, when every other Man's Humour might domineer over him?) But a *Liberty* to diſpoſe, and order as he liſts, his Perſon, Actions, Poſſeſſions, and his whole Property, within the Allowance of thoſe Laws, under which he is, and therein not to be ſubject to the Arbitrary Will of another, but freely follow his own.

58. The *Power*, then, *that Parents have* over their Children, ariſes from that Duty which is incumbent on them, to take care of their Off-ſpring, during the imperfect ſtate of Childhood. To inform the Mind, and govern the Actions of their yet ignorant Nonage, till Reaſon ſhall take its Place, and eaſe them of that Trouble, is what the Children want, and the Parents are bound to. For God having given Man an Underſtanding to direct his Actions, has allowed him a freedom of Will, and liberty of Acting, as properly belonging thereunto, within the bounds of that Law he is under. But whilſt he is in an Eſtate, wherein he has not *Underſtanding* of his own to direct his *Will*, he is not to have any *Will* of his own to follow: He that *underſtands* for him, muſt *will* for him too; he muſt preſcribe to his Will, and regulate his Actions; but when he comes to the Eſtate that made his *Father a Freeman*, the *Son is a Freeman* too.

59. This holds in all the Laws a Man is under, whether Natural or Civil. Is a Man under the Law of Nature? *What made him Free* of that Law? What gave him a free diſpoſing of his Property, according to his own Will, within the compaſs of that Law? I anſwer; a State of Maturity wherein he might be ſuppos'd capable to know that Law, that ſo he might keep his Actions within the Bounds of it. When he has acquired that State, he is preſumed to know how far that Law is to be his Guide, and how far he may make uſe of his *Freedom*, and ſo comes to have it; 'till then, ſome body elſe muſt guide him, who is preſumed to know, how far the Law allows a Liberty. If ſuch a State of Reaſon, ſuch an Age of Diſcretion *made him Free*, the ſame ſhall make his Son Free too. Is a Man under the Law of *England? What made him Free* of that Law? That is, to have the Liberty to diſpoſe of his Actions and Poſſeſſions according to his own Will, within the Permiſſion of that Law? A Capacity of knowing that Law. Which is ſuppoſed by that Law, at the Age of one and twenty Years, and in ſome Caſes ſooner. If this *made* the Father *Free*, it ſhall *make* the Son *Free* too. Till then we ſee the Law allows the Son to have no Will, but he is to be guided by the Will of his Father or Guardian, who is to underſtand for him. And if the Father die, and fail to ſubſtitute a Deputy in his Truſt; if he hath not provided a Tutor, to govern his Son, during his Minority, during his want of Underſtanding, the Law takes care to do it, ſome other muſt govern him, and be a Will to him, till he hath *attained to a State of Freedom*, and his Underſtanding be fit to take the Government of his Will. But after that, the Father and Son are equally *Free* as much as Tutor and Pupil after Nonage; equally Subjects of the ſame Law together, without any Dominion left in the Father over the Life, Liberty, or Eſtate of his Son, whether they be only in the State and under the Law of Nature, or under the poſitive Laws of an Eſtabliſh'd Government.

60. But if, through defects that may happen out of the ordinary courſe of Nature, any one comes not to ſuch a degree of Reaſon, wherein he might be ſuppoſed capable of knowing the Law, and ſo living within the Rules of it, he is *never capable of being a Free Man*, he is never let looſe to the diſpoſure of his own Will (becauſe he knows no bounds to it, has not Underſtanding, its proper Guide) but is continued under the Tuition and Government of others, all the time his own Underſtanding is uncapable of that Charge. And ſo *Lunaticks* and *Ideots* are never ſet free from the Government of their Parents; *Children, who are not as yet* *come*

come unto those Years whereat they may have; and Innocents which are excluded by a natural defect from ever having; Thirdly, *Madmen, which for the present cannot possibly have the use of right Reason to guide themselves, have for their Guide, the Reason that guideth other Men which are Tutors over them, to seek and procure their good for them, says* Hooker, Eccl. Pol. *lib.* 1. *Sect.* 7. All which seems no more than that Duty, which God and Nature has laid on Man, as well as other Creatures, to preserve their Off-spring, till they can be able to shift for themselves, and will scarce amount to an instance or proof of *Parents* Regal Authority.

61. Thus we are *born Free*, as we are born Rational; not that we have actually the Exercise of either: Age that brings one, brings with it the other too. And thus we see how *natural Freedom and Subjection to Parents* may consist together, and are both founded on the same Principle. A *Child* is *Free* by his Father's Title, by his Father's Understanding, which is to govern him, till he hath it of his own. The *Freedom of a Man at years of Discretion*, and the *Subjection* of a Child *to* his *Parents*, whilst yet short of that Age, are so consistent, and so distinguishable, that the most blinded Contenders for Monarchy, *by Right of Fatherhood*, cannot miss this *Difference*; the most obstinate cannot but allow their Consistency. For were their Doctrine all true, were the right Heir of *Adam* now known, and by that Title settled a Monarch in his Throne, invested with all the absolute unlimited Power Sir *R. F.* talks of; if he should die as soon as his Heir were Born, must not the *Child*, notwithstanding he were never so Free, never so much Sovereign, be in Subjection to his Mother and Nurse, to Tutors and Governors, till Age and Education brought him Reason and Ability to govern himself, and others? The Necessities of his Life, the Health of his Body, and the Information of his Mind would require him to be directed by the Will of others and not his own; and yet will any one think, that this Restraint and Subjection were inconsistent with, or spoiled him of that Liberty or Sovereignty he had a Right to, or gave away his Empire to those who had the Government of his Nonage? This Government over him only prepared him the better and sooner for it. If any body should ask me, when my Son is *of Age to be Free?* I shall answer, Just when his Monarch is of Age to govern. *But at what time*, says the judicious *Hooker*, Eccl. Pol. l. 1. Sect. 6. *a Man may be said to have attain'd so far forth the use of Reason, as sufficeth to make him capable of those Laws whereby he is then bound to guide his Actions; this is a great deal more easie for sense to discern, than for any one by Skill and Learning to determine.*

62. Commonwealths themselves take notice of, and allow, that there is a *time when Men* are to *begin to act like Free Men*, and therefore till that time require not Oaths of Fealty, or Allegiance, or other publick owning of, or Submission to the Government of their Countries.

63. The *Freedom* then of Man, and Liberty of acting according to his own Will, is *grounded on* his having *Reason*, which is able to instruct him in that Law he is to govern himself by, and make him know how far he is left to the Freedom of his own Will. To turn him loose to an unrestrain'd Liberty, before he has Reason to guide him, is not the allowing him the privilege of his Nature to be Free; but to thrust him out amongst Brutes, and abandon him to a State as wretched, and as much beneath that of a Man, as theirs. This is that which puts the *Authority* into the *Parents* hands to govern the *Minority* of their Children. God hath made it their business to imploy this Care on their Off-spring, and hath placed in them suitable Inclinations of Tenderness, and concern to temper this Power, to apply it, as his Wisdom designed it, to the Childrens good, as long as they should need to be under it.

64. But what reason can hence advance this care of the *Parents* due to their Off-spring into an *absolute Arbitrary Dominion* of the Father, whose Power reaches no farther, than by such a Discipline, as he finds most effectual, to give such Strength and Health to their Bodies, such vigour and rectitude to their Minds, as may best fit his Children to be most useful to themselves and others; and, if it be necessary to his Condition, to make them Work, when they are able, for their own Subsistence. But in this Power the *Mother* too has her share with the *Father*.

65. Nay this *Power* so little belongs to the *Father* by any peculiar right of Nature, but only as he is Guardian of his Children, that when he quits his care of them, he loses his Power over them, which goes along with their Nourishment

and

and Education, to which it is inſeparably annexed; and it belongs as much to the *Foſter-Father* of an expoſed Child, as to the Natural Father of another. So little Power does the bare *act of begetting* give a Man over his Iſſue; if all his Care ends there, and this be all the Title he hath to the Name and Authority of a Father. And what will become of this *Paternal Power* in that part of the World, where one Woman hath more than one Husband at a Time? Or in thoſe parts of *America*, where, when the Husband and Wife part, which happens frequently, the Children are all left to the Mother, follow her, and are wholly under her Care and Proviſion? If the Father die whilſt the Children are young, do they not naturally every where owe the ſame Obedience to their *Mother*, during their Minority, as to their Father were he alive? And will any one ſay, that the Mother hath a Legiſlative Power over her Children? that ſhe can make ſtanding Rules, which ſhall be of perpetual Obligation, by which they ought to regulate all the concerns of their Property, and bound their Liberty all the courſe of their Lives? Or can ſhe inforce the Obſervation of them with Capital Puniſhments? For this is the proper *Power of the Magiſtrate*, of which the Father hath not ſo much as the ſhadow. His Command over his Children is but Temporary, and reaches not their Life or Property: It is but a help to the weakneſs and imperfection of their Nonage, a Diſcipline neceſſary to their Education: And though a *Father* may diſpoſe of his own Poſſeſſions as he pleaſes, when his Children are out of danger of periſhing for Want, yet *his Power* extends not to the Lives or Goods, which either their own Induſtry, or anothers bounty has made theirs; nor to their Liberty neither, when they are once arrived to the infranchiſement of the Years of Diſcretion. The *Father's Empire* then ceaſes, and he can from thence forwards no more diſpoſe of the liberty of his Son, than that of any other Man: And it muſt be far from an abſolute or perpetual Juriſdiction, from which a Man may withdraw himſelf, having Licence from Divine Authority to *leave Father and Mother and cleave to his Wife*.

66. But though there be a time when a *Child* comes to be as *Free* from Subjection to the Will and Command of his Father, as the Father himſelf is Free from Subjection to the Will of any body elſe, and they are each under no other reſtraint, but that which is common to them both, whether it be the Law of Nature, or municipal Law of their Country: Yet this Freedom exempts not a Son from that *Honour* which he ought, by the Law of God and Nature, *to* pay his *Parents*. God having made the Parents Inſtruments in his great deſign of continuing the Race of Mankind, and the occaſions of Life to their Children; as he hath laid on them an obligation to Nouriſh, preſerve, and bring up their Off-ſpring; So he has laid on the Children a perpetual obligation of *honouring their Parents*, which containing in it an inward Eſteem and Reverence to be ſhewn by all outward Expreſſions, ties up the Child from any thing, that may ever injure or affront, diſturb, or endanger the Happineſs or Life of thoſe, from whom he received his; and engages him in all actions of Defence, Relief, Aſſiſtance and Comfort of thoſe, by whoſe means he entred into Being, and has been made capable of any Enjoyments of Life. From this Obligation no State, no Freedom can abſolve Children. But this is very far from giving Parents a Power of Command over their Children, or an Authority to make Laws and diſpoſe as they pleaſe, of their Lives or Liberties. 'Tis one thing to owe Honour, Reſpect, Gratitude and Aſſiſtance; another to require an abſolute Obedience and Submiſſion. The *Honour due to Parents*, a Monarch in his Throne owes his Mother, and yet this leſſens not his Authority, nor ſubjects him to her Government.

67. The ſubjection of a Minor places in the Father a temporary Government, which terminates with the Minority of the Child: and the *Honour due from a Child*, places in the Parents a perpetual Right to Reſpect, Reverence, Support and Compliance too, more or leſs, as the Father's Care, Coſt, and Kindneſs in his Education, has been more or leſs. This ends not with Minority, but holds in all Parts and Conditions of a Man's Life. The want of diſtinguiſhing theſe two Powers, *viz.* That which the Father hath in the Right of *Tuition*, during Minority; and the Right of *Honour* all his Life, may perhaps have cauſed a great part of the Miſtakes about this Matter. For to ſpeak properly of them, the firſt of theſe is rather the Privilege of Children, and Duty of Parents, than any Prerogative of paternal Power. The Nouriſhment and Education of their Children, is

a Chareg

a Charge ſo incumbent on Parents for their Children's Good, that nothing can abſolve them from taking Care of it. And tho' the *Power of commanding and chaſtiſing* them go along with it, yet God hath woven into the Principles of human Nature ſuch a Tenderneſs for their Off-ſpring, that there is little Fear that Parents ſhould uſe their Power with too much Rigour; the Exceſs is ſeldom on the ſevere ſide, the ſtrong byaſs of Nature drawing the other way. And therefore God Almighty when he would expreſs his gentle Dealing with the *Iſraelites*, he tells them, that tho' he chaſten'd them, *he chaſten'd them as a Man chaſtens his Son*, Deut. viii. 5. *i. e.* with Tenderneſs and Affection, and kept them under no ſeverer Diſcipline, than what was abſolutely beſt for them, and had been leſs Kindneſs to have ſlacken'd. This is that Power to which *Children* are commanded *Obedience*, that the Pains and Care of their Parents may not be increaſed, or ill rewarded.

68. On the other ſide, *Honour* and *Support* all that which Gratitude requires to return for the Benefits received by and from them is the indiſpenſible Duty of the Child, and the proper Privilege of the Parents. This is intended for the Parents Advantage, as the other is for the Child's; though Education, the Parents Duty, ſeems to have moſt Power, becauſe the Ignorance and Infirmities of Childhood ſtand in need of Reſtraint and Correction; which is a viſible Exerciſe of Rule, and a kind of Dominion. And that Duty which is comprehended in the Word *Honour*, requires leſs Obedience, though the Obligation be ſtronger on grown, than younger Children. For who can think the Command, *Children obey your Parents*, requires in a Man, that has Children of his own, the ſame Submiſſion to his Father, as it does in his yet young Children to him; and that by this Precept he were bound to obey all his Father's Commands, if, out of a Conceit of Authority, he ſhould have the Indiſcretion to treat him ſtill as a Boy?

69. The firſt part then of *Paternal Power*, or rather Duty, which is *Education*, belongs ſo to the Father, that it terminates at a certain ſeaſon; when the Buſineſs of Education is over it ceaſes of itſelf, and is alſo alienable before. For a Man may put the Tuition of his Son in other Hands; and he that has made his Son an *Apprentice* to another, has diſcharged him, during that time, of a great part of his Obedience both to himſelf and to his Mother. But all the *Duty of Honour*, the other part, remains never the leſs entire to them; nothing can cancel that: It is ſo inſeparable from them both, that the Father's Authority cannot diſpoſſeſs the Mother of this Right, nor can any Man diſcharge his Son from *honouring* her that bore him. But both theſe are very far from a Power to make Laws, and inforcing them with Penalties, that may reach Eſtate, Liberty, Limbs and Life. The Power of Commanding ends with Nonage; and though after that, *Honour* and Reſpect, Support and Defence, and whatſoever Gratitude can oblige a Man to, for the higheſt Benefits he is naturally capable of, be always due from a Son to his Parents; yet all this puts no Scepter into the Father's Hand, no ſovereign Power of Commanding. He has no Dominion over his Son's Property, or Actions; nor any Right, that his Will ſhould preſcribe to his Sons in all things; however it may become his Son in many things, not very inconvenient to him and his Family, to pay a Deference to it.

70. A Man may owe *Honour* and Reſpect to an ancient, or wiſe Man; Defence to his Child or Friend; Relief and Support to the Diſtreſſed; and Gratitude to a Benefactor, to ſuch a degree, that all he has, all he can do, cannot ſufficiently pay it: But all theſe give no Authority, no Right to any one, of making Laws over him from whom they are owing. And 'tis plain, all this is due not only to the bare Title of Father; not only becauſe, as has been ſaid, it is owing to the Mother too; but becauſe theſe Obligations to Parents, and the Degrees of what is required of Children, may be varied by the different Care and Kindneſs, Trouble and Expence, which is often employed upon one Child more than another.

71. This ſhews the Reaſon how it comes to paſs, that *Parents in Societies*, where they themſelves are Subjects, retain a *Power over their Children*, and have as much Right to their Subjection, as thoſe who are in the ſtate of Nature. Which could not poſſibly be, if all Political Power were only Paternal, and that in truth they were one and the ſame thing: For then, all Paternal Power being in

the Prince, the Subject could naturally have none of it. But these two *Powers, Political* and *Paternal,* are so perfectly distinct and separate; are built upon so different Foundations, and given to so different Ends, that every Subject that is a Father, has as much a Paternal Power over his Children, as the Prince has over his: And every Prince, that has Parents, owes them as much filial Duty and Obedience, as the meanest of his Subjects do to theirs; and can therefore contain not any part or Degree of that kind of Dominion, which a Prince or Magistrate has over his Subject.

72. Though the Obligation on the Parents to *bring up* their Children, and the Obligation on Children to *honour* their Parents, contain all the Power on the one Hand, and Submission on the other, which are proper to this Relation, yet there is *another Power* ordinarily *in the Father,* whereby he has a tie on the Obedience of his Children; which though it be common to him with other Men, yet the Occasions of shewing it, almost constantly happening to Fathers in their private Families, and the Instances of it elsewhere being rare, and less taken notice of, it passes in the World for a part of *Paternal Jurisdiction.* And this is the Power Men generally have to *bestow their Estates* on those who please them best. The Possession of the Father being the Expectation and Inheritance of the Children, ordinarily in certain Proportions, according to the Law and Custom of each Country; yet it is commonly in the Father's Power to bestow it with a more sparing or liberal Hand, according as the Behaviour of this or that Child hath comported with his Will and Humour.

73. This is no small Tie on the Obedience of Children: And there being always annexed to the Enjoyment of Land, a Submission to the Government of the Country, of which that Land is a part; it has been commonly suppos'd, That a *Father* could *oblige his Posterity to that Government,* of which he himself was a Subject, and that his Compact held them; whereas, it being only a necessary Condition annexed to the Land, and the Inheritance of an Estate which is under that Government, reaches only those who will take it on that Condition, and so is no natural Tie or Engagement, but a voluntary Submission. For *every Man's Children* being by Nature as *free* as himself, or any of his Ancestors ever were, may, whilst they are in that Freedom, choose what Society they will join themselves to, what Common-wealth they will put themselves under. But if they will enjoy the *Inheritance* of their Ancestors, they must take it on the same Terms their Ancestors had it, and submit to all the Conditions annex'd to such a Possession. By this Power indeed Fathers oblige their Children to Obedience to themselves, even when they are past Minority, and most commonly too subject them to this or that Political Power. But neither of these by any peculiar Right of *Fatherhood,* but by the Reward they have in their Hands to inforce and recompence such a Compliance; and is no more Power than what a *French Man* has over an *English Man,* who by the Hopes of an Estate he will leave him, will certainly have a strong Tie on his Obedience: And if when it is left him, he will enjoy it, he must certainly take it upon the Conditions annex'd to the *Possession of Land* in that Country where it lies, whether it be *France* or *England.*

74. To conclude then, though the *Father's Power* of commanding extends no farther than the Minority of his Children, and to a Degree only fit for the Discipline and Government of that Age; and though that *Honour* and *Respect,* and all that which the *Latins* called *Piety,* which they indispensibly owe to their Parents all their Life-time, and in all Estates, with all that Support and Defence is due to them, gives the Father no Power of Governing, *i. e.* making Laws and enacting Penalties on his Children; though by all this he has no Dominion over the Property or Actions of his Son: Yet 'tis obvious to conceive how easie it was, in the first Ages of the World, and in Places still, where the thinness of People gives Families leave to separate into unpossessed Quarters, and they have room to remove or plant themselves in yet vacant Habitations; for the *Father of the Family* to become the Prince of † it; he had been a Ruler from the beginning of the Infancy

† *It is no improbable Opinion therefore, which the* Arch-Philosopher *was of, That the chief Person in every Houshold was always, as it were, a King: So when Numbers of Houshalds joyn'd themselves in civil Societies together, Kings were the first kind of Governours amongst them, which is also, as*

fancy of his Children: and ſince without ſome Government it would be hard for them to live together, it was likelieſt it ſhould, by the expreſs or tacit Conſent of the Children when they were grown up, be in the Father, where it ſeemed without any Change barely to continue; when indeed nothing more was required to it, than the permitting the *Father* to exerciſe alone in his Family, that executive Power of the Law of Nature, which every free Man naturally hath, and by that Permiſſion reſigning up to him a Monarchical Power whilſt they remained in it. But that this was not by any *paternal Right*, but only by the Conſent of his Children, is evident from hence, That no Body doubts, but if a Stranger, whom Chance or Buſineſs had brought to his Family, had there kill'd any of his Children, or committed any other Fact, he might condemn and put him to death, or otherwiſe have puniſh'd him, as well as any of his Children; which it was impoſſible he ſhould do by virtue of any paternal Authority over one who was not his Child, but by vertue of that Executive Power of the Law of Nature, which, as a Man, he had a Right to: And he alone could puniſh him in his Family, where the Reſpect of his Children had laid by the Exerciſe of ſuch a Power, to give way to the Dignity and Authority they were willing ſhould remain in him, above the reſt of his Family.

75. Thus 'twas eaſie, and almoſt natural for Children by a tacit, and ſcarce avoidable Conſent, to make way for the *Father's Authority and Government.* They had been accuſtomed in their Childhood to follow his Direction, and to refer their little Differences to him; and when they were Men, who fitter to rule them? Their little Properties, and leſs Covetouſneſs, ſeldom afforded greater Controverſies; and when any ſhould ariſe, where could they have a fitter Umpire than he, by whoſe Care they had every one been ſuſtain'd and brought up, and who had a Tenderneſs for them all? 'Tis no wonder that they made no Diſtinction betwixt Minority and full Age; nor looked after one and twenty, or any other Age that might make them the free Diſpoſers of themſelves and Fortunes, when they could have no Deſire to be out of their Pupilage: The Government they had been under, during it, continued ſtill to be more their Protection than Reſtraint; And they could no where find a greater Security to their Peace, Liberties, and Fortunes, than in the *Rule of a Father.*

76. Thus the natural *Fathers of Families*, by an inſenſible Change, became the *politick Monarchs* of them too: And as they chanced to live long, and leave able and worthy Heirs, for ſeveral Succeſſions, or otherwiſe; ſo they laid the Foundations of Hereditary, or Elective Kingdoms, under ſeveral Conſtitutions and Manners, according as Chance, Contrivance, or Occaſions happen'd to mould them. But if Princes have their Titles in their Fathers Right, and it be a ſufficient Proof of the natural *Right of Fathers* to political Authority, becauſe they commonly were thoſe in whoſe Hands we find, *de facto*, the Exerciſe of Government: I ſay, if this Argument be good, it will as ſtrongly prove, that all Princes, nay Princes only, ought to be Prieſts, ſince 'tis as certain, that in the Beginning, *The Father of the Family was Prieſt, as that he was Ruler in his own Houſhold.*

---

as it ſeemeth, the reaſon why the Name of Fathers continued ſtill in them, who, of Fathers, were made Rulers; as alſo the ancient Cuſtom of Governours to do as Melchizedec, *and being Kings, to exerciſe the Office of Prieſts, which Fathers did, at the firſt grew perhaps by the ſame Occaſion. Howbeit, this is not the only kind of Regiment that has been received in the World. The Inconveniences of one kind have cauſed ſundry others to be deviſed; ſo that in a word, all publick Regiment of what kind ſoever, ſeemeth evidently to have riſen from the deliberate Advice, Conſultation and Compoſition between Men, judging it convenient and behoveful; there being no Impoſſibility in Nature conſidered by itſelf, but that Man might have lived without any publick Regiment.* Hooker's Eccl. P. L. 1. Sect. 10.

CHAP. VII.

Of Political or Civil Society.

77. GOD having made Man ſuch a Creature, that, in his own Judgment, it was not good for him to be alone, put him under ſtrong Obligations of Neceſſity, Convenience, and Inclination to drive him into *Society*, as well as fitted him with Underſtanding and Language to continue and enjoy it. The *firſt Society* was between Man and Wife, which gave beginning to that between Parents and Children; to which, in time, that between Maſter and Servant came to be added: And though all theſe might, and commonly did meet together, and make up but one Family, wherein the Maſter or Miſtreſs of it had ſome ſort of Rule proper to a Family; each of theſe, or all together, came ſhort of *political Society*, as we ſhall ſee, if we conſider the different Ends, Ties, and Bounds of each of theſe.

78. *Conjugal Society* is made by a voluntary Compact between Man and Woman; and tho' it conſiſt chiefly in ſuch a Communion and Right in one anothers Bodies as is neceſſary to its chief End, Procreation; yet it draws with it mutual Support and Aſſiſtance, and a Communion of Intereſts too, as neceſſary not only to unite their Care and Affection, but alſo neceſſary to their common Off-ſpring, who have a Right to be nouriſhed, and maintained by them, till they are able to provide for themſelves.

79. For the end of *Conjunction, between Male and Female*, being not barely Procreation, but the Continuation of the Species; this Conjunction betwixt Male and Female ought to laſt, even after Procreation, ſo long as is neceſſary to the Nouriſhment and Support of the young Ones, who are to be ſuſtained by thoſe that got them, till they are able to ſhift and provide for themſelves. This Rule, which the infinite wiſe Maker hath ſet to the Works of his Hands, we find the inferior Creatures ſteadily obey. In thoſe viviparous Animals which feed on Graſs, the *Conjunction between Male and Female* laſts no longer than the very Act of Copulation; becauſe the Teat of the Dam being ſufficient to nouriſh the Young, till it be able to feed on Graſs, the Male only begets, but concerns not himſelf for the Female or Young, to whoſe Suſtenance he can contribute nothing. But in Beaſts of Prey the *Conjunction* laſts longer: becauſe the Dam not being able well to ſubſiſt her ſelf, and nouriſh her numerous Off-ſpring by her own Prey alone, a more laborious, as well as more dangerous way of living, than by feeding on Graſs, the Aſſiſtance of the Male is neceſſary to the Maintenance of their common Family, which cannot ſubſiſt till they are able to prey for themſelves, but by the joynt Care of Male and Female. The ſame is to be obſerved in all Birds (except ſome domeſtick Ones, where Plenty of Food excuſes the Cock from feeding, and taking Care of the young Brood) whoſe Young needing Food in the Neſt, the Cock and Hen continue Mates, till the Young are able to uſe their Wing, and provide for themſelves.

80. And herein I think lies the chief, if not the only Reaſon, *why the Male and Female in Mankind are tyed to a longer Conjunction* than other Creatures, *viz.* Becauſe the Female is capable of conceiving, and *de facto* is commonly with Child again, and brings forth too a new Birth, long before the former is out of a Dependency for Support on his Parents Help, and able to ſhift for himſelf, and has all the Aſſiſtance is due to him from his Parents; whereby the Father, who is bound to take Care for thoſe he hath begot, is under an Obligation to continue in conjugal Society with the ſame Woman longer than other Creatures, whoſe Young being able to ſubſiſt of themſelves, before the time of Procreation returns again, the conjugal Bond diſſolves of it ſelf, and they are at Liberty, till *Hymen* at his uſual Anniverſary Seaſon ſummons them again to chuſe new Mates. Wherein one cannot but admire the Wiſdom of the great Creator, who having given to Man Foreſight, and an Ability to lay up for the future, as well as to ſupply the preſent Neceſſity, hath made it neceſſary, that *Society of Man and Wiſe ſhould be more laſting*, than of Male and Female amongſt other Creatures; that ſo their Induſtry might be encouraged, and their Intereſt better united, to make Proviſion and lay up

up Goods for their common Iſſue, which uncertain Mixture, or eaſy and frequent Solutions of conjugal Society would mightily diſturb.

81. But though theſe are Ties upon *Mankind*, which make the *Conjugal Bonds* more firm and laſting in Man, than the other Species of Animals; yet it would give one Reaſon to enquire, why this *Compact*, where Procreation and Education are ſecured, and Inheritance taken Care for, may not be made determinable, either by Conſent, or at a certain time, or upon certain Conditions, as well as any other voluntary Compacts, there being no Neceſſity in the Nature of the thing, nor to the Ends of it, that it ſhould always be for Life; I mean, to ſuch as are under no Reſtraint of any poſitive Law, which ordains all ſuch Contracts to be perpetual.

82. But the Husband and Wife, though they have but one common Concern, yet having different Underſtandings, will unavoidably ſometimes have different Wills too; it therefore being neceſſary that the laſt Determination, *i. e.* the Rule, ſhould be placed ſomewhere; it naturally falls to the Man's Share, as the abler and the ſtronger. But this reaching but to the things of their common Intereſt and Property, leaves the Wife in the full and free Poſſeſſion of what by Contract is her peculiar Right, and gives the Husband no more Power over her Life than ſhe has over his. The *Power of the Husband* being ſo far from that of an abſolute Monarch, that the *Wife* has in many Caſes a Liberty to ſeparate from him; where natural Right, or their Contract allows it, whether that Contract be made by themſelves in the State of Nature, or by the Cuſtoms or Laws of the Country they live in; and the Children upon ſuch Separation fall to the Father or Mother's Lot, as ſuch Contract does determine.

83. For all the Ends of *Marriage* being to be obtained under politick Government, as well as in the State of Nature, the Civil Magiſtrate doth not abridge the Right or Power of either naturally neceſſary to thoſe Ends, *viz.* Procreation and mutual Support and Aſſiſtance whilſt they are together; but only decides any Controverſy that may ariſe between Man and Wife about them. If it were otherwiſe, and that abſolute *Sovereignty* and Power of Life and Death naturally belong'd to the Husband, and were *neceſſary to the Society between Man and Wife*, there could be no Matrimony in any of thoſe Countries where the Husband is allow'd no ſuch abſolute Authority. But the Ends of Matrimony requiring no ſuch Power in the Husband, the Condition of *Conjugal Society* put it not in him, it being not at all neceſſary to that State. *Conjugal Society* could ſubſiſt and attain its Ends without it; nay, Community of Goods, and the Power over them, mutual Aſſiſtance and Maintenance, and other things belonging to *Conjugal Society*, might be varyed and regulated by that Contract which unites Man and Wife in that Society, as far as may conſiſt with Procreation and the bringing up of Children till they could ſhift for themſelves; nothing being neceſſary to any Society, that is not neceſſary to the Ends for which it is made.

84. The *Society betwixt Parents and Children*, and the diſtinct Rights and Powers belonging reſpectively to them, I have treated of ſo largely, in the foregoing Chapter, that I ſhall not here need to ſay any thing of it. And I think it is plain, that it is far different from a politick Society.

85. *Maſter* and *Servant* are Names as old as Hiſtory, but given to thoſe of far different Condition; for a Freeman makes himſelf a Servant to another, by ſelling him for a certain time, the Service he undertakes to do, in exchange for Wages he is to receive: And though this commonly puts him into the Family of his Maſter, and under the ordinary Diſcipline thereof; yet it gives the Maſter but a temporary Power over him, and no greater, than what is contained in the *Contract* between 'em. But there is another ſort of Servants, which by a peculiar Name we call *Slaves*, who being Captives taken in a juſt War, are by the Right of Nature ſubjected to the abſolute Dominion and arbitrary Power of their Maſters. Theſe Men having, as I ſay, forfeited their Lives, and with it their Liberties, and loſt their Eſtates; and being in the *State of Slavery*, not capable of any Property, cannot in that State be conſidered as any part of *Civil Society*; the chief End whereof is the Preſervation of Property.

86. Let us therefore conſider a *Maſter of a Family* with all theſe ſubordinate Relations of *Wife*, *Children*, *Servants*, and *Slaves*, united under the Domeſtick Rule of a Family; which, what Reſemblance ſoever it may have in its Order, Offices, and Number too, with a little Commonwealth, yet is very far from it, both in

in its Constitution, Power and End: Or if it must be thought a Monarchy, and the *Paterfamilias* the absolute Monarch in it, absolute Monarchy will have but a very shattered and short Power, when 'tis plain, by what has been said before, That the *Master of the Family* has a very distinct and differently limited *Power*, both as to Time and Extent, over those several Persons that are in it; for excepting the Slave (and the Family is as much a Family, and his Power as *Paterfamilias* as great, whether there be any Slaves in his Family or no) he has no Legislative Power of Life and Death over any of them, and none too but what a *Mistress of a Family* may have as well as he. And he certainly can have no absolute Power over the whole *Family*, who has but a very limitted one over every Individual in it. But how a *Family*, or any other Society of Men differ from that, which is properly *political Society*, we shall best see, by considering wherein *political Society* it self consists.

87. Man being born, as has been proved, with a Title to perfect Freedom, and an uncontrouled Enjoyment of all the Rights and Privileges of the Law of Nature, equally with any other Man, or Number of Men in the World, hath by Nature a Power, not only to preserve his Property, that is, his Life, Liberty and Estate, against the Injuries and Attempts of other Men; but to judge of, and punish the Breaches of that Law in others, as he is perswaded the Offence deserves, even with Death itself, in Crimes where the Heinousness of the Fact, in his Opinion, requires it. But because no *political Society* can be, nor subsist without having in itself the Power to preserve the Property, and in order thereunto, punish the Offences of all those of that Society; there, and there only is *political Society*, where every one of the Members hath quitted this natural Power, resign'd it up into the Hands of the Community in all Cases that exclude him not from appealing for Protection to the Law established by it. And thus all private Judgment of every particular Member being excluded, the Community comes to be Umpire, by settled standing Rules, indifferent, and the same to all Parties; and by Men having Authority from the Community, for the Execution of those Rules, decides all the Differences that may happen between any Members of that Society concerning any Matter of Right; and punishes those Offences which any Member hath committed against the Society, with such Penalties as the Law has established; whereby it is easie to discern, who are, and who are not, in *political Society* together. Those who are united into one Body, and have a common establish'd Law and Judicature to appeal to, with Authority to decide Controversies between them, and punish Offenders, are in *Civil Society* one with another: But those who have no such common Appeal, I mean on Earth, are still in the state of Nature, each being, where there is no other, Judge for himself, and Executioner; which is, as I have before shew'd it, the perfect *state of Nature*.

88. And thus the Commonwealth comes by a Power to set down what Punishment shall belong to the several Transgressions which they think worthy of it, committed amongst the Members of that Society, (which is the *Power of making Laws)* as well as it has the Power to punish any Injury done unto any of its Members, by any one that is not of it, (which is the *power of War and Peace*;) and all this for the Preservation of the Property of all the Members of that Society, as far as is possible. But though every Man who has enter'd into civil Society, and is become a member of any Commonwealth has thereby quitted his Power to punish Offences, against the Law of *Nature*, in prosecution of his own private Judgment, yet with the Judgment of Offences, which he has given up to the Legislative in all Cases, where he can appeal to the Magistrate, he has given a Right to the Commonwealth to imploy his Force, for the execution of the Judgments of the Commonwealth, whenever he shall be called to it; which indeed are his own Judgments, they being made by himself, or his Representative. And herein we have the original of the *legislative* and *executive Power* of civil Society, which is to judge by standing Laws, how far Offences are to be punished, when committed within the Commmonwealth; and also to determine, by occasional Judgments founded on the present Circumstances of the Fact, how far Injuries from without are to be vindicated; and in both these to imploy all the force of all the Members, when there shall be need.

89. Whereever therefore any number of Men are so united into one Society, as to quit every one his executive power of the Law of Nature, and to resign it to the

the publick, there and there only is a *political, or civil Society*. And this is done, whereever any number of Men, in the ſtate of Nature, enter into Society to make one People, one Body politick, under one ſupream Government; or elſe when any one joyns himſelf to, and incorporates with any Government already made. For hereby he authorizes the Society, or which is all one, the Legiſlative thereof, to make Laws for him, as the publick good of the Society ſhall require; to the Execution whereof, his own Aſſiſtance (as to his own Decrees) is due. And this *puts Men* out of a ſtate of Nature *into* that of a *Commonwealth*, by ſetting up a Judge on Earth, with Authority to determine all the Controverſies, and redreſs the Injuries, that may happen to any Member of the Commonwealth; which Judge is the Legiſlative, or Magiſtrates appointed by it. And whereever there are any number of Men, however aſſociated, that have no ſuch deciſive Power to appeal to, there they are ſtill in *the ſtate of Nature*.

90. Hence it is evident, that *abſolute Monarchy*, which by ſome Men is counted the only Government in the World, is indeed *inconſiſtent with civil Society*, and ſo can be no form of Civil-Government at all. For the *end of civil Society*, being to avoid, and remedy thoſe inconveniencies of the ſtate of Nature, which neceſſarily follow from every Man's being Judge in his own Caſe, by ſetting up a known Authority, to which every one of that Society may appeal upon any Injury received, or Controverſie that may ariſe, and which every one of the † Society ought to obey; whereever any Perſons are, who have not ſuch an Authority to appeal to, for the deciſion of any Difference between them, there thoſe Perſons are ſtill *in the ſtate of Nature*. And ſo is every *abſolute Prince* in reſpect of thoſe who are under his *Dominion*.

91. For he being ſuppos'd to have all, both legiſlative and executive Power in himſelf alone, there is no Judge to be found, no appeal lies open to any one, who may fairly, and indifferently, and with Authority decide, and from whoſe Deciſion Relief and Redreſs may be expected of any Injury or Inconveniency, that may be ſuffered from the Prince, or by his Order: So that ſuch a Man, however intitled, *Czar*, or *Grand Seignior*, or how you pleaſe, is as much *in the ſtate of Nature*, with all under his Dominion, as he is with the reſt of Mankind. For whereever any two Men are, who have no ſtanding Rule, and common Judge to appeal to on Earth, for the determination of Controverſies of Right betwixt them, there they are ſtill *in the ſtate of* * *Nature*, and under all the inconveniencies of it, with only this woful Difference to the Subject, or rather Slave of an abſolute Prince: That whereas, in the ordinary ſtate of Nature, he has a Liberty to judge of his Right, and according to the beſt of his Power, to maintain it; now whenever his Property is invaded by the will and order of his Monarch, he has not only no Appeal, as thoſe in Society ought to have, but as if he were degraded from the common ſtate of rational Creatures, is denied a Liberty to judge of, or to defend his Right; and ſo is expoſed to all the Miſery and Inconveniencies, that a Man can fear from one, who being in the unreſtrained ſtate of Nature, is yet corrupted with Flattery, and armed with Power.

92. For he that thinks *abſolute Power purifies Mens Bloods*, and corrects the baſeneſs of human Nature, need read but the Hiſtory of this, or any other Age to be convinced of the contrary. He that would have been inſolent and injurious in

† *The publick Power of all Society is above every Soul contained in the ſame Society; and the principal Uſe of that power is, to give Laws unto all that are under it, which Laws in ſuch Caſes we muſt obey, unleſs there be reaſon ſhew'd which may neceſſarily inforce, that the Law of Reaſon, or of God, doth injoyn the contrary,* Hook. Eccl. Pol. L. 1. Sect. 16.

* *To take away all ſuch mutual Grievances, Injuries and Wrongs,* i. e. ſuch as attend Men in the ſtate of Nature. *There was no way but only by growing into Compoſition and Agreement amongſt themſelves, by ordaining ſome kind of Government publick, and by yielding themſelves ſubject thereunto, that unto whom they granted Authority to rule and govern, by them the Peace, Tranquillity and happy Eſtate of the reſt might be procured. Men always knew that where Force and Injury was offered, they might be Defenders of themſelves; they knew that however Men may ſeek their own Commodity; yet if this were done with Injury unto others, it was not to be ſuffered, but by all Men, and all good Means to be withſtood. Finally, they knew that no Man might in reaſon take upon him to determine his own Right, and according to his own Determination proceed in Maintenance thereof, in as much as every Man is towards himſelf, and them whom he greatly affects, partial; and therefore that Strifes and Troubles would be endleſs, except they gave their common Conſent all to be ordered by ſome, whom they ſhould agree upon, without which Conſent there would be no reaſon that one Man ſhould take upon him to be Lord or Judge over another.* Hooker's Eccl. Pol. L. 1. Sect. 10.

the

the Woods of *America*, would not probably be much better in a Throne; where perhaps Learning and Religion ſhall be found out to juſtifie all, that he ſhall do to his Subjects, and the Sword preſently ſilence all thoſe that dare queſtion it. For what the *Protection of abſolute Monarchy* is, what kind of Fathers of their Countries it makes Princes to be, and to what a degree of Happineſs and Security it carries civil Society, where this ſort of Government is grown to perfection, he that will look into the late Relation of *Ceylon*, may eaſily ſee.

93. *In abſolute Monarchies* indeed, as well as other Governments of the World, the Subjects have an Appeal to the Law, and Judges to decide any Controverſies, and reſtrain any Violence that may happen betwixt the Subjects themſelves, one amongſt another. This every one thinks neceſſary, and believes he deſerves to be thought a declared Enemy to Society and Mankind, who ſhould go about to take it away. But whether this be from a true Love of Mankind and Society, and ſuch a Charity as we owe all one to another, there is Reaſon to doubt. For this is no more, than what every Man, who loves his own Power, Profit, or Greatneſs, may and naturally muſt do, keep thoſe Animals from hurting, or deſtroying one another, who labour and drudge only for his Pleaſure and Advantage; and ſo are taken care of, not out of any Love the Maſter has for them, but Love of himſelf, and the Profit they bring him. For if it be asked, what Security, *what Fence* is there, in ſuch a State, *againſt the Violence and Oppreſſion of this abſolute Ruler?* The very Queſtion can ſcarce be born. They are ready to tell you, that it deſerves Death only to ask after Safety. Betwixt Subject and Subject, they will grant, there muſt be Meaſures, Laws and Judges, for their mutual Peace and Security: But as for the *Ruler*, he ought to be *abſolute*, and is above all ſuch Circumſtances; becauſes he has Power to do more Hurt and Wrong, 'tis right when he does it. To ask how you may be guarded from Harm, or Injury, on that ſide where the ſtrongeſt Hand is to do it, is preſently the voice of Faction and Rebellion. As if when Men quitting the ſtate of Nature entered into Society, they agreed that all of them but one, ſhould be under the reſtraint of Laws, but that he ſhould ſtill retain all the Liberty of the ſtate of Nature, increaſed with Power, and made licentious by Impunity. This is to think, that Men are ſo fooliſh, that they take care to avoid what Miſchiefs may be done them by *Pole-Cats*, or *Foxes*; but are content, nay think it Safety, to be devoured by *Lions*.

94. But whatever Flatterers may talk to amuze Peoples Underſtandings, it hinders not Men from feeling; and when they perceive, that any Man in what Station ſoever, is out of the Bounds of the civil Society which they are of, and that they have no Appeal on Earth againſt any Harm, they may receive from him, they are apt to think themſelves in the ſtate of Nature, in reſpect of him, whom they find to be ſo; and to take Care as ſoon as they can, to have that *Safety and Security in civil Society*, for which it was firſt inſtituted, and for which only they entered into it. And therefore, though perhaps at firſt, (as ſhall be ſhewed more at large hereafter in the following part of this Diſcourſe) ſome one good and excellent Man having got a Preheminency amongſt the reſt, had this Difference paid to his Goodneſs and Vertue, as to a kind of natural Authority, that the chief Rule, with Arbitration of their Differences, by a tacit Conſent devolved into his Hands, without any other Caution, but the Aſſurance they had of his Uprightneſs and Wiſdom; yet when time, giving Authority, and (as ſome Men would perſwade us,) Sacredneſs to Cuſtoms, which the negligent, and unforeſeeing Innocence of the firſt Ages began, had brought in Succeſſors of another Stamp, the People finding their Properties not ſecure under the Government, as then it was, (whereas Government has no other end but the preſervation of * Property) could never be ſafe nor at reſt, *nor think themſelves in civil Society*, till the Legiſlature was placed in collective Bodies of Men, call them Senate, Parliament, or what you pleaſe. By which Means every ſingle Perſon became ſubject, equally with other the mea-

* *At the firſt, when ſome certain kind of Regiment was once appointed, it may be that nothing was then farther thought upon for the manner of governing, but all permitted unto their Wiſdom and Diſcretion, which were to Rule, till by Experience they found this for all Parts very inconvenient, ſo as the thing which they had deviſed for a Remedy, did indeed but increaſe the Sore, which it ſhould have cured. They ſaw, that* to live by one Man's Will, became the cauſe of all Mens Miſery. *This conſtrained them to come unto Laws, wherein all Men might ſee their Duty beforehand, and know the Penalties of tranſgreſſing them.* Hooker's Eccl. Pol. L. 1. Sect. 10.

neſt

neſt Men, to thoſe Laws, which he himſelf, as part of the Legiſlative, had eſtabliſhed; nor could any one, by his own Authority avoid the force of the Law, when once made; nor by any pretence of Superiority plead Exemption, thereby to licenſe his own, or the Miſcarriages of any of his Dependents. † *No Man in civil Society can be exempted from the Laws of it.* For if any Man may do, what he thinks fit, and there be no Appeal on Earth, for Redreſs or Security againſt any Harm he ſhall do: I ask, whether he be not perfectly ſtill in the ſtate of Nature, and ſo can be *no Part or Member of that civil Society*; unleſs any one will ſay, the ſtate of Nature and civil Society are one and the ſame thing, which I have never yet found any one ſo great a patron of Anarchy as to affirm.

CHAP. VIII.

Of the Beginning of Political Societies.

95. MEN being, as has been ſaid, by Nature, all free, equal, and independent, no one can be put out of this Eſtate, and ſubjected to the political Power of another, without his own Conſent. The only Way whereby any one deveſts himſelf of his natural Liberty, and puts on the *Bonds of civil Society* is by agreeing with other Men to joyn and unite into a Community, for their comfortable, ſafe, and peaceable Living one amongſt another, in a ſecure Enjoyment of their Properties, and a greater Security againſt any, that are not of it. This any number of Men may do, becauſe it injures not the Freedom of the reſt; they are left as they were in the Liberty of the ſtate of Nature. When any number of Men have ſo *conſented to make one Community or Government*, they are thereby preſently incorporated, and make *one Body politick*, wherein the *Majority* have a Right to act and conclude the reſt.

96. For when any number of Men have, by the conſent of every individual, made a *Community*, they have thereby made that *Community* one Body, with a Power to act as one Body, which is only by the Will and Determination of the *Majority*. For that which acts any Community, being only the conſent of the individuals of it, and it being neceſſary to that which is one Body to move one way; it is neceſſary the Body ſhould move that way whither the greater force carries it, which is the *conſent of the Majority*: Or elſe it is impoſſible it ſhould act or continue one Body, *one Community*, which the conſent of every individual that united into it, agreed that it ſhould; and ſo every one is bound by that conſent to be concluded by the *Majority*. And therefore we ſee, that in Aſſemblies, impowered to act by poſitive Laws, where no number is ſet by that poſitive Law which impowers them, the *Act of the Majority* paſſes for the Act of the whole, and of courſe determines, as having by the Law of Nature and Reaſon, the Power of the whole.

97. And thus every Man, by conſenting with others to make one Body Politick under one Government, puts himſelf under an Obligation, to every one of that Society, to ſubmit to the determination of the *Majority*, and to be concluded by it; or elſe this *original Compact*, whereby he with others incorporates into *one Society*, would ſignifie nothing, and be no Compact, if he be left Free, and under no other Ties, than he was in before in the State of Nature. For what appearance would there be of any Compact? What new Engagement if he were no farther tied by any decrees of the Society, than he himſelf thought fit, and did actually conſent to? This would be ſtill as great a Liberty, as he himſelf had before his Compact, or any one elſe in the State of Nature hath, who may ſubmit himſelf, and conſent to any acts of it if he thinks fit.

98. For if *the conſent of the Majority* ſhall not, in Reaſon, be received, as *the act of the whole*, and conclude every individual; nothing but the conſent of every in-

---

† *Civil Law being the Act of the whole Body politick, doth therefore over-rule each ſeveral part of the ſame Body.* Hooker ibid.

dividual can make any thing to be the act of the whole: But such a consent is next impossible ever to be had, if we consider the Infirmities of Health, and Avocations of Business, which in a Number, though much less than that of a Commonwealth, will necessarily keep many away from the publick Assembly. To which if we add the variety of Opinions, and contrariety of Interests, which unavoidably happen in all Collections of Men, the coming into Society upon such terms would be only like *Cato*'s coming into the Theatre, only to go out again. Such a Constitution, as this, would make the mighty *Leviathan* of a shorter Duration, than the feeblest Creatures; and not let it outlast the day it was born in: Which cannot be suppos'd, till we can think, that Rational Creatures should desire and constitute Societies only to be dissolved. For where the *majority* cannot conclude the rest, there they cannot act as one Body, and consequently will be immediately dissolved again.

99. Whosoever therefore out of a state of Nature unite into a *Community*, must be understood to give up all the Power, necessary to the ends for which they unite into Society, to the *majority* of the Community, unless they expresly agreed in any number greater than the Majority. And this is done by barely agreeing to *unite into one Political Society*, which is *all the Compact* that is, or needs be, between the Individuals, that enter into, or make up a *Commonwealth*. And thus that, which begins and actually *constitutes any Political Society*, is nothing but the consent of any number of Freemen capable of a majority to unite and incorporate into such a Society. And this is that, and that only, which did, or could give beginning to any *lawful Government* in the World.

100. To this I find two Objections made.

First, *That there are no Instances to be found in Story, of a Company of Men Independent, and equal one amongst another, that met together, and in this way began and set up a Government.*

Secondly, *'Tis impossible of Right, that Men should do so, because all Men being born under Government, they are to submit to that, and are not at liberty to begin a new one.*

101. To the first there is this to answer, That it is not at all to be wonder'd, that *History* gives us but a very little account of *Men, that lived together in the State of Nature*. The Inconveniencies of that Condition, and the Love, and want of Society no sooner brought any number of them together, but they presently united, and incorporated, if they designed to continue together. And if we may not suppose *Men* ever to have been *in the State of Nature*, because we hear not much of them in such a State, we may as well suppose the Armies of *Salmanasser*, or *Xerxes* were never Children, because we hear little of them, till they were Men, and imbodied in Armies. Government is every where antecedent to Records, and Letters seldom come in amongst a People, till a long continuation of Civil Society has, by other more necessary Arts, provided for their Safety, Ease, and Plenty. And then they begin to look after the History of their Founders, and search into their *Original*, when they have out-lived the memory of it. For 'tis with *Commonwealths* as with particular Persons, they are commonly *ignorant of their own Births and Infancies:* And if they know any thing of their *Original*, they are beholding, for it, to the accidental Records, that others have kept of it. And those that we have, of the beginning of any Polities in the World, excepting that of the *Jews*, where God himself immediately interpos'd, and which favours not at all paternal Dominion, are all either plain instances of such a beginning, as I have mentioned, or at least have manifest footsteps of it.

102. He must shew a strange inclination to deny evident matter of Fact, when it agrees not with his Hypothesis, who will not allow, that the *beginning* of *Rome* and *Venice* were by the uniting together of several Men free and independent one of another, amongst whom there was no natural Superiority or Subjection. And if *Josephus Acosta*'s word may be taken, he tells us, that in many parts of *America* there was no Government at all. *There are great and apparent Conjectures*, says he, *that these Men*, speaking of those of Peru, *for a long time had neither Kings nor Commonwealths, but lived in Troops, as they do this day in* Florida, *the* Cheriquanas, *those of* Brasil, *and many other Nations, which have no certain Kings, but as occasion is offered in Peace or War, they choose their Captains as they please*, l. 1. c. 25. If it be said, that every Man there was born subject to his Father, or the head of his Family. That the subjection due from a Child to a Father, took not away his Freedom of uniting

ting into what Political Society he thought fit, has been already proved. But be that as it will, these Men, 'tis evident, were actually *Free*; and whatever Superiority some Politicians now would place in any of them, they themselves claimed it not: but by consent were all *equal*, till by the same consent they set Rulers over themselves. So that their *Politick Societies* all *began* from a voluntary Union, and the mutual agreement of Men freely acting in the choice of their Governors, and forms of Government.

103. And I hope those who went away from *Sparta* with *Palantus*, mentioned by *Justin* l. 3. c. 4. will be allowed to have been *Freemen Independent* one of another, and to have set up a Government over themselves, by their own Consent. Thus I have given several Examples out of History, of *People Free and in the State of Nature*, that being met together incorporated and *began a Common-wealth*. And if the want of such instances be an Argument to prove that *Government* were not, nor could not be so *begun*, I suppose the Contenders for Paternal Empire were better let it alone, than urge it against natural Liberty. For if they can give so many instances, out of History, of *Governments begun* upon paternal Right, I think (though at best an Argument from what has been, to what should of right be, has no great force) one might, without any great danger, yield them the cause. But if I might advise them in the Case, they would do well not to search too much into the *Original of Governments*, as they have begun *de facto*, lest they should find at the foundation of most of them, something very little favourable to the design they promote, and such a Power as they contend for.

104. But to conclude, Reason being plain on our side, that Men are naturally Free, and the Examples of History shewing, that the *Governments* of the World, that were begun in Peace, had their beginning laid on that Foundation, and were *made by the Consent of the People*; There can be little room for doubt, either where the Right is, or what has been the Opinion, or Practice of Mankind, about the *first erecting of Governments*.

105. I will not deny, that if we look back as far as History will direct us, towards the *Original of Commonwealths*, we shall generally find them under the Government and Administration of one Man. And I am also apt to believe, that where a Family was numerous enough to subsist by itself, and continued entire together, without mixing with others, as it often happens, where there is much Land, and few People, the Government commonly began in the Father. For the Father having, by the Law of Nature, the same Power with every Man else to punish, as he thought fit, any Offences against that Law, might thereby punish his transgressing Children, even when they were Men, and out of their Pupilage; and they were very likely to submit to his Punishment, and all joyn with him against the Offender, in their turns, giving him thereby Power to Execute his Sentence against any transgression, and so in effect make him the Law-Maker, and Governor over all, that remained in Conjunction with his Family. He was fittest to be trusted; Paternal affection secured their Property, and Interest under his Care; and the Custom of obeying him, in their Childhood, made it easier to submit to him, rather than to any other. If therefore they must have one to rule them, as Government is hardly to be avoided amongst Men that live together; who so likely to be the Man, as he that was their common Father; unless Negligence, Cruelty, or any other defect of Mind, or Body made him unfit for it? But when either the Father died, and left his next Heir, for want of Age, Wisdom, Courage, or any other Qualities, less fit for Rule; or where several Familes met, and consented to continue together; There 'tis not to be doubted, but they used their natural Freedom, to set up him, whom they judged the ablest, and most likely, to Rule well over them. Conformable hereunto we find the People of *America*, who (living out of the reach of the Conquering Swords, and spreading domination of the two great Empires of *Peru* and *Mexico)* enjoy'd their own natural Freedom, though, *cæteris paribus*, they commonly prefer the Heir of their deceased King; yet if they find him any way weak, or uncapable, they pass him by, and set up the stoutest, and bravest Man for their Ruler.

106. Thus, though looking back as far as Records give us any account of peopling the World, and the History of Nations, we commonly find the *Government* to be in one Hand; yet it destroys not that which I affirm, *viz.* That the *Beginning of politick Society* depends upon the Consent of the Individuals, to joyn into,

and make one Society; who, when they are thus incorporated, might ſet up what Form of Government they thought fit. But this having given Occaſion to Men to miſtake, and think, that by Nature Government was monarchical, and belong'd to the Father, it may not be amiſs here to conſider, why People in the beginning generally pitch'd upon this Form, which though perhaps the Father's Preheminency might in the firſt Inſtitution of ſome Commonwealths, give a riſe to, and place in the beginning, the Power in one Hand; yet it is plain that the Reaſon, that continued the Form of *Government in a ſingle Perſon*, was not any Regard, or Reſpect to paternal Authority; ſince all petty *Monarchies*, that is, almoſt all Monarchies, near their Original, have been commonly, at leaſt upon occaſion, *Elective*.

107. Firſt then, in the beginning of things, the Father's Government of the Childhood of thoſe ſprung from him, having accuſtomed them to the *Rule of one Man*, and taught them that where it was exerciſed with Care and Skill, with Affection and Love to thoſe under it, it was ſufficient to procure and preſerve to Men all the political Happineſs they ſought for in Society. It was no wonder that they ſhould pitch upon, and naturally run into that Form of Government, which from their Infancy they had been all accuſtomed to; and which, by Experience, they had found both eaſie and ſafe. To which, if we add, that *Monarchy* being ſimple, and moſt obvious to Men, whom neither Experience had inſtructed in Forms of Government, nor the Ambition or Inſolence of Empire had taught to beware of the Encroachments of Prerogative, or the Inconveniencies of abſolute Power, which Monarchy in Succeſſion was apt to lay claim to, and bring upon them; it was not at all ſtrange, that they ſhould not much trouble themſelves, to think of Methods of reſtraining any Exorbitances of thoſe to whom they had given the Authority over them, and of balancing the Power of Government, by placing ſeveral parts of it in different Hands. They had neither felt the Oppreſſion of tyrannical Dominion, nor did the faſhion of the Age, nor their Poſſeſſions, or way of living, (which afforded little Matter for Covetouſneſs or Ambition) give them any Reaſon to apprehend or provide againſt it; and therefore 'tis no wonder they put themſelves into ſuch a *Frame of Government*, as was not only, as I ſaid, moſt obvious and ſimple, but alſo beſt ſuited to their preſent State and Condition; which ſtood more in need of Defence againſt foreign Invaſions and Injuries, than of Multiplicity of Laws. The Equality of a ſimple poor way of living, confining their Deſires within the narrow Bounds of each Man's ſmall Property, made few Controverſies, and ſo no need of many Laws to decide them, or Variety of Officers to ſuperintend the Proceſs, or look after the Execution of Juſtice, where there were but few Treſpaſſes, and few Offenders. Since then thoſe, who liked one another ſo well as to joyn into Society, cannot but be ſuppoſed to have ſome Acquaintance and Friendſhip together, and ſome Truſt one in another; they could not but have greater Apprehenſions of others, than of one another: And therefore their firſt Care and Thought cannot but be ſuppoſed to be, how to ſecure themſelves againſt foreign Force. 'Twas natural for them to put themſelves under a *Frame of Government*, which might beſt ſerve to that End; and chuſe the wiſeſt and braveſt Man to conduct them in their Wars, and lead them out againſt their Enemies, and in this chiefly be their *Ruler*.

108. Thus we ſee, that the *Kings* of the *Indians* in *America*, which is ſtill a Pattern of the firſt Ages in *Aſia* and *Europe*, whilſt the Inhabitants were too few for the Country, and want of People and Money gave Men no Temptation to enlarge their Poſſeſſions of Land, or conteſt for wider Extent of Ground, are little more than *Generals of their Armies*; and though they command abſolutely in War, yet at home and in time of Peace they exerciſe very little Dominion, and have but a very moderate Sovereignty, the Reſolutions of Peace and War being ordinarily either in the People, or in a Council. Though the War itſelf, which admits not of Plurality of Governours, naturally devolves the Command into the *King's ſole Authority*.

109. And thus in *Iſrael* it ſelf, the *chief Buſineſs of their Judges, and firſt Kings* ſeems to have been *to be Captains in War*, and Leaders of their Armies; which, (beſides what is ſignifyed by *going out and in before the People*, which was, to march forth to War, and home again in the Heads of their Forces) appears plainly in the Story of *Jephtha*. The *Ammonites* making War upon *Iſrael*, the *Gileadites* in fear

fear send to *Jephtha*, a Bastard of their Family whom they had cast off, and article with him, if he will assist them against the *Ammonites*, to make him their Ruler; which they do in these Words, *And the People made him Head and Captain over them*, Judg. xi. 11. which was, as it seems, all one as to be *Judge*. *And he judged Israel*, Judg. xii. 7. that is, was their *Captain-General six Years*. So when *Jotham* upbraids the *Shechemites* with the Obligation they had to *Gideon*, who had been their *Judge* and Ruler, he tells them, *He fought for you, and adventured his Life far, and delivered you out of the Hands of Midian*, Judg. ix. 17. Nothing mentioned of him, but what he did as a *General:* and indeed that is all is found in his History, or in any of the rest of the Judges. And *Abimelech* particularly is called *King*, tho' at most he was but their *General*. And when, being weary of the ill Conduct of *Samuel*'s Sons, the Children of *Israel* desired a *King*, *like all the Nations to judge them, and to go out before them, and to fight their Battels*, 1 Sam. viii. 20. God granting their Desire, says to *Samuel*, *I will send thee a Man, and thou shalt anoint him to be Captain over my People Israel, that he may save my People out of the Hands of the Philistines*, c. ix. v. 16. As if the only *Business of a King* had been to lead out their Armies, and fight in their Defence; and accordingly at his Inauguration pouring a Vial of Oyl upon him, declares to *Saul*, that *the Lord had anointed him to be Captain over his Inheritance*, c. x. v. 1. And therefore those, who after *Saul*'s being solemnly chosen and saluted *King* by the *Tribes* at *Mispah*, were unwilling to have him their King, make no other Objection but this, *How shall this Man save us?* v. 27. as if they should have said, This Man is unfit to be our *King*, not having Skill and Conduct enough in War, to be able to defend us. And when God resolved to transfer the Government to *David*, it is in these Words, *But now thy Kingdom shall not continue: The Lord hath sought him a Man after his own Heart, and the Lord hath commanded him to be Captain over his People*, c. xiii. v. 14. As if the whole *Kingly Authority* were nothing else but to be their *General:* And therefore the *Tribes* who had stuck to *Saul*'s Family, and opposed *David*'s Reign, when they came to *Hebron* with Terms of Submission to him, they tell him, amongst other arguments they had to submit to him as to their King, That he was in effect their *King* in *Saul*'s time, and therefore they had no reason but to receive him as their *King* now. *Also* (say they) *in time past, when Saul was King over us, thou wast he that leddest out and broughtest in Israel, and the Lord said unto thee, thou shalt feed my People Israel, and thou shalt be a Captain over Israel.*

110. Thus, whether *a Family* by degrees *grew up into a Commonwealth*, and the fatherly Authority being continued on to the elder Son, every one in his turn growing up under it, tacitly submitted to it, and the Easiness and Equality of it not offending any one, every one acquiesced, till time seemed to have confirmed it, and settled a right of Succession by Prescription; or whether several Families, or the Descendants of several Families, whom Chance, Neighbourhood, or Business brought together, uniting into Society, the need of a General, whose Conduct might defend them against their Enemies in War, and the great Confidence the Innocence and Sincerity of that poor but vertuous Age, (such as are almost all those which begin Governments, that ever come to last in the World) gave Men one of another, made the first Beginners of Commonwealths generally put the Rule into one Man's Hand, without any other express Limitation or Restraint, but what the Nature of the thing, and the End of Government required: Which ever of those it was that at first put the Rule into the Hand of a single Person, certain it is no body was intrusted with it but for the publick Good and Safety, and to those Ends in the Infancies of Commonwealths commonly used it. And unless those who had it had done so, young Societies could not have subsisted; without such nursing Fathers tender and careful of the Publick Weale, all Governments would have sunk under the Weakness and Infirmities of their Infancy, and the Prince and the People had soon perished together.

111. But though the *Golden Age* (before vain Ambition, and *amor sceleratus habendi*, evil Concupiscence had corrupted Mens Minds into a Mistake of true Power and Honour) had more Virtue, and consequently better Governours, as well as less vicious Subjects; and there was then *no stretching Prerogative* on the one side, to oppress the People; *nor* consequently on the other, any *Dispute about Privilege*, to lessen or restrain the Power of the Magistrate, and so no Contest betwixt Rulers and People about Governours or Government: Yet, when Ambition

tion and Luxury in future Ages * would retain and increaſe the Power, without doing the Buſineſs for which it was given; and aided by Flattery, taught Princes to have diſtinct and ſeparate Intereſts from their People, Men found it neceſſary to examine more carefully *the Original* and Rights *of Government*; and to find out ways to *reſtrain the Exorbitances*, and *prevent the Abuſes* of that Power, which they having intruſted in another's Hands only for their own Good they found was made uſe of to hurt them.

112. Thus we may ſee how probable it is, that People that were naturally free, and by their own Conſent either ſubmitted to the Government of their Father, or united together out of different Families to make a Government, ſhould generally put the *Rule into one Man's Hands*, and chuſe to be under the Conduct of a *ſingle Perſon*, without ſo much as by expreſs Conditions limiting or regulating his Power, which they thought ſafe enough in his Honeſty and Prudence. Though they never dream'd of Monarchy being *Jure Divino*, which we never heard of among Mankind, till it was revealed to us by the Divinity of this laſt Age; nor ever allowed paternal Power to have a Right to Dominion, or to be the Foundation of all Government. And thus much may ſuffice to ſhew, that as far as we have any Light from Hiſtory, we have reaſon to conclude, that all peaceful beginnings of *Government* have been *laid in the Conſent of the People.* I ſay *peaceful*, becauſe I ſhall have occaſion in another Place to ſpeak of Conqueſt, which ſome eſteem a way of beginning of Governments.

The other Objection I find urged againſt the beginning of Polities, in the way I have mentioned, is this, viz.

113. *That all Men being born under Government, ſome or other, it is impoſſible any of them ſhould ever be free, and at liberty to unite together, and begin a new one, or ever be able to erect a lawful Government.*

If this Argument be good; I ask, how came ſo many lawful Monarchies into the World? For if any body, upon this Suppoſition, can ſhew me any one Man in any Age of the World free to begin a lawful Monarchy; I will be bound to ſhew him ten other *free Men* at liberty, at the ſame time to unite and begin a new Government under a regal, or any other Form. It being Demonſtration, that if any one, *born under the Dominion* of another, may be ſo *free* as to have a Right to command others in a new and diſtinct Empire; every one that is *born under the Dominion* of an other may be ſo free too, and may become a Ruler, or Subject, of a diſtinct ſeparate Government. And ſo by this their own Principle, either all Men, however *born*, are *free*, or elſe there is but one lawful Prince, one lawful Government in the World. And then they have nothing to do but barely to ſhew us, which that is. Which when they have done, I doubt not but all Mankind will eaſily agree to pay Obedience to him.

114. Though it be a ſufficient Anſwer to their Objection to ſhew, that it involves them in the ſame Difficulties that it doth thoſe, they uſe it againſt; yet I ſhall endeavour to diſcover the weakneſs of this Argument a little farther.

All Men, ſay they, *are born under Government, and therefore they cannot be at Liberty to begin a new one. Every one is born a Subject to his Father, or his Prince, and is therefore under the perpetual tie of Subjection and Allegiance.* 'Tis plain Mankind never owned nor conſidered any ſuch natural *Subjection that they were born in*, to one or to the other that tied them, without their own Conſents, to a Subjection to them and their Heirs.

115. For there are no Examples ſo frequent in Hiſtory, both ſacred and prophane, as thoſe of Men withdrawing themſelves, and their Obedience, from the Juriſdiction they were born under, and the Family or Community they were bred up in, and *ſetting up new Governments* in other Places; from whence ſprang all that number of petty Commonwealths in the Beginning of Ages, and which always

---

* *At firſt, when ſome certain kind of Regiment was once approved, it may be nothing was then farther thought upon for the manner of governing, but all permitted unto their Wiſdom and Diſcretion which were to Rule, till by Experience they found this for all Parts very inconvenient, ſo as the thing which they had deviſed for a Remedy, did indeed but increaſe the Sore which it ſhould have cured. They ſaw, that* to live by one Man's Will, became the Cauſe of all Mens Miſery. *This conſtrained them to come unto Laws wherein all Men might ſee their Duty before hand, and know the Penalties of tranſgreſſing them.* Hooker's Eccl. Pol. L. 1. Sect. 10.

multiplied,

multiplied, as long as there was room enough, till the ſtronger, or more fortunate, ſwallowed the weaker; and thoſe great ones again breaking to Pieces, diſſolved into leſſer Dominions. All which are ſo many Teſtimonies againſt paternal Sovereignty, and plainly prove, That it was not the natural right of the *Father* deſcending to his Heirs, that made Governments in the Beginning, ſince it was impoſſible, upon that Ground, there ſhould have been ſo many little Kingdoms; all muſt have been but only one univerſal Monarchy, if Men had not been at *Liberty to ſeparate* themſelves from their Families, and the Government, be it what it will, that was ſet up in it, and go and make diſtinct Commonwealths and other Governments, as they thought fit.

116. This has been the practice of the World from its firſt beginning to this day; Nor is it now any more Hindrance to the freedom of Mankind, that they are *born under conſtituted and ancient Polities*, that have eſtabliſhed Laws, and ſet Forms of Government, than if they were born in the Woods, amongſt the unconfined Inhabitants, that run looſe in them. For thoſe, who would perſuade us, that *by being born under any Government, we are naturally Subjects to it*, and have no more any Title or Pretence to the freedom of the ſtate of Nature, have no other reaſon (bating that of paternal Power, which we have already anſwer'd) to produce for it, but only, becauſe our Fathers or Progenitors paſſed away their natural Liberty, and thereby bound up themſelves and their Poſterity to a perpetual Subjection to the Government, which they themſelves ſubmitted to. 'Tis true, that whatever Engagements or Promiſes any one has made for himſelf, he is under the Obligation of them, but *cannot* by any *Compact* whatſoever, *bind his Children or Poſterity.* For his Son, when a Man, being altogether as free as the Father, any *Act of the Father can no more give away the liberty of the Son*, than it can of any Body elſe: He may indeed annex ſuch Conditions to the Land, he enjoyed as a Subject of any Commonwealth, as may oblige his Son to be of that Community, if he will enjoy thoſe Poſſeſſions which were his Father's; becauſe that Eſtate being his Father's Property, he may diſpoſe, or ſettle it, as he pleaſes.

117. And this has generally given the occaſion to miſtake in this Matter; becauſe Commonwealths not permitting any part of their Dominions to be diſmembred, nor to be enjoyed by any but thoſe of their Community, the Son cannot ordinarily enjoy the Poſſeſſion of his Father, but under the ſame Terms his Father did; by becoming a member of the Society; whereby he puts himſelf preſently under the Government, he finds there eſtabliſhed, as much as any other Subject of that Commonwealth. And thus *the Conſent of Freemen, born under Government*, which only *makes them Members of it*, being given ſeparately in their Turns, as each comes to be of Age, and not in a Multitude together; People take no Notice of it, and thinking it not done at all, or not neceſſary, conclude they are naturally Subjects as they are Men.

118. But, 'tis plain, *Governments* themſelves underſtand it otherwiſe; they claim *no Power over the Son, becauſe of that they had over the Father*; nor look on Children as being their Subjects, by their Fathers being ſo. If a Subject of *England* have a Child, by an *Engliſh* Woman in *France*, whoſe Subject is he? Not the King of *England*'s; for he muſt have leave to be admitted to the Privileges of it. Nor the King of *France*'s: For how then has his Father a Liberty to bring him away, and breed him as he pleaſes? And whoever was judged as a *Traytor* or *Deſerter*, if he left, or warr'd againſt a Country, for being barely born in it of Parents that were Aliens there? 'Tis plain then, by the practice of Governments themſelves, as well as by the Law of right Reaſon, that *a Child is born a Subject of no Country or Government.* He is under his Father's Tuition and Authority, till he comes to Age of Diſcretion; and then he is a Freeman, at Liberty what Government he will put himſelf under; what Body politick he will unite himſelf to. For if an *Engliſhman*'s Son, born in *France*, be at Liberty, and may do ſo, 'tis evident there is no Tye upon him by his Father's being a Subject of this Kingdom; nor is he bound up, by any Compact of his Anceſtors. And why then hath not his Son, by the ſame Reaſon, the ſame Liberty, though he be born any where elſe? Since the Power that a Father hath naturally over his Children, is the ſame, where-ever they be born, and the Tyes of natural Obligations, are not bounded by the poſitive limits of Kingdoms and Commonwealths.

119. *Every*

119. *Every Man* being, as has been ſhewed, *naturally free*, and nothing being able to put him into Subjection to any earthly Power, but only his own *Conſent*, it is to be conſider'd, what ſhall be underſtood to be a *ſufficient Declaration* of a Man's *Conſent, to make him ſubject* to the Laws of any Government. There is a common diſtinction of an expreſs and a tacit Conſent, which will concern our preſent Caſe. No Body doubts but an expreſs *Conſent*, of any Man, entering into any Society, makes him a perfect member of that Society, a Subject of that Government. The Difficulty is, what ought to be look'd upon as a *tacit Conſent*, and how far it binds, *i. e.* how far any one ſhall be looked on to have conſented, and thereby ſubmitted to any Government, where he has made no Expreſſions of it at all. And to this I ſay, that every Man, that hath any Poſſeſſions, or Enjoyment, of any part of the Dominions of any Government, doth thereby give his *tacit Conſent*, and is as far forth obliged to Obedience to the Laws of that Government, during ſuch Enjoyment, as any one under it; whether this his Poſſeſſion be of Land, to him and his Heirs for ever, or a Lodging only for a Week; or whether it be barely travelling freely on the Highway; and in Effect, it reaches as far as the very being of any one within the Territories of that Government.

120. To underſtand this the better, it is fit to conſider, that every Man, when he, at firſt, incorporates himſelf into any Commonwealth, he, by his uniting himſelf thereunto, annexed alſo, and ſubmits to the Community thoſe Poſſeſſions, which he has, or ſhall acquire, that do not already belong to any other Government. For it would be a direct Contradiction, for any one, to enter into Society with others for the ſecuring and regulating of Property: And yet to ſuppoſe his Land, whoſe Property is to be regulated by the Laws of the Society, ſhould be exempt from the Juriſdiction of that Government, to which he himſelf, the Proprietor of the Land, is a Subject. By the ſame Act therefore, whereby any one unites his Perſon, which was before free, to any Commonwealth; by the ſame he unites his Poſſeſſions, which were before free, to it alſo; and they become, both of them, Perſon and Poſſeſſion, ſubject to the Government and Dominion of that Commonwealth, as long as it hath a Being. Whoever therefore, from thenceforth, by Inheritance, Purchaſe, Permiſſion, or otherways, *enjoys any part of the Land*, ſo annext to, and under the Government *of that Commonwealth, muſt take it with the Condition* it is under; that is, *of ſubmitting to the Government of the Commonwealth*, under whoſe Juriſdiction it is, as far forth as any Subject of it.

121. But ſince the Government has a direct Juriſdiction only over the Land, and reaches the Poſſeſſor of it, (before he has actually incorporated himſelf in the Society) only as he dwells upon, and enjoys that: The Obligation any one is under, by Virtue of ſuch Enjoyment, to *ſubmit to the Government, begins and ends with the Enjoyment*; ſo that whenever the Owner, who has given nothing but ſuch a *tacit Conſent* to the Government, will, by Donation, Sale, or otherwiſe, quit the ſaid Poſſeſſion, he is at Liberty to go and incorporate himſelf into any other Commonwealth; or to agree with others to begin a new one, *in vacuis locis*, in any part of the World, they can find free and unpoſſeſſed: Whereas he, that has once, by actual Agreement, and any *expreſs* Declaration, given his *Conſent* to be of any Commonweal, is perpetually and indiſpenſably obliged to be, and remain unalterably a Subject to it. and can never be again in the Liberty of the ſtate of Nature; unleſs, by any Calamity, the Government, he was under, comes to be diſſolved; or elſe by ſome publick Act cuts him off from being any longer a Member of it.

122. But ſubmitting to the Laws of any Country, living quietly, and enjoying Privileges and Protection under them, *makes not a Man a Member of that Society:* This is only a local Protection and Homage due to, and from all thoſe, who, not being in a ſtate of War, come within the Territories belonging to any Government, to all Parts whereof the force of its Law extends. But this no more *makes a Man a Member of that Society*, a perpetual Subject of that Commonwealth, than it would make a Man a Subject to another, in whoſe Family he found it convenient to abide for ſome time; though, whilſt he continued in it, he were obliged to comply with the Laws, and ſubmit to the Government, he found there. And thus we ſee, that *Foreigners*, by living all their Lives under another Government, and enjoying the Privileges and Protection of it, though they are bound, even in Conſcience, to ſubmit to its Adminiſtration, as far forth as any Deniſon; yet do not

not thereby come to be *Subjects or Members of that Commonwealth.* Nothing can make any Man so, but his actually entering into it by positive Engagement, and express Promise and Compact. This is that, which I think, concerning the beginning of political Societies, and that *Consent which makes any one a Member* of any Commonwealth.

CHAP. IX.

Of the Ends of Political Society and Government.

123. IF Man in the state of Nature be so free, as has been said; if he be absolute Lord of his own Person and Possessions, equal to the greatest and subject to no Body, why will he part with his Freedom? Why will he give up this Empire, and subject himself to the Dominion and Controul of any other Power? To which 'tis obvious to answer, that though in the state of Nature he hath such a Right, yet the Enjoyment of it is very uncertain, and constantly exposed to the Invasion of others. For all being Kings as much as he, every Man his Equal and the greater Part no strict Observers of Equity and Justice, the enjoyment of the Property he has in this State, is very unsafe, very unsecure. This makes him willing to quit this Condition, which however free, is full of Fears and continual Dangers: And 'tis not without Reason, that he seeks out, and is willing to joyn in Society with others, who are already united, or have a Mind to unite, for the mutual *Preservation* of their Lives, Liberties and Estates, which I call by the general Name, *Property.*

124. The great and *chief End* therefore, of Mens uniting into Commonwealths, and putting themselves under Government, *is the Preservation of their Property.* To which in the state of Nature there are many things wanting.

First, There wants an *establish'd*, settled, known *Law*, received and allowed by common Consent to be the Standard of right and wrong, and the common Measure to decide all Controversies between them. For though the Law of Nature be plain and intelligible to all rational Creatures; yet Men being biassed by their Interest, as well as ignorant for want of Study of it, are not apt to allow of it as a Law binding to them in the application of it to their particular Cases.

125. *Secondly*, In the state of Nature there wants *a known and indifferent Judge*, with Authority to determine all Differences according to the established Law. For every one in that State being both Judge and Executioner of the Law of Nature, Men being partial to themselves, Passion and Revenge is very apt to carry them too far, and with too much Heat, in their own Cases; as well as Negligence, and unconcernedness, to make them too remiss in others Mens,

126. *Thirdly*, In the state of Nature there often wants *Power* to back and support the Sentence when right, and to *give* it due *Execution.* They who by any Injustice offended, will seldom fail, where they are able, by Force to make good their Injustice; such Resistance many times makes the Punishment dangerous, and frequently destructive, to those who attempt it.

127. Thus Mankind, notwithstanding all the Privileges of the state of Nature, being but in an ill Condition, while they remain in it, are quickly driven into Society. Hence it comes to pass, that we seldom find any number of Men live any time together in this State. The Inconveniencies that they are therein exposed to, by the irregular, and uncertain exercise of the Power every Man has of punishing the transgressions of others, make them take Sanctuary under the establish'd Laws of Government, and therein seek *the preservation of their Property.* 'Tis this makes them so willingly give up every one his single Power of punishing, to be exercised by such alone, as shall be appointed to it, amongst them; and by such Rules as the Community, or those authorized by them to that purpose, shall agree on. And in this we have the original *right and rise of both the Legislative and Executive Power*, as well as of the Governments, and Societies themselves.

128. For in the State of Nature, to omit the liberty he has of innocent Delights, a Man has two Powers.

The firſt is to do whatſoever he thinks fit for the preſervation of himſelf, and others within the permiſſion of the *Law of Nature*; by which Law common to them all, he and all the reſt of *Mankind are one Community*, make up one Society, diſtinct from all other Creatures. And were it not for the Corruption and Vitiouſneſs of degenerate Men, there would be no need of any other; no Neceſſity that Men ſhould ſeparate from this great and natural Community, and by poſitive agreements combine into ſmaller and divided Aſſociations.

The other Power a Man has in the ſtate of Nature, is the *power to puniſh the Crimes* committed againſt that Law. Both theſe he gives up, when he joyns in a private, if I may ſo call it, or particular Political Society, and incorporates into any Commonwealth, ſeparate from the reſt of Mankind.

129. The firſt *Power, viz. of doing whatſoever he thought fit for the preſervation of himſelf*, and the reſt of Mankind, *he gives up* to be regulated by Laws made by the Society, ſo far forth as the preſervation of himſelf, and the reſt of that Society ſhall require; which Laws of the Society in many things confine the liberty he had by the Law of Nature.

130. *Secondly*, The *Power of puniſhing he wholly gives up*, and engages his natural Force, (which he might before imploy in the Execution of the Law of Nature, by his own ſingle Authority, as he thought fit) to aſſiſt the Executive Power of the Society, as the Law thereof ſhall require. For being now in a new State, wherein he is to enjoy many Conveniencies, from the Labour, Aſſiſtance, and Society of others in the ſame Community, as well as Protection from its whole Strength; he is to part alſo with as much of his natural Liberty, in providing for himſelf, as the Good, Proſperity, and Safety of the Society ſhall require; which is not only neceſſary, but juſt; ſince the other Members of the Society do the like.

131. But though Men when they enter into Society, give up the Equality, Liberty, and Executive Power they had in the State of Nature, into the hands of the Society, to be ſo far diſpoſed of by the Legiſlative, as the good of the Society ſhall require; yet it being only with an intention in every one the better to preſerve himſelf his Liberty and Property; (For no rational Creature can be ſuppoſed to change his condition with an intention to be worſe) the Power of the Society, or *Legiſlative* conſtituted by them, can *never be ſuppos'd to extend farther than the common good*; but is obliged to ſecure every ones Property, by providing againſt thoſe three defects above-mentioned, that made the State of Nature ſo unſafe and uneaſie. And ſo whoever has the Legiſlative or ſupream Power of any Commonwealth, is bound to govern by eſtabliſh'd *ſtanding Laws*, promulgated and known to the People, and not by Extemporary Decrees; by *indifferent* and upright *Judges*, who are to decide Controverſies by thoſe Laws; And to imploy the force of the Community at home, *only in the Execution of ſuch Laws*, or abroad to prevent or redreſs Foreign Injuries, and ſecure the Community from Inroads and Invaſion. And all this to be directed to no other *End*, but the *Peace*, *Safety*, and *publick good* of the People.

CHAP. X.

Of the Forms of a Commonwealth.

132. THE Majority having, as has been ſhew'd, upon Mens firſt uniting into Society, the whole Power of the Community, naturally in them, may imploy all that Power in making Laws for the Community from time to time, and executing thoſe Laws by Officers of their own appointing; and then the *Form* of the Government is a perfect *Democracy*: Or elſe may put the Power of making Laws into the hands of a few ſelect Men, and their Heirs or Succeſſors; and then it is an *Oligarchy*: Or elſe into the hands of one Man, and then it is a *Monarchy*: If to him and his Heirs, it is an *Hereditary Monarchy*: If to him only for Life, but upon his Death the Power only of nominating a Succeſſor to return to them; an *Elective Monarchy*. And ſo accordingly of theſe the Community may make compounded and mixed Forms of Government, as they think good. And if the Legiſlative Power be at firſt given by the Majority to one or more Perſons only for

for their Lives, or any limited time, and then the ſupream Power to revert to them again; when it is ſo reverted, the Community may diſpoſe of it again anew into what hands they pleaſe, and ſo conſtitute a new Form of Government. For the *Form of Government depending upon the placing the* ſupream Power, which is *the Legiſlative*, it being impoſſible to conceive that an inferior Power ſhould preſcribe to a ſuperior, or any but the ſupream make Laws, according as the Power of making Laws is placed, ſuch is the *Form of the Common-wealth*.

133. By *Commonwealth*, I muſt be underſtood all along to mean, not a Democracy, or any Form of Government, but *any Independent Community* which the *Latines* ſignified by the word *Civitas*, to which the word which beſt anſwers in our Language, is *Commonwealth*, and moſt properly expreſſes ſuch a Society of Men, which Community or City in *Engliſh* does not, for there may be ſubordinate Communities in a Government; and City amongſt us has a quite different Notion from Commonwealth: And therefore to avoid Ambiguity, I crave leave to uſe the word *Commonwealth* in that Senſe, in which I find it uſed by King *James the firſt*, and I take it to be its genuine ſignification; which if any Body diſlike, I conſent with him to change it for a better.

CHAP. XI.

Of the Extent of the Legiſlative Power.

134. THE great end of Mens entring into Society, being the Enjoyment of their Properties in Peace and Safety, and the great inſtrument and means of that being the Laws eſtabliſh'd in that Society; the *firſt and fundamental poſitive Law* of all Commonwealths, *is the eſtabliſhing of the Legiſlative* Power; as the *firſt and fundamental natural Law*, which is to govern even the Legiſlative it ſelf, *is the preſervation of the Society*, and (as far as will conſiſt with the publick good) of every perſon in it. This *Legiſlative* is not only *the ſupream Power* of the Commonwealth, but ſacred and unalterable in the hands where the Community have once placed it; nor can any Edict of any Body elſe, in what form ſoever conceived, or by what Power ſoever backed, have the force and obligation of a *Law*, which has not its *Sanction from* that *Legiſlative*, which the publick has choſen and appointed. For without this the Law could not have that, which is abſolutely neceſſary to its being a *Law*, * *the conſent of the Society*, over whom no Body can have a Power to make Laws, but by their own Conſent, and by Authority received from them; and therefore all the *Obedience*, which by the moſt ſolemn Ties any one can be obliged *to* Pay, ultimately terminates in this *Supream Power*, and is directed by thoſe Laws which it enacts: Nor can any Oaths to any foreign Power whatſoever, or any Domeſtick Subordinate Power, diſcharge any Member of the Society from his *Obedience to the Legiſlative*, acting purſuant to their Truſt; nor oblige him to any Obedience contrary to the Laws ſo enacted, or farther than they do allow; it being ridiculous to imagine one can be tied ultimately to *obey* any *Power* in the Society, which is not the *Supream*.

135. Though the *Legiſlative*, whether placed in one or more, whether it be always in being, or only by intervals, tho' it be the *ſupream* Power in every Commonwealth; yet,

Firſt, It is *not*, nor can poſſibly be abſolutely *Arbitrary* over the Lives and Fortunes of the People. For it being but the joint Power of every Member of the

---

* *The lawful Power of making Laws to Command whole Politick Societies of Men, belonging ſo properly unto the ſame intire Societies, that for any Prince or Potentate of what kind ſoever upon Earth, to exerciſe the ſame of himſelf, and not by expreſs Commiſſion immediately and perſonally received from God, or elſe by authority derived at the firſt from their Conſent, upon whoſe perſons they impoſe Laws, it is no better than mere* Tyranny. *Laws they are not therefore which publick approbation hath not made ſo.* Hooker's Eccl Pol. L. 1. Sect. 10. *Of this point therefore we are to Note, that ſith Men naturally have no full and perfect Power to Command whole Politick Multitudes of Men, therefore utterly without our Conſent, we could in ſuch ſort be at no Man's Commandment living. And to be commanded we do conſent when that Society, whereof we be a part, hath at any time before conſented, without revoking the ſame after by the like univerſal agreement.*

Laws therefore human, of what kind ſo ever, are available by conſent. Ibid.

Society given up to that Person, or Assembly, which is Legislator, it can be no more than those Persons had in a state of Nature before they enter'd into Society, and gave up to the Community. For no Body can transfer to another more Power, than he has in himself; and no Body has an absolute Arbitrary Power over himself, or over any other, to destroy his own Life, or take away the Life or Property of another. A Man, as has been proved, cannot subject himself to the Arbitrary Power of another; and having in the State of Nature no Arbitrary Power over the Life, Liberty, or Possession of another, but only so much as the Law of Nature gave him for the preservation of himself, and the rest of Mankind; this is all he doth, or can give up to the Commonwealth, and by it to the *Legislative Power*, so that the Legislative can have no more than this. Their Power in the utmost bounds of it, is *limited to the publick good* of the Society. It is a Power, that hath no other end but Preservation, and therefore can never † have a right to destroy, enslave, or designedly to impoverish the Subjects. The Obligations of the Law of Nature, cease not in Society, but only in may Cases are drawn closer, and have by human Laws known Penalties annexed to them, to inforce their Observation. Thus the Law of Nature stands as an Eternal Rule to all Men, *Legislators* as well as others. The *Rules* that they make for other Men's Actions, must, as well as their own, and other Men's Actions, be conformable to the Law of Nature, *i. e.* to the Will of God, of which that is a Declaration, and the *fundamental Law of Nature being the preservation of Mankind*, no Human Sanction can be good, or valid against it.

136. *Secondly*, * The *Legislative*, or supream Authority, cannot assume to its self a Power to Rule by Extemporary Arbitrary Decrees, but *is bound to dispense Justice*, and decide the Rights of the Subject *by promulgated standing Laws, and known Authoris'd Judges*. For the Law of Nature being unwritten, and so no where to be found but in the minds of Men, they who through Passion or Interest shall miscite, or misapply it, cannot so easily be convinced of their mistake where there is no establish'd Judge: And so it serves not, as it ought to determine the Rights, and fence the Properties of those that live under it, especially where every one is Judge, Interpreter, and Executioner of it too, and that in his own Case: And he that has right on his side, having ordinarily but his own single Strength, hath not force enough to defend himself from Injuries, or to punish Delinquents. To avoid these Inconveniencies, which disorder Mens Properties in the state of Nature, Men unite into Societies, that they may have the united strength of the whole Society to secure and defend their Properties, and may have *standing Rules* to bound it, by which every one may know, what is his. To this end it is that Men give up all their natural Power to the Society, which they enter into, and the Community put the Legislative Power into such hands as they think fit, with this Trust, that they shall be govern'd by *declared Laws*, or else their Peace, Quiet, and Property will still be at the same uncertainty, as it was in the state of Nature.

137. Absolute Arbitrary Power, or governing without *settled standing Laws*, can neither of them consist with the ends of Society and Government, which Men would not quit the freedom of the state of Nature for, and tie themselves up under, were it not to preserve their Lives, Liberties and Fortunes; and by

† *Two Foundations there are which bear up publick Societies, the one a natural inclination, whereby all Men desire sociable Life and Fellowship; the other an Order, expresly or secretly agreed upon, touching the manner of their union in living together; the latter is that which we call the Law of a Commonweal, the very Soul of a Politick Body, the parts whereof are by Law animated, held together, and set on work in such Actions as the common good requireth. Laws Politick, ordain'd for external order and regiment amongst Men, are never framed as they should be, unless presuming the will of Man to be inwardly Obstinate, Rebellious, and Averse from all Obedience to the sacred Laws of his Nature; in a word, unless presuming Man to be in regard of his depraved Mind, little better than a wild Beast, they do accordingly provide notwithstanding, so to frame his outward Actions, that they be no hindrance unto the common good, for which Societies are instituted. Unless they do this they are not perfect.* Hooker's Eccl. Pol. L. 1. Sect. 10.

* *Human Laws are measures in respect of Men whose Actions they must direct, howbeit such measures they are as have also their higher Rules to be measured by, which Rules are two, the Law of God, and the Law of Nature; so that Laws Human must be made according to the general Laws of Nature, and without contradiction to any positive Law of Scripture, otherwise they are ill made.* Ibid. L. 3. Sect. 9.

To constrain Men to any thing inconvenient doth seem unreasonable Ibid. L. 1. Sect. 10.

stated

ſtated Rules of Right and Property to ſecure their Peace and Quiet. It cannot be ſuppos'd that they ſhould intend, had they a Power ſo to do, to give to any one, or more, an *abſolute Arbitrary Power* over their Perſons and Eſtates, and put a force into the Magiſtrates hand to execute his unlimited Will arbitrarily upon them. This were to put themſelves into a worſe condition than the ſtate of Nature, wherein they had a Liberty to defend their Right againſt the Injuries of others, and were upon equal terms of force to maintain it, whether invaded by a ſingle Man, or many in Combination. Whereas by ſuppoſing they have given up themſelves to the *abſolute Arbitrary Power* and Will of a Legiſlator, they have diſarmed themſelves, and armed him, to make a prey of them when he pleaſes. He being in a much worſe condition, who is expoſed to the Arbitrary Power of one Man, who has the Command of 100000, than he that is expos'd to the Arbitrary Power of 100000 ſingle Men; no Body being ſecure, that his Will, who has ſuch a Command, is better, than that of other Men, though his force be 100000 times ſtronger. And therefore whatever form the Commonwealth is under, the ruling Power ought to govern by *declared* and *received Laws*, and not by extemporary Dictates and undetermin'd Reſolutions. For then Mankind will be in a far worſe condition, than in the ſtate of Nature, if they ſhall have armed one, or a few Men with the joint Power of a Multitude, to force them to obey at pleaſure the exorbitant and unlimited decrees of their ſudden Thoughts, or unreſtrain'd, and till that moment unknown Wills, without having any meaſures ſet down which may guide and juſtify their Actions. For all the Power the Government has, being only for the good of the Society, as it ought not to be *Arbitrary* and at Pleaſure, ſo it ought to be exerciſed by *eſtabliſhed and promulgated Laws*; that both the People may know their Duty, and be ſafe and ſecure within the limits of the Law; and the Rulers too kept within their due Bounds, and not be tempted, by the Power they have in their hands, to imploy it to ſuch Purpoſes, and by ſuch Meaſures, as they would not have known, and own not willingly.

138. *Thirdly*, The *ſupream Power cannot take* from any Man any part of his *Property* without his own Conſent. For the preſervation of Property being the end of Government, and that for which Men enter into Society, it neceſſarily ſuppoſes and requires, that the People ſhould *have Property*, without which they muſt be ſuppos'd to loſe that, by entering into Society, which was the end for which they entered into it, too groſs an abſurdity for any Man to own. *Men* therefore *in Society having Property*, they have ſuch a right to the Goods, which by the Law of the Community are theirs, that no Body hath a right to take their Subſtance or any part of it from them, without their own Conſent; without this they have no *Property* at all. For I have truly no *Property* in that, which another can by right take from me, when he pleaſes, againſt my Conſent. Hence it is a miſtake to think, that the *Supream or Legiſlative Power* of any Common-wealth, can do what it will, and diſpoſe of the Eſtates of the Subject *Arbitrarily*, or take any part of them at Pleaſure. This is not much to be fear'd in Governments where the *Legiſlative* conſiſts, wholly or in part, in Aſſemblies which are variable, whoſe Members upon the diſſolution of the Aſſembly, are Subjects under the common Laws of their Country, equally with the reſt. But in Governments, were the *Legiſlative* is in one laſting Aſſembly always in Being, or in one Man, as in abſolute Monarchies, there is danger ſtill, that they will think themſelves to have a diſtinct intereſt, from the reſt of the Community; and ſo will be apt to increaſe their own Riches and Power, by taking what they think fit from the People. For a Man's *Property* is not at all ſecure, though there be good and equitable Laws to ſet the bounds of it, between him and his fellow Subjects, if he who Commands thoſe Subjects, have Power to take from any private Man, what part he pleaſes of his *Property*, and uſe and diſpoſe of it as he thinks good.

139. But *Government* into whatſoever hands it is put, being as I have before ſhew'd, intruſted with this Condition, and *for this End*, that Men might have and ſecure their *Properties*, the Prince, or Senate, however it may have Power to make Laws, for the regulating of *Property*, between the Subjects one amongſt another, yet can never have a Power to take to themſelves the whole, or any part of the Subjects *Property*, without their own Conſent. For this would be in effect to leave them no *Property* at all. And to let us ſee, that even *abſolute Power*, where

where it is neceſſary, is *not Arbitrary* by being abſolute, but is ſtill limited by that Reaſon, and confined to thoſe Ends, which required it in ſome Caſes to be abſolute, we need look no farther than the common practice of Martial Diſcipline. For the preſervation of the Army, and in it of the whole Commonwealth, requires an *abſolute Obedience* to the Command of every ſuperior Officer, and it is juſtly Death to diſobey or diſpute the moſt dangerous or unreaſonable of them; but yet we ſee, that neither the Serjeant, that could Command a Soldier to march up to the mouth of a Cannon, or ſtand in a Breach, where he is almoſt ſure to periſh, can command that Soldier to give him one Penny of his Money; nor the *General*, that can condemn him to Death for deſerting his Poſt, or for not obeying the moſt deſperate Orders, can yet with all his *abſolute Power* of Life and Death, diſpoſe of one Farthing of that Soldier's Eſtate, or ſeize one jot of his Goods; whom yet he can command any Thing, and hang for the leaſt Diſobedience. Becauſe ſuch a blind Obedience is neceſſary to that end, for which the Commander has his Power, *viz.* the preſervation of the reſt; but the diſpoſing of his Goods has nothing to do with it.

140. 'Tis true, Governments cannot be ſupported without great Charge, and 'tis fit every one who enjoys his ſhare of the Protection, ſhould pay out of his Eſtate his proportion for the maintenance of it. But ſtill it muſt be with his own Conſent, *i. e.* the Conſent of the Majority, giving it either by themſelves, or their Repreſentatives choſen by them. For if any one ſhall claim a *Power to lay* and levy *Taxes* on the People, by his own Authority, and without ſuch conſent of the People, he thereby invades the *Fundamental Law of Property*, and ſubverts the end of Government. For what Property have I in that, which another may by right take, when he pleaſes to himſelf?

141. *Fourthly*, The *Legiſlative cannot transfer the Power of making Laws* to any other hands. For it being but a delegated Power from the People, they who have it, cannot paſs it over to others. The People alone can appoint the Form of the Commonwealth, which is by Conſtituting the Legiſlative, and appointing in whoſe hands that ſhall be. And when the People have ſaid, we will ſubmit to Rules, and be govern'd by *Laws* made by ſuch Men, and in ſuch Forms, no Body elſe can ſay other Men ſhall make *Laws* for them; nor can the People be bound by any *Laws*, but ſuch as are Enacted by thoſe whom they have Choſen, and Authorized to make *Laws* for them. The Power of the *Legiſlative* being derived from the People by a poſitive voluntary Grant and Inſtitution, can be no other, than what that poſitive Grant conveyed, which being only to make *Laws*, and not to make *Legiſlators*, the *Legiſlative* can have no Power to transfer their Authority of making Laws, and place it in other hands.

142. Theſe are the *Bounds* which the truſt, that is put in them by the Society, and the Law of God and Nature, have *ſet to the Legiſlative* Power of every Commonwealth, in all Forms of Government.

Firſt, They are to govern by *promulgated eſtabliſh'd Laws*, not to be varied in particular Caſes, but to have one Rule for Rich and Poor, for the Favourite at Court, and the Country Man at Plough.

Secondly, Theſe *Laws* alſo ought to be deſigned *for* no other end ultimately, but *the good of the People.*

Thirdly, They muſt *not raiſe Taxes* on the *Property of the People, without the Conſent of the People*, given by themſelves, or their Deputies. And this properly concerns only ſuch Governments where the *Legiſlative* is always in Being, or at leaſt where the People have not reſerv'd any part of the Legiſlative to Deputies, to be from time to time choſen by themſelves.

Fourthly, The *Legiſlative* neither muſt *nor can transfer the Power of making Laws* to any Body elſe, or place it any where, but where the People have.

CHAP.

CHAP. XII.

Of the Legiſlative, Executive, and Federative Power of the Commonwealth.

143. THE *Legiſlative* Power is that, which has a right *to direct how the Force of the Commonwealth* ſhall be imploy'd for preſerving the Community and the Members of it. But becauſe thoſe Laws which are conſtantly to be Executed, and whoſe force is always to continue, may be made in a little time; therefore there is no need, that the *Legiſlative* ſhould be always in Being, not having always buſineſs to do. And becauſe it may be too great a temptation to human frailty apt to graſp at Power, for the ſame Perſons, who have the Power of making Laws, to have alſo in their hands the Power to execute them, whereby they may exempt themſelves from Obedience to the Laws they make, and ſuit the Law, both in its making, and execution, to their own private advantage, and thereby come to have a diſtinct intereſt from the reſt of the Community, contrary to the end of Society and Government: Therefore in well order'd Commonwealths, where the good of the whole is ſo conſidered, as it ought, the *Legiſlative* Power is put into the hands of divers Perſons, who duly Aſſembled, have by themſelves, or jointly with others, a Power to make Laws, which when they have done, being ſeparated again, they are themſelves ſubject to the Laws, they have made; which is a new and near tie upon them, to take Care, that they make them for the publick good.

144. But becauſe the Laws, that are at once, and in a ſhort time made, have a conſtant and laſting Force, and need a *perpetual Execution*, or an attendance thereunto: Therefore 'tis neceſſary there ſhould be a *Power always in Being*, which ſhould ſee to the *Execution* of the Laws that are made, and remain in Force. And thus the *Legiſlative* and *Executive Power* come often to be ſeparated.

145. There is another *Power* in every Commonwealth, which one may call *natural*, becauſe it is that which anſwers to the Power every Man naturally had before he entered into Society. For though in a Commonwealth the Members of it are diſtinct Perſons ſtill in reference to one another, and as ſuch are governed by the Laws of the Society; yet in reference to the reſt of Mankind, they make one Body, which is, as every Member of it before was, ſtill in the ſtate of Nature with the reſt of Mankind. Hence it is, that the Controverſies that happen between any Man of the Society with thoſe that are out of it, are managed by the Publick; and an injury done to a Member of their Body, engages the whole in the reparation of it. So that under this Conſideration, the whole Community is one Body in the ſtate of Nature, in reſpect of all other States or Perſons out of its Community.

146. This therefore contains the Power of War and Peace, Leagues and Alliances, and all the Tranſactions, with all Perſons and Communities without the Commonwealth, and may be called *Federative*, if any one pleaſes. So the thing be underſtood, I am indifferent as to the Name.

147. Theſe two Powers, *Executive* and *Federative*, though they be really diſtinct in themſelves, yet one comprehending the *Execution* of the Municipal Laws of the Society *within* its ſelf, upon all that are parts of it; the other the management of the *ſecurity and intereſt of the publick without*, with all thoſe that it may receive benefit or damage from, yet they are always almoſt united. And though this *Federative Power* in the well or ill management of it be of great moment to the Commonwealth, yet it is much leſs capable to be directed by antecedent, ſtanding, poſitive Laws, than the *Executive*; and ſo muſt neceſſarily be left to the Prudence and Wiſdom of thoſe, whoſe hands it is in, to be managed for the publick good. For the *Laws* that concern Subjects one amongſt another, being to direct their Actions, may well enough *precede* them. But what is to be done in reference to *Foreigners*, depending much upon their Actions, and the variation of deſigns and intereſts, muſt be *left* in great part *to* the *Prudence* of thoſe, who have this Power committed to them, to be managed by the beſt of their Skill, for the advantage of the Commonwealth.

148. Though,

148. Though, as I said, the *Executive* and *Federative Power* of every Community be really distinct in themselves, yet they are hardly to be separated, and placed at the same time, in the hands of distinct Persons. For both of them requiring the force of the Society for their Exercise, it is almost impracticable to place the Force of the Commonwealth in distinct, and not subordinate hands; or that the *Executive* and *Federative Power* should be *placed* in Persons, that might act separately, whereby the Force of the Publick would be under different Commands, which would be apt sometime or other to cause Disorder and Ruine.

CHAP. XIII.

Of the Subordination of the Powers of the Commonwealth.

149. Though in a constituted Commonwealth, standing upon its own Basis, and acting according to its own Nature, that is, acting for the preservation of the Community, there can be but *one supream Power*, which is *the Legislative*, to which all the rest are and must be Subordinate, yet the Legislative being only a Fiduciary Power to act for certain ends, there remains still *in the People a supream Power to remove or alter the Legislative*, when they find the *Legislative* act contrary to the trust reposed in them. For all *Power given with trust* for the attaining an *end*, being limited by that end, whenever that *end* is manifestly neglected, or opposed, the *trust* must necessarily be *forfeited*, and the Power devolve into the Hands of those that gave it, who may place it anew where they shall think best for their safety and security. And thus the *Community* perpetually *retains a supream Power* of saving themselves from the attempts and designs of any body, even of their Legislators, whenever they shall be so foolish, or so wicked, as to lay and carry on designs against the Liberties and Properties of the Subject. For no Man or Society of Men, having a Power to deliver up their *Preservation*, or consequently the means of it, to the absolute Will and arbitrary Dominion of another; when ever any one shall go about to bring them into such a slavish Condition, they will always have a right to preserve, what they have not a Power to part with; and to rid themselves of those, who invade this Fundamental, Sacred, and unalterable Law of *Self-preservation*, for which they enter'd into Society. And thus the *Community* may be said in this respect to be *always the supream Power*, but not as considered under any Form of Government, because this Power of the People can never take place till the Government be dissolved.

150. In all Cases, whilest the Government subsists, the *Legislative is the supream Power*. For what can give Laws to another, must needs be superior to him; and since the Legislative is no otherwise Legislative of the Society, but by the right it has to make Laws for all the parts, and for every Member of the Society, prescribing Rules to their Actions, and giving power of Execution, where they are transgressed, the *Legislative* must needs be the *Supream*, and all other Powers in any Members or parts of the Society, derived from and subordinate to it.

151. In some Commonwealths where the *Legislative* is not always in Being, and the *Executive* is vested in a single Person, who has also a share in the Legislative; there that single Person in a very tolerable Sense may also be called *Supream*, not that he has in himself all the supream Power, which is that of Law-making: But because he has in him the *supream Execution*, from whom all inferiour Magistrates derive all their several subordinate Powers, or at least the greatest part of them; having also no Legislative superiour to him, there being no Law to be made without his Consent, which cannot be expected should ever subject him to the other part of the Legislative, *he* is properly enough in this Sense *Supream*. But yet it is to be observed, that though *Oaths of Allegiance* and Fealty are taken to him, 'tis not to him as supream Legislator, but as *supream Executor* of the Law, made by a joint Power of him with others; *Allegiance* being nothing but an *Obedience according to Law*, which when he violates, he has no right to Obedience, nor can claim it otherwise than as the publick Person vested with the Power of the Law, and

and ſo is to be conſider'd as the Image, Phantom, or Repreſentative of the Commonwealth, acted by the will of the Society, declared in its Laws; and thus he has no Will, no Power, but that of the Law. But when he quits this Repreſentation, this publick Will, and acts by his own private Will, he degrades himſelf, and is but a ſingle private Perſon without Power, and without Will, that has any Right to *Obedience*; the Members owing no *Obedience* but to the publick Will of the Society.

152. The *executive Power* placed any where but in a Perſon, that has alſo a Share in the Legiſlative, is viſibly ſubordinate and accountable to it, and may be at pleaſure changed and diſplaced; ſo that it is not the *ſupream Executive Power*, that is exempt from *Subordination*, but the *ſupreme Executive Power* veſted in one, who having a Share in the Legiſlative, has no diſtinct ſuperior Legiſlative to be ſubordinate and accountable to, farther than he himſelf ſhall joyn and conſent; ſo that he is no more ſubordinate than he himſelf ſhall think fit, which one may certainly conclude will be but very little. Of other *miniſterial and ſubordinate Powers* in a Commonwealth, we need not ſpeak, they being ſo multiply'd with infinite Variety, in the different Cuſtoms and Conſtitutions of diſtinct Commonwealths, that it is impoſſible to give a particular Account of them all. Only thus much, which is neceſſary to our preſent Purpoſe, we may take Notice of concerning them, that they have no manner of Authority any of them, beyond what is by poſitive Grant and Commiſſion, delegated to them, and are all of them accountable to ſome other Power in the Commonwealth.

153. It is not neceſſary, no nor ſo much as convenient, that the *Legiſlative* ſhould be *always in Being*. But abſolutely neceſſary that the Executive Power ſhould, becauſe there is not always need of new Laws to be made, but always need of Execution of the Laws that are made. When the *Legiſlative* hath put the *Execution* of the Laws, they make, into other Hands, they have a Power ſtill to reſume it out of thoſe Hands, when they find Cauſe, and to puniſh for any mall-adminiſtration againſt the Laws. The ſame holds alſo in regard of the *federative* Power, that and the *Executive* being both *miniſterial* and *ſubordinate to the Legiſlative*, which as has been ſhew'd in a conſtituted Commonwealth, is the ſupream. The *Legiſlative* alſo in this Caſe being ſuppos'd to conſiſt of ſeveral Perſons; (for if it be a ſingle Perſon, it cannot but be always in Being, and ſo will as Supream, naturally have the Supream Executive Power, together with the Legiſlative) may *aſſemble and exerciſe their Legiſlature*, at the Times, that either their original Conſtitution, or their own Adjournment appoints, or when they pleaſe; if neither of theſe hath appointed any time, or there be no other Way preſcribed to convoke them. For the ſupream Power being placed in them by the People, 'tis always in them, and they may exerciſe it when they pleaſe, unleſs by their original Conſtitution they are limited to certain Seaſons, or by an Act of their ſupream Power, they have adjourned to a certain time; and when that time comes, they have a Right to *aſſemble* and act again.

154. If the *Legiſlative*, or any part of it be made up of *Repreſentatives* choſen for that time by the People, which afterwards return into the ordinary ſtate of Subjects, and have no Share in the Legiſlature but upon a new Choice, this Power of chuſing muſt alſo be exerciſed by the People, either at certain appointed Seaſons, or elſe when they are ſummon'd to it; and in this latter Caſe, the Power of convoking the Legiſlative, is ordinarily placed in the Executive, and has one of theſe two Limitations in reſpect of time: That either the original Conſtitution requires their *aſſembling* and *acting* at certain Intervals, and then the executive Power does nothing but miniſterially iſſue Directions for their electing and aſſembling, according to due Forms: Or elſe it is left to his Prudence to call them by new Elections, when the Occaſions or Exigencies of the Publick require the Amendment of old, or making of new Laws, or the redreſs or prevention of any Inconveniencies, that lie on, or threaten the People.

155. It may be demanded here, What if the Executive Power being poſſeſſed of the Force of the Commonwealth, ſhall make uſe of that Force to hinder the *meeting* and *acting of the Legiſlative*, when the original Conſtitution, or the publick Exigencies require it? I ſay uſing Force upon the People without Authority, and contrary to the Truſt put in him, that does ſo, is a ſtate of War with the People, who have a Right to *reinſtate* their *Legiſlative in the Exerciſe* of their Power. For

having erected a Legislative, with an Intent they should exercise the Power of making Laws, either at certain set times, or when there is need of it, when they are hinder'd by any Force from, what is so necessary to the Society, and wherein the safety and Preservation of the People consists, the People have a Right to remove it by Force. In all States and Conditions the true remedy of *Force* without Authority, is to oppose *Force* to it. The use of *Force* without Authority, always puts him that uses it into a *state of War*, as the Aggressor, and renders him liable to be treated accordingly.

156. The *Power of assembling and dismissing the Legislative*, placed in the Executive, gives not the Executive a superiority over it, but is a fiduciary Trust placed in him, for the safety of the People, in a Case where the uncertainty, and variableness of human Affairs could not bear a steady fixed Rule. For it not being possible, that the first framers of the Government should, by any foresight, be so much Masters of future Events, as to be able to prefix so just periods of Return and Duration to the *Assemblies of the Legislative*, in all times to come, that might exactly answer all the Exigencies of the Commonwealth; the best Remedy could be found for this Defect, was to trust this to the Prudence of one who was always to be present, and whose Business it was to watch over the publick Good. Constant *frequent Meetings of the Legislative*, and long Continuations of their Assemblies, without necessary Occasion, could not but be burthensome to the People, and must necessarily in time produce more dangerous Inconveniencies, and yet the quick turn of Affairs might be sometimes such as to need their present Help: Any Delay of their *convening* might endanger the publick; and sometimes too their Business might be so great, that the limitted time of their sitting might be too short for their Work, and rob the publick of that Benefit which could be had only from their mature Deliberation. What then could be done in this Case to prevent the Community from being exposed some time or other to eminent Hazard, on one side or the other, by fixed Intervals and Periods, set to the *meeting and acting of the Legislative*, but to intrust it to the Prudence of some, who being present, and acquainted with the state of publick Affairs, might make use of this Prerogative for the publick Good? And where else could this be so well placed as in his Hands, who was intrusted with the Execution of the Laws for the same End? Thus supposing the Regulation of Times for the *assembling and sitting of the Legislative*, not settled by the original Constitution, it naturally fell into the Hands of the Executive, not as an arbitrary Power depending on his good Pleasure, but with this trust always to have it exercised only for the publick Weal, as the Occurrences of Times and change of Affairs might require. Whether *settled Periods of their convening*, or *a Liberty* left to the Prince for *convoking the Legislative*, or perhaps a Mixture of both, hath the least Inconvenience attending it, 'tis not my Business here to inquire, but only to shew, that though the Executive Power may have the Prerogative of *convoking* and *dissolving* such *Conventions of the Legislative*, yet it is not thereby superior to it.

157. Things of this World are in so constant a Flux, that nothing remains long in the same State. Thus People, Riches, Trade, Power, change their Stations, flourishing mighty Cities come to ruine, and prove in time neglected desolate Corners, whilst other unfrequented Places grow into populous Countries, fill'd with Wealth and Inhabitants. But things not always changing equally, and private Interest often keeping up Customs and Privileges, when the Reasons of them are ceased, it often comes to pass, that in Governments, where part of the Legislative consists of *Representatives* chosen by the People, that in tract of time this *Representation* becomes very *unequal* and disproportionate to the Reasons it was at first establish'd upon. To what gross Absurdities the following of Custom, when Reason has left it, may lead, we may be satisfied, when we see the bare Name of a Town, of which there remains not so much as the Ruines, where scarce so much Housing as a Sheepcoat, or more Inhabitants than a Shepherd is to be found, sends *as many Representatives* to the grand Assembly of Law-makers, as a whole County numerous in People, and powerful in Riches. This Strangers stand amazed at, and every one must confess needs a Remedy. Though most think it hard to find one, because the Constitution of the Legislative being the original and supream Act of the Society, antecedent to all positive Laws in it, and depending wholly on the People, no inferior Power

can

can alter it. And therefore the *People*, when the *Legislative* is once constituted, *having* in such a Government as we have been speaking of, *no Power* to act as long as the Government stands; this Inconvenience is thought incapable of a Remedy.

158. *Salus Populi Suprema Lex*, is certainly so just and fundamental a Rule, that he, who sincerely follows it, cannot dangerously err. If therefore the Executive, who has the Power of convoking the Legislative, observing rather the true Proportion, than Fashion of *Representation*, regulates, not by old Custom, but true Reason, the *Number of Members*, in all Places, that have a Right to be distinctly represented, which no part of the People however incorporated can pretend to, but in Proportion to the Assistance which it affords to the Publick, it cannot be judg'd to have set up a new Legislative, but to have restored the old and true one, and to have rectified the Disorders, which Succession of time had insensibly, as well as inevitably introduced. For it being the Interest, as well as Intention of the People, to have a fair and *equal Representative*; whoever brings it nearest to that, is an undoubted Friend to, and Establisher of the Government, and cannot miss the Consent and Approbation of the Community. *Prerogative* being nothing but a Power in the Hands of the Prince, to provide for the publick Good, in such Cases, which depending upon unforeseen and uncertain Occurrences, certain and unalterable Laws could not safely direct; whatsoever shall be done manifestly for the good of the People, and the establishing the Government upon its true Foundations, is and always will be just *Prerogative*. The Power of erecting new Corporations, and therewith *new Representatives*, carries with it a Supposition, that in time the *Measures of Representation* might vary, and those Places have a just Right to be represented which before had none; and by the same Reason, those cease to have a Right, and be too inconsiderable for such a Privilege, which before had it. 'Tis not a Change from the present State, which perhaps Corruption or Decay has introduced, that makes an Inroad upon the Government, but the Tendency of it to injure or oppress the People, and to set up one Part, or Party, with a Distinction from, and an unequal Subjection of the rest. Whatsoever cannot but be acknowledged to be of Advantage to the Society, and People in general, upon just and lasting Measures, will always, when done, justifie itself; and whenever the People shall chuse their *Representatives upon* just and undeniably *equal Measures*, suitable to the original Frame of the Government, it cannot be doubted to be the Will and Act of the Society, whoever permitted or caused them so to do.

CHAP. XIV.

Of PREROGATIVE.

159. WHERE the Legislative and Executive Power are in distinct Hands, (as they are in all moderated Monarchies, and well-framed Governments) there the Good of the Society requires, that several things should be left to the Discretion of him, that has the Executive Power. For the Legislators not being able to foresee and provide by Laws, for all that may be useful to the Community, the Executor of the Laws having the Power in his Hands, has by the common Law of Nature a Right to make use of it for the good of the Society, in many Cases, where the municipal Law has given no Direction, till the Legislative can conveniently be assembled to provide for it. Many things there are, which the Law can by no means provide for, and those must necessarily be left to the Discretion of him that has the executive Power in his Hands, to be ordered by him as the publick Good and Advantage shall require: Nay, 'tis fit that the Laws themselves should in some Cases give way to the executive Power, or rather to this fundamental Law of Nature and Government, *viz.* That as much as may be, *all* the Members of the Society are to be preserved. For since many Accidents may happen, wherein a strict and rigid Observation of the Laws may do harm; (as not to pull down an innocent Man's House to stop the Fire, when the next to it is burning) and a Man may come sometimes within the

reach of the Law, which makes no Diſtinction of Perſons, by an Action that may deſerve Reward and Pardon; 'tis fit the Ruler ſhould have a Power, in many Caſes, to mitigate the Severity of the Law, and pardon ſome Offenders: For the *End of Government* being *the Preſervation of all*, as much as may be, even the Guilty are to be ſpared, where it can prove no Prejudice to the Innocent.

160. This Power to act according to Diſcretion, for the Publick Good, without the Preſcription of the Law, and ſometimes even againſt it, *is* that which is called *Prerogative.* For ſince in ſome Governments the Law-making Power is not always in Being, and is uſually too numerous, and ſo too ſlow, for the Diſpatch requiſite to Execution: and becauſe alſo it is impoſſible to foreſee, and ſo by Laws to provide for all Accidents and Neceſſities that may concern the Publick; or to make ſuch Laws as will do no harm, if they are executed with an inflexible Rigour, on all Occaſions, and upon all Perſons that may come in their way, therefore there is a Latitude left to the Executive Power, to do many things of Choice which the Laws do not preſcribe.

161. This Power, whilſt employed for the Benefit of the Community, and ſuitably to the Truſt and Ends of the Government, *is undoubted Prerogative*, and never is queſtioned. For the People are very ſeldom or never ſcrupulous or nice in the Point; they are far from examining *Prerogative*, whilſt it is in any tolerable Degree employ'd for the uſe it was meant, that is, for the Good of the People, and not manifeſtly againſt it. But if there comes to be a *Queſtion* between the Executive Power and the People, about a thing claimed as a *Prerogative*; the Tendency of the Exerciſe of ſuch *Prerogative* to the Good or Hurt of the People will eaſily decide that Queſtion.

162. It is eaſie to conceive, that in the Infancy of Governments, when Commonwealths differed little from Families in Number of People, they differ'd from them too but little in Number of Laws: And the Governours, being as the Fathers of them, watching over them for their Good, the Government was almoſt all *Prerogative.* A few eſtabliſh'd Laws ſerv'd the Turn, and the Diſcretion and Care of the Ruler ſupply'd the reſt. But when Miſtake or Flattery prevailed with weak Princes to make uſe of this Power for private Ends of their own, and not for the publick Good, the People were fain by expreſs Laws to get Prerogative determin'd in thoſe Points wherein they found Diſadvantage from it: And thus declared *Limitations of Prerogative* were by the People found neceſſary in Caſes which they and their Anceſtors had left, in the utmoſt Latitude, to the Wiſdom of thoſe Princes, who made no other but a right uſe of it, that is, for the Good of their People.

163. And therefore they have a very wrong Notion of Government, who ſay, that the People have *incroach'd upon the Prerogative*, when they have got any part of it to be defined by poſitive Laws. For in ſo doing they have not pulled from the Prince any thing that of right belong'd to him, but only declared, that that Power which they indefinitely left in his or his Anceſtors Hands, to be exerciſed for their Good, was not a thing whch they intended him when he uſed it otherwiſe. For the End of Government being the good of the Community, whatſoever Alterations are made in it, tending to that End, cannot be an *Incroachment* upon any body, ſince no body in Government can have a right tending to any other end. And thoſe only are *Incroachments* which prejudice or hinder the publick good. Thoſe who ſay otherwiſe, ſpeak as if the Prince had a diſtinct and ſeparate Intereſt from the Good of the Community, and was not made for it, the Root and Source from which ſpring almoſt all thoſe Evils and Diſorders which happen in Kingly Governments. And indeed if that be ſo, the People under his Government are not a Society of rational Creatures, entred into a Community for their mutual Good; they are not ſuch as have ſet Rulers over themſelves, to guard, and promote that good; but are to be looked on as an Herd of inferior Creatures under the Dominion of a Maſter, who keeps them and works them for his own Pleaſure or Profit. If Men were ſo void of Reaſon, and brutiſh, as to enter into Society upon ſuch Terms, *Prerogative* might indeed be, what ſome Men would have it, an arbitrary Power to do things hurtful to the People.

164. But ſince a rational Creature cannot be ſuppoſed when free, to put himſelf into Subjection to another, for his own Harm: (Though where he finds a good

good and wiſe Ruler, he may not perhaps think it either neceſſary or uſeful, to ſet preciſe Bounds to his Power in all things) *Prerogative* can be nothing but the Peoples permitting their Rulers to do ſeveral things of their own free Choice, where the Law was ſilent, and ſometimes too againſt the direct Letter of the Law, for the publick good; and their acquieſcing in it when ſo done. For as a good Prince, who is mindful of the Truſt put into his Hands, and careful of the Good of his People, cannot have too much *Prerogative*, that is, Power to do good: So a weak and ill Prince, who would claim that Power which his Predeceſſors exerciſed without the Direction of the Law, as a Prerogative belonging to him by Right of his Office, which he may exerciſe at his pleaſure, to make or promote an Intereſt diſtinct from that of the publick, gives the People an Occaſion to claim their Right, and limit that Power, which, whilſt it was exerciſed for their Good, they were content ſhould be tacitly allowed.

165. And therefore he that will look into the *Hiſtory of England*, will find, that *Prerogative* was always *largeſt* in the Hands of our wiſeſt and beſt Princes, becauſe the People obſerving the whole Tendency of their Actions to be the publick good, conteſted not what was done without Law to that end; or if any human Frailty or Miſtake (for Princes are but Men, made as others) appear'd in ſome ſmall Declinations from that end; yet 'twas viſible, the main of their Conduct tended to nothing but the Care of the publick. The People therefore finding reaſon to be ſatisfyed with theſe Princes, whenever they acted without or contrary to the Letter of the Law, acquieſced in what they did, and, without the leaſt Complaint, let them inlarge their *Prerogative* as they pleaſed, judging rightly, that they did nothing herein to the prejudice of their Laws, ſince they acted conformable to the Foundation and End of all Laws, the publick good.

166. Such God-like Princes indeed had ſome Title to arbitrary Power, by that Argument, that would prove abſolute Monarchy the beſt Government, as that which God himſelf governs the Univerſe by; becauſe ſuch Kings partake of his Wiſdom and Goodneſs. Upon this is founded that ſaying, That the Reigns of good Princes have been always moſt dangerous to the Liberties of their People. For when their Succeſſors, managing the Government with different Thoughts, would draw the Actions of thoſe good Rulers into Precedent, and make them the Standard of their *Prerogative*, as if what had been done only for the good of the People, was a Right in them to do, for the Harm of the People, if they ſo pleaſed; it has often occaſioned Conteſt, and ſometimes publick Diſorders, before the People could recover their original Right, and get that to be declared not to be *Prerogative*, which truly was never ſo: Since it is impoſſible that any body in the Society ſhould ever have a Right to do the People Harm; though it be very poſſible, and reaſonable, that the People ſhould not go about to ſet any Bounds to the *Prerogative* of thoſe Kings or Rulers, who themſelves tranſgreſſed not the Bounds of the publick Good. For *Prerogative is nothing but the Power of doing publick Good without a Rule.*

167. The Power of *calling Parliaments* in *England*, as to preciſe Time, Place, and Duration, is certainly a *Prerogative* of the King, but ſtill with this truſt, that it ſhall be made uſe of for the good of the Nation, as the Exigencies of the Times, and Variety of Occaſions ſhall require. For it being impoſſible to foreſee which ſhould always be the fitteſt place for them to aſſemble in, and what the beſt Seaſon; the Choice of theſe was left with the Executive Power, as might be moſt ſubſervient to the publick Good, and beſt ſuit the Ends of Parliaments.

168. The old Queſtion will be asked in this Matter of *Prerogative*. But *who ſhall be Judge* when this Power is made a right uſe of? I anſwer: Between an Executive Power in Being, with ſuch a Prerogative, and a Legiſlative that depends upon his Will for their convening, there can be no *Judge on Earth:* As there can be none between the Legiſlative and the People, ſhould either the Executive, or the Legiſlative, when they have got the Power in their Hands, deſign, or go about to enſlave or deſtroy them. The People have no other Remedy in this, as in all other Caſes where they have no Judge on Earth, but to *appeal to Heaven.* For the Rulers, in ſuch Attempts, exerciſing a Power the People never put into their Hands, (who can never be ſuppoſed to conſent that any body ſhould rule over them for their harm) do that which they have not a Right to do. And where the Body of the People, or any ſingle Man is deprived of their Right, or is under the

the Exercise of a Power without Right, and have no Appeal on Earth, then they have a Liberty to appeal to Heaven, whenever they judge the Cause of sufficient Moment. And therefore tho' the *People cannot* be *Judge*, so as to have by the Constitution of that Society any superior Power, to determine and give effective Sentence in the Case; yet they have, by a Law antecedent and paramount to all positive Laws of Men, reserv'd that ultimate Determination to themselves which belongs to all Mankind, where there lies no Appeal on Earth, *viz.* to judge, whether they have just Cause to make their Appeal to Heaven. And this Judgment they cannot part with, it being out of a Man's Power so to submit himself to another, as to give him a Liberty to destroy him; God and Nature never allowing a Man so to abandon himself, as to neglect his own Preservation: And since he cannot take away his own Life, neither can he give Another power to take it. Nor let any one think, this lays a perpetual Foundation for Disorder; for this operates not, till the Inconveniency is so great that the Majority feel it, and are weary of it, and find a Necessity to have it amended. But this the Executive Power, or wise Princes never need come in the Danger of: And 'tis the thing of all others, they have most need to avoid, as of all others the most perilous.

CHAP. XV.

Of Paternal, Political, and Despotical Power, consider'd together.

169. THough I have had occasion to speak of these separately before, yet the great Mistakes of late about Government, having, as I suppose, arisen from confounding these distinct Powers one with another, it may not, perhaps, be amiss to consider them here together.

170. *First* then, *paternal* or *parental Power* is nothing but that which Parents have over their Children, to govern them for the Childrens good, till they come to the use of Reason, or a State of Knowledge, wherein they may be supposed capable to understand that Rule, whether it be the Law of Nature, or the municipal Law of their Country, they are to govern themselves by: Capable, I say, to know it, as well as several others, who live as Freemen under that Law. The Affection and Tenderness which God hath planted in the Breasts of Parents towards their Children, makes it evident, that this is not intended to be a severe arbitrary Government, but only for the Help, Instruction, and Preservation of their Offspring. But happen it as it will, there is, as I have proved, no reason why it should be thought to extend to Life and Death, at any time over their Children, more than over any body else; neither can there be any pretence why this *parental Power* should keep the Child when grown to a Man, in subjection to the Will of his Parents, any farther than the having received Life and Education from his Parents, obliges him to Respect, Honour, Gratitude, Assistance, and Support all his Life to both Father and Mother. And thus, 'tis true, the *Paternal* is a natural *Government*, but not at all extending it self to the Ends and Jurisdictions of that, which is Political. The *Power of the Father doth not reach* at all to the *Property* of the Child, which is only in his own disposing.

171. *Secondly*, *Political Power* is that Power, which every Man having in the state of Nature, has given up into the hands of the Society, and therein to the Governours, whom the Society hath set over itself, with this express or tacit Trust, That it shall be imployed for their good, and the preservation of their Property: Now this *Power*, which every Man has *in the state of Nature*, and which he parts with to the Society, in all such Cases, where the Society can secure him, is to use such means, for the preserving of his own Property, as he thinks good, and Nature allows him; and to punish the Breach of the Law of Nature in others so, as (according to the best of his Reason) may most conduce to the preservation of himself, and the rest of Mankind. So that the *end and measure of this Power*, when in every Man's hands in the state of Nature, being the preservation of all of his Society, that is, all Mankind in general, it can have no other *end or measure*, when in the hands of the Magistrate, but to preserve the Members of that

that Society in their Lives, Liberties, and Poſſeſſions; and ſo cannot be an Abſolute, Arbitrary Power over their Lives and Fortunes, which are as much as poſſible to be preſerved; but a *Power to make Laws*, and annex ſuch *Penalties* to them, as may tend to the preſervation of the whole, by cutting off thoſe Parts, and thoſe only, which are ſo corrupt, that they threaten the ſound and healthy, without which no ſeverity is lawful. And this *Power has its Original only from Compact* and Agreement, and the mutual Conſent of thoſe who make up the Community.

172. *Thirdly, Deſpotical Power* is an Abſolute, Arbitrary Power one Man has over another, to take away his Life, whenever he pleaſes. This is a Power, which neither Nature gives, for it has made no ſuch diſtinction between one Man and another; nor Compact can convey, for Man not having ſuch an Arbitrary Power over his own Life, cannot give another Man ſuch a Power over it; but it is the *effect only of Forfeiture*, which the Aggreſſor makes of his own Life, when he puts himſelf into the ſtate of War with another. For having quitted Reaſon, which God hath given to be the Rule betwixt Man and Man, and the common bond whereby human kind is united into one Fellowſhip and Society; and having renounced the way of Peace which that teaches, and made uſe of the Force of War, to compaſs his unjuſt ends upon another; where he has no right, and ſo revolting from his own Kind to that of Beaſts, by making Force, which is theirs, to be his Rule of Right, he renders himſelf liable to be deſtroyed by the injur'd Perſon, and the reſt of Mankind, that will join with him in the execution of Juſtice, as any other wild Beaſt, or noxious Brute with whom Mankind can have neither Society nor Security. And thus *Captives*, taken in a juſt and lawful War, and ſuch only, are *ſubject to a Deſpotical Power*, which as it ariſes not from Compact, ſo neither is it capable of any, but is the ſtate of War continued. For what Compact can be made with a Man that is not Maſter of his own Life? What Condition can he perform? And if he be once allowed to be Maſter of his own Life, the *Deſpotical, Arbitrary Power* of his Maſter ceaſes. He that is Maſter of himſelf, and his own Life, has a right too to the means of preſerving it; ſo that *as ſoon as Compact enters, Slavery ceaſes*, and he ſo far quits his abſolute Power, and puts an end to the ſtate of War, who enters into Conditions with his Captive.

173. *Nature gives* the firſt of theſe, *viz. Paternal Power to Parents* for the Benefit of their Children during their Minority, to ſupply their want of Ability, and underſtanding how to manage their Property. (By *Property* I muſt be underſtood here, as in other places, to mean that Property which Men have in their Perſons as well as Goods) *Voluntary Agreement gives* the ſecond, *viz. Political Power to Governours* for the Benefit of their Subjects, to ſecure them in the Poſſeſſion and Uſe of their Properties. And *Forfeiture gives* the third *Deſpotical Power to Lords* for their own Benefit, over thoſe who are ſtripp'd of all Property.

174. He, that ſhall conſider the diſtinct riſe and extent, and the different ends of theſe ſeveral Powers, will plainly ſee, that *paternal Power* comes as far ſhort of that of the *Magiſtrate*, as *Deſpotical* exceeds it; and that *abſolute Dominion*, however placed, is ſo far from being one kind of civil Society, that it is as inconſiſtent with it, as Slavery is with Property. *Paternal Power* is only where Minority makes the Child incapable to manage his Property; *Political* where Men have Property in their own Diſpoſal; and *Deſpotical* over ſuch as have no Property at all.

CHAP. XVI.

Of CONQUEST.

175. THough Governments can originally have no other Riſe than that before mentioned, nor *Polities* be *founded on* any thing but *the Conſent of the People*; yet ſuch has been the Diſorders Ambition has fill'd the World with, that in the noiſe of War, which makes ſo great a part of the Hiſtory of Mankind, *this Conſent* is little taken notice of: And therefore many have miſtaken the Force of Arms, for the Conſent of the People; and reckon Conqueſt as one of the Originals

Originals of Government. But *Conquest* is as far from setting up any Government, as demolishing an House is from building a new one in the Place. Indeed it often makes way for a new Frame of a Commonwealth, by destroying the former; but, without the Consent of the People, can never erect a new one.

176. That the *Aggressor*, who puts himself into the state of War with another, and *unjustly invades* another Man's Right, *can*, by such an unjust War, *never* come to *have a right over the Conquered*, will be easily agreed by all Men, who will not think, that Robbers and Pyrates have a Right of Empire over whomsoever they have Force enough to master, or that Men are bound by Promises, which unlawful Force extorts from them. Should a Robber break into my House, and with a Dagger at my Throat, make me seal Deeds to convey my Estate to him, would this give him any Title? Just such a Title by his Sword, has an *unjust Conquerour*, who forces me into Submission. The Injury and the Crime is equal, whether committed by the wearer of a Crown, or some petty Villain. The Title of the Offender, and the Number of his Followers make no difference in the Offence, unless it be to aggravate it. The only difference is, Great Robbers punish little ones, to keep them in their Obedience, but the great ones are rewarded with Laurels and Triumphs, because they are too big for the weak hands of Justice in this World, and have the Power in their own Possession, which should punish Offenders. What is my Remedy against a Robber, that so broke into my House? *Appeal* to the Law for Justice. But perhaps Justice is deny'd, or I am crippled and cannot stir, Robbed and have not the means to do it. If God has taken away all means of seeking Remedy, there is nothing left but patience. But my Son, when able, may seek the Relief of the Law, which I am denied: He or his Son may renew his *Appeal*, till he recover his Right. But the Conquered, or their Children have no Court, no Arbitrator on Earth to appeal to. Then they may *Appeal*, as *Jephtha* did *to Heaven*, and repeat their *Appeal*, till they recovered the native Right of their Ancestors, which was, to have such a Legislative over them, as the Majority should approve, and freely acquiesce in. If it be objected, this would cause endless trouble; I answer, No more than Justice does, where she lies open to all that appeal to her. He that troubles his Neighbour without a Cause, is punished for it by the Justice of the Court he appeals to. And he that *appeals to Heaven*, must be sure he has Right on his side; and a Right too that is worth the Trouble and Cost of the Appeal, as he will answer at a Tribunal, that cannot be deceived, and will be sure to retribute to every one according to the Mischiefs he hath created to his Fellow Subjects; that is, any part of Mankind. From whence 'tis plain, that he that *Conquers in an unjust War can thereby have no Title to the Subjection and Obedience of the Conquered.*

177. But supposing Victory favours the right side, let us consider a *Conquerour in a lawful War*, and see what Power he gets, and over whom.

First, 'Tis plain he *gets no Power by his Conquest over those that Conquered with him.* They that fought on his side cannot suffer by the Conquest, but must at least be as much Freemen as they were before. And most commonly they serve upon Terms, and on Condition to share with their Leader, and enjoy a part of the Spoil, and other Advantages that attend the Conquering Sword: Or at least have a part of the subdued Country bestowed upon them. And *the conquering People are not I hope to be Slaves by Conquest*, and wear their Laurels only to shew they are Sacrifices to their Leaders Triumph. They that found absolute Monarchy upon the Title of the Sword make their Heroes, who are the Founders of such Monarchies, arrant *Draw-can-Sirs*, and forget they had any Officers and Soldiers that fought on their Side in the Battles they won, or assisted them in the subduing, or shared in possessing the Countries they master'd. We are told by some, that the *English* Monarchy is founded in the *Norman* Conquest, and that our Princes have thereby a Title to absolute Dominion: Which if it were true, (as by the History it appears otherwise) and that *William* had a Right to make War on this Island; yet his Dominion by Conquest could reach no farther than to the *Saxons* and *Britains*, that were then Inhabitants of this Country. The *Normans* that came with him, and helped to conquer, and all descended from them, are Freemen and no Subjects by Conquest; let that give what Dominion it will. And if I, or any Body else shall claim Freedom, as derived from them, it will be very hard to prove the contrary: And 'tis plain, the Law that has made no distinction between

tween the one and the other, intendsnot there ſhould be any Difference in their Freedom or Privileges

178. But ſuppoſing, which ſeldom happens, that the Conquerors and conquered never incorporate into one People, under the ſame Laws and Freedom. Let us ſee next *what Power a lawful Conqueror has over the Subdued:* And that I ſay is purely deſpotical. He has an abſolute Power over the Lives of thoſe, who by an unjuſt War have forfeited them; but not over the Lives or Fortunes of thoſe, who ingaged not in the War, nor over the Poſſeſſions even of thoſe, who were actually engaged in it.

179. *Secondly*, I ſay then the *Conqueror* gets no Power but only over thoſe, who have actually aſſiſted, concurr'd, or conſented to that unjuſt Force, that is uſed againſt him. For the People having given to their Governours no Power to do an unjuſt thing, ſuch as is to make an unjuſt War, (for they never had ſuch a Power in themſelves:) They ought not to be charged, as guilty of the Violence and Unjuſtice, that is committed in an Unjuſt War, any farther, than they actually abet it; no more, than they are to be thought guilty of any Violence or Oppreſſion their Governours ſhould uſe upon the People themſelves, or any part of their Fellow Subjects, they having impowered them no more to the one, than to the other. Conquerours, 'tis true, ſeldom trouble themſelves to make the diſtinction, but they willingly permit the Confuſion of War to ſweep all together; but yet this alters not the Right: For the Conqueror's Power over the Lives of the Conquered, being only becauſe they have uſed Force to do, or maintain an Injuſtice, he can have that Power only over thoſe, who have concurred in that Force, all the reſt are innocent; and he has no more Title over the People of that Country, who have done him no Injury, and ſo have made no forfeiture of their Lives, than he has over any other, who without any Injuries or Provocations, have lived upon fair Terms with him.

180. *Thirdly*, The *Power a Conquerour gets* over thoſe he overcomes *in a juſt War, is perfectly deſpotical*; he has an abſolute Power over the Lives of thoſe, who by putting themſelves in a ſtate of War, have forfeited them; but he has not thereby a Right and Title to their Poſſeſſions. This I doubt not, but at firſt Sight will ſeem a ſtrange Doctrine, it being ſo quite contrary to the practice of the World; there being nothing more familiar in ſpeaking of the Dominion of Countries, than to ſay ſuch an one conquer'd it. As if Conqueſt, without any more ado, convey'd a Right of Poſſeſſion. But when we conſider, that the Practice of the ſtrong and powerful, how univerſal ſoever it may be, is ſeldom the rule of Right, however it be one part of the Subjection of the Conquered, not to argue againſt the Conditions, cut out to them by the Conquering Sword.

181. Though in all War there be uſually a complication of Force and Damage, and the Aggreſſor ſeldom fails to harm the Eſtate, when he uſes Force againſt the Perſons of thoſe he makes War upon; yet 'tis the uſe of Force only that puts a Man into the ſtate of War. For whether by Force he begins the Injury, or elſe having quietly, and by fraud, done the Injury, he refuſes to make Reparation and by Force maintains it, (which is the ſame thing, as at firſt to have done it by Force) 'tis the unjuſt uſe of Force, that makes the War. For he that breaks open my Houſe, and violently turns me out of Doors; or having peaceably got in, by Force keeps me out, does in Effect the ſame thing; ſuppoſing we arein ſuch a ſtate, that we have no common Judge on Earth, whom I may appeal to, and to whom we are both obliged to ſubmit: For of ſuch I am now ſpeaking. 'Tis the *unjuſt uſe of Force* then, that *puts a Man into the ſtate of War* with another, and thereby he, that is guilty of it, makes a forfeiture of his Life. For quitting Reaſon, which is the Rule given between Man and Man, and uſing Force the way of Beaſts, he becomes liable to be deſtroyed by him he uſes Force againſt, as any ſavage ravenous Beaſt, that is dangerous to his Being.

182. But becauſe the miſcarriages of the Father are no faults of the Children, and they may be rational and peaceable, notwithſtanding the brutiſhneſs and injuſtice of the Father; the Father, by his Miſcarriages and Violence, can forfeit but his own Life, but involves not his Children in his Guilt or Deſtruction. His Goods, which Nature that willeth the preſervation of all Mankind as much as is poſſible, hath made to belong to the Children to keep them from periſhing, do ſtill continue to belong to his Children. For ſuppoſing them not to have joyn'd in

in the War, either through Infancy, Abſence, or Choice, they have done nothing to forfeit them: *nor has the Conqueror any Right* to take them away, by the bare Title of having ſubdued him, that by Force attempted his Deſtruction; though perhaps he may have ſome Right to them, to repair the Damages, he has ſuſtained by the War, and the Defence of his own Right; which how far it reaches to the poſſeſſions of the Conquered, we ſhall ſee by and by. So that he that *by Conqueſt has a Right over a Man's Perſon* to deſtroy him if he pleaſes, has *not* thereby a Right over *his Eſtate* to poſſeſs and enjoy it. For it is the brutal Force the Aggreſſor has uſed, that gives his Adverſary a Right to take away his Life, and deſtroy him if he pleaſes, as a noxious Creature, but 'tis Damage ſuſtain'd that alone gives him Title to another Man's Goods: For though I may kill a Thief that ſets on me in the Highway, yet I may not (which ſeems leſs) take away his Money, and let him go; this would be Robbery on my ſide. His Force, and the ſtate of War he put himſelf in, made him forfeit his Life, but gave me no Title to his Goods. The *Right* then of *Conqueſt extends only to the Lives* of thoſe who joyn'd in the War, *not to their Eſtates*, but only in order to make Reparation for the Damages received, and the Charges of the War, and that too with Reſervation of the right of the innocent Wife and Children.

183. Let the *Conqueror* have as much Juſtice on his Side, as could be ſuppoſed, he *has* no *Right* to ſeize more than the vanquiſhed could forfeit; his Life is at the Victor's Mercy, and his Service, and Goods he may appropriate, to make himſelf Reparation; but he cannot take the Goods of his Wife and Children; they too had a Title to the Goods he enjoy'd, and their Shares in the Eſtate he poſſeſſed. For Example, I in the ſtate of Nature (and all Commonwealths are in the ſtate of Nature one with another) have injured another Man, and refuſing to give Satisfaction, it comes to a ſtate of War, wherein my defending by Force, what I had gotten unjuſtly, makes me the Aggreſſor. I am conquered: My Life, 'tis true, as forfeit, is at mercy, but not my Wives and Childrens. They made not the War, nor aſſiſted in it. I could not forfeit their Lives, they were not mine to forfeit. My Wife had a Share in my Eſtate, that neither could I forfeit. And my Children alſo, being born of me, had a Right to be maintained out of my Labour or Subſtance. Here then is the Caſe; The Conqueror has a Title to Reparation for Damages received, and the Children have a Title to their Father's Eſtate for their Subſiſtence. For as to the Wife's ſhare, whether her own Labour, or Compact gave her a Title to it, 'tis plain, her Husband could not forfeit what was hers. What muſt be done in the Caſe? I anſwer; The fundamental Law of Nature being, that all, as much as may be, ſhould be preſerved, it follows, that if there be not enough fully to *ſatisfie* both, *viz.* for the *Conqueror's Loſſes*, and Childrens Maintenance, he that hath, and to ſpare, muſt remit ſomething of his full Satisfaction, and give way to the preſſing and preferable Title of thoſe, who are in Danger to periſh without it.

184. But ſuppoſing the *Charge* and *Damages of the War* are to be made up to the Conqueror, to the utmoſt Farthing; and that the Children of the Vanquiſhed, ſpoiled of all their Father's Goods, are to be left to ſtarve and periſh; yet the ſatisfying of what ſhall, on this Score, be due to the Conqueror, will ſcarce give him a *Title to any Countrey he ſhall conquer*. For the Damages of War can ſcarce amount to the value of any conſiderable Tract of Land, in any part of the World, where all the Land is poſſeſſed, and none lies waſte. And if I have not taken away the Conqueror's Land, which, being vanquiſhed, it is impoſſible I ſhould; ſcarce any other Spoil I have done him, can amount to the Value of mine, ſuppoſing it equally cultivated, and of an Extent any way coming near, what I had over run of his. The deſtruction of a Years Product or two, (for it ſeldom reaches four or five) is the utmoſt Spoil, that uſually can be done. For as to Money, and ſuch Riches, and Treaſure taken away, theſe are none of Natures Goods, they have but a phantaſtical imaginary Value: Nature has put no ſuch upon them: They are of no more account by her Standard, than the Wampompeke of the *Americans* to an *European* Prince, or the Silver Money of *Europe* would have been formerly to an *American*. And five Years product is not worth the perpetual Inheritance of Land, where all is poſſeſſed, and none remains waſte, to be taken up by him, that is diſſeiz'd: Which will be eaſily granted, if one do but take away the imaginary value of Money, the diſproportion being more, than between five

and

and five hundred. Though, at the same time, half a Years product is more worth than the Inheritance, where there being more Land, than the Inhabitants possess, and make use of, any one has Liberty to make use of the Waste: But there Conquerors take little Care to possess themselves of the *Lands of the Vanquished*. No Damage therefore, that Men in the state of Nature (as all Princes and Governments are in reference to one another) suffer from one another, can give a Conqueror Power to dispossess the Posterity of the Vanquished, and turn them out of that Inheritance, which ought to be the Possession of them and their Descendants to all Generations. The Conqueror indeed will be apt to think himself Master: And 'tis the very Condition of the Subdued not to be able to dispute their Right. But if that be all, it gives no other Title than what bare Force gives to the stronger over the weaker: And, by this reason, he that is strongest will have a Right to whatever he pleases to seize on.

185. Over those then that joyned with him in the War, and over those of the subdued Country that opposed him not, and the Posterity even of those that did, the Conqueror, even in a just War, hath, by his Conquest no *Right of Dominion:* They are free from any Subjection to him, and if their former Government be dissolved, they are at Liberty to begin and erect another to themselves.

186. The Conqueror, 'tis true, usually, by the Force he has over them, compels them, with a Sword at their Breasts, to stoop to his Conditions, and submit to such a Government as he pleases to afford them; but the Enquiry is, What Right he has to do so? If it be said, they submit by their own Consent, then this allows their own *Consent* to be *necessary to give the Conqueror a Title to rule* over them. It remains only to be considered, whether *Promises extorted by Force*, without Right, can be thought Consent, and *how far they bind*. To which I shall say, they *bind not at all*; because whatsoever another gets from me by Force, I still retain the Right of, and he is obliged presently to restore. He that forces my Horse from me, ought presently to restore him, and I have still a Right to retake him. By the same Reason, he that *forced a Promise* from me, ought presently to restore it, *i. e.* quit me of the Obligation of it; or I may resume it my self, *i. e.* chuse whether I will perform it. For the Law of Nature laying an Obligation on me only by the Rules she prescribes, cannot oblige me by the Violation of her Rules: Such is the extorting any thing from me by Force. Nor does it at all alter the Case to say, *I gave my Promise*, no more than it excuses the Force, and passes the Right, when I put my Hand in my Pocket, and deliver my Purse my self to a Thief, who demands it with a Pistol at my Breast.

187. From all which it follows, that the *Government of a Conqueror*, imposed by Force on the Subdued, against whom he had no Right of War, or who joyned not in the War against him, where he had Right, *has no Obligation* upon them.

188. But let us suppose, that all the Men of that Community being all Members of the same Body politick, may be taken to have joyn'd in that unjust War wherein they are subdued, and so their Lives are at the Mercy of the Conqueror.

189. I say, this concerns not their Children who are in their Minority. For since a Father hath not, in himself, a Power over the Life or Liberty of his Child, no act of his can possibly forfeit it. So that the Children, whatever may have happened to the Fathers, are Freemen, and the absolute Power of the *Conqueror* reaches no farther than the Persons of the Men that were subdued by him, and dies with them; and should he govern them as Slaves, subjected to his absolute arbitrary Power, he *has no such Right of Dominion over their Children*. He can have no Power over them but by their own Consent, whatever he may drive them to say or do; and he has no lawful Authority, whilst Force, and not Choice, compels them to Submission.

190. Every Man is born with a double Right: *First*, A *Right of Freedom to his Person*, which no other Man has a Power over, but the free Disposal of it lies in himself. *Secondly*, A *Right* before any other Man, *to inherit* with his Brethren his *Father's Goods*.

191. By the first of these, a Man is *naturally free* from Subjection to any Government, tho' he be born in a place under its Jurisdiction. But if he disclaim the lawful Government of the Country he was born in, he must also quit the Right that belong'd to him by the Laws of it, and the Possessions there descending to him from his Ancestors, if it were a Government made by their Consent.

192. By the ſecond, the *Inhabitants* of any Country, who are deſcended, and derive a Title to their Eſtates from thoſe who are ſubdued, and had a Government forced upon them againſt their free Conſents, *retain a Right to the Poſſeſſion of their Anceſtors*, though they conſent not freely to the Government, whoſe hard Conditions were by Force impoſed on the Poſſeſſors of that Country. For the firſt *Conqueror never having had a Title to the Land* of that Country, the People who are the Deſcendants of, or claim under thoſe who were forced to ſubmit to the Yoke of a Government by Conſtraint, have always a Right to ſhake it off, and free themſelves from the Uſurpation or Tyranny which the Sword hath brought in upon them, till their Rulers put them under ſuch a Frame of Government as they willingly and of choice conſent to. Who doubts but the *Græcian* Chriſtians, Deſcendants of the ancient Poſſeſſors of that Country, may juſtly caſt off the *Turkiſh* Yoke which they have ſo long groaned under, whenever they have an Opportunity to do it? For no Government can have a Right to Obedience from a People who have not freely conſented to it; which they can never be ſuppoſed to do, till either they are put in a full ſtate of Liberty, to chuſe their Government and Governors, or at leaſt till they have ſuch ſtanding Laws, to which they have by themſelves or their Repreſentatives given their free Conſent, and alſo till they are allow'd their due Property, which is ſo to be Proprietors of what they have, that no body can take away any part of it without their own Conſent, without which, Men under any Government are not in the ſtate of Freemen, but are direct Slaves under the Force of War.

193. But granting that the *Conqueror* in a juſt War has a Right to the Eſtates, as well as Power over the Perſons, of the Conquered; which, 'tis plain, he *hath* not: Nothing of *abſolute Power* will follow from hence, in the Continuance of the Government: Becauſe the Deſcendants of theſe being all Freemen, if he grants them Eſtates and Poſſeſſions to inhabit his Country, (without which it would be worth nothing) whatſoever he grants them, they have, ſo far as it is granted, *Property* in. The Nature whereof is, that *without a Man's own Conſent* it *cannot be taken from him*.

194. Their *Perſons* are *free* by a native Right, and their *Properties*, be they more or leſs, are *their own, and at their own diſpoſe*, and not at his; or elſe it is no *Property*. Suppoſing the Conqueror gives to one Man a thouſand Acres, to him and his Heirs for ever; to another he lets a thouſand Acres for his Life, under the Rent of 50*l.* or 500*l. per Ann.* Has not the one of theſe a Right to his thouſand Acres for ever, and the other, during his Life, paying the ſaid Rent? And hath not the Tenant for Life a *Property* in all that he gets over and above his Rent, by his Labour and Induſtry during the ſaid Term, ſuppoſing it be double the Rent? Can any one ſay, the King, or Conqueror, after his Grant, may by his Power of Conqueror take away all, or part of the Land from the Heirs of one, or from the other during his Life, he paying the Rent? Or can he take away from either, the Goods or Money they have got upon the ſaid Land, at his pleaſure? If he can, then all free and voluntary *Contracts* ceaſe, and are void in the World; there needs nothing to diſſolve them at any time, but Power enough: And all the *Grants* and *Promiſes* of *Men in Power*, are but Mockery and Colluſion. For can there be any thing more ridiculous than to ſay, I give you and yours this for ever; and that in the ſureſt and moſt ſolemn way of conveyance can be deviſed: And yet it is to be underſtood, that I have Right, if I pleaſe, to take it away from you again to Morrow?

195. I will not diſpute now whether Princes are exempt from the Laws of their Country; but this I am ſure, they owe Subjection to the Laws of God and Nature. No Body, no Power, can exempt them from the Obligations of that eternal Law. Thoſe are ſo great, and ſo ſtrong, in the Caſe of *Promiſes*, that Omnipotency itſelf can be tyed by them. *Grants*, *Promiſes*, and *Oaths*, are *Bonds* that *hold the Almighty*: Whatever ſome Flatterers ſay to Princes of the World, who all together, with all their People joyned to them, are, in Compariſon of the Great God, but as a Drop of the Bucket, or a Duſt on the Balance, inconſiderable, nothing!

196. The ſhort of the *Caſe in Conqueſt* is this, The Conqueror, if he have a juſt Cauſe, has a deſpotical Right over the Perſons of all, that actually aided, and concurred in the War againſt him, and a Right to make up his Damage and Coſt

out

out of their Labour and Eſtates, ſo he injure not the Right of any other. Over the reſt of the People, if there were any that conſented not to the War, and over the Children of the Captives themſelves, or the Poſſeſſons of either, he has no Power; and ſo can have, *by vertue of Conqueſt, no lawful Title* himſelf *to Dominion* over them, or derive it to his Poſterity; but is an Aggreſſor, if he attempts upon their Properties, and thereby puts himſelf in a ſtate of War againſt them, and has no better a Right of Principality, he, nor any of his Succeſſors, than *Hingar*, or *Hubba*, the *Danes* had here in *England*; or *Spartacus*, had he conquered *Italy*, would have had; which is to have their Yoke caſt off, as ſoon as God ſhall give thoſe under their Subjection Courage and Opportunity to do it. Thus, notwithſtanding whatever Title the Kings of *Aſſyria* had over *Judah*, by the Sword, God aſſiſted *Hezekiah* to throw off the Dominion of that conquering Empire. *And the Lord was with Hezekiah, and he proſpered; wherefore he went forth, and he rebelled againſt the King of Aſſyria, and ſerved him not*, 2 Kings xviii. 7. Whence it is plain, that ſhaking off a Power, which Force, and not Right hath ſet over any one, though it hath the Name of *Rebellion*, yet is no Offence before God, but is that which he allows and countenances, though even Promiſes and Covenants, when obtain'd by Force, have intervened. For 'tis very probable, to any one that reads the Story of *Ahaz* and *Hezekiah* attentively, that the *Aſſyrians* ſubdued *Ahaz*, and depoſed him, and made *Hezekiah* King in his Father's Lifetime; and that *Hezekiah* by Agreement had done him Homage, and paid him Tribute all this time.

CHAP. XVII.

Of USURPATION.

197. AS Conqueſt may be called a foreign Uſurpation, ſo Uſurpation is a kind of domeſtick Conqueſt, with this Difference, that an Uſurper can never have Right on his ſide, it being no *Uſurpation*, but where one is got into the *Poſſeſſion of what another has Right to*. This, ſo far as it is *Uſurpation*, is a Change only of Perſons, but not of the Forms and Rules of the Government: For if the Uſurper extend his Power beyond what of Right belonged to the lawful Princes, or Governors of the Commonwealth, 'tis *Tyranny* added to *Uſurpation*.

198. In all lawful Governments, the Deſignation of the Perſons, who are to bear Rule, is as natural and neceſſary a part as the Form of the Government itſelf, and is that which had its Eſtabliſhment originally from the People; the Anarchy being much alike, to have no Form of Government at all; or to agree, that it ſhall be monarchical, but to appoint no way to deſign the Perſon that ſhall have the Power, and be the Monarch. Hence all Commonwealths, with the Form of Government eſtabliſhed, have Rules alſo of appointing thoſe, who are to have any ſhare in the publick Authority, and ſettled Methods of conveying the Right to them. For the Anarchy is much alike to have no Form of Government at all; or to agree that it ſhall be monarchical, but to appoint no way to know or deſign the Perſon that ſhall have the Power, and be the Monarch. Whoever gets into the Exerciſe of any part of the Power, by other ways than what the Laws of the Community have preſcribed, hath no Right to be obeyed, though the Form of the Commonwealth be ſtill preſerved; ſince he is not the Perſon the Laws have appointed, and conſequently not the Perſon the People have conſented to. Nor can ſuch an *Uſurper*, or any deriving from him, ever have a Title, till the People are both at liberty to conſent, and have actually conſented to allow, and confirm in him the Power he hath till then uſurped.

CHAP

CHAP. XVIII.

Of TYRANNY.

199. AS Usurpation is the Exercise of Power, which another hath a Right to; so *Tyranny is the Exercise of Power beyond Right*, which no body can have a Right to. And this is making use of the Power any one has in his Hands, not for the Good of those who are under it, but for his own private separate Advantage. When the Governor, however intituled, makes not the Law, but his Will, the Rule; and his Commands and Actions are not directed to the Preservation of the Properties of his People, but the Satisfaction of his own Ambition, Revenge, Covetousness, or any other irregular Passion.

200. If one can doubt this to be Truth, or Reason, because it comes from the obscure Hand of a Subject, I hope the Authority of a King will make it pass with him. King *James* the First, in his Speech to the Parliament 1603, tells them thus, *I will ever prefer the Weal of the Publick, and of the whole Commonwealth, in making of good Laws and Constitutions, to any particular and private Ends of mine. Thinking ever the Wealth and Weal of the Commonwealth to be my greatest Weal and worldly Felicity; a Point wherein a lawful King doth directly differ from a Tyrant. For I do acknowledge, that the special and greatest point of Difference that is between a rightful King, and an usurping Tyrant, is this, That whereas the proud and ambitious Tyrant doth think, his Kingdom and People are only ordained for Satisfaction of his Desires and unreasonable Appetites; the righteous and just King doth by the contrary acknowledge himself to be ordained for the procuring of the Wealth and Property of his People.* And again, in his Speech to the Parliament 1609, he hath these Words, *The King binds himself by a double Oath, to the Observation of the fundamental Laws of his Kingdom. Tacitly, as by being a King, and so bound to protect as well the People, as the Laws of his Kingdom, and expresly by his Oath at his Coronation; so as every just King, in a settled Kingdom, is bound to observe that Paction made to his People, by his Laws in framing his Government agreeable thereunto, according to that Paction which God made with* Noah *after the Deluge. Hereafter, Seed-time and Harvest, and Cold and Heat, and Summer and Winter, and Day and Night, shall not cease while the Earth remaineth. And therefore a King governing in a settled Kingdom, leaves to be a King, and degenerates into a Tyrant, as soon as he leaves off to rule according to his Laws.* And a little after, *Therefore all Kings that are not Tyrants, or perjured, will be glad to bound themselves within the Limits of their Laws. And they that perswade them the contrary, are Vipers, and Pests both against them and the Commonwealth.* Thus that learned King, who well understood the Notions of things, makes the Difference betwixt a *King* and a *Tyrant* to consist only in this, That one makes the Laws the Bounds of his Power, and the Good of the Publick, the End of his Government; the other makes all give way to his own Will and Appetite.

201. 'Tis a Mistake to think this Fault is proper only to Monarchies; other Forms of Government are lyable to it, as well as that. For wherever the Power, that is put in any Hands for the Government of the People, and the Preservation of their Properties is applied to other Ends, and made use of to impoverish, harass, or subdue them to the arbitrary and irregular Commands of those that have it: There it presently becomes *Tyranny* whether those that thus use it are one or many. Thus we read of the Thirty Tyrants at *Athens*, as well as One at *Syracuse*; and the intolerable Dominion of the *Decemviri* at *Rome* was nothing better.

202. *Where-ever Law ends, Tyranny begins*, if the Law be transgressed to another's harm. And whosoever in Authority exceeds the Power given him by the Law, and makes use of the Force, he has under his Command, to compass that upon the Subject, which the Law, allows not, ceases in that to be a Magistrate, and acting without Authority, may be opposed, as any other Man, who by force invades the Right of another. This is acknowledged in subordinate Magistrates. He that hath Authority to seize my Person in the Street, may be opposed as a Theif and a Robber, if he indeavours to break into my House to execute a Writ,

notwithstanding

notwithſtanding that I know, he has ſuch a Warrant, and ſuch a Legal Authority, as will impower him to Arreſt me abroad. And why this ſhould not hold in the higheſt, as well as in the moſt Inferiour Magiſtrate, I would gladly be informed. Is it reaſonable, that the Eldeſt Brother, becauſe he has the greateſt part of his Father's Eſtate, ſhould thereby have a Right to take away any of his younger Brother's Portions? Or that a Rich Man, who poſſeſſed a whole Country, ſhould from thence have a Right to ſeize, when he pleaſed, the Cottage and Garden of his poor Neighbour? The being rightfully poſſeſſed of great Power and Riches exceedingly beyond the greateſt part of the Sons of *Adam*, is ſo far from being an Excuſe, much leſs a Reaſon, for Rapine and Oppreſſion, which the endamaging another without Authority is, that it is a great Aggravation of it. For the enceeding the Bounds of Authority, is no more a Right in a great, than a petty Officer; no more juſtifiable in a King than a Conſtable: But is ſo much the worſe in him, in that he has more truſt put in him, has already a much greater ſhare than the reſt of his Brethren, and is ſuppoſed, from the advantages of his Education, Imployment, and Counſellors, to be more knowing in the meaſures of Right and Wrong.

203. May the *Commands* then *of a Prince be Oppoſed?* May he be reſiſted as often as any one ſhall find himſelf aggrieved, and but imagine he has not Right done him? This will unhinge and overturn all Polities, and inſtead of Government and Order, leave nothing but Anarchy and Confuſion.

204. To this I anſwer: That *Force* is to be *oppoſed* to nothing, but to unjuſt and unlawful *Force*; whoever makes any oppoſition in any other Caſe, draws on himſelf a juſt Condemnation both from God and Man; and ſo no ſuch Danger or Confuſion will follow, as is often ſuggeſted. For,

205. *Firſt*, As in ſome Countries, the Perſon of the Prince by the Law is Sacred; and ſo whatever he commands or does, his Perſon is ſtill free from all Queſtion or Violence, not liable to Force, or any Judicial Cenſure or Condemnation. But yet oppoſition may be made to the illegal Acts of any inferiour Officer, or other commiſſioned by him; unleſs he will by actually putting himſelf into a ſtate of War with his People, diſſolve the Government, and leave them to that Defence, which belongs to every one in the ſtate of Nature. For of ſuch things who can tell what the end will be? And a Neighbour Kingdom has ſhewed the World an odd Example. In all other Caſes the *Sacredneſs* of the *Perſon exempts him from all Inconveniencies*, whereby he is ſecure, whilſt the Government ſtands, from all violence and harm whatſoever; Than which there cannot be a wiſer Conſtitution. For the harm he can do in his own Perſon not being likely to happen often, nor to extend it ſelf far; nor being able by his ſingle ſtrength to ſubvert the Laws, nor oppreſs the Body of the People, ſhould any Prince have ſo much Weakneſs, and ill Nature as to be willing to do it, the Inconveniency of ſome particular miſchiefs, that may happen ſometimes, when a heady Prince comes to the Throne, are well recompenced, by the peace of the Publick, and ſecurity of the Government, in the Perſon of the Chief Magiſtrate, thus ſet out of the reach of danger: It being ſafer for the Body, that ſome few private Men ſhould be ſometimes in danger to ſuffer, than that the Head of the Republick ſhould be eaſily, and upon ſlight occaſions expoſed.

206. *Secondly*, But this Privilege belonging only to the King's Perſon, hinders not, but they may be queſtioned, oppoſed, and reſiſted, who uſe unjuſt Force, though they pretend a Commiſſion from him, which the Law authorizes not. As is plain in the Caſe of him, that has the King's Writ to Arreſt a Man, which is a full Commiſſion from the King; and yet he that has it cannot break open a Man's Houſe to do it, nor execute this Command of the King upon certain Days, nor in certain Places, though this Commiſſion have no ſuch exception in it, but they are the Limitations of the Law, which if any one tranſgreſs, the King's Commiſſion excuſes him not. For the King's Authority being given him only by the Law, he cannot impower any one to act againſt the Law, or juſtifie him, by his Commiſſion in ſo doing. The *Commiſſion*, or *Command of any Magiſtrate, where he has no Authority*, being as *void* and inſignificant, as that of any private Man. The difference between the one and the other, being that the Magiſtrate has ſome Authority ſo far, and to ſuch ends, and the private Man has none at all. For 'tis not the *Commiſſion*, but the *Authority*, that gives the Right of acting; and *againſt* *the*

the Laws there can be no Authority. But, notwithstanding such Resistance, the King's Person and Authority are still both secured, and so *no danger to Governor or Government.*

207. *Thirdly,* Supposing a Government wherein the Person of the Chief Magistrate is not thus Sacred; yet this *Doctrine* of the lawfulness of *resisting* all unlawful exercises of his Power, *will not* upon every slight occasion indanger him, or *imbroil the Government.* For where the injured Party may be relieved, and his Damages repaired by Appeal to the Law, there can be no pretence for Force, which is only to be used where a Man is intercepted from appealing to the Law. For nothing is to be accounted Hostile Force, but where it leaves not the remedy of such an Appeal. And 'tis such *Force* alone, that *puts* him that uses it *into a state of War,* and makes it lawful to resist him. A Man with a Sword in his Hand demands my Purse in the High-way, when perhaps I have not 12 *d.* in my Pocket; This Man I may lawfully kill. To another I deliver 100 *l.* to hold only whilst I alight, which he refuses to restore me, when I am got up again, but draws his Sword to defend the possession of it by Force, if I endeavour to retake it. The mischief this Man does me, is a hundred, or possibly a thousand times more, than the other perhaps intended me, (whom I killed before he really did me any) and yet I might lawfully kill the one, and cannot so much as hurt the other lawfully. The Reason whereof is plain; because the one using *Force,* which threatned my Life, I could not have *time to appeal* to the Law to secure it: And when it was gone, 'twas too late to appeal. The Law could not restore Life to my dead Carcass: The Loss was irreparable; which to prevent, the Law of Nature gave me a Right to *destroy* him, who had put himself into a state of War with me, and threatened my Destruction. But in the other Case, my Life not being in danger, I may have the *benefit of appealing* to the Law, and have Reparation for my 100 *l.* that way.

208. *Fourthly,* But if the unlawful acts done by the Magistrate, be maintained (by the Power he has got) and the remedy which is due by Law, be by the same Power obstructed; yet the *Right of Resisting,* even in such manifest Acts of Tyranny, *will not* suddenly, or on slight occasions, *disturb the Government.* For if it reach no farther than some private Mens Cases, though they have a right to defend themselves and to recover by force, what by unlawful Force is taken from them; yet the Right to do so, will not easily ingage them in a Contest, wherein they are sure to perish; it being as impossible for one, or a few oppressed Men to *disturb the Government,* where the Body of the People do not think themselves concerned in it, as for a raving mad Man, or heady Malecontent to overturn a well-setled State; the People being as little apt to follow the one, as the other.

209. But if either these illegal Acts have extended to the Majority of the People; or if the Mischief and Oppression has light only on some few, but in such Cases, as the Precedent, and Consequences seem to threaten all, and they are perswaded in their Consciences, that their Laws, and with them their Estates, Liberties, and Lives are in danger, and perhaps their Religion too, how they will be hindered from resisting illegal force, used against them, I cannot tell. This is an *Inconvenience,* I confess, *that attends all Governments* whatsoever, when the Governours have brought it to this pass, to be generally suspected of their People; the most dangerous state which they can possibly put themselves in; wherein they are the less to be pitied, because it is so easie to be avoided; It being as impossible for a Governor, if he really means the good of his People, and the preservation of them, and their Laws together, not to make them see and feel it; as it is for the Father of a Family, not to let his Children see he loves, and takes care of them.

210. But if all the World shall observe Pretences of one kind, and Actions of another; Arts used to elude the Law, and the trust of Prerogative (which is an Arbitrary Power in some things left in the Prince's hand to do good, not harm to the People) employed, contrary to the end, for which it was given: If the People shall find the Ministers and subordinate Magistrates chosen suitable to such ends, and favoured, or laid by proportionably, as they promote, or oppose them: If they see several Experiments made of arbitrary Power, and that Religion underhand favoured, (though publickly proclaimed against) which is readiest to introduce it; and the Operators in it supported, as much as may be; and when that

that cannot be done, yet approved ſtill, and liked the better: If a *long Train of Actings ſhew the Councils* all tending that way, how can a Man any more hinder himſelf from being perſwaded in his own Mind, which way things are going; or from caſting about how to ſave himſelf, than he could from believing the Captain of the Ship he was in, was carrying him, and the reſt of the Company to *Algiers*, when he found him always ſteering that Courſe, though croſs Winds, Leaks in his Ship, and want of Men and Proviſions did often force him to turn his Courſe another way for ſome time, which he ſteadily returned to again, as ſoon as the Wind, Weather, and other Circumſtances would let him?

CHAP. XIX.

Of the Diſſolution of Government.

211. HE that will with any clearneſs ſpeak of the *Diſſolution of Government*, ought in the firſt place to diſtinguiſh between the *Diſſolution of the Society*, and the *Diſſolution of the Government*. That which makes the Community, and brings Men out of the looſe ſtate of Nature, into *one Politick Society*, is the Agreement which every one has with the reſt to incorporate, and act as one Body, and ſo be one diſtinct Commonwealth. The uſual, and almoſt only way whereby *this Union is diſſolved*, is the Inroad of Foreign Force making a Conqueſt upon them. For in that Caſe, (not being able to maintain and ſupport themſelves, as *one intire* and *independent Body)* the Union belonging to that Body which conſiſted therein, muſt neceſſarily ceaſe, and ſo every one return to the ſtate he was in before, with a liberty to ſhift for himſelf, and provide for his own Safety as he thinks fit in ſome other Society. Whenever the *Society is diſſolved*, 'tis certain the Government of that Society cannot remain. Thus Conquerours Swords often cut up Governments by the Roots, and mangle Societies to pieces, ſeparating the ſubdued or ſcattered Multitude from the Protection of, and Dependence on that Society which ought to have preſerved them from violence. The World is too well inſtructed in, and too forward to allow of this way of diſſolving of Governments to need any more to be ſaid of it; and there wants not much Argument to prove that where the *Society is diſſolved*, the Government cannot remain; that being as impoſſible, as for the Frame of an Houſe to ſubſiſt, when the Materials of it are ſcattered, and diſſipated by a Whirl-wind; or jumbled into a confuſed heap by an Earth-quake.

212. Beſides this over-turning from without, *Governments are diſſolved from within*,

Firſt, When the *Legiſlative* is *altered*. Civil Society being a ſtate of Peace, amongſt thoſe who are of it, from whom the ſtate of War is excluded by the Umpirage, which they have provided in their Legiſlative, for the ending all Differences, that may ariſe amongſt any of them, 'tis in their *Legiſlative*, that the Members of a Commonwealth are united, and combined together into one coherent living Body. This *is the Soul that gives Form, Life, and Unity* to the Commonwealth: From hence the ſeveral Members have their mutual Influence, Sympathy, and Connexion: And therefore when the *Legiſlative* is broken, or *diſſolved*, Diſſolution and Death follows. For the *Eſſence and Union of the Society* conſiſting in having one Will, the Legiſlative, when once eſtabliſhed by the Majority, has the declaring, and as it were keeping of that Will. The *Conſtitution of the Legiſlative* is the firſt and fundamental Act of Society, whereby proviſion is made for the *Continuation of their Union*, under the Direction of Perſons, and Bonds of Laws, made by Perſons authorized thereunto, by the Conſent and Appointment of the People, without which no one Man, or number of Men, amongſt them, can have Authority of making Laws, that ſhall be binding to the reſt. When any one or more, ſhall take upon them to make Laws, whom the People have not appointed ſo to do, they make Laws without Authority, which the People are not therefore bound to Obey; by which means they come again to be out of Subjection, and may conſtitute to themſelves a *new Legiſlative*, as they think beſt, being in full liberty to reſiſt the force of thoſe, who without Authority would impoſe any thing upon them. Every one is at the disposure of his own Will, when those who had by the delegation of the Society, the declaring of the publick Will, are excluded from it, and others usurp the Place, who have no such Authority or Delegation.

213. This being usually brought about by such in the Commonwealth, who misuse the Power they have; it is hard to consider it aright, and know at whose door to lay it, without knowing the Form of Government in which it happens. Let us suppose then the Legislative placed in the Concurrence of three distinct Persons.

1. A single hereditary Person having the constant, supream, executive Power, and with it the Power of Convoking and Dissolving the other two within certain Periods of Time.

2. An Assembly of Hereditary Nobility.

3. An Assembly of Representatives chosen *pro tempore*, by the People: Such a Form of Government supposed, it is evident,

214. *First*, That when such a single Person, or Prince sets up his own arbitrary Will in place of the Laws, which are the will of the Society, declared by the Legislative, then the *Legislative is changed*. For that being in effect the Legislative, whose Rules and Laws are put in execution, and required to be obeyed; when other Laws are set up, and other Rules pretended, and inforced, than what the Legislative, constituted by the Society, have enacted, 'tis plain, that the *Legislative is changed*. Whoever introduces new Laws, not being thereunto authorized by the fundamental appointment of the Society, or subverts the old, disowns and overturns the Power by which they were made, and so sets up a *new Legislative*.

215. *Secondly*, When the Prince hinders the Legislative from assembing in its due time, or from acting freely, pursuant to those ends, for which it was constituted, the *Legislative is altered*. For 'tis not a certain number of Men, no, nor their meeting, unless they have also Freedom of debating, and Leisure of perfecting, what is for the good of the Society, wherein the Legislative consists; when these are taken away or altered, so as to deprive the Society of the due exercise of their Power, the *Legislative* is truly altered. For it is not Names, that constitute Governments, but the Use and Exercise of those Powers, that were intended to accompany them, so that he, who takes away the Freedom, or hinders the acting of the Legislative in its due Seasons, in effect takes *away the Legislative*, and *puts an end to the Government*.

216. *Thirdly*, When by the arbitrary Power of the Prince, the Electors, or ways of Election are altered, without the Consent, and contrary to the common Interest of the People, there also the *Legislative is altered*. For if others, than those whom the Society hath authorized thereunto, do chuse, or in another Way, than what the Society hath prescribed, those chosen are not the Legislative appointed by the People.

217. *Fourthly*, the Delivery also of the People into the Subjection of a foreign Power, either by the Prince, or by the Legislative, is certainly a *Change of the Legislative*, and so a *Dissolution of the Government*. For the end why People entered into Society being to be preserved one intire, free, independent Society, to be governed by its own Laws; this is lost, whenever they are given up into the Power of another.

218. Why in such a Constitution as this, the *Dissolution of the Government* in these Cases is to be imputed to the Prince, is evident; because he having the Force, Treasure and Offices of the State to imploy, and often perswading himself, or being flattered by others, that as supream Magistrate he is uncapable of controul; he alone is in a Condition to make great Advances toward such Changes, under pretence of lawful Authority, and has it in his Hands to terrifie or suppress Opposers, as factious, seditious, and Enemies to the Government: Whereas no other part of the Legislative, or People is capable by themselves to attempt any alteration of the Legislative, without open and visible Rebellion, apt enough to be taken notice of, which when it prevails, produces Effects very little different from foreign Conquest. Besides the Prince in such a form of Government, having the Power of dissolving the other parts of the Legislative, and thereby rendering them private Persons, they can never in Opposition to him, or without his Concurrence, alter the Legislative by a Law, his Consent being necessary to

 give

give any of their Decrees that Sanction. But yet so far as the other parts of the Legislative any Way contribute to any Attempt upon the Government, and do either promote, or not, what lies in them, hinder such Designs, they are guilty, and partake in this, which is certainly the greatest Crime Men can be guilty of one towards another.

219. There is one Way more whereby such a Government may be dissolved, and that is, when he who has the supream executive Power, neglects and abandons that Charge, so that the Laws already made can no longer be put in Execution. This is demonstratively to reduce all to Anarchy, and so effectually *to dissolve the Government*. For Laws not being made for themselves, but to be by their execution, the Bonds of the Society, to keep every part of the Body politick in its due Place and Function, when that totally ceases, the *Government* visibly *ceases*, and the People become a confused Multitude, without Order or Connexion. Where there is no longer the administration of Justice, for the securing of Mens Rights, nor any remaining Power within the Community to direct the Force, or provide for the Necessities of the Publick, there certainly is *no Government left*. Where the Laws cannot be executed, it is all one, as if there were no Laws, and a Government without Laws, is, I suppose, a Mystery in Politicks, unconceivable to human Capacity, and inconsistent with human Society.

220. In these and the like Cases, *when the Government is dissolved*, the People are at Liberty to provide for themselves, by erecting a new Legislative, differing from the other, by the change of Persons, or Form, or both, as they shall find it most for their Safety and Good. For the *Society* can never, by the Fault of another, lose the Native and Original Right it has to preserve it self, which can only be done by a settled Legislative, and a fair and impartial execution of the Laws made by it. But the state of Mankind is not so miserable that they are not capable of using this Remedy, till it be too late to look for any. To tell *People* they *may provide for themselves*, by erecting a new Legislative, when by Oppression, Artifice, or being delivered over to a foreign Power, their old one is gone, is only to tell them, they may expect Relief, when it is too late, and the evil is past Cure. This is in effect no more, than to bid them first be Slaves, and then to take care of their Libety; and when their Chains are on, tell them, they may act like Freemen. This, if barely so, is rather Mockery, than Relief; and Men can never be secure from Tyranny, if there be no means to escape it, till they are perfectly under it: And therefore it is, that they have not only a Right to get out of it, but to prevent it.

221. There is therefore Secondly another Way whereby *Governments are dissolved*, and that is, when the Legislative, or the Prince either of them act contrary to their Trust.

First, The *Legislative acts against the Trust* reposed in them, when they endeavour to invade the Property of the Subject, and to make themselves, or any part of the Community, Masters, or arbitrary Disposers of the Lives, Liberties, or Fortunes of the People.

222. The Reason why Men enter into Society, is the preservation of their Property; and the End why they chuse and authorize a Legislative, is, that there may be Laws made, and Rules set, as Guards and Fences to the Properties of all the Members of the Society, to limit the Power, and moderate the Dominion of every part and member of the Society. For since it can never be supposed to be the will of the Society, that the Legislative should have a Power to destroy that, which every one designs to secure, by entering into Society, and for which the People submitted themselves to Legislators of their own making, whenever the *Legislators endeavour to take away, and destroy the property of the People*, or to reduce them to Slavery under arbitrary Power, they put themselves into a state of War with the People, who are thereupon absolved from any farther Obedience, and are left to the common Refuge, which God hath provided for all Men, against Force and Violence. Whensoever therefore the *Legislative* shall transgress this fundamental Rule of Society; and either by Ambition, Fear, Folly or Corruption, *endeavour to grasp* themselves, *or put into the Hands of any other an absolute Power* over the Lives, Liberties, and Estates of the People; By this breach of Trust they *forfeit the Power*, the People had put into their Hands, for quite contrary ends, and it devolves to the People, who have a Right to resume their original Liberty,

and, by the eſtabliſhment of a new Legiſlative, (ſuch as they ſhall think fit) provide for their own Safety and Security, which is the end for which they are in Society. What I have ſaid here, concerning the Legiſlative in general, holds true alſo concerning the ſupreme Executor, who having a double Truſt put in him, both to have a part in the Legiſlative, and the ſupreme Execution of the Law, acts againſt both, when he goes about to ſet up his own arbitrary Will, as the Law of the Society. He *acts* alſo *contrary to his Truſt*, when he either imploys the Force, Treaſure, and Offices of the Society, to corrupt the *Repreſentatives*, and gain them to his Purpoſes; or openly pre-ingages the *Electors*, and preſcribes to their Choice, ſuch, whom he has by Sollicitations, Threats, Promiſes, or otherwiſe won to his Deſigns; and imploys them to bring in ſuch, who have promiſed before-hand, what to Vote, and what to Enact. Thus to regulate Candidates and Electors, and new model the ways of Election, what is it but to cut up the Government by the Roots, and poiſon the very Fountain of publick Security? For the People having reſerved to themſelves the Choice of their *Repreſentatives*, as the Fence to their Properties, could do it for no other end, but that they might always be freely choſen, and ſo choſen, freely act and adviſe, as the neceſſity of the Commonwealth, and the publick Good ſhould, upon examination, and mature Debate, be judged to require. This, thoſe who give their Votes before they hear the Debate, and have weighed the Reaſons on all ſides, are not capable of doing. To prepare ſuch an Aſſembly as this, and endeavour to ſet up the declared Abettors of his own Will, for the true *Repreſentatives* of the People, and the Law-makers of the Society, is certainly as great a *breach of Truſt*, and as perfect a Declaration of a Deſign to ſubvert the Government, as is poſſible to be met with. To which, if one ſhall add Rewards and Puniſhments viſibly imploy'd to the ſame end, and all the Arts of perverted Law made uſe of, to take off and deſtroy all, that ſtand in the way of ſuch a Deſign, and will not comply and conſent to betray the Liberties of their Country, 'twill be paſt doubt what is doing. What Power they ought to have in the Society, who thus imploy it contrary to the Truſt went along with it in is firſt Inſtitution, is eaſie to determine; and one cannot but ſee, that he, who has once attempted any ſuch thing as this, cannot any longer be truſted.

223. To this perhaps it will be ſaid, that the People being ignorant, and always diſcontented, to lay the foundation of Government in the unſteady Opinion and uncertain Humour of the People, is to expoſe it to certain Ruin; And *no Government will be able long to ſubſiſt*, if the People may ſet up a new Legiſlative, whenever they take offence at the old one. To this I anſwer, quite the contrary. People are not ſo eaſily got out of their old Forms, as ſome are apt to ſuggeſt. They are hardly to be prevailed with to amend the acknowledg'd Faults, in the Frame they have been accuſtom'd to. And if there be any original Defects, or adventitious ones introduced by time, or Corruption; 'tis not an eaſie thing to get them changed, even when all the World ſees there is an Opportunity for it. This Slowneſs and Averſion in the People to quit their old Conſtitutions, has, in the many Revolutions which have been ſeen in this Kingdom, in this and former Ages ſtill kept us to, or, after ſome interval of fruitleſs Attempts, ſtill brought us back again to our old Legiſlative of King, Lords and Commons: And whatever Provocations have made the Crown be taken from ſome of our Princes Heads, they never carried the People ſo far, as to place it in another Line.

224. But 'twill be ſaid, this *Hypotheſis* lays a *ferment for* frequent *Rebellion*. To which I Anſwer,

Firſt, No more than any other *Hypotheſis*. For when the People are made miſerable, and find themſelves *expoſed to the ill Uſage of arbitrary Power*, cry up their Governors, as much as you will, for Sons of *Jupiter*, let them be Sacred and Divine, deſcended, or authoriz'd from Heaven; give them out for whom or what you pleaſe, the ſame will happen. *The People generally ill treated*, and contrary to right, will be ready upon any Occaſion to eaſe themſelves of a Burden, that ſits heavy upon them. They will wiſh, and ſeek for the Opportunity, which in the change, weakneſs and accidents of human Affairs, ſeldom delays long to offer it ſelf. He muſt have lived but a little while in the World, who has not ſeen Examples of this in his time; and he muſt have read very little, who cannot produce Examples of it in all ſorts of Governments in the World.

225. *Secondly*,

225. *Secondly*, I anſwer, ſuch *Revolutions happen* not upon every little Miſmanagement in publick Affairs. *Great Miſtakes* in the ruling Part, many wrong and inconvenient Laws, and all the *Slips* of human Frailty will be *born by the People* without Mutiny or Murmur. But if a long train of Abuſes, Prevarications and Artifices, all tending the ſame Way, make the Deſign viſible to the People, and they cannot but feel, what they lie under, and ſee, whither they are going; 'tis not to be wonder'd, that they ſhould then rouze themſelves, and endeavour to put the rule into ſuch Hands, which may ſecure to them the ends for which Government was at firſt erected; and without which, ancient Names, and ſpecious Forms, are ſo far from being better, that they are much worſe, than the ſtate of Nature, or pure Anarchy; the Inconveniencies being all as great and as near, but the Remedy farther off and more difficult.

226. *Thirdly*, I anſwer, That *this Doctrine* of a Power in the People of providing for their Safety a-new, by a new Legiſlative, when their Legiſlators have acted contrary to their Truſt, by invading their Property, is *the beſt Fence againſt Rebellion*, and the probableſt Means to hinder it. For *Rebellion* being an Oppoſition, not to Perſons, but Authority, which is founded only in the Conſtitutions and Laws of the Government; thoſe whoever they be, who by Force break through, and by Force juſtifie their Violation of them, are truly and properly *Rebels*. For when Men by entering into Society and Civil-Government, have excluded Force, and introduced Laws for the preſervation of Property, Peace, and Unity amongſt themſelves, thoſe who ſet up Force again in Oppoſition to the Laws, do *rebellare*, that is, bring back again the ſtate of War, and are properly Rebels: Which they who are in Power, (by the Pretence they have to Authority, the temptation of Force they have in their Hands, and the Flattery of thoſe about them) being likelieſt to do; the propereſt Way to prevent the Evil, is to ſhew them the Danger and Injuſtice of it, who are under the greateſt Temptation to run into it.

227. In both the forementioned Caſes, when either the Legiſlative is changed, or the Legiſlators act contrary to the End for which they were conſtituted; thoſe who are guilty are *guilty of Rebellion*. For if any one by Force takes away the eſtabliſh'd Legiſlative of any Society, and the Laws by them made, purſuant to their Truſt, he thereby takes away the Umpirage, which every one had conſented to, for a peaceable deciſion of all their Controverſies, and a Bar to the ſtate of War amongſt them. They, who remove, or change the Legiſlative, take away this deciſive Power, which no Body can have, but by the appointment and conſent of the People; and ſo deſtroying the Authority, which People did, and no Body elſe can ſet up, and introducing a Power, which the People hath not authoriz'd, they actually *introduce a ſtate of War*, which is that of Force without Authority: And thus by removing the Legiſlative eſtabliſh'd by the Society, (in whoſe Deciſions the People acquieſced and united, as to that of their own Will) they unty the Knot, and *expoſe the People anew to the ſtate of War*. And if thoſe, who by Force take away the Legiſlative, are *Rebels*, the *Legiſlators* themſelves, as has been ſhewn, can be no leſs eſteemed ſo; when they, who were ſet up for the protection, and preſervation of the People, their Liberties and Properties, ſhall by Force invade and endeavour to take them away; and ſo they putting themſelves into a ſtate of War with thoſe, who made them the Protectors and Guardians of their Peace, are properly, and with the greateſt Aggravation, *Rebellantes*, Rebels.

228. But if they, who ſay *it lays a Foundation for Rebellion*, mean that it may occaſion civil Wars, or inteſtine Broils, to tell the People they are abſolved from Obedience, when illegal Attempts are made upon their Liberties or Properties, and may oppoſe the unlawful Violence of thoſe, who were their Magiſtrates, when they invade their Properties contrary to the Truſt put in them; and that therefore this Doctrine is not to be allow'd, being ſo deſtructive to the Peace of the World. They may as well ſay upon the ſame Ground, that honeſt Men may not oppoſe Robbers or Pirats, becauſe this may occaſion diſorder or bloodſhed. If any *Miſchief* come in ſuch Caſes, it is not to be charged upon him who defends his own Right, but *on him, that invades* his Neighbours. If the innocent honeſt Man muſt quietly quit all he has for Peace ſake, to him, who will lay violent Hands upon it, I deſire it may be conſider'd, what a kind of Peace there will be in the

the World, which consists only in Violence and Rapine; and which is to be maintain'd only for the benefit of Robbers and Oppressors. Who would not think it an admirable Peace betwixt the Mighty and the Mean, when the Lamb, without Resistance, yielded his Throat to be torn by the imperious Wolf? *Polyphemus*'s Den gives us a perfect Pattern of such a Peace, and such a Government, wherein *Ulysses* and his Companions had nothing to do, but quietly to suffer themselves to be devour'd. And no doubt *Ulysses*, who was a prudent Man, preach'd up *passive Obedience*, and exhorted them to a quiet Submission, by representing to them of what concernment Peace was to Mankind; and by shewing the Inconveniencies might happen, if they should offer to resist *Polyphemus*, who had now the Power over them.

229. The end of Government is the good of Mankind; and which is *best for Mankind*, that the People should be always expos'd to the boundless will of Tyranny, or that the Rulers should be sometimes liable to be oppos'd, when they grow exorbitant in the use of their Power, and imploy it for the destruction, and not the preservation of the Properties of their People?

230. Nor let any one say, that mischief can arise from hence, as often as it shall please a busie head, or turbulent spirit, to desire the alteration of the Government. 'Tis true, such Men may stir, whenever they please, but it will be only to their own just Ruine and Perdition. For till the mischief be grown general, and the ill designs of the Rulers become visible, or their attempts sensible to the greater part, the People, who are more disposed to suffer, than right themselves by Resistance, are not apt to stir. The examples of particular Injustice, or Oppression of here and there an unfortunate Man, moves them not. But if they universally have a perswasion, grounded upon manifest Evidence, that designs are carrying on against their Liberties, and the general course and tendency of things cannot but give them strong suspicions of the evil intention of their Governors, who is to be blamed for it? Who can help it, if they, who might avoid it, bring themselves, into this suspicion? Are the People to be blamed, if they have the sence of rational Creatures, and can think of things no otherwise, than as they find and feel them? And is it not rather *their Fault*, who puts things into such a posture, that they would not have them thought to be as they are? I grant, that the Pride, Ambition, and Turbulency of private Men have sometimes caused great Disorders in Commonwealths, and Factions have been fatal to States and Kingdoms. But whether *the mischief* hath *oftener* begun *in the Peoples Wantonness*, and a desire to cast off the lawful Authority of their Rulers; or *in the Rulers Insolence*, and Endeavours to get, and exercise an Arbitrary Power over their People; whether Oppression, or Disobedience gave the first rise to the Disorder, I leave it to impartial History to determine. This I am sure, whoever, either Ruler or Subject, by force goes about to invade the Rights of either Prince or People, and lays the foundation for *overturning* the Constitution and Frame of *any Just Government*, is highly guilty of the greatest Crime, I think, a Man is capable of, being to answer for all those mischiefs of Blood, Rapine, and Desolation, which the breaking to pieces of Governments bring on a Country. And he who does it, is justly to be esteemed the common Enemy and Pest of Mankind; and is to be treated accordingly.

231. That *Subjects* or *Foreigners* attempting by force on the Properties of any People, may be *resisted* with force, is agreed on all hands. But that *Magistrates*, doing the same thing, may be *resisted*, hath of late been denied: As if those who had the greatest Privileges and Advantages by the Law, had thereby a Power to break those Laws, by which alone they were set in a better place than their Brethren: Whereas their Offence is thereby the greater, both as being ungrateful for the greater share they have by the Law, and breaking also that Trust, which is put into their hands by their Brethren.

232. Whosoever uses *force without Right*, as every one does in Society, who does it without Law, puts himself into a *state of War* with those, against whom he so uses it, and in that state all former Ties are cancelled, all other Rights cease, and every one has a right to defend himself, and *to resist the Aggressor*. This is so evident, that *Barclay* himself, that great Assertor of the Power and Sacredness of Kings, is forced to confess, That it is lawful for the People, in some

ſome Caſes, to *reſiſt* their King; and that too in a Chapter, wherein he pretends to ſhew, that the Divine Law ſhuts up the People from all manner of Rebellion. Whereby it is evident, even by his own Doctrine, that, ſince they may in ſome Caſes *reſiſt*, all reſiſting of *Princes* is not Rebellion. His words are theſe. *Quod ſiquis dicat, Ergone populus tyrannicæ crudelitati & furori jugulum ſemper præbebit? Ergone multitudo civitates ſuas fame, ferro, & flammâ vaſtari, ſeque, conjuges, & liberos fortunæ ludibrio & tyranni libidini exponi, inque omnia vitæ pericula omneſque miſerias & moleſtiás à Rege deduci patientur? Num illis quod omni animantium generi eſt à naturâ tributum, denegari debet, ut ſc. vim vi repellant, ſeſeq; ab injuriâ tueantur? Huic breviter reſponſum ſit, Populo univerſo negari defenſionem, quæ juris naturalis eſt, neque ultionem quæ præter naturam eſt adverſus Regem concedi debere. Quapropter ſi Rex non in ſingulares tantum perſonas aliquot privatum odium exerceat, ſed corpus etiam Reipublicæ, cujus ipſe caput eſt,* i. e. *totum populum, vel inſignem aliquam ejus partem immani & intolerandâ ſævitiâ ſeu tyrannide divexet; populo, quidem hoc caſu reſiſtendi ac tuendi ſe ab injuriâ poteſtas competit, ſed tuendi ſe tantum, non enim in principem invadendi: & reſtituendæ injuræ illatæ, non recedendi à debitâ reverentiâ propter acceptam injuriam. Præſentem denique impetum propulſandi non vim præteritam ulciſcendi jus habet. Horum enim alterum à naturâ eſt, ut vitam ſcilicet corpuſque tueamur. Alterum vero contra naturam, ut inferior de ſuperiori ſupplicium ſumat. Quod itaque populus malum, antequam factum ſit, impedire poteſt, ne fiat, id poſtquam factum eſt, in Regem authorem ſceleris vindicare non poteſt: Populus igitur hoc ampliùs quam privatus quiſpiam habet: Quod huic, vel ipſis adverſariis judicibus, excepto Buchanano, nullum niſi in patientia remedium ſupereſt. Cùm ille ſi intolerabilis tyrannus eſt (modicum enim ferre omnino debet) reſiſtere cum reverentiâ poſſit,* Barclay *contra Monarchom.* L. 3. c. 8.

In *Engliſh* thus.

233. *But if any one ſhould ask, muſt the People then always lay themſelves open to the Cruelty and Rage of Tyranny? Muſt they ſee their Cities pillaged, and laid in Aſhes, their Wives and Children expoſed to the Tyrant's Luſt and Fury, and themſelves and Families reduced by their King to Ruine, and all the Miſeries of Want and Oppreſſion, and yet ſit ſtill? Muſt Men alone be debarred the common Privilege of oppoſing Force with Force, which Nature allows ſo freely to all other Creatures for their preſervation from Injury? I anſwer: Self-defence is a part of the Law of Nature; nor can it be denied the Community, even againſt the King himſelf: But to revenge themſelves upon him, muſt by no means be allowed them; it being not agreeable to that Law. Wherefore if the King ſhall ſhew an hatred, not only to ſome particular Perſons, but ſets himſelf againſt the Body of the Commonwealth, whereof he is the Head, and ſhall, with intolerable ill Uſage, cruelly tyrannize over the whole, or a conſiderable part of the People, in this caſe the People have a right to reſiſt and defend themſelves from Injury: But it muſt be with this Caution, that they only defend themſelves, but do not attack their Prince: They may repair the Damages received, but muſt not for any provocation exceed the bounds of due Reverence and Reſpect. They may repulſe the preſent Attempt, but muſt not revenge paſt Violences. For it is natural for us to defend Life and Limb, but that an Inferiour ſhould puniſh a Superiour, is againſt Nature. The miſchief which is deſigned them, the People may prevent before it be done, but when it is done, they muſt not revenge it on the King, though Author of the Villany. This therefore is the Privilege of the People in general, above what any private Perſon hath; that particular Men are alloweed by our Adverſaries themſelves,* (Buchanan *only excepted) to have no other Remedy but Patience; but the Body of the People may with Reſpect reſiſt intolerable Tyranny; for when it is but moderate, they ought to endure it.*

234. Thus far that great Advocate of Monarchical Power allows of *Reſiſtance.*

235. 'Tis true, he has annexed two Limitations to it, to no purpoſe:

Firſt, He ſays, it muſt be with Reverence.

Secondly, It muſt be without Retribution, or Puniſhment; and the Reaſon he gives is, *Becauſe an Inferiour cannot puniſh a Superiour.*

Firſt,

First, How to *resist Force without striking again*, or how to *strike with Reverence*, will need some Skill to make intelligible. He that shall oppose an Assault only with a Shield to receive the Blows, or in any more respectful Posture, without a Sword in his hand, to abate the Confidence and Force of the Assailant, will quickly be at an end of his *Resistance*, and will find such a defence serve only to draw on himself the worse Usage. This is as ridiculous a way of *resisting*, as *Juvenal* thought it of fighting; *ubi tu pulsas, ego vapulo tantum*. And the Success of the Combat will be unavoidably the same he there describes it:

——Libertas pauperis hæc est:
Pulsatus rogat, & pugnis concisus, adorat,
Ut liceat paucis cum dentibus inde reverti.

This will always be the event of such an imaginary *Resistance*, where Men may not strike again. He therefore *who may resist, must be allowed to strike*. And then let our Author, or any Body else join a knock on the Head, or a cut on the Face, with as much *Reverence* and *Respect* as he thinks fit. He that can reconcile blows and Reverence, may, for ought I know, deserve for his Pains, a Civil, Respectful, Cudgeling whereever he can meet with it.

Secondly, As to his Second, *An Inferiour cannot punish a Superiour*; that's true, generally speaking, whilst he is his Superiour. But to resist Force with Force, being *the state of War* that *levels the Parties*, cancels all former relation of Reverence, Respect, and *Superiority*: And then the odds that remains, is, That he, who opposes the unjust Aggressor, has this *Superiority* over him, that he has a Right, when he prevails, to punish the Offender, both for the Breach of the Peace, and all the Evils that followed upon it. *Barclay* therefore, in another place, more coherently to himself, denies it to be lawful to *resist* a King in any Case. But he there assigns two Cases, whereby a King may Un-king himself. His Words are,

Quid ergo, nulline casus incidere possunt quibus populo sese erigere atque in Regem impotentius dominantem arma capere & invadere jure suo suâque authoritate liceat? Nulli certe quamdiu Rex manet. Semper enim ex divinis id obstat, Regem honorificato; & qui potestati resistit, Dei ordinationi resistit: *Non aliàs igitur in eum populo potestas est quam si id committat propter quod ipso jure rex esse desinat. Tunc enim se ipse principatu exuit atque in privatis constituit liber: Hoc modo populus & superior efficitur, reverso ad eum sc. jure illo quod ante regem inauguratum in interregno habuit. At sunt paucorum generum commissa ejusmodi quæ hunc effectum pariunt. At ego cum plurima animo perlustrem, duo tantum invenio, duos, inquam, casus quibus rex ipso facto ex Rege non regem se facit & omni honore & dignitate regali atque in subditos potestate destituit; quorum etiam meminit* Winzerus. *Horum unus est, Si regnum disperdat, quemadmodum de Nerone fertur, quod is nempe senatum populumque Romanum, atque adeo urbem ipsam ferro flammaque vastare, ac novas sibi sedes quærere decrevisset. Et de Caligula, quod palam denunciarit se neque civem neque principem senatui amplius fore, inque animo habuerit interempto utriusque ordinis Electissimo quoque* Alexandriam *commigrare, ac ut populum uno ictu interimeret, unam ei cervicem optavit. Talia cum rex aliquis meditatur & molitur serio, omnem regnandi curam & animum ilico abjicit, ac proinde imperium in subditos amittit, ut dominus servi pro derelicto habiti dominium.*

236. *Alter casus est, Si rex in alicujus clientelam se contulit, ac regnum quod liberum à majoribus & populo traditum accepit, alienæ ditioni mancipavit. Nam tunc quamvis forte non eâ mente id agit populo plane ut incommodet: Tamen quia quod præcipuum est regiæ dignitatis amisit, ut summus scilicet in regno secundum Deum sit, & solo Deo inferior, atque populum etiam totum ignorantem vel invitum, cujus libertatem sartam & tectam conservare debuit, in alterius gentis ditionem & potestatem dedidit; hâc velut quadam regni ab alienatione effecit, ut nec quod ipse in regno imperium habuit retineat, nec in eum cui collatum voluit, juris quicquam transferat; atque ita eo facto liberum jam & suæ potestatis populum relinquit, cujus rei exemplum unum annales Scotici suppeditant.* Barclay contra Monarchom. L. 3. c. 16.

Which

Which in *English* runs thus.

237. *What then, Can there no Case happen wherein the People may of Right, and by their own Authority help themselves, take Arms, and set upon their King, imperiously domineering over them? None at all, whilst he remains a King.* Honour the King, *and* he that resists the Power, resists the Ordinance of God; *are Divine Oracles that will never permit it. The People therefore can never come by a Power over him, unless he does something that makes him cease to be a King. For then he divests himself of his Crown and Dignity, and returns to the state of a private Man, and the People become Free and Superiour, the Power which they had in the* Interregnum, *before they Crown'd him King, devolving to them again. But there are but few miscarriages which bring the matter to this State. After considering it well on all sides, I can find but two. Two Cases there are, I say, whereby a King,* ipso facto, *becomes no King; and loses all Power and Regal Authority over his People; which are also taken notice of by* Winzerus.

The first is, If he endeavour to overturn the Government, that is, if he have a purpose and design to ruine the Kingdom and Commonwealth, as it is recorded of Nero, *that he resolved to cut off the Senate and People of* Rome, *lay the City waste with Fire and Sword, and then remove to some other Place. And of* Caligula, *that he openly declar'd, that he would be no longer a Head to the People or Senate, and that he had it in his thoughts to cut off the worthiest Men of both Ranks, and then retire to* Alexandria: *And he wisht that the People had but one Neck, that he might dispatch them all at a blow. Such designs as these, when any King harbours in his thoughts, and seriously promotes, he immediately gives up all care and thought of the Commonwealth: and consequently forfeits the Power of Governing his Subjects, as a Master does the Dominion over his Slaves whom he hath abandon'd.*

238. *The other Case is, When a King makes himself the dependent of another, and subjects his Kingdom which his Ancestors left him, and the People put free into his hands, to the Dominion of another. For however perhaps it may not be his intention to prejudice the People; yet because he has hereby lost the principal part of Regal Dignity,* viz. *to be next and immediately under God, Supream in his Kingdom; and also because he betray'd or forced his People, whose liberty he ought to have carefully preserved into the Power and Dominion of a Foreign Nation. By this as it were alienation of his Kingdom, he himself loses the Power he had in it before, without transferring any the least right to those on whom he would have bestowed it; and so by this act sets the People free, and leaves them at their own disposal. One Example of this is to be found in the* Scotch *Annals.*

239. In these Cases *Barclay* the great Champion of Absolute Monarchy, is forced to allow, That a King may be *resisted,* and *ceases to be a King.* That is, in short, not to multiply Cases, In whatsoever he has *no Authority*, there he is *no King*, and may be *resisted:* For wheresoever the *Authority ceases, the King ceases too,* and becomes like other Men who have no Authority. And these two Cases he instances in, differ little from those above-mention'd, to be destructive to Governments, only that he has omitted the Principle from which his Doctrine flows; and that is, The Breach of Trust, in not preserving the Form of Government agreed on, and in not intending the end of Government itself, which is the publick Good and preservation of Property. When a King has dethron'd himself, and put himself in a State of War with his People, what shall hinder them from prosecuting him who is no King, as they would any other Man, who has put himself into a state of War with them? *Barclay*, and those of his Opinion, would do well to tell us. This farther I desire may be taken notice of out of *Barclay*, that he says, *The Mischief that is designed them, the People may prevent before it be done,* whereby he allows *Resistance* when Tyranny is but in design. *Such Designs as these* (says he) *when any King harbours in his thoughts and seriously promotes, he immediately gives up all Care and Thought of the Commonwealth*; so that according to him the neglect of the publick Good is to be taken as an Evidence of such *Design*, or at least for a sufficient Cause of *Resistance.* And the reason of all, he gives in these Words, *Because he betray'd or forced his People whose Liberty he ought carefully to have preserved.* What he adds *into the Power and Dominion of a Foreign Nation,* signifies nothing, the Fault and Forfeiture lying in the Loss of their *Li-*

berty, which he *ought to have preserved*, and not in any Distinction of the Persons to whose Dominion they were subjected. The Peoples Right is equally invaded, and their Liberty lost, whether they are made Slaves to any of their own, or a *Foreign Nation*; and in this lies the Injury, and against this only have they the Right of Defence. And there are Instances to be found in all Countries, which shew, that 'tis not the change of Nations in the Persons of their Governours, but the change of Government, that gives the Offence. *Bilson*, a Bishop of our Church, and a great Stickler for the Power and Prerogative of Princes, does, if I mistake not, in his Treatise of *Christian Subjection*, acknowledge, That *Princes may forfeit their Power*, and their Title to the Obedience of their Subjects; and if there needed Authority in a Case where reason is so plain, I could send my Reader to *Bracton*, *Fortescue*, and the Author of *the Mirrour*, and others, Writers that cannot be suspected to be ignorant of our Government, or Enemies to it. But I thought *Hooker* alone might be enough to satisfy those Men, who relying on him for their Ecclesiastical Polity, are by a strange Fate carryed to deny those Principles upon which he builds it. Whether they are herein made the Tools of cunninger Workmen, to pull down their own Fabrick, they were best look. This I am sure, their Civil Policy is so new, so dangerous, and so destructive to both Rulers and People, that as former Ages never could bear the broaching of it; so it may be hoped, those to come, redeem'd from the Impositions of these *Egyptian* Under-Taskmasters, will abhor the Memory of such servile Flatterers, who whilst it seem'd to serve their turn, resolv'd all Government into absolute Tyranny, and would have all Men born to, what their mean Souls fitted them for, Slavery.

240. Here, 'tis like, the common Question will be made, *Who shall be Judge*, whether the Prince or Legislative act contrary to their Trust? This, perhaps, ill affected and factious Men may spread amongst the People, when the Prince only makes use of his due Prerogative. To this I reply; *The People shall be Judge*; for who shall be *Judge* whether his Trustee or Deputy acts well, and according to the Trust reposed in him, but he who deputes him, and must, by having deputed him, have still a Power to discard him, when he fails in his Trust? If this be reasonable in particular Cases of private Men, why should it be otherwise in that of the greatest moment, where the Welfare of Millions is concerned, and also where the Evil, if not prevented, is greater, and the Redress very difficult, dear, and dangerous?

141. But farther, this Question, *(Who shall be Judge?)* cannot mean, that there is no Judge at all. For where there is no Judicature on Earth, to decide Controversies amongst Men, *God* in Heaven is *Judge*. He alone, 'tis true, is Judge of the Right. But *every Man* is *Judge* for himself, as in all other Cases, so in this, whether another hath put himself into a state of War with him, and whether he should appeal to the Supreme Judge, as *Jeptha* did.

242. If a Controversie arise betwixt a Prince and some of the People, in a matter, where the Law is silent, or doubtful, and the thing be of great Consequence, I should think the proper *Umpire*, in such a Case, should be the Body of the *People*. For in Cases where the Prince hath a Trust reposed in him, and is dispensed from the common ordinary Rules of the Law; there, if any Men find themselves aggrieved, and think the Prince acts contrary to, or beyond that Trust, who so proper to *judge* as the Body of the *People*, (who, at first, lodg'd that Trust in him) how far they meant it should extend? But if the Prince, or whoever they be in the Administration, decline that way of Determination, the Appeal then lies no where but to Heaven. Force between either Persons, who have no known Superior on Earth, or which permits no Appeal to a Judge on Earth, being properly a state of War, wherein the Appeal lies only to Heaven, and in that State the *injured Party must judge* for himself, when he will think fit to make use of that Appeal, and put himself upon it.

243. To conclude, The *Power that every Individual gave the Society*, when he entered into it, can never revert to the Individuals again, as long as the Society lasts, but will always remain in the Community; because without this, there can be no Community, no Commonwealth, which is contrary to the original Agreement: So also when the Society hath placed the Legislative in any Assembly

Aſſembly of Men, to continue in them and their Succeſſors, with Direction and Authority for providing ſuch Succeſſors, *the Legiſlative can never revert to the People* whilſt that Government laſts: Becauſe having provided a Legiſlative with Power to continue for ever, they have given up their Political Power to the Legiſlative, and cannot reſume it. But if they have ſet Limits to the Duration of their Legiſlative, and made this ſupreme Power in any Perſon, or Aſſembly, only temporary: Or elſe, when by the Miſcarriages of thoſe in Authority, it is forfeited; upon the Forfeiture, or at the Determination of the Time ſet, *it reverts to the Society*, and the People have a Right to act as Supreme, and continue the Legiſlative in themſelves; or erect a new Form, or under the old Form place it in new Hands, as they think good.

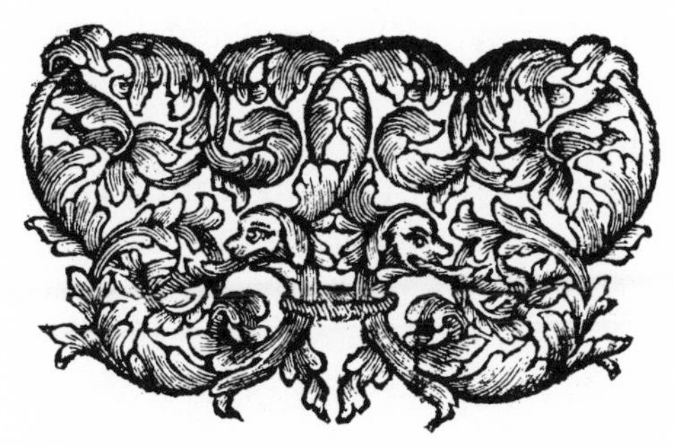

"Algernon Sidney, the honest republican, who foreshadowed the institutional form in which this idea was destined to develop"
-Frothingham

THE birth of Sidney, his education and connection with the court, the honors bestowed on his family, and the offices they held, should have attached him to the party of Charles I at the beginning of the civil wars. The hatred to arbitrary power, which appeared innate in him, induced him, at the age of twenty-one, to support the parliament...He was at that period attached to the Independents, who aiding the ambitious views of Cromwell, were desirous of establishing a republican form of government. When Cromwell, however, assumed the sovereignty under the title of Protector, Sidney retired to private life. Secluded in the family seat at Penshurst, he composed his first 'Discourse on Government'...

Discourse on Government

"Sidney...connecting himself with the Duke of Monmouth, the lords Essex, Russell, Shaftesbury, Grey, was implicated with them, and apprehended on a charge of being concerned in the Rye-house plot, the object of which was to destroy the king, and occasion a general revolt. On this point historians differ, but even those who consider the conspiracy as proved, confess that a spirit of revenge directed openly the violent proceedings of which Sidney was a victim. The laws were unjustly violated. A single person stepped forward as his accusor; to supply the place of a second witness the manuscript of his 'Discourse on Government', found among his papers, was produced, and this very production, which had been long previously composed, which had never been published, nor communicated to anyone, was, in the opinion of a sanguinary judge, considered a sufficent motive for his condemnation. Sidney was then 61. After having defended himself with great warmth, during his trial, he gloried dying a martyr in the cause of liberty...He was beheaded, on Tower Hill, 1683. After the revolution of 1688, the sentence against him was declared illegal, in the first parliament of William and Mary..."

The above excerpts are from "Historic Gallery and Biographical Review", Volume VII - London 1819

Algernon Sidney

"DISCOURSES CONCERNING GOVERNMENT"

HAVING lately seen a book, intitled 'Patriarcha,' written by Sir Robert Filmer, concerning the universal and undistinguished right of all kings, I thought a time of leisure might be well employed in examining his doctrine, and the questions arising from it; which seem so far to concern all mankind, that besides the influence upon our future life, they may be said to comprehend all that in this world deserves to be cared for...Whilst Filmer's business is to overthrow liberty and truth, he, in his passage, modestly professeth 'not to meddle with mysteries of state,' or 'arcana imperii.' He renounces those inquiries through an implicit faith, which never entered into the head of any but fools, and such as, through a carelessness of the point in question, acted as if they were so... Who will wear a shoe that hurts him, because the shoemaker tells him it is well made? or who will live in a house that yields no defence against the extremities of weather, because the mason or carpenter assures him it is a very good house? Such as have reason, understanding, or common sense, will, and ought to make use of it in those things that concern themselves, and their posterity, and suspect the words of such as are interested in deceiving or persuading them not to see with their own eyes, that they may be more easily deceived. This rule obliges us so far to search into matters of state, as to examine the original principles of government in general, and of our own in particular. We cannot distinguish truth from falsehood, right from wrong, or know what obedience we owe to the magistrate, or what we may justly expect from him, unless we know what he is, why he is, and by whom he is made to be what he is. These perhaps may be called 'mysteries of state,' and some would persuade us they are to be esteemed 'arcana' but whoever confesses himself to be ignorant of them, must acknowledge that he is incapable of giving any judgment upon things relating to the superstructure: and in so doing evidently shews to others, that they ought not at all to hearken to what he says...It is an eternal truth, that a weak or wicked prince can never choose a wise council, nor receive any benefit by one that is imposed upon him, unless they have a power of acting without him; which would render the government in effect aristocratical, and would probably displease our author as much as if it were so in name also. Good and wise counsellors do not grow up like mushrooms: great judgment is required in choosing and preparing them.

.mplicit faith
elongs to fools;
nd truth is
omprehended
y examining
inciples"

The above excerpts are from "The Works of Algernon Sidney", London 1772. Marginal notes are by Sidney.

"To depend upon the will of a man is slavery."

"This, as he thinks, is farther sweetened, by asserting, that he does not inquire what the rights of a people are, but from whence: not considering, that while he denies they can proceed from the laws of natural liberty, or any other root than 'the grace and bounty of the prince,' he declares they can have none at all. For, as liberty solely consists in an independency upon the will of another, and by the name of slave we understand a man, who can neither dispose of his person nor goods, but enjoys all at the will of his master, there is no such thing in nature as a slave, if those men or nations are not slaves, who have no other title to what they enjoy, than the grace of the prince, which he may revoke whenever he pleases. But there is more than ordinary extravagance in his assertion, that 'the greatest liberty in the world is for a people to live under a monarch,' when his whole book is to prove, that this monarch has his right from God and nature, is endowed with an unlimited power of doing what he pleases, and can be restrained by no law. If it be liberty to live under such a government, I desire to know what is slavery....

"God leaves to man the choice of forms in government; and those who constitute one form may abrogate it."

"...Is there any absurdity in saying, that, since God in goodness and mercy to mankind hath, with an equal hand, given to all the benefit of liberty, with some measure of understanding how to employ it, it is lawful for any nation, as occasion shall require, to give the exercise of that power to one or more men, under certain limitations and conditions; or to retain it to themselves, if they think it good for them? If this may be done, we are at an end of all controversies concerning one form of government established by God, to which all mankind must submit; and we may safely conclude, that having given to all men, in some degree, a capacity of judging what is good for themselves, he hath granted to all likewise a liberty of inventing such forms as please them best, without favouring one more than another....

"We say in general, 'he that institutes, may also abrogate;' more especially when the institution is not only by, but for himself. If the multitude therefore do institute, the multitude may abrogate; and they themselves, or those who succeed in the same right, can only be fit judges of the performance of the ends of the institution. Our author may perhaps say, the public peace may be hereby disturbed: but he ought to know, there can be no peace, where there is no justice; nor any justice, if the government instituted for the good of a nation be turned to its ruin....

"Reason leads them to this: no one man or family is able to provide that which is requisite for their convenience or security, whilst every one has an equal right to every thing, and none ac-

The above excerpts are from "The Works of Algernon Sidney", London, 1772.
The marginal notes are by Sidney.

"Such as enter into society, must in some degree diminish their liberty."

knowledges a superior to determine the controversies, that upon such occasions must continually arise, and will probably be so many and great, that mankind cannot bear them. Therefore, though I do not believe, that Bellarmine said, 'a commonwealth 'could not exercise its power;' for he could not be ignorant, that Rome and Athens did exercise theirs, and that all the regular kingdoms in the world are commonwealths; yet there is nothing of absurdity in saying, that man cannot continue in the perpetual and entire fruition of the liberty that God hath given him. The liberty of one is thwarted by that of another; and whilst they are all equal, none will yield to any, otherwise than by a general consent. This is the ground of all just governments; for violence or fraud can create no right; and the same consent gives the form to them all how much soever they differ from each other. Some small numbers of men, living within the precincts of one city, have, as it were, cast into a common stock, the right which they had of governing themselves and children, and by common consent joining in one body, exercised such power over every single person as seemed beneficial to the whole; and this men call perfect 'democracy.' Others chose rather to be governed by a select number of such as most excelled in wisdom and virtue; and this, according to the signification of the word, was called 'aristocracy.' When one man excelled all others, the government was put into his hands under the name of 'monarchy.' But the wisest, best, and by far the greatest part of mankind, rejecting these simple species, did form governments mixed or composed of the three, . . . which commonly received their respective denomination from the part that prevailed, and did deserve praise or blame, as they were well or ill proportioned. . . . If men are naturally free, such as have wisdom and understanding will always frame good governments; but if they are born under the necessity of a perpetual slavery, no wisdom can be of use to them; but all must for ever depend on the will of their lords, how cruel, mad, proud, or wicked, soever they be.

"No man comes to command many, unless by consent or by force."

"But because I cannot believe God hath created man in such a state of misery and slavery. . . . I am led to a certain conclusion that every father of a family is free, and exempt from the domination of any other, as the seventy-two that went from Babel were. It is hard to comprehend how one man can come to be master of many, equal to himself in right, unless it be by consent, or by force. . . . This subduing by force we call conquest; but as he that forceth must be stronger than those that are forced, to talk of one man who in strength exceeds many millions of men, is to go beyond the extravagance of fables and romances. This wound is not cured by saying, that he first conquers one, and then more, and with their help others; for as to matter of fact, the first news we hear of Nimrod is, that he reigned over a great multitude, and built vast

The above excerpts are from "The Works of Algernon Sidney", London, 1772.
The marginal notes are by Sidney.

cities; and we know of no kingdom in the world, that did not begin with a greater number than any one man could possibly subdue. If they who chose one to be their head, did under his conduct subdue others, they were fellow-conquerors with him; and nothing can be more brutish, than to think, that by their virtue and valour they had purchased perpetual slavery to themselves, and their posterity...He that persists in doing injustice, aggravates it, and takes upon himself all the guilt of his predecessors...

"The ancients chose those to be kings, who excelled in the virtues that are most beneficial to civil society"

"But if governments arise from the consent of men, and are instituted by men according to their own inclinations, they do therein seek their own good; for the will is ever drawn by some real good, or the appearance of it. This is that which man seeks by all the regular or irregular motions of his mind. Reason and passion, virtue and vice, do herein concur, though they differ vastly in the objects, in which each of them thinks this good to consist. A people therefore that sets up kings, dictators, consuls, pretors, or emperors, does it not, that they may be great, glorious, rich or happy, but that it may be well with themselves, and their posterity...

"The Liberty of a people is the Gift of God and nature"

"If any man ask, how nations come to have the power of doing these things, I answer, that liberty being only an exemption from the dominion of another, the question ought not to be, how a nation can come to be free, but how a man comes to have a dominion over it; for till the right of dominion be proved and justified, liberty subsists, as arising from the nature and being of a man...

"The creature having nothing, and being nothing but what the Creator makes him, must owe all to him, and nothing to any one from whom he has received nothing. Man therefore must be naturally free, unless he be created by another power than we have yet heard of...This liberty therefore must continue, till it be either forfeited or willingly resigned...Resignation is a public declaration of their assent to be governed by the person to whom they resign; that is, they do by that act constitute him to be their governor. This necessarily puts us upon the inquiry, why they do resign, how they will be governed, and proves the governor to be their creature; and the right of disposing the government must be in them, or they who receive it can have none.

"The only ends for which governments are constituted, and obedience rendered to them, are the obtaining of justice and protection; and they who cannot provide for both give the people a right of taking such ways as best please themselves, in order to their own safety."

The above excerpts are from "The Works of Algernon Sidney", London 1772.
Marginal notes are by Sidney.

MONTESQUIEU

"THE SPIRIT OF LAWS"

BLACKSTONE

"THE COMMENTARIES ON THE LAWS OF ENGLAND"

"...without liberty and equality, there cannot exist that tranquillity of mind which results from the assurance of every citizen that his own personal safety and rights are secure. This, I think, is a sentiment of the celebrated Montesquieu, and it is the end and design of all free and lawful governments."

- Samuel Adams, Address to the Massachusetts Legislature, 1794

"It is the observation of the celebrated Montesquieu, that if the crime of treason be indeterminate, this alone is sufficent to make any government degenerate into arbitrary power..."

- James Wilson, "Of Crimes, Immediately Against the Community"
Lectures on Law, 1790-2

"Apply yourself, without delay, to the study of the law of nature. I would recommend to your persual Grotius, Puffendorf, Locke, Montesquieu..."

- Alexander Hamilton, "The Farmer Refuted", 1775

"I very cheerfully express my approbation of the proposed edition of Blackstone's Commentaries..."

- James Madison, 1821

"I hear that they have sold nearly as many of Blackstone's Commentaries in America as in England."

- Edmund Burke, March 22, 1775
Address before Parliament

"... the three great departments of power should be separate and distinct. The oracle who is always consulted and cited on this subject is the celebrated Montesquieu ... "

James Madison
Federalist Papers
No. 47

Voltaire and Montesquieu

WRITERS with an ingenious turn for the discovery of analogies have compared him to Voltaire, who was born but a few years after Montesquieu. Voltaire was undoubtedly a man of rare genius and unequaled skill when it came to the work of destruction. To demolish ancient things was the task in which he excelled and which he delighted to perform. His bitterness against the social system of which the Church was an integral part displayed itself with all the venom of personal enmity: it was flavored with the passion of revenge rather than a desire to promote right and to prevent wrong. In his early youth, he had been subjected to personal indignities at the hands of blue-blooded men who considered it the privilege of their caste to disregard the claims of those whose pedigree was not as long as their own. The friend of Frederick II never forgot the humiliation of his early life. The Church was the ally and prop of the social scheme which permitted these wrongs, hence the Church must pay the penalty. His rage increased with the years, until he boasted, in the heat of his madness, that one man might destroy the religion which twelve men had founded.

"But Montesquieu had no personal reasons for disliking either Church or State. In the rich soil of his generous nature, no seed had been

The above excerpts are from the special introduction by Frederick R. Coudert to "The Spirit of Laws" -- published by the Colonial Press, 1900

sown from which hatred could grow. He was a lover of the human race and sought to promote its happiness. He meant to cure, not to kill: he hoped to make, not to mar; he sought to repair and to improve, not to tear down and to destroy.

"Persian Letters" viewed with suspicion

"Montesquieu became famous in a day. His 'Persian Letters', written when he was thirty years of age, charmed, delighted and irritated his countrymen, and especially his countrywomen, who were quite as ready and able as the male part of the population to make a writer's fame.

"The Persian visitors whom he invented and whose comments upon the society and the religion of France he gives to the public, were very free in their criticisms of what they saw, and it is not to be wondered at that the guardians of public morals looked with suspicion and alarm upon the trenchant wit of the Gascon sage, who dared to criticize abuses and to laugh at practices which time had rendered venerable.

Montesquieu delves at the roots of history

"The 'Causes of the Greatness and Decline of the Romans', next issued from Montesquieu's pen, would have assured his fame had the 'Spirit of Laws' not belittled it by its own superiority. His Treatise on the Romans is marked by the same perseverance and research as his book on the Laws. He delves at the roots of History to learn how from general causes events have grown. He is no believer in chance: there is a Philosophy of History with its rules and principles and they must be studied and found before we can know the nature and reason of Things. 'It is not chance that rules the world', he says; 'witness the Romans, who had a constant succession of triumphs while they managed their government on a certain plan, and an uninterrupted series of reverses when it was conducted on another'.

"Spirit of Laws"

"Upon this theory, he has examined symptoms to ascertain causes, and has, with a beauty of style that well became the dignity of his subject, first taught men that the records of the past might be found to contain sermons as well as traditions, lessons as well as facts, and materials for prophecy mingled with the dust of ages.

"When the 'Spirit of Laws' appeared, the work upon which his title to the admiration of posterity must depend, he was well known to the literary world as the author of the "Persian Letters', but it is not clear that he was much helped by the celebrity thus acquired.

The above excerpts are from the special introduction by Frederick R. Coudert to "The Spirit of Laws" -- published by the Colonial Press, 1900

"Although the success of the 'Spirit of Laws' was not immediate in France, it was not long in doubt. In England, intelligent opinion immediately seized upon the work, and received it with enthusiasm. This was due in a great measure to the fact that the author, had been a close student and admirer of the British Constitution, had adopted the shortest road to the British heart by his intelligent tribute to the superiority of that vague, shadowy, and unwritten charter of British liberty.

"It is curious to note how Montesquieu was at first alone of his immediate circle to realize and adequately measure the value of the 'Spirit of Laws'. Whether the long and faithful labor of years had satisfied him that he could not have thus striven in vain or the equipoise of his trained mind allowed him to judge as correctly as though he were passing on the performance of a stranger he knew from the outset that the book would win him renown.

Foundation of the Spirit of Laws - "in the nature of things"

"The foundation of the work was the attempt to find those common principles and emotions which, operating upon men of every climate and degree of civilization, produce certain results. He was satisfied that those principles existed, and if found, would afford a scientific explanation of what without their aid would seem to be chaotic and inexplicable. Or, to come nearer to his own language, he rejoiced to find in 'the nature of things' the explanation of so many different laws and customs.

"The close of his life was marked by the same kindly and gentle philosophy that he had exhibited from the beginning. He appears to have been a devout and consistent Christian, although making but few professions and preferring to lock up in his own heart the sentiments that he entertained on the most important problems that can occupy the mind of man. He was not only a believer in, but a great admirer of, the morality of the Gospel. He declared that he could not share the humility of the atheists, but preferred to believe that his soul was immortal.

"Much and lavish praise waited upon the 'Spirit of Laws' but the tribute paid by Voltaire during Montesquieu's own life-time is the one which best expresses in fewest words the opinion of his admirers. It is all the more precious because Voltaire never loved him and he himself was never reckoned among Voltaire's friends. 'The human family had lost its title deeds - Montesquieu found them and restored them to their owner'. "

The above excerpts are from the special introduction by Frederick R. Coudert to "The Spirit of Laws" - published by Colonial Press - 1900

THE SPIRIT OF LAWS

LAWS, in their most general signification, are the necessary relations arising from the nature of things. In this sense all beings have their laws: the Deity His laws, the material world its laws, the intelligences superior to man their laws, the beasts their laws, man his laws. They who assert that a blind fatality produced the various effects we behold in this world talk very absurdly; for can any thing be more unreasonable than to pretend that a blind fatality could be productive of intelligent beings? There is, then, a prime reason; and laws are the relations subsisting between it and different beings, and the relations of these to one another.

Law is necessary

"God is related to the universe, as Creator and Preserver; the laws by which He created all things are those by which He preserves them. He acts according to these rules, because He knows them; He knows them, because He made them; and He made them, because they are in relation to his Wisdom and power...

God

"In every government there are three sorts of power:

Three branches

"The legislative; the executive in respect to things dependent on the law of nations; and the executive in regard to matters that depend on the civil law. By virtue of the first, the prince or magistrate enacts temporary or perpetual laws, and amends or abrogates those that have already been enacted. By the second, he makes peace or war, sends or receives embassies, establishes the public security, and provides against invasions. By the third, he punishes criminals, or determines the disputes that arise between individuals. The latter we shall call the judiciary power, and the other simply the executive power of the state. The political liberty of the subject is a tranquillity of mind arising from the opinion each person has of his safety. In order to have this liberty, it is requisite the government be so constituted as one man need not be afraid of another. When the legislative and executive powers are united in the same person, or in the same body of magistrates, there can be no liberty; because apprehensions

Legislative, Judiciary, Executive

Requisite of Liberty

The above excerpts are from Montesquieu's "The Spirit of Laws", as published by the Colonial Press - 1900

may arise, lest the same monarch or senate should enact tyrannical laws, to execute them in a tyrannical manner.

Separation of powers fundamental

"Again, there is no liberty, if the judiciary power be not separated from the legislative and executive. Were it joined with the legislative, the life and liberty of the subject would be exposed to arbitrary control; for the judge would be then the legislator. Were it joined to the executive power, the judge might behave with violence and oppression.

"There would be an end of everything, were the same man or the same body, whether of the nobles or of the people, to exercise those three powers, that of enacting laws, that of executing the public resolutions, and of trying the causes of individuals...

"Hence it is that many of the princes of Europe, whose aim has been levelled at arbitrary power, have constantly set out with uniting in their own persons all the branches of magistracy, and all the great offices of state...

"The judiciary power ought not to be given to a standing senate; it should be exercised by persons taken from the body of the people at certain times of the year, and consistently with a form and manner prescribed by law, in order to erect a tribunal that should last only so long as necessity requires...

"The other two powers may be given rather to magistrates or permanent bodies, because they are not exercised on any private subject; one being no more than the general will of the state, and the other the execution of that general will.

Fixed judgments

"But though the tribunals ought not to be fixed, the judgments ought; and to such a degree as to be ever conformable to the letter of the law. Were they to be the private opinion of the judge, people would then live in society, without exactly knowing the nature of their obligations...

Representative government

"As in a country of liberty, every man who is supposed a free agent ought to be his own governor; the legislative power should reside in the whole body of the people. But since this is impossible in large states, and in small ones is subject to many inconveniences, it is fit the people should transact by their representatives what they cannot transact by themselves.

The above excerpts are from Montesquieu's "The Spirit of Laws", as published by the Colonial Press - 1900

Local self-government

"The inhabitants of a particular town are much better acquainted with its wants and interests than with those of other places; and are better judges of the capacity of their neighbors than of that of the rest of their countrymen. The members, therefore, of the legislature should not be chosen from the general body of the nation; but it is proper that in every considerable place a representative should be elected by the inhabitants.

Advantages of the Republic

"The great advantage of representatives is, their capacity of discussing public affairs. For this the people collectively are extremely unfit, which is one of the chief inconveniences of a democracy.

"It is not at all necessary that the representatives who have received a general instruction from their constituents should wait to be directed on each particular affair, as is practised in the diets of Germany. True it is that by this way of proceeding the speeches of the deputies might with greater propriety be called the voice of the nation; but, on the other hand, this would occasion infinite delays; would give each deputy a power of controlling the assembly; and, on the most urgent and pressing occasions, the wheels of government might be stopped by the caprice of a single person....

Faults of ancient republics

"One great fault there was in most of the ancient republics, that the people had a right to active resolutions, such as require some execution, a thing of which they are absolutely incapable. They ought to have no share in the government but for the choosing of representatives, which is within their reach. For though few can tell the exact degree of men's capacities, yet there are none but are capable of knowing in general whether the person they choose is better qualified than most of his neighbors.

Duty of representative body

"Neither ought the representative body to be chosen for the executive part of government, for which it is not so fit; but for the enacting of laws, or to see whether the laws in being are duly executed, a thing suited to their abilities, and which none indeed but themselves can properly perform....

"The legislative power is therefore committed to the body of the nobles, and to that which represents the people, each having their assemblies and deliberations apart, each their separate views and interests.

Judiciary least

"Of the three powers above mentioned, the judiciary is in some measure next to nothing: there remain, therefore, only two;

The above excerpts are from Montesquieu's "The Spirit of Laws", as published by the Colonial Press - 1900

and as these have need of a regulating power to moderate them, the part of the legislative body composed of the nobility is extremely proper for this purpose. . . .

'ower in the ands of a ingle ndividual

"The executive power ought to be in the hands of a monarch, because this branch of government, having need of despatch, is better administered by one than by many: on the other hand, whatever depends on the legislative power is oftentimes better regulated by many than by a single person.

:nd of iberty

"But if there were no monarch, and the executive power should be committed to a certain number of persons selected from the legislative body, there would be an end then of liberty; by reason the two powers would be united, as the same persons would sometimes possess, and would be always able to possess, a share in both. . . .

Vecessary alance

"Were the executive power not to have a right of restraining the encroachments of the legislative body, the latter would become despotic; for as it might arrogate to itself what authority it pleased, it would soon destroy all the other powers.

"But it is not proper, on the other hand, that the legislative power should have a right to stay the executive. For as the execution has its natural limits, it is useless to confine it; besides, the executive power is generally employed in momentary operations. The power, therefore, of the Roman tribunes was faulty, as it put a stop not only to the legislation, but likewise to the executive part of government; which was attended with infinite mischief.

lights of the egislative

"But if the legislative power in a free state has no right to stay the executive, it has a right and ought to have the means of examining in what manner its laws have been executed; an advantage which this government has over that of Crete and Sparta, where the Cosmi and the Ephori gave no account of their administration. . . .

xecutive 'eto

"The executive power, pursuant of what has been already said, ought to have a share in the legislature by the power of rejecting; otherwise it would soon be stripped of its prerogative. But should the legislative power usurp a share of the executive, the latter would be equally undone.

The above excerpts are from Montesquieu's "The Spirit of Laws", as published by the Colonial Press - 1900

A system of check and balance

"If the prince were to have a part in the legislature by the power of resolving, liberty would be lost. But as it is necessary he should have a share in the legislature for the support of his own prerogative, this share must consist in the power of rejecting. The change of government at Rome was owing to this, that neither the senate, who had one part of the executive power, nor the magistrates, who were intrusted with the other, had the right of rejecting, which was entirely lodged in the people. Here, then, is the fundamental constitution of the government we are treating of. The legislative body being composed of two parts, they check one another by the mutual privilege of rejecting. They are both restrained by the executive power, as the executive is by the legislative. These three powers should naturally form a state of repose or inaction. But as there is a necessity for movement in the course of human affairs, they are forced to move, but still in concert..."

The above excerpts are from Montesquieu's "The Spirit of Laws", as published by the Colonial Press - 1900

LAWS

Indestructible Foundation Grounded in Christianity

IN the year of our Lord one thousand seven hundred and forty-eight, Montesquieu, wisest in his age of the reflecting statesmen of France, apprized the cultivated world, that a free, prosperous and great people was forming in the forests of America, which England had sent forth her sons to inhabit... The age could have learnt, from the school of Voltaire, to scoff at its past; but the studious and observing Montesquieu discovered 'the title deeds of humanity', as they lay buried under the rubbish of privileges, conventional charters, and statutes. His was a generous nature that disdained the impotence of epicureanism, and found no resting-place in doubt. He saw that society, notwithstanding all its revolutions, must repose on principles that do not change; that Christianity, which seems to aim only at the happiness of another life, also constitutes man's blessedness in this. He questioned the laws of every nation to unfold to him the truth that had inspired them; and behind the confused masses of positive rules, he recognized the anterior existence and reality of justice."

The above excerpts are from George Bancroft's "History of the United States" - 1850

William Blackstone

AMONG those who have risen to eminence by the profession of the law, none have obtained a more extended and durable reputation than Sir William Blackstone...He seems from the first to have made up his mind to follow the profession of the law...At Oxford he had diligently progressed in the study of the classics, mathematics, and, before he was twenty, had compiled a Treatise on the Elements of Architecture...In 1750, he took his degree of Doctor on Civil Law, and thereby became a member of the convocation...Although his hopes of advancement at Westminster Hall had been disappointed, and although he had sufficent employment at Oxford to make his time pass without tedium, and sufficent revenue to free him from anxiety, he was not deterred from attempting 'things unattempted yet in prose or rhyne'.

"He formed the design of reducing into system the common law, which had hitherto lain in scattered fragments in the reports, or in large masses in the Institutes of Coke...of treating with elegance a subject on which the graces of composition had never before been bestowed - of teaching, in a place where it had never before been taught, a science which no one there desired to learn...Too much gratitude cannot be paid to him by lawyers, for this gratuitous and invaluable present to his profession.

"Mr. Viner having bequeathed a large sum of money, and a larger abridgement of law, to the University of Oxford, for the purpose of instituting a professorship of common law, it became necessary to appoint a professor. All eyes were turned towards Dr. Blackstone as the fittest person for that office, and he was accordingly, on the 20th of October 1758, unanimously elected first Vinerian Professor. He lost no time in entering upon the duties of his professorship, and on the 25th of the same month delivered his Introductory Lecture on the Study of the Law, now prefixed to the Commentaries, which for elegance of composition is perhaps not excelled...

"In 1765 appeared the first volume of the Commentaries...It may be inferred that he was no enthusiast either in religion or in politics; in the former he was a sincere believer in Christianity, from a profound investigation of its evidences; in the latter he was what would be called a Conservative, friendly to mild but authoritative government, inimical to the agitations of pretended patriots..."

The above excerpts are from W. N. Welsby's "Lives of Eminent English Judges" - 1846

THE COMMENTARIES

OF THE NATURE OF LAWS IN GENERAL. Meaning of law. - Law, in its most general and comprehensive sense, signifies a rule of action; and is applied indiscriminately to all kinds of action, whether animate or inanimate, rational or irrational. Thus we say, the laws of motion, of gravitation, of optics, or mechanics, as well as the laws of nature and of nations. And it is that rule of action, which is prescribed by some superior, and which the inferior is bound to obey.

Law-Order of Universe

LAW AS ORDER OF THE UNIVERSE. - Thus when the Supreme Being formed the universe, and created matter out of nothing, He impressed certain principles upon that matter, from which it can never depart, and without which it would cease to be. When He put the matter into motion, He established certain laws of motion, to which all movable bodies must conform. And, to descend from the greatest operations to the smallest, when a workman forms a clock, or other piece of mechanism, he establishes at his own pleasure certain arbitrary laws for its direction; as that the hand shall describe a given space in a given time; to which law as long as the work conforms, so long it continues in perfection, and answers the end of its formation. If we further advance, from mere inactive matter to vegetable and animal life, we shall find them still governed by laws; more numerous indeed, but equally fixed and invariable. The whole progress of plants, from the seed to the root, and from thence to the seed again; the method of animal nutrition, digestion, secretion and all other branches of vital economy; - are not left to chance, or the will of the creature itself, but are performed in a wondrous involuntary manner, and guided by unerring rules laid down by the great Creator.

Human Conduct in Relation to Law

LAW AS A RULE OF HUMAN ACTION. This, then, is the general signification of law, a rule of action dictated by some superior being; and, in those creatures that have neither the power to think, nor to will, such laws must be invariably obeyed, so long as the creature itself subsists, for its existence depends on the obedience. But laws, in their more confined sense, and in which it is our present business to consider them, denote the rules, not of action in general, but of human action or conduct: that is, the precepts by which man, the

The above excerpts are from William Blackstone's "Commentaries" - 1765, Jones Ed. 1915

noblest of all sublunary beings, a creature endowed with both reason and free will, is commanded to make use of those faculties in the general regulation of his behavior. Man, considered as a creature, must necessarily be subject to the laws of his Creator, for he is entirely a dependent being. A being independent of any other, has no rule to pursue, but such as he prescribes to himself; but a state of dependence will inevitably oblige the inferior to take the will of him, on whom he depends, as the rule of his conduct; not indeed in every particular, but in all those points wherein his dependence consists. This principle, therefore, has more or less extent and effect, in proportion as the superiority of the one and the dependence of the other is greater or less, absolute or limited. And consequently, as man depends absolutely upon his Maker for everything, it is necessary that he should in all points conform to his Maker's will.

Man subject to Creator

LAW OF NATURE. - This will of his Maker is called the law of nature. For as God, when He created matter, and endued it with a principle of mobility, established certain rules for the perpetual direction of that motion; so, when He created man, and endued him with free will to conduct himself in all parts of life, He laid down certain immutable laws of human nature, whereby that free will is in some degree regulated and restrained, and gave him also the faculty of reason to discover the purport of those laws.

Law of Nature

"Considering the Creator only a Being of infinite power, He was able unquestionably to have prescribed whatever laws He pleased to His creature, man, however unjust or severe. But as he is also a Being of infinite wisdom, He has laid down only such laws as were founded in those relations of justice, that existed in the nature of things antecedent to any positive precept. These are the eternal, immutable laws of good and evil, to which the Creator Himself in all his Dispensations conforms; and which He has enabled human reason to discover, so far as they are necessary for the conduct of human actions. Such, among others, are these principles: that we should live honestly, should hurt nobody, and should render to everyone his due; to which three general precepts Justinian has reduced the whole doctrine of law. But if the discovery of these first principles of the law of nature depended only upon the due exertion of right reason, and could not otherwise be obtained than by a chain of metaphysical disquisitions, mankind would have wanted some inducement to have quickened their inquiries, and the greater part of the world would have rested content in mental indolence, and ignorance its inseparable companion. As, therefore,

Creator: Being of Infinite Power

The above excerpts are from William Blackstone's "Commentaries" - 1765, Jones Ed. 1915

Creator: Being of Infinite Goodness

the Creator is a Being, not only of infinite power, and wisdom, but also of infinite goodness, He has been pleased so to contrive the constitution and frame of humanity, that we should want no other prompter than to inquire after and pursue the rule of right, but only our own self-love, that universal principle of action. For He has so intimately connected, so inseparably interwoven the laws of eternal justice with the happiness of each individual, that the latter cannot be attained but by observing the former; and, if the former be punctually obeyed, it cannot but induce the latter. In consequence of which mutual connection of justice and human felicity, He has not perplexed the law of nature with a multitude of abstracted rules and precepts, referring merely to the fitness or unfitness of things, as some have vainly surmised; but has graciously reduced the rule of obedience to this one paternal precept, 'that man should pursue his own true and substantial happiness.' This is the foundation of what we call ethics, or natural law. For the several articles into which it is branched in our systems, amount to no more than demonstrating, that this or that action tends to man's real happiness, and therefore very justly concluding that the performance of it is a part of the law of nature; or, on the other hand, that this or that action is destructive to man's real happiness, and therefore that the law of nature forbids it.

Law of Nature is to Man True and Substantial Happiness

God's Law Superior to Human Law

"This law of nature, being coeval with mankind and dictated by God Himself, is of course superior in obligation to any other. It is binding over all the globe in all countries, and at all times: no human laws are of any validity, if contrary to this; and such of them as are valid derive all their force, and all their authority, mediately or immediately, from this original. But in order to apply this to the particular exigencies of each individual, it is still necessary to have recourse to human reason; whose office it is to discover, as was before observed, what the law of nature directs in every circumstance of life; by considering, what method will tend most effectually to our own substantial happiness. And if our reason were always, as in our first ancestor before his transgression, clear and perfect, unruffled by passions, unclouded by prejudice, unimpaired by disease or intemperance, the task would be pleasant and easy; we should need no other guide but this. But every man now finds the contrary in his own experience; that his reason is corrupt, and his understanding full of ignorance and error.

Office of Human Reason to Discover the Laws of Nature

REVEALED LAW. - This has given manifold occasion for the benign interposition of divine providence; which, in compassion

The above excerpts are from William Blackstone's "Commentaries" - 1765, Jones Ed. 1915

Revealed Law

to the frailty, the imperfection, and the blindness of human reason, hath been pleased, at sundry times and in divers manners, to discover and enforce its laws by an immediate and direct revelation. The doctrines thus delivered we call the revealed or divine law, and they are to be found only in the Holy Scriptures. These precepts, when revealed, are found upon comparison to be really a part of the original law of nature, as they tend in all their consequences to man's felicity. But we are not from thence to conclude that the knowledge of these truths was attainable by reason, in its present corrupted state; since we find that, until they were revealed, they were hid from the wisdom of the ages. As then the moral precepts of this law are indeed of the same original with those of the law of nature, so their intrinsic obligation is of equal strength and perpetuity. Yet undoubtedly the revealed law is of infinitely more authenticity than that moral system, which is framed by ethical writers, and denominated the natural law. Because one is the law of nature, expressly declared so to be by God Himself; the other is only what, by the assistance of human reason, we imagine to be that law. If we could be as certain of the latter as we are of the former, both would have an equal authority; but, till then, they can never be put in any competition together.

Revealed Law Superior to the Morality of Human Ethics

All Human laws Depend on (1) Law of Nature and (2) Law of Revelation

"Upon these two foundations, the law of nature and the law of revelation, depend all human laws; that is to say, no human laws should be suffered to contradict these. There are, it is true, a great number of indifferent points, in which both the divine law and the natural leave a man at his own liberty; but which are found necessary for the benefit of society to be restrained within certain limits. And herein it is that human laws have their greatest force and efficacy: for, with regard to such points as are not indifferent, human laws are only declaratory of, and act in subordination to the former. To instance in the case of murder: this is expressly forbidden by the divine, and demonstrably by the natural law; and from these prohibitions arises the true unlawfulness of this crime. Those human laws that annex a punishment to it do not at all increase its moral guilt, or superadd any fresh obligation <u>in foro conscientiae</u> (in the court of conscience) to abstain from its perpetration. Nay, if any human law should allow or enjoin us to commit it, we, are bound to transgress that human law, or else we must offend both the natural and the divine. But with regard to matters that are in themselves indifferent, and are not commanded or forbidden by those superior laws; such, for

The above excerpts are from William Blackstone's "Commentaries" - 1765, Jones Ed. 1915

Emphasis by Blackstone

instance, as exporting of wool into foreign countries; here the inferior legislature has scope and opportunity to interpose, and to make that action unlawful which before was not so.

Treaties - Leagues - Intercourse of Nations - Resort to Law of God and Law of Nature

LAW OF NATIONS. - If man were to live in a state of nature, unconnected with other individuals, there would be no occasion for any other laws, than the law of nature and the law of God. Neither could any other law possibly exist; for a law always supposes some superior who is to make it; and in a state of nature we are all equal, without any other superior but Him who is the author of our being. But man was formed for society; and, as is demonstrated by the writers on this subject, is neither capable of living alone, nor indeed has the courage to do it... Hence arises a third kind of law to regulate this mutual intercourse called 'the law of nations'; which, as none of these states will acknowledge a superiority in the other, cannot be dictated by any; but depends entirely upon the rules of natural law, or upon mutual compacts, treaties, leagues, and agreements between these several communities: in the construction also of which compacts we have no other rule to resort to, but the law of nature; being the only one to which both communities are equally subject...

Civil Law Governs the Nation

MUNICIPAL LAW. - Thus much I thought it necessary to premise concerning the law of nature, the revealed law, and the law of nations, before I proceeded to treat more fully of the principal subject of this section, municipal or civil law; that is, the rule by which the particular districts, communites, or nations are governed; being thus defined by Justinian ...the civil law is that which each nation has established for itself. I call it municipal law, in compliance with common speech; for, though strictly that expression denotes the particular customs of one single municipium or free town...

DEFINITION OF MUNICIPAL LAW. - Municipal law, thus understood, is properly defined to be 'a rule of civil conduct, prescribed by the supreme power in a state, commanding what is right and prohibiting what is wrong'...

NATURE OF CIVIL GOVERNMENT. - This may lead us into a short inquiry concerning the nature of society and civil government;

The above excerpts are from William Blackstone's "Commentaries" - 1765, Jones Ed. 1915

and the natural, inherent right that belongs to the sovereignty of a state, wherever that sovereignty be lodged, of making and enforcing laws.

FOUNDATIONS OF SOCIETY. - The only true and natural foundations of society are the wants and fears of individuals...

Government preserves society

ESTABLISHMENT OF GOVERNMENT. - For when civil society is once formed, government at the same time results of course, as necessary to preserve and to keep that society in order...

Sovereignty Belongs to a Supreme Authority

SOVEREIGNTY. - How the several forms of government we now see in the world at first actually began, is a matter of great uncertainty, and has occasioned infinite disputes. It is not my business or intention to enter into any of them. However they began, or by what right soever they subsist, there is and must be in all of them a supreme, irresistible, absolute, uncontrolled authority, in which the jura summi imperii, or the rights of sovereignty reside. And this authority is placed in those hands, wherein (according to the opinion of the founders of such respective states, either expressly given, or collected from their tacit approbation) the qualities requisite for supremacy, wisdom, goodness, and power, are the most likely to be found.

Division of authority must conform to the sovereign power

LAWS MADE BY SOVEREIGN. - By the sovereign power, as was before observed, is meant the making of laws; for wherever that power resides, all others must conform to, and be directed by it... For it is at any time in the option of the legislature to alter that form and administration by a new edict or rule, and to put the execution of the laws into whatever hands it pleases; by constituting one, or a few, or many executive magistrates, and all the other powers of the state must obey the legislative power in the execution of their several functions, or else the constitution is at an end.

Democracy Aristocracy Monarchy

FORMS OF GOVERNMENT. - The political writers of antiquity will not allow more than three regular forms of government; the first, when the sovereign power is lodged in an aggregate assembly consisting of all the free members of a community, which is called a democracy; the second, when it is lodged in a council, composed of select members, and then it is styled an aristocracy; the last,

The above excerpts are from William Blackstone's "Commentaries" - 1765, Jones Ed. 1915

when it is entrusted in the hands of a single person, and then it takes the name of monarchy. All other species of government, they say, are either corruptions of, or reducible to, these three.

Strengths and Weaknesses

MERITS and DEMERITS OF DIFFERENT FORMS of government. - In a democracy, where the right of making laws resides in the people at large, public virtue, or goodness of intention, is more likely to be found, than either of the other qualities of government. Popular assemblies are frequently foolish in their contrivance, and weak in their execution; but generally mean to do the thing that is right and just, and have always a degree of patriotism or public spirit. In aristocracies there is more wisdom to be found, than in the other frames of government; being composed, or intended to be composed, of the most experienced citizens; but there is less honesty than in a republic, and less strength than in a monarchy. A monarchy is indeed the most powerful of any; for by the entire conjunction of the legislative and executive powers all the sinews of government are knit together, and united in the hand of the prince; but then there is imminent danger of his employing that strength to improvident or oppressive purposes. Thus these three species of government have, all of them, their several perfections and imperfections. Democracies are usually the best calculated to direct the end of a law; aristocracies to invent the means by which that end shall be obtained; and monarchies to carry those means into execution...

Sovereign Authority Prescribes Civil Action

LEGISLATIVE POWER SUPREME. - Having thus cursorily considered the three usual species of government...I proceed to observe, that, as the power of making laws constitutes the supreme authority, so wherever the supreme authority in any state resides, it is the right of that authority to make laws; that is, in the words of our definition, to prescribe the rule of civil action. And this may be discovered from the very end and institution of civil states. For a state is a collective body, composed of a multitude of individuals, united for their safety and convenience, and intending to act together as one man...It can therefore be no otherwise produced than by a political union; by the consent of all persons to submit their own private wills to the will of one man, or of one or more assemblies of men, to whom the supreme authority is entrusted; and this will of that one man, or assemblage of men, is in different states, according to their different constitutions, understood to be law."

The above excerpts are from William Blackstone's "Commentaries" - 1765, Jones Ed. 1915

Part Three

LOCAL SELF - GOVERNMENT

"So is the kingdom of God, as if a man should cast seed into the ground; And should sleep, and rise night and day, and the seed should spring and grow up, he knoweth not how. For the earth bringeth forth fruit of herself; first the blade, then the ear, after that the full corn in the ear."

- Mark 4:26 - 28

"...All the churches, in those primitive times, were independent bodies; or none of them subject to the jurisdiction of any other. For, though the churches which were founded by the apostles themselves frequently had the honor shown them to be consulted in difficult and doubtful cases, yet they had no judicial authority, no control, no power of giving laws..."

- Johann Mosheim, "Ecclesiastical History", 1726

"Our popular government lay in embryo on board the Mayflower, all-environed with its only possible preservatives, popular intelligence and popular virtue. The idea born there, and embodied in a civil constitution... grew with the growth of the colonies, gradually expelling from the thoughts and affections of the people all other theories of civil government, until finally it enthroned itself in the national mind, and then embodied itself in our national government."

- Wellman, "Polity of the Pilgrim Church", 1856

"...you seem to have supposed a greater ignorance, at the commencement of the contest with G. Britain, of the doctrines of self-government, than was the fact. The controversial papers of the epoch show it. The date of the Virginia Declaration of Rights would itself be a witness. The merit of the founders of our Republics lies in the more accurate views and the practical application of the doctrines. The rights of man as the foundation of just Government had been long understood; but the superstructures projected had been sadly defective."

- James Madison, Letter to N. P. Trist, February, 1830

SELF - GOVERNMENT

CHRISTIANITY:

Basis of American Idea of Local Self-Government

Two great elements:

(1) Local Self-Government

(2) National Union

THE polity of the United States is original and peculiar. It is obviously made up of two great elements or divisions of power - that of the States and of the nation; and the beginnings of these are as obviously found in the colonies and their union. The motto on the seal of the United States gives the genealogy, - E PLURIBUS UNUM. The circumstances connected with the origin of each one of the many satisfactorily explain why there were colonies and now are States, unequal in size, population, wealth, and political weight...In the general progress and development of civilization, there is ever a providential ordering of events, superior to and the master of circumstances. This moves on through the working of great ideas, or the hidden forces, which joined with climate and soil, mould society and direct its tendencies. These ideas were fulfilling their mission when theories of vital consequence to the human race, pronounced in the Old World Utopian, were carried out in the New World, and their influence fixed society on a new basis. Indications of their presence are seen at every step of progress. The preamble to an early American Bill of Rights runs, 'The free fruition of such liberties, immunities, and privileges as humanity, civility, and Christianity call for, as due to every man, in his place and proportion, without impeachment or infringement, hath ever been, and ever will be, the tranquillity and stability of churches and commonwealths; and the denial or deprival thereof, the disturbance, if not the ruin of both.' Here is seen, in the early American lawmakers, the influence of the Christian element. The legislation of several of the colonies, establishing a system of public instruction for youth, shows the high aim of basing commonwealths on intelligence, or on the general education of the people. On viewing this class of facts, in connection with the results that have been attained, a philosophic inquirer, penetrating beneath the incidental and transient elements of error and of wrong, which, in American history, as in other

Christian Element

People trained for a century and a half in the nature of sovereignty

The above excerpts are from Richard Frothingham's "Rise of the Republic" - 1890

he
Grand
laxim"

histories, are mingled with the progress of Truth and Right, declares that the grand maxim on which civil and political society in the United States rests is, 'that Providence has given to every human being the degree of reason necessary to direct himself in the affairs which interest him exclusively' (De Tocqueville). After the people had been trained for a century and a half in the exercise of these powers in purely local spheres, there rose at length, as the product of rare public virtue, and to supply the needs of the nation, the polity of a republican government based on the principle of the sovereignty of the people...

iversity
nd
nity

"I do not purpose to study the Why of the E Pluribus Unum; but an order of facts that seem to show the How it came to pass, - a class of events that mark the continuous blending of Diversity and Unity in the formation of the public opinion, that evolved The One from the many; or, how the United States came to be the United States, free from the benumbing influences of centralization on the one hand, and from the fatal dangers of disintegration on the other.

wo
lain Elements
cting
1
larmony

"At every stage in the progress towards this result, the two main elements of the national life are found acting in harmony. It may be useful to preface the narrative by a glance at the origin and progress of the Idea of Local Self-Government, which developed into the State, and at the Idea of Union, which developed into the nation.

he
lement
f
elf-Government

LOCAL SELF-GOVERNMENT. - The self-government which developed and is recognized in the Republic is not simply a custom, in the units termed municipalities or States, of managing their local affairs; but a degree of freedom in the individual to engage in the various pursuits of life, unrecognized elsewhere at the period when the Republic was formed, and yet unknown where centralization prevails, whether he chooses to act by himself or in association for civil or religious purposes; and this self-government exists in union with the fulfilment of every obligation demanded by the nation. The theme in hand, however, requires references to institutions of a purely political nature. The idea of Local Self-government was historical at the time of the colonization of North America. Among the Germanic ancestors of the emigrants, the custom was so general for the inhabitants of a district to control their local affairs, that it has been said, 'One leading principle pervaded the primeval polity of the Goths: where the law was administered, the law was made'; and they filled all Europe for five hundred years with the fame of their exploits, and were the first nation beyond the Danube to receive Christianity.

rimeval Polity
f
ocal
elf-Government

The above excerpts are from Richard Frothingham's "Rise of the Republic" - 1890

"In ancient England, local self-government is found in connection with the political and territorial divisions of tythings, hundreds, burghs, counties, and shires, in which the body of the inhabitants had a voice in managing their own affairs. Hence it was the germinal idea of the Anglo-Saxon polity.

Self-perpetuating bodies weaken local self-government

"In the course of events, the crown deprived the body of the people of this power of local rule, and vested it in a small number of persons in each locality, ... and were thus self-perpetuating bodies. In this way, the ancient freedom of the municipalities was undermined, and the power of the ruling classes was installed in its place. Such was the nature of the local self-government in England, not merely during the period of the planting of her American colonies (1607 to 1732), but for a century later; and it was the same in other countries. It was a noble form robbed of its life-giving spirit.

"It has been said by Guizot, that, 'when there scarcely remained traces of popular assemblies, the remembrance of them, of the right of freemen to deliberate and transact their business together, resided in the minds of men as a primitive tradition, and a thing which might come about again.' These assemblies reappeared, and old rights were again enjoyed, when the emigrants to the soil now the United States began to frame the laws under which they were to live.

"Mayflower Compact - 1620"

"An instance of this occurred (1620) on board the 'Mayflower', as she was bearing the Pilgrims from Southampton to Plymouth. Some of the passengers, termed strangers, said, that, as their patent did not apply to New England, there would be no authority to exercise powers of government; and, when they got on shore, they would use their own liberty. To curb this riotous spirit, forty-one of the band, when at Cape Cod, signed the well-known covenant, by which they mutually and solemnly combined themselves into a 'civil body politic', for the better ordering and preservation of the object, and by virtue thereof to frame, enact, and obey such just and equal laws as from time to time should be thought most meet and convenient for the general good of the colony: in the expectation that this form of government might be as firm as any patent, and in some respects more sure. They declared that their enterprise was undertaken for the glory of God, for the advance of the Christian faith, and for the honor of their king and country. This was a covenant to provide a code of laws and a public authority, or a local government, not in the spirit of sovereignty, but of subordination to it, or as loyal subjects of the king."

Covenant establishes first "Civil Body Politic" in America

The above excerpts are from Richard Frothingham's "Rise of the Republic" - 1890

THE PARENT COLONIES

VIRGINIA COLONY

"...the agitation for a colony was primarily a commercial one."

- Edward Eggleston, "History of the United States", 1888

"Virginia was a continuation of English society...a love for England and English institutions..."

- George Bancroft, "History of the United States", 1859

NEW ENGLAND COLONY

"...religion being their chief motive of their retreating into these parts..."

- Daniel Neal, "History of the Puritans", 1731

"The settlement of New England...was instigated by a detestation of civil and ecclesiastical tyranny..."

- Alexander Hamilton

"The exalted feelings which determined the Pilgrims to seek in a New World, through the perils and sufferings to be encountered, the liberty, religious and civil, denied them in the old; and the fruits of their heroic virtues, in the multiplied blessings now enjoyed by their expanding posterity, cannot fail to inspire admiration and gratitude..."

- James Madison

THE ORIGINAL AND PARENT COLONIES

Key to the Chart

" ... He (James) divided that portion of North America, which stretches from the thirty-fourth to the fifty-fifth degree of latitude, into two districts nearly equal; the one called the first or south colony of Virginia, the other, the second or north colony (April 10, 1616). (This date is apparently a misprint in the Robertson history; Bancroft gives April, 1606.) He authorized Sir Thomas Gates, Sir George Summers, Richard Hakluyt, and their associates, mostly resident in London, to settle any part of the former ..." (William Robertson, "History of the Discovery and Settlement of America", Book IX) See Pg. 155 of text.

"... The two provinces of Virginia and New England forms a regular and connected story. The former in the south, and the latter in the north, may be considered as the original and parent colonies, in imitation of which and under whose shelter, all the others have been successively planted and reared." (William Robertson) See "History of Virginia" in text.

" ... The two most distinctive and most chracteristic lines of development which English forms of government have followed ... are the two lines that have led through New England on the one hand and through Virginia on the other ..." (John Fiske, "Civil Government") See Pg. 276 of text.

"... an aristocratic type of society was developed in Virginia as naturally as a democratic type was developed in New England." (John Fiske, "Civil Government") See Pg. 277 of text.

" ... the political life of New England was in a manner built up out of the political life of the towns, so the political life of Virginia was built up out of the political life of the counties ..." (John Fiske, "Civil Government") See Pg. 278 of text.

NEW ENGLAND COLONY

"Religion being the chief motive of their retreating into these parts, that was settled in the first place ..." (Neal, "History of the Puritans", Pg. 299) See Bradford's "History of Plymouth Plantation" and "History of New England" in text.

1620. "They were poor and friendless, separatists from the Church and exiles from England; but they bore with them the seeds of a great nation and of a great system of government ... the vanguard of a great column, bearing a civilization and a system of government which was to confront that other system founded far away to the south on the rivers of Virginia, and which, after a conflict of two centuries and a half, was destined to prevail throughout the length and breadth of a continent ..." (Henry Cabot Lodge, "English Colonies in America", 1881)

" ... great equality existed among the emigrants who settled on the shores of New England. The germ of aristocracy was never planted in that part of the Union. The only influence which obtained there was that of intellect..." (De Tocqueville, "Democracy in America")

VIRGINIA COLONY

"... The vast treasure of gold and silver drawn by the Spaniards from Mexico and Peru produced a belief in the English mind that a colony planted at any place on the American coast might find gold ... The American (Indian) women are described as 'wearing great plates of gold covering their whole bodies like armor ... In every cottage pearls are to be found, and in some houses a peck' ... The banqueting houses are built of crystal, 'with pillars of massive silver, some of gold'.... Thus grotesque and misleading were many of the glimpses that Europe got of the New World as the mists of ignorance slowly lifted from it ... English beginnings in America were thus made in a time abounding in bold enterprises - enterprises brilliant in conception, but in the execution of which there was often a lack of foresight and practical wisdom." (Edward Eggleston, "The Beginners of a Nation", Pages 12, 15, 20 - 1896) See "History of Virginia" in text.

"The intercourse between Spain and England ... the study of the Spanish language ... and the translation of several histories of America into English, diffused gradually through the nation a more distinct knowledge of the policy of Spain in planting its colonies, and of the advantages which it derived from them .... Almost every eminent leader of the age aimed at distinguishing himself by naval exploits. That service, and the ideas connected with it, the discovery of unknown countries, the establishment of distant colonies, and the enriching of commerce by new commodities, became familiar to persons of rank. In consequence of all those concurring causes, the English began seriously to form plans of settling colonies in those parts of America which hitherto they had only visited ..." (William Robertson "History of the Discovery and Settlement of America", Book IX, Pg. 396) See "History of Virginia", Pg. 151 of text.

"... Virginia was a continuation of English society ... a love for England and English institutions ... The aristocracy of Virginia was, from its origin, exclusively a landed aristocracy; its germ lay in the manner in which rights to the soil had been obtained ..." (George Bancroft, "History of the United States", Pg. 190)

ORIGINAL AND PARENT COLONIES

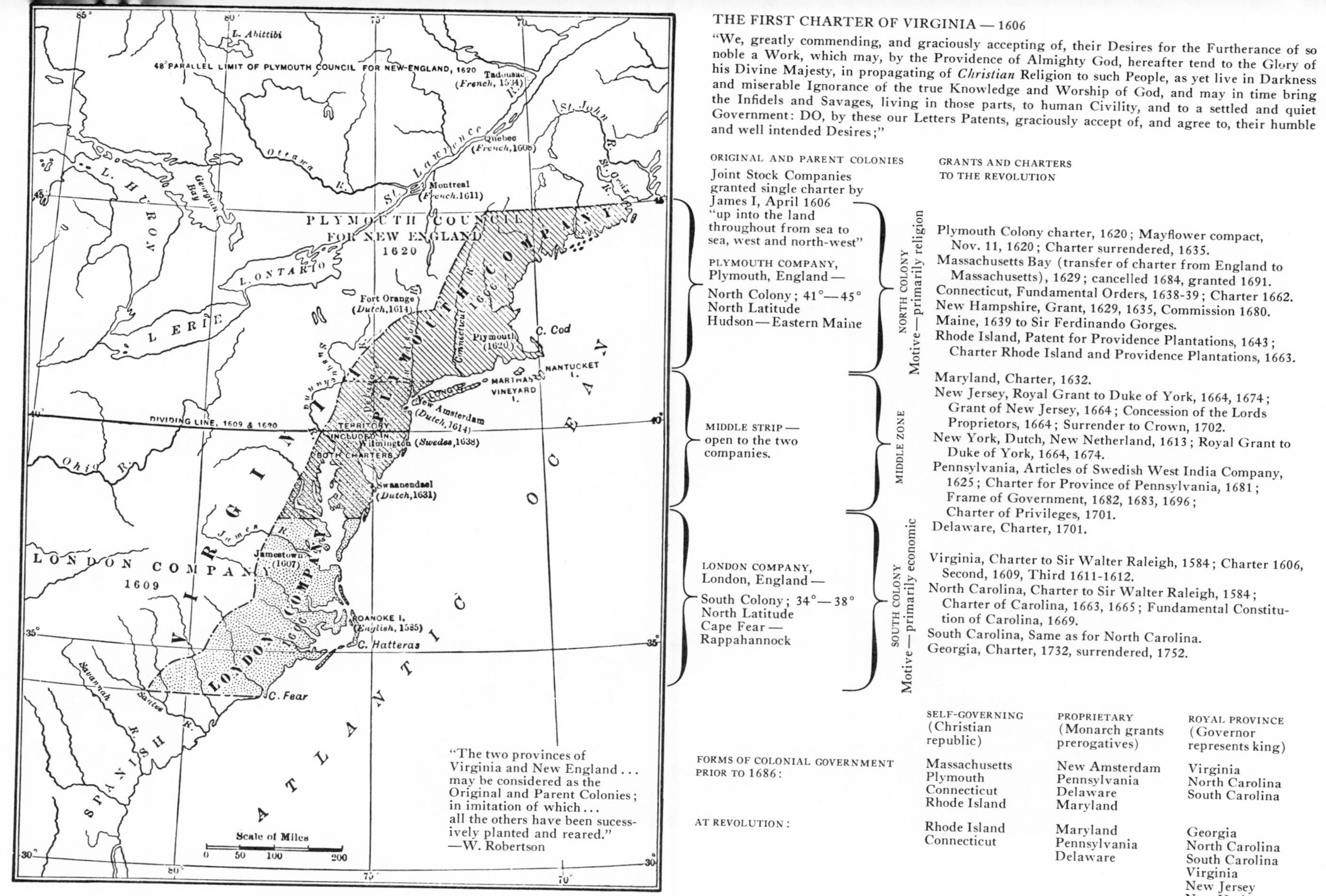

THE FIRST CHARTER OF VIRGINIA — 1606

"We, greatly commending, and graciously accepting of, their Desires for the Furtherance of so noble a Work, which may, by the Providence of Almighty God, hereafter tend to the Glory of his Divine Majesty, in propagating of *Christian* Religion to such People, as yet live in Darkness and miserable Ignorance of the true Knowledge and Worship of God, and may in time bring the Infidels and Savages, living in those parts, to human Civility, and to a settled and quiet Government: DO, by these our Letters Patents, graciously accept of, and agree to, their humble and well intended Desires;"

ORIGINAL AND PARENT COLONIES		GRANTS AND CHARTERS TO THE REVOLUTION
Joint Stock Companies granted single charter by James I, April 1606 "up into the land throughout from sea to sea, west and north-west" PLYMOUTH COMPANY, Plymouth, England — North Colony; 41°—45° North Latitude Hudson — Eastern Maine	NORTH COLONY Motive — primarily religion	Plymouth Colony charter, 1620; Mayflower compact, Nov. 11, 1620; Charter surrendered, 1635. Massachusetts Bay (transfer of charter from England to Massachusetts), 1629; cancelled 1684, granted 1691. Connecticut, Fundamental Orders, 1638-39; Charter 1662. New Hampshire, Grant, 1629, 1635, Commission 1680. Maine, 1639 to Sir Ferdinando Gorges. Rhode Island, Patent for Providence Plantations, 1643; Charter Rhode Island and Providence Plantations, 1663.
MIDDLE STRIP — open to the two companies.	MIDDLE ZONE	Maryland, Charter, 1632. New Jersey, Royal Grant to Duke of York, 1664, 1674; Grant of New Jersey, 1664; Concession of the Lords Proprietors, 1664; Surrender to Crown, 1702. New York, Dutch, New Netherland, 1613; Royal Grant to Duke of York, 1664, 1674. Pennsylvania, Articles of Swedish West India Company, 1625; Charter for Province of Pennsylvania, 1681; Frame of Government, 1682, 1683, 1696; Charter of Privileges, 1701. Delaware, Charter, 1701.
LONDON COMPANY, London, England — South Colony; 34°—38° North Latitude Cape Fear — Rappahannock	SOUTH COLONY Motive — primarily economic	Virginia, Charter to Sir Walter Raleigh, 1584; Charter 1606, Second, 1609, Third 1611-1612. North Carolina, Charter to Sir Walter Raleigh, 1584; Charter of Carolina, 1663, 1665; Fundamental Constitution of Carolina, 1669. South Carolina, Same as for North Carolina. Georgia, Charter, 1732, surrendered, 1752.

	SELF-GOVERNING (Christian republic)	PROPRIETARY (Monarch grants prerogatives)	ROYAL PROVINCE (Governor represents king)
FORMS OF COLONIAL GOVERNMENT PRIOR TO 1686:	Massachusetts Plymouth Connecticut Rhode Island	New Amsterdam Pennsylvania Delaware Maryland	Virginia North Carolina South Carolina
AT REVOLUTION:	Rhode Island Connecticut	Maryland Pennsylvania Delaware	Georgia North Carolina South Carolina Virginia New Jersey New York Massachusetts New Hampshire

SIR WALTER RALEIGH

"...men of rank and men of business...formed an association to establish colonies in America..."

- William Robertson, 1777
"History of the Discovery and Settlement of America"

VIRGINIA COLONY

THE intercourse between Spain and England, during the reign of Philip and Mary; the resort of the Spanish nobility to the English court, while Philip resided there; the study of the Spanish language, which became fashionable; and the translation of several histories of America into English, diffused gradually through the nation a more distinct knowledge of the policy of Spain in planting its colonies, and of the advantages which it derived from them.

"When hostilities commenced between Elizabeth and Philip, the prospect of annoying Spain by sea opened a new career to the enterprising spirit of the English nobility... Among them, Sir Humphry Gilbert, of Compton in Devonshire, ought to be mentioned with the distinction due to the conductor of the first English colony to America... he was deemed a proper person to be employed in establishing a new colony, and easily obtained from the queen letters patent (June 11, 1578), vesting in him sufficent powers for this purpose.

The first charter granted for English colonization of America 1578

"As this is the first charter to a colony granted by the crown of England, the articles in it merit particular attention, as they unfold the ideas of that age with respect to the nature of such settlements. Elizabeth authorizes him to discover and take possession of all remote and barbarous lands, unoccupied by any Christian prince or people. She vests in him, his heirs and assigns for ever, the full right of property in the soil of those countries whereof he shall take possession. She permits such of her subjects as were willing to accompany Gilbert in his voyage, to go and settle in the countries which he shall plant. She empowers him, his heirs and assigns, to dispose of whatever portion of those lands he shall judge meet, to persons settled there, in fee simple, according to the laws of England. She ordains, that all the lands granted to Gilbert shall hold of the crown of England by homage, on payment of the fifth part of the gold or silver ore found there. She confers upon him, his heirs and assigns, the complete jurisdiction and royalties, as well marine as other, within the said lands and seas thereunto adjoining; and as their common safety and interest would render good government necessary in their new settlements, she gave Gilbert, his heirs and assigns, full power to convict, punish, pardon, govern, and rule, by their good discretion and policy, as well in causes capital or criminal as civil, both marine and other, all persons who shall, from time to time, settle within the said

'All the schemes for colonization were carried on by the funds of individuals without any public aid" -Robertson

The above excerpts are from William Robertson's "History of the Discovery and Settlement of America", Book IX, Harper & Bros. 1835 Edition.

countries, according to such statutes, laws, and ordinances, as shall be by him, his heirs and assigns, devised and established for their better government. She declared, that all who settled there should have and enjoy all the privileges of free denizens and natives of England, any law, custom, or usage to the contrary notwithstanding....

First attempts to colonize end in disaster 1580

..."His own character, and the zealous efforts of his half brother Walter Ralegh, who even in his early youth displayed those splendid talents, and that undaunted spirit, which create admiration and confidence, soon procured him a sufficient number of followers. But his success was not suited either to the sanguine hopes of his countrymen, or to the expense of his preparations. Two expeditions, both of which he conducted in person, ended disastrously (1580). In the last he himself perished, without having effected his intended settlement on the continent of America,...

Walter Raleigh secures patent to colonize 1584

"But the miscarriage of a scheme, in which Gilbert had wasted his fortune, did not discourage Ralegh. He adopted all his brother's ideas; and applying to the Queen, in whose favour he stood high at that time, he procured a patent (March 26, 1584), with jurisdiction and prerogatives as ample as had been granted unto Gilbert. Ralegh, no less eager to execute than to undertake the scheme, instantly despatched two small vessels (April 27), under the command of Amadas and Barlow, two officers of trust, to visit the countries which he intended to settle, and to acquire some previous knowledge of their coasts, their soil, and productions....

Country is named VIRGINIA

..."Amadas and Barlow returned to England (Sept. 15), with two of the natives, and gave such splendid descriptions of the beauty of the country, the fertility of the soil, and the mildness of the climate, that Elizabeth, delighted with the idea of occupying a territory superior, so far, to the barren regions towards the north hitherto visited by her subjects, bestowed on it the name of Virginia; as a memorial that this happy discovery had been made under a virgin queen.

Raleigh prepares to take possession of Virginia

"Their report encouraged Ralegh to hasten his preparations for taking possession of such an inviting property. He fitted out a squadron of seven small ships, under the command of Sir Richard Greenville, a man of honourable birth, and of courage so undaunted as to be conspicuous even in that gallant age. But the spirit of that predatory war which the English carried on against Spain, mingled with this scheme of settlement; and on this account, as well as from unacquaintance with a more direct and shorter course to North America, Greenville sailed by the West India islands. He spent some time in cruising among these, and in taking prizes; so that it was towards

The above excerpts are from William Robertson's "History of the Discovery and Settlement of America", Book IX, Harper & Bros. 1835 Edition

Roanoke settled 1585

the close of June before he arrived on the coast of North America... But as, unfortunately, he did not advance far enough towards the north, to discover the noble bay of Chesapeak, he established the colony (Aug. 25), which he left on the island of Roanoke, an incommodious station, without any safe harbour, and almost uninhabited.

Search for gold and silver

"This colony consisted only of one hundred and eighty persons, under the command of Captain Lane.... Their chief employment, during a residence of nine months, was to obtain a more extensive knowledge of the country; and their researches were carried on with greater spirit, and reached further than could have been expected from a colony so feeble, and in a station so disadvantageous. But from the same impatience of indigent adventurers to acquire sudden wealth which gave a wrong direction to the industry of the Spaniards in their settlements, the greater part of the English seem to have considered nothing as worthy of attention but mines of gold and silver. These they sought for wherever they came: these they inquired after with unwearied eagerness. The savages soon discovered the favourite objects which allured them, and artfully amused them with so many tales concerning pearl fisheries, and rich mines of various metals, that Lane and his companions wasted their time and activity on the chimerical pursuit of these, instead of labouring to raise provisions for their own subsistence....

Raising of provisions neglected

"The colony, reduced to the utmost distress, and on the point of perishing with famine, was preparing to disperse into different districts of the country in quest of food, when Sir Francis Drake appeared with his fleet (June 1), returning from a successful expedition against the Spaniards in the West Indies...at their joint request, as they were worn out with fatigue and famine, he carried them home to England (June 19)....

Fatigue and famine

"A few days after Drake departed from Roanoke, a small bark, despatched by Ralegh with a supply of stores for the colony, landed at the place where the English had settled; but on finding it deserted by their countrymen they returned to England. The bark was hardly gone, when Sir Richard Greenville appeared with three ships. After searching in vain for the colony which he had planted, without being able to learn what had befallen it, he left fifteen of his crew to keep possession of the island. This handful of men was soon overpowered and cut in pieces by the savages.

Roanoke deserted

"Though all Ralegh's efforts to establish a colony in Virginia had hitherto proved abortive, and had been defeated by a succession of disasters and disappointments, neither his hopes nor resources

The above excerpts are from William Robertson's "History of the Discovery and Settlement of America", Book IX, Harper & Bros. 1835 Edition

Roanoke recolonized by Raleigh 1587

were exhausted. Early in the following year (1587), he fitted out three ships, under the command of Captain John White, who carried thither a colony more numerous than that which had been settled under Lane. On their arrival in Virginia, after viewing the face of the country covered with one continued forest, which to them appeared an uninhabited wild, as it was occupied only by a few scattered tribes of savages, they discovered that they were destitute of many things which they deemed essentially necessary towards their subsistence in such an uncomfortable situation; and with one voice, requested White, their commander, to return to England, as the person among them most likely to solicit, with efficacy, the supply on which depended the existence of the colony. White landed in his native country at a most unfavourable season for the negotiation which he had undertaken. He found the nation in universal alarm at the formidable preparations of Philip II. to invade England,... The unfortunate colony in Roanoke received no supply, and perished miserably by famine, or by the unrelenting cruelty of those barbarians by whom they were surrounded.

Colony perishes

"During the remainder of Elizabeth's reign, the scheme of establishing a colony in Virginia was not resumed.... But the succession of the Scottish line to the crown of England (1603) hastened its approach. James was hardly seated on the throne before he discovered his pacific intentions, and he soon terminated the long war which had been carried on between Spain and England, by an amicable treaty. From that period, uninterrupted tranquillity continued during his reign. Many persons of high rank, and of ardent ambition, to whom the war with Spain had afforded constant employment, and presented alluring prospects not only of fame but of wealth, soon became so impatient of languishing at home without occupation or object, that their invention was on the stretch to find some exercise for their activity and talents. To both these North America seemed to open a new field, and schemes of carrying colonies thither became more general and more popular.

Gosnold reaches America by a shorter route

"A voyage undertaken by Bartholomew Gosnold, in the last year of the Queen, facilitated as well as encouraged the execution of these schemes. He sailed from Falmouth in a small bark with thirty-two men. Instead of following former navigators in their unnecessary circuit by the West India isles and the Gulf of Florida, Gosnold steered due west as nearly as the winds would permit, and was the first English commander who reached America by this shorter and more direct course.... He and his companions were so much delighted every where with the inviting aspect of the country, that notwithstanding the smallness of their number, a part of them consented

The above excerpts are from William Robertson's "History of the Discovery and Settlement of America", Book IX, Harper & Bros., 1835 Edition

to remain there. But when they had leisure to reflect upon the fate of former settlers in America, they retracted a resolution formed in the first warmth of their admiration; and Gosnold returned to England in less than four months from the time of his departure.

"This voyage however inconsiderable it may appear, had important effects. The English now discovered the aspect of the American continent to be extremely inviting far to the north of the place where they had formerly attempted to settle. The coast of a vast country, stretching through the most desirable climates, lay before them. The richness of its virgin soil promised a certain recompense to their industry. In its interior provinces unexpected sources of wealth might open, and unknown objects of commerce might be found. Its distance from England was diminished almost a third part by the new course which Gosnold had pointed out. Plans for establishing colonies began to be formed in different parts of the kingdom;...

James I establishes the districts of the <u>South Colony</u> and a <u>North Colony</u>

"James, who prided himself on his profound skill in the science of government, and who had turned his attention to consider the advantages which might be derived from colonies,... was now no less fond of directing the active genius of his English subjects towards occupations not repugnant to his own pacific maxims, and listened with a favourable ear to their application. But as the extent as well as value of the American continent began now to be better known, a grant of the whole of such a vast region to any one body of men, however respectable, appeared to him an act of impolitic and profuse liberality. For this reason he divided that portion of North America, which stretches from the thirty-fourth to the fifty-fifth degree of latitude, into two districts nearly equal; the one called the first or south colony of Virginia, the other, the second or north colony (April 10, 1616). He authorized Sir Thomas Gates, Sir George Summers, Richard Hakluyt, and their associates, mostly resident in London, to settle any part of the former which they should choose, and vested in them a right of property to the land extending along the coast fifty miles on each side of the place of their first habitation, and reaching into the interior country a hundred miles. The latter district he allotted, as the place of settlement to sundry knights, gentlemen, and merchants of Bristol, Plymouth, and other parts in the west of England, with a similar grant of territory....

"Without hesitation or reluctance the proprietors of both colonies prepared to execute their respective plans; and under the authority of a charter, which would now be rejected with disdain as a violent

The above excerpts are from William Robertson's "History of the Discovery and Settlement of America", Book IX, Harper & Bros 1835 Edition

invasion of the sacred and inalienable rights of liberty, the first permanent settlements of the English in America were established....

105 men sail for Virginia

..."Though many persons of distinction became proprietors in the company which undertook to plant a colony in Virginia, its funds seem not to have been considerable, and its first effort was certainly extremely feeble. A small vessel of a hundred tons, and two barks, under the command of Captain Newport, sailed (Dec. 19) with a hundred and five men destined to remain in the country. Some of these were of respectable families, particularly a brother of the Earl of Northumberland, and several officers who had served with reputation in the reign of Elizabeth. Newport, I know not for what reason, followed the ancient course by the West Indies, and did not reach the coast of North America for four months (April 26, 1607). But he approached it with better fortune than any former navigator; for, having been driven, by the violence of a storm, to the northward of Roanoke, the place of his destination, the first land he discovered was a promontory which he called Cape Henry, the southern boundary of the Bay of Chesapeak.

Settlement of James Town 1607

"The English stood directly into that spacious inlet, which seemed to invite them to enter; and as they advanced, contemplated, with a mixture of delight and admiration, that grand reservoir, into which are poured the waters of all the vast rivers, which not only diffuse fertility through that district of America, but open the interior parts of the country to navigation, and render a commercial intercourse more extensive and commodious than in any other region of the globe. Newport, keeping along the southern shore, sailed up a river which the natives called Powhatan, and to which he gave the name of James River. After viewing its banks, during a run of above forty miles from its mouth, they all concluded that a country, where safe and convenient harbours seemed to be numerous, would be a more suitable station for a trading colony than the shoaly and dangerous coast to the south, on which their countrymen had formerly settled. Here then they determined to abide; and having chosen a proper spot for their residence, they gave this infant settlement the name of James Town,...

Violent animosities among leaders of the Colony

"But however well chosen the situation might be, the members of the colony were far from availing themselves of its advantages. Violent animosities had broke out among some of their leaders, during their voyage to Virginia. These did not subside on their arrival there. The first deed of the council, which assumed the government in virtue of a commission brought from England under the seal of the company, and opened on the day after they landed,

The above excerpts are from William Robertson's "History of the Discovery and Settlement of America", Book IX, Harper & Bros. 1835 Edition

was an act of injustice. Captain Smith, who had been appointed a member of the council, was excluded from his seat at the board,... This diminution of his influence, and restraint on his activity, was an essential injury to the colony,... For soon after they began to settle, the English were involved in a war with the natives, ...

Smith warring with Indians

"To this was added a calamity still more dreadful; the stock of provisions left for their subsistence, on the departure of their ships for England (June 15), was so scanty and of such bad quality, that a scarcity, approaching almost to absolute famine, soon followed. Such poor unwholesome fare brought on diseases, the violence of which was so much increased by the sultry heat of the climate, and the moisture of a country covered with wood, that before the beginning of September one half of their number died, and most of the survivors were sickly and dejected. ... Every eye was now turned towards Smith, and all willingly devolved on him that authority of which they had formerly deprived him....

Famine and disease reduce Colony

Danger to James Town subsides under leadership of Captain Smith

"He instantly adopted the only plan that could save them from destruction. He began by surrounding James Town with such rude fortifications as were a sufficient defence against the assaults of savages. He then marched, at the head of a small detachment, in quest of their enemies. Some tribes he gained by caresses and presents, and procured from them a supply of provisions. Others he attacked with open force; and defeating them on every occasion, whatever their superiority in numbers might be, compelled them to impart to him some portion of their winter stores. As the recompense of all his toils and dangers, he saw abundance and contentment reestablished in the colony, and hoped that he should be able to maintain them in that happy state, until the arrival of ships from England in the spring; but in one of his excursions he was surprised by a numerous body of Indians, and in making his escape from them, after a gallant defence, he sunk to the neck in a swamp, and was obliged to surrender. Though he knew well what a dreadful fate awaits the prisoners of savages, his presence of mind did not forsake him. He showed those who had taken him captive a mariner's

The above excerpts are from William Robertson's "History of the Discovery and Settlement of America", Book IX, Harper & Bros. 1835 Edition

Pocahuntas saves Captain Smith

compass, and amused them with so many wonderful accounts of its virtues as filled them with astonishment and veneration, which began to operate very powerfully in his favour. They led him, however, in triumph through various parts of the country, and conducted him at last to Powhatan, the most considerable Sachim in that part of Virginia. There the doom of death being pronounced, he was led to the place of execution, . . . The favourite daughter of Powhatan rushed in between him and the executioner, and by her entreaties and tears prevailed on her father to spare his life. The beneficence of his deliverer, whom the early English writers dignify with the title of the Princess Pocahuntas, did not terminate here; she soon after procured his liberty, and sent from time to time seasonable presents of provisions

Smith returns to a scene of despair

"Smith, on his return to James Town, found the colony reduced to thirty-eight persons, who, in despair were preparing to abandon a country which did not seem destined to be the habitation of Englishmen. He employed caresses, threats, and even violence, in order to prevent them from executing this fatal resolution. With difficulty he prevailed on them to defer it so long, that the succour anxiously expected from England arrived. Plenty was instantly restored; a hundred new planters were added to their number; and an ample stock of whatever was requisite for clearing and sowing the ground was delivered to them.

"Every useful occupation were totally neglected"

"But an unlucky incident turned their attention from that species of industry which alone could render their situation comfortable. In a small stream of water that issued from a bank of sand near James Town, a sediment of some shining mineral substance, which had some resemblance of gold, was discovered. At a time when the precious metals were conceived to be the peculiar and only valuable productions of the New World, when every mountain was supposed to contain a treasure, and every rivulet was searched for its golden sands, this appearance was fondly considered as an infallible indication of a mine. Every hand was eager to dig; large quantities of this glittering dust were amassed. From some assay of its nature, made by an artist as unskilful as his companions were credulous, it was pronounced to be extremely rich. 'There was now,' says Smith, 'no talk, no hope, no work, but dig gold, wash gold, refine gold.' With this imaginary wealth the first vessel returning to England was loaded, while the culture of the land and every useful occupation were totally neglected.

. . . "The colony still depended for subsistence chiefly on supplies from the natives; as, after all the efforts of their own industry, hardly thirty acres of ground were yet cleared so as to be capable

The above excerpts are from William Robertson's "History of the Discovery and Settlement of America", Book IX, Harper & Bros. 1835 Edition

James revises his charter to London Company 1609

New powers of the company - more explicit and complete

Delaware appointed governor of Virginia

of culture. By Smith's attention, however, the stores of the English were so regularly filled that for some time they felt no considerable distress; and at this juncture a change was made in the constitution of the company... James... granted them a new charter (May 23, 1609), with more ample privileges... he vested the government entirely in a council residing in London... the new council was to appoint Lord Delaware governor... But as he could not immediately leave England, the council despatched Sir Thomas Gates and Sir George Summers... A violent hurricane separated the vessel in which Gates and Summers had embarked from the rest of the fleet, and stranded it on the coast of Bermudas (Aug. 11). The other ships arrived safely at James Town. But the fate of their commanders was unknown. Their commission for new modelling the government, and all other public papers, were supposed to be lost... Smith was not in a condition at this juncture to assert his own rights, or to act with his wonted vigour. By an accidental explosion of gunpowder, he had been so miserably scorched and mangled that he was incapable of moving, and under the necessity of committing himself to the guidance of his friends, who carried him aboard one of the ships returning to England...

The above excerpts are from William Robertson's "History of the Discovery and Settlement of America", Book IX, Harper & Bros. 1835 Edition

"Wildest anarchy" follows Smith's departure

"After his departure, every thing tended fast to the wildest anarchy. Faction and discontent had often risen so high among the old settlers that they could hardly be kept within bounds. The spirit of the new comers was too ungovernable to bear any restraint. Several among them of better rank were such dissipated hopeless young men, as their friends were glad to send out in quest of whatever fortune might betide them in a foreign land. Of the lower order many were so profligate, or desperate, that their country was happy to throw them out as nuisances in society. Such persons were little capable of the regular subordination, the strict economy, and persevering industry, which their situation required. The Indians observing their misconduct, and that every precaution for sustenance or safety was neglected, not only withheld the supplies of provisions which they were accustomed to furnish, but harassed them with continual hostilities. All their subsistence was derived from the stores which they had brought from England; these were soon consumed; then the domestic animals sent out to breed in the country were devoured; and by this inconsiderate waste, they were reduced to such extremity of famine,... In less than six months, of five hundred persons whom Smith left in Virginia, only sixty remained; and these so feeble and dejected that they could not have survived for ten days, if succour had not arrived from a quarter whence they did not expect it.

Neglect of sustenance and safety destructive to Colonists

"When Gates and Summers were thrown ashore on Bermudas, fortunately not a single person on board their ship perished. A considerable part of their provisions and stores too, was saved, and in that delightful spot, Nature, with spontaneous bounty, presented to them such a variety of her productions, that a hundred and fifty people subsisted in affluence for ten months on an uninhabited island. Impatient, however, to escape from a place where they were cut off from all intercourse with mankind, they set about building two barks with such tools and materials as they had, and by amazing efforts of perseverance and ingenuity they finished them. In these they embarked, and steered directly towards Virginia, in hopes of finding an ample consolation for all their toils and dangers in the embraces of their companions, and amidst the comforts of a flourishing colony.

Gates and Summers arrive in a destitute James Town

"After a more prosperous navigation than they could have expected in their ill constructed vessels, they landed at James Town (May 23). But instead of that joyful interview for which they fondly looked, a spectacle presented itself which struck them with horror. They beheld the miserable remainder of their countrymen emaciated with famine and sickness, sunk in despair, and in their figure and looks

The above excerpts are from William Robertson's "History of the Discovery and Settlement of America", Book IX, Harper & Bros. 1835 Edition

James Town is abandoned

rather resembling spectres than human beings. As Gates and Summers, in full confidence of finding plenty of provisions in Virginia, had brought with them no larger stock than was deemed necessary for their own support during the voyage, their inability to afford relief to their countrymen added to the anguish with which they viewed this unexpected scene of distress. Nothing now remained but instantly to abandon a country where it was impossible to subsist any longer; and though all that could be found in the stores of the colony when added to what remained of the stock brought from Bermudas, did not amount to more than what was sufficient to support them for sixteen days, at the most scanty allowance, they set sail, in hopes of being able to reach Newfoundland, where they expected to be relieved by their countrymen employed at that season in the fishery there.

Lord Delaware arrives and reestablishes Colony

"But it was not the will of Heaven that all the labour of the English, in planting this colony, as well as all their hopes of benefit from its future prosperity, should be for ever lost. Before Gates and the melancholy companions of his voyage had reached the mouth of James River, they were met by Lord Delaware with three ships, that brought a large recruit of provisions, a considerable number of new settlers, and every thing requisite for defence or cultivation. By persuasion and authority he prevailed on them to return to James Town, where they found their fort, their magazines, and houses entire, which Sir Thomas Gates, by some happy chance, had preserved from being set on fire at the time of their departure.

"A society so feeble and disordered in its frame required a tender and skilful hand to cherish it, and restore its vigour. This it found in Lord Delaware: he searched into the causes of their misfortunes, as far as he could discover them, amidst the violence of their mutual accusations; but instead of exerting his power in punishing crimes that were past, he employed his prudence in healing their dissensions, and in guarding against a repetition of the same fatal errors....

"Under such an administration, the colony began once more to assume a promising appearance; when unhappily for it, a complication of diseases brought on by the climate obliged Lord Delaware to quit the country (March 28, 1611); the government of which he committed to Mr. Percy.

"He was soon superseded by the arrival (May 10) of Sir Thomas Dale; in whom the company had vested more absolute authority than in any of his predecessors, empowering him to rule by martial law.... But

The above excerpts are from William Robertson's "History of the Discovery and Settlement of America", Book IX, Harper & Bros. 1835 Edition

London Company empowers Dale to rule by martial law

however unconstitutional or oppressive this may appear, it was adopted by the advice of Sir Francis Bacon, the most enlightened philosopher, and one of the most eminent lawyers of the age. The company, well acquainted with the inefficacy of every method which they had hitherto employed for restraining the unruly mutinous spirits which they had to govern, eagerly adopted a plan that had the sanction of such high authority to recommend it. Happily for the colony, Sir Thomas Dale, who was intrusted with this dangerous power, exercised it with prudence and moderation....

"By the severe discipline of martial law, the activity of the colonists was forced into a proper direction, and exerted itself in useful industry. This, aided by a fertile soil and favourable climate, soon enabled them to raise such a large stock of provisions, that they were no longer obliged to trust for subsistence to the precarious supplies which they obtained or extorted from the Indians.... Sir Thomas Dale concluded a treaty with one of their most powerful and warlike tribes, situated on the river Chickahominy, in which they consented to acknowledge themselves subjects to the King of Great Britain, to assume henceforth the name of Englishmen, to send a body of their warriors to the assistance of the English as often as they took the field against any enemy, and to deposite annually a stipulated quantity of Indian corn in the storehouses of the colony....

Evil results from practice of communism in James Town

"During the interval of tranquillity procured by the alliance with Powhatan, an important change was made in the state of the colony. Hitherto no right of private property in land had been established. The fields that were cleared had been cultivated by the joint labour of the colonists; their product was carried to the common storehouses, and distributed weekly to every family, according to its number and exigencies. A society, destitute of the first advantages resulting from social union, was not formed to prosper. Industry, when not excited by the idea of property in what was acquired by its own efforts, made no vigorous exertion. The head had no inducement to contrive, nor the hand to labour. The idle and improvident trusted entirely to what was issued from the common store; the assiduity even of the sober and attentive relaxed, when they perceived that others were to reap the fruit of their toil; and it was computed, that the united industry of the colony, did not accomplish as much work in a week as might have been performed in a day, if each individual had laboured on his own account. In order to remedy this, Sir Thomas Dale divided a considerable portion of the land into small lots, and granted one of these to each individual in full property. From the moment that industry had the

Communism ends with a grant of land to each individual

The above excerpts are from William Robertson's "History of the Discovery and Settlement of America", Book IX, Harper & Bros. 1835 Edition

certain prospect of a recompense, it advanced with rapid progress. The articles of primary necessity were cultivated with so much attention as secured the means of subsistence....

"The industrious spirit which began to rise among the planters was soon directed towards a new object; and they applied to it for some time with such inconsiderate ardour as was productive of fatal consequences. The culture of tobacco, which has since become the staple of Virginia, and the source of its prosperity, was introduced about this time (1616), into the colony. As the taste for that weed continued to increase in England, notwithstanding the zealous declamations of James against it, the tobacco imported from Virginia came to a ready market....

Other crops neglected for tobacco planting

"Allured by the prospect of such a certain and quick return, every other species of industry was neglected. The land which ought to have been reserved for raising provisions, and even the streets of James Town, were planted with tobacco. Various regulations were framed to restrain this ill directed activity. But, from eagerness for present gain, the planters disregarded every admonition. The means of subsistence became so scanty, as forced them to renew their demands upon the Indians, who seeing no end of those exactions, their antipathy to the English name revived with additional rancour, and they began to form schemes of vengeance.... Meanwhile the colony, notwithstanding this error in its operations, and the cloud that was gathering over its head, continued to wear an aspect of prosperity....

The first women arrive in James Town 1619

"As few women had hitherto ventured to encounter the hardships which were unavoidable in an unknown and uncultivated country, most of the colonists, constrained to live single, considered themselves as no more than sojourners in a land to which they were not attached by the tender ties of a family and children. In order to induce them to settle there, the company took advantage of the apparent tranquillity in the country, to send out a considerable number of young women of humble birth indeed, but of unexceptionable character, and encouraged the planters, by premiums and immunities, to marry them. These new companions were received with such fondness, and many of them so comfortably established, as invited others to follow their example; and by degrees thoughtless adventurers, assuming the sentiments of virtuous citizens and of provident fathers of families, became solicitous about the prosperity of a country which they now considered as their own.

Adventurers assume the sentiments of citizens

The above excerpts are from William Robertson's "History of the Discovery and Settlement of America", Book IX, Harper & Bros. 1835 Edition

Introduction of African slavery by Dutch

"As the colonists began to form more extensive plans of industry, they were unexpectedly furnished with means of executing them with greater facility. A Dutch ship from the coast of Guinea, having sailed up James River, sold a part of her cargo of Negroes to the planters; and as that hardy race was found more capable of enduring fatigue under a sultry climate than Europeans, their number has been increased by continual importation; their aid seems now to be essential to the existence of the colony, and the greater part of field labour in Virginia is performed by servile hands.

First legislative assembly in America 1619

... "To Englishmen the summary and severe decisions of martial law, however tempered by the mildness of their governors, appeared intolerably oppressive; and they longed to recover the privileges to which they had been accustomed under the liberal form of government in their native country. In compliance with this spirit, Sir George Yeardly, in the year 1619 (June), called the first general assembly that was ever held in Virginia; and the numbers of the people were now so increased, and their settlements so dispersed, that eleven corporations appeared by their representatives in this convention, where they were permitted to assume legislative power, and to exercise the noblest functions of free men. The laws enacted in it seem neither to have been many nor of great importance; but the meeting was highly acceptable to the people, as they now beheld among themselves an image of the English constitution, which they reverenced as the most perfect model of free government.

Government of colony in imitation of Great Britain

"In order to render this resemblance more complete, and the rights of the planters more certain, the company issued a charter of ordinance (July 24), which gave a legal and permanent form to the government of the colony. The supreme legislative authority in Virginia, in imitation of that in Great Britain, was divided and lodged partly in the governor, who held the place of the sovereign; partly in a council of state named by the company, which possessed some of the distinctions, and exercised some of the functions belonging to the peerage; partly in a general council or assembly composed of the representatives of the people, in which were vested powers and privileges similar to those of the House of Commons.

A degree of local self-government

"In both these councils all questions were to be determined by the majority of voices, and a negative was reserved to the governor; but no law or ordinance, though approved of by all the three members of the legislature, was to be of force until it was ratified in England by a general court of the company, and returned under its seal. Thus the constitution of the colony was fixed, and the members of it are henceforth to be considered, not merely as servants of a commercial company dependent on the will and orders of their superior, but as free men and citizens.

The above excerpts are from William Robertson's "History of the Discovery and Settlement of America", Book IX, Harper & Bros. 1835 Edition

. . . "But while the colony continued to increase so fast that settlements were scattered, not only along the banks of James and York rivers, but began to extend to the Rapahannock, and even to the Potowmack, the English, relying on their own numbers, and deceived by this appearance of prosperity, lived in full security. They neither attended to the movements of the Indians, nor suspected their machinations;. . . The Indians, whom they commonly employed as hunters, were furnished with fire arms, and taught to use them with dexterity. They were permitted to frequent the habitations of the English at all hours, and received as innocent visitants whom there was no reason to dread. This inconsiderate security enabled the Indians to prepare for the execution of that plan of vengeance, which they meditated with all the deliberate forethought which is agreeable to their temper. . . .

Indian massacre 1622

"On the morning of the day consecrated to vengeance (March 22), each was at the place of rendezvous appointed, while the English were so little aware of the impending destruction that they received with unsuspicious hospitality several persons sent by Opechancanough, under pretext of delivering presents of venison and fruits, but in reality to observe their motions. . . . In one hour nearly a fourth part of the whole colony was cut off, almost without knowing by whose hands they fell. . . . In some settlements not a single Englishman escaped. Many persons of prime note in the colony, and among these several members of the council, were slain. The survivors, overwhelmed with grief, astonishment, and terror, abandoned all their remote settlements, and, crowding together for safety to James Town, did not occupy a territory of greater extent than had been planted soon after the arrival of their countrymen in Virginia. Confined within those narrow boundaries, they were less intent on schemes of industry than on thoughts of revenge. Every man took arms. A bloody war against the Indians commenced; and, bent on exterminating the whole race, neither old nor young were spared. . . . This atrocious deed, which the perpetrators laboured to represent as a necessary act of retaliation, was followed by some happy effects. It delivered the colony so entirely from any dread of the Indians, that its settlements began again to extend, and its industry to revive.

Settlers retaliate

"But unfortunately at this juncture the state of the company in England, in which the property of Virginia and the government of the colony settled there were vested, prevented it from seconding the efforts of the planters, by such a reinforcement of men, and such a supply of necessaries, as were requisite to replace what they had lost. The company was originally composed of many adventurers, and increased so fast by the junction of new members, allured

The above excerpts are from William Robertson's "History of the Discovery and Settlement of America", Book IX, Harper & Bros. 1835 Edition

General courts of London Company become a popular assembly

by the prospect of gain, or the desire of promoting a scheme of public utility, that its general courts formed a numerous assembly. The operation of every political principle and passion, that spread through the kingdom, was felt in those popular meetings, and influenced their decisions. As towards the close of Jame's reign more just and enlarged sentiments with respect to constitutional liberty were diffused among the people, they came to understand their rights better and to assert them with greater boldness....

"As the king did not often assemble the great council of the nation in parliament, the general courts of the company became a theatre on which popular orators displayed their talents; the proclamations of the crown, and acts of the privy council, with respect to the commerce and police of the colony, were canvassed there with freedom, and censured with severity, ill suited to the lofty ideas which James entertained of his own wisdom, and the extent of his prerogative. In order to check this growing spirit of discussion, the ministers employed all their address and influence to gain as many members of the company as might give them the direction of their deliberations. But so unsuccessful were they in this attempt, that every measure proposed by them was reprobated by a vast majority, and sometimes without any reason but because they were the proposers of it.

James undertakes to reform the London Company

"James, little favourable to the power of any popular assembly, and weary of contending with one over which he had laboured in vain to obtain an ascendant, began to entertain thoughts of dissolving the company, and new modelling its constitution. Pretexts, neither unplausible nor destitute of some foundation, seemed to justify this measure. The slow progress of the colony, the large sums of money expended, and great number of men who had perished in attempting to plant it, the late massacre by the Indians, and every disaster that had befallen the English from their first migration to America, were imputed solely to the inability of a numerous company to conduct an enterprise so complex and arduous....The present state of its affairs, as well as the wishes of the people, seemed to call for the interposition of the crown; and James, eager to display the superiority of his royal wisdom, in correcting those errors into which the company had been betrayed by inexperience in the arts of government, boldly undertook the work of reformation (May 9, 1623)....

"But here James and his ministers encountered a spirit of which they seem not to have been aware. They found the members of the company unwilling tamely to relinquish rights of franchises,

The above excerpts are from William Robertson's "History of the Discovery and Settlement of America", Book IX, Harper & Bros. 1835 Edition

embers of
ondon
ompany
sist and
ject the
ill of the
ng

conveyed to them with such legal formality, that upon faith in their validity they had expended considerable sums; and still more averse to the abolition of a popular form of government, in which every proprietor had a voice, in order to subject a colony, in which they were deeply interested, to the dominion of a small junto absolutely dependent on the crown. Neither promises nor threats could induce them to depart from these sentiments; and in a general court (Oct. 20), the king's proposal was almost unanimously rejected, and a resolution taken to defend to the utmost their chartered rights, if these should be called in question in any court of justice. James, highly offended at their presumption in daring to oppose his will, directed (Nov. 10) a writ of quo warranto to be issued against the company, that the validity of its charter might be tried in the Court of King's Bench;...

mes
ssolves
ndon
ompany
24

"The lawsuit in the King's Bench did not hang long in suspense. It terminated, as was usual in that reign, in a decision perfectly consonant to the wishes of the monarch. The charter was forfeited, the company was dissolved (June, 1624), and all the rights and privileges conferred upon it returned to the King, from whom they flowed....In the course of eighteen years ten different persons presided over the province as chief governors. No wonder that, under such administration, all the efforts to give vigour and stability to the colony should prove abortive, or produce only slender effects. These efforts, however, when estimated according to the ideas of that age, either with respect to commerce or to policy, were very considerable, and conducted with astonishing perseverance.

"Above a hundred and fifty thousand pounds were expended in this first attempt to plant an English colony in America; and more than nine thousand persons were sent out from the mother country to people this new settlement. At the dissolution of the company, the nation, in return for this waste of treasure and of people, did not receive from Virginia an annual importation of commodities exceeding twenty thousand pounds in value; and the colony was so far from having added strength to the state by an increase of population, that in the year one thousand six hundred and twenty-four, scarcely two thousand persons survived; a wretched remnant of the numerous emigrants who had flocked thither with sanguine expectations of a very different fate.

... "Soon after the final judgment in the Court of King's Bench against the company, James appointed a council of twelve persons (Aug. 26), to take the temporary direction of affairs in

The above excerpts are from William Robertson's "History of the Discovery and Settlement of America", Book IX, Harper & Bros. 1835 Edition

Virginia that he might have leisure to frame with deliberate consideration proper regulations for the permanent government of the colony. Pleased with such an opportunity of exercising his talents as a legislator, he began to turn his attention towards the subject; but death prevented him from completing his plan.

Charles I appoints Yardley governor with arbitrary powers to rule

"Charles I., on his accession to the throne (March 27, 1625), adopted all his father's maxims with respect to the colony in Virginia. He declared it to be a part of the empire annexed to the crown, and immediately subordinate to its jurisdiction: he conferred the title of Governor on Sir George Yardely, and appointed him, in conjunction with a council of twelve, and a secretary, to exercise supreme authority there, and enjoined them to conform, in every point, to such instructions as from time to time they might receive from him. From the tenor of the king's commission, as well as from the known spirit of his policy, it is apparent that he intended to invest every power of government, both legislative and executive, in the governor and council, without recourse to the representatives of the people, as possessing a right to enact laws for the community, or to impose taxes upon it.

All local self-government violated

"Yardely and his council, who seem to have been fit instruments for carrying this system of arbitrary rule into execution, did not fail to put such a construction on the words of their commission as was most favourable to their own jurisdiction. During a great part of Charles's reign, Virginia knew no other law than the will of the Sovereign. Statutes were published and taxes imposed, without once calling the representatives of the people to authorize them by their sanction. At the same time that the colonists were bereaved of their political rights, which they deemed essential to freemen and citizens, their private property was violently invaded. A proclamation was issued, by which, under pretexts equally absurd and frivolous, they were prohibited from selling tobacco to any person but certain commissioners appointed by the king to purchase it on his account; and they had the cruel mortification to behold the sovereign, who should have afforded them protection, engross all the profits of their industry, by seizing the only valuable commodity which they had to vend, and retaining the monopoly of it in his own hands....

"Colonists were bereaved of their political rights

"The murmurs and complaints which such a system of administration excited, were augmented by the rigour with which Sir John Harvey, who succeeded Yardely in the government of the colony, enforced every act of power (1627). Rapacious, unfeeling,

The above excerpts are from William Robertson's "History of the Discovery and Settlement of America", Book IX, Harper & Bros. 1835 Edition

olonists
ize Harvey
nd return
m to
ngland

and haughty, he added insolence to oppression, and neither regarded the sentiments nor listened to the remonstrances of the people under his command. The colonists, far from the seat of government, and overawed by authority derived from a royal commission, submitted long to his tyranny and exactions. Their patience was at last exhausted; and in a transport of popular rage and indignation, they seized their governor, and sent him a prisoner to England, accompanied by two of their number, whom they deputed to prefer their accusations against him to the king.

harles
fuses to
ear grievances
Virginians

"But this attempt to redress their own wrongs, by a proceeding so summary and violent as is hardly consistent with any idea of regular government, and can be justified only in cases of such urgent necessity as rarely occur in civil society, was altogether repugnant to every notion which Charles entertained with respect to the obedience due by subjects to their sovereign. To him the conduct of the colonists appeared to be not only a usurpation of his right to judge and to punish one of his own officers, by an open and audacious act of rebellion against his authority. Without deigning to admit their deputies into his presence, or to hear one article of their charge against Harvey, the king instantly sent him back to his former station, with an ample renewal of all the powers belonging to it. But though Charles deemed this vigorous step necessary in order to assert his own authority, and to testify his displeasure with those who had presumed to offer such an insult to it, he seems to have been so sensible of the grievances under which the colonists groaned, and of the chief source from which they flowed, that soon after (1639) he not only removed a governor so justly odious to them, but named as a successor Sir William Berkeley, a person far superior to Harvey in rank and abilities, and still more distinguished, by possessing all the popular virtues to which the other was a stranger.

erkeley
named
overnor
1639

"Under his government the colony in Virginia remained, with some short intervals of interruption, almost forty years; and to his mild and prudent administration its increase and prosperity are in a great measure to be ascribed. It was indebted, however, to the king himself for such a reform of its constitution and policy, as gave a different aspect to the colony, and animated all its operations with new spirit. Though the tenor of Sir William Berkeley's commission was the same with that of his predecessor, he received instructions under the great seal, by which he was empowered to declare, that in all its concerns, civil as well as ecclesiastical, the colony was to be governed according to the laws of England. . . .

The above excerpts are from William Robertson's "History of the Discovery and Settlement of America", Book IX, Harper Bros. 1835 Edition

Virginia remains loyal to monarchy

..."Even after monarchy was abolished, after one King had been beheaded, and another driven into exile, the authority of the crown continued to be acknowledged and revered in Virginia (1650). Irritated at this open defiance of its power, the parliament issued an ordinance, declaring, that as the settlement in Virginia had been made at the cost and by the people of England, it ought to be subordinate to and dependent upon the English commonwealth, and subject to such laws and regulations as are or shall be made in parliament; that, instead of this dutiful submission, the colonists had disclaimed the authority of the state, and audaciously rebelled against it; that on this account they were denounced notorious traitors, and not only all vessels belonging to natives of England, but those of foreign nations, were prohibited to enter their ports, or carry on any commerce with them.

The Commonwealth subdues royalist Virginia

"It was not the mode of that age to wage a war of words alone. The efforts of a high spirited government in asserting its own dignity were prompt and vigorous. A powerful squadron, with a considerable body of land forces, was despatched to reduce the Virginians to obedience. After compelling the colonies in Barbadoes and the other islands to submit to the commonwealth, the squadron entered the Bay of Chesapeak (1651). Berkeley, with more courage than prudence, took arms to oppose this formidable armament; but he could not long maintain such an unequal contest. His gallant resistance, however, procured favourable terms to the people under his government. A general indemnity for all past offences was granted; they acknowledged the authority of the commonwealth, and were admitted to a participation of all the rights enjoyed by citizens....

Commonwealth parliament prohibits and restricts trade of colonists

"Not satisfied with taking measures to subject the colonies, the commonwealth turned its attention towards the most effectual mode of retaining them in dependence on the parent state, and of securing to it the benefit of their increasing commerce. With this view the parliament framed two laws, one of which expressly prohibited all mercantile intercourse between the colonies and foreign states, and the other ordained that no production of Asia, Africa, or America, should be imported into the dominions of the commonwealth but in vessels belonging to English owners, or to the people of the colonies settled there, and navigated by an English commander, and by crews of which the greater part must be Englishmen....

"Under governors appointed by the commonwealth, or by Cromwell when he usurped the supreme power, Virginia remained almost nine years in perfect tranquillity. During that period,

The above excerpts are from William Robertson's "History of the Discovery and Settlement of America", Book IX, Harper & Bros. 1835 Edition

Under Cromwell adherents to monarchy settle in Virginia

many adherents to the royal party, and among these some gentlemen of good families, in order to avoid danger and oppression, to which they were exposed in England, or in hopes of repairing their ruined fortunes, resorted thither. Warmly attached to the cause for which they had fought and suffered, and animated with all the passions natural to men recently engaged in a fierce and long protracted civil war, they, by their intercourse with the colonists, confirmed them in principles of loyalty, and added to their impatience and indignation under the restraints imposed on their commerce by their new masters.

Virginia renounces Commonwealth and hoists standard of Charles II

"On the death of Matthews, the last governor named by Cromwell, the sentiments and inclination of the people, no longer under the control of authority, burst out with violence. They forced Sir William Berkeley to quit his retirement; they unanimously elected him governor of the colony: and as he refused to act under a usurped authority, they boldly erected the royal standard, and acknowledging Charles II. to be their lawful sovereign, proclaimed him with all his titles; and the Virginians long boasted, that as they were the last of the king's subjects who renounced their allegiance, they were the first who returned to their duty.

Parliament under Charles II extends oppressive acts instituted by Commonwealth

"Happily for the people of Virginia, a revolution in England, no less sudden than unexpected, seated Charles on the throne of his ancestors, and saved them from the severe chastisement to which their premature declaration in his favour must have exposed them. On receiving the first account of this event, the joy and exultation of the colony were universal and unbounded. These, however, were not of long continuance. Gracious but unproductive professions of esteem and good will were the only return made by Charles to loyalty and services which in their own estimation were so distinguished that no recompense was beyond what they might claim. If the king's neglect and ingratitude disappointed all the sanguine hopes which their vanity had founded on the merit of their past conduct, the spirit which influenced parliament in its commercial deliberations opened a prospect that alarmed them with respect to their future situation. In framing regulations for the encouragement of trade, which, during the convulsions of civil war, and amidst continual fluctuations in government, had met with such obstruction that it declined in every quarter; the House of Commons, instead of granting the colonies that relief which they expected from the restraints in their commerce imposed by the commonwealth and Cromwell, not only adopted all their ideas concerning this branch of legislation, but extended them further.

The above excerpts are from William Robertson's "History of the Discovery and Settlement of America", Book IX, Harper & Bros. 1835 Edition

Act of Navigation designed for monopoly of commerce

"This produced the act of navigation, the most important and memorable of any in the statute-book with respect to the history of English commerce. By it, besides several momentous articles foreign to the subject of this work, it was enacted, that no commodities should be imported into any settlement in Asia, Africa, or America, or exported from them, but in vessels of English or plantation built, whereof the master and three-fourths of the mariners shall be English subjects, under pain of forfeiting ship and goods; that none but natural born subjects, or such as have been naturalized, shall exercise the occupation of merchant or factor in any English settlement, under pain of forfeiting their goods and chattels; that no sugar, tobacco, cotton, wool, indigo, ginger, or woods used in dyeing, of the growth or manufacture of the colonies, shall be shipped from them to any other country but England;... Soon after (1663), the act of navigation was extended, and additional restraints were imposed, by a new law, which prohibited the importation of any European commodity into the colonies, but what was laden in England in vessels navigated and manned as the act of navigation required.... In prosecution of those favourite maxims, the English legislature proceeded a step further. As the act of navigation had left the people of the colonies at liberty to export the enumerated commodities from one plantation to another without paying any duty (1672), it subjected them to a tax equivalent to what was paid by the consumers of these commodities in England.

Virginia's appeals for relief ignored by Charles and Parliament

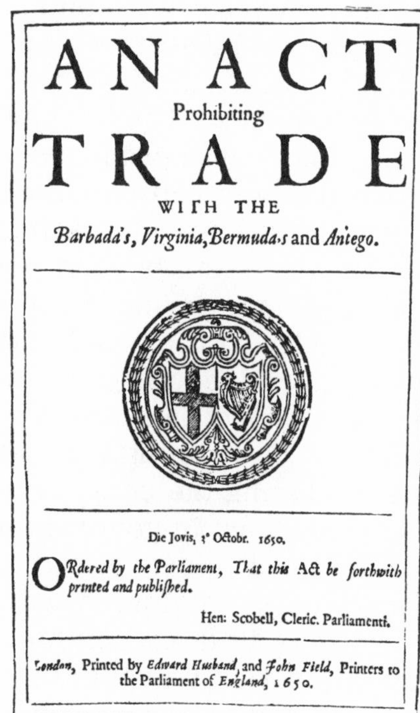

AN ACT
Prohibiting
TRADE
WITH THE
Barbada's, Virginia, Bermuda's and *Antego.*

Die Jovis, 3° Octobr. 1650.

ORdered by the Parliament, That this Act be forthwith printed and published.

Hen: Scobell, Cleric. Parliamenti.

London, Printed by *Edward Husband*, and *John Field*, Printers to the Parliament of *England*, 1650.

"By these successive regulations, the plan of securing to England a monopoly of the commerce with its colonies, and of shutting up every other channel into which it might be diverted, was perfected, and reduced into complete system...

"Hardly was the act of navigation known in Virginia, and its effects begun to be felt, when the colony remonstrated against it as a grievance, and petitioned earnestly for relief.... The Virginians, seeing no prospect of obtaining exemption from the act, set themselves to evade it; and found means, notwithstanding the vigilance with which they were watched,...

The above excerpts are from William Robertson's "History of the Discovery and Settlement of America", Book IX, Harper & Bros. 1835 Edition

Charles violates individual property rights in Virginia

"Charles had imprudently imitated the example of his father, by granting such large tracts of land in Virginia to several of his courtiers, as tended to unsettle the distribution of property in the country, and to render the title of the most ancient planters to their estates precarious and questionable. From those various causes, which in a greater or less degree affected every individual in the colony, the indignation of the people became general, and was worked up to such a pitch, that nothing was wanting to precipitate them into the most desperate acts but some leader qualified to unite and to direct their operations.

Nathaniel Bacon appears as leader of the indignant colonists

"Such a leader they found in Nathaniel Bacon, a colonel of militia, who, though he had been settled in Virginia only three years, had acquired, by popular manners, an insinuating address, and the consideration derived from having been regularly trained in England to the profession of law, such general esteem that he had been admitted into the council, and was regarded as one of the most respectable persons in the colony. Bacon was ambitious, eloquent, daring, and, prompted either by honest zeal to redress the public wrongs, or allured by hopes of raising himself to distinction and power, he mingled with the malecontents; and by his bold harangues and confident promises of removing all their grievances, he inflamed them almost to madness.

"Bacon's Rebellion"

"As the devastations committed by the Indians was the calamity most sensibly felt by the people, he accused the governor of having neglected the proper measures for repelling the invasions of the savages, and exhorted them to take arms in their own defence, and to exterminate that odious race. Great numbers assembled, and chose Bacon to be their general. He applied to the governor for a commission, confirming this election of the people, and offering to march instantly against the common enemy. Berkeley, accustomed by long possession of supreme command to high ideas of the respect due to his station, considered this tumultuary armament as an open insult to his authority, and suspected that, under specious appearances, Bacon concealed most dangerous designs. Unwilling, however, to give farther provocation to an incensed multitude by a direct refusal of what they demanded, he thought it prudent to negotiate in order to gain time; and it was not until he found all endeavours to soothe them ineffectual, that he issued a proclamation, requiring them in the king's name, under the pain of being denounced rebels, to disperse.

"But Bacon, sensible that he had now advanced so far as rendered it impossible to recede with honour or safety, instantly took the only resolution that remained in his situation. At the head of a

The above excerpts are from William Robertson's "History of the Discovery and Settlement of America", Book IX, Harper & Bros. 1835 Edition

Bacon forces commission from council to fight Indians

chosen body of his followers, he marched rapidly to James Town, and surrounding the house where the governor and council were assembled, demanded the commission for which he had formerly applied. Berkeley, with the proud indignant spirit of a cavalier, disdaining the requisitions of a rebel, peremptorily refused to comply, and calmly presented his naked breast to the weapons which were pointed against it. The council, however, foreseeing the fatal consequences of driving an enraged multitude, in whose power they were, to the last extremities of violence, prepared a commission constituting Bacon general of all the forces in Virginia, and by their entreaties prevailed on the governor to sign it.

Commission declared null and void

"Bacon with his troops retired in triumph. Hardly was the council delivered by his departure from the dread of present danger, when, by a transition not unusual in feeble minds, presumptuous boldness succeeded to excessive fear. The commission granted to Bacon was declared to be null, having been extorted by force; he was proclaimed a rebel, his followers were required to abandon his standard, and the militia ordered to arm, and to join the governor.

"Enraged at conduct which he branded with the name of base and treacherous, Bacon, instead of continuing his march towards the Indian country, instantly wheeled about, and advanced with all his forces to James Town....

James Town reduced to ashes

"Berkeley, meanwhile, having collected some forces, made inroads into different parts of the colony where Bacon's authority was recognized. Several sharp conflicts happened with various success. James Town was reduced to ashes, and the best cultivated districts in the province were laid waste, sometimes by one party and sometimes by the other. But it was not by his own exertions that the governor hoped to terminate the contest. He had early transmitted an account of the transactions in Virginia to the king, and demanded such a body of soldiers as would enable him to quell the insurgents whom he represented as so exasperated by the restraint imposed on their trade, that they were impatient to shake off all dependence on the parent state.

Charles II sends troops to suppress Virginia

"Charles, alarmed at a commotion no less dangerous than unexpected, and solicitous to maintain his authority over a colony the value of which was daily increasing and more fully understood, speedily despatched a small squadron with such a number of regular troops as Berkeley had required. Bacon and his followers received information of this armament, but were not intimidated at its approach. They boldly determined to oppose it with open

The above excerpts are from William Robertson's "History of the Discovery and Settlement of America", Book IX, Harper & Bros. 1835 Edition

force, and declared it to be consistent with their duty and allegiance, to treat all who should aid Sir William Berkeley as enemies, until they should have an opportunity of laying their grievances before their sovereign.

acon's ebellion erminated 577

"But while both parties prepared, with equal animosity, to involve their country in the horrors of civil war (1677), an event happened, which quieted the commotion almost as suddenly as it had been excited. Bacon, when ready to take the field, sickened and died.... Thus terminated an insurrection, which, in the annals of Virginia, is distinguished by the name of Bacon's rebellion....

he ppressive nd arbitrary le mained

"From that period to the Revolution in 1688, there is scarcely any memorable occurrence in the history of Virginia. A peace was concluded with the Indians. Under several successive governors, administration was carried on in the colony with the same arbitrary spirit that distinguished the latter years of Charles II. and the precipitate councils of James II. The Virginians, with a constitution which in form resembled that of England, enjoyed hardly any portion of the liberty which that admirable system of policy is framed to secure. They were deprived even of the last consolation of the oppressed, the power of complaining, by a law which, under severe penalties, prohibited them from speaking disrespectfully of the governor, or defaming, either by words or writing, the administration of the colony. Still, however, the laws restraining their commerce were felt as an intolerable grievance, and they nourished in secret a spirit of discontent, which, from the necessity of concealing it, acquired a greater degree of acrimony. But notwithstanding those unfavourable circumstances, the colony continued to increase.... "

The above excerpts are from William Robertson's "History of the Discovery and Settlement of America", Book IX, Harper & Bros. 1835 Edition

Capitol and Royal Governors Palace at Williamsburg

NEW ENGLAND COLONY

Plymouth 1620 - 1630

THE Pilgrims suffered, like their predecessors, from the prevailing unskillfulness in colony-planting. They had escaped from the horrors of the Mayflower, but how much better was the wild land than the wild sea; the rude, overcrowded forest cabins than the too populous ship? 'All things stared upon them with a weather beaten face,' says Bradford. The horrors of the first winter in Virginia were repeated; here, as at Jamestown, nearly all were ill at once, and nearly half of the people died before the coming of spring. The same system of partnership with mercenary shareholders or 'adventurers' in England that had brought disaster in Virginia was tried with similar results at Plymouth. and a similar attempt at communism in labor and supply was made, this time under the most favorable conditions, among a people conscientious and bound together by strong religious enthusiasm. It resulted, as such sinking of personal interest must ever result, in dissensions and insubordination, in unthrift and famine. The colony was saved from the prolonged misery that makes the early history of Virginia horrible by the wise head and strong hand of its leader. William Bradford, who had been chosen governor on the death of Carver, a few months after the arrival at Plymouth, had been a youth but eighteen years old when he fled with the rest of the Scrooby church to Holland. He was bred to husbandry and had inherited some property. In Holland he became a silk worker and on attaining his majority set up for himself in that trade. He was still a young man when first chosen governor of the little colony, and he ruled New Plymouth almost continuously till his death - that is, for about thirty-seven years. He was of a magnanimous temper, resolute but patient, devotedly religious, but neither intolerant nor austere. He had a genius for quaintly vivid expression in writing that marked him as a man endowed with the literary gift, which comes as Heaven pleases where one would least look for it.

Plymouth attempts Communism with same disastrous results as Jamestown

Wise and strong leadership of William Bradford

Collective farming source of suffering and want

"After two years of labor in common had brought the colony more than once to the verge of ruin, Bradford had the courage and wisdom to cut the knot he could not untie. During the scarce springtime of

The above excerpts are from Edward Eggleston's "The Beginners of a Nation" - 1896

1623, he assigned all the detached persons in the colony to live with families, and then temporarily divided the ancient Indian field on which the settlement had been made among the several families in proportion to their number, leaving every household to shift for itself or suffer want. 'Any general want or suffering hath not been among them since to this day.' he writes years afterward. The assignment was a revolutionary stroke, in violation of the contract with the shareholders, and contrary to their wishes. But Bradford saw that it was a life-and-death necessity to be rid of the pernicious system, even at the cost of cutting off all support from England. In his history he draws a very clear picture of the evils of communism as he had observed them.

"the pernicious system"

"Why should the historian linger thus over the story of this last surviving remnant of the 'Brownist'? Why have we dwelt upon the little settlement that was never very flourishing, that consisted at its best of only a few thousand peaceful and agricultural people, and that after seventy years was merged politically in its more vigorous neighbor the colony of Massachusetts Bay? Historical importance does not depend on population. Plymouth was the second step in the founding of a great nation. When Bradford and the other leaders had at last successfully extricated the little settlement from its economical difficulties, it became the sure forerunner of a greater Puritan migration. This tiny free state on the margin of a wilderness continent, like a distant glimmering pharos, showed the persecuted Puritans in England the fare-way to a harbor. Men who undertake a great enterprise rarely find their anticipations fulfilled; they are fortunate if their general aim is reached at last in any way. The Pilgrims had migrated, hoping to be 'stepping-stones to others,' as they phrased it. They thought that many like-minded in matters of religion would come to them out of England, but the Separatist movement had been worn out by persecution. There were few open dissenters left, and the Pilgrims, by their long exile, had lost all close relations with their own country. Among those that came to Plymouth from England were some whose coming tended to dilute the religious life and lower the moral standards of the colony. The fervor of the Pilgrims themselves abated something of its intensity in the preoccupations incident to pioneer life. The hope of expanding their religious organization by the rapid growth of the colony was not fulfilled; discontented Puritans were not eager to settle under the government of Separatists, and ten years after their migration the Plymouth colony contained little more than three hundred people.

James Town and Plymouth "The Two Original and Parent Colonies"

"None the less the hope of the Pilgrims was realized; they became stepping-stones to thousands of others. Captain John Smith laughed at the 'humorous ignorances' of these 'Brownist' settlers,

The above excerpts are from Edward Eggleston's "The Beginners of a Nation" - 1896

Plymouth colonists remained where others returned

but, humorous or not, ignorant or not, the 'Brownists' remained on the coast while other emigrants retreated. In spite of their terrible suffering none of the Pilgrims went back. This is the capital fact in their history. A new force had been introduced into colonization. Henceforth persecuted or discontented religionists, prompted by a motive vastly more strenuous and enduring than cupidity, were to bear the main brunt of breaking a way into the wilderness.

"Religion being the chief motive of their retreating into these parts" - Neal

"The first effect of the slender success at Plymouth was to stimulate speculative and merely adventurous migration. From 1607 until the arrival of the Pilgrims in 1620 no English colony had landed on the northern coast; but after the Pilgrims came, fish-drying and fur-buying stations began to appear on the banks of the Piscataqua and the coast eastward in 1622 and 1623. These tiny settlements were germs of New Hampshire and Maine, the only New England plantations begun without any admixture of religious motives. A commercial colony was tried in Massachusetts Bay as early as 1622, but it failed. There were other like attempts. In 1624 some men of Dorchester, headed by John White, the 'Patriarch' Puritan clergyman, sent out a colony to Cape Ann. The members of this company were to grow maize to supply fishing ships, and in the season the same men were to lend a hand on board the ships, which would thus be saved the necessity for carrying double crews. But this plausible scheme proved a case of seeking strawberries in the sea and red herrings in the wood. Farmers were but lubbers at codfishing, and salt-water fishermen were clumsy enough in the cornfield. Losses of several sorts forced the Dorchester Company to dissolve. Four members of their futile colony, encouraged by a message from White, remained on Cape Ann. Removing to the present site of Salem, they waited at the risk of their lives for the coming of a new colony from England.

The adventurer in New England

"Solitary adventurers of the sort known on nearly every frontier were presently to be found in several places. The scholarly recluse was represented by Blackstone, who had selected for his secluded abode a spot convenient to a spring of good water where the town of Boston was afterward planted; the inevitable Scotch adventurer was on an island in Boston Harbor; Samuel Maverick, a pattern of frontier hospitality and generosity, took up his abode on Noddle's Island; while the rollicking and scoffing libertine was found in Thomas Morton, who with some rebellious bond servants got possession of a fortified house in what is now Braintree. Here Morton welcomed renegade servants from Plymouth and elsewhere. He wrote ribald verses which he posted

The above excerpts are from Edward Eggleston's "The Beginners of a Nation" - 1896

on his Maypole, and devised Maydances in which the saturnine Indian women participated. He broke all the commandments with delight, carried on a profitable trade in selling firearms to the savages in defiance of royal proclamations, and wrought whatever other deviltry came within his reach, until his neighbors could no longer endure the proximity of so dangerous a firebrand. Little Captain Standish, whom Morton derisively dubbed 'Captain Shrimp, descended on this kingdom of misrule at last and broke up the perpetual carnival, sending Morton to England.

"The settlement of New England was thus beginning sporadically and slowly. If the Massachusetts Puritans had not come, these feeble and scattered plantations might have grown into colonies after a long time, as such beginnings did in New Hampshire and Maine, and later in North Carolina, but having no strong neighbor to support them, it is likely that they would all have been driven away or annihilated by some inevitable collision with the Indians. . . .

Charter granted Massachusetts Bay Colony 1628

"The evolution of the Massachusetts government may now be traced through its several stages. A company was formed, partly of Dorchester man, but chiefly of residents of London. This company secured a patent to lands in Massachusetts Bay from the Council for New England. . . . In March, 1628, they secured a liberal charter from the king, which gave them the right to establish in Massachusetts a government subordinate to the company. The plan was to settle a government in the form rendered familiar by that of the Virginia Company. . . .

Colonists foresee dangers with government of colony in England

Government is established in colony

'Winthrop and his coterie of gentlemen appear to have been dissatisfied with the prospect of living under a government directed from England, and thus subject to English stockholders and liable to interference from the court. . . . The annulling of the charter of the Virginia Company on frivolous pretexts had shown how easily the Massachusetts charter might meet the same fate in a reign far more devoted to arbitrary government than that of James and entirely hostile to Puritanism. . . . It was at this juncture probably that Cradock conceived his ingenious plan. . . . The meetings of the company might therefore be held in Massachusetts, where the puritanism of its proceedings would attract less attention. . . . the company and the colony would thus be merged into one, and the charter. . . would perhaps be beyond the reach of writs and judgments.

". . . The preamble states the object of this migration. It was not civil liberty, the end that political Puritans had most

The above excerpts are from Edward Eggleston's "The Beginners of a Nation" - 1896

Object of Puritan migration under Winthrop

in view, and certainly there is no hint of a desire for religious liberty. Even the conversion of the Indian is not uppermost in this solemn resolve. 'God's glory and the church's good' are the words used... The whole pledge is couched in language befitting men who feel themselves engaged in a religious enterprise of the highest importance... The next year the charter crossed the wide seas, and in 1630 a court of the company was held in the wilderness at Charlestown... From the point of view of our later age, the removal of the charter government to America is the event of chief importance in this migration of Winthrop's company. The ultimate effect of this brilliant stroke was so to modify a commercial corporation that it became a colonial government as independent as possible of control from England. By the admission of a large number of the colonists to be freemen - that is, to vote as stockholders in the affairs of the company, which was now the colony itself, and a little later by the development of a second chamber - the government became representative..."

Transformation by degrees into a small republic

The above excerpts are from Edward Eggleston's "The Beginners of a Nation" - 1896

CRADLE OF NEW ENGLAND

Scrooby

THIS devoted band (the Separatists) ordinarily met at Mr. Brewster's mansion 'on the Lord's-day which was a manor of the bishop's, and with great love he entertained them when they came, making provision for them, to his great charge, and continued to do so while they could stay in England'. Mr. Brewster was a gentlemen of fortune; he was educated at Cambridge, and was now living on his manorial estate at Scrooby, Nottinghamshire. Governor Bradford, who was originally one of the church, and whose birthplace and residence was at Austerfield in the vicinity, states distinctly, that Mr. Brewster's house was 'a manor of the bishop's'... The Brewsters were residents at Scrooby: the manor place which they occupied originally belonged to the Archbishops of York, and had been leased to Sir Samuel Sandys, son of Dr. Sandys the Archbishop, in 1586. The Brewster family were now tenants of Sir Samuel, and were occupants of the mansion of the Sandys. This fact serves both as an identification of the place, and as an explanation of the circumstance, that the Sandys took great interest, at a subsequent period, in promoting the settlement of the Pilgrims, under the direction of Mr. Brewster, on the shores of the Atlantic. Scrooby must henceforward be regarded as the cradle... Here the

The above excerpts are from "The Works of John Robinson"
Robert Ashton, 1851

choice and noble spirits, at the head of whom were Brewster and Bradford, first learned the lessons of truth and freedom. Here, under the faithful ministrations of the pastors, they were nourished and strengthened to that vigorous and manly fortitude which braved all dangers, and here too they acquired that moral and spiritual courage which enabled them to sacrifice their homes, property and friends, and expatriate themselves to distant lands, rather than abandon their principles and yield to the attempted usurpations on the liberty of their consciences."

The above excerpts are from "The Works of John Robinson"
Robert Ashton, 1851

NEW ENGLAND CULTURE

Background

THROUGHOUT the reign of James the First, it (the Puritan Party) controlled the House of Commons, composed chiefly of the landed gentry of the kingdom...

"The aggregate property of that Puritan House of Commons, was computed to be three times as great as that of the Lords. The statesmen of the first period of that Parliament which by and by dethroned Charles the First, had been bred in the luxury of the landed aristocracy of the realm...

"The supposition of any necessary connection between Puritanism and what is harsh and rude in taste and manners, will not even stand the test of an observation of the character of men who figured in its ranks, when the lines came to be most distinctly drawn."

The above excerpts are from "History of New England" - Palfrey

"Upon the whole, it has been computed that the four settlements of New England, viz. Plymouth, the Massachusetts Bay, Connecticut, and New Haven, all which were accomplished before the beginning of the civil wars, drained England of four or five hundred thousand pounds in money (a very great sum in those days); and if the persecution of the Puritans had continued twelve years longer, it is thought that a fourth part of the riches of the kingdom would have passed out of it through this channel."

The above excerpt is from the "History of the Puritans", Daniel Neal, 1731

THE PILGRIM WANTED INDIVIDUAL LIBERTY

Puritan aims:
Reformation of church and national governments by compulsion

Pilgrim aims:
Liberty of local self-government as natural right and non-compulsive

IN the old world on the other side of the ocean, the Puritan was a Nationalist, believing that a Christian nation is a Christian church, and demanding that the Church of England should be thoroughly reformed; while the Pilgrim was a Separatist, not only from the Anglican Prayer-book and Queen Elizabeth's episcopacy, but from all national churches. Between them there was sharp contention... The Pilgrim wanted liberty for himself and his wife and little ones, and for his brethren, to walk with God in a Christian life as the rules and motives of such a life were revealed to him from God's Word. For that he went into exile; for that he crossed the ocean; for that he made his home in a wilderness. The Puritan's idea was not liberty, but right government in church and state - such government as should not only permit him, but also compel other men to walk in the right way."

The above excerpts are from Leonard Bacon's "Genesis of the New England Churches" - 1874

THE SIGNIFICANCE OF PILGRIM ENDURANCE

NOTHING can be trivial which relates to the voyage of the 'Mayflower' or the first four years' experience of the Colony.

"There is importance in every event which in any degree affected the question whether the settlement should be maintained or abandoned; for reading between the lines of that question there is seen within it another, as to whether posterity should behold an Anglo-Saxon state on the American continent. Had Plymouth been deserted by the Pilgrim Fathers in 1621 - 22, Massachusetts Bay would have remained desolate, and even Virginia would doubtless have been abandoned. Then, before new colonization could be organized, France would have made good her claim by pushing down our Atlantic coast until she met Spain ascending from the south, - unless, indeed, Holland had retained her hold at the centre... Such were some of the momentous issues that were largely decided by the apparently little things which make up the Pilgrim history... Sir Thomas Hutchinson, whose tastes would not have led him to an undue estimation of the uncourtly and unchartered settlers at Plymouth, thus spoke of them in his History: 'These were the founders of the Colony at New Plymouth. The settlement of this Colony occasioned the settlement of Massachusetts Bay, which was the source of all the other Colonies in New England. Virginia was in a dying state, and seemed to revive and flourish from the example of New England'."

The above excerpts are from John A. Goodwin's "The Pilgrim Republic" - 1888

GOD'S children are like stars that shine brightest in the darkest skies; like the chamomile, which, the more it is trodden down, the faster it spreads and grows.

"The glories of Christianity in England are to be traced in the sufferings of confessors and martyrs in the sixteenth and seventeenth centuries; and it was under the influence of Christian principles, imbibed at this very period, that the Mayflower brought over the band of Pilgrims to Plymouth... We should never forget that the prison, the scaffold, and the stake were stages in the march of civil and religious liberty which our forefathers had to travel, in order that we might attain our present liberty...

"Before our children remove their religious connections... before they leave the old paths of God's Word... before they barter their birthright for a mess of pottage - let us place in their hands this chronicle of the glorious days of the suffering Churches, and let them know that they are the sons of the men 'of whom the world was not worthy', and whose sufferings for conscience' sake are here monumentally recorded."

- John Overton Choules, August 12, 1843
Preface to the 1844 reprint of Neal's "History of the Puritans", 1731

THEN I proclaimed a fast there, at the river of Ahava, that we might afflict ourselves before our God, to seek of him a right way for us, and for our little ones, and for all our substance. For I was ashamed to require of the king a band of soldiers and horsemen to help us against the enemy in the way: because we had spoken unto the king, saying, The hand of our God is upon all them for good that seek him; but his power and his wrath is against all them that forsake him."

- Ezra 8:21-22

ROBINSON'S FAREWELL COUNSEL

"The arrangements for the departure of the emigrants being completed, the whole congregation met for humiliation and prayer on the 21st of July, 1620, when Mr. Robinson preached, with deep emotion, from Ezra 8:21-22. The close of his discourse is thus given by Mr. Winslow: 'We are now ere long to part asunder, and the Lord knoweth whether ever he should live to see our faces again. But whether the Lord had appointed it or not, he charged us before God and his blessed angels, to follow him no further than he followed Christ; and if God should reveal any thing to us by any other instrument of his, to be as ready to receive it, as ever we were to receive any truth by his ministry; for he was very confident the Lord had more truth and light yet to break forth out of his holy word. He took occasion also miserably to bewail the state and condition of the Reformed churches who were come to a period in religion, and would go no further than the instruments of their reformation. As for example, the Lutherans, they could not be drawn to go beyond what Luther saw; for whatever part of God's will he had further imparted and revealed to Calvin, they will rather die than embrace it. And so also, saith he, you see the Calvinists, they stick where he left them, a misery much to be lamented; for though they were precious shining lights in their times, yet God had not revealed his whole will to them; and were they now living, saith he, they would be as ready and willing to embrace further light, as that they had received. Here also he put us in mind of our church covenant, at least that part of it whereby we promise and covenant with God and one another to receive whatsoever light or truth shall be made known to us from his written Word; but withal exhorted us to take heed what we received for truth, and well to examine and compare it and weigh it with other Scriptures of truth before we received it. For saith he, it is not possible the Christian world should come so lately out of such thick antichristian darkness, and that full perfection of knowledge should break forth at once."

The above excerpts are from William B. Sprague's "Annals of the American Pulpit" - 1857

HISTORY "OF PLIMOTH PLANTATION"

WILLIAM BRADFORD

AND first of ye occasion and indusments ther unto; the which that I may truly unfould, I must begine at ye very roote & rise of ye same. The which I shall endevor to manefest in a plaine stile, with singuler regard unto ye simple trueth in all things, at least as near as my slender judgmente can attaine the same...

Scrooby

"But that I may come more near my intendmente; when as by the travell & diligence of some godly & zealous preachers, & Gods blessing on their labours, as in other places of ye land, so in ye North parts, many became inlightened by ye word of God, and had their ignorance & sins discovered unto them, and begane by his grace to reforme their lives, and make conscience of their ways, the worke of God was no sooner manifest in them, but presently they were both scoffed and scorned by ye prophane multitude, and ye ministers urged with ye yoak of subscription, or els must be silenced; and ye poore people were so vexed with apparators, & pursuants, & ye comissarie courts, as truly their affliction was not smale; which, notwithstanding, they bore sundrie years with much patience, till they were occasioned (by ye continuance & encrease of these troubls, and other means which ye Lord raised up in those days) to see further into things by the light of ye word of God... So many therfore of these proffessors as saw ye evill of these things, in thes parts, and whose harts ye Lord had touched wth heavenly Zeale for his trueth, they shooke of this yoake of antichristian bondage, and as ye Lords free people, joyned them selves (by a covenant of the Lord) into a church estate, in ye felowship of ye gospell, to walke in all his wayes, make known or to be made known unto them, according to their best endeavours, whatsoever it should cost them, the Lord assisting them. And that it cost them something this ensewing historie will declare...

"Of their departure into Holland and their troubls ther aboute, with some of ye many difficulties they found and mete withall.

"Being thus constrained to leave their native soyle and countrie, their lands & livings, and all their freinds & famillier acquaintance,

The above excerpts are from the original manuscript, written 1647, (1901 Edition)

it was much, and thought marvelous by many. But to goe into a countrie they knew not (but hearsay), wher they must learne a new language, and get their livings they knew not how, it being a dear place, & subjecte to ye misseries of warr, it was by many thought an adventure almost desperate, a case intolerable, & a misserie worse then death. Espetially seeing they were not aquainted with trads nor traffique, (by which yt countrie doth subsiste,) but had only been used to a plaine countrie life, & ye inocente trade of husbandrey. But these things did not dismay them (though they did some times trouble them) for their desires were sett on ye ways of God, & to injoye his ordinances; but they rested on his providence, & knew whom they had beleeved. Yet this was not all, for though they could not stay, yet were ye not suffered to goe, but ye ports & havens were shut against them, so as they were faine to seeke secrete means of conveance, & to bribe & fee ye mariners, & give exterordinarie rates for their passages. And yet were they often times betrayed (many of them), and both they & their goods intercepted & surprised, and therby put to great trouble & charge, of which I will give an instance or tow, & omitte the rest.

"Ther was a large companie of them purposed to get passage at Boston in Lincoln-shire, and for that end had hired a shipe wholy to them selves, & made agreement with the maister to be ready at a certaine day, and take them and their goods in, at a conveniente place, wher they accordingly would all attende in readines. So after long waiting, & large expences, though he kepte not day with them, yet he came at length & tooke them in, in ye night. But when he had them & their goods abord, he betrayed them, haveing before hand complotted with ye serchers & other officers so to doe; who tooke them, and put them into open boats,

Betrayal

& ther rifled & ransaked them, searching them to their shirts for money, yea even ye women furder then became modestie; and then caried them back into ye towne, & made them a spectackle & wonder to ye multitude, which came flocking on all sids to behould them. Being thus first, by the chatchpoule officers, rifled, & stripte of their money, books, and much other goods, they were presented to ye magestrates, and messengers sente to informe ye lords of ye Counsell of them; and so they were comited to ward. Indeed ye magestrats used them courteously, and shewed them what favour they could; but could not deliver them, till order came from ye Counsell table. But ye issue was that after a months imprisonmente, ye greatest parte were dismiste, & sent to ye places from whence they came; but 7. of ye principall were still kept in prison, and bound over to ye Assises.

The above excerpts are from the original manuscript, written 1647, (1901 Edition)

"The nexte spring after, ther was another attempte made by some of these & others, to get over at an other place. And it so fell out, that they light of a Dutchman at Hull, having a ship of his owne belonging to Zealand; they made agreemente with him, and acquainted him with their condition, hoping to find more faithfullnes in him, then in ye former of their owne nation. He bad them not fear, for he would doe well enough. He was by appointment to take them in betweene Grimsbe & Hull, wher was a large comone a good way distante from any towne. Now aganst the prefixed time, the women & children, with ye goods, were sent to ye place in a small barke, which they had hired for yt end; and ye men were to meete them by land. But it so fell out, that they were ther a day before ye shipe came, & ye sea being rough, and ye women very sicke, prevailed with ye seamen to put into a creeke hardby, wher they lay on ground at lowwater. The nexte morning ye shipe came, but they were fast, & could not stir till aboute noone. In ye mean time, ye shipe maister, perceiving how ye matter was, sente his boate to be getting ye men abord whom he saw ready, walking aboute ye shore. But after ye first boat full was gott abord, & she was ready to goe for more, the mr espied a greate company, both horse & foote, with bills, & gunes, & other weapons; for ye countrie was raised to take them. Ye Dutchman seeing yt, swore his countries oath, 'sacremente,' and having ye wind faire, waiged his Ancor, hoysed sayles, & away. But ye poore men which were gott abord, were in great distress for their wives and children, which they saw thus to be taken, and were left destitute of their helps; and them selves also, not having a cloath to shifte them with, more then they had on their baks, & some scarce a peney aboute them, all they had being abord ye barke. It drew tears from their eyes, and any thing they had they would have given to have been a shore againe; but all in vaine, ther was no remedy, they must thus sadly part. And afterward endured a fearfull storme at sea, being 14. days or more before yey arived at their porte, in 7. wherof they neither saw son, moone, nor stars, & were driven near ye coast of Norway; the mariners them selves often despairing of life; and once with shriks & cries gave over all, as if ye ship had been foundred in ye sea, & they sinking without recoverie. But when mans hope & helpe wholy failed, ye Lords power & mercie appeared in ther recoverie; for ye ship rose againe, & gave ye mariners courage againe to manage her. And if modestie woud suffer me, I might declare with what fervente prayres they cried unto ye Lord in this great distres, (espetialy some of them,) even without any great distraction, when ye water rane into their mouthes & ears; & the mariners cried out,

Next Attempt

Fearful Storm

The above excerpts are from the original manuscript, written 1647, (1901 Edition)

"We sinke, we sinke; they cried (if not with mirakelous, yet with a great hight or degree of devine faith), Yet Lord thou canst save, yet Lord thou canst save; with shuch other expressions as I will forbeare. Upon which ye ship did not only recover, but shortly after ye violence of ye storme begane to abate, and ye Lord filed their afflicted minds with shuch comforts as every one canot understand, and in ye end brought them to their desired Haven, wher ye people came flockeing admiring their deliverance, the storme having ben so longe & sore, in which much hurt had been don, as ye masters freinds related unto him in their congrattulations.

"But to returne to ye others wher we left. The rest of ye men yt were in greatest danger, made shift to escape away before ye troope could surprise them; those only staying yt best might, to be assistante unto ye women. But pitifull it was to see ye heavie case of these poore women in this distress; what weeping & crying on every side, some for their husbands, that were caried away in ye ship as is before related; others not knowing what should become of them, & their litle ones; others againe melted in teares, seeing their poore litle ones hanging aboute them, crying for feare, and quaking with could. Being thus aprehended, they were hurried from one place to another, and from one justice to another, till in ye ende they knew not what to doe with them; for to imprison so many women & innocent children for no other cause (many of them) but that they must goe with their husbands, semed to be unreasonable and all would crie out of them; and to send them home againe was as difficult, for they aledged, as ye trueth was, they had no homes to goe to, for they had either sould, or otherwise disposed of their houses & livings. To be shorte, after they had been thus turmolyed a good while, and conveyed from one constable to another, they were glad to be ridd of them in ye end upon any termes; for all were wearied & tired with them. Though in ye mean time they (poore soules) indured miserie enough; and thus in ye end necessitie forste a way for them.

Plight of Women and Children

"But yt I be not tedious in these things, I will omitte ye rest, though I might relate many other notable passages and troubles which they endured & underwente in these their wanderings & travells both at land & sea; but I hast to other things. Yet I may not omitte ye fruite that came hearby, for by these so publick troubls, in so many eminente places, their cause became famouss, & occasioned many to looke into ye same; and their godly cariage & Christian behaviour was such as left a deep impression in the minds of many. And though some few shrunk

Cause Became Famous

The above excerpts are from the original manuscript, written 1647, (1901 Edition)

at these first conflicts & sharp beginings, (as it was no marvell,) yet many more came on with fresh courage, & greatly animated others. And in ye end, notwithstanding all these stormes of oppossition, they all gatt over at length, some at one time & some at an other, and some in one place & some in an other, and mette togeather againe according to their desires, with no small rejoycing.

"Of their setling in Holand, & their maner of living, & entertainmente ther.

Faith and Patience Conquer Grim Poverty

"Being now come into ye Low Countries, they saw many goodly & fortified cities, strongly walled and garded with troopes of armed men. Also they heard a strange & uncouth language, and beheld ye differente maners & customes of ye people, with their strange fashons and attires; all so farre differing from yt of their plaine countrie villages (wherin they were bred, & had so longe lived) as it seemed they were come into a new world. But these were not ye things they much looked on, or long tooke up their thoughts; for they had other work in hand, & an other kind of warr to wage & maintaine. For though they saw faire & bewtifull cities, flowing with abundance of all sorts of welth & riches, yet it was not longe before they saw the grime & grisly face of povertie coming upon them like an armed man, with whom they must bukle & incounter, and from whom they could not flye; but they were armed with faith & patience against him, and all his encounters; and though they were sometimes foyled, yet by Gods assistance they prevailed and got ye victorie.

One Year Stay in Amsterdam

"Now when Mr. Robinson, Mr. Brewster, & other principall members were come over, (for they were of ye last, & stayed to help ye weakest over before them,) such things were thought on as were necessarie for their setling and best ordering of ye church affairs. And when they had lived at Amsterdam aboute a year, Mr. Robinson, their pastor, and some others of best discerning, seeing how Mr. John Smith and his companie was allready fallen in to contention with ye church yt was ther before them, & no means they could use would doe any good to cure ye same, and also that ye flames of contention were like to breake out in yt anciente church it selfe (as affterwards lamentably came to pass); which things they prudently foreseeing, thought it was best to remove, before they were any way engaged with ye same; though they well knew it would be much to ye prejudice of their outward estats, both at presente & in licklyhood in ye future; as indeed it proved to be.

The above excerpts are from the original manuscript, written 1647 (1901 Edition)

Their remoovall to Leyden.

Remove to Leyden

"For these & some other reasons they removed to Leyden, a fair & bewtifull citie, and of a sweete situation, but made more famous by ye universitie wherwith it is adorned, in which of late had been so many learned men. But wanting that traffike by sea which Amsterdam injoyes, it was not so beneficiall for their outward means of living & estats. But being now hear pitchet they fell to such trads & imployments as they best could; valewing peace & their spirituall comforte above any other riches whatsoever. And at lenght they came to raise a competente & comforteable living, but with hard and continuall labor.

Pilgrim Character Seen in Their Formative Period

"Being thus setled (after many difficulties) they continued many years in a comfortable condition, injoying much sweete & delightefull societie & spirituall comforte togeather in ye wayes of God, under ye able ministrie, and prudente governmente of Mr. John Robinson, & Mr. William Brewster, who was an assistante unto him in ye place of an Elder, unto which he was now called & chosen by the church. So as they grew in knowledge & other gifts & graces of ye spirite of God, & lived togeather in peace, & love, and holines; and many came unto them from diverse parts of England, so as they grew a great congregation. And if at any time any differences arose, or offences broak out (as it cannot be, but some time ther will, even amongst ye best of men) they were ever so mete with, and nipt in ye head betims, or otherwise so well composed, as still love, peace, and communion was continued; or els ye church purged of those that were incurable & incorrigible, when, after much patience used, no other means would serve, which seldom came to pass. Yea such was ye mutuall love, & reciprocall respecte that this worthy man had to his flocke, and his flocke to him, that it might be said of them as it once was of yt famouse Emperour Marcus Aurelious, and ye people of Rome, that it was hard to judge wheather he delighted more in haveing shuch a people, or they in haveing such a pastor. His love was greate towards them, and his care was all ways bente for their best good, both for soule and body; for besids his singuler abilities in devine things (wherin he excelled), he was also very able to give directions in civill affaires, and to foresee dangers & inconveniences; by wch means he was very helpfull to their outward estats, & so was every way as a commone father unto them....

"But seeing it is not my purpose to treat of ye severall passages that befell this people whilst they thus lived in ye Low Countries, (which might worthily require a large treatise

The above excerpts are from the original manuscript, written 1647, (1901 Edition)

of it selfe,) but to make way to shew ye begining of this plantation, which is that I aime at; yet because some of their adversaries did, upon ye rumore of their removall, cast out slanders against them, as if that state had been wearie of them, & had rather driven them out (as ye heathen historians did faine of Moyses & ye Isralits when they went out of Egipte), then yt it was their owne free choyse & motion, I will therfore mention a perticuler or too to shew ye contrary, and ye good acceptation they had in ye place wher they lived. And first though many of them weer poore, yet ther was none so poore, but if they were known to be of yt congregation, the Dutch (either bakers or others) would trust them in any reasonable matter when yey wanted money. Because they had found by experience how carfull they were to keep their word, and saw them so painfull & dilligente in their callings; yea, they would strive to gett their custome, and to imploy them above others, in their worke, for their honestie & diligence....

The Dutch Valued Pilgrim Honesty and Diligence

"Showing ye reasons & causes of their remooval.

"After they had lived in this citie about some 11. or 12. years, (which is ye more observable being ye whole time of yt famose truce between that state & ye Spaniards,) and sundrie of them were taken away by death, & many others begane to be well striken in years, the grave mistris Experience haveing taught them many things, those prudent governours with sundrie of ye sagest members begane both deeply to apprehend their present dangers, & wisely to foresee ye future, & thinke of timly remedy. In ye agitation of their thoughts, and much discours of things hear aboute, at length they began to incline to this conclusion, of remoovall to some other place. Not out of any newfanglednes, or other such like giddie humor, by which men are oftentimes transported to their great hurt & danger, but for sundrie weightie & solid reasons; some of ye cheefe of which I will hear breefly touch. And first, they saw & found by experience the hardnes of ye place & countrie to be such, as few in comparison would come to them, and fewer that would bide it out, and continew with them. For many yt came to them, and many more yt desired to be with them, could not endure yt great labor and hard fare, with other inconveniences which they underwent & were contented with. But though they loved their persons, approved their cause, and honoured their sufferings, yet they left them as it weer weeping, as Orpah did her mother in law Naomie, or as those Romans did Cato in Utica, who desired to be excused & borne with, though they could not all be Catoes. For many,

Hardships in Holland Discouraging to the Pilgrims

The above excerpts are from the original manuscript, written 1647, (1901 Edition)

though they desired to injoye ye ordinances of God in their puritie, and ye libertie of the gospell with them, yet, alass, they admitted of bondage, with danger of conscience, rather then to indure these hardships; yea, some preferred & chose ye prisons in England, rather then this libertie in Holland, with these afflictions. But it was thought that if a better and easier place of living could be had, it would draw many, & take away these discouragments. Yea, their pastor would often say, that many of those wo both wrate & preached now against them, if they were in a place wher they might have libertie and live comfortably, they would then practise as they did.

"They saw that though ye people generally bore all these difficulties very cherfully, & with a resolute courage, being in ye best & strength of their years, yet old age began to steale on many of them, (and their great & continuall labours, with other crosses and sorrows, hastened it before ye time,) so as it was not only probably thought, but apparently seen, that within a few years more they would be in danger to scatter, by necessities pressing them, or sinke under their burdens, or both. And therfore according to ye devine proverb, yt a wise man seeth ye plague when it cometh, & hideth him selfe, Pro. 22. 3., so they like skillfull & beaten souldiers were fearfull either to be intrapped or surrounded by their enimies, so as they should neither be able to fight nor flie; and therfor thought it better to dislodge betimes to some place of better advantage & less danger, if any such could be found. Thirdly; as necessitie was a taskmaster over them, so they were forced to be such, not only to their servants, but in a sorte, to their dearest chilldren; the which as it did not a litle wound ye tender harts of many a loving father & mother, so it produced likwise sundrie sad & sorowful effects. For many of their children, that were of best dispositions and gracious inclinations, haveing lernde to bear ye yoake in their youth, and willing to bear parte of their parents burden, were, often times, so oppressed with their hevie labours, that though their minds were free and willing, yet their bodies bowed under ye weight of ye same, and became decreped in their early youth; the vigor of nature being consumed in ye very budd as it were. But that which was more lamentable, and of all sorowes most heavie to be borne, was that many of their children, by these occasions, and ye great licentiousnes of youth in yt countrie, and ye manifold temptations of the place, were drawne away by evill examples into extravagante & dangerous courses, getting ye raines off their neks, & departing from their parents. Some became souldiers, others tooke upon them farr viages by

Trials Take Toll of Health and Vigor

The above excerpts are from the original manuscript, written 1647, (1901 Edition)

sea, and other some worse courses, tending to dissolutnes & the danger of their soules, to ye great greefe of their parents and dishonour of God. So that they saw their posteritie would be in danger to degenerate & be corrupted.

Pilgrim Aspires to Propogate the Gospel

"Lastly, (and which was not least,) a great hope & inward zeall they had of laying some good foundation, or at least to make some way therunto, for ye propagating & advancing ye gospell of ye kingdom of Christ in those remote parts of ye world; yea, though they should be but even as stepping-stones unto others for ye performing of so great a work.

"These, & some other like reasons, moved them to undertake this resolution of their removall; the which they afterward prosecuted with so great difficulties, as by the sequell will appeare.

Savage Dangers, Lack of Sustenance Threaten Pilgrim in Any New Land

"The place they had thoughts on was some of those vast & unpeopled countries of America, which are frutfull & fitt for habitation, being devoyd of all civill inhabitants, wher ther are only salvage & brutish men, which range up and downe, litle otherwise then ye wild beasts of the same. This proposition being made publike and coming to ye scaning of all, it raised many variable opinions amongst men, and caused many fears & doubts amongst them selves.... For ther they should be liable to famine, and nakednes, & ye wante, in a maner, of all things. The chang of aire, diate, & drinking of water, would infecte their bodies with sore sicknesses, and greevous diseases. And also those which should escape or overcome these difficulties, should yett be in continuall danger of ye salvage people, who are cruell, barbarous, & most trecherous, being most furious in their rage, and merciles wher they overcome; not being contente only to kill, & take away life, but delight to tormente men in ye most bloodie maner that may be;.... It was furder objected, that it would require greater sumes of money to furnish such a voiage, and to fitt them with necessaries, then their consumed estats would amounte too; and yett they must as well looke to be seconded with supplies, as presently to be trasported. Also many presidents of ill success, & lamentable misseries befalne others in the like designes, were easie to be found, and not forgotten to be aledged; besids their owne experience, in their former troubles & hardships in their removall into Holand, and how hard a thing it was for them to live in that strange place, though it was a nieghbour countrie, & a civill and rich comone wealth.

"It was answered, that all great & honourable actions are accompanied with great difficulties, and must be both enterprised and

The above excerpts are from the original manuscript, written 1647, (1901 Edition)

overcome with answerable courages. It was granted ye dangers were great, but not desperate; the difficulties were many, but not invincible. For though their were many of them likly, yet they were not cartaine; it might be sundrie of ye things feared might never befale; others by providente care & ye use of good means, might in a great measure be prevented; and all of them, through ye help of God, by fortitude and patience, might either be borne, or overcome. True it was, that such attempts were not to be made and undertaken without good ground & reason; not rashly or lightly as many have done for curiositie or hope of gaine, &c. But their condition was not ordinarie; their ends were good & honourable; their calling lawfull, & urgente; and therfore they might expecte ye blessing of God in their proceding. Yea, though they should loose their lives in this action, yet might they have comforte in the same, and their endeavors would be honourable. They lived hear but as men in exile, & in a poore condition; and as great miseries might possibly befale them in this place, for ye 12. years of truce were now out, & ther was nothing but beating of drumes, and preparing for warr, the events wherof are allway uncertaine. Ye Spaniard might prove as cruell as the salvages of America, and ye famine and pestelence as sore hear as ther, & their libertie less to looke out for remedie. After many other perticuler things answered & aledged on both sids, it was fully concluded by ye major parte, to put this designe in execution, and to prosecute it by the best means they could.

Dangers Great - Not Desperate; Difficulties many - Not Invincible

"Shewing what means they used for preparation to this waightie vioag.

"And first after thir humble praiers unto God for his direction & assistance, & a generall conferrence held hear aboute, they consulted what perticuler place to pitch upon, & prepare for....

"On ye other hand, for Virginia it was objected, that if they lived among ye English wch wear ther planted, or so near them as to be under their government, they should be in as great danger to be troubled and persecuted for the cause of religion, as if they lived in England, and it might be worse. And if they lived too farr of, they should neither have succour, nor defence from them.

"But at length ye conclusion was, to live as a distincte body by them selves, under ye generall Government of Virginia; and by their freinds to sue to his majestie that he would be pleased to

The above excerpts are from the original manuscript, written 1647 , (1901 Edition)

grant them freedome of Religion; and yt this might be obtained, they wear putt in good hope by some great persons, of good ranke & qualitie, that were made their freinds. Whereupon 2. were chosen & sent in to England (at ye charge of ye rest) to sollicite this matter, who found the Virginia Company very desirous to have them goe thither, and willing to grante them a patent, with as ample priviliges as they had, or could grant to any, and to give them the best furderance they could. And some of ye cheefe of yt company douted not to obtaine their suite of ye king for liberty in Religion, and to have it confirmed under ye kings broad seale, according to their desires. But it prooved a harder peece of worke then they tooke it for;....

Pilgrims Doubt Freedom of Religion in Virginia

Seek Guarantee of Religious Liberty

"Seeing therfore the course was probable, they must rest herein on Gods providence, as they had done in other things.

"Upon this resolution, other messengers were dispatched, to end with ye Virginia Company as well as they could. And to procure a patent with as good and ample conditions as they might by any good means obtaine. As also to treate and conclude with such merchants and other freinds as had manifested their forwardnes to provoke too and adventure in this vioage. For which end they had instructions given them upon what conditions they should proceed with them, or els to conclude nothing without further advice....

Request Patent of Merchants in England

"Conscerning ye agreements and artickles between them, and such marchants & others as adventured moneys; with other things falling out aboute making their provissions.

"....Aboute this time also they had heard, both by Mr. Weston and others, yt sundrie Honbl: Lords had obtained a large grante from ye king, for ye more northerly parts of that countrie, derived out of ye Virginia patente, and wholy secluded from their Governmente, and to be called by another name, viz. New-England. Unto which Mr. Weston, and ye cheefe of them, begane to incline it was best for them to goe, as for other reasons, so cheefly for ye hope of present profite to be made by ye fishing that was found in yt countrie....

New England Offered for Settlement

"But now another difficultie arose, for Mr. Weston and some other that were for this course, either for their better advantage or rather for ye drawing on of others, as they pretended, would have some of those conditions altered yt were first agreed on at Leyden.

The above excerpts are from the original manuscript, written 1647, (1901 Edition)

Pilgrims' Agents Forced to Accept Changes in First Commitment

To which ye 2. agents sent from Leyden (or at least one of them who is most charged with it) did consente; seeing els yt all was like to be dashte, & ye opportunitie lost, and yt they which had put of their estats and paid in their moneys were in hazard to be undon. They presumed to conclude with ye marchants on those termes, in some things contrary to their order & comission, and without giving them notice of ye same; yea, it was conceled least it should make any furder delay; which was ye cause afterward of much trouble & contention.

"It will be meete I here inserte these conditions, which are as foloweth.

> "1. The adventurers & planters doe agree, that every person that goeth being aged 16. years & upward, be rated at 10li., and ten pounds to be accounted a single share.
>
> '2. That he that goeth in person, and furnisheth him selfe out with 10li. either in money or other provissions, be accounted as haveing 20li. in stock, and in ye divission shall receive a double share.
>
> "3. The persons transported & ye adventurers shall continue their joynt stock & partnership together, ye space of 7. years, (excepte some unexpected impedimente doe cause ye whole company to agree otherwise,) during which time, all profits & benifits that are gott by trade, traffick, trucking, working, fishing, or any other means of any person or persons, remaine still in ye comone stock until ye division.
>
> "4. That at their coming ther, they chose out such a number of fitt persons, as may furnish their ships and boats for fishing upon ye sea; imploying the rest in their severall faculties upon ye land; as building houses, tilling, and planting ye ground, & makeing shuch comodities as shall be most usefull for ye collonie.
>
> "5. That at ye end of ye 7. years, ye capitall & profits, viz. the houses, lands, goods and chatles, be equally divided betwixte ye adventurers, and planters; wch done, every man shall be free from other of them of any debt or detrimente concerning this adventure.

Conditions

The above excerpts are from the original manuscript, written 1647, (1901 Edition)

"6. Whosoever cometh to ye colonie herafter, or putteth any into ye stock, shall at the ende of ye 7. years be alowed proportionably to ye time of his so doing.

"7. He that shall carie his wife & children, or servants, shall be alowed for everie person now aged 16. years & upward, a single share in ye division, or if he provid them necessaries, a duble share, or if they be between 10. year old and 16., then 2. of them to be reconed for a person, both in trasportation and division.

"8. That such children as now goe, & are under ye age of ten years, have noe other shar in ye devision, but 50. acers of unmanured land.

"9. That such persons as die before ye 7. years be expired, their executors to have their parte or sharr at ye devision, proportionably to ye time of their life in ye collonie.

"10. That all such persons as are of this collonie, are to have their meate, drink, apparell, and all provissions out of ye comon stock & goods of ye said collonie.

hange
n
greement

"The cheefe & principall differences betwene these & the former conditions, stood in those 2. points; that ye houses, & lands improved, espetialy gardens & home lotts should remaine undevided wholy to ye planters at ye 7. years end. 2ly, yt they should have had 2. days in a weeke for their owne private imploymente, for ye more comforte of them selves and their families, espetialy such as had families....

"I have bene ye larger in these things, and so shall crave leave in some like passages following, (thoug in other things I shal labour to be more contracte,) that their children may see with what difficulties their fathers wrastled in going throug these things in their first beginings, and how God brought them along notwithstanding all their weaknesses & infirmities. As allso that some use may be made hereof in after times by others in such like waightie imployments; and herewith I will end this chapter.

The above excerpts are from the original manuscript, written 1647, (1901 Edition)

"Of their departure from Leyden, and other things ther aboute, with their arivall at South hamton, were they all mete togeather, and tooke in ther provissions.

"At length, after much travell and these debats, all things were got ready and provided. A smale ship was bought, & fitted in Holand, which was intended as to serve to help to transport them, so to stay in ye cuntrie and atend upon fishing and shuch other affairs as might be for ye good & benefite of ye colonie when they came ther. Another was hired at London, of burden about 9. score; and all other things gott in readines. So being ready to departe, they had a day of solleme humiliation, their pastor taking his texte from Ezra 8. 21. 'And ther at ye river, by Ahava, I proclaimed a fast, that we might humble ourselves before our God, and seeke of him a right way for us, and for our children, and for all our substance.' Upon which he spente a good parte of ye day very profitably, and suitable to their presente occasion....

Preparation for Voyage

"At their parting Mr. Robinson write a leter to ye whole company, which though it hath already bene printed, yet I thought good here likwise to inserte it;....

Letter to the Pilgrims from John Robinson

"Lovinge Christian friends, I doe hartily & in ye Lord salute you all, as being they with whom I am presente in my best affection, and most ernest longings after you, though I be constrained for a while to be bodily absente from you....And though I doubt not but in your godly wisdoms, you both foresee & resolve upon yt which concerneth your presente state & condition, both severally & joyntly, yet have I thought it but my duty to add some furder spurr of provocation unto them, who rune allready, if not because you need it, yet because I owe it in love & dutie. And first, as we are daly to renew our repentance with our God, espetially for our sines known, and generally for our unknowne trespasses, so doth ye Lord call us in a singuler maner upon occasions of shuch difficultie & danger as lieth upon you, to a both more narrow search & carefull reformation of your ways in his sight; least he, calling to remembrance our sines forgotten by us or unrepented of, take advantage against us, & in judgmente leave us for ye same to be swalowed up in one danger or other; wheras, on the contrary, sine being

The above excerpts are from the original manuscript, written 1647, (1901 Edition)

taken away by ernest repentance & ye pardon therof from ye Lord sealed up unto a mans conscience by his spirite, great shall be his securitie and peace in all dangers, sweete his comforts in all distresses, with hapie deliverance from all evill, whether in life or in death.

"Now next after this heavenly peace with God & our owne consciences, we are carefully to provide for peace with all men what in us lieth, espetially with our associats, & for yt watchfullnes must be had, that we neither at all in our selves doe give, no nor easily take offence being given by others. Woe be unto ye world for offences, for though it be necessarie (considering ye malice of Satan & mans corruption) that offences come, yet woe unto ye man or woman either by whom ye offence cometh, saith Christ, Mat. 18. 7. And if offences in ye unseasonable use of things in them selves indifferent, be more to be feared then death itselfe, as ye Apostle teacheth, 1. Cor. 9. 15. How much more in things simply evill, in which neither honour of God nor love of man is thought worthy to be regarded. Neither yet is it sufficiente yt we keepe our selves by ye grace of God from giveing offence, exepte withall we be armed against ye taking of them when they be given by others. For how unperfect & lame is ye work of grace in yt person, who wants charritie to cover a multitude of offences, as ye scriptures speake. Neither are you to be exhorted to this grace only upon ye comone grounds of Christianitie, which are, that persons ready to take offence, either wante charitie, to cover offences, of wisdome duly to waigh humane frailtie; or lastly, are grosse, though close hipocrites, as Christ our Lord teacheth, Mat. 7. 1, 2, 3, as indeed in my owne experience, few or none have bene found which sooner give offence, then shuch as easily take it; neither have they ever proved sould & profitable members in societies, which have nurished this touchey humor. But besids these, ther are diverse motives provoking you above others to great care & conscience this way: As first, you are many of you strangers, as to ye persons, so to ye infirmities one of another, & so stand in neede of more watchfullnes this way, least when shuch things fall out in men & women as you suspected not, you be inordinatly affected with them; which doth require at your hands much wisdome & charitie for ye covering & preventing of incident offences that way. And lastly, your intended course of civill comunitie will minister continuall occasion of

Relation with Others

The above excerpts are from the original manuscript, written 1647, (1901 Edition)

offence, & will be as fuell for that fire, excepte you dilligently quench it with brotherly forbearance. And if taking of offence causlesly or easilie at mens doings be so carefuly to be aboyded, how much more heed is to be taken yt we take not offence at God him selfe, which yet we certainly doe so ofte as we doe murmure at his providence in our crosses, or beare impatiently shuch afflictions as wherwith he pleaseth to visite us. Store up therfore patience against ye evill day, without which we take offence at ye Lord him selfe in his holy & just works.

Need of Self Discipline

"A 4. thing ther is carfully to be provided for, to witte, that with your comone imploymentes you joyne comone affections truly bente upon ye generall good, avoyding as a deadly plague of your both comone & spetiall comfort all retirednes of minde for proper advantage, and all singularly affected any maner of way; let every man represe in him selfe & ye whol body in each person, as so many rebels against ye comone good, all private respects of mens selves, not sorting with ye generall conveniencie. And as men are carfull not to have a new house shaken with any violence before it be well setled & ye parts firmly knite, so be you, I beseech you, brethren, much more carfull, yt the house of God which you are, and are to be, be not shaken with unnecessarie novelties or other oppositions at ye first setling therof.

Civil Affairs

"Lastly, wheras you are become a body politik, using amongst your selves civill governmente, and are not furnished with any persons of spetiall eminencie above ye rest, to be chosen by you into office of government, let your wisdome & godlines appeare, not only in chusing shuch persons as doe entirely love and will promote ye comone good, but also in yeelding unto them all due honour & obedience in their lawfull administrations; not behoulding in them ye ordinarinesse of their persons, but Gods ordinance for your good, not being like ye foolish multitud who more honour ye gay coate, then either ye vertuous minde of ye man, or glorious ordinance of ye Lord. But you know better things, & that ye image of ye Lords power & authoritie which ye magistrate beareth, is honourable, in how meane persons soever. And this dutie you both may ye more willingly and ought ye more conscionably to performe, because you are at least for ye present to have only them for your ordinarie governours, which your selves shall make choyse of for that worke.

The above excerpts are from the original manuscript, written 1647, (1901 Edition)

"Sundrie other things of importance I could put you in minde of, and of those before mentioned, in more words, but I will not so farr wrong your godly minds as to thinke you heedless of these things, ther being also diverce among you so well able to admonish both them selves & others of what concerneth them. These few things therfore, & ye same in few words, I doe ernestly comend unto your care & conscience, joyning therwith my daily incessante prayers unto ye Lord, yt he who hath made ye heavens & ye earth, ye sea and all rivers of waters, and whose providence is over all his workes, espetially over all his dear children for good, would so guide & gard you in your wayes, as inwardly by his Spirite, so outwardly by ye hand of his power, as yt both you & we also, for & with you, may have after matter of praising his name all ye days of your and our lives. Fare you well in him in whom you trust, and in whom I rest.

"An unfained wellwiller of your hapie
success in this hopefull voyage,

John Robinson."

"This letter, though large, yet being so frutfull in it selfe, and suitable to their occation, I thought meete to inserte in this place.

"All things being now ready, & every bussines dispatched, the company was caled togeather, and this letter read amongst them, which had good acceptation with all, and after fruit with many. Then they ordered & distributed their company for either shipe, as they conceived for ye best. And chose a Govr & 2. or 3. assistants for each shipe, to order ye people by ye way, and see to ye dispossing of there provissions, and shuch like affairs. All which was not only with ye liking of ye maisters of ye ships, but according to their desires. Which being done, they sett sayle from thence aboute ye 5. of August;...."

"Of their vioage, & how they passed ye sea, and of their safe arrivall at Cape Codd.

"....After they had injoyed faire winds and weather for a season, they were incountred many times with crosse winds, and mette with many feirce stormes, with which ye shipe was shroundly shaken, and her upper works made very leakie; and one of the maine beames

The above excerpts are from the original manuscript, written 1647, (1901 Edition)

in ye midd ships was bowed & craked, which put them in some fear that ye shipe could not be able to performe ye vioage. So some of ye cheefe of ye company, perceiveing ye mariners to feare ye suf- fisiencie of ye shipe, as appeared by their mutterings, they entred into serious consulltation with ye mr. & other officers of ye ship, to consider in time of ye danger; and rather to returne then to cast them selves into a desperate & inevitable perill. And truly ther was great distraction & differance of opinion amongst ye mariners them selves; faine would they doe what could be done for their wages sake, (being now halfe the seas over,) and on ye other hand they were loath to hazard their lives too desperatly. But in ex- amening of all opinions, the mr. & others affirmed they knew ye ship to be stronge & firme under water; and for the buckling of ye maine beame, ther was a great iron scrue ye passengers brought out of Holland, which would raise ye beame into his place; ye which being done, the carpenter & mr. affirmed that with a post put under it, set firme in ye lower deck, & otherways bounde, he would make it sufficiente. And as for ye decks & uper workes they would calke them as well as they could, and though with ye workeing of ye ship they would not longe keepe stanch, yet ther would otherwise be no great danger, if they did not overpress her with sails. So they comited them selves to ye will of God, & resolved to proseede. In sundrie of these stormes the winds were so feirce, & ye seas so high, as they could not beare a knote of saile, but were forced to hull, for diverce days togither.....But to omite other things, (that I may be breefe,) after longe beating at sea they fell with that land which is called Cape Cod; the which being made & certainly knowne to be it, they were not a litle joyfull....

Perils of Sea Voyage

"But hear I cannot but stay and make a pause, and stand half amased at this poore peoples presente condition; and so I thinke will the reader too, when he well considers ye same. Being thus passed ye vast ocean, and a sea of troubles before in their preparation (as may be remembred by yt which wente before), they had now no freinds to wellcome them, nor inns to entertaine or refresh their weatherbeaten bodys, no houses or much less townes to repaire too, to seeke for succoure. It is recorded in scripture as a mercie to ye apostle & his shipwraked company, yt the barbarians shewed them no smale kindnes in refreshing them, but these savage bar- barians, when they mette with them (as after will appeare) were readier to fill their sids full of arrows then otherwise. And for ye season it was winter, and they that know ye winters of yt cun- trie know them to be sharp & violent, & subjecte to cruell & feirce stormes, deangerous to travill to known places, much more to serch an unknown coast. Besids, what could they see but a hidious

Landing in a Desolate Wilderness in Winter

The above excerpts are from the original manuscript, written 1647, (1901 Edition)

& desolate wildernes, full of wild beasts & wild men? and what multituds ther might be of them they knew not. Nether could they, as it were, goe up to ye tope of Pisgah, to vew from this willdernes a more goodly cuntrie to feed their hops; for which way soever they turnd their eys (save upward to ye heavens) they could have litle solace or content in respecte of any outward objects. For sumer being done, all things stand upon them with a wetherbeaten face; and ye whole countrie, full of woods & thickets, represented a wild & savage heiw. If they looked behind them, ther was ye mighty ocean which they had passed, and was now as a maine barr & goulfe to seperate them from all ye civill parts of ye world. If it be said they had a ship to sucour them, it is trew; but what heard they daly from ye mr. & company? but yt with speede they should looke out a place with their shallop, wher they would be at some near distance; for ye season was shuch as he would not stirr from thence till a safe harbor was discovered by them wher they would be, and he might goe without danger; and that victells consumed apace, but he must & would keepe sufficient for them selves & their returne. Yea, it was muttered by some, that if they gott not a place in time, they would turne them & their goods ashore & leave them. Let it also be considred what weake hopes of supply & succoure they left behinde them, yt might bear up their minds in this sade condition and trialls they were under; and they could not but be very smale. It is true, indeed, ye affections & love of their brethren at Leyden was cordiall & entire towards them, but they had litle power to help them, or them selves; and how ye case stode betweene them & ye marchants at their coming away, hath allready been declared. What could now sustaine them but ye spirite of God & his grace? May not & ought not the children of these fathers rightly say: Ourfaithers were Englishmen which came over this great ocean, and were ready to perish in this willdernes; but they cried unto ye Lord, and he heard their voyce, and looked on their adversitie, &c. Let them therfore praise ye Lord, because he is good, & his mercies endure for ever. Yea, let them which have been redeemed of ye Lord, shew how he hath delivered them from ye hand of ye oppressour. When they wandered in ye deserte willdernes out of ye way, and found no citie to dwell in, both hungrie, & thirstie, their sowle was overwhelmed in them. Let them confess before ye Lord his loving kindnes, and his wonderfull works before ye sons of men.

"Showing how they sought out a place of habitation, and what befell them theraboute.

The above excerpts are from the original manuscript, written 1647, (1901 Edition)

"Being thus arrived at Cap-Cod ye 11. of November, and necessitie calling them to looke out a place for habitation, (as well as the maisters & mariners importunitie,) they having brought a large shalop with them out of England, stowed in quarters in ye ship, they now gott her out & sett their carpenters to worke to trime her up; but being much brused & shatered in ye shipe wth foule weather, they saw she would be longe in mending....

The 2. Booke.

"The rest of this History (if God give me life, & opportunitie) I shall, for brevitis sake, handle by way of annalls, noteing only the heads of principall things, and passages as they fell in order of time, and may seeme to be profitable to know, or to make use of. And this may be as ye 2. Booke.

Mutineers "Strangers" not Pilgrims

"I shall a litle returne backe and begine with a combination made by them before they came ashore, being ye first foundation of their govermente in this place; occasioned partly by ye discontented & mutinous speeches that some of the strangers amongst them had let fall from them in ye ship - That when they came a shore they would use their owne libertie; for none had power to comand them, the patente they had being for Virginia, and not for New-england, which belonged to an other Goverment, with which ye Virginia Company had nothing to doe. And partly that shuch an acte by them done (this their condition considered) might be as firme as any patent, and in some respects more sure. The forme was as followeth.

The Mayflower Compact

"In ye name of God, Amen. We whose names are underwriten, the loyall subjects of our dread soveraigne Lord, King James, by ye grace of God, of Great Britaine, Franc, & Ireland king, defender of ye faith, &c., haveing undertaken, for ye glorie of God, and advancemente of ye Christian faith, and honour of our king & countrie, a voyage to plant ye first colonie in ye Northerne parts of Virginia, doe by these presents solemnly & mutualy in ye presence of God, and one of another, covenant & combine our selves togeather into a civill body politick, for our better ordering & preservation & furtherance of ye ends aforesaid; and by vertue hearof to enacte, constitute, and frame such just & equall lawes, ordinances, acts, constitutions, & offices, from time to time, as shall be thought most meete & convenient for ye generall good of ye Colonie, unto which we promise all due

The above excerpts are from the original manuscript, written 1647, (1901 Edition)

> submission and obedience. In witnes wherof we have hereunder subscribed our names at Cap-Codd ye 11. of November, in ye year of ye raigne of our soveraigne lord, King James, of England, France, & Ireland ye eighteenth, and of Scotland ye fiftie fourth. Ano:Dom. 1620.

Government Formed and Officers Elected

"After this they chose, or rather confirmed, Mr. John Carver (a man godly & well approved amongst them) their Governour for that year. And after they had provided a place for their goods, or comone store, (which were long in unlading for want of boats, foulnes of winter weather, and sicknes of diverce,) and begune some small cottages for their habitation, as time would admitte, they mette and consulted of lawes & orders, both for their civill & military Govermente, as ye necessitie of their condition did require, still adding therunto as urgent occasion in severall times, and as cases did require.

Half of Colony Perish

"In these hard & difficulte beginings they found some discontents & murmurings arise amongst some, and mutinous speeches & carriags in other; but they were soone quelled & overcome by ye wisdome, patience, and just & equall carrage of things by ye Govr and better part, wch clave faithfully togeather in ye maine. But that which was most sadd & lamentable was, that in 2. or 3. moneths time halfe of their company dyed, espetialy in Jan: & February, being ye depth of winter, and wanting houses & other comforts; being infected with ye scurvie & other diseases, which this long vioage & their inacomodate condition had brought upon them; so as ther dyed some times 2. or 3. of a day, in ye foresaid time; that of 100. & odd persons, scarce 50. remained. And of these in ye time of most distres, ther was but 6. or 7. sound persons, who, to their great comendations be it spoken, spared no pains, night nor day, but with abundance of toyle and hazard of their owne health, fetched them woode, made them fires, drest them meat, made their beads, washed their lothsome cloaths, cloathed & uncloathed them; in a word, did all ye homly & necessarie offices for them wch dainty & quesie stomacks cannot endure to hear named; and all this willingly & cherfully, without any grudging in ye least, shewing herein their true love unto their freinds & bretheren. A rare example & worthy to be remembred. Tow of these 7. were Mr. William Brewster, ther reverend Elder, & Myles Standish, ther Captein & military comander, unto whom my selfe, & many others, were much beholden in our low & sicke condition. And yet the Lord so upheld these persons, as in this generall calamity they were not at all infected either with sicknes, or lamnes. And what I have said of these, I may say of many others who dyed in this generall vissitation, & others

Unselfish Assistance to Needy

Self-Reliant Leaders

The above excerpts are from the original manuscript, written 1647, (1901 Edition)

yet living, that whilst they had health, yea, or any strength continuing, they were not wanting to any that had need of them. And I doute not but their recompence is with ye Lord....

Establish Friendly Relations with Indians

"All this while ye Indians came skulking about them, and would sometimes show them selves aloofe of, but when any aproached near them, they would rune away. And once they stoale away their tools wher they had been at worke, & were gone to diner. But about ye 16. of March a certaine Indian came bouldly amongst them, and spoke to them in broken English, which they could well understand, but marvelled at it. At length they understood by discourse with him, that he was not of these parts, but belonged to ye eastrene parts, wher some English-ships came to fhish, with whom he was aquainted, & could name sundrie of them by their names, amongst whom he had gott his language. He became profitable to them in aquainting them with many things concerning ye state of ye cuntry in ye east-parts wher he lived, which was afterwards profitable unto them; as also of ye people hear, of their names, number, & strength; of their situation & distance from this place, and who was cheefe amongst them. His name was Samaset; he tould them also of another Indian whos name was Squanto, a native of this place, who had been in England & could speake better English then him selfe. Being, after some time of entertainmente & gifts, dismist, a while after he came againe, & 5. more with him, & they brought againe all ye tooles that were stolen away before, and made way for ye coming of their great Sachem, called Massasoyt; who, about 4. or 5. days after, came with the cheefe of his freinds & other attendance, with the aforesaid Squanto. With whom, after frendly entertainment, & some gifts given him, they made a peace with him (which hath now continued this 24. years) in these terms.

Indian Speaks English Language

Massasoyt and Squanto

"1. That neither he nor any of his, should injurie or doe hurte to any of their peopl.

"2. That if any of his did any hurte to any of theirs, he should send ye offender, that they might punish him.

Pilgrim & Indian Compact Governs Relations

"3. That if any thing were taken away from any of theirs, he should cause it to be restored; and they should doe ye like to his.

"4. If any did unjustly warr against him, they would aide him; if any did warr against them, he should aide them.

"5. He should send to his neighbours confederats, to certifie them of this, that they might not wrong them, but might be likewise comprised in ye conditions of peace.

The above excerpts are from the original manuscript, written 1647, (1901 Edition)

"6. That when ther men came to them, they should leave their bows & arrows behind them....

".... The spring now approaching, it pleased God the mortalitie begane to cease amongst them, and ye sick and lame recovered apace, which put as it were new life into them; though they had borne their sadd affliction with much patience & contentednes, as I thinke any people could doe. But it was ye Lord which upheld them, and had beforehand prepared them; many having long borne ye yoake, yea from their youth. Many other smaler maters I omite, sundrie of them having been allready published in a Jurnall made by one of ye company; and some other passages of jurneys and relations allredy published, to which I referr those that are willing to know them more perticulerly. And being now come to ye 25. of March I shall begine ye year 1621.

Unshakeable Faith in God

"They now begane to dispatch ye ship away which brought them over, which lay tille aboute this time, or ye begining of Aprill....

"Afterwards they (as many as were able) began to plant ther corne, in which servise Squanto stood them in great stead, showing them both ye maner how to set it, and after how to dress & tend it. Also he tould them excepte they gott fish & set with it (in these old grounds) it would come to nothing, and he showed them yt in ye midle of Aprill they should have store enough come up ye brooke, by which they begane to build, and taught them how to take it, and wher to get other provissions necessary for them; all which they found true by triall & experience. Some English seed they sew, as wheat & pease, but it came not to good, eather by ye badnes of ye seed, or latenes of ye season, or both, or some other defecte....

Squanto Aids Pilgrims

"After this, ye 18. of Sepembr: they sente out ther shalop to the Massachusets, with 10. men, and Squanto for their guid and interpreter, to discover and veiw that bay, and trade with ye natives; the which they performed, and found kind entertainement. The people were much affraid of ye Tarentins, a people to ye eastward which used to come in harvest time and take away their corne, & many times kill their persons. They returned in saftie, and brought home a good quanty of beaver, and made reporte of ye place, wishing they had been ther seated; (but it seems ye Lord, who assignes to all men ye bounds of their habitations, had apoynted it for an other use). And thus they found ye Lord to be with them in all their ways, and to blesse their outgoings & incomings, for which let his holy name have ye praise for ever, to all posteritie.

Exploring Neighborhood

The above excerpts are from the original manuscript, written 1647, (1901 Edition)

"They begane now to gather in ye small harvest they had, and to fitte up their houses and dwellings against winter, being all well recovered in health & strenght, and had all things in good plenty; for as some were thus imployed in affairs abroad, others were excersised in fishing, aboute codd, & bass, & other fish, of which yey tooke good store, of which every family had their portion. All ye somer ther was no wante. And now begane to come in store of foule, as winter aproached, of which this place did abound when they came first (but afterward decreased by degrees). And besids water foule, ther was great store of wild Turkies, of which they tooke many, besids venison, &c. Besids they had aboute a peck a meale a weeke to a person. or now since harvest, Indean corne to yt proportion. Which made many afterwards write so largly of their plenty hear to their freinds in England, which were not fained, but true reports.

Promising Harvest

"In Novembr, about yt time twelfe month that them selves came, ther came in a small ship to them unexpected or loked for, in which came Mr. Cushman (so much spoken of before) and with him 35. persons to remaine & live in ye plantation; which did not a litle rejoyce them.... So they were all landed; but ther was not so much as bisket-cake or any other victialls for them, neither had they any beding, but some sory things they had in their cabins, nor pot, nor pan, to drese any meate in; nor overmany cloaths, for many of them had brusht away their coats & cloaks at Plimoth as they came. But ther was sent over some burching-lane suits in ye ship, out of which they were supplied. The plantation was glad of this addition of strenght, but could have wished that many of them had been of beter condition, and all of them beter furnished with provissions; but yt could not now be helpte.

Ship Arrives with 35 Persons

New Arrivals Without Provisions

"In this ship Mr. Weston sent a large leter to Mr. Carver, ye late Gover, now deseased, full of complaints & expostulations aboute former passagess at Hampton; and ye keeping ye shipe so long in ye country, and returning her without lading, &c., which for brevitie I omite....

"This ship (caled ye Fortune) was speedily dispatcht away, being laden with good clapbord as full as she could stowe, and 2. hoggsheads of beaver and otter skins, which they gott with a few trifling comodities brought with them at first, being alltogeather unprovided for trade; neither was ther any amongst them that ever saw a beaver skin till they came hear, and were informed by Squanto. The fraight was estimated to be worth near 500li. Mr. Cushman returned backe also with this ship, for so Mr. Weston & ye rest

Pilgrims Ship Clapboard-Beaver and other Skins to England

The above excerpts are from the original manuscript, written 1647, (1901 Edition)

had apoynted him, for their better information. And he doubted not, nor them selves neither, but they should have a speedy supply; considering allso how by Mr. Cushmans perswation, and letters received from Leyden, wherin they willed them so to doe, they yeelded to ye afforesaid conditions, and subscribed them with their hands. But it proved other wise, for Mr. Weston, who had made yt large promise in his leter, (as is before noted,) that if all ye rest should fall of, yet he would never quit ye bussines, but stick to them, if they yeelded to ye conditions, and sente some lading in ye ship; and of this Mr. Cushman was confident, and confirmed ye same from his mouth, & serious protestations to him selfe before he came. But all proved but wind, for he was ye first and only man that forsooke them, and that before he so much as heard of ye returne of this ship, or knew what was done; (so vaine is ye confidence in man.)....

Vinter
ood
ationed

"After ye departure of this ship, (which stayed not above 14. days,) the Gover & his assistante haveing disposed these late comers into severall families, as yey best could, tooke an exacte accounte of all their provissions in store, and proportioned ye same to ye number of persons, and found that it would not hould out above 6. months at halfe alowance, and hardly that. And they could not well give less this winter time till fish came in againe. So they were presently put to half alowance, one as well as an other, which begane to be hard, but they bore it patiently under hope of supply....

More
ersons
rrive
Vithout
rovisions

"Now in a maner their provissions were wholy spent, and they looked hard for supply, but none came. But about ye later end of May, they spied a boat at sea, which at first they thought had beene some French-man; but it proved a shalop which came from a ship which Mr. Weston & an other had set out a fishing, at a place called Damarins-cove, 40. leagues to ye eastward of them, wher were yt year many more ships come a fishing. This boat brought 7. passengers and some letters, but no vitails, nor any hope of any. Some part of which I shall set downe....

"Sundry other things I pass over, being tedious & impertinent.

n Extreme
Iunger they
'urn to their
eligion for
omfort

"All this was but could comfort to fill their hungrie bellies, and a slender performance of his former late promiss; and as litle did it either fill or warme them, as those ye Apostle James spake of, by him before mentioned. And well might it make them remember what ye psalmist saith, Psa. 118. 8. 'It is better to trust in the Lord, then to have confidence in man.' And Psa. 146. 'Put not you trust in princes' (much less in ye marchants) 'nor in ye sone of man,

The above excerpts are from the original manuscript, written 1647, (1901 Edition)

for ther is no help in them. v. 5. 'Blesed is he that hath ye God of Jacob for his help, whose hope is in ye Lord his God.' And as they were now fayled of suply by him and others in this their greatest neede and wants, which was caused by him and ye rest, who put so great a company of men upon them, as ye former company were, without any food, and came at shuch a time as they must live almost a whole year before any could be raised, excepte they had sente some; so, upon ye pointe they never had any supply of vitales more afterwards (but what the Lord gave them otherwise); for all ye company sent at any time was allways too short for those people yt came with it....

Reliance on Help from England Again Fails

"Thus all ther hops in regard of Mr. Weston were layed in ye dust, and all his promised helpe turned into an empttie advice, which they apprehended was nether lawfull nor profitable for them to follow. And they were not only thus left destitute of help in their extreme wants, haveing neither vitails, nor any thing to trade with, but others prepared & ready to glean up what ye cuntrie might have afforded for their releefe. As for those harsh censures & susspitions intimated in ye former and following leters, they desired to judg as charitably and wisly of them as they could, waighing them in ye ballance of love and reason; and though they (in parte) came from godly & loveing freinds, yet they conceived many things might arise from over deepe jealocie and fear, togeather with unmeete provocations, though they well saw Mr. Weston pursued his owne ends, and was imbittered in spirite....

Plymouth Colony Further Burdened by Weston

"All these things they pondred and well considered, yet concluded to give his men frendly entertainmente; partly in regard of Mr. Weston him selfe, considering what he had been unto them, & done for them, & to some, more espetially; and partly in compassion to ye people, who were now come into a willdernes, (as them selves were,) and were by ye ship to be presently put a shore, (for she was to cary other passengers to Virginia, who lay at great charge,) and they were alltogeather unacquainted & knew not what to doe. So as they had received his former company of 7. men, and vitailed them as their owne hitherto, so they also received these (being aboute 60. lusty men), and gave housing for them selves and their goods; and many being sicke, they had ye best means ye place could aford them. They stayed hear ye most parte of ye somer till ye ship came back againe from Virginia. Then, by his direction, or those whom he set over them, they removed into ye Massachusset Bay, he having got a patente for some part ther, (by light of ther former discovery in

The above excerpts are from the original manuscript, written 1647, (1901 Edition)

Jnruly Settlers Without Good Government

leters sent home). Yet they left all ther sicke folke hear till they were setled and housed. But of ther victails they had not any, though they were in great wante, nor any thing els in recompence of any courtecie done them; neither did they desire it, for they saw they were an unruly company, and had no good govermente over them, and by disorder would soone fall into wants if Mr. Weston came not ye sooner amongst them; and therfore, to prevente all after occasion, would have nothing of them.

'amine .ets In

"Amids these streights, and ye desertion of those from whom they had hoped for supply, and when famine begane now to pinch them sore, they not knowing what to doe, the Lord, (who never fails his,) presents them with an occasion, beyond all expectation. This boat which came from ye eastward brought them a letter from a stranger, of whose name they had never heard before, being a captaine of a ship come ther a fishing....

upplies from 'irginia Ship Aid Plymouth Colony

"By this boat ye Govr returned a thankfull answer, as was meete, and sent a boate of their owne with them, which was piloted by them, in which Mr. Winslow was sente to procure what provissions he could of ye ships, who was kindly received by ye foresaid gentill-man, who not only spared what he could, but writ to others to doe ye like. By which means he gott some good quantitie and returned in saftie, by which ye plantation had a duble benefite, first, a present refreshing by ye food brought, and secondly, they knew ye way to those parts for their benifite hearafter. But what was gott, & this small boat brought, being devided among so many, came but to a litle, yet by Gods blesing it upheld them till harvest. It arose but to a quarter of a pound of bread a day to each person; and ye Govr caused it to be dayly given them, otherwise, had it been in their owne custody, they would have eate it up & then starved. But thus, with what els they could get, they made pretie shift till corne was ripe....

/4 lb. of read per Day er Person rith Harvest

ood hortage ontinues

"Now ye wellcome time of harvest aproached, in which all had their hungrie bellies filled. But it arose but to a litle, in comparison of a full years supplie; partly by reason they were not yet well aquainted with ye maner of Indean corne, (and they had no other,) allso their many other imployments, but cheefly their weaknes for wante of food, to tend it as they should have done. Also much was stolne both by night & day, before it became scarce eatable, & much more afterward. And though many were well whipt (when they were taken) for a few ears of corne, yet hunger made others (whom conscience did not restraine) to venture. So as it well appeared yt famine must still insue ye next year allso, if not some way prevented, or supplie should faile, to which they durst not

The above excerpts are from the original manuscript, written 1647, (1901 Edition)

trust. Markets there was none to goe too, but only ye Indeans, and they had no trading comodities. Behold now another providence of God; a ship comes into ye harbor, one Captain Jons being cheefe therin. They were set out by some marchants to discovere all ye harbors betweene this & Virginia, and ye shoulds of Cap-Cod, and to trade along ye coast wher they could. This ship had store of English-beads (which were then good trade) and some knives, but would sell none but at dear rates, and also a good quantie togeather. Yet they weere glad of ye occasion, and faine to buy at any rate; they were faine to give after ye rate of cento per cento, if not more, and yet pay away coat-beaver at 3s. perli, which in a few years after yeelded 20s. By this means they were fitted againe to trade for beaver & other things, and intended to buy what corne they could....

Trading with Another Ship

"Shortly after harvest Mr. Westons people who were now seated at ye Massachusets, and by disorder (as it seems) had made havock of their provissions, begane now to perceive that want would come upon them....

"It may be thought strang that these people should fall to these extremities in so short a time, being left competently provided when ye ship left them, and had an addition by that moyetie of corn that was got by trade, besids much they gott of ye Indans wher they lived, by one means & other. It must needs be their great disorder, for they spent excesseivly whilst they had, or could get it; and, it may be, wasted parte away among ye Indeans (for he yt was their cheef was taxed by some amongst them for keeping Indean women, how truly I know not). And after they begane to come into wants, many sould away their cloathes and bed coverings; others (so base were they) became servants to ye Indeans, and would cutt them woode & fetch them water, for a cap full of corne; others fell to plaine stealing, both night & day, from ye Indeans, of which they greevosly complained. In ye end, they came to that misery, that some starved & dyed with could & hunger....

Weston's Settlement Again in Want

"This was ye end of these that some time bosted of their strength, (being all able lustie men,) and what they would doe & bring to pass, in comparison of ye people hear, who had many women & children and weak ons amongst them; and said at their first arivall, when they saw the wants hear, that they would take an other course, and not to fall into shuch a condition, as this simple people were come too. But a mans way is not in his owne power; God can make ye weake to stand; let him also that standeth take heed least he fall....

Pilgrim Relied on God

The above excerpts are from the original manuscript, written 1647, (1901 Edition)

How to Raise More Corn?

"All this whille no supply was heard of, neither knew they when they might expecte any. So they begane to thinke how they might raise as much corne as they could, and obtaine a beter crope then they had done, that they might not still thus languish in miserie. At length, after much debate of things, the Govr (with ye advise of ye cheefest amongest them) gave way that they should set corne every man for his owne perticuler, and in that regard trust to them selves; in all other things to goe on in ye generall way as before. And so assigned to every family a parcell of land, according to the proportion of their number for that end, only for present use (but made no devission for inheritance), and ranged all boys & youth under some familie. This had very good success; for it made all hands very industrious, so as much more corne was planted then other waise would have bene by any means ye Govr or any other could use, and saved him a great deall of trouble, and gave farr better contente. The women now wente willingly into ye feild, and tooke their litle-ons with them to set corne, which before would aledg weaknes, and inabilitie; whom to have compelled would have bene thought great tiranie and oppression.

Initiative of Individual Farming Replaces the Inadequacy of Collective Farming

"The experience that was had in this comone course and condition, tried sundrie years, and that amongst godly and sober men, may well evince the vanitie of that conceite of Platos & other ancients, applauded by some of later times; - that ye taking away of propertie, and bringing in comunitie into a comone wealth, would make them happy and florishing; as if they were wiser then God. For this comunitie (so farr as it was) was found to breed much confusion & discontent, and retard much imploymet that would have been to their benefite and comforte. For ye yong-men that were most able and fitte for labour & service did repine that they should spend their time & streingth to worke for other mens wives and children, with out any recompence. The strong, or man of parts, had no more in devission of fictails & cloaths, then he that was weake and not able to doe a quarter ye other could; this was thought injuestice. The aged and graver men to be ranked and equalised in labours, and victails, cloaths, &c., with ye meaner & yonger sorte, thought it some indignite & disrespect unto them. And for mens wives to be commanded to doe service for other men, as dresing their meate, washing their cloaths, &c., they deemd it a kind of slaverie, neither could many husbands well brooke it. Upon ye poynte all being to have alike, and all to doe alike, they thought them selves in ye like condition, and one as good as another; and so, if it did not cut of those relations that God hath set amongest men, yet it did at least much diminish and take of ye mutuall respects that should be preserved amongst them.

Plymouth Plantation Knew and Experienced the Injustice of Collectivism

The above excerpts are from the original manuscript, written 1647, (1901 Edition)

And would have bene worse if they had been man of another condition. Let none objecte this is men's corruption, and nothing to ye course it selfe. I answer, seeing all men have this corruption in them, God in his wisdome saw another course fiter for them.

"But to returne. After this course setled, and by that their core was planted, all ther victails were spente, and they were only to rest on Gods providence; at night not many times knowing wher to have a bitt of any thing ye next day. And so, as one well observed, had need to pray that God would give them their dayly brade, above all people in ye world. Yet they bore these wants with great patience & allacritie of spirite, and that for so long a time as for ye most parte of 2. years;....

Rest on God's Providence

"They haveing but one boat left and she not over well fitted, they were devided into severall companies, 6. or 7. to a gangg or company, and so wente out with a nett they had bought, to take bass & such like fish, by course, every company knowing their turne. No sooner was ye boate discharged of what she brought, but ye next company tooke her and wente out with her. Neither did they returne till they had cauight something, though it were 5. or 6. days before, for they knew ther was nothing at home, and to goe home emptie would be a great discouragemente to ye rest. Yea, they strive who should doe best. If she stayed longe or got litle, then all went to seeking of shel-fish, which at low-water they digged out of ye sands. And this was their living in ye somer time, till God sente ym beter; & in winter they were helped with ground-nuts and foule. Also in ye somer they gott now & then a dear; for one or 2. of ye fitest was apoynted ro range ye woods for yt end, & what was gott that way was devided amongst them.

"At length they received some leters from ye adventurers, too long and tedious hear to record, by which they heard of their furder crosses and frustrations;....

"This ship was brought by Mr. John Peirce, and set out at his owne charge, upon hope of great maters. These passengers, & ye goods the company sent in her, tooke in for fraught, for which they agreed with him to be delivered hear. This was he in whose name their first patente was taken, by reason of aquaintance, and some aliance that some of their freinds had with him. But his name was only used in trust. But when he saw they were hear hopfully thus seated, and by ye success God gave them had obtained ye favour of ye Counsell of New-England, he goes and

Attempt by John Pierce to Thwart Success of Plymouth Colony

The above excerpts are from the original manuscript, written 1647, (1901 Edition)

sues to them for another patent of much larger extente (in their names), which was easily obtained. But he mente to keep it to him selfe and alow them what he pleased, to hold of him as tenants, and sue to his courts as cheefe Lord, as will appear by that which follows. But ye Lord marvelously crost him; for after this first returne, and ye charge above mentioned, when shee was againe fitted, he pesters him selfe and taks in more passengers, and those not very good to help to bear his losses, and sets out ye 2. time....

Prayer for Rain

"*I may not here omite how, notwithstand all their great paines & industrie, and ye great hops of a large cropp, the Lord seemed to blast, & take away the same, and to threaten further & more sore famine unto them, by a great drought which continued from ye 3. weeke in May, till about ye midle of July, without any raine, and with great heat (for ye most parte), insomuch as ye corne begane to wither away, though it was set with fishe, the moysture wherof helped it much. Yet at length it begane to languish sore, and some of ye drier grounds were partched like withered hay, part wherof was never recovered. Upon which they sett a parte a solemne day of humilliation, to seek ye Lord by humble & fervente prayer, in this great distrese. And he was pleased to give them a gracious & speedy answer, both to their owne, & the Indeans admiration, that lived amongest them. For all ye morning, and greatest part of the day, it was clear weather & very hotte, and not a cloud or any signe of raine to be seen, yet toward evening it begane to overcast, and shortly after to raine, with shuch sweete and gentle showers, as gave them cause of rejoyceing, & blesing God. It came, without either wind, or thunder, or any violence, and by degreese in yt abundance, as that ye earth was thorowly wete and soked therwith. Which did so apparently revive & quicken ye decayed corne & other fruits, as was wonderfull to see, and made ye Indeans astonished to behold; and afterwards the Lord sent them shuch seasonable showers, with enterchange of faire warme weather, as, through his blessing, caused a fruitfull & liberall harvest, to their no small comforte and rejoycing. For which mercie (in time conveniente) they also sett aparte a day of thanksgiveing. This being overslipt in its place, I thought meet here to inserte ye same....

The above excerpts are from the original manuscript, written 1647, (1901 Edition)

"About 14. days after came in this ship, caled ye Anne, wherof Mr. William Peirce was mr., and aboute a weeke or 10. days after came in ye pinass which in foule weather they lost at sea, a fine new vessell of about 44. tune, which ye company had builte to stay in the cuntrie. They brought about 60. persons for ye generall, some of them being very usefull persons, and became good members to ye body, and some were ye wives and children of shuch as were hear allready. And some were so bad, as they were faine to be at charge to send them home againe ye next year. Also, besids these ther came a company, that did not belong to ye generall body, but came one their perticuler, and were to have lands assigned them, and be for them selves, yet to be subjecte to ye generall Goverment; which caused some diferance and disturbance amongst them, as will after appeare....

60 Persons Arrive on the Anne

"These passengers, when they saw their low & poore condition a shore, were much danted and dismayed, and according to their diverse humores were diversly affected; some wished them selves in England againe; others fell a weeping, fancying their own miserie in what yey saw now in others; other some pitying the distress they saw their freinds had been long in, and still were under; in a word, all were full of sadnes. Only some of their old freinds rejoysed to see them, and yt it was no worse with them, for they could not expecte it should be better, and now hoped they should injoye better days togeather. And truly it was no marvell they should be thus affected, for they were in a very low condition, many were ragged in aparell, & some litle beter then halfe naked; though some yt were well stord before, were well enough in this regard. But for food they were all alike, save some yt had got a few pease of ye ship yt was last hear. The best dish they could presente their freinds with was a lobster, or a peece of fish, without bread or any thing els but a cupp of fair spring water. And ye long continuance of this diate, and their labours abroad, had something abated ye freshnes of their former complexion. But God gave them health and strength in a good measure; and shewed them by experience ye truth of yt word, Deut. 8. 3. 'Yt man liveth not by bread only, but by every word yt proceedeth out of ye mouth of ye Lord doth a man live.'

Newcomers Ill Prepared on Arrival from Plymouth

"When I think how sadly ye scripture speaks of the famine in Jaakobs time, when he said to his sonns, 'Goe buy us food, that we may live and not dye.' Gen. 42. 2. and 43. 1, that the famine was great, or heavie in the land; and yet they had such great herds, and store of catle of sundrie kinds, which, besids flesh, must needs produse other food, as milke, butter & cheese, &c., and yet it was counted a sore affliction; theirs hear must needs

The above excerpts are from the original manuscript, written 1647, (1901 Edition)

be very great, therfore, who not only wanted the staffe of bread, but all these things, and had no Egipte to goe too. But God fedd them out of ye sea for ye most parte, so wonderfull is his providence over his in all ages; for his mercie endureth for ever.

"On ye other hand the old planters were affraid that their corne, when it was ripe, should be imparted to ye new-comers, whose provissions wch they brought with them they feared would fall short before ye year wente aboute (as indeed it did). They came to ye Govr and besought him that as it was before agreed that they should set corne for their perticuler, and accordingly they had taken extraordinary pains ther aboute, that they might freely injoye the same, and they would not have a bitte of ye victails now come, but waite till harvest for their owne, and let ye new-comers injoye what they had brought; they would have none of it, excepte they could purchase any of it of them by bargaine or exchainge. Their requeste was granted them, for it gave both sides good contente; for ye new-comers were as much afraid that ye hungrie planters would have eat up ye provissions brought, and they should have fallen into ye like condition.

Provisions Subject only to Bargain on Exchange by Mutual Agreement

"This ship was in a shorte time laden with clapbord, by ye help of many hands. Also they sente in her all ye beaver and other furrs they had, & Mr. Winslow was sent over with her, to informe of all things, and procure such things as were thought needfull for their presente condition. By this time harvest was come, and in stead of famine, now God gave them plentie, and ye face of things was changed, to ye rejoysing of ye harts of many, for which they blessed God. And ye effect of their particuler planting was well seene, for all had, one way & other, pretty well to bring ye year aboute, and some of ye abler sorte and more industrious had to spare, and sell to others, so as any generall wante or famine hath not been amongst them since to this day....

Effect on the System of Individual Enterprise Puts End to Famine and General Want

"The time of new election of ther officers for this year being come, and ye number of their people increased, and their troubls and occasions therwith, the Govr desired them to chainge ye persons, as well as renew ye election; and also to adde more Assistans to ye Govr for help & counsell, and ye better carrying on of affairs. Showing that it was necessarie it should be so. If it was any honour or benefite, it was fitte others should be made pertakers of it; if it was a burthen, (as doubtles it was,) it was but equall others should help to bear it; and yt this was ye end of Añuall Elections. The issue was, that as before ther was but one Assistante, they now chose 5. giving the Govr a duble voyce; and aftwards they increased them to 7. which course hath continued to this day....

Annual Election of 1624 – Purpose: To Have Rotation in Office and More Persons Take Responsibility in Government

The above excerpts are from the original manuscript, written 1647, (1901 Edition)

Ample Harvest Proves Wisdom of Individual Planting his own Crop

Corn More Precious than Silver

System of Barter

Request to Reap the Benefits of their own Labors by Being Given the Same Acre in Continuance

Inequity of Annual Tenure Abolished

"These things premised, I shall now prosecute ye procedings and afairs here. And before I come to other things I must speak a word of their planting this year; they having found ye benifite of their last years harvest, and setting corne for their particuler, having therby with a great deale of patience overcome hunger & famine. Which maks me remember a saing of Senecas, Epis: 123. That a great parte of libertie is a well governed belly, and to be patiente in all wants. They begane now highly to prise corne as more pretious then silver, and those that had some to spare begane to trade one with another for smale things, by ye quarte, potle, & peck, &c.; for money they had none, and if any had, corne was prefered before it. That they might therfore encrease their tillage to better advantage, they made suite (116) to the Govr to have some portion of land given them for continuance, and not by yearly lotte, for by that means, that which ye more industrious had brought into good culture (by much pains) one year, came to leave it ye nexte, and often another might injoye it; so as the dressing of their lands were the more sleighted over, & to lese profite. Which being well considered, their request was granted. And to every person was given only one acrre of land, to them & theirs, as nere ye towne as might be, and they had no more till ye 7. years were expired. The reason was, that they might be kept close together both for more saftie and defence, and ye better improvement of ye generall imployments. Which condition of theirs did make me often thinke, of what I had read in Plinie of ye Romans first beginnings in Romulus time. How every man contented him selfe with 2. Acres of land, and had no more assigned them. And chap. 3. It was thought a great reward, to receive at ye hands of ye people of Rome a pinte of corne. And long after, the greatest presente given to a Captaine yt had gotte a victory over their enemise, was as much ground as they could till in one day. And he was not counted a good, but a dangerous man, that would not contente him selfe with 7. Acres of land. As also how they did pound their corne in morters, as these people were forcte to doe many years before they could get a mille....

Craftsman Constructs Boats

Salt Making Discouraging Factor

"The ship-carpenter that was sent them, was an honest and very industrious man, and followed his labour very dilligently, and made all that were imployed with him doe ye like; he quickly builte them 2 very good & strong shalops (which after did them greate service), and a great and strong lighter, and had hewne timber for 2. catches;.... But he whom they sent to make salte was an ignorante, foolish, self-willd fellow;.... For he could not doe any thing but boyle salt in pans, & yet would make them yt were joynd with him beleeve ther was so grat a misterie in it as was not easie to be attained, and made them doe many unnecessary things to blind their eys, till they discerned his sutltie....

The above excerpts are from the original manuscript, written 1647, (1901 Edition)

"The 3d. eminente person (which ye letters before mention) was ye minister which they sent over, by name Mr. John Lyford, of whom & whose doing I must be more large, though I shall abridg things as much as I can. When this man first came a shore, he saluted them with that reverence & humilitie as is seldome to be seen, and indeed made them ashamed, he so bowed and cringed unto them, and would have kissed their hands if they would have (118) suffered him; yea, he wept & shed many tears, blessing God that had brought him to see their faces; and admiring ye things they had done in their wants, &c. as if he had been made all of love, and ye humblest person in ye world. And all ye while, (if we may judg by his after cariags) he was but like him mentioned in Psa: 10. 10. That croucheth & boweth, that heaps of poore may fall by his might. Or like to that dissembling Ishmaell, who, when he had slaine Gedelia, went out weeping and mette them yt were coming to offer incense in ye house of ye Lord; saing, Come to Gedelia, when he ment to slay them....

Minister Sent Over from Company in England

"I must hear speake a word also of Mr. John Oldom, who was a copartner with him in his after courses. He had bene a cheefe sticler in ye former faction among ye perticulers, and an intelligencer to those in England. But now, since the coming of this ship and he saw ye supply that came, he tooke occasion to open his minde to some of ye cheefe amongst them heere, and confessed he had done them wrong both by word & deed, & writing into England; but he now saw the eminente hand of God to be with them, and his blesing upon them, which made his hart smite him, neither should those in England ever use him as an instrumente any longer against them in any thing; he also desired former things might be forgotten, and that they would looke upon him as one that desired to close with them in all things, with such like expressions. Now whether this was in hipocrisie, or out of some sudden pange of conviction (which I rather thinke), God only knows. Upon it they shew all readynes to imbrace his love, and carry towards him in all frendlynes, and called him to counsell with them in all cheefe affairs, as ye other, without any distruct at all.

John Oldom Wrongly Informs of Pilgrims to Faction in England

John Oldom Avers True Friendship to Pilgrims and is Taken into their Confidence

"Thus all things seemed to goe very comfortably and smothly on amongst them, at which they did much rejoyce; but this lasted not (119) long, for both Oldom and he grew very perverse, and shewed a spirite of great malignancie, drawing as many into faction as they could;....

Oldom and Liford Start Faction

"At lenght when ye ship was ready to goe, it was observed Liford was long in writing, & sente many letters, and could not forbear to comunicate to his intimats such things as made them laugh in

The above excerpts are from the original manuscript, written 1647, (1901 Edition)

their sleeves, and thought he had done ther errand sufficiently. The Govr and some other of his freinds knowing how things stood in England, and what hurt these things might doe, tooke a shalop and wente out with the ship a league or 2. to sea, and caled for all Lifords & Oldums letters. Mr. William Peirce being mr. of ye ship, (and knew well their evill dealing both in England & here,) afforded him all ye assistance he could. He found above 20. of Lyfords letters, many of them larg, and full of slanders, & false accusations, tending not only to their prejudice, but to their ruine & utter subversion. Most of the letters they let pas, only tooke copys of them, but some of ye most materiall they sent true copyes of them, and kept ye originalls, least he should deney them, and that they might produce his owne hand against him. . . . This ship went out towards eving, and in the night ye Govr retured. They were somwaht blanke at it, but after some weeks, when they heard nothing, they then were as briske as ever, thinking nothing had been knowne, but all was gone currente, and that the Govr went but to dispatch his owne letters. The reason why the Govr & rest concealed these things the longer, was to let things ripen, that they (120) might ye better discover their intents and see who were their adherents. . . .

Liford and Oldom Write Many Letters for Ship to Take to England

Plot to Discredit Colony Uncovered by Governor in Examination of the Letters

"It was now thought high time (to prevent further mischeefe) to calle them to accounte; so ye Govr called a courte and sumoned the whol company to appeare. And then charged Lyford & Oldom with such things as they were guilty of. But they were stiffe, & stood resolutly upon ye deneyall of most things, and required proofe. . . .

"Lyford denyed that he had any thing to doe with them in England, or knew of their courses, and made other things as strange that he was charged with. Then his letters were prodused & some of them read, at which he was struck mute. But Oldam begane to rage furiously, because they had intercepted and opened his letters, threatening them in very high language, and in a most audacious and mutinous maner stood up & caled upon ye people, saying, My maisters, wher is your harts? now shew your courage, you have oft complained to me so & so; now is ye time, if you will doe any thing, I will stand by you, &c. Thinking yt every one (knowing his humor) that had soothed and flattered him, or other wise in their discontente uttered any thing unto him, would now side wth him in open rebellion. But he was deceived, for not a man opened his mouth, but all were silent, being strucken with the injustice of ye thing. Then ye Govr turned his speech to Mr. Lyford, and asked him if he thought they had done evill to open

Conspirators Confronted with Evidence

The above excerpts are from the original manuscript, written 1647, (1901 Edition)

his letters; but he was silente, & would not say a word, well knowing what they might reply. Then ye Govr shewed the people he did it as a magistrate, and was bound to it by his place, to prevent ye mischeefe & ruine that this conspiracie and plots of theirs would bring on this poor colony....

Trial - Admission of Guilt - Conviction

"After their triall & conviction, the court censured them to be expeld the place; Oldame presently, though his wife & family had liberty to stay all winter, or longer, till he could make provission to remove them comfortably. Lyford had liberty to stay 6. months. It was, indeede, with some eye to his release, if he caried him selfe well in the meane time, and that his repentance proved sound. Lyford acknowledged his censure was farr less then he deserved....

Company Withholds Further Supply and Subsistence

"(134) This storme being thus blowne over, yet sundrie sad effects followed ye same; for the Company of Adventurers broake in peeces here upon, and ye greatest parte wholy deserted ye colony in regarde of any further supply, or care of their subsistance....

"And I shall first inserte some part of their letters as followeth; for I thinke it best to render their minds in ther owne words....

".... The former course for the generalitie here is wholy dissolved from what it was; and wheras you & we were formerly sharers and partners, in all viages & deallings, this way is now no more, but you and we are left to bethinke our sellves what course to take in ye future, that your lives & our monies be not lost.

"The reasons and causes of this allteration have been these. First and mainly, ye many losses and crosses at sea, and abuses of seamen, wch have caused us to rune into so much charge, debts, & ingagements, as our estats & means were not able to goe on without impoverishing our selves, except our estats had been greater, and our associats cloven beter unto us. 2ly, as here hath been a faction and siding amongst us now more then 2. years, so now there is an uter breach and sequestration amongst us, and in too parts of us a full dissertion and forsaking of you, without any intente or purpose of medling more with you. And though we are perswaded the maine cause of this their doing is wante of money, (for neede wherof men use to make many excuses,) yet other things are pretended, as that you are Brownists, &c. Now what use you or we ought to make of these things, it remaineth to be considered, for we know ye hand of God to be in all these things, and no doubt he would admonish some thing therby, and to looke what is amise. And allthough it be now too late for us or you to prevent & stay

The above excerpts are from the original manuscript, written 1647, (1901 Edition)

these things, yet it is not to late to exercise patience, wisdom, and conscience in bearing them, and in caring our selves in & under them for ye time to come.

"(136) And as we our selves stand ready to imbrace all occasions that may tend to ye furthrance of so hopefull a work, rather admiring of what is, then grudging for what is not; so it must rest in you to make all good againe. And if in nothing else you can be approved, yet let your honestie & conscience be still approved, & lose not one jote of your innocencie, amids your crosses & afflictions. And surly if you upon this allteration behave your selves wisly, and goe on fairly, as men whose hope is not in this life, you shall need no other weapon to wound your adversaries; for when your righteousnes is revealled as ye light, they shall cover their faces with shame, that causlesly have sought your overthrow.

"Now we thinke it but reason, that all such things as ther apertaine to the generall, be kept & preserved togeather, and rather increased dayly, then any way be dispersed or imbeseled away for any private ends or intents whatsoever. And after your necessities are served, you gather togeather such comodities as ye cuntrie yeelds, & send them over to pay debts & clear ingagements hear, which are not less then 1400li. And we hope you will doe your best to free our ingagements, &c. Let us all indeavor to keep a faire & honest course, and see what time will bring forth, and how God in his providence will worke for us. We still are perswaded you are ye people that must make a plantation in those remoate places when all others faile and returne. And your experience of Gods providence and preservation of you is such as we hope your harts will not faile you, though your freinds should forsake you (which we our selves shall not doe whilst we live, so long as your honestie so well appereth). Yet surly help would arise from some other place whilst you waite on God, with uprightnes, though we should leave you allso.

"And lastly be you all intreated to walke circumspectly, and carry your selves so uprightly in all your ways, as yt no man may make just exceptions against you. And more espetially that ye favour and countenance of God may be so toward you, as yt you may find abundante joye & peace even amids tribulations, that you may say with David, Though my father & mother should forsake me, yet ye Lord would take me up.

"We have sent you hear some catle, cloath, hose, shoes, leather, &c., but in another nature then formerly, as it stood us in hand to doe; we have comitted them to ye charge & custody of Mr. Allerton

The above excerpts are from the original manuscript, written 1647, (1901 Edition)

and Mr. Winslow, as our factours, at whose discretion they are to be sould, and comodities to be taken for them, as is fitting. And by how much ye more they will be chargable unto you, the better they had need to be husbanded, &c. Goe on, good freinds, comfortably, pluck up your spirits, and quitte your selves like men in all your difficulties, that notwithstanding all displeasure and threats of men, yet ye work may goe on you are aboute, and not be neglected. Which is so much for ye glorie of God, and the furthrance of our countrie-men, as that a man may with more comforte (137) spend his life in it, then live ye life of Mathusala, in wasting ye plentie of a tilled land, or eating ye fruite of a growne tree. Thus with harty salutations to you all, and harty prayers for you all, we lovingly take our leaves, this 18. of Des: 1624.

Your assured freinds to our powers,
J. S. W. C. T. F. R. H. &c.

Pilgrims Pay High Interest on Goods Brought into Colony

"By this leter it appears in what state ye affairs of ye plantation stood at this time. These goods they bought, but they were at deare rates, for they put 40. in ye hundred upon them, for profite and adventure, outward bound; and because of ye vnture of ye paiment homeward, they would have 30. in ye 100. more, which was in all 70. pr. cent; a thing thought unreasonable by some, and too great an oppression upon ye poore people, as their case stood. The catle were ye best goods, for ye other being ventured ware, were neither at ye best (some of them) nor at ye best prises. Sundrie of their freinds disliked these high rates, but coming from many hands, they could not help it....

Standish Seeks Re-Establishment of Former Covenant or Fair Termination of Same

"In ye bigger of these ships was sent over Captine Standish from ye plantation, wth leters & instructions, both to their freinds of ye company which still clave to them, and also to ye Honourable Counsell of New-England. To ye company to desire yt seeing that they ment only to let them have goods upon sale, that they might have them upon easier termes, for they should never be able to bear such high intrest, or to allow so much per cent; also that what they would doe in yt way that it might be disburst in money, or such goods as were fitte and needfull for them, & bought at best hand; and to acquainte them with ye contents of his leters to ye Counsell above said, which was to this purpose, to desire their favour & help; that such of ye adventurers as had thus forsaken & deserted them, might be brought to some order, and not to keepe them bound, and them selves be free. But that they might either stand to ther former covenants, or ells come to some faire end, by dividente, or composition. But he came in a very bad time, for ye Stat was full of trouble, and ye plague

The above excerpts are from the original manuscript, written 1647, (1901 Edition)

very hote in London, so as no bussines could be done; yet he spake with some of ye Honourd Counsell, who promised all helpfullnes to ye plantation which lay in them....and so returned passenger in a fhishing ship, haveing prepared a good way for ye compossition that was afterward made....

Standish Returns from England

"About ye begining of Aprill they heard of Captain Standish his arrivall, and sent a boat to fetch him home, and ye things he had brought. Welcome he was, but ye news he broughte was sadd in many regards; not only in regarde of the former losses, before related, which their freinds had suffered, by which some in a maner were undon, others much disabled from doing any further help, and some dead of ye plague, but also yt Mr. Robinson, their pastor, was dead, which struck them with much sorrow & sadnes, as they had cause. His and their adversaries had been long & continually plotting how they might hinder his coming hither, but ye Lord had appointed him a better place;....

All Help under Original Provisions of Covenant at an End

"All which things (before related) being well weighed and laied togither, it could not but strick them with great perplexitie; and to looke humanly on ye state of things as they presented them selves at this time, it is a marvell it did not wholy discourage them, and sinck them. But they gathered up their spirits, and ye Lord so helped them, whose worke they had in hand, as now when they were at lowest they begane to rise againe, and being striped (in a maner) of all humane helps and hops, he brought things aboute other wise, in his devine providence, as they were not only upheld & sustained, but their proccedings both honoured and imitated by others; as by ye sequell will more appeare, if ye Lord spare me life & time to declare ye same.

Pilgrims Set Themselves Entirely to their own Industry

"Having now no fishing busines, or other things to intend, but only their trading & planting, they sett them selves to follow the same with ye best industrie they could. The planters finding their corne, what they could spare from ther necessities, to be a comoditie, (for they sould it at 6s. a bushell,) used great dilligence in planting ye same. And ye Gover and such as were designed to manage the trade, (for it was retained for ye generall good, (141) and none were to trade in perticuler,) they followed it to the best advantage they could;....

Pilgrims Send Allerton to England to Represent Them in Business Affairs

"This year they sent Mr. Allerton into England, and gave him order to make a composition with ye adventurers, upon as good termes as he could (unto which some way had ben made ye year before by Captaine Standish); but yet injoyned him not to conclud absolutly till they knew ye termes, and had well considered of

The above excerpts are from the original manuscript, written 1647, (1901 Edition)

them; but to drive it to as good an issew as he could, and referr ye conclusion to them. Also they gave him a comission under their hands & seals to take up some money, provided it exeeded not such a sume specified, for which they engaged them selves, and gave him order how to lay out ye same for ye use of ye plantation. . . .

Pilgrims Secure Loan in England at 30%

"At ye usuall season of ye coming of ships Mr. Allerton returned, and brought some usfull goods with him, according to ye order given him. For upon his commission he tooke up 200li. which he now gott at 30. per cent. The which goods they gott safly home, and well conditioned, which was much to the comfort & contente of ye plantation. He declared unto them, allso, how, with much adoe and no small trouble, he had made a composition with ye adventurers, by the help of sundrie of their faithfull freinds ther, who had allso tooke much pains ther about. The agreement or bargen he had brought a draught of, with a list of ther names ther too annexed, drawne by the best counsell of law they could get, to make it firme. The heads wherof I shall here inserte.

Allerton Buys Needed Supplies with Money Borrowed

Prospective Agreement Arranged with Adventurers for Colony's Approval

"To all Christian people, greeting, &c. Wheras at a meeting ye 26. of October last past, diverse & sundrie persons, whose names to ye one part of these presents are subscribed in a schedule hereunto annexed, Adventurers to New-Plimoth in New-England in America, were contented and agreed, in consideration of the sume of one thousand and eight hundred pounds sterling to be paid, (in maner and forme folling,) to sell, and make sale of all & every ye stocks, shares, lands, marchandise, and chatles, what soever, to ye said adventurers, and other ther fellow adventurers to New Plimoth aforesaid, any way accruing, or belonging to ye generalitie of ye said adventurers aforesaid; as well by reason of any sume or sumes of money, or marchandise, at any time heretofore adventured or disbursed by them, or other wise howsoever; for ye better expression and setting forth of which said agreemente, the parties to these presents subscribing, doe for (144) them selves severally, and as much as in them is, grant, bargan, alien, sell, and transfere all & every ye said shares, goods, lands, marchandice, and chatles to them belonging as aforesaid, unto Isaack Alerton, one of ye planters resident at Plimoth afforesaid, assigned, and sent over as agente for ye rest of ye planters ther, ... And therfore ye said Isaack Allerton doth, for him, his heirs & assigns, covenant, promise, & grant too & with ye adven: whose names are here unto subscribed, ther heirs, &c. well & truly to pay, or cause to be payed, unto ye said adven: or 5. of them which were, at yt meeting

Agreement: Plymouth Colony to be Free and Clear of all Encumbrance Under Original Contract with "Merchants Adventurers Co.," by Payment of 1800 pounds Sterling

The above excerpts are from the original manuscript, written 1647, (1901 Edition)

afforsaid, nominated & deputed, viz. John Pocock, John Beachamp, Robert Keane, Edward Base, and James Sherley, marchants, their heirs, &c. too and for ye use of ye generallitie of them, the sume of 1800li. of lawfull money of England, at ye place appoynted for ye receipts of money, on the west side of ye Royall Exchaing in London, by 200li. yearly, and every year, on ye feast of St. Migchell, the first paiment to be made Ano: 1628. &c. Allso ye said Isaack is to indeavor to procure & obtaine from ye planters of N. P. aforesaid, securitie, by severall obligations, or writings obligatory, to make paiment of ye said sume of 1800li. in forme afforsaid, according to ye true meaning of these presents. In testimonie wherof to this part of these presents remaining with ye said Isaack Allerton, ye said subscribing adven: have sett to their names, &c. And to ye other part remaining with ye said adven: the said Isaack Allerton hath subscribed his name, ye 15. Novbr. Ano: 1626. in ye 2. year of his Majesties raigne.

Agreement Confirmed by Parties Thereto

"This agreemente was very well liked of, & approved by all ye plantation, and consented unto; though they knew not well how to raise ye payment, and discharge their other ingagements, and supply the yearly wants of ye plantation, seeing they were forced for their necessities to take up money or goods at so high intrests. Yet they undertooke it, and 7. or 8. of ye cheefe of ye place became joyntly bound for ye paimente of this 1800li. (in ye behalfe of ye rest) at ye severall days. In which they rane a great adventure, as their present state stood, having many other heavie burthens allready upon them, and all things in an uncertaine condition amongst them.

A Burdensome Undertaking

So ye next returne it was absolutly confirmed on both sids, and ye bargen fairly ingrossed in partchmente and in many things put into better forme, by ye advice of ye learnedest counsell they could gett; and least any forfeiture should fall on ye whole for none paimente at any of ye days, it rane thus: to forfite 30s. a weeke if they missed ye time; and was concluded under their hands & seals, as may be seen at large by ye deed it selfe.

"(145) Now though they had some untowarde persons mixed amongst them from the first, which came out of England, and more afterwards by some of ye adventurers, as freindship or other affections led them, - though sundrie were gone, some for Virginia, and some to other places, - yet diverse were still mingled amongst them, about whom ye Gover & counsell with other of their cheefe freinds had serious consideration, how to setle things in regard of this new bargen or purchas made, in respecte of ye distribution of things both for ye presente and future. For ye present, excepte peace and union were preserved, they should be able to doe nothing, but indanger to over throw all, now that other tyes

The above excerpts are from the original manuscript, written 1647, (1901 Edition)

& bonds were taken away. Therfore they resolved, for sundrie reasons, to take in all amongst them, that were either heads of families, or single yonge men, that were of ability, and free, (and able to governe them selvs with meete descretion, and their affairs, so as to be helpfull in ye comone-welth,) into this partnership or purchass....

Each Individual to Share in Payment of Debts

"So they caled ye company togeather, and conferred with them, and came to this conclusion, that ye trade should be managed as before, to help to pay the debts; and all such persons as were above named should be reputed and inrouled for purchasers; single free men to have a single share, and every father of a familie to be alowed to purchass so many shares as he had persons in his family; that is to say, one for him selfe, and one for his wife, and for every child that he had living with him, one. As for servants, they had none, but what either their maisters should give them out of theirs, or their deservings should obtaine from ye company afterwards. Thus all were to be cast into single shares according to the order abovesaid; and so every one was to pay his part according to his proportion towards ye purchass, & all other debts, what ye profite of ye trade would not reach too; viz. a single man for a single share, a maister of a famalie for so many as he had. This gave all good contente....

Payment on Debts made through Allerton

"They now sent (with ye returne of ye ships) Mr. Allerton againe into England, giveing him full power, under their hands & seals, to conclude the former bargaine with ye adventurers; and sent ther bonds for ye paimente of the money. Allso they sent what beaver they could spare to pay some of their ingagementes, & to defray his chargs; for those deepe interests still kepte them low....

"Before they sent Mr. Allerton away for England this year, ye Gover and some of their cheefe freinds had serious consideration, not only how they might discharge those great ingagments which lay so heavily upon them, as is affore mentioned, but also how they might (if possiblie they could) devise means to help some of their freinds and breethren of Leyden over unto them, who desired so much to come to them, ād they desired as much their company. To effecte which, they resolved to rune a high course, and of great adventure, not knowing otherwise how to bring it aboute. Which was to hire ye trade of ye company for certaine years, and in that time to undertake to pay that 1800li. and all ye rest of ye debts that then lay upon ye plantation, which was aboute some 600li. more; and so to set them free, and returne

The above excerpts are from the original manuscript, written 1647, (1901 Edition)

the trade to ye generalitie againe at ye end of ye terme. Upon which resolution they called ye company togeither, and made it clearly appear unto all what their debts were, and upon what terms they would undertake to pay them all in such a time, and sett them clear....So after some agitation of the thing wth ye company, it was yeelded unto, and the agreemente made upon ye conditions following.

Plan for Payment of Colony's Debts

"Articles of agreemente betweene ye collony of New-Plimoth of ye one partie, and William Bradford, Captein Myles Standish, Isaack Allerton, &c. one ye other partie; and shuch others as they shall thinke good to take as partners and undertakers with them, concerning the trade for beaver & other furrs & comodities, &c.; made July, 1627.

"First, it is agreed and covenanted betweexte ye said parties, that ye afforsaid William Bradford, Captain Myles Standish, & Isaack Allerton, &c. have undertaken, and doe by these presents, covenante and agree to pay, discharge, and acquite ye said collony of all ye debtes both due for ye purchass, or any other belonging to them, at ye day of ye date of these presents.

Company Formed

"(153) Secondly, ye above-said parties are to have and freely injoye ye pinass latly builte, the boat at Manamett, and ye shalop, called ye Bass-boat, with all other implements to them belonging, that is in ye store of ye said company; with all ye whole stock of furrs, fells, beads, corne, wampampeak, hatchets, knives, &c. that is now in ye storre, or any way due unto ye same upon accounte.

"3ly. That ye above said parties have ye whole trade to them selves, their heires and assignes, with all ye privileges therof, as ye said collonie doth now, or may use the same, for 6. full years, to begine ye last of September next insuing.

"4ly. In furder consideration of ye discharge of ye said debtes, every severall purchaser doth promise and covenante yearly to pay, or cause to be payed, to the above said parties, during ye full terme of ye said 6. years, 3. bushells of corne, or 6li. of tobaco, at ye undertakers choyse.

"5ly. The said undertakers shall dureing ye afforesaid terme bestow 50li. per annum, in hose and shoese, to be brought over for ye collonies use, to be sould unto them for corne at 6s. per bushell.

"6ly. That at ye end of ye said terme of 6. years, the whole trade shall returne to ye use and benefite of ye said collonie, as before.

The above excerpts are from the original manuscript, written 1647, (1901 Edition)

"Lastly, if ye afforesaid undertakers, after they have aquainted their freinds in England with these covenants, doe (upon ye first returne) resolve to performe them, and undertake to discharge ye debtes of ye said collony, according to ye true meaning & intente of these presents, then they are (upon such notice given) to stand in full force; otherwise all things to remaine as formerly they were, and a true accounte to be given to ye said collonie, of the disposing of all things according to the former order....

"After Mr. Allertons arivall in England, he aquainted them with his comission and full power to conclude ye forementioned bargan & purchas; upon (154) the view wherof, and ye delivery of ye bonds for ye paymente of ye money yearly, (as is before mentioned,) it was fully concluded, and a deede fairly ingrossed in partchmente was delivered him, under their hands & seals confirming the same....

"(157) Mr. Allerton having setled all things thus in a good and hopfull way, he made hast to returne in ye first of ye spring to be hear with their supply for trade, (for ye fishermen with whom he came used to sett forth in winter & be here betimes.) He brought a resonable supply of goods for ye plantation, and without those great interests as before is noted; and brought an accounte of ye beaver sould, and how ye money was disposed for goods, & ye paymente of other debtes, having paid all debts abroad to others, save to Mr. Sherley, Mr. Beachamp, & Mr. Andrews; from whom likwise he brought an accounte which to them all amounted not to above 400li. for which he had passed bonds. Allso he had payed the first paymente for ye purchass, being due for this year, viz. 200li. and brought them ye bonde for ye same cansselled; so as they now had no more foreine debtes but ye abovesaid 400li. and odde pownds, and ye rest of ye yearly purchass monie. Some other debtes they had in ye cuntrie, but they were without any intrest, & they had wherwith to discharge them when they were due. To this pass the Lord had brought things for them. Also he brought them further notice that their freinds, the abovenamed, & some others that would joyne with them in ye trad & purchass, did intend for to send over to Leyden, for a competente number of them, to be hear the next year without fayle, if ye Lord pleased to blesse their journey. He allso brought them a patente for Kenebeck, but it was so straite & ill bounded, as they were faine to renew & inlarge it the next year, as allso that which they had at home, to their great charge, as will after appeare....

Payment on Debts Made

Affairs Improve

"Mr. Allerton safly arriving in England, and delivering his leters to their freinds their, and aquainting them with his instructions, found good acceptation with them, and they were very forward &

The above excerpts are from the original manuscript, written 1647, (1901 Edition)

willing to joyne with them in ye partnership of trade, & in ye charge to send over ye Leyden people; a company wherof were allready come out of Holand, and prepared to come over, and so were sent away before Mr. Allerton could be ready to come. They had passage with ye ships that came to Salem, that brought over many godly persons to begine ye plantations & churches of Christ ther, & in ye Bay of Massachussets; so their long stay & keeping back (164) was recompensed by ye Lord to ther freinds here with a duble blessing, in that they not only injoyed them now beyond ther late expectation, (when all their hops seemed to be cutt of,) but, with them, many more godly freinds & Christian breethren, as ye begining of a larger harvest unto ye Lord, in ye increase of his churches & people in these parts, to ye admiration of many, and allmost wonder of ye world; that of so small beginings so great things should insue, as time after manifested; and that here should be a resting place for so many of ye Lords people, when so sharp a scourge came upon their owne nation. But it was ye Lords doing, & it ought to be marvellous in our eyes....

New Colonists Arrive from Leyden

"(165) That I may handle things together, I have put these 2. companies that came from Leyden in this place; though they came at 2. severall times, yet they both came out of England this year. The former company, being 35. persons, were shiped in May, and arived here aboute August. The later were shiped in ye begining of March, and arived hear ye later end of May, 1630. Mr. Sherleys 2. letters, ye effect wherof I have before related, (as much of them as is pertinente,) mentions both. Their charge, as Mr. Allerton brought it in afterwards on accounte, came to above 550li. besids ther fetching hither from Salem & ye Bay, wher they and their goods were landed; viz. their transportation from Holland to England, & their charges lying ther, and passages hither, with clothing provided for them. For I find by accounte for ye one company, 125. yeards of karsey, 127. ellons of linen cloath, shoes, 66. pr, with many other perticulers. The charge of ye other company is reckoned on ye severall families, some 50li., some 40li., some 30li., and so more or less, as their number & expencess were. And besids all this charg, their freinds & bretheren here were to provid corne & other provissions for them, till they could reap a crope which was long before. Those that came in May were thus maintained upward of 16. or 18. months, before they had any harvest of their owne, & ye other by proportion. And all they could doe in ye mean time was to gett them some housing, and prepare them grounds to plant on, against the season. And this charg of maintaining them all this while was litle less then ye former sume. These things I note more perticulerly, for sundry regards. First,

Colony Maintains Newcomers until the Next Harvest

The above excerpts are from the original manuscript, written 1647, (1901 Edition)

to shew a rare example herein of brotherly love, and Christian care in performing their promises and covenants to their bretheren, too, & in a sorte beyonde their power; that they should venture so desperatly to ingage them selves to accomplish this thing, and bear it so cheerfully; for they never demanded, much less had, any repaymente of all these great sumes thus disbursed. 2ly. It must needs b e that ther was more then of man in these acheevements, that should thus readily stire up ye harts of shuch able frinds to joyne in partnership with them in shuch a case, and cleave so faithfullie to them as these did, in so great adventures; and the more because the most of them never saw their faces to this day; ther being neither kindred, aliance, or other acquaintance or relations betweene any of them, then hath been before mentioned; it must needs be therfore the spetiall worke and hand of God. 3ly. That these poore people here in a wilderness should, notwithstanding, be inabled in time to repay all these ingagments, and many more unjustly brought upon them through the unfaithfullnes of some, and many other great losses which they sustained, which will be made manifest, if ye Lord be pleased to give life and time. In ye mean time, I cannot but admire his ways and workes towards his servants, and humbly desire to blesse his holy name for his great mercies hithertoo.

"(166) The Leyden people being thus come over, and sundry of ye generalitie seeing & hearing how great ye charg was like to be that was that way to be expended, they begane to murmure and repine at it, notwithstanding ye burden lay on other mens shoulders; espetially at ye paying of ye 3. bushells of corne a year, according to ye former agreemente, when ye trad was lett for ye 6. years aforesaid. But to give them contente herein allso, it was promised them, that if they could doe it in ye time without it, they would never demand it of them; which gave them good contente. And indeed it never was paid, ...

Allerton Exceeds Instructions Given him by Colony

"Concerning ye rest of Mr. Allertons instructions, in which they strictly injoyned him not to exceed above yt 50li. in ye goods before mentioned, not to bring any but trading comodities, he followed them not at all, but did the quite contrarie; bringing over many other sorts of retaile goods, selling what he could by the way on his owne accounte, and delivering the rest, which he said to be theirs, into ye store; and for trading goods brought but litle in comparison; excusing the matter, they had laid out much about ye Laiden people, & patent, &c. And for other goods, they had much of them of ther owne dealings, without present disbursemente, & to like effect. And as for passing his bounds & instructions, he laid it on Mr. Sherley, ...

The above excerpts are from the original manuscript, written 1647, (1901 Edition)

"By this it appears that ther was a kind of concurrance betweene Mr. Allerton and them in these things, and that they gave more regard to his way & course in these things, then to ye advise from hence; which made him bould to presume above his instructions, and to rune on in ye course he did, to their greater hurt afterwards, as will appear. These things did much trouble them hear, but they well knew not how to help it, being loath to make any breach or contention hear aboute;....An other more secrete cause was herewith concurrente; Mr. Allerton had maried ye daughter of their Reverend Elder, Mr. Brewster (a man beloved & honoured amongst them, and who tooke great paines in teaching & dispenceing ye word of God unto them), whom they were loath to greeve or any way offend, so as they bore with much in that respecte. And with all Mr. Allerton carried so faire with him, and procured such leters from Mr. Sherley to him, with shuch applause of Mr. Allertons wisdom, care, and faithfullnes, in ye bussines; and as things stood none were so fitte to send aboute them as he; and if any should suggest other wise, it was rather out of envie, or some other sinister respecte then other wise. Besids, though private gaine, I doe perswade my selfe, was some cause to lead Mr. Allerton aside in these beginings, yet I thinke, or at least charitie caries me to hope, that he intended to deale faithfully with them in ye maine,....

Winslow Replaces Allerton as Agent for Colony

"At length they, having an oppertunitie, resolved to send Mr. Winslow, with what beaver they had ready, into England, to see how ye squars wente, being very jeolouse of these things, & Mr. Allertons courses; and writ shuch leters, and gave him shuch instructions, as they thought meet; and if he found things not well, to discharge Mr. Allerton for being any longer agent for them, or to deal any more in ye bussines, and to see how ye accounts stood, &c....

Winslow Re-establishes Good Trade

"Mr. Winslow, whom they had sent over, sent them over some supply as soone as he could; and afterwards when he came, which was something longe by reason of bussines, he brought a large supply of suitable goods with him, by which ther trading was well carried on....

Winslow's Letter Confirms Extent of Allerton's Mishandling of Colony's Affairs in England

"Sr: It fell out by Gods providence, yt I received and brought your leters pr Mr. Allerton from Bristoll, to London; and doe much feare what will be ye event of things. Mr. Allerton intended to prepare ye ship againe, to set forth upon fishing. Mr. Sherley, Mr. Beachamp, & Mr. Andrews, they renounce all perticulers, protesting but for us they would never have adventured one penie into those parts; Mr. Hatherley stands inclinable to either. And wheras you write that he and Mr. Allerton

The above excerpts are from the original manuscript, written 1647, (1901 Edition)

have taken ye Whit-Angell (ship) upon them, for their partners here, they professe they neiver gave any such order, nor will make it good; if them selves will cleare ye accounte & doe it, all shall be well. What ye evente of these things will be, I know not. The Lord so directe and assiste us, as he may not be dishonoured by our divissions. I hear (pr a freind) that I was much blamed for speaking wt I heard in ye spring of ye year, concerning ye buying & setting forth of yt ship; sure, if I should not have tould you what I heard so peremtorly reported (which report I offered now to prove at Bristoll), I should have been unworthy my implоymente. And concerning ye comission so long since given to Mr. Allerton, the truth is, the thing we feared is come upon us; for Mr. Sherley & ye rest have it, and will not deliver it, that being ye ground of our agents credite to procure great sumes. But I looke for bitter words, hard thoughts, and sower looks, from sundrie, as well for writing this, as reporting ye former. I would I had a more thankfull implоymente; but I hope a good conscience shall make it comefortable, &c....

"(187) Concerning Mr. Allerton's accounts, they were so larg and intrecate, as they could not well understand them, much less examine & correcte them, without a great deale of time & help, and his owne presence, which was now hard to gett amongst them; and it was 2. or 3. years before they could bring them to any good pass, but never make them perfecte....

Colony Must Pay Thousands of Pounds Sterling as Result of Allerton's Unauthorized Commitments

"Into these deepe sumes had Mr. Allerton rune them in tow years, for in ye later end of ye year 1628. all their debts did not amounte to much above 400li., as was then noted; and now come to so many thousands....

Colony Prospers

Trade Increases

Plowing and Tillage of Land Expands

"Though ye partners were thus pluged into great ingagments, & oppresed with unjust debts, yet ye Lord prospered their trading, that they made yearly large returnes, and had soone wound them selves out of all, if yet they had otherwise been well delt with all; as will more appear here after. (192) Also ye people of ye plantation begane to grow in their owtward estats, by reason of ye flowing of many people into ye cuntrie, espetially into ye Bay of ye Massachusets; by which means corne & catle rose to a great prise, by wch many were much inriched, and comodities grue plentifull; and yet in other regards this benefite turned to their hurte, and this accession of strength to their weaknes. For now as their stocks increased, and ye increse vendible, ther was no longer any holding them togeather, but now they must of necessitie goe to their great lots; they could not other wise keep their

The above excerpts are from the original manuscript, written 1647, (1901 Edition)

katle; and having oxen growne, they must have land for plowing & tillage. And no man now thought he could live, except he had catle and a great deale of ground to keep them; all striving to increase their stocks. By which means they were scatered all over ye bay, quickly, and ye towne, in which they lived compactly till now, was left very thine, and in a short time allmost desolate....

Population "Scattered all over the Bay"

"Having had formerly converse and famliarity with ye Dutch,.... they, seeing them seated here in a barren quarter, tould them of a river called by them ye Fresh River, but now is known by ye name of Conightecute-River, which they often comended unto them for a fine place both for plantation and trade, and wished them to make use of it. But their hands being full otherwise, they let it pass. But afterwards ther coming a company of banishte Indeans into these parts, that were drivene out from thence by the potencie of ye Pequents, which usurped upon them, and drive them from thence, they often sollisited them to goe thither, and they should have much trad, espetially if they would keep a house ther. And having now good store of comodities, and allso need to looke out wher they could advantage them selves to help them out of their great ingagments, they now begane to send that way to discover ye same, and trade with ye natives. They found it to be a fine place, but had no great store of trade; but ye Indeans excused ye same in regard of ye season, and the fear ye Indans were in of their enemise. So they tried diverse times, not with out profite, but saw ye most certainty would be by keeping a house ther, to receive ye trad when it came down out of ye inland. These Indeans, not seeing them very forward to build ther, solisited them of ye Massachusets in like sorte (for their end was to be restored to their countrie againe); but they in ye Bay being but latly come, were not fitte for ye same; but some of their cheefe made a motion to joyne wth the partners here, to trad joyntly with them in yt river, the which they were willing to imbrace, and so they should have builte, and put in equall stock togeather. A time of meeting was appointed at ye Massachusets, and some of ye cheefe here was appointed to treat with them, and went accordingly; but they cast many fears of deanger & loss and the like, which was perceived to be the maine obstacles, though they alledged they were not provided of trading goods. But those hear offered at presente to put in sufficiente for both, provided they would become ingaged for ye halfe, and prepare against ye nexte year. They confessed more could not be offered, but thanked them, and tould them they had no mind to it. They then answered, they hoped it would be no offence unto (197) them, if them sellves wente on without them, if they saw it meete. They said ther was no reason they should;

Dutch Recommend that Pilgrims Establish Plantation in Connecticut River Area

Pilgrims Ask Massachusetts Bay to Join in Connecticut Venture

Offer to Advance Supplies and Trading Goods

The above excerpts are from the original manuscript, written 1647, (1901 Edition)

Massachusetts Bay Colony Declines

and thus this treaty broake of, and those here tooke conveniente time to made a begining ther; and were ye first English that both discovered that place, and built in ye same, though they were litle better then thrust out of it afterward as may appeare.

Dutch Now Resist Plans of Pilgrims by Building Fort

"But ye Dutch begane now to repente, and hearing of their purpose & preparation, indeoured to prevente them, and gott in a litle before them, and made a slight forte, and planted 2. peeces of ordnance, thretening to stopp their passage. But they having made a smale frame of a house ready, and haveing a great new-barke, they stowed their frame in her hold, & bords to cover & finishe it, having nayles & all other provisions fitting for their use.... When they came up ye river, the Dutch demanded what they intended, and whither they would goe; they answered, up ye river to trade (now their order was to goe and seat above them). They bid them strike, & stay, or els they would shoote them; & stood by ther ordnance ready fitted. They answered they had comission from ye Govr of Plimoth to goe up ye river to such a place, and if they did shoote, they must obey their order and proceede; they would not molest them, but would goe one. So they passed along, and though the Dutch threatened them hard, yet they shoot not. Coming to their place, they clapt up their house quickly, and landed their provissions, and left ye companie appoynted, and sent the barke home; and afterwards palisadoed their house aboute, and fortified them selves better.... They did ye Dutch no wrong, for they took not a foote of any land they bought, but went to ye place above them, and bought that tracte of land which belonged to these Indeans which they carried with them, and their friends, with whom ye Dutch had nothing to doe....

Dutch Refuse to let Pilgrim Party Pass Fort

Pilgrims Proceed Unharmed; Land Provisions and Erect Trading Post

Pilgrims Pay Indians for Land

Remunerative Trade Improves Status of Colony

"It pleased ye Lord to inable them this year to send home a great quantity of beaver, besids paing all their charges, & debts at home, which good returne did much incourage their freinds in England. They sent in beaver 3366li. waight, and much of it coat beaver, which yeeled 20s. pr pound, & some of it above; and of otter-skines 346. sould also at a good prise. And thus much of ye affairs of this year....

"Mr. Winslow was very wellcome to them in England, and ye more in regard of ye large returne he brought with him, which came all safe to their hands, and was well sould. And he was borne in hand, (at least he so apprehended,) that all accounts should be cleared before his returne, and all former differences ther aboute well setled. And so he writ over to them hear, that he hoped to cleare ye accounts, and bring them over with him;

The above excerpts are from the original manuscript, written 1647, (1901 Edition)

and yt the accounte of ye White Angele (ship contracted for by Allerton) would be taken of, and all things fairly ended....

English Merchants Fail to Render Accounting but Colonists Continue to Make Shipments to Them

"Mr. Ed: Winslow was chosen Govr this year. In ye former year, because they perceived by Mr. Winslows later letters that no accounts would be sente, they resolved to keep ye beaver, and send no more, till they had them, or came to some further agreemente. At least they would forbear till Mr. Winslow came over, that by more full conferance with him they might better understand what was meete to be done. But when he came, though he brought no accounts, yet he perswaded them to send ye beaver, & was confident upon ye receite of yt beaver, & his letters, they should have accounts ye nexte year; and though they thought his grounds but weake, that gave him this hope, & made him so confidente, yet by his importunitie they yeelded, & sent ye same, ther being a ship at ye latter end of year, by whom they sente 1150li. waight of beaver, and 200. otter skins, besids sundrie small furrs, as 55. minks, 2. black foxe skins, &c. ...

"That which made them so desirous to bring things to an end was partly to stope ye clamours and aspertions raised & cast upon them hereaboute; though they conceived them selves to sustaine the greatest wrong, and had most cause of complainte; and partly because they feared ye fall of catle, in which most parte of their estats lay. And this was not a vaine feare; for they fell indeede before they came to a conclusion, and that so souddanly, as a cowe that but a month before was worth 20li., and would so have passed in any paymente, fell now to 5li. and would yeeld no more; and a goate that wente at 3li. or 50s. would not yeeld but 8. or 10s. at most. All men feared a fall of catle, but it was thought it would be by degrees; and not to be from ye highest pitch at once to ye lowest, as it did, which was greatly to ye damage of many, and ye undoing of some. An other reason was, they many of them grew aged, (and indeed a rare thing it was that so many partners should all live together so many years as these did,) and saw many changes were like to befall; so as they were loath to leave these intanglements upon their children and posteritie, who might be driven to remove places, as they had done; yea, them.selves might doe it yet before they dyed. But this bussines must yet rest; ye next year gave it more ripnes, though it rendred them less able to pay, for ye reasons afforesaid.

Low Price of Cattle Renders more Difficult the Final Settlement of Allerton's Unauthorized Obligations

"Mr. Sherley being weary of this controversie, and desirous of an end, (as well as them selves,) write to Mr. John Atwode and Mr. William Collier, 2. of ye inhabitants of this place, and of

The above excerpts are from the original manuscript, written 1647, (1901 Edition)

his speatiall aquaintance, and desired them to be a means to bring this bussines to an end, by advising & counselling the partners hear, by some way to bring it to a composition, by mutuall agreemente. And he write to them selves allso to yt end, as by his letter may apear; so much therof as concernse ye same I shall hear relate....

"Being thus by this leter, and allso by Mr. Atwodes & Mr.Colliers mediation urged to bring things to an end, (and ye continuall clamors from ye rest,) and by none more urged then by their own desires, they tooke this course (because many scandals had been raised upon them). They apoynted these 2. men before mentioned to meet on a certaine day, and called some other freinds on both sids, and Mr. Free-man, brother in law to Mr. Beachamp, and having drawne up a collection of all ye remains of ye stock, in what soever it was, as housing, boats, bark, and all implements belonging to ye same, as they were used in ye time of ye trad, were they better or worce, with ye remaines of all comodities, as beads, knives, hatchetts, cloth, or any thing els, as well ye refuse as ye more vendible, with all debts, as well those yt were desperate as others more hopefull; and having spent diverce days to bring this to pass, having ye helpe of all bookes and papers, which either any of them selves had, or Josias Winslow, who was their accountante; and they found ye sume in all to arise (as ye things were valued) to aboute 1400li. And they all of them tooke a voluntary but a sollem oath, in ye presence one of an other, and of all their frends, ye persons abovesaid yt were now presente, that this was all that any of them knew of, or could remember; and Josias Winslow did ye like for his parte....

Inventory of Property

Appraisal

Agreement Reached

"Marvilous it may be to see and consider how some kind of wickednes did grow & breake forth here, in a land wher the same was so much witnesed against, and so narrowly looked unto, & severly punished when it was knowne; as in no place more, or so much, that I have knowne or heard of; insomuch as they have been somewhat censured, even by moderate and good men, for their severitie in punishments. And yet all this could not suppress ye breaking out of sundrie notorious sins....I say it may justly be marveled at, and cause us to fear & tremble at the consideration of our corrupte natures, which are so hardly bridled, subdued, & mortified; nay, cannot by any other means but ye powerfull worke & grace of Gods spirite. But (besids this) one reason may be, that ye Divell may carrie a greater spite against the churches of Christ and ye gospell hear, by how much ye more they indeaour to preserve holynes and puritie amongst them, and strictly punisheth the contrary when it ariseth either in church or comone wealth;....

The above excerpts are from the original manuscript, written 1647, (1901 Edition)

Reasons for Difficulties

"But it may be demanded how came it to pass that so many wicked persons and profane people should so quickly come over into this land, & mixe them selves amongst them? seeing it was religious men yt begane ye work, and they came for religions sake. I confess this may be marveilled at, at least in time to come, when the reasons therof should not be knowne; and ye more because here was so many hardships and wants mett withall. I shall therfore indeavor to give some answer hereunto. And first, according to yt in ye gospell, it is ever to be remembred that wher ye Lord begins to sow good seed, ther ye envious man will endeavore to sow tares. 2. Men being to come over into a wildernes, in which much labour & servise was to be done aboute building & planting, &c., such as wanted help in yt respecte, when they could not have such as yey would, were glad to take such as they could; and so, many untoward servants, sundry of them proved, that were thus brought over, both men & women kind; who, when their times were expired, became families of them selves, which gave increase hereunto. 3. An other and a maine reason hearof was, that men, finding so many godly disposed persons willing to come into these parts, some begane to make a trade of it, to transeport passengers & their goods, and hired ships for that end; and then, to make up their fraight and advance their profite, cared not who ye persons were, so they had money to pay them. And by this means the cuntrie became pestered with many unworthy persons, who, being come over, crept into one place or other. 4. Againe, the Lords blesing usually following his people, as well in outward as spirituall things, (though afflictions be mixed withall,) doe make many to adhear to ye people of God, as many followed Christ, for ye loaves sake, Iohn 6. 26. and a mixed multitud came into ye willdernes with ye people of God out of Eagipte of old, Exod. 12. 38; so allso ther were sente by their freinds some under hope yt they would be made better; others that they might be eased of such burthens, and they kept from shame at home yt would necessarily follow their dissolute courses. And thus, by one means or other, in 20. years time, it is a question whether ye greater part be not growne ye worser.

"(250) I am now come to ye conclusion of that long & tedious bussines betweene ye partners hear, & them in England, the which I shall manifest by their owne letters as followeth, in such parts of them as are pertinente to ye same....

"I am to begine this year whith that which was a mater of great saddnes and mouring unto them all. Aboute ye 18. of Aprill dyed their Reved Elder, and my dear & loving friend, Mr. William Brewster; a man that had done and suffered much for ye Lord

The above excerpts are from the original manuscript, written 1647, (1901 Edition)

Jesus and ye gospells sake, and had bore his parte in well and woe with this poore persecuted church above 36. years (254) in England, Holand, and in this wildernes, and done ye Lord & them faithfull service in his place & calling. And notwithstanding ye many troubls and sorrows he passed throw, the Lord unheld him to a great age....

Pilgrim Longevity

"I cannot but here take occasion, not only to mention, but greatly to admire ye marvelous providence of God, that notwithstanding ye many changes and hardships that these people wente throwgh, and ye many enemies they had and difficulties they mette with all, that so many of them should live to very olde age! It was not only this reved mans condition, (for one swallow maks no summer, as they say,) but many more of them did ye like, some dying aboute and before this time, and many still living, who attained to 60. years of age, and to 65. diverse to 70. and above, and some nere 80. as he did. It must needs be more then ordinarie, and above naturall reason, that so it should be; for it is found in experience, that chaing of aeir, famine, or unholsome foode, much drinking of water, sorrows & troubls, &c., all of them are enimies to health, causes of many diseaces, consumers of naturall vigoure and ye bodys of men, and shortners of life. And yet of all these things they had a large parte, and suffered deeply in ye same. They wente from England to Holand, wher they found both worse air and dyet then that they came from; from thence (induring a long imprisonmente, as it were, in ye ships at sea) into New-England; and how it hath been with them hear hath allready beene showne; and what crosses, troubls, fears, wants, and sorrowes they had been lyable unto, is easie to conjecture; so as in some sorte they may say with ye Apostle, 2. Cor: 11. 26, 27. they were in journeyings often, in perils of waters, in perills of robers, in perills of their owne nation, in perils among ye heathen, in perills in ye willdernes, in perills in ye sea, in perills among false breethern, in wearines & painfullnes, in watching often, in hunger and thirst, in fasting often, in could and nakednes. What was it then that upheld them? It was Gods vissitation that preserved their spirits. Job 10. 12. Thou hast given me life and grace, and thy vissitation hath preserved my spirite. He that upheld ye Apostle upheld them. They were persecuted, but not forsaken, cast downe, but perished not. 2. Cor: 4. 9. As unknowen, and yet knowen; as dying, and behold we live; as chastened, and yett not kiled. 2. Cor: 6. 9. God, it seems, would have all men to behold and observe such mercies and works of his providence as these are towards his people, that they in like cases might be incouraged to depend upon God in their trials, &

The above excerpts are from the original manuscript, written 1647, (1901 Edition)

also blese his name when they see his goodnes towards others. Man lives not by bread only, Deut: 8. 3. It is not by good & dainty fare, by peace, & rest, and harts ease, in injoying ye contentments and good things of this world only, that preserves health and prolongs life. God in such examples would have ye world see & behold that he can doe it without them; and if ye world will shut ther eyes, and take no notice therof, yet he would have his people to see and consider it. Daniell could be better liking with pulse then others were with ye kings dainties. Jaacob, though he wente from one nation to another people, and passed throw famine, fears, & many afflictions, yet he lived till old age, and dyed sweetly, & rested in ye Lord, as infinite others of Gods servants have done, and still shall doe, (through Gods goodnes,) notwithstanding all ye malice of their enemies; when ye branch of ye wicked shall be cut of before his day, Job. 15. 32. and ye bloody and deceitfull men shall not live out halfe their days. Psa: 55. 23....

Anno Dom: 1646

"This year Mr. Edward Winslow went into England, upon this occation: some discontented persons under ye govermente of the Massachusets sought to trouble their peace, and distrube, if not innovate, their govermente, by laying many (270) scandals upon them; and intended to prosecute against them in England, by petitioning & complaining to the Parlemente. Allso Samuell Gorton & his company made complaints against them; so as they made choyse of Mr. Winslow to be their agente, to make their defence, and gave him comission & instructions for that end; in which he so carried him selfe as did well answer their ends, and cleared them from any blame or dishonour, to the shame of their adversaries....

The above excerpts are from the original manuscript, written 1647, (1901 Edition)

THE "MAYFLOWER."

THE INDEPENDENTS

PILGRIMS OF THE MAYFLOWER WERE NOT PURITANS

"...the Rev. Mr. John Robinson, of Leyden, the father of the Independents, whose numerous congregations being on the decline, by their aged members dying off and their children marrying into Dutch families, they consulted how to preserve their church and religion; and at length...resolved to remove into some part of America...the adventurers were about one hundred and twenty, who, having joined their other ship, sailed for New England, August 5; but one of their vessels proved leaky, they left it, and embarked in one vessel, which arrived at Cape Cod November 9, 1620."

- Daniel Neal, "History of the Puritans", 1731

"...They had sought refuge in Holland, where their minds were braced and their scriptural views confirmed...

"The reasonings of the Independents were broad and more comprehensive than those of their predecessors...

"Abandoning the partial and unsatisfactory ground which had been taken by the Puritans, they entrenched themselves behind the nature of man and the character of Christianity and would enter into no compromise which endangered the highest and best interests of the human family...to form and propagate their opinions, they honestly contended. Hence their claims on the gratitude and admiration of posterity. The principles for which Locke and succeeding philosophers triumphantly pleaded were brought forth to public view, and instilled in the national mind..."

- Price, "History of Non-conformity".

HARVARD COLLEGE

AFTER God had carried us safe to New England, and wee had builded our houses, provided necessaries for our liveli-hood, rear'd convenient places for Gods worship, and settled the Civill Government: One of the next things we longed for, and looked after was to advance Learning, and perpetuate it to Posterity, dreading to leave an illiterate Ministery to the Churches, when our present Ministers shall lie in the Dust. And as wee were thinking and consulting how to effect this great Work; it pleased God to stir up the heart of one Mr. Harvard (a godly Gentlemen and a lover of Learning, there living amongst us) to give the one halfe of his Estate...towards the erecting of a Colledge, and all his Library...

"Rules, and Precepts that are observed in the Colledge...Let every Student be plainly instructed, and earnestly pressed to consider well, the maine end of his life and studies is, to know God and Jesus Christ which is eternall life, John 17:3 and therefore to lay Christ in the bottome, as the only foundation of all found knowledge and Learning..."

- "Old South Leaflets", Taken from a letter dated Boston, Sept. 26, 1642

INFLUENCE OF THE PLYMOUTH SETTLEMENT

Effect Of The Pilgrims On The Puritans

IN 1628 occured a movement of vital consequence to Plymouth. The various English claims around Boston and Salem had been absorbed or superseded by the Massachusetts Bay Company, which strong corporation had a grant from the Council for New England of all the territory from three miles south of Charles River to three miles north of the Marrimack, and reaching from the Atlantic to the Pacific... The new Company's grant was confirmed by the King in a charter of unprecedented liberality in the matter of self-government by the Company (but not intentionally by the people). Many members of the new body were men of wealth and education; some had titles, and several had influential connections. It was expected that the corporation and its officers would continue in England; and with this idea, in 1628 it sent over to Naumkeag (Salem) John Endicott as a sort of deputy-governor, with a body of working-men. Endicott found already on his territory some eight settlements, ranging from single households to the village at Naumkeag under Conant... Endicott's people, living through their first winter largely upon meats preserved in the unwholesome salt already noticed, and having imperfect housing, suffered a mortality like that of the Pilgrims in their first season. Soon a cry for help went out to Plymouth. Through Roger Conant, Endicott must have learned of Plymouth's 'good physician,' Dr. Fuller, and Bradford was entreated to send him to Salem. Fuller hastened to the sufferers, and repeated his journey both that year and the next...

dicott
nt to
lem

"Fuller had long been a Congregational deacon, and the deacons in that Church, even though laymen, were as carefully selected and as formally ordained as were the clergy. Our medical deacon seems to have been strong as a theologian. In Salem the Episcopal form of worship had been the only one known from the beginning in 1625-6; and Endicott and his fellows, as Puritans, not only adhered to it, but no one who saw them depart from England supposed that they would ever do otherwise. While warring against disease, Deacon Fuller also assailed Endicott's Puritanism, and with more decided results.

ilgrim Fuller
ssails
ndicott's
uritanism

"At the end of this visit Endicott sent Governor Bradford a letter expressing his thanks for it; and also exhibiting the Puritan prejudice with which he had theretofore regarded Separatists and 'Brownists,' but which he had found groundless. On this point he said: -

The above excerpts are from John A. Goodwin's "The Pilgrim Republic" - 1888

Groundless prejudice of Pilgrims

"'I acknowledge myself much bound to you for your kind love and care in sending Mr. Fuller among us, and rejoice much that I am by him satisfied touching your judgments of the outward form of God's worship. It is, as far as I can yet gather, no other than is warranted by the evidences of truth, and the same which I have professed and maintained ever since the Lord in mercy revealed himself unto me; being far from the common report that hath been spread of you touching that particular.'

Prevailing influence of Pilgrim independency

"Thus Endicott came to Salem as an Episcopalian, and so remained for his first year; and the Separatists of Plymouth (still miscalled Brownists) were 'everywhere spoken against'. But Endicott was about to take the lead in a remarkable change....

"Thus after an unquestioned sway of some four years was Episcopacy slain in the house of its friends, and Independency exalted to its place. Yet so odious was the term Separatist, or Separation, that the Salem clergy, while clinging to the thing, indignantly disowned its name. But their Independency, at that trial of it, had a far shorter tenancy than the rule it had supplanted. In 1630 arrived Winthrop with a great company, who had after embarkation written a farewell message to the Puritan friends unable to accompany them, and had addressed it 'To the Rest of their brethren in and of the Church of England,' therein declaring themselves 'members of the same body,' who should 'unfeignedly grieve for any sorrow that shall ever betide her,... our dear mother;' yet these immigrants turned their backs on this 'dear mother' as soon as they came within the influence of Higginson, Skelton, and Endicott....

Genial spirit of Pilgrims supplants bigoted sternness of Puritans

"The religious despotism which so despotically ruled the Bay Colony often exerted a malign influence on the comparatively liberal Plymouth; but the Independency of the latter not only survived, but extended itself until Congregationalism became the 'standing order,' even in Massachusetts and its child Connecticut. Massachusetts, led by an aristocracy, social and religious, and acting under the King's charter, was in many respects the opposite of the Congregationalist Plymouth, whose yeomen and artisans were fortunate in the fact that royalty and nobility had thus far ignored their self-authorized little democracy. That the incorporated, highly connected Colonists at the Bay often assumed airs of superiority over the almost friendless plebeian State beside them, was natural; as also was it that the sturdy commonsense and liberal leanings of the weaker body should finally permeate the other, so that after two generations of rivalry the more

The above excerpts are from John A. Goodwin's "The Pilgrim Republic" - 1888

genial spirit of the Pilgrims should supplant the bigoted sternness of the Puritans."

The above excerpts are from John A. Goodwin's "The Pilgrim Republic" - 1888

Influence of Plymouth

Pilgrims were Separatists

One salient fact in the history of the Massachusetts Bay colony is the dominant influence of the example of Plymouth. The Puritans of the Massachusetts colony were not Separatists. No one had been more severe in controversy with the Separatists than some of the Puritans who remained in the Church of England. They were eagerly desirous not to be confounded with these schismatics....

Puritans Originally were not Separatists

Pilgrim Independency Became Model

"It is to be remembered that these Puritans did not agree among themselves. Puritanism was of many shades. There were some, like the Brownes whom Endicott sent out of the colony, that were even unwilling to surrender the prayer book. The greater part of the earlier Puritans had desired to imitate the Presbyterianism of Scotland and Geneva, and in Elizabeth's time they had organized presbyteries. Nothing seemed more probable beforehand than the revival in New England of the presbyteries of the days of Cartwright. But what happened was unexpected even by the Puritans. The churches of Massachusetts were formed on the model of John Robinson's Independency.

By Coming to America Puritans Found Themselves Utterly Free

"There must have been a certain exhilarant reaction in the minds of the Puritans when at last they were clear of the English coast and free from the authority that had put so many constraints upon them. There were preachings and expoundings by beloved preachers with no fear of pursuivants. The new religious freedom was delightful to intoxication. 'Every day for ten weeks together,' writes one passenger, they had preaching and exposition. On one ship the watches were set by the Puritan captain with the accompaniment of psalm-singing. Those who all their lives long had made outward and inward compromises between their ultimate convictions and their obligations to antagonistic authority found themselves at length utterly free. It was not that action was freed from the restraint of fear, so much as that thought itself was freed from the necessity for politic compromises. Every ship thus became a seminary for discussion. Every man now indulged in the unwonted privilege of thinking his bottom thought. The tendency to swing to an extreme is all

The above excerpts are from Edward Eggleston's "The Beginners of a Nation" - 1896

Objections to Old Order Clearly Seen

Puritans Came to Agree with Pilgrim Independence

Pilgrim Toleration not easily Communicated

but irresistible in the minds of men thus suddenly liberated. To such enthusiasts the long-deferred opportunity to actualize ultimate ideals in an ecclesiastical vacuum would be accepted with joy. What deductions such companies would finally make from the hints in the New Testament was uncertain. The only sure thing was that every vestige of that which they deemed objectionable in the English church would be repressed, obliterated, in their new organization. With the evils and the abuses of English church more and more exaggerated in their thoughts, the sin of separation readily came to seem less heinous than before. There was no longer any necessity for professing loyalty to the church nor any further temptation to think ill of those at Plymouth, who, like themselves had suffered much to avoid what both Separatist and Puritans deemed unchristian practices. Thus the church discipline and the form of government in Massachusetts borrowed much from Plymouth, but the mildness and semi-toleration - the 'toleration of tolerable opinions' - which Robinson had impressed on the Pilgrims was not so easily communicated to their new neighbors who had been trained in another school.

The above excerpts are from Edward Eggleston's "The Beginners of a Nation" - 1896

THE INDEPENDENTS INSTRUCTED JOHN LOCKE

THE character of Mr. Locke's writings cannot be well understood, without considering the circumstances of the writer. Educated among the English Dissenters, during the short period of their political ascendency, he early imbibed the deep piety and ardent spirit of liberty which actuated that body of men... Sects, founded on the right of private judgment, naturally tend to purify themselves from intolerance, and in time learn to respect, in others, the freedom of thought, to the exercise of which they owe their own existence.

John Locke instructed by the Independents

"By the Independent divines who were his instructors, our philosopher was taught those principles of religious liberty which they were the first to disclose to the world...

"Dr. Owen, the Independent, was Dean of Christchurch in 1651, when Locke was admitted a member of that college..."

The above excerpts are from "The Miscellaneous Works" of Sir James Mackintosh, 1851

PLYMOUTH

Spirit of the First Settlement

Prospect of futurity

"We live in the past by a knowledge of its history"

Relating past to present

First scene of our history

LET us rejoice that we behold this day.

"Let us be thankful that we have lived to see the bright and happy breaking of the auspicious morn, when commences the third century of the history of New England. Auspicious indeed, - bringing a happiness beyond the common allotment of Providence to men, - full of present joy, and gilding with bright beams the prospect of futurity, is the dawn that awakens us to the commemoration of the landing of the Pilgrims...

"It is a noble faculty of our nature which enables us to connect our thought, our sympathies, and our happiness with what is distant in place or time; and, looking before and after, to hold communion at once with our ancestors and our posterity. Human and mortal although we are, we are nevertheless not mere insulated beings, without relation to the past or the future. Neither the point of time, nor the spot of earth, in which we physically live, bounds our rational and intellectual enjoyments. We live in the past by a knowledge of its history; and in the future by hope and anticipation. By ascending to an association with our ancestors; by contemplating their example and studying their character; by partaking their sentiments, and imbibing their spirit; by accompanying them in their toils, by sympathizing in their sufferings, and rejoicing in their successes and their triumphs; we seem to belong to their age, and to mingle our own existence with theirs...

"And in like manner, by running along the line of future time, by contemplating the probable fortunes of those who are coming after us, by attempting something which may promote their happiness, and leave some not dishonorable memorial of ourselves for their regard, when we shall sleep with the fathers, we protract our own earthly being, and seem to crown whatever is future, as well as all that is past, into the narrow compass of our earthly existence... Standing in this relation to our ancestors and our posterity, we are assembled on this memorable spot, to perform the duties which that relation and the present occasion impose upon us. We have come to this Rock, to record here our homage for our Pilgrim Fathers... We feel that we are on the spot where the first scene of our history was laid; where the hearths and altars of New England were first placed; where Christianity, and civilization, and let-

The above excerpts are from Daniel Webster's "A Discourse delivered at Plymouth, on the 22nd of December, 1820 by Daniel Webster", Vol. I, The Works of Daniel Webster - 1851

ters made their first lodgement, in a vast extent of country, covered with a wilderness, and peopled by roving barbarians....

Love of country

"Different, indeed, most widely different, from all these instances of emigration and plantation, were the condition, the purposes, and the prospects of our fathers, when they established their infant colony upon this spot.... A new existence awaited them here; and when they waw these shores, rough, cold, barbarous, and barren, as then they were, they beheld their country. That mixed and strong feeling, which we call love of country, and which is, in general, never extinguished in the heart of man, grasped and embraced its proper object here. Whatever constitutes country, except the earth and the sun, all the moral causes of affection and attachment which operate upon the heart, they had brought with them to their new abode. Here were now their families and friends, their homes, and their property. Before they reached the shore, they had established the elements of a social system, and at a much earlier period had settled their forms of religious worship.

National sentiments

"At the moment of their landing, therefore, they possessed institutions of government, and institutions of religion: and friends and families, and social and religious institutions, framed by consent, founded on choice and preference, how nearly do these fill up our whole idea of country!

The making of a nation

"The morning that beamed on the first night of their repose saw the Pilgrims already at home in their country. There were political institutions, and civil liberty, and religious worship. Poetry has fancied nothing, in the wanderings of heroes, so distinct and characteristic. Here was man, indeed, unprotected, and unprovided for, on the shore of a rude and fearful wilderness; but it was politic, intelligent, and educated man. Everything was civilized but the physical world. Institutions, containing in substance all that ages had done for human government, were organized in a forest.

The Pilgrim was politic, intelligent and educated

"Cultivated mind was to act on uncultivated nature; and, more than all, a government and a country were to commence, with the very first foundations laid under the divine light of the Christian religion. Happy auspices of a happy futurity! Who would wish that his country's existence had otherwise begun? Who would desire the power of going back to the ages of fable? Who would wish for an origin obscured in the darkness of antiquity? Who would wish for other emblazoning of his country's heraldry,

First foundations Christian

The above excerpts are from "The Works of Daniel Webster" - 1851, Vol. I

or other ornaments of her genealogy, than to be able to say, that her first existence was with intelligence, her first breath the inspiration of liberty, her first principle the truth of divine religion?....

True morality Christian

"Lastly, our ancestors established their system of government on morality and religious sentiment. Moral habits, they believed, cannot safely be trusted on any other foundation than religious principle, nor any government be secure which is not supported by moral habits. Living under the heavenly light of revelation, they hoped to find all the social dispositions, all the duties which men owe to each other and to society, enforced and performed. Whatever makes men good Christians, makes them good citizens....

"Her eyes look toward the sea. Forever she beholds upon its waves the incoming 'Mayflower'; she sees the Pilgrims land. They vanish, but she, the monument of their faith, remains, and tells their story to the world. This our generation too shall pass away, and its successors for centuries-to-come; but she will stand, and, overlooking our forgotten memory, will still speak of them and of their foundation of the Republic on the Plymouth Rocks of Liberty, Law, Morality, and Education."

- John D. Long

Statue of Faith
Pilgrim Monument

To know our responsibility

"If the blessings of our political and social condition have not been too highly estimated, we cannot well overrate the responsibility and duty which they impose upon us. We hold these institutions of government, religion, and learning, to be transmitted, as well as enjoyed. We are in the line of conveyance, through which whatever has been obtained by the spirit and efforts of our ancestors is to be communicated to our children.

To avoid disaster

"We are bound to maintain public liberty, and, by the example of our own systems, to convince the world that order and law, religion and morality, the rights of conscience, the rights of persons, and the rights of property, may all be preserved and secured, in the most perfect manner, by a government entirely and purely elective. If we fail in this, our disaster will be signal, and will furnish an argument, stronger than has yet been found, in support of those opinions which maintain that government can rest safely on nothing but power and coercion....

The above excerpts are from "The Works of Daniel Webster" - 1851, Vol. I

SABBATH IN THE COMMON HOUSE AT PLYMOUTH.

The American culture

"The cause of science and literature also imposes upon us an important and delicate trust.... If, almost on the day of their landing, our ancestors founded schools and endowed colleges, what obligations do not rest upon us, living under circumstances so much more favorable both for providing and for using the means of education? Literature becomes free institutions. It is the graceful ornament of civil liberty, and a happy restraint on the asperities which political controversies sometimes occasion. Just taste is not only an embellishment of society, but it rises almost to the rank of the virtues, and diffuses positive good throughout the whole extent of its influence. There is a connection between right feeling and right principles, and truth in taste is allied with truth in morality....

Truth in truth allied with morality

"Finally, let us not forget the religious character of our origin. Our fathers were brought hither by their high veneration for the Christian religion. They journeyed by its light, and labored in its hope. They sought to incorporate its principles with the elements of their society, and to diffuse its influence through all their institutions, civil, political, or literary. Let us cherish these sentiments, and extend this influence still more widely; in the full conviction, that that is the happiest society which partakes in the highest degree of the mild and peaceful spirit of Christianity."

Our Founding Fathers and the Christian Religion

The above excerpts are from "The Works of Daniel Webster" - 1851, Vol. I

LIFE, LIBERTY & PROPERTY

"And tis' not without Reason, that he seeks out, and is willing to joyn in Society with others, who are already united, or have a Mind to unite, for the mutual PRESERVATION of their Lives, Liberties and Estates, which I call by the general Name, PROPERTY."

- John Locke, "Of the Ends of Political Society and Government", 1690

"It is observable that, though many have disregarded life and contemned liberty, yet there are few men who do not agree that property is a valuable acquisition...Those who ridicule the ideas of right and justice, faith and truth, among men, will put a high value upon money. Property is admitted to have an existence even in the savage state of nature...And if property is necessary for the support of savage life, it is by no means less so in civil society. The utopian schemes of levelling, and a community of goods, are as visionary and impracticable as those which vest all property in the Crown are arbitrary, despotic, and in our government, unconstitutional."

- Samuel Adams, 1768

"We hold these Truths to be self-evident, that all Men are created equal, that they are endowed by their Creator with certain unalienable Rights, that among these are Life, Liberty, and the Pursuit of Happiness - That to secure these Rights, Governments are instituted among Men..."

- "A Declaration by the Representatives of the United States of America"
The Declaration of Independence, 1776

"PROPERTY...In the former sense, a man's land, or merchandise, or money, is called his property. In the latter sense, a man has a property in his opinions and the free communication of them. He has a property of peculiar value in his religious opinions, and in the profession and practice dictated by them...He has an equal property in the free use of his faculties, and free choice of the objects on which to employ them. In a word, as a man is said to have a right to his property, he may be equally said to have a property in his rights. Where an excess of power prevails, property of no sort is duly respected. No man is safe in his opinions, his person, his faculties, or his possessions. Where there is an excess of liberty, the effect is the same...Government is instituted to protect property of every sort...This being the end of government...Conscience is the most sacred of all property; other property depending in part on positive law, the exercise of that being a natural and unalienable right...A just security to property is not afforded by that government, under which unequal taxes oppress one species of property and reward another species..."

- James Madison, "Property", 1792

"In studying the laws which were promulgated at this first era of the American republics, it is impossible not to be struck by the remarkable acquaintance with the science of government, and the advanced theory of legislation which they display... In the laws of Connecticut, as well as in all those of New England, we find the germ and gradual development of that township independence which is the life and mainspring of American liberty of the present day ..."

-De Tocqueville

OCTOBER 8, 1635... settlements had been commenced, by emigrants from the environs of Boston, at Hartford, and Windsor, and Wethersfield; and in the last days of the pleasantest of the autumnal months, a company of sixty pilgrims, women and children being of the number, began their march to the west. Never before had the forests of America witnessed such a scene. But the journey was begun too late in the season: the winter was so unusually early and severe, that provisions could not arrive by way of the river; imperfect shelter had been provided; cattle perished in great numbers; and the men suffered such privations, that many of them, in the depth of winter, abandoned their newly-chosen homes, and waded through the snows to the sea-board.

APRIL 26, 1636... Yet, in the opening of next year, a government was organized, and civil order established; and the budding of the trees and the springing of the grass were signals for a greater emigration to the Connecticut. Some smaller parties had already made their way to the new Hesperia of Puritanism. In June, the principal caravan began its march, led by Thomas Hooker, 'the light of the Western Churches'. There were of the company about one hundred souls; many of them persons accustomed to affluence and the ease of European life. They drove before them numerous herds of cattle; and thus they traversed on foot the pathless forests of Massachusetts... Never again was there such a pilgrimage from the sea-side 'to the delightful banks' of the Connecticut. The emigrants had been gathered from among the most valued citizens, the earliest settlers, and the oldest churches of the Bay..."

The above excerpts are from George Bancroft's "History of the United States" - 1850

THE FIRST AMERICAN CONSTITUTION: 1638

"FUNDAMENTAL ORDERS OF CONNECTICUT"

Three Self-Governing Independent Connecticut Towns Form and Establish the First Written Constitution

THE same year, witnessed the preliminary proceedings, very imperfectly recorded, of one of the most interesting events in all civil history - the establishment of a written constitution for the government of the Colony; the 'first written constitution', it has been called, 'in the history of nations'.

Towns elect delegates to frame laws

"The common affairs of these towns along the River had at first been conducted by a provisional government under Massachusetts authority. But the term of that commission having expired, a General Court of the towns took its place.

"At some time in 1638 a General Court was elected for the purpose of framing a body of laws for the permanent government of the Colony.

"The deliberations of the assembly thus chosen have perished. We know only the result, which arrived at the authority of Fundamental Laws on the 14th of January, 1639.

Recognition of the origin of law

"That Charter of public rule was a document far in advance of anything the world had ever seen, in its recognition of the origin of all civil authority as derived, under God, from the agreement and covenant of the whole body of the governed.

"Such a 'combination and Confederation together... to be guided and governed according to such Lawes, Rules, Orders, and decrees as shall be made, ordered & decreed,' marks a reckoning point in the history and science of government.

The above excerpts are from "History of the First Church in Hartford - 1633-1883" by George Leon Walker, 1884

Governing principle learned in religious matters

"But the chief interest in this matter, so far as the present chronicle is concerned, is not a scientific one, or even a historic one, reckoned from the point of the concerns of civil administration only. The interest of the subject, as connected with this Church survey, now in hand, is twofold: It is, first, that the form of civil government here established was simply an extension to the domain of secular affairs of the principles already adopted in religious matters - the mutual covenant and agreement of those associated, as under God the ultimate law. And, second, and more particularly, because of the agency in leading on to the establishment of this principle in the Fundamental Laws of this Colony, of the wise and far-sighted Pastor of this Church. We are indebted for the discovery of definite evidence of this agency - though it might have been antecedently conjectured from all that we know of the man who exercised it - to the skill and research of the distinguished antiquarian scholar, J. H. Trumbull.

Volume found in Windsor, Connecticut

"The evidence lay undiscovered more than two and a quarter centuries in a little, almost undecipherable volume of manuscript, written by a young man - Mr. Henry Wolcott, Jr., born January, 1610 - in the neighbor town of Windsor. The volume contains notes in cipher of sermons and lectures preached by Rev. Messrs. Warham and Huit of Windsor, and Rev. Messrs. Hooker and Stone of Hartford. In it is found an abstract of Mr. Hooker's lecture given on 'Thursday, May 31, 1638, at an adjourned session, probably of the April Court; and apparently designed to lead the way to the general recognition of the great truths which were soon to be successfully incorporated in the Fundamental Laws.' The following is the deciphered abstract of the sermon:

<u>TEXT:</u> Sermon May 31, 1638

Deuteronomy 1: 13. 'Take you wise men, and understanding, and known among your tribes, and I will make them rulers over you.' Captains over thousands, and captains over hundreds - over fifties - over tens, etc.

<u>DOCTRINE:</u>

I. That the choice of public magistrates belongs unto the people by God's own allowance.

II. The privilege of election which belongs unto the people, therefore, must not be exercised according to their humors, but according to the blessed will and law of God.

III. They who have power to appoint officers and magistrates, it is their power, also, to set the bounds of the power and place unto which they call them.

The above excerpts are from "History of the First Church in Hartford - 1633-1883" by George Leon Walker, 1884

REASONS:

I. Because the foundation of authority is laid, firstly, in the free consent of the people.

II. Because, by a free choice the hearts of the people will be more inclined to the love of the persons (chosen), and more ready to yield (obedience).

III. Because of that duty and engagement of the people.

USES:

The lesson taught is threefold: -

I. There is matter of thankful acknowledgment in the (appreciation) of God's faithfulness towards us and the permission of these measures that God doth commend and vouchsafe.

II. Of reproof - to dash the conceits of all those that shall oppose it.

III. Of exhortation - to persuade us as God hath given us liberty, to take it.

And lastly. As God hath spared our lives, and given us them in liberty, so to seek the guidance of God, and to choose in God and for God.'

"The doctrine was adapted to the auditors and to the time. It was harmonious with the experiences and the teachings of Providence in which the hearers had been led. But its statement was a novelty in politics, not the less. Dr. Badon says of it: 'That sermon by Thomas Hooker from the pulpit of the First Church in Hartford, is the earliest known suggestion of a fundamental law, enacted not by royal charter, nor by concession from any previously existing government, but by the people themselves - a primary and supreme law by which the government is constituted, and which not only provides for the free choice of magistrates by the people, but also 'sets the bounds and limitations of the power and place to which each magistrate is called.'

"Eight months later, the fundamental laws embodying these principles for the first time in human history, were 'sentenced, ordered, and decreed'. It is impossible not to recognize the Master hand. The Pastor of the Hartford Church was Connecticut's great Legislator, also.

The above excerpts are from "History of the First Church in Hartford - 1633-1883" by George Leon Walker, 1884

CONNECTICUT REPUBLIC

Early Model of the American Republic of Self-Governing Independent States

First written constitution in history that created a civil government

AT the opening session of the General Court, May 31, 1638, Mr. Hooker preached a sermon of wonderful power, in which he maintained that 'the foundation of authority is laid in the free consent of the people, that the choice of public magistrates belongs unto the people by God's own allowance', and that 'they who have power to appoint officers and magistrates have the right also to set the bounds and limitations of the power and place unto which they call them'. On the 14th of January, 1639, all the freemen of the three towns assembled at Hartford, and adopted a written constitution in which the hand of the great preacher is clearly discernible. It is worthy of note that this document contains none of the conventional references to a 'dread sovereign' or a 'gracious king', nor the slightest allusion to the British or any other government outside of Connecticut itself, nor does it prescribe any condition of church-membership for the right of suffrage. It was the first written constitution known to history, that created a government, and it marked the beginnings of American democracy, of which Thomas Hooker deserves more than any other man to be called the father.

Early model for the United States of America

"The government of the United States today is in lineal descent more nearly related to that of Connecticut than to that of any of the other thirteen colonies. The most noteworthy features of the Connecticut republic was that it was a federation of independent towns, and that all attributes of sovereignty not expressly granted to the General Court remained, as of original right, in the towns...

Results of the normal and unthwarted development of a Christian republic

"This little federal republic was allowed to develop peacefully and normally; its constitution was not violently wrenched out of shape like that of Massachusetts at the end of the seventeenth century. It silently grew till it became the strongest political structure on the continent, as was illustrated in the remarkable military energy and the unshaken financial credit of Connecticut during the Revolutionary War; and in the chief crisis of the Federal Convention of 1787 Connecticut, with her compromise which secured equal state representation in one branch of the national government and popular representation in the other, played the controlling part."

The above excerpts are from John Fiske's "Beginnings of New England" - 1889

FUNDAMENTAL ORDERS Of Connecticut

Inhabitants of Windsor, Herteford & Wethersfield form a union

FORASMUCH as it has pleased the Almighty God by the wise disposition of his divine prudence so to order and dispose of things that we the inhabitants and residents of Windsor, Harteford and Wethersfield are now cohabiting and dwelling in and upon the River of Conectecotte and the lands thereunto adjoining; and well knowing where a people are gathered together the word of God requires that to maintain the peace and union of such a people there should be an orderly and decent government established according to God, to order and dispose of the affairs of the people at all seasons as occasion shall require; do therefore associate and conjoin ourselves to be as one Public State or commonwealth; and do, for ourselves and our successors and such as shall be adjoined to us at any time hereafter, enter into combination and confederation together, to maintain and preserve the liberty and purity of the gospel of our Lord Jesus which we now profess, as also the discipline of the Churches, which according to the truth of the said gospel is now practiced amongst us; as also in our civil affairs to be guided and governed according to such laws, rules, orders and decrees as shall be made, ordered and decreed, as follows:

Two general assemblies

Annual elections

Qualifications for citizenship

"1. It is ordered, sentenced and decreed, that there shall be yearly two general Assemblies or Courts, the one on the second Thursday in April, the other the second Thursday in September, following; the first shall be called the Court of Election, wherein shall be yearly chosen from time to time so many magestrates and other public officers as shall be found requisite: Whereof one to be chosen governor for the year ensueing and until another be chosen, and no other magestrate to be chosen for more than one year; provided always there be six chosen besides the governor; which being chosen and sworn according to an oath recorded for that purpose shall have power to administer justice according to the laws here established, and for want thereof according to the rule of the word of God; which choice shall be made by all that are admitted freemen and have taken the Oath of Fidelity, and do cohabit within this jurisdiction, (having been admitted inhabitants by the major part of the town wherein they live), or the major part of such as shall be then present.

The above excerpts are from "Old South Leaflets", No. 8

Vote by ballot

"2. It is ordered, sentenced and decreed, that the election of the aforesaid magestrates shall be on this manner: every person present and qualified for choice shall bring in (to the persons deputed to receive them) one single paper with the name of him written in it whom he desires to have Governor, and he that hath the greatest number of papers shall be Governor for that year. And the rest of the magestrates or public officers to be chosen in this manner: The secretary for the time being shall first read the names of all that are to be put to choice and then shall severally nominate them distinctly, and every one that would have the person nominated to be chosen shall bring one single paper written upon, and he that would not have him chosen shall bring a blank: and every one that has more written papers than blanks shall be a magistrate for that year; which papers shall be recalled and told by one or more that shall be then chosen by the court and sworn to be faithful therein; but in case there should not be six chosen as aforesaid, besides the Governor, out of those which are nominated, then he or they which have the most written papers shall be a magistrate or magestrates for the ensueing year, to make up the foresaid number.

Nomination method

"3. It is ordered, sentenced and decreed, that the secretary shall not nominate any person, nor shall any person be chosen newly into the magestracy which was not propounded in some General Court before, to be nominated the next election; and to that end it shall be lawful for each of the towns aforesaid by their deputies to nominate any two whom they conceive fit to be put to election; and the Court may add so many more as they judge requisite.

Limitation on term of office

Qualifications for public office

"4. It is ordered, sentenced and decreed that no person be chosen Governor above once in two years, and that the Governor be always a member of some approved congregation, and formerly of the magestracy within this jurisdiction; and all the magestrates freemen of this commonwealth: and that no magestrate or other public officer shall execute any part of his or their office before they are severally sworn, which shall be done in the face of the Court if they be present, and in case of absence by some deputed for that purpose.

Representative system

"5. It is ordered, sentenced and decreed, that to the aforesaid Court of Election the several towns shall send their deputies and when the elections are ended they may proceed in any public service as at other courts. Also the other General Court in September shall be for making of laws, and any other public occasion, which concerns the good of the commonwealth.

The above excerpts are from "Old South Leaflets", No. 8

Due notice given in calling Assemblies

"6. It is ordered, sentenced and decreed, that the Governor shall, either by himself or by the secretary, send out summons to the constables of our town for the calling of these two standing courts one month at least before their several times: And also if the Governor and the greatest part of the magestrates see cause upon any special occasion to call a general court, they may give order to the secretary so to do within fourteen days warning; and if urgent necessity so require, upon a shorter notice, giving sufficient grounds for it to the deputies when they meet, or else be questioned for the same; And if the Governor and major part of magestrates shall either neglect or refuse to call the two general standing courts or either of them, as also at other times when the occasions of the commonwealth require, the freemen thereof, or the major part of them, shall petition to them so to do: if then it be either denied or neglected the said freemen or the major part of them shall have power to give order to the constables of the several towns to do the same, and so may meet together, and choose to themselves a moderator, and may proceed to do any act of power, which any other general court may.

Sovereignty resides in the Individual

"7. It is ordered, sentenced and decreed that after there are warrants given out for any of the said general courts, the constable or constables of each town shall forthwith give notice distinctly to the inhabitants of the same, in some public assembly or by going or sending from house to house, that at a place and time by him or them limited and set, they meet and assemble themselves together to elect and choose certain deputies to be at the general court then following to agitate the affairs of the commonwealth; which said deputies shall be chosen by all that are admitted inhabitants in the several towns and have taken the oath of fidelity; provided that none be chosen a deputy for any general court which is not a freeman of this commonwealth.

System devised to preserve the rights of the People through their representative Assemblies

"The foresaid deputies shall be chosen in manner following: every person that is present and qualified as before expressed, shall bring the names of such, written in several papers, as they desire to have chosen for that employment, and these 3 or 4, more or less, being the number agreed on to be chosen for that time, that have greatest number of papers written for them shall be deputies for that court; whose names shall be endorsed on the back side of the warrant and returned into the court, with the constable or constables hand unto the same.

The above excerpts are from "Old South Leaflets", No. 8

Proportional representation

"8. It is ordered, sentenced and decreed, that Wyndsor, Hartford and Wethersfield shall have power, each town, to send four of their freemen as deputies to every general court; and whatsoever other towns shall be hereafter added to this jurisdiction, they shall send so many deputies as the court shall judge meet, a reasonable proportion to the number of freemen that are in the said towns being to be attended therein; which deputies shall have the power of the whole town to give their votes and allowance to all such laws and orders as may be for the public good, and unto which the said towns are to be bound.

Rights, obligations and authority of representative

"9. It is ordered and decreed, that the deputies thus chosen shall have power and liberty to appoint a time and a place of meeting together before any general court to advise and consult of all such things as may concern the good of the public, as also to examine their own elections, whether according to the order, and if they or the greatest part of them find any election to be illegal they may seclude such for present from their meeting, and return the same and their reasons to the court; and if it prove true, the court may fine the party or parties so intruding and the town, if they see cause, and give out a warrant to go to a new election in a legal way, either in part or in whole. Also the said deputies shall have power to fine any that shall be disorderly at their meetings, or for not coming in due time or place according to appointment; and they may return the said fines into the court if it be refused to be paid, and the treasurer to take notice of it, and to estreat or levy the same as he does other fines.

Extent of Assembly jurisdiction

"10. It is ordered, sentenced and decreed, that every general court, except such as through neglect of the Governor and the greatest part of magestrates the freemen themselves do call, shall consist of the Governor, or some one chosen to moderate the court, and 4 other magestrates at least, with the major part of the deputies of the several towns legally chosen; and in case the freemen or major part of them, through neglect or refusal of the Governor and major part of the magestrates, shall call a court, it shall consist of the major part of freemen that are present or their deputies, with a moderator chosen by them: In which said general courts shall consist the supreme power of the commonwealth, and they only shall have power to make laws or repeal them, to grant leaves, to admit of freemen dispose of lands undisposed of, to several towns or persons, and also shall have power to call either court or magestrate or any other person whatsoever into question for any misdemeanor.

The above excerpts are from "Old South Leaflets", No. 8

and may for just causes displace or deal otherwise according to the nature of the offence; and also may deal in any other matter that concerns the good of this commonwealth, except election of magestrates, which shall be done by the whole body of freemen. In which court the Governor or moderator shall have power to order the court to give liberty of speach, and silence unseasonable and disorderly speaking, to put all things to vote, and in case the vote be equal to have the casting voice. But none of these courts shall be adjourned or dissolved without the consent of the major part of the court.

Parliamentary procedure provided

"11. It is ordered, sentenced and decreed, that when any general court upon the occasions of the commonwealth have agreed upon any sum or sums of money to be levied upon the several towns within this jurisdiction, that a committee be chosen to set out and appoint what shall be the proportion of every town to pay of the said levy, provided the committees be made up of an equal number out of each town. 14th January, 1638, the 11 Orders abovesaid are voted."

Proportionate taxation with equal representation

The above excerpts are from "Old South Leaflets", No. 8

MASSACHUSETTS BODY OF LIBERTIES

"As early as 1639 people had begun to complain that too much power was vested in the discretion of the magistrate, and they clamoured for a code of laws; but as Winthrop says, the magistrates and ministers were 'not very forward in this matter', for they preferred to supplement the common law of England by decisions based on the Old Testament rather than by a body of statutes. It was not until 1641, after a persistent struggle, that the deputies won a decisive victory over the assistants and secured for Massachusetts a definite code of laws: 'The Body of Liberties' drawn up by Rev. Nathaniel Ward of Ipswich."

John Fiske in "The Beginnings of New England"

THE free fruition of such liberties Immunities and priveledges as humanitie, Civilitie, and Christianitie call for as due to every man in his place and proportion without impeachment and Infringement hath ever bene and ever will be the tranquillitie and Stabilitie of Churches and Commonwealths. And the deniall or deprivall thereof, the disturbance if not the ruine of both. We hould it therefore our dutie and safetie whilst we are about the further establishing of this Government to collect and expresse all such freedomes as for present we forsee may concerne

Preamble to "BODY OF LIBERTIES"

The above excerpts are from "Old South Leaflets", No. 164

us, and our posteritie after us, And to ratify them with our sollemne consent.

"Wee doe therefore this day religiously and unanimously decree and confirme these following Rites, liberties and priviledges concerneing our Churches, and Civill State to be respectively impartiallie and inviolably enjoyed and observed throughout our Jurisdiction for ever.

LAW ONE

"No mans life shall be taken away, no mans honour or good name shall be stayned, no mans person shall be arested, restrayned, banished, dismembred, nor any wayes punished, no man shall be deprived of his wife or children, no mans goods or estaite shall be taken away from him, nor any way indammaged under colour of law or Countenance of Authoritie, unlesse it be by vertue or equitie of some expresse law of the Country waranting the same, established by a generall Court and sufficiently published, or in case of the defect of a law in any partecular case by the word of God. And in Capitall cases, or in cases concerning dismembring or banishment according to that word to be judged by the Generall Court.

LAW TWO

"Every person within this Jurisdiction, whether Inhabitant or forreiner shall enjoy the same justice and law, that is generall for the plantation, which we constitute and execute one towards another without partialitie or delay.

LAW THREE

"No man shall be urged to take any oath or subscribe any articles, covenants or remonstrance, of a publique and Civill nature, but such as the Generall Court hath considered, allowed and required.

LAW FOUR

"No man shall be punished for not appearing at or before any Civill Assembly, Court, Councell, Magistrate, or Officer, nor for the omission of any office or service, if he shall be necessarily hindred by any apparent Act or providence of God, which he could neither foresee nor avoid. Provided that this law shall not prejudice any person of his just cost or damage, in any civill action.

LAW FIVE

"No man shall be compelled to any publique worke or service unlesse the presse be grounded upon some act of the generall Court, and have reasonable allowance therefore.

LAW SIX

"No man shall be pressed in person to any office, worke, warres or other publique service, that is necessarily and suffitiently exempted by any naturall or personall impediment, as by want of years, greatnes of age, defect of minde, fayling of sences, or impotencie of Lymbes.

The above excerpts are from "Old South Leaflets", No. 164

LAW SEVEN

"No man shall be compelled to goe out of the limits of this plantation upon any offensive warres which this Comonwealth or any of our freinds or confederats shall volentarily undertake. But onely upon such vindictive and defensive warres in our owne behalfe or the behalfe of our freinds and confederats as shall be enterprized by the Counsell and consent of a Court generall, or by authority derived from the same.

LAW EIGHT

"No mans Cattel or goods of what kinde soever shall be pressed or taken for any publique use or service, unlesse it be by warrant grounded upon some act of the generall Court, nor without such reasonable prices and hire as the ordinarie rates of the Countrie do afford. And if his Cattle or goods shall perish or suffer damage in such service, the owner shall be sufficiently recompenced.

LAW NINE

"No monopolies shall be granted or allowed amongst us, but of such new Inventions that are profitable to the Countrie, and that for a short time.

LAW TEN

"All our lands and heritages shall be free from all fines and licenses upon Alienations, and from all hariotts, wardships, Liveries, Primer-seisins, yeare day and wast, Escheates, and forfeitures, upon the deaths of parents or Ancestors, be they naturall, casuall or Juditiall.

LAW ELEVEN

"All persons which are of the age of 21 yeares, and of right understanding and meamories, whether excommunicate or condemned shall have full power and libertie to make there wills and testaments, and other lawfull alienations of theire lands and estates.

LAW TWELVE

"Every man whether Inhabitant or fforreiner, free or not free shall have libertie to come to any publique Court, Councel, or Towne meeting, and either by speech or writeing to move any lawfull, seasonable, and materiall question, or to present any necessary motion, complaint, petition, Bill or information, whereof that meeting hath proper cognizance, so it be done in convenient time, due order, and respective manner.

LAW THIRTEEN

"No man shall be rated here for any estaite or revenue he hath in England, or in any forreine partes till it be transported hither.

LAW FOURTEEN

"Any Conveyance or Alienation of land or other estaite whatsoever, made by any woman that is married, any childe under age, Ideott or distracted person, shall be good if it be passed and ratified by the consent of a generall Court.

The above excerpts are from "Old South Leaflets", No. 164

LAW FIFTEEN

"All Covenous or fraudulent Alienations or Conveyances of lands, tenements, or any heriditaments, shall be of no validitie to defeate any man from due debts or legacies, or from any just title, clame or possession, of that which is so fraudulently conveyed.

LAW SIXTEEN

"Every Inhabitant that is an howse holder shall have free fishing and fowling in any great ponds and Bayes, Coves and Rivers, so farre as the sea ebbes and flowes within the presincts of the towne where they dwell, unlesse the free men of the same Towne or the Generall Court have otherwise appropriated them, provided that this shall not be extended to give leave to any man to come upon others proprietie without there leave.

LAW SEVENTEEN

"Every man of or within this Jurisdiction shall have free libertie, notwithstanding any Civill power to remove both himselfe, and his familie at their pleasure out of the same, provided there be no legall impediment to the contrarie....

LAW NINETY-SIX

"Howsoever these above specified rites, freedomes Immunities, Authorites and priveledges, both Civill and Ecclesiastical are expressed onely under the name and title of Liberties, and not in the exact forme of Laws or Statutes, yet we do with one consent fullie Authorise, and earnestly intreate all that are and shall be in Authoritie to consider them as laws, and not to faile to inflict condigne and proportionable punishments upon every man impartiallie, that shall infringe or violate any of them.

LAW NINETY-SEVEN

"Wee likewise give full power and libertie to any person that shall at any time be denyed or deprived of any of them, to commence and prosecute their suite, Complaint or action against any man that shall so doe in any Court that hath proper Cognizance or judicature thereof.

LAW NINETY-EIGHT

"Lastly because our dutie and desire is to do nothing suddainlie which fundamentally concerne us, we decree that these rites and liberties, shall be Audably read and deliberately weighed at every Generall Court that shall be held, within three yeares next insueing, And such of them as shall not be altered or repealed they shall stand so ratified, That no man shall infringe them without due punishment.

"And if any Generall Court within these next thre yeares shall faile or forget to reade and consider them as abovesaid. The Governor and Deputy Governor for the time being, and every Assistant present at such Courts, shall forfeite 20sh. a man,

The above excerpts are from "Old South Leaflets", No. 164

and everie Deputie 10sh, a man for each neglect, which shall be paid out of their proper estate, and not by the Country or the Townes which choose them, and whensoever there shall arise any question in any Court amonge the Assistants and Associates thereof about the explanation of these Rites and liberties, The Generall Court onely shall have power to interprett them."

The above excerpts are from "Old South Leaflets", No. 164

FUNDAMENTAL PRINCIPLES

Sacredness of Life, Liberty, Property, Reputation.

Fundamental principles relating to local self-government

Life, Liberty and Property - Foundation of local self-government

Old World policy of control and regulation of prices abandoned by colonists

THE Body of Liberties... under ninety-eight heads or propositions, - making with the preamble and close, a hundred sections, - first lays down those fundamental principles relating to the sacredness of life, liberty, property, and reputation, which are the special subject-matter of a Bill of Rights. It then goes on to prescribe general rules of judicial proceedings to define the privileges and duties of freemen; to provide for justice to women, children, servants, and foreigners, and for gentle treatment of the brute creation; to declare capital offences, in ten specifications; and to describe the liberties and prerogatives of the churches... Ward was capable of the great business to which he was set... When... he announced the principle that life, liberty, or property was not to be invaded except by virtue of express law, established by the local authority and sufficently published, a step was taken than which none could be more important towards creating at once a prosperous and an independent commonwealth... It was almost a Declaration of Independence... The opinions of the present age respecting the proper province of law are not altogether the same as were current at the time of the colonization of New England. In all the Colonies, orders were made for the regulation of the prices of commodities and labor. This legislation was fluctuating, because experience could not fail speedily to show the inutility or mischief of each particular provision. The theory of a public control over the terms of private contracts is plausible; and, till experiments prosecuted in every promising direction had exposed its unsoundness, the idea was not abandoned that some new devise would remedy the manifest defects of those which had preceded. But the error was not native in New England, nor did it linger longest in that country. It was embodied in the statutes of the mother country at least as early as the fourteenth century; it continued in good credit there at least to the latest days of the Stuarts, long after it had been abandoned by the practical wisdom of the colonists..."

The above excerpts are from John Palfrey's "History of New England", Vol. II - 1865

"THERE IS A TWOFOLD LIBERTY"

THERE is a twofold liberty, natural (I mean as our nature is now corrupt) and civil or federal. The first is common to man with beasts and other creatures. By this, man as he stands in relation to man simply, hath liberty to do what he lists: it is a liberty to evil as well as to good. This liberty is incompatible and inconsistent with authority, and cannot endure the least restraint of the most just authority. The exercise and maintaining of this liberty makes men grow more evil, and in time to be worse than brute beasts: omnes sumus licentia deteriores. This is that great enemy of truth and peace, that wild beast, which all the ordinances of God are bent against, to restrain and subdue it.

"The other kind of liberty I call civil or federal; it may also be termed moral, in reference to the covenant between God and man, in the moral law, and the politic covenants and constitutions, amongst men themselves. This liberty is the proper end and object of authority, and cannot subsist without it; and it is a liberty to that only which is good, just, and honest. This liberty you are to stand for, with the hazard (not only of your goods, but) of your lives, if need be. Whatsoever crosseth this is not authority, but a distemper thereof. This liberty is maintained and exercised in a way of subjection to authority; it is of the same kind of liberty wherewith Christ hath made us free..."

- John Winthrop, "Little Speech on Liberty", 1645

MIDDLE COLONY

WHEREAS the glory of Almighty God and the good of mankind is the reason and end of government, and therefore government itself is a venerable ordinance of God, and forasmuch as it is principally devised and intended by the Proprietary and Governor and freemen of Pennsylvania and territories thereunto belonging, to make and establish such laws as shall best preserve true Christian and civil liberty, in opposition to all unchristian, licentious, and unjust practices, whereby God may have his due, Caesar his due, and the people their due..."

- From the Great Law, first Legislative Act in the Colony.

"William Penn...founded all his institutions on the double basis of liberty and property; he moreover established an absolute toleration; it was his wish that every man who believed in God should partake of the rights of a citizen; and that every man who adored Him as a Christian, of whatever sect he might be, should be a partaker in authority..."

- "Biographical Review", London, 1819

"Penn...as the friend of Algernon Sidney,...never ceased to intercede, through his friends at court, for the persecuted...On the accession of James he was received by that prince with favour...That it really was great, appears from his obtaining a promise of pardon for his friend Mr. Locke, which that illustrious man declined..."

- Sir James Mackintosh, "Miscellaneous Works", 1851

"The immortal memory of Penn, who subdued the ferocity of savages by his virtues, and enlightened the civilized world by his institutions."

- James Madison

In 1668, Penn became a Quaker

WILLIAM Penn possessed more influence with the ruling class of England than did any other of the followers of Fox. His joining the Friends in 1668 is a memorable event in the history of their Society. The son of Admiral Sir William Penn, the conqueror of Jamaica, and of his wife Margaret, daughter of John Jasper, of Amsterdam, he was born in London Oct. 14, 1644, the year in which Fox began to preach to his neighbors in Leicestershire...while a student at Oxford, the young Penn chanced to hear the preaching of Thomas Loe, a Quaker, and so impressed was he by it that he ceased to attend the religious services of his College. For this he was expelled from the University. His father, after a brief impulse of anger which this disgrace caused, sent him to Paris, and in that gay capital the impressions made by the Quaker preacher were nearly effaced. From Paris he went to Saumur and became a pupil of Moses Amyrault, a learned professor of the French Reformed Church. At the conclusion of his studies he travelled in France and Italy, and in 1664 returned to England...While in Ireland, Penn again came under the influence of the preaching of Loe, and in his heart became a Quaker. He was shortly afterwards arrested with others at a Quaker meeting... Penn wrote industriously in the cause, and endeavored by personal solicitation at Court to obtain for the Quakers more liberal treatment. Imprisoned in the Tower for heresy, he passed his time in writing 'No Cross, No Crown'..."

The above excerpts are from Frederick D. Stone's "The Founding of Pennsylvania" - 1884, Winsor's, Vol. III

PENNSYLVANIA

'enn inherits rom his ather large noney :laims on he crown

IN September, 1670, his father died, leaving him an ample fortune, besides large claims on the Government. But the temptations of wealth had no influence on Penn. He continued to defend the faith he had embraced, and in the latter part of the year was again in Newgate. There he wrote "The Great Case of Liberty of Conscience Debated". Had his services to humanity been no greater than those rendered by the pen they would have secured for him a lasting remembrance; but the experience he gained in defending the principles of the Friends was fitting him for higher responsibilities. His mind, which was naturally bright, had been improved by study. In such rough schools of statesmanship as the Old Bailey, Newgate, and the Tower, he imbibed broad and liberal views of what was necessary for the welfare of mankind, which in the end prompted him to attempt a practical interpretation of the philosophy of More and Harrington...

670 - In Newgate, mprisoned 'or defending Quaker faith

n settlement of government claim, Penn planned to obtain land in America

"Penn conceived the idea of obtaining a grant of land in America in settlement of a debt of f16, 000 due the estate of his father from the Crown. We have no evidence showing when this thought first took form in his mind, but his words and actions prove that it was not prompted in order to better his worldly condition. Certain it is that the eyes of the Friends had long been turned to what is now Pennsylvania as a spot upon which they might find refuge from persecution. In 1660, when George Fox first thought of a Quaker settlement in America, he wrote on this subject to Josiah Coale, who was then with the Susquehanna Indians north of Maryland. The reply from Maryland is dated 'eleventh month, 1660', and reads, -

"'Dear George, - As concerning Friends buying a piece of land of the Susquehanna Indians, I have spoken of it to them, and told them what thou said concerning it; but their answer was that there is no land that is habitable or fit for situation beyond Baltimore's liberty till they come to or near the Susquehanna's fort'.

"In 1681 Penn, in writing about his province, said: 'This I can say, that I had an opening of joy as to these parts in the year 1661 at

The above excerpts are from Frederick D. Stone's "The Founding of Pennsylvania" - 1884, Winsor's, Vol. III

Oxford twenty years since. The interest which centred in West Jersey caused the scheme to slumber, until revived by Penn in 1680.

"The petition to the King was presented about the 1st of June, 1680. It asked for a tract of land 'lying North of Maryland, on the East bounded with Delaware River, on the West limited as Maryland is, and Northward to extend as far as plantable, which is altogether Indian. This, 'his Majty being graciously disposed to gratify,' was referred to the Lords of Trade and Plantations, and if it should meet with their approval, they were to consider 'such restrictions, limitations, and other Clauses as were fitting to be inserted in the Grant.

1681 - Charter granted to Penn and his successors with general powers of government - a proprietary

"The proceedings which followed prevented the issue of the charter for some time.... The charter as granted gave to Penn and his successors all the territory between the fortieth and forty-second degrees of latitude, extending through five degrees of longitude west from the Delaware River, with the exception of that part which would fall within a circle drawn twelve miles around New Castle, the northern segment of which was to form the boundary between Penn's province and the Duke of York's colonies of Delaware. It was supposed that such a circle would be intersected on the west by the fortieth degree of latitude, the proposed boundary between Pennsylvania and Maryland. This erroneous opinion was the cause of a prolonged litigation. The allegiance of the Proprietary and of the inhabitants was reserved to the Crown. The right to govern was vested in Penn. He could appoint officers, and with the consent of the people make such laws as were necessary; but to insure their unison with those of England they were to be submitted to the Crown within five years for approval. He could raise troops for the defence of his province, and collect taxes and duties; but the latter were to be in addition to those ordered by Parliament. He could pardon all crimes except treason and wilful murder, and grant reprieves in such cases until the pleasure of the King should be known. The Bishop of London had the power to appoint a chaplain on the petition of twenty of the inhabitants, and an agent was to reside near the Court to explain any misdemeanor that might be committed.

Laws to be agreeable to the laws of England

"The charter was signed March 4, 1681, and on the next day Penn wrote to Robert Turner, -

"'After many waitings, watchings, solicitings, and disputes in Council, this day my country was confirmed to me under the

The above excerpts are from Frederick D. Stone's "The Founding of Pennsylvania", 1884, Winsor's, Vol. III

Great Seal of England, with large powers and privileges, by the name of Pennsilvania, a name the King would have given in honor of my father. I chose New Wales, being as this a pretty hilly country,....for I feared lest it should be looked as a vanity in me and not as a respect in the King, as it truly was, to my father, whom he often mentions with praise. Thou mayst communicate my graunt to friends, and expect shortly my proposals; 't is a clear and just thing; and my God, that has given it me through many difficulties, will, I believe, bless and make it the seed of a nation. I shall have a tender care to the government, that it will be well laid at first.'

Penn's hope that God "will bless and make it the seed of a nation."

"On the 2d of April a royal proclamation, addressed to those who were already settled within the province, informed them of the granting of the patent, and its character. Six days afterwards Penn prepared a letter to be read to the settlers by his representative, couched in language of friendship and affection. He told them frankly that government was a business he had never undertaken, but that it was his wish to do it uprightly. You are 'at the mercy of no governor,' he said, 'who comes to make his fortune great; you shall be governed by laws of your own making, and live a free and, if you will, a sober and industrious people.' On the same day he gave to his kinsman, William Markham, whom he had selected to be his deputy-governor, and who was to precede him to Pennsylvania, instructions regarding the first business to be transacted....

Penn's views on government - terms for acquiring land

"Soon after the confirmation of his charter, Penn issued a pamphlet, in which the essential parts of that instrument were given, together with an account of the country and the views he entertained for its government. The conditions on which he proposed to dispose of land were, a share of five thousand acres free from any Indian incumbrance for £100, and one shilling English quit-rent for one hundred acres, the quit-rent not to begin until after 1684. Those who hired were to pay one penny per acre for lots not exceeding two hundred acres. Fifty acres per head were allowed to the masters of servants, and the same quantity was given to every servant when his time should expire. A plan for building cities was also suggested, in which all should receive lots in proportion to their investments.

Unselfish, religious motives

"The unselfishness and purity of Penn's motives, and the religious feelings with which he was inspired, are evident from his letters. On the 12th of April, 1681, he wrote to three of his friends, -

The above excerpts are from Frederick D. Stone's "The Founding of Pennsylvania", 1884, Winsor's, Vol. III

"That the will of one man may not hinder the good of an whole country"

"'Having published a paper with relation to my province in America (at least what I thought advisable to publish), I here inclose one that you may know and inform others of it. I have been these thirteen years the servant of truth and Friends, and for my testimony sake lost much not only the greatness and preferments of this world, but f16, 000 of my estate, that had I not been what I am I had long ago obtained. But I murmur not; the Lord is good to me, and the interest his truth has given me with his people may more than repair it; for many are drawn forth to be concerned with me: and perhaps this way of satisfaction has more the hand of God in it than a downright payment. . . . For the matter of liberty and privilege, I propose that which is extraordinary, and to leave myself and successors no power of doing mischief, - that the will of one man may not hinder the good of an whole country. But to publish those things now and here, as matters stand, would not be wise, and I was advised to reserve that until I came there.'

Philadelphia

"To another he wrote, - 'And because I have been somewhat exercised at times about the nature and end of government among men, it is reasonable to expect that I should endeavor to establish a just and righteous one in this province, that others may take example by it, - truly this my heart desires. For the nations want a precedent. . . . I do, therefore, desire the Lord's wisdom to guide me, and those that may be concerned with me, that we do the thing that is truly wise and just.

"The nations want a precedent"

"And again, - 'For my country, I eyed the Lord in obtaining it, and more was I drawn inward to look to him, and to owe it to his hand and power than to any other way. I have so obtained it, and desire to keep it that I may not be unworthy of his love, . . .

Quakers were attracted to Penn's province

"The scheme grew apace, and, as Penn says, 'many were drawn forth to be concerned with him.' His prominence as a Quaker attracted the attention of Quakers in all quarters. He had travelled in their service in Wales, and from thence some of the first settlers came. Two visits to Holland and Germany had made him known to the Mennonites and like religious bodies there. His pamphlet was reprinted at Amsterdam, and the seed sown soon brought forth abundantly. By July 11, 1681, matters had so

The above excerpts are from Frederick D. Stone's "The Founding of Pennsylvania", 1884, Winsor's, Vol. III

far progressed that it was necessary to form a definite agreement between Penn and the purchasers, and a paper known as 'Certain Conditions or Concessions' was executed.

Free trade with Indians maintained - refusal to sell a monopoly, even for £ 6,000

"By this time also (July, 1681) troubles with Lord Baltimore were anticipated in England, and some of the adventurers were deterred from purchasing. Penn at once began negotiations for the acquirement of the Duke of York's interest on the Delaware. Meanwhile, in the face of all these rumors, Penn refused to part with any of his rights, except on the terms and in the spirit which he had announced. Six thousand pounds were offered for a monopoly of the Indian trade, but he declined it; 'I would not,' are his words, 'so defile what came to me clean.'

"William Crispin, John Bezar, and Nathaniel Allen were commissioned by Penn (Sept. 30, 1681) to assist Markham. They were to select a site for a town, and superintend its laying out. William Haige was subsequently added to the number. By them he sent to the Indians a letter of an affectionate character, and another to be read to the Swedes by their ministers.

"The first commissioners probably sailed on the 'John Sarah,' which cleared for Pennsylvania in October. She is supposed to have been the first vessel to arrive there after Penn received his grant.

Further land acquisitions

"On August 24, 1682, Penn acquired from the Duke of York the town of New Castle and the country twelve miles around it, and the same day the Duke conveyed to him the territory lying south of New Castle, reserving for himself one half the rents. The first of these gifts professed to have been made on account of the Duke's respect for the memory of Sir William Penn. A deed was also obtained from the Duke (August 20) for any right he might have to Pennsylvania as a part of New Netherland.

"Having completed his business in England, Penn prepared to sail for America. On the 4th of August, from his home at Worminghurst, he addressed to his wife and children a letter of singular beauty, manliness, and affection. It is evident from it that he appreciated the dangers before him, as well as the responsibilities which he had assumed. To his wife, who was the daughter of Sir William Springett, he wrote: 'Remember thy mother's example when thy father's public-spiritedness had worsted his estate, which is my case.' To his children, fearing he would see them no more, he said: 'And as for you who are likely to be concerned in the government of Pennsylvania

The above excerpts are from Frederick D. Stone's "The Founding of Pennsylvania", 1884, Winsor's, Vol. III

and my parts of East Jersey, especially the first, I do charge you before the Lord God and His holy angels, that you be lowly, diligent, and tender, fearing God, loving the people, and hating covetousness.' To both, in closing, he wrote: 'So farewell to my thrice-dearly beloved wife and children. Yours as God pleaseth, in that which no waters can quench, no time forget, nor distance wear away.'

Three ships, with Penn and many Quakers, sailed for Pennsylvania

"On the 30th of August he wrote to all faithful friends in England, and the next day there 'sailed out of the Downs three ships bound for Pennsylvania, on board of which was Mr. Pen, with a great many Quakers who go to settle there.' Such was the announcement in the London Gazette of September 4, of the departure of those who were to found one of the most prosperous of the British colonies in America....

Government traced to a divine origin

"The attention which Penn gave to the constitution of his province was a duty which had for him a particular interest. His thoughts had necessarily dwelt much on the subject, and his experience had made him acquainted with the principles of the law and the abuses of government. The drafts of this paper which have been preserved show how deeply it was considered. Henry Sidney, Sir William Jones, and Counsellor Bamfield were consulted, and portions of it were framed in accordance with the wishes of the Quakers. In the Introduction to this remarkable paper, the ingenuousness of its author is clearly discernible. Recognizing the necessity of government, and tracing it to a divine origin, Penn continues, -

Penn deplored bias, passion and sinister interests affecting all governments extant

"'For particular frames and models, it will become me to say little, and comparatively I will say nothing. My reasons are, first, that the age is too nice and difficult for it, there being nothing the wits of men are more busy and divided upon .... Men side with their passions against their reason, and their sinister interests have so strong a bias upon their minds, that they lean to them against the good of the things they know.

"'I do not find a model in the world that time, place, and some singular emergencies have not necessarily altered, nor is it easy to frame a civil government that shall serve all places alike. I know what is said by the several admirers of monarchy, aristocracy, and democracy, which are the rule of one, a few, and many, and are the three common ideas of government when men discourse on that subject. But I choose to solve the controversy with this small distinction, and it belongs to all three, - any government is free to the people under it

The above excerpts are from Frederick D. Stone's "The Founding of Pennsylvania", 1884, Winsor's, Vol. III

(whatever be the frame) where the laws rule and the people are a party to those laws; and more than this is tyranny, oligarchy, or confusion...Liberty without obedience is confusion, and obedience without liberty is slavery.'

..."Care or the virtuous education of youth"

"The good men of a nation, he argues, should make and keep its government, and laws should bind those who make laws necessary. As wisdom and virtue are qualities that descend not with worldly inheritances, care should be taken for the virtuous education of youth.

April 25, 1682

Penn's Frame of government established

"The Frame of Government which followed these remarks was signed by Penn on the 25th of April, 1682. By this Act the Government was vested in the governor and freemen, in the form of a provincial council and an assembly. The provincial council was to consist of seventy-two members. The first election of councilmen was to be held on the 20th of February, 1682-83, and they were to meet on the 10th of the following month. One-third of the number were to retire each year when their successors were chosen. An elaborate scheme was devised for forming the council into committees to attend to the various duties.

All freemen or their chosen representatives had a voice in the government

"The assembly for the first year was to consist of all the freemen of the province, and after that two hundred were to be annually chosen. They were to meet on April 20; the governor was to preside over the council. Laws were to originate with the latter, and the chief duty of the assembly was to approve such legislation..."

The above excerpts are from Frederick D. Stone's "The Founding of Pennsylvania" - 1884, Winsor's, Vol. III

"When the purchase was agreed, great promises passed between us of kindness and good neighborhood, and that the Indians and English must live in love as long as the sun gave light."

- William Penn, 1683

THE GOVERNMENTS OF THE PARENT COLONIES

TWO DISTINCT SYSTEMS DEVELOP IN AMERICA

"We have seen that in Massachusetts the principal part of the public administration lies in the township. It forms the common centre of the interests and affections of the citizens. But this ceases to be the case as we descend to States in which knowledge is less generally diffused, and where the township consequently offers fewer guarantees of a wise and active administration. As we leave New England, therefore, we find that the importance of the town is gradually transferred to the county, which becomes the centre of administration, and the intermediate power between the Government and the citizen."

- Alexis De Tocqueville, "Democracy in America", 1838

THE CENTRIFUGAL AND CENTRIPETAL POLITICAL POWERS

Key to the Chart

1 "... The principal voice was that of the people, or of the whole body of Christians; for even the apostles themselves inculcated, by their example, that nothing of any moment was to be done or determined on but with the knowledge and consent
7 of the brotherhood. The assembled people elected their own rulers and teachers, or by their free consent received such as
were nominated to them ... In a word, the people did every thing that is proper for those in whom the supreme power of
the community is vested ... Among all members of the church, of whatever class or condition, there was the most perfect
equality." (Mosheim, "Ecclesiastical History", Murdock;s Translation, Vol. I, Pg. 68) See Pg. 28 of text.

" ... All the churches, in those primitive times, were independent bodies; or none of them subject to the jurisdiction of ar
10 other. For, though the churches which were founded by the apostles themselves frequently had the honor shown them to be
consulted in difficult and doubtful cases, yet they had no judicial authority, no control, no power of giving laws. On the
contrary, it is clear as the noonday, that all Christian churches had equal rights, and were in all respects on a footing of
equality. Nor does there appear, in this first century, any vestige of that consociation of the churches of the same provinc
which gave rise to ecclesiastical councils and to metropolitans ..." ("Mosheim's Ecclesiastical History", Vol. I, Pg. 72)
See "Polity of the Primitive Christian Churches", Pg. 16 of text.

14 1620. "... It was here that the government based on the will of the governed was <u>first</u> established on the American coast.
(North American Review, I, Pg. 336)

"... Thus, then, were these wide districts first settled, and with their very earliest texture were thus interwoven the thread
10 of congregational dissent. The name of Independents they eschewed. Their especial features were a rejection of episcopacy, of the use of 'common prayer', and of the ceremonies of the Church. Each congregation of worshippers, united by
12 a willing bond or covenant, submitting themselves to a pastor of their own choice, and exercising discipline, through
certain ruling elders, according to what they quaintly termed 'the scriptural platform', formed a separate 'church', which
could have no alliance, save that of friendly alliance, with other 'churches', nor own any submission except to their
common Lord. For this, which they esteemed a more perfect reformation, they had left their native land, and become
settlers in the wilderness..." ("Protestant Episcopal Church in America", Pg. 66, Samuel, Lord Bishop of Oxford.)

"... Did the apostles institute any national church?"... ("Genesis of the New England Churches", Leonard Bacon)
See "Polity of the Primitive Christian Churches", Pg. 23 of text.

2 1620. "... for ye glorie of God and advancemente of ye Christian faith, ... doe by these presents solemnly and mutual
4 in ye presence of God, and one of another, covenant and combine our selves togeather into a civill body politick..."
(Bradford's "History of Plymouth Plantation"). See Pg. 204 of text, also Pg. 150.

1 "During some years they appear not to have acquired right by any legal conveyance to the territory which they had occupie
2 At length ... they obtained a grant of property from the council of the New Plymouth Company, but were never incorporated as a body politic by royal charter. Unlike all the other settlements in America, this colony must be considered merel
13 as a voluntary association, held together by the tacit consent of its members to recognize the authority of laws, and to sub-
14 mit to the jurisdiction of magistrates, framed and chosen by themselves ..." ("History of the Discovery and Settlement of
America", Book X, William Robertson). See Mayflower Compact, Pg. 204 of text.

8 "Then ... congregational parishes comprise two organizations. The 'society' ... the 'church'. ("Pilgrim Republic",
9 John A. Goodwin)

"... There is nothing, either, in this primitive constitution of the church, to prevent the members of several churches unit
ing their prayers and labors in carrying forward some enterprise of Christian benevolence. They may even form a society t
11 accomplish such an object, but not to exercise any authority over the local churches. No organization that takes any thing
12 away from the completeness of a local church, or in any degree forms a complement to it, or to its authority, has any war
rant in Scripture ... The primitive churches were distinct, complete, independent, local, or, as we now denominate then
Congregational churches..." ("Church Polity of the Pilgrims", Pg. 43-44, J. W. Wellman) See Pg. 16 of text.

8 "... The society was purely voluntary, and every church so constituted was strictly independent of all others in the conduc
10 of its worship, the admission of its members, the exercise of its discipline, the choice of its officers, and the entire manag
11 ment of its affairs. They were, in a word, independent republics ..." ("Church Polity of the Pilgrims", Pg. 53.)

"... An oligarchical government in the church cannot promote republicanism in the state ..." ("Church Polity of the Pilgrims", Pg. 132, Wellman) See Montesquieu on "Republicanism of Christianity", Pg. 27 of text.

4 "In a New England township the people directly govern themselves; the government is the people, or, to speak with entire
6 cision, it is all the male inhabitants of one and twenty years of age and upwards." ("Civil Government", Pg. 19, John Fis
See Pg. 271 of text, "Township and County".

3 "In county matters and state matters they speak for the town, and if it is a party to a lawsuit they represent it in court; for
5 the New England town is a legal corporation, and as such can hold property, and sue and be sued." ("Civil Government",
4 Pg. 21, John Fiske). See "Township and County", Pg. 272 of text.

1644. "... the first attempt was made at the Federal system, which more than a century later became the central prin-
13 ciple in the formation of the United States ..." ("English Colonies in America", Pg. 351, Henry Cabot Lodge.)

1 "The dread and redoubtable sovereign, when traced to his ultimate and genuine source, has been found as he ought to have
7 been found, in the free and independent man." ("Works of James Wilson", Bird Wilson Edition.)

"Church organization which vests all ecclesiastical power in the assembled brotherhood of each local church" -(Webster's
12 Collegiate Dictionary, 1948).

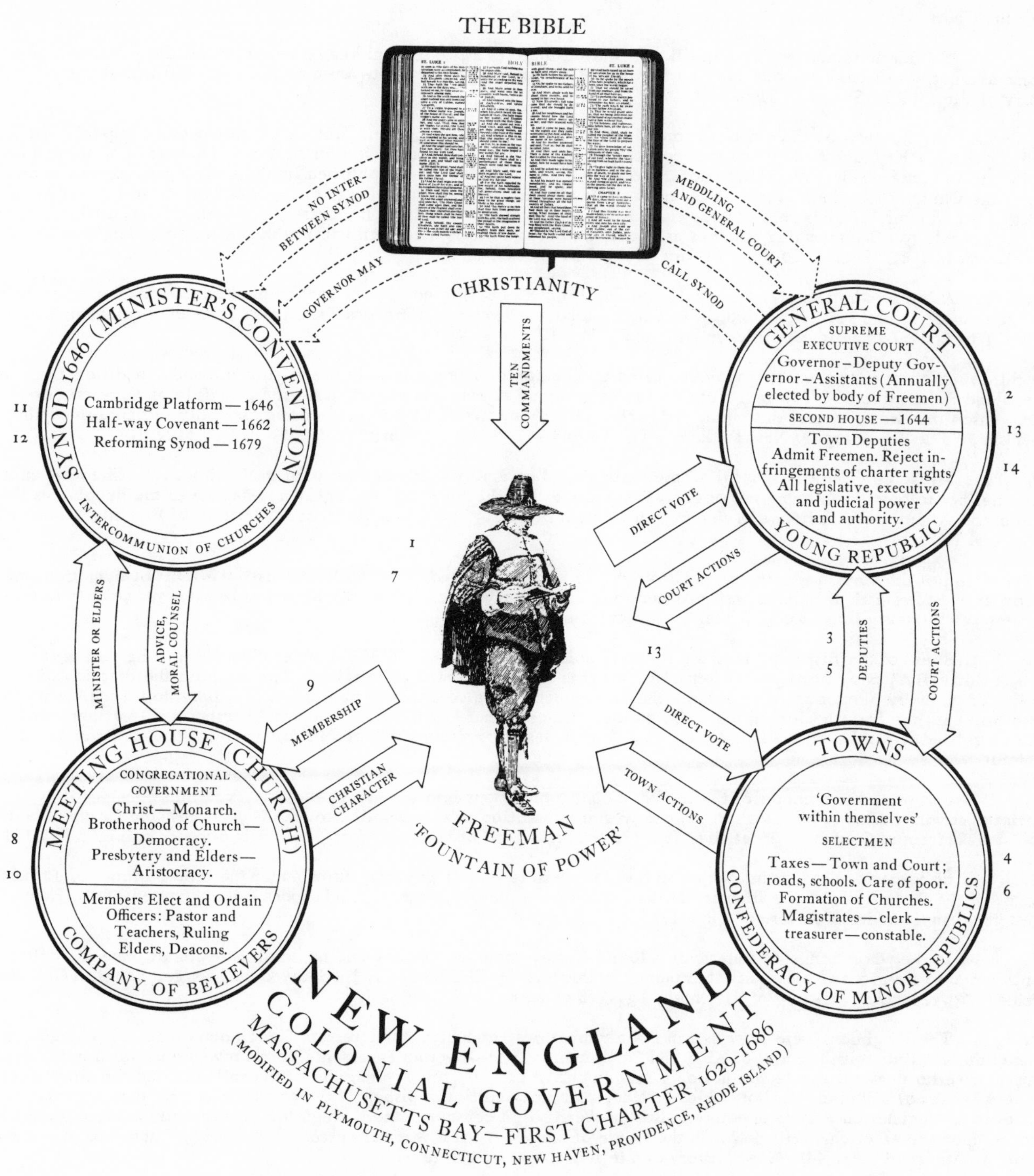

"The government and patent should be settled in New England" August, 1629

"Not birth, nor wealth, nor learning, nor skill in war, was to confer political power;. but *personal character,*—goodness of the highest type,—goodness of that purity and force which only the faith of Jesus Christ is competent to create."—Palfrey.

Franchise: 'To the end the body of the commons may be preserved of honest and good men' it was 'ordered and agreed, that, for the time to come, no man shall be admitted to the freedom of this body politic, but such as are members of some of the churches within the limits of the same.' — Mass. Col. Records.

The Centrifugal and Centripetal Political Powers

THE CENTRIPETAL AND CENTRIFUGAL POLITICAL POWERS

Key to the Chart

1578. "... Elizabeth authorizes ... that all who settled there (Virginia) should have and enjoy all the privileges of free
1 denizens and natives of England, any law, custom, or usage to the contrary notwithstanding ..." (William Robertson,
"History of Virginia") See Pg. 151 of text.

1606. "... On the petition of certain 'firm and hearty lovers' of colonization, James I chartered two companies the Londo
and Plymouth.... For each colony separate councils, appointed by the King, were instituted in England, and these councils
were in turn to name resident councillors for the colonies ... Religion was established in accordance with the forms and doc-
1 trines of the Church of England ... 'Who (ever) shall dwell and inhabit within every and any of said several colonies and
plantations, and every of their children ... shall have and enjoy all liberties, franchises, and immunities, within any of ou
2 other dominions, to all intents and purposes as if they had been abiding and born within this our realm of England ..."
(Henry Cabot Lodge, "English Colonies in America", Pgs. 2 and 3)

1619. "... A few hundred sturdy, liberty-loving Englishmen, bearing up against unexampled hardships, living the rudest a
6 most exposed lives, and striving for sudden fortune by tobacco-growing, constituted the great State of Virginia in 1619 ..."
(Henry Cabot Lodge, "English Colonies in America", Pg. 10)

"The third method of nation-making may be called the Teutonic or preeminently the English method. It differs from the
12 Oriental and Roman methods ... in a feature of most profound significance; it contains the principle of representation ...
for this reason that we must call the method of nation making by means of a representative assembly the English method ..."
(John Fiske, "The Beginnings of New England", Pg. 16 and 21) See "The Christian Idea", Pg. 10 of text.

3 1619. "... Sir George Yeardly ... called the first general assembly that was ever held in Virginia.... The laws enacted i
it seem neither to have been many nor of great importance; but the meeting was highly acceptable to the people, as they no
7 beheld among themselves an image of the English Constitution ..." (William Robertson, "History of Virginia", Book IX)
See Pg. 164 in text.

2 "... The head of the Church was the royal Governor, to whom belonged, nominally at least, the right of induction, while th
supervision of ecclesiastical matters was intrusted to a commissary appointed by the Bishop of London and paid from the royal
4 quit-rents ..." (Henry Cabot Lodge, "English Colonies in America")

1622. "... Some of the first records of the reviving colony (Jamestown) are of a happier character. The first seven laws
2 (amongst thirty-five) passed two years afterwards, provide for the interests of religion. They require the erection of a house
5 worship ... on every plantation; they enforce the attendance of the colonists at public worship; provide for uniformity of fait
and worship with the English Church; prescribe the observance of her holydays ... and enjoin respectful treatment and the pa
11 ment of a settled stipend to the colonial clergy ..." ("Protestant Episcopal Church in America", Pg. 24, Samuel, Lord Bish
of Oxford)

1652. "... and when the humours of the mother-country broke out into the great rebellion, Virginia continued loyal ... T
6 expatriated cavaliers fled to her as a refuge; and with a population now multiplied to 20,000, she resisted Cromwell's arms .
("Protestant Episcopal Church in America", Pg. 37, Samuel, Lord Bishop of Oxford) See "History of Virginia", Pg. 171 in t

1652. "... at no period did Virginia enjoy so large a measure of self-government as under the Protectorate ... for under th
guidance of the Puritan Party, the liberties of the people were quietly, legally, and successfully affirmed ..." (Henry Cabo
Lodge, "English Colonies in America", Pg. 17)

1687. "... In the whole range of American colonial history there are to be found no administration at once so contemptibl
1 so sordid, and so injurious as those inflicted upon Virginia ... by Charles II ..." (Henry Cabot Lodge, "English Colonies in
America", Pg. 24) See "History of Virginia", Pg. 175 of text.

1688. "... The Virginians were Royalists in their sympathies, and firm supporters of Church and State ... The governmen
3 was upon the familiar British model of King and Parliament. The Governor represented the Crown, and was a most importan
4 and very powerful personage. He was not only the executive officer, the commander of the militia, and the admiral of the
7 navy, but he was also lord chancellor, chief-justice, and practically the bishop of the province ... He possessed the veto
power as to all legislation ... He appointed also the sheriffs and coroners, and through the former often exerted a decisive
10 influence upon the elections. His power in the House of burgesses itself was very great ..." (Henry Cabot Lodge, "English
Colonies in America", Pg. 44) See "History of Virginia", Pg. 164 in text.

2 "... The Established Church was one of the appendages of the Virginian aristocracy. They controlled the vestries and the
ministers, and the parish church stood not infrequently on the estate of the great planter who had built and managed it ..."
8 (Henry Cabot Lodge, "English Colonies in America", Pg. 57)

" ... the county was an area for the administration of justice. There were usually in each county eight justices of the peac
7 and their court was the counterpart of the Quarter Sessions in England. They were appointed by the governor, but it was
customary for them to nominate candidates for the governor to appoint, so that practically the court filled its own vacancies
8 and was a close corporation, like the parish vestry. Such an arrangement tended to keep the general supervision and control
9 of things in the hands of a few families ..." (John Fiske, "Civil Government", Pg. 66) See "Township & County", Pg. 27
of text.
13

"...In church government supreme authority resides in a body of bishops, and not in any individual ..." (Webster's Colle-
2 giate Dictionary, 1948).

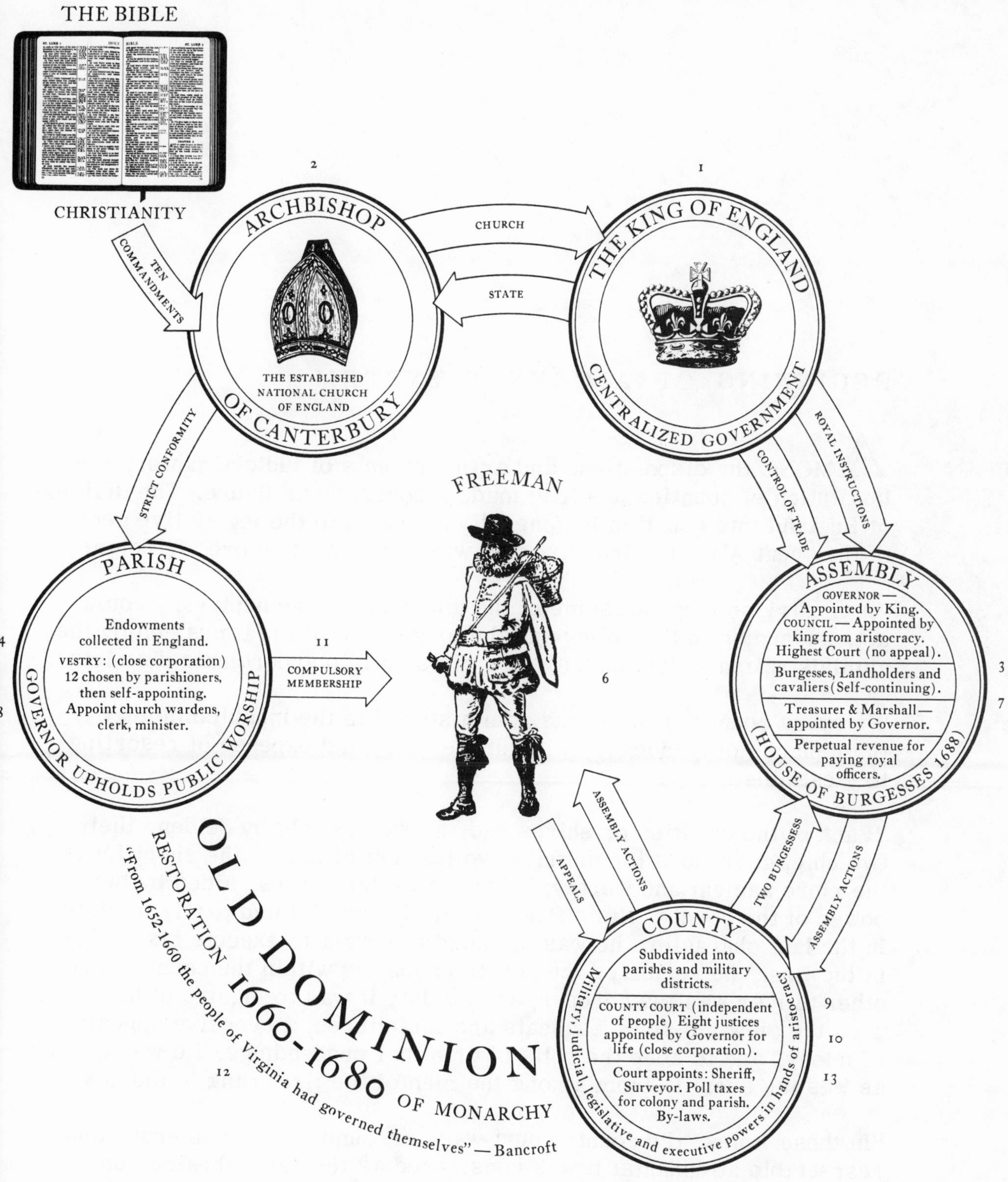

Usurping Assembly and government. 1662: 'The people, at the usual places of election,' could not elect burgesses, but only present their grievances to the adjourned assembly. 1670: 'None but freeholders and housekeepers shall here-after have a voice in the election of any burgesses.' The majority of the people of Virginia were disfranchised.

"Virginia was a continuation of English society . . . they came under the auspices of the nobility, the church, and the mercantile interests of England; they brought with them an attachment to monarchy, a reverence for the Anglican church, a love for England and English institutions." —Bancroft

The Centripetal and Centrifugal Political Powers

BEGINNING OF A COUNTY SYSTEM

AMONG the dispositions and arrangements of judicial power, the institution of counties has long made a conspicuous figure. The division of England into counties is generally ascribed to the legislative genius of the great Alfred... but part of it was performed before his reign.

"A country so large as some of the kingdoms of the heptarchy could not, according to the policy and the exigencies of the times, enjoy the administration of justice without a division into subordinate districts...

"In every county, justice was administered to the inhabitants near their places of residence, without the delay and expense of resorting to Westminster.

"Each of the counties or shires had, as we are told by Selden, their two chief governors for distributive justice: of these, the sheriff was the more ancient and worthy; being, in certain cases, aided by the power of the county. His office was partly judicial and partly ministerial. In the last character, he was the king's servant to execute his writs: in the first, he regulated the courts of justice within the county. The other officer was the coroner, whose duty it was to inquire of homicide upon the view, to seize escheats and forfeitures, to receive appeals of felony, and to keep the rolls of criminal proceedings. He was chosen, as was the sheriff, from among the men of the first rank in the county.

"In those times, the county court was surrounded with numerous and respectable attendants: it was considered as the great theatre, on which the justice and the power of the county were displayed. In those times, justice was administered principally in the county establishments; and it was only in cases of uncommon magnitude or difficulty, that recourse was had to that judicial tribunal, whose jurisdiction extended over the whole kingdom. In those times, the proceedings and decisions of the courts were simple and unembarrassed..."

- James Wilson, "Lectures on Law", 1790-91

TOWNSHIP & COUNTY

The New England Township

New England was settled by Church Congregations

OF the various kinds of government to be found in the United States, we may begin by considering that of the New England township. As we shall presently see, it is in principle of all known forms of government the oldest as well as the simplest. Let us observe how the New England township grew up. When people from England first came to dwell in the wilderness of Massachusetts Bay, they settled in groups upon small irregular-shaped patches of land, which soon came to be known as townships. There were several reasons why they settled thus in small groups, instead of scattering about over the country and carving out broad estates for themselves. In the first place, their principal reason for coming to New England was their dissatisfaction with the way in which church affairs were managed in the old country. They wished to bring about a reform in the church, in such wise that the members of a congregation should have more voice than formerly in the church government, and that the minister of each congregation should be more independent than formerly of the bishop and of the civil government... Hence it was quite natural that they should come in congregations, led by the favourite ministers... This migration, therefore, was a movement not of individuals or of separate families, but of church congregations, and it continued to be so as the settlers made their way inland and westward. The first river towns of Connecticut were founded by congregations coming from Dorchester, Cambridge, and Watertown. This kind of settlement was favoured by the government of Massachusetts, which made grants of land, not to individuals but to companies of people who wished to live together and attend the same church.

Migration by congregation

"In the second place, the soil of New England was not favourable to the cultivation of great quantities of staple articles, such as rice or tobacco, so that there was nothing to tempt people to undertake extensive plantations. Most of the people lived on small farms, each family raising but little more than enough food for its own support; and the small size of the farms made it possible to have a good many in a compact neighborhood... Thus the early settlers of New England came to live in townships. A township would consist of about as many farms as could be disposed within convenient distance from the meetinghouse, where all the inhabitants, young and old, gathered every

Small self-supporting farms

Geography determined size of township

The above excerpts are from John Fiske's "Civil Government in the United States" - 1890

Sunday, coming on horseback or afoot. The meeting-house was thus centrally situated, and near it was the town pasture or 'common,' with the schoolhouse and the blockhouse, or rude fortress for defence against the Indians. Among the people who thus tilled the farms and built up the villages of New England, the differences in what we should call social position, though noticeable, were not extreme....

Little emphasis on social position

"All had for many generations been more or less accustomed to self-government and to public meetings for discussing local affairs. That self-government, especially as far as church matters were concerned, they were stoutly bent upon maintaining and extending. Indeed, that was what they had crossed the ocean for. Under these circumstances they developed a kind of government which we may describe in the present tense, for its methods are pretty much the same today that they were two centuries ago.

Public meetings customary

"In a New England township the people directly govern themselves; the government is the people, or, to speak with entire precision, it is all the male inhabitants of one and twenty years of age and upwards. The people tax themselves. Once each year, usually in March, but sometime as early as February or as late as April, a 'town-meeting,' is held, at which all the grown men of the township are expected to be present and to vote, while any one may introduce motions or take part in the discussion....

New England primary assembly

"The principal executive magistrates of the town are the selectmen. They are three, five, seven, or nine in number, according to the size of the town and the amount of public business to be transacted. The odd number insures a majority decision in case of any difference of opinion among them. They have the general management of the public business. They issue warrants for the holding of town-meetings, and they can call such a meeting at any time during the year when there seems to be need for it, but the warrant must always specify the subjects which are to be discussed and acted on at the meeting. The selectmen also lay out highways, grant licenses, and impanel jurors; they may act as health officers and issue orders regarding sewerage, the abatement of nuisances, or the isolation of contagious diseases; in many cases they act as assessors of taxes, and as overseers of the poor. They are the proper persons to listen to complaints if anything goes wrong in the town. In county matters and state matters they speak for the town, and if it is a party to a lawsuit they represent it in court; for the New England town is a legal corporation, and as such can hold property, and sue and be sued.

Selectmen principal executives

New England town a legal corporation

The above excerpts are from John Fiske's "Civil Government in the United States" - 1890

In a certain sense the selectmen may be said to be 'the government' of the town during the intervals between the town-meetings.

Town-clerk

"An officer no less important than the selectmen is the town-clerk. He keeps the record of all votes passed in the town-meeting....

Town-treasurer

"Every town has also its treasurer, who receives and takes care of the money coming in from the taxpayers, or whatever money belongs to the town....

Constables

"Every town has one or more constables, who serve warrants from the selectmen and writs from the law courts. They pursue criminals and take them to jail. They summon jurors....

Other officers

"Where the duties of the selectmen are likely to be too numerous, the town may choose three or more assessors of taxes to prepare the tax lists; and three or more overseers of the poor, to regulate the management of the village almshouse and confer with other towns upon such questions as often arise concerning the settlement and maintenance of homeless paupers.

Free Public Schools 1647

"Every town has its school committee. In 1647 the legislature of Massachusetts enacted a law with the following preamble: 'It being one chief project of that old deluder, Satan, to keep men from the knowledge of the Scriptures, as in former times by keeping them in an unknown tongue, so in these latter times by persuading from the use of tongues, that so at least the true sense and meaning of the original might be clouded and corrupted with false glosses of deceivers; to the end that learning may not be buried in the graves of our forefathers, in church and commonwealth, the Lord assisting our endeavours;' it was therefore ordered that every township containing fifty families or householders should forthwith set up a school in which children might be taught to read and write, and that every township containing one hundred families or householders should set up a school in which boys might be fitted for entering Harvard College. Even before this statute, several towns, as for instance Roxbury and Dedham, had begun to appropriate money for free schools; and these were the beginnings of a system of public education which has come to be adopted throughout the United States.

Leading to higher education

Each town selects school committee

"The school committee exercises powers of such a character as to make it a body of great importance. The term of service of the members is three years, one third being chosen annually. The number of members must therefore be some multiple of three. The slow change in the membership of the board insures

The above excerpts are from John Fiske's "Civil Government in the United States" - 1890

Duties:
1) visit schools
2) choose textbooks
2) select teachers

that a large proportion of the members shall always be familiar with the duties of the place. The school committee must visit all the public schools at least once a month, and make a report to the town every year. It is for them to decide what text-books are to be used. They examine candidates for the position of teacher and issue certificates to those whom they select....

Local government under the eyes of the people

"Within its proper sphere, government by town-meeting is the form of government most effectively under watch and control. Everything is done in the full daylight of publicity. The specific objects for which public money is to be appropriated are discussed in the presence of everybody, and any one who disapproves of any of these objects, or of the way in which it is proposed to obtain it, has an opportunity to declare his opinions. Under this form of government people are not so liable to bewildering delusions as under other forms. I refer especially to the delusion that 'the Government' is a sort of mysterious power, possessed of a magic inexhaustible fund of wealth, and able to do all manner of things for the benefit of 'the People.' Some such notion as this, more often implied than expressed, is very common, and it is inexpressibly dear to demagogues. It is the prolific root from which springs that luxuriant crop of humbug upon which political tricksters thrive as pigs fatten upon corn. In point of fact no such government, armed with a magic fund of its own, has ever existed upon the earth. No government has ever yet used any money for public purposes which it did not first take from its own people, - unless when it may have plundered it from some other people in victorious warfare.

"The People" only source of public money

"Political training of no small value"

"The inhabitant of a New England town is perpetually reminded that 'the Government' is 'the People'. Although he may think loosely about the government of his state or the still more remote government at Washington, he is kept pretty close to the facts where local affairs are concerned, and in this there is a political training of no small value.

Educational value of the Town-Meeting

"In the kind of discussion which it provokes, in the necessity of facing argument with argument and of keeping one's temper under control, the town-meeting is the best political training school in existence. Its educational value is far higher than that of the newspaper, which, in spite of its many merits as a diffuser of information, is very apt to do its best to bemuddle and sophisticate plain facts. The period when town-meetings were most important from the wide scope of their transactions was the period of earnest and sometimes stormy discussion that ushered in our Revolutionary

The above excerpts are from John Fiske's "Civil Government in the United States" - 1890

war. Country towns were then of more importance relatively than now; one country town - Boston - was at the same time a great political centre; and its meetings were presided over and addressed by men of commanding ability, among whom Samuel Adams, 'the man of the town meeting, ' was foremost. In those days great principles of government were discussed with a wealth of knowledge and stated with masterly skill in town meeting.

Principles of government discussed

"The town-meeting is to a very limited extent a legislative body; it can make sundry regulations for the management of its local affairs. Such regulations are known by a very ancient name, 'by-laws.' By is an Old Norse word meaning 'town', and it appears in the names of such towns as Derby and Whitby in the part of England overrun by the Danes in the ninth and tenth centuries. Bylaws are town laws.

"By-Laws are town laws

"To complete our sketch of the origin of the New England town, one point should here be briefly mentioned in anticipation of what will have to be said hereafter; but it is a point of so much importance that we need not mind a little repetition in stating it.

"We have seen what a great part taxation plays in the business of government, and we shall presently have to treat of county, state, and federal governments, all of them wider in their sphere than the town government. In the course of history, as nations have gradually been built up, these wider governments have been apt to absorb or supplant and crush the narrower governments, such as the parish or township; and this process has too often been destructive to political freedom. Such a result is, of course, disastrous to everybody; and if it were unavoidable, it would be better that great national governments need never be formed. But it is not unavoidable. There is one way of escaping it, and that is to give the little government of the town some real share in making up the great government of the state. That is not an easy thing to do, as is shown by the fact that most peoples have failed in the attempt. The people who speak the English language have been the most successful, and the device by which they have overcome the difficulty is REPRESENTATION. The town sends to the wider government a delegation of persons who can represent the town and its people. They can speak for the town, and have a voice in the framing of laws and imposition of taxes by the wider government....

Building a nation by absorption of local governments

Result:

Destruction of freedom

Solution:

Representation

"Observe now that the township is to be regarded in two lights. It must be considered not only in itself, but as part of a greater whole. We began by describing it as a self-governing body,

Two aspects

The above excerpts are from John Fiske's "Civil Government in the United States" - 1890

but in order to complete our sketch we were obliged to speak of it as a body which has a share in the government of the state and the nation. The latter aspect is as important as the former.

The County in its Beginnings

The county in Massachusetts

"The first English settlers in America were familiar with the county as a district for the administration of justice, and they brought with them coroners, sheriffs, and quarter sessions. In 1635 the General Court of Massachusetts appointed four towns - Boston, Cambridge, Salem, and Ipswich - as places where courts should be held quarterly. In 1643 the colony, which then included as much of New Hampshire as was settled, was divided into four 'shires', - Suffolk, Essex, Middlesex, and Norfolk, the latter lying then to the northward and including the New Hampshire towns. The militia was then organized, perhaps without consciousness of the analogy, after a very old English fashion; the militia of each town formed a company, and the companies of the shire formed a regiment. The county was organized from the beginning as a judicial district, with its court-house, jail, and sheriff. After 1697 the court, held by the justices of the peace, was called the Court of General Sessions. It could try criminal causes not involving the penalty of death or banishment, and civil causes in which the value at stake was less than forty shillings. It also had control over highways going from town to town; and it apportioned the county taxes among the several towns. The justices and sheriff were appointed by the governor, as in England by the king.

County sphere of government

The Old Virginia County

Local government in Virginia

"By common consent of historians, the two most distinctive and most characteristic lines of development which English forms of government have followed, in propagating themselves throughout the United States, are the two lines that have led through New England on the one hand and through Virginia on the other. We have seen what shape local government assumed in New England; let us now observe what shape it assumed in the Old Dominion.

"The first point to be noticed in the early settlement of Virginia is that people did not live so near together as in New England. This was because tobacco, cultivated on large estates was a

The above excerpts are from John Fiske's "Civil Government in the United States" - 1890

Migration by individual

source of wealth....They came not in organized groups or congregations, but as a multitude of individuals. Land was granted to individuals, and sometimes these grants were of enormous extent....

Geography factor in plantation system

"A glance at the map of Virginia shows to what a remarkable degree it is intersected by navigable rivers. This fact made it possible for plantations, even at a long distance from the coast, to have each its own private wharf, where a ship from England could unload its cargo of tools, cloth, or furniture, and receive a cargo of tobacco in return. As the planters were thus supplied with most of the necessaries of life, there was no occasion for the kind of trade that builds up towns....

Slavery

"The cultivation of tobacco upon large estates caused a great demand for cheap labour, and this was supplied partly by bringing negro slaves from Africa, partly by bringing criminals from English jails. The latter were sold into slavery for a limited term of years, and were known as 'indentured white servants'. So great was the demand for labour that it became customary to kidnap poor friendless wretches on the streets of seaport towns in England and ship them off to Virginia to be sold into servitude....

Founders of Virginia and New England compared

"In this rural community the owners of plantations came from the same classes of society as the settlers of New England; they were for the most part country squires and yeomen. But while in New England there was no lower class of society sharply marked off from the upper, on the other hand in Virginia there was an insurmountable distinction between the owners of plantations and the so-called 'mean whites' or 'white trash'. This class was originally formed of men and women who had been indentured white servants, and was increased by such shiftless people as now and then found their way to the colony, but could not win estates or obtain social recognition. With such a sharp division between classes, an aristocratic type of society was developed in Virginia as naturally as a democratic type was developed in New England.

No town-meetings

Parish system

"In Virginia there were no town-meetings. The distances between plantations cooperated with the distinction between classes to prevent the growth of such an institution. The English parish, with its church-wardens and vestry and clerk, was reproduced in Virginia under the same name, but with some noteworthy peculiarities. If the whole body of ratepayers had assembled in vestry meeting, to enact by-laws and assess taxes, the course of development would have been like that of the New England town-meeting. But instead of this the vestry, which exercised the chief authority in the parish, was composed of twelve

The above excerpts are from John Fiske's "Civil Government in the United States" - 1890

chosen men. This was not government by a primary assembly, it was representative government.

Differs from a New England primary assembly

"At first the twelve vestrymen were elected by the people of the parish, and thus resembled the selectmen of New England; but after a while 'they obtained the power of filling vacancies in their own number', so that they became what is called a 'close corporation', and the people had nothing to do with choosing them. Strictly speaking, that was not representative government; it was a step on the road that leads towards oligarchical or despotic government.

Vestrymen tax and govern Virginia parish

"It was the vestry, thus constituted, that apportioned the parish taxes, appointed the churchwardens, presented the minister for induction into office, and acted as overseers of the poor. The minister presided in all vestry meetings....

Local government by the few

"With the local government thus administered, we see that the larger part of the people had little directly to do. Nevertheless in these small neighbourhoods government was in full sight of the people. Its proceedings went on in broad daylight and were sustained by public sentiment....

Virginia county counterpart of New England township

"The difference, however, between the New England township and the Virginia parish, in respect of self-government, was striking enough. We have now to note a further difference. In New England, as we have seen, the township was the unit of representation in the colonial legislature; but in Virginia the parish was not the unit of representation. The county was that unit. In the colonial legislature of Virginia the representatives sat not for parishes, but for counties. The difference is very significant. As the political life of New England was in a manner built up out of the political life of the towns, so the political life of Virginia was built up out of the political life of the counties. This was partly because the vast plantations were not grouped about a compact village nucleus like the small farms at the North, and partly because there was not in Virginia that Puritan theory of the church according to which each congregation is a self-governing democracy. The conditions which made the New England town-meeting were absent. The only alternative was some kind of representative government, and for this the county was a small enough area....

Comparison with Puritan government

"In Virginia, as in England and in New England, the county was an area for the administration of justice. There were usually in each county eight justices of the peace, and their court was

The above excerpts are from John Fiske's "Civil Government in the United States" - 1890

County courts in Virginia self-perpetuating

the counterpart of the Quarter Sessions in England. They were appointed by the governor, but it was customary for them to nominate candidates for the governor to appoint, so that practically the court filled its own vacancies and was a close corporation, like the parish vestry.

"If now we sum up the contrasts between local government in Virginia and that in New England, we observe: -

Local governments contrasted

"1. That in New England the management of local affairs was mostly in the hands of town officers, the county being superadded for certain purposes, chiefly judicial; while in Virginia the management was chiefly in the hands of county officers, though certain functions, chiefly ecclesiastical, were reserved to the parish.

Selection of public officers contrasted

"2. That in New England the local magistrates were almost always, with the exception of justices, chosen by the people; while in Virginia, though some of them were nominally appointed by the governor, yet in practice they generally contrived to appoint themselves - in other words the local boards practically filled their own vacancies and were self-perpetuating.

Jefferson lauds New England townships

"These differences are striking and profound. There can be no doubt that, as Thomas Jefferson clearly saw, in the long run the interests of political liberty are much safer under the New England system than under the Virginia system. Jefferson said, 'Those wards, called townships in New England, are the vital principle of their governments, and have proved themselves the wisest invention ever devised by the wit of man for the perfect exercise of self-government, and for its preservation.'....

"Court-day" and town-meeting

"We must, however, avoid the mistake of making too much of this contrast. As already hinted, in those rural societies where people generally knew one another, its effects were not so far-reaching as they would be in the more complicated society of today. Even though Virginia had not the town-meeting, 'it had its familiar court-day,' which 'was a holiday for all the countryside,' especially in the fall and spring....

"For seventy years or more before the Declaration of Independence the matters of general public concern, about which stump speeches were made on Virginia court-days, were very similar to those that were discussed in Massachusetts town-meetings when representatives were to be chosen for the legislature. Such questions generally related to some real or alleged encroachment upon popular liberties by the royal governor, who, being

The above excerpts are from John Fiske's "Civil Government in the United States" - 1890

appointed and sent from beyond sea, was apt to have ideas and purposes of his own that conflicted with those of the people. This perpetual antagonism to the governor, who represented British imperial interference with American local self-government, was an excellent schooling in political liberty, alike for Virginia and for Massachusetts. When the stress of the Revolution came, these two leading colonies cordially supported each other, and their political characteristics were reflected in the kind of achievements for which each was especially distinguished. The Virginia system, concentrating the administration of local affairs in the hands of a few county families, was eminently favourable for developing skilful and vigorous leadership. And while in the history of Massachusetts during the Revolution we are chiefly impressed with the wonderful degree in which the mass of the people exhibited the kind of political training that nothing in the world except the habit of parliamentary discussion can impart; on the other hand, Virginia at that time gave us - in Washington, Jefferson, Henry, Madison, and Marshall, to mention no others - such a group of consummate leaders as the world has seldom seen equalled.

Virginia system: Produces great leaders

Massachusetts: Produces politically trained citizenry

"... South Carolina was settled from half a century to a century later than Massachusetts and Virginia, and by two distinct streams of immigration. The lowlands near the coast were settled by Englishmen and by French Huguenots, but the form of government was purely English. There were parishes, as in Virginia, but popular election played a greater part in them. The vestrymen were elected yearly by all the taxpayers of the parish. The minister was also elected by his people, and after 1719 each parish sent its representatives to the colonial legislature, though in a few instances two parishes were joined together for the purpose of choosing representatives. The system was thus more democratic than in Virginia; and in this connection it is worth while to observe that parochial libraries and free schools were established as early as 1712, much earlier than in Virginia.

South Carolina: In lowlands, parish system

"During the first half of the eighteenth century a very different stream of immigration, coming mostly along the slope of the Alleghanies from Virginia and Pennsylvania, and consisting in great part of Germans, Scotch Highlanders, and Scotch-Irish, peopled the upland western regions of South Carolina. For some time this territory had scarcely any civil organization. It was a kind of 'wild West.' There were as yet no counties in the colony. There was just one sheriff for the whole colony, who 'held his office by patent from the Crown.' A court sat in Charleston, but the arm of justice was hardly long enough to reach offenders in the mountains....

In uplands, little civil organization

District system established 1768

The above excerpts are from John Fiske's "Civil Government in the United States" - 1890

"In order to put a stop to this lynch law, the legislature in 1768 divided the back country into districts, each with its sheriff and court-house, and the judges were sent on circuit through these districts. The upland region with its districts was thus very differently organized from the lowland region with its parishes, and the effect was for a while almost like dividing South Carolina into two states....

"We come now to Maryland. The early history of local institutions in this state is a fascinating subject of study. None of the American colonies had a more distinctive character of its own, or reproduced old English usages in a more curious fashion. There was much in colonial Maryland, with its lords of the manor, its bailiffs and seneschals, its courts baron and courts leet, to remind one of the England of the thirteenth century. But of these ancient institutions, long since extinct, there is but one that needs to be mentioned in the present connection. In Maryland the earliest form of civil community was called, not a parish or township, but a hundred. This curious designation is often met with in English history, and the institution which it describes, though now almost everywhere extinct, was once almost universal among men....

<u>Maryland</u>: and the hundred

"...Our English forefathers seem to have been organized, like other barbarians, in clans, brotherhoods, and tribes; and the brotherhood was in some way connected with the furnishing a hundred warriors to the host. In the tenth century we find England covered with small districts known as hundreds. Several townships together made a hundred, and several hundreds together made a shire. The hundred was chiefly notable as the smallest area for the administration of justice....

"By the thirteenth century the importance of the hundred had much diminished. The need for any such body, intermediate between township and county, ceased to be felt, and the functions of the hundred were gradually absorbed by the county. Almost everywhere in England, by the reign of Elizabeth, the hundred had fallen into decay. It is curious that its name and some of its peculiarities should have been brought to America, and should in one state have remained to the present day. Some of the early settlements in Virginia were called hundreds, but they were practically nothing more than parishes, and the name soon became obsolete, except upon the map, where we still see, for example, Bermuda Hundred. But in Maryland the hundred flourished and became the political unit, like the township in New England. The hundred was the militia district, and the district for the assessment of taxes. In the earliest times it was also

Political unit like the township

The above excerpts are from John Fiske's "Civil Government in the United States" - 1890

the representative district; delegates to the colonial legislature sat for hundreds. But in 1654 this was changed, and representatives were elected by counties. The officers of the Maryland hundred were the high constable, the commander of militia, the tobacco-viewer, the overseer of roads, and the assessor of taxes. The last-mentioned officer was elected by the people, the others were all appointed by the governor. The hundred had also its assembly of all the people, which was in many respects like the New England town-meeting....

In 1654 county system established

"We next come to the great middle colonies, Pennsylvania and New York. The most noteworthy feature of local government in Pennsylvania was the general election of county officers by popular vote. The county was the unit of representation in the colonial legislature, and on election days the people of the county elected at the same time their sheriffs, coroners, assessors, and county commissioners. In this respect Pennsylvania furnished a model which has been followed by most of the states since the Revolution, as regards the county governments. It is also to be noted that before the Revolution, as Pennsylvania increased in population, the townships began to participate in the work of government, each township choosing its overseers of the poor, highway surveyors, and inspectors of elections.

Pennsylvania: County system and Township system

"New York had from the very beginning the rudiments of an excellent system of local self-government. The Dutch villages had their assemblies, which under the English rule were developed into town-meetings, though with less ample powers than those of New England. The governing body of the New York town consisted of the constable and eight overseers, who answered in most respects to the selectmen of New England. Four of the overseers were elected each year in town-meeting, and one of the retiring overseers was at the same time elected constable. In course of time the elective offices came to include assessors and collectors, town-clerk, highway surveyors, fence-viewers, pound-masters, and overseers of the poor. At first the town-meetings seem to have been held only for the election of officers, but they acquired to a limited extent the power of levying taxes and enacting by-laws. In 1703 a law was passed requiring each town to elect yearly an officer to be known as the 'supervisor,' whose duty was 'to compute, ascertain, examine, oversee, and allow the contingent, publick, and necessary charges' of the county. For this purpose the supervisors met once a year at the county town. The principle was the same as that of the levy court in Delaware. This board of supervisors was a strictly representative government, and formed a strong contrast to the close corporation by which county affairs were administered in Virginia."...

New York: Town-meeting system

The above excerpts are from John Fiske's "Civil Government in the United States" - 1890

LOCAL SELF-GOVERNMENT OF THE COLONIES

1643 - 1776

"To understand political Power, right, and derive it from its Original, we must consider, what State all Men are naturally in, and that is, a STATE OF PERFECT FREEDOM to order their Actions, and dispose of their Possessions, and Persons as they think fit, within the bounds of the Law of Nature, without asking leave, or depending upon the Will of any other Man..."

- John Locke, "Of Civil-Government", 1690

"In a MORAL view, self government increases, instead of impairing, the security, the liberty, and the dignity of the MAN; in a POLITICAL view, self government increases, instead of impairing, the security, the liberty, and the dignity, of the CITIZEN."

- James Wilson, "Lectures on Law", 1790-91

"...still there is the great and perpetual law of self-preservation, to which every natural person or corporate body hath an inherent right to recur. This being the law of the Creator, no human law can be of force against it..."

- Samuel Adams, Boston Gazette, March 29, 1773

S.W. View of the STATE-HOUSE, in BOSTON.

"...Every art and every instrument was made use of to prevent the meetings of the towns in the country, but to no purpose. It is no wonder that a measure calculated to promote a correspondence and free communication among the people should awaken their apprehensions; for they well knew it must detect their falsehood..."

- Samuel Adams, Letter to Arthur Lee, 1773

LOCAL SELF-GOVERNMENT
1643 to 1776

'he dawning f inherent ights arouses orces of pposition

At this period, the local governments were dealing with certain opinions that were pronounced to be heresy by the Church, and to be faction by the State; and in doing this, in the dawning of a recognition of an inherent right of the people to criticise public measures and to enjoy freedom in religion, there were seen in America specimens of the errors and the intolerance which were characteristic of the age. Aggrieved parties appealed for redress from local decisions to the Lords of Trade; charged that the colonies were aiming at sovereignty; and some petitioned for the appointment of a general governor....

lassachusetts naintains ppeals to ngland rom local ulings nconsistent

"The Governor and Company of Massachusetts, in an official communication from the Lords Commissioners of the 15th of May, 1646, were summoned to answer complaints of this nature. In their reply, they aver, that, though removed out of their native country, they still had dependence on it, and owed allegiance and subjection to it according to their charter; but said that they had not admitted appeals to the Lords of Trade because they believed the practice could not stand with the liberty and power that had been granted to them, and that they believed it would not be allowed by the commissioners because it would be destructive to all government. The court also prepared an elaborate Declaration, and appointed Edward Winslow of Plymouth, who had been imprisoned by the former commission, to take care of it. This vigilant and capable public servant, on arriving in England, found that the faction, in the usual manner of unscrupulous partisans, had used falsehoods and manufactured pretexts to gain their ends....

ong arliament cquiesces

"Still there was a lurking jealousy of popular power in the minds of the Lords of Trade. Winslow advised the colonies, that there were designs maturing against their liberties; and an act of parliament, a little later, manifested this fact. The Massachusetts General Court, in 1651, addressing this body as 'the supreme authority,' thanked it for stopping appeals to the Commission, and plead earnestly that the frame of their government might not be changed, but that they might continue to live under magistrates of their own choosing, and laws of their own making, not repugnant to the laws of England, as they had 'governed themselves above this twenty-three years.' This plea proved effectual, and the colonies were allowed, by the celebrated Long Parliament, the boon of neglect from the mother country, or, rather, the favor of an acquiescence in their claim to the enjoyment of local self-government.

The above excerpts are from Richard Frothingham's "The Rise of the Republic", 1890
See "The Memorial History of Boston", J. Winsor, 1880

Oliver Cromwell

"Nor was the political relation of the colonies changed during the rule of Oliver Cromwell, a great hero of the Teuton race, who rose to be a connecting link between Luther and Washington, all of like stock and intuitions. Though Cromwell, with wonderful sagacity, dealt roughly with the factions which threatened to rend the land, yet he inaugurated a reign of personal liberty and national glory such as England never saw before. He was the first of her statesmen who had a true sense of the value of the colonies to the mother country. It did not disturb him that the colonists held the Navigation Act to be contrary to their charters, as it was contrary to their natural rights; for he saw that with a claim of local government that was sometimes untenable, yet there existed a devotion to the country or the sovereignty that was genuine and serviceable; and where there was this allegiance, he forebore to intermeddle with the internal affairs of the colonies. Under his administration, New England and Virginia enjoyed free commerce and self-government....

Local self-government and commerce continue

"The restoration of the monarchy dissipated these visions of a commonwealth. On the 25th of May, 1660, Charles II. landed at Dover to ascend the throne of his ancestors.... Sir Edward Hyde, who had just been created Earl of Clarendon, and subsequently was the father-in-law of the Duke, was the Lord Chancellor and the chief minister. This bland and wily courtier, high church and high tory in his principles and of smooth speech, aimed to re-invest royalty with all its functions. His policy in relation to the colonies was definite and steadily pursued though in a foxlike manner, during the seven years in which he held power. He strove to bring them into a close dependence on the prerogative.

Schemes to enforce prerogative power

"This was an epoch in the history of the colonies. In that day of dishonor and shame to the people of England, when individual and municipal liberties were grossly violated, when profligacy, public and private, held carnival, it is not strange that a colonial polity, which, in its political organizations and in its educational aims, embodied an aspiration of human advancement, was scorned by the reckless rulers who wielded the sovereignty. This polity was pronounced to be republican. It was held, that, unless the government of the colonies were changed, 'they would harden in their constitution and grow on near to a commonwealth, towards which they were already well nigh ripened.' It was determined to check this tendency, by centralizing in the crown several functions that were exercised by the people; and to the end, that England, as the mother country, might have the full commercial benefit of her colonial possessions, it was determined

England determined to change republican governments of colonies

The above excerpts are from Richard Frothingham's "The Rise of the Republic", 1890.

ʼlonstrous ɑonopolies ʼs. ɑdividual ʼursuits

to enforce the mercantile system, with its absurd restrictions on individual pursuits, - its monstrous monopolies and downright robberies. This was an attempt to install a rule based on privilege, on the ruins of a polity in which were working the elements of equality and freedom that are the germinal forces of American institutions.

ʼouncil o oversee ʼolonies

"On the 4th of July, 1660, at a court at Whitehall, at which were present the King, the Duke of York, and the Lord Chancellor, an order was passed constituting ten Lords of the Council, or any three or more of them, a board to meet twice a week, and receive petitions and papers relating to the plantations in America; and, on the 7th of November, the king, by a commission, created 'A Council for Foreign Plantations.' This council were required by their instructions to correspond with the governors of the colonies, and to devise means to bring them into a more certain civil and uniform government.

ʼrosperity ʼxcites envy

"The confusions of the time afforded abundant material upon which to found complaints against the colonies, and especially against New England.... Besides, the London merchants were disturbed by the enterprise of New England. Its prosperity excited envy in the other colonies; and its 'commonwealth notions' supplied a field in which zealous placemen might show their zeal for the crown....

ʼolonial ʼerritory ɑade ʼrincipality

"A short time after the grant of the charters of Connecticut and Rhode Island, the prodigal Charles II, bestowed (March 12, 1664) on his brother, the Duke of York, a principality, consisting of a portion of the territory of New England and the whole of New Netherland, - a territory extending from the banks of the Delaware to the St. Croix.... The Council for Foreign Plantations, to put him in possession of his American dominions, created a special commission. England and the United Netherlands were at peace, and this measure demanded an act of war. It was determined to devolve on the same commission the duty of regulating the internal affairs of New England, a design which for years had been in contemplation....

ʼVar ʼesigns

"The commissioners were empowered to reduce New Netherland.... They were also empowered to hear and determine complaints in all civil, criminal, and military cases, 'according to their good and sound discretion.'

"On the 23d of July, 1664, a portion of the fleet designed to reduce New Netherland arrived at Boston, - the first time ships of

The above excerpts are from Richard Frothingham's "The Rise of the Republic", 1890

Original Colonies become a geographical unit

the royal navy had been seen in that harbor. The commissioners were on board. The local authorities proffered them respect, and tendered to them the hospitality of a residence....In September, Manhattan capitulated, and thenceforth New Netherland was called New York. In October, the Swedes on the Delaware surrendered; and then the flag of England floated along the whole line of the Atlantic coast from New France to Florida, and the original colonies attained a geographical unity.

"Meanwhile the General Court of Massachusetts deliberated on the very grave matter of the commission. The debates as to the course that ought to be pursued were uncommonly earnest. The reverend elders who were in town were called in to give their advice; a day of fasting and prayer was appointed, and a petition to the king was adopted....If this commission was valid, its discretion would be installed above the local law, and thus would supersede the charter. In fact, its creation was an unwarrantable exercise of the prerogative, and, as a precedent, dangerous to English liberties, and a violation of colonial rights....

"In the sight of God and man"

"The committee, who had guided the action of the General Court, prepared a narrative of their proceedings, which occupies over a hundred pages of the Colonial Records....They claimed 'full and absolute power of governing all the people of this place,' according to such laws as they should make, 'being not repugnant to the laws of England.' They averred that they had 'above thirty years enjoyed the aforesaid power and privilege of government within themselves, as their undoubted right in the sight of God and man.' They said, 'We keep ourselves within our line, and meddle not with matters abroad. A just dependence upon and subjection to your majesty, according to our Charter, it is far from our hearts to disacknowledge. We so highly prize your favorable aspect, though at this great distance, as we would gladly do any thing that is in our power to purchase a continuance of it....It is a great unhappiness to be reduced to so hard a case as to have no other testimony of our subjection and loyalty offered us but this; viz, to destroy our own being, which nature teaches us to preserve; or to yield up our liberties, which are far dearer to us than our lives, and which, had we any fear of being deprived of, we had never wandered from our fathers' house into these ends of the earth'....

"Our liberties - dearer to us than our lives"

"This remarkable state-paper exhibits the ability and the statesmanship of the colony in a favorable light....It constitutes a clean political record. The action it narrates was not aimed against the sovereignty, but against an undeniable stretch of power by the

The above excerpts are from Richard Frothingham's "The Rise of the Republic", 1890

Steady adherence to local self-government

administration which superseded, in many respects, the authority and powers granted by the charter; and that action was prosecuted by the General Court, not in an obstinate or a perverse spirit, but in a modest and steady adherence to what they believed, and what really were, their just rights and privileges....

"I cannot but think that much error has crept into American history by not keeping in view the difference between opposition to the measures of an administration and resistance to the supreme power of the empire or to the sovereignty. The immigrants, in spite of what they had suffered in their native land, bore towards it a noble affection, receiving its stripes as from a mother....

1684 to 1690

Twelve Colonies - 1688:

Twelve of the thirteen original colonies were then (1688) founded. Contemporary descriptions, printed in separate tracts, or in general compilations, serve to show their progress, relative importance, and reputation. Carolina was already famed for its product of rice; but, including the great territory subsequently called Georgia, it contained only about eight thousand Europeans. They were divided between the flourishing colony of South Carolina, of which Charleston was the chief settlement, and the settlements in the county of Albemarle, which were the beginnings of the colony of North Carolina. Carolina was receiving large accessions of the persecuted Huguenots.

The Carolinas

Virginia

"The splendid domain of Virginia, celebrated for its crops of tobacco, had a population of over fifty thousand, who lived on plantations far apart from each other; the nearest approach to a town being a cluster of buildings located around 'The State House' at Jamestown. They had neither printing-press, public schools, nor college. It was written of Virginia, that, 'as it came out of the hands of God, it was certainly one of the best countries in the world;' but as it respected well-built towns, well-educated children, and an industrious and thriving people, it was certainly 'one of the poorest, miserablest, and worst countries in all America that was inhabited by Christians.'

The above excerpts are from Richard Frothingham's "The Rise of the Republic", 1890

Maryland

Pennsylvania

"In Maryland, also, the people did not gather in towns. This colony invited settlers by promising 'toleration in religion to all who professed faith in Christ.' Pennsylvania had been founded only six years. The large influence of William Penn and the mild virtues of Quakerism attracted emigrants. The city of Philadelphia was described as increasing rapidly, and as a place scarcely to be paralleled for a favorable location.

New Jersey

Delaware

"New Jersey, then divided into East and West New Jersey, and its neighbors, 'The Delaware Counties,' were characterized as having air, soil, ports, and harbors not inferior to those of any other colony. Several towns had been founded, which were said to be in a flourishing condition. These four prosperous colonies had reached a population of forty-seven thousand.

New York

"The colony of New York contained twenty thousand inhabitants. The city was described as having five hundred houses, built of fair Dutch brick, and as being famous for pleasure and great business activity.

Plymouth Colony
Connecticut
Rhode Island
Massachusetts
New Hampshire

"The New England colonies had a population of seventy-five thousand. Plymouth continued to be a backward colony; Connecticut and Rhode Island had become models of peace, progress, and self-government; Massachusetts had purchased the Province of Maine, and was rapidly growing in importance; New Hampshire, constituted in 1680 an independent colony, had but four towns. These colonies enjoyed the educational influences of the town, the public school, the college, the congregational church, the public meeting, and the general assembly. The spirit of commercial enterprise was so active, and the cause of religion, as viewed by earnest souls, seemed in comparison to be so languid, that the generation who were about leaving the stage mourned over the departing glory of New England, and prophesied that she had seen her best days. But it can now be seen, that, in the inner life of religion, the original spirit was only accepting new forms. New England outwardly was moving forward with a steady step towards wealth and power, with freedom as the enlivening principle of its pursuits, and the accumulation of property, landed and personal, as the invigorating nerve of its enterprise....

"This glance at the twelve colonies, 'The English Empire in America,' serves to show their relative importance at the interesting period of the Revolution of 1688. They were applying the principle of local self-government. It was, under their situation, a necessity. It was not practicable for the parliament to legislate on the various little wants of each colony, - to care for the making

The above excerpts are from Richard Frothingham's "The Rise of the Republic", 1890

Local affairs: The concern of local governments

of roads, the building of churches, and the maintenance of schools, or to frame a remedy for the inconveniences or evils that a change of circumstances daily brought forth. All this was provided for under the general powers of government conveyed by the crown to each colony, either directly, as in the charters which were granted to Massachusetts, Connecticut, and Rhode Island, or through the medium of the proprietors of the soil, as in Maryland, Pennsylvania, Delaware, New Jersey, and the two Carolinas, or by instructions sent by the crown to the governors, as in Virginia, New Hampshire, and New York, which were called royal provinces.

Each Colony chose local laws adapted to its need

"Each colony manifested a similar spirit of freedom in exercising these powers. In each the popular will was expressed through the representative assembly. Each adopted so much of the English statute law, and claimed the benefit of so much of the common law, as seemed to be suited to the condition of its inhabitants. While all recognized their subordination to the acts of parliament which expressly named the colonies, and bound them as integral parts of the empire in a general system framed for all, and for the benefit of all, they also recognized the common law, which united the colonies to the parent State by the general ties of allegiance and dependency. In this spirit each community framed its local law. Each was strongly attached to the form which it had adopted, and thought it to be the best....In each the people were governed by magistrates whom they selected, and by the laws which they framed. Thus organized, the twelve colonies contained the elements of our country as it is today.

Schemes against the growth of republicanism

"This self-government was regarded by the supreme power as a growth of republicanism, as it really was. To meet and to check this element, the Clarendon ministry (1660 to 1667), as has been stated, devised the scheme of bringing the colonies more under the control of the prerogative; and this continued to be the policy of the Government. On the fall of Clarendon, the administration known as the Cabal wielded, for six years (1667-1673), the sovereignty. The Council for Foreign Plantations was enlarged (March 20, 1671), and the Duke of York and several high personages were created members. The Danby ministry succeeded the Cabal (1673-1679) when the Cavaliers obtained complete power. During this period, Charles II. gave Virginia away to two of his courtiers for thirty-one years, and he renewed (1674) the Duke of York's patent. He dissolved the Council for Foreign Plantations, and appointed (March 12, 1675) a committee of the Privy Council to consider matters connected with the American colonies. They were directed to sit once a week, and report their proceedings to the

The above excerpts are from Richard Frothingham's "The Rise of the Republic", 1890

council. This arrangement continued not only till the close of the reign of Charles, but through that of his successor.

American affairs incite tyrannical intentions

"The subject of American affairs occupied the attention of the Government largely during this period. The several administrations shrunk from a decisive interference with the internal affairs of the colonies. When it was judged that events required bold action, the debates in the Privy Council were earnest. 'The question was considered thoroughly whether the council should introduce there the same government that was established in England, or should subject the colonists to the rule of a governor and council, who should have all authority in their hands, without being obliged to observe any other laws than those which should be prescribed in England.'

Royal prerogative to thwart Colonial assemblies

"'It was resolved that the governor and council should not be obliged to call assemblies from the country to make taxes and to regulate other important matters, but that they should do what they should judge proper, rendering an account only to his Britannic majesty.' This was the opinion of the Duke of York. He held that the colonies did not need general assemblies, and ought not to have them. This view prevailed....

James II overthrown

"The tyranny of James II. had fallen upon his English and his transatlantic subjects alike: neither were of a temper tamely to submit to it, and both were delighted to welcome the advent of William and Mary. When the report reached Boston that the Prince of Orange had landed in England, an uprising against the existing rule was planned and consummated. The general-governor, Sir Edmund Andros, and some of his associates, were imprisoned; and a provisional government, in the name of William and Mary, was established....The revolution extended to the Carolinas. In all the colonies, their right of local government had been violated. In all, William and Mary were joyfully proclaimed.

William and Mary proclaimed

"There was then a period of confusion and of transition....

1690 to 1760

The population of the colonies, in seventy years, increased from two hundred thousand to a million and a half. It was described as 'a mixture of English, Scotch, Irish, French, Dutch, Germans and

The above excerpts are from Richard Frothingham's "The Rise of the Republic", 1890

Swedes'. Only small groups of Irish and Scotch were seen in the colonies in the seventeenth century; but, in the reigns of Anne and George I, oppression and scarcity of food drove large numbers of them to America. They were termed Scotch-Irish. They were generally Presbyterians; and wherever they settled, they adopted the usages of the Church of Scotland. Germans also emigrated in large numbers, and chiefly into Maryland and Pennsylvania. The African race rapidly multiplied, by fresh importations as well as by natural increase....

Ruthless power exerted in Colonial affairs

"All the colonies exercised powers of government under authority derived from the crown. In seven of them, the forms remained the same as they were at the close of the former period. Virginia and New York continued royal governments; and Maryland and Pennsylvania retained their proprietary character, the three lower counties of the latter becoming the independent province of Delaware. Connecticut and Rhode Island were permitted to resume their charters. The crown decreed important territorial and political changes in the five other colonies. It granted to Massachusetts a charter which included the Plymouth jurisdiction, and embraced the 'Province of Maine;' but took from the people the election of the governor. It constituted the towns of New Hampshire a separate province; united into one colony East and West New Jersey; divided Carolina into the two colonies of North Carolina and South Carolina; and it founded Georgia, - giving to these five colonies royal governments. The rights conveyed by charters and royal instructions were necessarily vague and indefinite; but under each form the people shared in the control of local affairs through representative assemblies....

"The colonies, moulded and directed by a race of freemen, continued to be treated by the mother country in the autocratic spirit which has been described. The revolution, pronounced the most beneficent of all revolutions for England, proved little more than a succession of an unnatural policy for America. The colonial administration of William and Mary embodied a zealous attachment to the prerogative and a stern exercise of arbitrary power. Royal officials, who had been imprisoned by the colonists for their oppressions, were installed governors and judges. The same spirit controlled the colonial action during most of the reigns of Queen Anne and George I. and George II. At times, decisions were wisely taken, as was the case when Sir Robert Walpole declined to tax America. But, in the main, Great Britain, like an unnatural parent, treated her colonies, during seventy years, as aliens and rivals....

The above excerpts are from Richard Frothingham's "The Rise of the Republic", 1890

"Natural right" fundamental to Americans

"The events having a bearing on the idea of union embraces many facts which show the condition of self-government. The development of this principle was seen in social life, as the American, imbued with a spirit of individual freedom, went on quietly creating his own proper sphere of action as the unit of a free State. He was met by laws enacted by parliament forbidding him to manufacture certain articles and restricting him in the petty detail of trade. This incited him to reason on the natural right of labor to choose its fields, and to enjoy its earnings.

Protest against foreign control of American business

"(The succession of acts discouraging the American from manufacturing, - too often related to need more than a reference - provoked sharp queries. In the 'Boston Gazette' of April 29, 1765, is the following: 'Whose natural right is infringed by the erection of an American windmill, or the occupation of a watermill on a man's own land, provided he does not flood his neighbors?.... A colonist cannot make a button, a horseshoe, nor a hob-nail, but some sooty ironmonger or respectable button-maker of Britain shall bawl and squall that his honor's worship is most egregiously maltreated, injured, cheated, and robbed by the rascally American republicans.')

Individual liberty and self-government not inconsistent with "duty to the nation"

"His conclusions, after a manner, justified the practice which ignored such laws as violated the most sacred rights of mankind. It is easy now to see that this was a part of the process in America of solving the problem, how a large measure of individual liberty may be combined with obedience to every requirement of just law, how a high degree of self-government may exist and be consistent with the performance of every patriotic duty to the nation. Again, it is easy to see that this development of individual freedom was quietly undermining the old paternal theory of government. This was based on the idea that the body of the people do not possess the capacity to take care of their own personal concerns, but require to be controlled in their dress, diet, business, and opinions. I can, however, only thus casually refer to the social side of this subject, - the theme in hand requiring an adherence to facts more strictly political.

Civil liberties were promised the prospective pioneer

"The fidelity of the colonists to the principle of local self-government was constant through the whole of this period (1690 to 1760). It is an interesting fact, that Europeans, by advertisements in tracts and newspapers, were promised, on their arrival and settlement in America, a share in making the laws under which they were to live. This formed, to many, one of the inducements to leave their native land, and meet the hardships in the life of a pioneer. The promise was vague in its terms; but there were no

The above excerpts are from Richard Frothingham's "The Rise of the Republic", 1890

such exceptions in the charters or the advertisements as that immigrants, in their new homes, should not be allowed to make their own clothes, should not work up their rags into paper, should not carry the wool which they might grow over a river to a market, should not sell a hat to each other. And even after the acts severely restrictive on labor were passed, it might have been said, to do away with the unfavorable impression, that they were in a great measure inoperative in the colonies. It was held out as an inducement to emigrate, that the lands were so productive as to render it certain that industry would enable the emigrant to better his condition, and that he would enjoy large civil liberties.

English traditional rights dear to Colonists

"The colonies held these liberties under general powers derived from the crown. As time rolled on, they were more and more prized, as they were embodied in their free institutions. Ardent as was the attachment of the people of each colony to its local polity, still they went beyond it to meet and satisfy the great sentiment of country. They claimed to be in partnership with a noble empire. They regarded their connection with the mother country to be a fountain of good. They looked upon the English Constitution as their own. It was said in the press, 'Our Constitution is English, which is another name for free and happy; and is without doubt the perfectest model of civil government that has ever been in the world'. The colonists claimed the advantage of the great moral discoveries of Habeas Corpus and Trial by Jury, of a Popular Representation and a Free Press. It was through the provisions of law that had grown up under their local governments that these discoveries, fraught with perennial blessings, were brought to their doors. In a word, they aimed to preserve their liberties and also to preserve their union with Great Britain. The banner of St. George was to the subject in the colonial age what the flag of the Stars and Stripes is to the citizen of the United States.

Rights brought home through their local governments

Royal aim - to remodel local governments

"The royal governors, in dealing with the representative branches of their several governments, came directly in contact with this development of self-government. They regarded some of the pretensions set up by the general assemblies as invasions of the royal prerogative. They characterized the colonies as imbued with pernicious political principles, as animated by a spirit of disobedience to law, and as aiming at throwing off their dependence on the crown. They were continually invoking a vigorous assertion of the prerogative, or of the power of parliament, by remodelling the local governments, and with a view of checking the growth of popular power.

The above excerpts are from Richard Frothingham's "The Rise of the Republic", 1890

To restrain the press and deny writ of habeas corpus

"These representations were sent to successive British ministers, who were always sensitive on the point of sovereignty, and were zealous for the prerogative or for the parliament, as the tory or the whig schools predominated. Their spirit in dealing with the rising colonies is seen in the royal instructions, which aimed to restrain the liberty of the press, thus denying to the colonists freedom of mind, and in refusing to allow them the writ of habeas corpus, which deprived them of the great guard of personal liberty. It is seen in the instructions that were given to the governors, from time to time, to maintain the prerogative; in the successive measures brought forward in parliament to override the charters, and to enlarge the powers of the Board of Trade; and in the conclusion that was reached to revise the local governments. At length, in 1750, at a meeting of the Privy Council, the Lords of Trade were directed to propose such measures as would retain and establish the prerogative in its utmost extent throughout the colonies. All branches of the home government determined to shape the colonies into new modes of being, and no other pattern was thought of than that of England.

"And exercise of the royal prerogative by the governors, which was regarded by the assemblies to be illegal, evoked in the colonies a sturdy defence of the rights that they held to be constitutional. The struggles between these branches were at times severe and acrimonious. A glance at a few of the issues raised, will show the political situation when the crown invited the assemblies to deliberate on the great question of union.

Issue - representation

"In New Hampshire, the issue turned on the question of representation, which the crown held was a privilege that it might give or withhold at its pleasure, but which the colonies held was a right to which they were entitled under the law....

Issue - control of salary and tenure of royal governors

"In Massachusetts, the issue for many years was mainly on the salary of the governors, royal instructions directing that they should be settled and made permanent, so that the governors might be independent of successive assemblies; while the assemblies held that the grants should be made annually, in order to insure responsibility. (The same party who maintained the charter-privileges in the time of Charles II. and James II. continued to be the advocates of popular rights under their successors. Minot remarks (Hist. of Mass. i. 51), 'From this period (1683) we may date the origin of the two parties, - the patriots and prerogative men, - between whom controversy scarcely intermitted and war never ended until the separation of the two countries.')....

The above excerpts are from Richard Frothingham's "The Rise of the Republic", 1890

"In New York, the controversies between the two branches had been carried on with great heat; and the governors repeatedly represented that the assembly and the people aimed to throw off his majesty's authority. In no colony was the claim of the assembly to be a free deliberative body put forth earlier or maintained with more intelligence and tenacity than it was in Virginia. Although there had been great political tranquillity in South Carolina, yet its governor complained that the whole power was in the hands of the people....

Feudal concept encounters "the great idea" of government

"The governors came over with high ideas of their own importance, and with not a little of the feudal spirit, which regarded the possessors of power as the holders of so much personal property that they might turn to their own private uses; while the assemblies were imbued with the spirit of the great idea, that government is an agency or trust, which was to be exercised for the common good. It is, however, not necessary to maintain that the governors were always wrong in their positions, or that the assemblies were always right in their methods; but it was the steady aim of the governors, of their superiors and the end of their own action to check the growth of popular power, while it was the object of the assemblies to defend their constitutional rights. They were met by the indefinite, imperious, and mysterious claims of the royal prerogative, which were urged by needy governors with an arrogance and conceit that made the claims doubly offensive. This was occurring constantly through the colonial age. It is difficult to say precisely what the prerogative was. As defined by the great jurist of that age, it was something out of the ordinary course of common law, and inherent in the royal dignity.

Blackstone defines prerogative

"(Blackstone began to read lectures on law in 1753. He thus defines the prerogative: 'By the word prerogative we usually understand that special preeminence which the king hath over and above all other persons, and out of the ordinary course of common law, in right of his regal dignity. It signifies in its etymology something that is required and demanded before or in preference to others. And hence it follows that it must be in its nature singular and excentrical; that it can only be applied to those rights and capacities which the king enjoys alone in contradistinction to others, and not to those which he enjoys in common with any of his subjects; for, if once any prerogative of the crown could be held in common with the subjects, it would cease to be prerogative any longer. And therefore, Finch lays it down as a maxim, that the prerogative is that law in the case of the king, which is law in no case of the subject.' - Commentaries, i. 239)

The above excerpts are from Richard Frothingham's "The Rise of the Republic", 1890

Prerogative hostile to principle of local self-government

"As a practical thing, embodied in royal instructions and applied to the detail of affairs, it embraced well nigh the whole field of administration. It was in theory utterly hostile to the principle of local self-government. In meeting it, the members of the assemblies often manifested a zeal and an ability worthy of admiration. In doing this, they were ever mindful to keep in view their readiness to recognize a just claim for the prerogative. Indeed, whether the colonists spoke through the assembly or the press, the liberty which they defended never meant an absence of law. A sentence of the press runs, 'It would fill us with the deepest shame and grief, could we be justly charged with really opposing that sacred ordinance from heaven, civil government.'

Affairs of civil government circulated in the press

"The executive speeches and the replies of the assemblies elicited in these local contests were widely circulated in the press. The newspapers had a too intimate connection with the formation of public sentiment to allow their appearance to pass without remark. The first permanent newspaper in the colonies was established in Boston in 1704, and in about a half a century journals were printed in ten of the thirteen colonies. This is the most efficient instrument used in the political world; for 'nothing but a newspaper can drop the same thought into a thousand minds at the same moment. It soon began to play a great part in American history. The springs of this history are not to be found so much in the foresight and wise planning of a few, however great and essential may have been individual worth and influence, as in the impulses and aims of the many.

The prime office of a responsible press

"At epochs in public affairs, the body of the people, at the call of some great right, or by the commission of some great wrong, have instinctively and spontaneously joined in a common effort, when society has been impelled forward by a master-passion, until the culmination of great crises. In these periods, the newspaper has been a powerful agency, not merely by passionate appeals, but by virtue of its prime office of collecting and circulating intelligence; by disseminating the facts that enabled the public opinion of one community or political centre to act on other communities. In thus adding to the momentum, the newspaper chronicles the progress of popular movements, and, after its temporary office, it remains to do historical service. It is a dial which measures and marks the play of the inner forces of society, as the meter marks the passage of the sources of light. The pages of an unfettered press are a mirror which reflects the past of a collective life, when it was stirred by fear, when it glowed with hope, when it was inspired into heroic action by the presence and the power of great ideas....

The above excerpts are from Richard Frothingham's "The Rise of the Republic", 1890

Stamp used in 1765

1760 to 1766.

Plan of George III for America

The ministry of George III. decided on a policy with regard to America more in harmony with English ideas and objects than with wisdom and justice. This policy, so far as it was developed in the Stamp Act, was an assertion by parliament of the right to tax the colonies by a body in which they were not represented; and the attempt to execute this act evoked out of the prevalent diversity a sentiment of union, and called forth a congress for a redress of grievances....

Scheme to mold America into uniformity with un-American ideas

"The men in power regarded England as the head and heart of the whole empire, as omnipotent in the matter of government; and they aimed to make every other part of the empire 'the mere instrument or conduit of conveying nourishment and vigor' to the head. A policy based substantially on this idea had long been urged by the Lords of Trade. It amounted to the construction of a new colonial map. It embraced an alteration of territorial boundaries, a remodelling of the local constitutions, an abridgment of popular power, and an introduction of the aristocratic or hereditary element. It contemplated, in fact, the moulding of America into uniformity with England. It included an execution of the Navigation Act, which had never been enforced, of laws of trade which had remained dead letters on the statute-book, the collection of a revenue, and the establishment of a standing army. The ministry of the Earl of Bute, based on prerogative and power, decided in favor of this policy, and successive administrations endeavored to carry it out in part or in the whole.

Arbitrary laws create alarm

"The measures embodying this scheme were not adopted at once.... The orders issued after the Peace of Paris, directing an execution of the Sugar Act, the Navigation Act, and the arbitrary laws of trade created great alarm in the colonies. This was protested against by the community generally. It was suggested that the merchants in the colonies should hold meetings, choose committees to memorialize the general assemblies to act on the subject of the Sugar Act, and that these committees should open a correspondence with each other, and thus endeavor 'to promote a union or a coalition of all their councils'; an idea carried out nine years later in the celebrated organization of committees of cor-

The above excerpts are from Richard Frothingham's "The Rise of the Republic", 1890

respondence. This suggestion met with favor. The merchants of several towns in Massachusetts, New York, and Rhode Island held meetings, corresponded with each other, and adopted memorials to the assemblies; and representations were sent to England against the Sugar Act. All this proved of no avail. The act, about to expire, was renewed and made more obnoxious, and other duties were imposed.

Protest by Colonial communities

"Meantime reports multiplied that the home government was devising a system of 'inland taxation', that the method was to be stamp tax, and that the internal police of the colonies was to be altered. Charles Townshend was advanced to the place of First Lord of Trade. He was as zealous for an alteration of the local governments as when he first became a member of this Board. The Chancellor of the Exchequer, George Grenville, declined to bring forward this part of the Bute policy, though fully resolved on the measure of taxation. On the 9th of March, 1764, he read in the House of Commons a series of resolutions declaring the intention of the government to raise a revenue in America by a duty on stamped paper; announcing, however, that final action on the question would be delayed, with the view of allowing the colonists an opportunity of suggesting other modes of laying a tax....

The Declaratory Resolves

"The Declaratory Resolves, the heralds of the famous Stamp Act, caused great sensation in the colonies. The American mind was soon occupied with the profound questions of government, natural rights, and constitutional law. As the discussion went on in the public meeting, the press, and the general assemblies, the people became divided in sentiment. The opposers of the measures of the administration were termed Whigs, Patriots, and Sons of Liberty; and the supporters of the administration were called Loyalists, Tories, and Friends of Government. Each party could point to men of learning, talents, and integrity, as actors or sympathizers, who believed in the justice of certain leading principles and objects, and sought by joint endeavor to promote them; and each party had to endure the evils inflicted on the cause by its own selfish, unscrupulous, rash, and violent members. Both sides claimed to act under the British Constitution, and to be loyal to the crown. Both regarded with pride their connection with the mother-country: nor did the Whigs, until after hostilities commenced, aim at a dissolution of this connection.

American mind alert to natural rights and constitutional law

Whigs and Tories debate

"The Whigs, traced by the lineage of principles, had an ancestry in Buchanan and Languet, in Milton, Locke, and Sidney, or the political school whose utterances are inspired and imbued with

The above excerpts are from Richard Frothingham's "The Rise of the Republic", 1890

Whig principles traced to "The Christian Idea of Man"

the Christian idea of man. Their leading principle was republicanism as it was embodied in the free institutions of the colonies. The sentiment of their advocates on freedom and equality shows that they instinctively grasped the principle which has most thoroughly leavened modern opinion, and promises to modify most deeply the constitution of society and the politics of states. Their platform was summed up in the Declaration of Independence, and became the American theory of government. Most of the men who figured in the grand political centre of the congress that adopted this measure, appear as prominent Whigs in the action of their respective localities during the stages which led to it; and this remark is applicable to the members of the convention that framed the Federal Constitution. In order to understand a revolution, it is necessary to consider it at its origin and at its termination. The Whigs, at the origin of this movement, were in a minority in some of the colonies. When they organized into a party, it had powerful opponents in them all; but it grew in numbers until it embraced substantially the whole people. This, therefore, was the national party. To it posterity are indebted for the mighty historic influence of American Union.

Tories maintain prerogative power of the State - "The Pagan Idea of Man"

"The Tories had for their leading principle the supremacy of law, and for their leading object continual dependence on England. Their chief men in each colony were most of the circle of officials appointed by the crown, and many persons of wealth and high social position. They were numerous in every colony, and had seven or eight journals in their interest. It is not easy to generalize accurately as to them. Some of the royal governors sent from England were imbued with high-toned Tory ideas, and held the self-government that had grown up as equivalent to mob-law; while Americans who took this side deplored the adoption of some of the ministerial measures, though they held that submission to them was due to the loyalty which they owed to the sovereign and the reverence which was due to parliament. Hence they gradually became defenders of arbitrary power.

"At the date of the passage of the Declaratory Resolves, the Whigs were not united into a party; and eight years elapsed before the celebrated organization of committees of correspondence.

"The intelligence of the intention to impose a direct internal tax on the colonies was soon followed by important action. A writer remarks, that 'the American people entered at once into one vast arena for the purpose of mutual defence and national concert'. It is more precise to say, that the portion of the people, soon to be known as Sons of Liberty, felt alike grieved at the contemplated

The above excerpts are from Richard Frothingham's "The Rise of the Republic," 1890

aggression on the custom of self-taxation, which was held as guaranteed by the British Constitution. This is evinced in independent and spontaneous utterances in various colonies....

Public sentiment against Stamp Act

"The Stamp Act found a public sentiment in the colonies prepared to oppose it as an internal tax. All parties regarded it in this light. Some were in favor of yielding obedience to it as the law; but the Whigs, though a portion of them involuntarily hesitated at the idea of resisting the execution of an act of parliament, soon became united in the view that submission would be a badge of slavery.

"The newspapers abound with detail relative to a passive resistance to the new policy, - the movement in favor of domestic manufactures and of a non-importation agreement....

"The Sons of Liberty"

"Meantime, 'The Sons of Liberty' - a term that grew into use soon after the publication of Barre's speech - were entering into associations to resist, by all lawful means, the execution of the Stamp Act. They were long kept secret, which occasioned loyalists to say, that there was a private union among a certain sect of republican principles from one end of the continent to the other. As they increased in numbers, they grew in boldness and publicity, announcing in the newspapers their committees of correspondence, and interchanging solemn pledges of support. The Virginia resolves, as circulated in the press, declaring that no obedience was due to the Stamp Act, strengthened the purpose of these associations....

The Liberty Tree

"As a great concourse gathering under the elm, subsequently named Liberty Tree, marched through the streets, the words 'Liberty, Property, and No Stamps' passed from mouth to mouth. They proved to be talismanic words. They were echoed in processions formed in other places for similar purposes. In some cases, the unhappy stamp distributors were compelled to stand high before the people and shout, 'Liberty, Property, and No Stamps.' These words became a favorite toast, and stood as a motto at the head of the press....

Continental union urged

"Meanwhile the Sons of Liberty, through their committees of correspondence, urged a continental Union; pledged a mutual support in case of danger; in some instances stated the numbers of armed men that might be relied on; and thus evinced a common determination to resist the execution of the Stamp Act....

"The above narrative of the proceedings in the colonies, growing out of the attempt of the ministry to carry out the new policy, shows

The above excerpts are from Richard Frothingham's "The Rise of the Republic", 1890

how the two political schools regarded union when it was in American hands, and was urged for American objects.

Ridicule of union by Tories

"The party of the prerogative met the proposition to hold a congress with ridicule, or denounced it as disloyal.... This school aimed to keep America weak, by fostering the isolation of the colonies, or it aimed at such a unity by a consolidation of popular functions as would repress the republican element. It held that the government in England had unlimited power over the colonies, and that they ought not even to unite in a petition without its permission.

Undoubted right to communicate with neighbors

"The Whigs held that the colonies, though subordinate, were under a limited government; that they had an undoubted right to join in petitions; and that union was the most efficient means to obtain a redress of grievances. Hence the attempt to unite the merchants, by committees of correspondence, in protests against the injustice of the acts of Trade; the proposition for joint action in the earliest organized movement in opposition to the contemplated Stamp Act; the cordial reception of the Massachusetts proposal for a congress; the associations of the Sons of Liberty, pledging to each other their lives in the support of their rights; and the inspiring cry for 'A continental union'. It is not without significance that at that time the term 'America' was used as applied to a people, and the term 'country' as applied to America. The inspiration of the thought which those terms expressed is seen in the language in which Christopher Gadsden urged his countrymen to lift above all merely provincial names the name of American. Thus union had become a sentiment, a moral power, and began to influence the course of events.... The stern words in which Gadsden connected a refusal to unite with infamy, show the strength of the conviction of the popular leaders respecting union. In many ways, the public mind, especially through the press, grew familiar with the idea that the colonies were linked together in a common destiny.

American industry subjected to arbitrary restrictions

"I have alluded but cursorily to the passive resistance to the new policy by the non-importation agreement, and by fostering domestic manufactures, when the watchword was Frugality and Industry. Then Americans asserted, practically, the right of labor to choose its fields and enjoy its fruits; when even liberal thinkers advocated the most vexatious restrictions on industrial pursuits, and the old colonial system was so triumphant, that Chatham declared he would not allow a hobnail to be manufactured in America. Otis averred that 'one single act of parliament had set people a-thinking, in six months, more than they had done in their whole lives before'.

"The thought was, that Americans might clothe themselves with their own hands, and be independent of a foreign supply. The

The above excerpts are from Richard Frothingham's "The Rise of the Republic", 1890

members of the assemblies were urged to set the example. 'I have in my younger days,' wrote Dulany, 'seen fine sights, and been captivated by their dazzling pomp and glittering splendor; but the sight of our representatives, all adorned in complete dresses of their own leather and flax and wool, manufactured by the art and industry of the inhabitants of America, would excite not the gaze of admiration, the flutter of an agitated imagination, or the momentary amusement of a transient scene; but a calm, solid, heartfelt delight'. The daughters of America entered into this movement with a spirit that gave inspiration to the cause....

America - "the school of Christian knowledge"

"Meantime the prosperity and progress of the colonies continued to elicit foreshadowings of the future of America. Ezra Stiles, one of the gifted Americans of his age, anticipated the independence of his country. He said that there would be a provincial confederacy formed on free suffrage, which in time would grow into an imperial dominion; Watson, Vicar of Yorkshire, in a sermon on American colleges, adopting the thought that all arts and sciences were travelling westward, speculated on what America would be as a powerful and independent state, - the school of Christian knowledge and of liberal science....

1766 to 1770.

Stamp used in 1765

Repeal of Stamp Act

Thoughtful minds questioned whether the repeal of the Stamp Act, 'on European rather than American reasons', was worthy of the rejoicings that burst spontaneously, in full chorus, from the heart of a grateful people. The Repeal was accompanied by the famous Declaratory Act, that parliament had the right to bind the colonies in all cases whatsoever. The great champion of Repeal, William Pitt, asserted for parliament this right of governing, as emphatically as he denied the right to tax. It was said, however, that this act was but laying down an abstraction. Against it were the declarations of the thirteen colonies, that the people had inherent rights, and that the powers of the king and the parliament were limited by the Constitution.

Declaratory Act asserts Parliament's supremacy

"Some urged, that the new declaration might be, and ought to be, met by a fresh assertion, by each colony, of what it regarded as its rights. But the appeals for a continuation of agitation against

The above excerpts are from Richard Frothingham's "The Rise of the Republic", 1890

an abstraction proved of little account. The Sons of Liberty dissolved their association, and, in a great measure, ceased their operations. The masses are moved more by feeling than by reasoning, and the paramount feeling was that of gratitude. It was said that the Repeal hushed into silence every clamor, and composed every wave of popular disorder into a smooth and peaceful calm. The colonies cheerfully and gratefully acknowledged their dependence on the crown of Great Britain.

Parliament to remodel local governments

"The Repeal was regarded by the king as a fatal compliance. It proved only a pause in the attempt to carry out the new policy. Soon after, to the astonishment and sorrow of the liberal world, William Pitt accepted a peerage, and entered the House of Lords; when Charles Townshend became the leader of the House of Commons.... He continued to favor the policy of remodelling the local governments, which he urged when a member of the Board of Trade.... Townshend became the master spirit of the cabinet that succeeded the Rockingham ministry....

America

1) To pay heavy duties

2) Quarter British troops

3) Yield to writs of assistance

"The Townshend Revenue Acts, the chief of which was introduced into parliament the 13th of May, 1767, received the royal assent the 29th of June, and was to go into effect on the 20th of November. These acts, in brief, imposed duties on glass, paper, painters' colors, and tea; established a board of customs at Boston to collect the revenue throughout America; and legalized writs of assistance. The preamble of the act imposing duties stated that they were laid for raising a revenue to provide for the support of civil government in the provinces, and for their general defence. It was designed that the governors, judges, and attorneys should be rendered independent of the local assemblies. The extent to which parliament interfered with these bodies was seen in the law suspending the New York assembly from the exercise of the powers of legislation until it should comply with the act requiring it to provide quarters for British troops.

For purpose of asserting British sovereignty

"The new duties were imposed not on commercial grounds, but for political reasons; not to regulate trade, but for revenue and to assert British sovereignty. The scheme was thoroughly dissected by the press. Its aggression on the ancient self-government was pointed out. The line between external and internal taxation - between the spheres of the colonial or local and the imperial - was not clearly defined; yet it was the theory of the Whigs, that each colony, as an integral part of the nation, had a general assembly, which, though subordinate, was a free, deliberative body; and, while parliament had the right to make the laws for England, these assemblies, with the council, had the right to make the laws bearing

The above excerpts are from Richard Frothingham's "The Rise of the Republic", 1890

exclusively on America; and that the king was the common executive, whose rightful prerogative was in force in each colony as it was in England.

New scheme more dangerous than the Stamp Act

"This law-making power regulated 'the internal police'; which meant, that it provided for the elective franchise, representation, trial by jury, the habeas corpus, the concerns of order, education, and religion. This power was the custodian of the municipalities; and they, in the fine words of Mirabeau, 'are the basis of the social state, the safety of every day, the security of every fireside, the only possible way of interesting the entire people in the government, and of securing all rights'. Now the new scheme was regarded by Americans as more dangerous to their liberties than the Stamp Act, because it was an aggression on the old usages, grown into a right, of fashioning the 'internal police'. A British official, who knew America by personal observation, described the situation, politically, as he remarked, that the operation of the Stamp Act, on colonial ideas 'would have been by sap'; but the Townshend scheme 'was attacking them by storm every day'.

"The father of the new acts, Charles Townshend, died before they went into effect; and their execution devolved on Lord North, appointed chancellor of the exchequer....

Sons of Liberty aroused to action

European mob action denounced as un-American

"It was then said that 'American liberty must be entirely of American fabric'. A new movement, as it was termed, began. The popular leaders enjoined the people to avoid mobs, confusions, tumults, - the terrible spirit of disorder that was a part of the action against the Stamp Act, and which was like the European popular action, - spasmodic, dangerous, and ruinous. This advice was given, in line upon line, in the press. On the day the new acts went into effect, there was posted under 'Liberty Tree', in Boston, a paper calling on the 'Sons of Liberty' to rise and fight for their rights, and saying that they would be joined by legions. This incident drew from James Otis, the moderator of a meeting held in the town on that day, a spirited denunciation of mobs. He said, that, 'were the burdens of the people ever so heavy, or their grievances ever so great, no possible circumstances, though ever so oppressive, could be supposed sufficient to justify private tumults and disorders, either to their consciences before God, or legally before men; that their forefathers, in the beginning of the reign of Charles I., for fifteen years together, were continually offering up prayers to their God, and petitions to their king for redress of grievances, before they would betake themselves to any forcible measures; that to insult and tear each other in pieces was to act like madmen'.

The above excerpts are fromRichard Frothingham's "The Rise of the Republic", 1890

American method of political agitation

"This speech was printed in the newspapers, and was heartily indorsed. 'Our cause,' it was said, 'is a cause of the highest dignity: it is nothing less than to maintain the liberty with which Heaven itself has made us free. I hope it will not be disgraced in any colony by a single rash step. We have constitutional methods of seeking redress, and they are the best methods'. The Whigs, with these views, entered upon the work of 'defending the liberties of their common country'. Aiming to avoid any thing like insurrection, and repelling the idea of revolution, they unfurled their banner under the noble aegis of law. They based their action on social order. They hoped to build up their cause on the foundation of an intelligent public opinion. This was a new and an American method of political agitation.

Whigs aim to cement inter-Colonial action

"The Whigs, in this spirit, aimed at concert of action. They did not fail to profit by such union as was reached in the Stamp Act, and they sought opportunities to cement and perpetuate it. When the air was full of rejoicing on account of the repeal, a learned divine of Boston, Jonathan Mayhew, in a note addressed to James Otis, proposed that the Massachusetts assembly should send congratulatory letters to the other assemblies on the favorable aspect of things, expressing warm friendship, and a desire to cultivate union among them by all practical methods; remarking, that the communion of colonies, like the communion of churches, might be of great use, and that on some future occasion union might be the only means of perpetuating their liberties. The benefit of keeping up a friendly correspondence among the patriots was urged in public meetings and in the press. The appeals of the popular leaders have an elevation of sentiment so common and so continuous as to constitute a feature of the revolutionary struggle. Thus 'The Farmer's Letters', addressed to 'The American People', imbued with a sentiment of union - say, 'You are assigned by Divine Providence, in the appointed order of things, the protector of unborn ages, whose fate depends on your virtue.'

Jonathan Mayhew urges warm friendship among Colonies

Self-sustaining economy

"The earliest movement, in reference to the new scheme, was a renewal of the non-importation agreement. At a town meeting held at Boston, October 28, 1767, in which James Otis presided, statements were read to the effect, that one town, the past year, made thirty thousand yards of cloth; that Lynn turned out forty thousand pairs of women's shoes; that a circle of agreeable ladies had agreed to lay aside the use of ribbons: and a subscription was started to promote economy, industry, and manufacture. The proceedings, under the heading 'Save your money, and you save your country'. were printed in the journals, and made a great noise in England.

The above excerpts are from Richard Frothingham's "The Rise of the Republic", 1890

Massachusetts leads

"It was circulated in the newspapers, that, whenever 'the cause of American freedom was to be vindicated', the province of Massachusetts Bay, 'as it had hitherto done, must first kindle the sacred flame that must illuminate and warm the continent'. Its legislature came together in its second session, Dec. 30, 1767, in the Town House, or State House....

Samuel Adams author of protests to England

"On opening the session, Governor Bernard summoned the members of the House to the council chamber, but in his address to them, did not refer to the new acts. They were, however, read in the House, and referred to a committee on the state of the province. They reported an elaborate letter written by Samuel Adams, to be sent to the agent of the colony in London, and intended for the ministers....

"The same committee reported letters to several noblemen in England, and a petition to the king, prepared by Samuel Adams....

"It was next proposed, in the spirit of the prevailing sentiment of union, to inform the other assemblies of these measures....

Circular letter to sister Colonies

"This Circular Letter states that the House had taken into serious consideration the several acts of parliament and their consequences; and, in the view that all possible care should be taken that the several assemblies should harmonize with each other, it freely communicated their mind to their sister colonies, on a common concern, in the same manner as they would be glad to receive in return the sentiments of any similar assembly. Then the positions that had been taken, in the papers which had been adopted, were tersely recapitulated....

"The House, by a special committee, informed the Governor of the adoption of this letter, and stated that a copy of it would be laid before him as soon as a draft could be made, and copies also of other papers, if he should desire them. A few days after, he summoned the members into the council chamber, when, on proroguing the House, he delivered a speech, in which he sharply censured them for their doings, saying there were men to whose being everlasting contention was necessary, but that time would soon pull the masks off those false patriots who were sacrificing their country to the gratification of their passions....

"At this point in the communion of the colonies, the king appeared on the stage, and as a direct consequence of the course of the Tories. They represented that the Whigs meant to resist by force the execution of the revenue acts: in fact, that their real object was independence; and that British troops were required to prevent

The above excerpts are from Richard Frothingham's "The Rise of the Republic", 1890

an insurrection in Boston, which might extend through the colonies. Governor Bernard of Massachusetts was conspicuous in this bald mis-representation.... Bernard characterized the Circular Letter as designed to pave the way for a confederacy, and calculated to inflame the continent; and, presented in this light, it naturally alarmed the ministers....

George III exerts despotic power

"The king, then giving unusual attention to American affairs, judged that the exigency required special measures; and, without any regard to the limitations of law, it was determined that one royal order should require the Massachusetts assembly to rescind its Circular Letter, and that another order should require the other assemblies to treat it with contempt, - imposing the penalty of dissolution in case of non-compliance with these orders.... The monarchical office was the most powerful political machine in Europe. In the colonies the king's name was a tower of strength; and hence this entrance of George III. into the arena added vastly to the interest and importance of the American question.

Americans and American property seized

"Meantime, the people of Massachusetts had elected a new assembly, containing most of the members of the last, and nearly all the popular leaders. It convened when events - driftings toward revolution - were creating intense excitement in this colony, and attracting more and more the attention of the other colonies. A British naval force was moored in Boston Harbor. It was the common report that an army was to be stationed in this town to overawe the citizens and execute the odious policy. The seizure of Americans by a press-gang from the ships, and of the sloop 'Liberty', owned by Hancock, for a violation of the revenue laws, bred a riot. This occasioned one of those public meetings in the spirit of fidelity to the cause of liberty, and yet under the law, which henceforward characterized the revolutionary history of Boston and of Massachusetts. Governor Bernard, in this case, dealt with a distressed community in a spirit of candor and conciliation, for which he met with grateful acknowledgments. While doing this, he received a dispatch from Lord Hillsborough, terming the Circular Letter of the last House inflammatory, tending to create unwarrantable combinations, and to excite unjustifiable opposition to the authority of parliament; and containing the royal order for the assembly to rescind the resolution on which it was based, on the penalty of a dissolution in case of a refusal....

Warships in Boston harbor

Emergency meeting

"This message placed George III. in a novel position before an American assembly. There was no debate at this time; but the news of the message spread through the community, and in the afternoon, as the gallery and both of the doors of the hall were open. There

The above excerpts are from Richard Frothingham's "The Rise of the Republic", 1890

Otis speaks

were present great numbers of the citizens. The message was read again; when James Otis took the floor, and spoke two hours on public affairs....

"The question occupied the minds of the House for nine days, during which the members were guided by a special committee, and were inspired by the answers received from the other assemblies. The Governor, in a second message, communicated the threat to dissolve the House in case of non-compliance; in a third, he pressed a decision; in a fourth, he declined to grant a recess.... On the 30th of June, the speaker informed the House that the committee were ready to report, when the gallery was ordered to be cleared; the door was locked and notice was sent to the council that the House was entering on a debate of importance....

Shall the circular letter be rescinded?

"A letter addressed to Lord Hillsborough was read. It stated the origin and purpose of the Circular Letter; that the House was the representative of the commons of the province, as the British House was of the British commons; that perhaps no requisitions from the throne, of the nature then made, had been known since the Revolution; and it expressed the hope that a petition to the king might not be deemed inconsistent with the British constitution, nor a Letter, acquainting their fellow-subjects with what they had done, be judged an inflammatory proceeding. The letter was read twice, adopted, and ordered to be sent to Lord Hillsborough. Then the question was put, 'Whether this House will rescind the resolution of the last House which gave birth to their Circular Letter to the several houses of representatives and burgesses of the other colonies on this continent.' The vote was taken by yeas and nays, and was printed in the newspapers in the order of counties....

Vote:

92 - not to rescind

17 - to obey king

"Ninety-two answered nay, and among them were several who usually voted on the side of the administration, while only seventeen answered yea.... The House then adopted an answer to the messages of the Governor, saying that they regarded the Circular Letter moderate and innocent, respectful to the authority of parliament, and dutiful to the king.... After stating the vote refusing to comply with the royal command, they concluded: 'In all this we have been actuated by a conscientious, and finally a clear and determined sense of duty to God, to our king, our country, and to our latest posterity; and we most ardently wish and humbly pray that in your future conduct your Excellency may be influenced by the same principles.' This action was in the spirit of fidelity to self-government manifested by a former Massachusetts assembly when it triumphantly resisted an illegal commission of Charles II....

The above excerpts are from Richard Frothingham's "The Rise of the Republic", 1890

"These proceedings created profound sensation in this colony and in other colonies. It was said that the question was the greatest which had ever occupied the attention of an American legislature; that the brave and virtuous behavior of the assembly in the sacred cause of liberty and their country gave general satisfaction; and that the vote not to rescind elicited as evident tokens of joy as were manifested on the fall of Louisburg or the conquest of Canada; and that the 'Illustrious Ninety-Two' was the toast in all companies. 'May the same noble zeal', a New Yorker wrote, 'spread itself from town to town and colony to colony, till we become united as one man in this glorious resolution, - never to surrender our inherent rights and privileges.'

All assemblies placed under royal order

"And now the other royal order, requiring the assemblies not to notice the Massachusetts Circular Letter, appeared in the newspapers in a dispatch sent by Lord Hillsborough to the Governor of Rhode Island.... This dispatch was first commented on as addressed only to the Governor of Rhode Island, but it proved to be a general circular to the governors; and it had the effect to put the king before all the assemblies in the same attitude as he stood in towards the Massachusetts House. It provoked severe comment. ...

Colonies no longer disconnected

"The reply of North Carolina, dates Nov. 10, 1768, is in the 'Boston Evening Post' of May 15, 1769, accompanied by the following remark: 'The above letter completes the answers to our Circular Letter. The colonies, no longer disconnected, form one body; a common sensation possesses the whole; the circulation is complete, and the vital fluid returns from whence it was sent out.'

"The people manifested their approval of the doings of their representatives by votes of thanks, by joyful demonstrations and reelections....

"The general approval of the Circular Letter and the growing spirit of union filled the hearts of the Boston patriots with joy; so that Cooper and Adams said it was the most glorious day they ever saw.

Rights attained only in America

"This political action kept remarkably true to social order, carried on under the banner of law, was an unusual spectacle in the political world. England had not attained to the right of public meeting or the freedom of the press or publicity in the law-making body. In France, for a century and a half the people had not appeared on the public stage; and in Germany there was but a glim-

The above excerpts are from Richard Frothingham's "The Rise of the Republic", 1890

Tory feared agency of a free public opinion

mer here and there of free discussion of political measures. In the colonies, Whig and Tory regarded this embodiment of public opinion as a new and powerful political agency. The Tory feared it more than he did the greatest disorders; for he saw that the sentiment thus put forth on the nature of government very often met with the approbation of the body of the people, and could not be counteracted. The Whig, on subsequently revolving the steps of progress towards the Revolution, viewed the spark in every American that blazed in the public meeting as 'that almost divine spirit that evidenced the approach of an independent and free republic in America'.

The People knew their privileges and duties

"The proceedings growing out of the Circular Letter are certainly remarkable.... The action of the assemblies is that of freemen knowing their privileges and duties. They concurred in a spirited assertion of the inherent rights of political discussion, of free interchange of thought, of an untrammelled legislature, - in a word, of their right to enjoy the national heritage of English law, not merely for themselves, but for their posterity; and with the thought, as an inspiration, that they were acting not merely for their country, but for humanity. They asked that their municipal freedom and self-government, which were felt to be fountains of a rich public life, might be spared from the benumbing influences of centralization; and thus that the public liberty developed on American soil, out of the roots of a grand historic past, might be respected as a sacred possession....

Municipal freedom and self-government

"The memorials and petitions were delivered by the agents of the colonies into the hands of Lord Hillsborough. Owing to various causes not needed to be dwelt upon here, reasoning which seemed conclusive, and loyalty urged with a fervid sincerity, proved of no avail. The petitions, it was said, were from a distempered and a delirious people. Some did not reach the royal ear. Some met with cold neglect. All were thrown in the faces of the colonists. The misrepresentations of unscrupulous politicians working for selfish ends, or of conservatives jealous of the republican idea, outweighed the noble appeals of millions of loyal subjects.

Military force ordered to Boston

"The proceedings in Massachusetts attracted in England the greatest attention, elicited the severest comment, and, because a military force had been ordered to Boston to support the stand of the administration, created the greatest solicitude.... The king, on opening parliament, characterized the action of Boston as a subversion of the Constitution and evincing a disposition to

The above excerpts are from Richard Frothingham's "The Rise of the Republic", 1890

throw off dependence on Great Britain. The indictment against the colonies was presented in sixty papers laid before parliament....

"The king's speeches, the parliamentary documents, and the debates and a flood of letters circulating broadcast in the American newspapers, revealed the hot temper of England, and filled the colonies with indignation....

An example to be made of Massachusetts

"The administration determined to make an example of Massachusetts, as the ring-leading province in political mischief, by transporting its popular leaders to England to be tried for their lives in the king's bench. Such was the purport of an elaborate despatch which Lord Hillsborough sent to Governor Bernard, directing an inquiry to be instituted into the conduct of any persons who had committed any overt act of resistance to the laws. This step was the occasion of a flood of reports contained in letters printed in the newspapers. Thus a great issue was created that affected all the colonies; for the proposed action touched the individual unit of society. Because this was man, it had rank and position on American soil which power was bound to respect. The word now was that Massachusetts or Boston represented a common cause and ought to be sustained.

Americans to be tried for their lives in the king's bench

British scheme to divide

"There was no adequate step taken to meet the threatened aggression until the House of Burgesses of Virginia convened in May. This colony, in opposing the administration, was co-equal with Massachusetts in guilt or in merit; but while the bayonet was pointed at the one, blandishment was devised for the other, - it being a cardinal object of the government to divide the colonies, and thus paralyze their efforts....

Virginia Burgesses

"The burgesses included in their ranks illustrious men; for Richard Henry Lee, Patrick Henry, Peyton Randolph, Archibald Carey, and Washington, were of their number; all of whom were in former assemblies. Thomas Jefferson, at the age of twenty-six, was a member for the first time....

"Virginia Resolves" assert rights of Colonies and individuals

"It was the report among the Burgesses that the Governor would be gratified if they would maintain silence on political questions. The popular leaders, however, had revolved the grave issue that had sprung up, and came prepared to play a great part. They adopted a series of resolves declaring that the sole right of imposing taxes on the inhabitants of the colony was constitutionally vested in the House of Burgesses, with the consent of the Council and His Majesty, or his Governor for the time being; that it was an undoubted privilege to petition the Sovereign, and procure the

The above excerpts are from Richard Frothingham's "The Rise of the Republic", 1890

concurrence of the other colonies; that all trials for treason ought to be conducted in the courts of the colony, and that the seizing of any persons suspected of crime, and transporting them to places beyond seas, would deprive them of the inestimable privilege of being tried by a jury from the vicinage; and that a dutiful and loyal address be presented to His Majesty to beseech him to quiet the minds of the inhabitants of that colony, by averting the dangers and miseries that might ensue from the seizing and carrying beyond sea any person residing in America, to be tried in any other manner than by the ancient mode of proceeding.

Royal governor dissolves House of Burgesses

"These resolves were calm in manner, concise, simple, and effective, and so perfect in form and substance that time finds no omission to regret and no improvement to suggest. They were viewed by one of the Burgesses as nothing more than a necessary and manly assertion of social privileges founded in reason, guaranteed by the English Constitution, and rendered sacred by the possession of two hundred years. But Lord Botetourt looked on them as abominable, and dissolved the House.

Resolves sent to other Colonial assemblies

"The speaker, Peyton Randolph, sent the resolves to the other assemblies, accompanied by a brief Circular Letter expressing a belief that the importance of the subject would be sufficient to engage immediate attention, and that the circumstances of America would evince the propriety of the action of the Burgesses. This generous action, spread through the colonies in the newspapers, elicited expressions of admiration and gratitude....

To make common cause

"Well might there have been this gratitude; for Virginia invited all the colonies to make common cause with Massachusetts when king and parliament had laid a heavy hand upon her, and the presence of an army and a fleet attested that complete submission was decreed as her lot.

Assemblies "agreed in essentials"

"The assemblies, as they convened, responded heartily to the Virginia resolves....The assemblies agreed in essentials. The harmony was so inspiring that it was said, 'The whole continent from New England to Georgia seems firmly fixed: like a strong, well-constructed arch, the more weight there is laid upon it the firmer it stands; and thus with Americans, the more we are loaded the more we are united.' Thus grandly was the aegis of the inchoate union cast over the personal liberty of Americans. Thus fixed was the determination to claim as a birthright trial by jury.

The above excerpts are from Richard Frothingham's "The Rise of the Republic", 1890

Burgesses meet in private residence - vote to carry out "non-importation"

"When Lord Botetourt dissolved the House of Burgesses, the members immediately went to Anthony Hay's residence, chose Peyton Randolph moderator, discussed the situation, and decided to unite into an association to carry out the non-importation agreement. On the next day articles submitted by Washington were adopted and signed, - his name being near the head of the list. The journals circulated these proceedings; and thus this patriotic movement received a powerful impulse.... After the decisive action of the Burgesses, the Whigs pressed the movement vigorously; assemblies thanked the merchants for their patriotism in adopting it; colony after colony, including Rhode Island, entered into it; and when it was adopted by North Carolina, it was said: 'This completes the chain of union throughout the continent for the measure of non-importation and economy.' It was patriotism not to use certain European articles of luxury, not to import slaves or to buy them of importers.

Patriots use and wear American manufactures

"It was patriotism to grow flax and wool, to spin and weave to make clothes and wear them. Ingenuous youth received the honors of their Alma Mater, and legislators appeared in their halls, clothed in American apparel. The Daughters of Liberty vied with each other in their spinning-matches and homespun gowns. Such attire was of more lustre than all the gems that sparkle in the mine, for it spoke fidelity to a just cause. The Americans saw in this harmony a proof that 'all the colonies had the same ideas of liberty'. The saying was current in London that industry and economy were universal in America, where the farmer strutted in homespun and cast an indignant look at the meanness of soul that hoped for superior distinction by indulging in the manufactures of a country that exulted in enslaving the colonies.

Partial repeal of Townshend Act

"The ministers postponed the design of altering the American constitutions. Lord North, in April, 1770, based a motion for a partial repeal of the Townshend Revenue Act on the petition of the merchants of London. He urged the abolition of the duties on glass, paper, and painter's colors, on the ground that they were uncommercial, while he justified the retention of the duty on tea as necessary to assert the supremacy of parliament. Such was the judgment of the king who held that 'there must always be one tax to keep up the right'. Hence the Act was repealed (April 12, 1770) only in part. The Declaratory Act, asserting the right to legislate for the colonies in all cases whatsoever, and the tax on tea, remained on the statute book.

Partial repeal unsatisfactory

"The popular leaders regarded this partial repeal as insidious and unsatisfactory, - settling nothing and boding evil. They urged a rigid adherence to the non-importation agreement as the

The above excerpts are from Richard Frothingham's "The Rise of the Republic", 1890

most effectual method to obtain a redress of grievances. Above all, they commended union as absolutely essential to the salvation of America.

Differences on fundamentals between England and America

"The attempt of the ministry to check the republican element, to abridge English liberties in America, had the effect to throw the colonists back on themselves; to move them to reflect on the scope and tendency of the ideas they had applied, on the institutions they had reared and the position they had attained; and to reveal the fact that there were marked differences on fundamentals between the views held by the statesmen in England and in America....

America "united in public opinion and conviction"

"The movement elicited by the Townshend Revenue Acts resulted in a settled public opinion and conviction by a free people, as to the nature and value of their rights. This was embodied in the utterances of public bodies and the press. Many were circulated in the journals and in pamphlets in England, and the ability they evinced elicited high praise....Many were translated and circulated on the continent....Generous tributes from abroad flowed in upon the patriots. A London letter reads: 'Your late conduct is noble indeed; every ray is splendid with asserted right and vindicated freedom.' Another wrote: 'The whole Christian world owe you much thanks. The star rising out of your wilderness will become a great luminary and enlighten the whole earth.' A Paris letter, urging a continuance of the 'noble struggle for liberty', runs: 'I imagine I see illustrious statesmen, eloquent orators, wise historians, and learned philosophers rising up among you, whose generous souls have espoused the interests of humanity, and are spreading the blessings of liberty throughout the world around them.' These praises, circulated by the press, might be read in every home in America. They could hardly fail to strengthen the conviction of the patriots that their stand for liberty and law was appreciated, - that it would be approved by the wise and good, and that they would be justified in maintaining it at every cost.

"In the tribute just cited, it is said that the patriots had embraced the cause of humanity....The earliest utterances of the patriots are inspired by the thought that Providence had set them to defend the rights and liberties of mankind; and in their proud day of triumph they said, 'Let it be remembered that it had ever been the pride and boast of America that the rights for which she contended were the rights of human nature.' Their noble array of utterances warrant the remark that they viewed 'mankind toiling and suffering, separated by oceans, divided by language, and severed by national enmity, yet evermore tending under a

The above excerpts are from Richard Frothingham's "The Rise of the Republic", 1890

divine control towards the fulfilment of that inscrutable purpose for which the world was created, and man placed in it, bearing the image of God.' Native gifts developed in labors in behalf of such a cause. Men thus grew in stature; each colony had its roll of honor, and said and did things that made a mark on the age....

Stamp used in 1765

March, 1770 to August, 1773.

England becomes all Tory in views and sentiment toward America

The successive British administrations, since the beginning of the controversy of the colonies with the mother-country, had been composed of members of several parties; but at length the Tory party attained power, as it ruled England, with brief intervals, for half a century. It was imbued with low views of human nature, high-toned principles of government, unsound doctrines of political economy, and a disposition to stretch the prerogative and to gratify the pride of dominion. Out of its ranks George III. formed a cabinet 'to deal with Wilkes and America'. The premier, Lord North, about forty years of age, was a scholar of elegant taste, of eminent ability as a debater, and had administrative talents which qualified him for his place. He voted for the Stamp Act and against its repeal, and was the first to move the expulsion of Wilkes. One of his sayings then circulated in the press was, that he never could acquiesce in the absurd opinion that all men were equal; another, that the question between England and her colonies was no less than sovereignty on the one side and independence on the other, when simple justice by England might have adjourned, at least for years, all thought of independence.

Aim: "to bind three million free men"

"The Tory party, in partially repealing the Townshend Revenue Acts, only paused in the execution of the Bute policy. It was fully embodied in the Declaratory Act of 1766, that the king's majesty, with the advice of parliament, had, and of right ought to have, full power to make laws of sufficient validity to bind the people of America in all cases whatever, - 'a resolution', Lord Chatham said, 'for England's right to do what the Treasury pleased with three millions of freemen'. It was also embodied in the tax on tea retained to keep up the right....

"It might have been wise to have simply aimed to render the imperial authority independent in its proper sphere, while leaving the local authorities free to act in their spheres, just as the

The above excerpts are from Richard Frothingham's "The Rise of the Republic", 1890

Two independent spheres of government acting as one, not understood in England

officers of the United States are independent of the State and municipal authorities; but the object of putting the civil list on a new basis, - arrogantly avowed from ministerial benches, and steadily pursued by the men in power, - was to repress the republican spirit, by shaping the local governments according to English ideas. Thus the minister aimed to impose a polity on a people, instead of recognizing and protecting the polity developed by them, and which was a natural outgrowth. Such a purpose was war on their dearly prized local self-government; and it was prosecuted in the same spirit of persecution of the liberal element in America which characterized the course of the party in England.

"It was as suicidal a policy as it would be for an American administration to aim at impairing the municipal liberties, which are perennial fountains of a noble public life. On this object the vigilant eye of patriotism kept steadily fixed.

American Whigs:

Adherents to the school of John Locke

"The ministers, in carrying out this policy, now resorted to an extraordinary use of Royal Instructions, which, for three years, played an important part in American politics. A rule of action, to meet a current question in England, was concisely stated in the following terms: 'The law is above the king; and the crown, as well as the subject is bound by it as much during the recess as in the session of parliament; because no point of time nor emergent circumstance can alter the Constitution, or create a right not antecedently inherent. These only draw forth into action the power that before existed, but was quiescent. There is no such prerogative in any hour or moment of time as vests the semblance of legislative power in the crown.' This doctrine seems to have been accepted by the American Whigs; for their utterances are imbued with the sentiment inculcated by the school of Locke, that the freedom of a people under government is to have standing rules to live by, so that the government may be one of laws, and not of men.

Royal Instructions issued with force of law

"Without much regard to this rule, or indeed to any law, the ministers, after the repeal of the Townshend Acts, issued to the governors a series of extraordinary instructions. They came under the king's sign manual, with the privy seal annexed.... The first instruction was adopted in the Privy Council on the 6th of July, 1770. This may be fixed on as the time when Royal Instructions began their mission.

"In framing these instructions, little, if any, regard was paid to customs, forms, and prejudices in the colonies as old as their existence, which had become unwritten law, and were therefore, at least, worthy of consideration.... The instructions required

The above excerpts are from Richard Frothingham's "The Rise of the Republic", 1890

Assemblies dissolved - local governments shackled

the dissolution of assemblies; their removal to unusual places of meeting, as in South Carolina to Beaufort, and in Massachusetts to Cambridge; negatived arbitrarily the choice of speakers; provided for the maintenance of local officers; and thus entirely ignored the local legislation for the support of government, and even directed the executive to refuse his assent to tax-bills because they taxed the officers of government....

"The ministry seemed bent on giving full force to the Declaratory Act, and governing the colonies in all cases whatever; and their arbitrary practices grated harshly on a people habituated to the ways of freedom.

Colonists persistent in stating their rights

"These practices were manfully, and in general successfully, met. In some cases they provoked deeds of violence.... In brief, the claim that the king's instructions had the force of law, or that the people were under a personal government, was everywhere contested. Its nature and tendency were exposed in papers issued by public meetings, by general assemblies, and the press, often marked by keen analysis and strong reasoning. Indeed, the vein of Americanism was so wide and deep, that, outside of official circles, these instructions had scarcely more than quasi-defenders.... 'Not to oppose', Arthur Lee wrote, 'this most pernicious system, would be crime; to oppose it unsuccessfully, would be misfortune only.' The colonial judgment on this insidious phase of centralization was as intelligent as it was just.

Adherence to non-importation urged

"Meantime word had gone through the colonies to adhere to the non-importation agreement, as the best means to procure a repeal of the tax on tea, and a redress of grievances; on the ground that this would distress the commerce of England and aid the opponents of the administration. Fidelity to this agreement came to be looked upon as vital to the salvation of the cause, - in fact, as a test of patriotism. 'Let us be united', a Philadelphia broadside runs: 'the eyes of all Europe, nay, of the whole world, are fixed upon us'. In general, the patriots carried out the agreement in good faith; but the Tories, and selfish men among the Whigs, would not respect it, when personal violence was used to compel its observance.

"Its enemies charged upon the patriots as a body the delinquencies really belonging to the few. It was alleged that Virginia and Massachusetts were growing rich at the expense of their neighbors. In this period of mistrust the merchants of the city of New York sent out a Circular to the principal commercial places, proposing to confine the agreement of non-importation to the single

The above excerpts are from Richard Frothingham's "The Rise of the Republic", 1890

article of tea, and that trade should be free in all other articles. The proposition fell upon the patriots like the news of some public calamity. It created a panic. The excitement was general and intense. The proposal was met by indignant remonstrances....

Tories exult - foresee disunion

"Thus the American cause was in the presence of varied internal strife. It was feared by the patriots that two evils would be likely to grow out of this confusion and bloodshed, that might prove irremediable, - loss of character in England, and the destruction of that confidence at home that was essential to success. It was exultingly said by the Tories, who rejoiced at the dissension and weakness, that the union was well broken, and that it would require a miracle to restore it. It is wonderful that men now living saw this spectacle, were born when the thirteen colonies seemed destined to reproduce only the petty autonomy of ancient Greece, and to suffer as the penalty border wars, chronic impotence, or subjection to foreign sway.

"The non-importation agreement was broken, to the infinite joy of the Tories in America and in England. Then no general issue remained to stir the colonies....

"The popular leaders, however, kept on exposing the danger of admitting Royal Instructions to have the force of law, and earnestly urged renewed effort in behalf of American liberty. They never yielded to the fatal heresy of a personal government, or to the sweep of power covered by the Declaratory Act. They saw in the halcyon sky the cloud no bigger than a man's hand, which contained the thunderbolt of civil war; and, in the storm which they predicted, they could see shelter only in the fold of union. It is not easy to imagine how political insight could have been more penetrating as to causes, or foresight more accurate as to results.

Samuel Adams - writer on constitutional law

"Among these leaders Samuel Adams was pre-eminent. He had been steadily rising in reputation in Massachusetts and abroad. There had been no decline in his zeal, no pause in his labor. He gave to the cause the whole of his time. A wide correspondence, voluminous writing in the press, and masterly state papers attest his intelligence, industry, and influence. He was now directing public attention, through the press, to the theory and practice of the ministry. While he restated the old argument against the right of parliament to tax, he closely examined the foundations of the claim of the ministers to govern by Royal Instructions. He had grasped the idea that the king, lords, and

The above excerpts are from Richard Frothingham's "The Rise of the Republic", 1890

commons, as well as the colonies, were subject to the authority and bound by the limitations of constitutional law. In applying this idea, he did not appeal to what might quite as likely be human fancy or passion, or the political capital of arrant demagogues, as the State's collected will; but he appealed to a supreme law which the nation had made, and which it was expected the temporary agents would ever respect and preserve: as the trial by jury, the habeas corpus, Magna Charta, - expressions of the general reason, organic, and therefore inviolable.

Adams cites Coke on Magna Charta

"For illustration: when his opponents, in controverting his position urged that Magna Charta was but an act of parliament, which king, lords, and commons, as the sovereignty, might amend as they could any ordinary act, he would make the grand answer: 'This view made Magna Charta of no greater consequence than a corporation of button-makers; whereas Lord Coke held that it was declaratory of the principal grounds of the fundamental laws and liberties of England.' His appeal could hardly have been more forcible had there been established the American custom of a written constitution, which, to all, was a supreme law: even this, however, is of little value in the presence of a dead constitutional morality.

American convictions

"The appeal of Samuel Adams was to such constitutional law as was grounded in the hearts of the nation, and which Americans loved and respected. While he emphatically denied that the just supremacy of parliament was questioned, specifying as an illustration the general concession of the right to regulate the trade of the empire, - and as earnestly disclaimed the intention of calling in question the sovereignty, specifying the facts attesting the loyalty to the crown, - he contended for the preservation to each colony of its old right to make its laws of a domestic nature, and held that the people, as Americans, were members of one body, or of the nation; and while they were bound to fight for the king, they were entitled to be recognized as co-equal sharers with the English people in English liberties.

"The aggressions on popular rights in Massachusetts required continued service at his hands, in private consultations, in public meetings, in the general assembly, and in preparing matter for the press; and it is doing no injustice to others to say that he was the centre around which all the movements of the patriots turned. Still his eye was ever upon the whole American field. He urged that the cause of one colony was the cause of all the colonies, and that it was only through united councils that the continent could expect to maintain its rights. His great theme

The above excerpts are from Richard Frothingham's "The Rise of the Republic", 1890

from the beginning of the controversy had been a union of the colonies.

Samuel Adams proposes Committees of Correspondence

"In handling it, he was comprehensive in principle, method, and object, looking ever for the better time in the future. 'Let us forget', he now wrote to the South Carolina patriots, of the non-importation agreement, 'there ever was so futile a combination, and awaken an attention to our first grand object, and shew that we are united in constitutional principles.' Union was his paramount thought. The need of it never seemed so great. The method he suggested was for the patriots in each town or county in every colony to hold legal meetings, and choose substantial citizens to act as committees of correspondence, with a view to secure concert of action; and for the Massachusetts towns to adopt the measure, and then, through the assembly, to propose it to the other colonies in the hope that they would adopt it....

Feudal and paternalistic policies

"At this period Lord Hillsborough was succeeded at the head of the American department by Lord Dartmouth, who had the reputation of being an amiable and good man, and well disposed towards the colonies. Hopes were indulged that he might reverse the policy of his predecessor. But this policy had deeper roots than personal preferences: it grew out of feudal ideas; and the new secretary was a disciple of the school which had these ideas for its platform. He looked with unfeigned distrust on the measure of popular power exercised by the colonists....He had a paternal desire to do for them, joined to a repugnance to recognizing a polity which fostered the capacity to do for themselves. If he did not originate, he certainly did not hesitate to send out the worst Royal Instruction that was issued in the king's name....

Uncertainty and apathy

"Samuel Adams selected this instruction as the occasion for rousing the patriots, for healing divisions, and for organization, by forming committees of correspondence, saying: 'This country must shake off its intolerable burdens at all events; every day strengthens our oppressors, and weakens us. If each town would declare its sense of these matters, I am persuaded our enemies would not have it in their power to divide us....I wish we could rouse the continent.' Such appeals, however, failed to renew the agitation. Town meetings were called in Boston to consider public affairs, but they were neither so large nor so enthusiastic as the meetings of previous years. Nor were the patriots agreed as to what the next step ought to be. This apathy and disunion in the town was typical of the political situation in the colonies.

The above excerpts are from Richard Frothingham's "The Rise of the Republic", 1890

"The rights of colonists as men, Christians and subjects"

- Samuel Adams

"A town meeting was called in Faneuil Hall, to consider the question of the salaries of the judges.... In the afternoon, Samuel Adams moved 'that a committee of correspondence be appointed, to consist of twenty-one persons, to state the rights of the colonies, and of this province in particular, as men, as Christians, and as subjects; to communicate and publish the same to the several towns in this province and to the world, as the sense of this town, with the infringements and violations thereof that have been, or from time to time may be, made; also requesting of each town a free communication of their sentiments on this subject.'

Boston inaugurates Committee of Correspondence

"Though this motion was opposed by some of the patriots, including three of the representatives to the General Court, on the ground that its failure might hurt the cause, yet it was adopted. This inaugurated the system of local committees of correspondence. They multiplied and widened under successive impulses, until they constituted the accredited organs of the party that founded the Republic of the United States. 'They may be called', a contemporary wrote, 'the corner-stone of our revolution, or new empire'. Hence the action of Boston proved the beginning of the first national party of the country.

"The committee was composed of citizens who had rendered service to the cause, and who coveted no other reward than to see their work prosper.... This Report, after long deliberation, was adopted. Six hundred copies were ordered to be printed in a pamphlet, and a copy was directed to be sent to every town in the province. A copy was also sent to prominent Whigs in other colonies.

Boston platform of Christian, civil rights

"This paper was the most radical exposition of rights and grievances - the most systematic presentation of the American cause - that had been adopted by a public meeting. It covered well-nigh the whole ground of natural and constitutional rights. It gave to principles, which had been held as abstractions, a practical significance. It considered the relations of man not only as a citizen, but as a Christian, and claimed for him that equality which is the cardinal principle of Christianity. It claimed for him, under law, the position to which he is entitled, - the right to make the laws under which he lives, to select his field of labor and enjoy its fruits, and thus claimed fair play for the industrial energy which has contributed so much to the growth and glory of the country. Its bold theory, incisive criticism, and solid reasoning were admirably calculated to strengthen and direct public opinion.

"The committee, as they sent out this Report, were not disheartened by the doubts of the Whigs nor the jeers of the Tories, by

The above excerpts are from Richard Frothingham's "The Rise of the Republic", 1890

Samuel Adams' "faith that the cause would make friends"

the spectacle presented in the colonies of ill-nature and disunion in some quarters, nor by the general apathy on the question with the mother-country. The great popular leader at their council board in Faneuil Hall, Samuel Adams, held the faith that the cause would make friends, and rise; and he infused his spirit into those near him. His steps can be traced day by day. A warm patriot in Plymouth, James Warren, on getting the Report, wrote to Adams: 'I shall not fail to exert myself to have as many towns as possible meet, but fear the bigger part of them will not. They are dead; and the dead can't be raised without a miracle.' Adams was prompt to reply: 'I am very sorry to find any thing in your letter that discovers the least approach towards despair. Nil desperandum. That is a motto for you and for me. All are not dead; and where there is a spark of patriotic fire, we will rekindle it.' To another he wrote: 'If our enemies should see the flame bursting in different parts of the country, and distant from each other, it might discourage their attempts to damp and quench it.' The originators of this measure did not, as is the modern practice, attend the meetings in the country and speak in favor of the Report. It was its own orator.

Plymouth first to respond

"The patriots of Plymouth were the earliest to follow Boston in choosing a committee of correspondence. In a few weeks the committees so multiplied, and the expression of sentiment was so inspiring, as to exceed the expectation of the friends of the measure. The Boston committee began to print in the newspapers the letters and proceedings elicited by the Boston Report, which, being often elaborate, proved too strong a draft on the space at the command of the conductors....

Patriotic letters

"A few sentences from these patriotic responses will shew the spirit of the whole. One says: 'May every town in this province and every colony on the continent be awakened to a sense of danger, and unite in the glorious cause of liberty.' Another urges that all 'should stand firm as one man to support and maintain their just rights and liberties'....and another responds: 'It becomes us to rely no longer on an arm of flesh, but on the arm of that all-powerful God who is able to unite the numerous inhabitants of this extensive country as a band of brothers in one common cause'....

The press

"This movement was commended in the press as the most likely of any plan ever devised to establish the rights of all the colonies, and thus secure peace and harmony; for it was reasoned, if the ministers see America united and determined, they will give up their vain pretensions. Hence union was enjoined in passionate

The above excerpts are from Richard Frothingham's "The Rise of the Republic", 1890

terms. It was represented to be the voice of Freedom; that she was saying to Americans: -

'If you're united in one faithful band,
Like everlasting mountains you shall stand,
Whose bases rest on God's almighty hand.'

Massachusetts' hope that the continent would adopt plan

"The result of the movement, so far as relates to Massachusetts, was all that could have been expected, and nearly all that could have been desired.... This faith, however, was not based on what might be attempted or might be done on the few thousand square miles of territory that was known as Massachusetts, but on the hope that the patriots of the other colonies would adopt the organization, and 'that it would extend to every town of any consequence throughout America'; in the language of the time, that a continent would adopt the organization.

Royal governor belittles plan

"The spread of the movement, the expression of public sentiment, and the indications of a renewal of union, were observed with deep interest by Governor Hutchinson of Massachusetts, who was the strongest man on the Tory side here; indeed, so varied were his talents, and so high was his personal character, that he was ranked among the greatest and best men in America.... He condemned the committees of correspondence as not warranted by the Constitution; declared the doctrines set forth by the towns dangerous; and presented the whole question between Great Britain and her colonies in a manner uncommonly satisfactory to his political friends....

New York and South do not cooperate

"Meantime the movement of the towns in Massachusetts attracted more and more attention in the other colonies. The Boston Report was printed in full in Southern newspapers.... But the patriots did not choose committees of correspondence. It was said in Boston, 'They are still and quiet at the South, and at New York they laugh at us.'... Passionate words were not enough. The general apathy continued. A case of violated right bearing on the people of all the colonies was needed.

Royal Instruction alarms Rhode Island

"Lord Dartmouth supplied the want in a fresh Royal Instruction, dated the 4th of September, 1772... It was directed to the Governor of Rhode Island. It created, under the sign manual of the king, a commission to hold its sessions in that colony, and to inquire into the circumstances of the burning of His Majesty's schooner 'Gaspee'. This commission... was instructed that the offence was high treason, or levying war against the king; and was directed to order the arrest of the parties charged with this crime... The commission was also instructed to deliver the

The above excerpts are from Richard Frothingham's "The Rise of the Republic", 1890

parties thus arrested to Admiral Montagu... to send them to England. This was a bold Royal Instruction. It violated the fundamental of trial by jury, which... distinguished the English from all the nations of the earth. It affected the personal liberty of the individual, and bore alike on all the colonies....

King's court starts hearing in Rhode Island

"Several patriots of Rhode Island sent extracts from this instruction to Samuel Adams, and asked his advice; who, after consultation with a few friends, sent a reply recommending the Rhode Island patriots to send a circular to the other colonies calling for assistance... The commission held its first session in Newport, in January, 1773, and drew all eyes on Rhode Island, which, for a time, seemed destined to be the theatre of great events. The Royal Instructions were laid before its assembly by Governor Wanton, but that body did not issue a circular calling for aid... This tameness provoked Nathaniel Greene, the future general, to say that the assembly appeared to have lost its ancient public virtue, and to have sunk into an acquiescence in ministerial mandates.

Virginia patriots meet

"The Virginia House of Burgesses now (March 4, 1773) convened. As nothing particularly exciting had occurred in that colony for a considerable time, the people seemed to fall into a state of insensibility to their political situation; but the Rhode Island court of inquiry demanded attention. A few of the younger members, Patrick Henry, Richard Henry Lee, Thomas Jefferson, Francis L. Lee, Dabney Carr, and others, met at the Raleigh Tavern to consult on the state of things.... They agreed upon a set of resolves, and Jefferson was requested to present them to the assembly. But he desired that Dabney Carr, a new member, should do this, in order that his great worth and talents might be made known to the House. Accordingly Carr, a brilliant young lawyer, on the 12th of March moved the resolves, in a speech imbued with feeling, imagination, and patriotism, which was listened to with delight. He was followed by Richard Henry Lee and Patrick Henry, in impressive speeches. The resolutions were unanimously adopted.

Virginia establishes Committee of Correspondence

Eleven members were designated a committee of correspondence to communicate with the other colonies, to obtain authentic information of the doings of the administration, and especially respecting the Rhode Island court of inquiry, and to report the result to the Burgesses....

Massachusetts welcomes Virginia's action

"The action of Virginia was an inspiration to the cause, and especially to the Massachusetts patriots. Their appeal for organization had been doing its work four months; and, however gratifying the results might have been within the province, their plan had not been adopted in any other, - not one town outside of Massachusetts, I think, choosing a committee of correspondence...

The above excerpts are from Richard Frothingham's "The Rise of the Republic", 1890

ifferent plans esting on one rinciple

"In the Virginia plan, the immediate constituents of the committee were the assembly; in the Massachusetts plan, they were the legal voters: in one plan the unit was the colony; in the other the unit was the individual....

Five more assemblies appoint Committees

"The journals soon announced the assemblies, which adopted the 'plan of union proposed by the patriotic House of Burgesses', by choosing committees....In this spirit five assemblies promptly responded to the action of Virginia. Their resolutions, in stating the object of the committees, were generally a transcript of those of Virginia; and were sent to the assemblies in circular letters, usually signed by the speakers. Thus six colonies, under the general issue created by the last Royal Instruction, exchanged assurances of cooperation, and, as Jefferson characterizes their action, appointed 'committees of national correspondence'.

Seven Colonies do not act

"The hearty welcome of this action, and the earnest language of the popular leaders, shew how much it was desired that the remaining seven colonies should join in the plan of deliverance, which, it was said, 'Heaven itself seemed to have dictated to the noble Virginians.' No recommendation of it was more generous than that of the patriots of Massachusetts; nor was any action more prompt and efficient in following this lead than that of the Boston committee....

King's court adjourns to avert crisis

"The 'new union' and its embodiment in corresponding committees was closely watched by royal officers, and largely dwelt upon in their letters. It was plain that the strict execution of the instruction creating the court of inquiry would bring on a crisis....The commission then adjourned. The design of transporting Americans to England was given up. This was the close of the issue of Royal Instructions. It was their mission to rouse a spirit which inaugurated the organization of the popular party.

Right to trial by jury attained

"The patriots had cast the aegis of their inchoate union over the personal liberty of Americans, by securing trial by jury. They triumphed when less than half the assemblies had chosen committees of correspondence. The other assemblies - some because they did not happen to meet - did not choose until another issue arose. In fact political agitation subsided, in the spring, when it was seen that the arbitrary commission did not act; and the public mind became calm when it was abandoned....

"As Samuel Adams reviewed the events of this period about three years later, he remarked that, notwithstanding all that had been said and done, real union had not been reached. It is easy now to see that this was the fact. The cause needed an

The above excerpts are from Richard Frothingham's "The Rise of the Republic", 1890

Tea Act revives issue of local self-government

impulse other than form or personal leadership could give. It needed another aggression, something startling, that should stir feeling, quicken the public pulse, and create a popular tide, which in the nature of a providential current should bear the popular party onward beyond the possibility of a reaction. It was soon supplied by George III. in the Tea Act. It was the case over again of Joseph and his brethren: their design was evil, but it was overruled for good.

Sentiment - intelligent public opinion- and organization

"The popular party was prepared to take advantage of such an impulse. In meeting the Stamp Act, they evoked a sentiment of union; in meeting the Townshend Acts, they created and embodied an intelligent public opinion; and Royal Instructions.had produced the fruit of an organization in the committees of correspondence, municipal and legislative, ready to widen out to the breadth of a common union. In this action Massachusetts and Virginia, like two sagacious leaders, went hand in hand. The venerated characters whose names are connected with this step had nothing narrow or selfish in their plans or objects. They embraced common principles. They were impelled onward by great ideas. They aimed to unite all of similar political faith, wherever they were, in the bonds of a common brotherhood.

Co-leadership

"So much has been written about these famous committees, and especially on the credit due to Massachusetts and Virginia in forming them, that nothing need be added. The narrative now brought down to the month of August, 1773, shews the results effected under the issue of Royal Instructions.

"Moral effect of pledge of union

"The action of the House of Burgesses followed a season of mutual crimination and disunion; and the prompt acceptance of its invitation by five assemblies was an earnest of harmony and future concert. This, contrasted with the recent division and strife, was like the passage from death to life. Its salutary effect on the cause is attested by abundant contemporary evidence: and it ever afterwards occupied a high place in the minds of the actors as a spring of events.... The value of the movement, up to this time, was in the moral effect of the pledge of union.

To guide public sentiment

"The Boston committee held stated meetings. It kept up a correspondence with the committees chosen by other towns. It prepared and circulated political matter. It matured political measures. It thus performed the service which is expected of the committees representing modern parties, by aiming to create and guide public sentiment. The precise character of the work of the committee is seen in its records, which are in fine preservation....

The above excerpts are from Richard Frothingham's "The Rise of the Republic", 1890

American cause of Justice higher obligation than fidelity to England

"But love of liberty under law was the reigning principle. The high-toned theories of government, the course of the ministry, the arrogance of its champions, its practices with the assemblies, its scorn of popular rights, its treatment of petitions, tended to weaken the attachment to the mother-country. Salient aggressions roused ardent natures to utter thoughts that were the dawnings of a sentiment of nationality. They nurtured the idea that devotion to the cause of justice was a higher obligation than fidelity to the old flag when it was used to cover despotic power. They revolved the saying of a great patriot, that freedom and security, under Providence, depended on themselves. They reasoned that continued regard of the just complaints of the people might have 'the valuable tendency to make the next effort for freedom savor more of that virtue and valor for which Englishmen in former ages had been justly renowned, and might turn the Great People to call on the name of the Lord, and to seek a redress of their grievances with the spear and lance at that glorious seat of justice where Moses brought the Egyptians and Samson the Philistines.'...

Salutary faith in divine justice

August, 1773 to August, 1774.

Americans shun English Tea

When Lord Dartmouth took charge of the American department, the king sent to Lord North a sketch of such alterations in the administration of its affairs as he thought essential to give efficacy to the government. The first-fruit of this advice was probably the Rhode Island commission. The king's next measure related to the duty on Tea. This was inoperative. The Americans would not buy teas shipped from England: they would not live without tea; and hence illicit importations came in freely from Holland. The affairs of the East-India Company were in great confusion, and a portion of its financial troubles was alleged to be owing to the loss of the American trade in tea. The king now suggested a plan to relieve the corporation, and at the same time try the question with America.

Financial loss in England

Parliament votes subsidy to tea shippers

"Lord North in the House of Commons proposed (April 27, 1773) 'to allow the company to export such portion of the tea then in their warehouses, to British America, as they should think proper, duty free.' He moved two resolutions, providing that on all teas imported to any British Plantations in America after the 10th of May, 1773, 'a drawback be allowed of all the duties of customs paid upon the importation of such teas,' which left the company to pay the threepence tax on the teas imported into America; and

The above excerpts are from Richard Frothingham's "The Rise of the Republic", 1890

the resolutions provided that this importation should be made under licenses from the commissioners of the Treasury.

"They have no idea that any people can act from any other principle but that of interest"

-Franklin

"The measure roused no opposition, occasioned little, if any, debate, and was adopted. It was carried to the House of Lords on the 6th of May, adopted there also, and on the 10th received the royal assent. The ministry thought it a wise scheme to take off so much duty on tea as was paid in England, as this would allow the company to sell tea cheaper in America than foreigners could supply it; and to confine the duty here, to keep up the exercise of the right of taxation. 'They,' Franklin wrote, 'have no idea that any people can act from any other principle but that of interest; and they believe that three pence on a pound of tea, of which one does not perhaps drink ten pounds in a year, is sufficient to overcome all the patriotism of an American.'...

"For if any one shall claim a Power to lay and levy Taxes on the People, by his own Authority, and without such consent of the People, he thereby invades the Fundamental Law of Property, and subverts the end of Government. For what Property have I in that, which another may by right take, when he pleases to himself?"
-John Locke

"The opposition to arbitrary power was never founded so much on knowledge and principle, was never so firm and systematic, as it was at the time of the passage of this Act.... The directors, however, in August obtained licenses from the Lords of the Treasury, and soon dispatched ships loaded with teas to the four ports of Boston, Charleston, New York, and Philadelphia....

"The scheme was pronounced an attempt to establish the right of parliament to tax the colonies and to give the East-India Company the monoply of the colonial market. As it bore on all the colonies, it diverted attention from the local issues, raised the past three years by Royal Instructions, to the original, general, and profound question of taxation. This had been argued in the court of public opinion: the verdict on it had been made up, and judgment had been rendered. The determination of the Americans not to pay a tax levied by a body in which they were not represented was as fixed as the purpose of the king to collect the duty on tea.... The Americans of today will say that their ancestors showed great intelligence in being alive to these weighty considerations founded on right and justice, when the dominant party in England was dead to them, and a heroic spirit in acting up to their convictions. The scheme suddenly roused more indignation than had been created by the Stamp Act. 'All America was in a flame.' The mighty surge of passion plainly meant resistance.

Colonists believed there was a British constitution with limits on arbitrary power

"The resistance contemplated was in general such action as might be necessary to thwart by lawful methods this ministerial measure. The idea had been grasped in America that there was a Constitution which limited the power of kings, lords, and commons.... The conviction was deep and general that the claim of

The above excerpts are from Richard Frothingham's "The Rise of the Republic", 1890

Colonies realized British system found wanting in peaceful means of redress

parliament to tax was against natural equity and against the Constitution. But political science had not devised the peaceable mode of obtaining redress in such cases in the manner suggested by Otis, - an idea embodied subsequently in the powers vested in the Supreme Court of the United States, and familiar to the American mind. This tribunal declares such legislation void. The only way then to defeat an odious scheme to collect an illegal tax was to follow the methods, as circumstances might dictate, of popular demonstration, which had long been customary in England, and thus render the law inapplicable....

"Would not submit to wrong"

"The efficiency that could not come from general organization was supplied by the ripeness and fixedness of public opinion on the assumption involved in the claim of taxation and the Declaratory Act, and the stern determination of the people not to submit to it. They did not rise up against the paltry duty because they were poor and could not pay, but because they were free and would not submit to wrong....

Tea ships enroute to four ports

"There was now the power of an intelligent public opinion behind the determination to baffle the attempt to establish the tea duty. The manifestations in each of the four ports to which the teas were consigned, printed in the newspapers, constituted strong assurances that the patriots in each felt, talked, and acted in a similar spirit, and that the teas would not be allowed to be sold, even if they were permitted to be landed. The decisive tone in each warrants the remark that the question as to which should be the first to thwart the ministerial scheme depended on the port selected for the earliest consignment. Before this was certainly known, there were great popular demonstrations.

"The patriots of Philadelphia, early in October, circulated an 'Address to the Tea Commissioners', in which it was said that the eyes of all were fixed on them as on men who had it in their power to ward off the most dangerous stroke that had ever been meditated against the liberties of America, and it appealed to them in passionate terms to decline to act....

Patriots meet in Philadelphia Boston New York Charleston

"The Boston patriots held great and exciting public meetings in Faneuil Hall, adopted the Philadelphia resolves, and requested the consignees to resign; but met with a peremptory refusal. The New York patriots held a meeting in City Hall, highly approved of the action of their brethren of Philadelphia and Boston 'in support of the common liberties of America', and voted that the tea under any circumstances should not be landed there. The Charleston patriots, at a meeting in their Great Hall, received

The above excerpts are from Richard Frothingham's "The Rise of the Republic", 1890

the resignation of the consignees with rounds of applause, and returned them many thanks....

All eyes on Boston

"In Boston, the course of the consignees, in refusing to resign, fixed all eyes upon the town. The aspect became so threatening that the legislative committee of correspondence were summoned to meet. They sent a Circular (October 21) to the other committees, reviewing in a calm tone, but in strong terms, the question between the colonies and Great Britain.... The patriots of Boston were unwearied in their efforts to produce the resignation of the consignees, and in this they were aided by some of their political opponents....In a long, anxious, and irritating contest with the officers of the crown, the Bostonians stood forth, 'like their native rocks, angular, sharp, and defiant'. Their proceedings gave great joy to the patriots in the other colonies. On the reception in Philadelphia of the news of the first meeting, the bells were rung, and the merchants greeted the resolves with hearty cheers. Still there were doubts expressed whether the love of money would not prove stronger than love of the cause. A Philadelphia letter printed in Boston runs: 'All we fear is that you will shrink at Boston. May God give you virtue enough to save the liberties of your country.'

Tea ships arrive in Boston

Patriots on guard to prevent unloading of tea

"In this way the progress of events served to fix attention more and more on Boston; and its patriots could see in expressions from other colonies that they were relied on to act with firmness and efficiency. When the struggle to compel the consignees to resign had gone on nearly a month, a vessel containing the tea arrived (November 28th) in the harbor, and in a few days two others, which the patriots directed to be moored near the first, that one guard might serve for all, their object being to prevent the cargoes from being landed. They now concentrated their efforts to have the teas sent back in the ships that brought them....

"The ships with the tea in them could not pass the castle without a permit from the Governor. He would not grant one before they were regularly cleared at the custom house, and the collector declined to give a clearance until the vessels were discharged of articles subject to duty. All the efforts of the patriots in their long struggle had produced from the consignees only a repetition of the original peremptory answer, 'No resignation', and a refusal to return the teas. A vessel twenty days after her arrival in port was liable to seizure for the non-payment of the duties; and this would be the case of the 'Dartmouth' on the sixteenth day of December....A great meeting, held two days before, stood adjourned to this day (December 16th,) which was

The above excerpts are from Richard Frothingham's "The Rise of the Republic", 1890

Patriots held town-meeting in "Old South"

Thursday. Business in town was generally suspended. The inhabitants in the morning flocked to 'The Old South Meeting House', still standing. They were joined by people from the country for twenty miles around. The gathering consisted of nearly seven thousand, - 'merchants, yeomen, gentlemen, - respectable for their rank, and venerable for their age and character.' The forenoon was occupied mostly with dealing with Francis Rotch, the owner of the 'Dartmouth', who was informed that he was expected to procure a pass from the Governor and proceed on this day with his vessel on his voyage for London. The meeting adjourned to three o'clock in the afternoon....

"In the afternoon Rotch was at Milton, the country seat of Governor Hutchinson. He went there to ask once more for a pass to enable his ship with the tea in her to get by the castle.... After a little time Hutchinson sternly repeated his refusal to grant the pass, saying that he could not do it consistently with the rules of government and his duty to the king, unless the vessel was properly cleared....

"This meeting can do no more to save the country"

-Samuel Adams

"About six o'clock Rotch returned to the Old South, which was dimly lighted with candles and filled with people, many also standing in the streets. He stated the result of his application to the Governor for a pass. On slight manifestations of disorder, Thomas Young rose and said that Rotch was a good man who had done all that was in his power to gratify the people; and they were enjoined to do no harm to his person or his property. He was then asked 'whether he would send his vessel back with the tea in her, under the circumstances.' He replied, 'he could not possibly comply, as he apprehended compliance would prove his ruin'; and confessed that, 'if called upon by the proper officers, he should attempt, for his own security, to land the tea.' Samuel Adams then said: 'This meeting can do nothing more to save the country.' A war-whoop was now sounded at the door, which was answered from the galleries. The shouting became tremendous....

From words to action

"As the party from whom rose the war-whoop passed the church, numbers naturally followed on; and the throng went directly to Griffin's Wharf, now Liverpool, at the foot of Purchase Street, off which were moored the three vessels which contained the tea. A resolute band had guarded them day and night. John Hancock was one of the guard this evening. The party in disguise, - probably his friend Joseph Warren was among them, - whooping like Indians, went on board the vessels, and, warning their officers and those of the customhouse to keep out of the way,

The above excerpts are from Richard Frothingham's "The Rise of the Republic", 1890

unlaid the hatches, hoisted the chests of tea on deck, cut them open, and hove the tea overboard. They proved quiet and systematic workers. No one interfered with them. No other property was injured; no person was harmed; no tea was allowed to be carried away; and the silence of the crowd on shore was such that the noise of breaking the chests was distinctly heard by them. 'The whole', Hutchinson wrote, 'was done with very little tumult'. The town was never more still of a Saturday night than it was at ten o'clock that evening. The men from the country carried great news to their villages. Joy, as for deliverance from calamity, now burst in full chorus from the American heart. The local exultation was extreme. 'You cannot imagine', Samuel Adams wrote, 'the height of joy that sparkes in the eyes and animates the countenances as well as the hearts of all we meet on this occasion.' 'This', John Adams said, 'is the most magnificent movement of all. There is a dignity, a majesty, a sublimity, in this last effort of the patriots, that I greatly admore.' 'We', John Scollay, one of the selectmen and an actor, wrote, 'do console ourselves that we have acted constitutionally', - namely, did no more than was necessary, under the circumstances, to defeat the design of landing the teas.

Object of arbitrary taxation quietly hoisted into Boston Harbor

The Tea Party

"The exultation was scarcely less outside of Massachusetts.... The Tea Act had the effect to make this question of taxation a living issue.... The popular leaders now sought to give direction to a great movement; or to take advantage of a happy disposition in the public mind and extend the organization of committees of correspondence.... The popular party, in their several municipalities, proceeded independently in forming committees....

Philadelphia resolute - ships return tea to England

"The resistance to the ministerial scheme in this way was general, systematic, and thorough. The newspapers contain much matter relative to the reception of the cargoes at the ports to which the tea was consigned. In Philadelphia, at an hour's notice, five thousand met, and resolved that a cargo should not be landed, but should go back in the same bottom. The captain and the consignees bowed to the popular will, and a vast concourse escorted them to the tea ship and saw her sail.

The above excerpts are from Richard Frothingham's "The Rise of the Republic", 1890

New York and Charleston stand firm and won

"In New York, it was announced in the Tory organ that arrangements were made to have the tea sent back in the same ship, and thus New York be secured 'a succession of that blessed tranquillity which they enjoyed under the present wise and serene administration'. In Charleston a great meeting on the arrival of the cargo appointed a committee, - on which were Christopher Gadsden, Charles Pinckney, and Charles Cotesworth Pinckney, - to inform the captain that the teas must go back; but the ship was delayed beyond the twenty days, when the collector seized the vessel and stored the tea in a damp cellar, where it was destroyed. There were similar dealings with the teas in other places. The scheme was thoroughly defeated.

An American congress advocated

"The unity of spirit and harmony of action of the popular party once more excited the liveliest hopes. Samuel Adams, reflecting on the increasing intercourse between the colonies, remarked that old jealousies had been removed, and harmony subsisted between them, and said that the institution of committees of correspondence would be attended with great and good consequences. The friend always by his side, Joseph Warren, enthusiastic over the prospect of union, wrote: 'We can never enough adore that Almighty Disposer who has, as it were, by general inspiration awakened a whole continent to a sense of their danger.' The ardent hoped to see a congress grow out of the movement. This measure was earnestly advocated in the press. 'It is now time', a writer says, 'for the colonies to have a grand congress to complete the system for the American independent commonwealth, as it is so evident that no other plan will secure the rights of this people; for this would unite all Americans by an indissoluble bond of union, and thereby make them formidable and superior to any kingdom upon earth.'...

"The expression in favor of a congress produced no regular call for the election of delegates during the spring of 1774. The journals for months after the complete defeat of the execution of the Tea Act show little political agitation outside of Massachusetts.... Even here the agitation was limited....

"Samuel Adams apprehended the situation. His utterances show that he hoped rather than expected that the ministers would alter their policy; and in the case of their persistence in it, he saw as a consequence no other result than separation and independence. Still his record as clearly shows that, so far from welcoming the bloody work of revolution, he involuntarily shrunk from it. He continued for a year to express warm affection for the mother-country. He stood, however, firm in his conviction of what public duty demanded. It was in vain to expect that the people would

The above excerpts are from Richard Frothingham's "The Rise of the Republic", 1890

be contented with partial or temporary relief, or be amused with court promises. Their opposition to unconstitutional measures had grown into system; colony communed freely with colony; there was among the colonies a common affection, - the communis sensus; the whole continent had become united in sentiment and in opposition to tyranny.

"The condition of equal liberty"

"However, the old good-will and affection for the parent country was not lost; if she returned to her former moderation, the former love would return; for the people wanted nothing more than permanent union with her on the condition of equal liberty. This is all they had for ten years been contending for, and nothing short of this would or ought to satisfy them. This was his position stated in his own words. It was a defensive one. He had faith in the republican idea; appreciated the value of its embodiment in American institutions; sought their preservation; and for their protection would have been satisfied with the national power which grandly met the natural sentiment of country. As the reports came that the government was maturing severe penal measures, and that fleets and armies were to be sent over to enforce them, his faith in God and his countrymen rose....

England decides to punish America for refusing arbitrary taxation

"The period of suspense terminated during the first week in May, when the newspapers became burdened with details shewing the feeling roused in England by the destruction of the tea. It was pronounced by the king a subversion of the Constitution; by Lord North, the culmination of years of riot and confusion; by parliament, actual rebellion flowing from ideas of independence. The opposition bowed to the storm, Lord Chatham uttered rebuke, and Colonel Barre conceded the necessity of punishment. Lord Dartmouth was the most moderate in his speech, terming the proceeding a commotion, but was anxious that the offenders should be punished. The bold stroke of the Boston patriots stirred an intense nationality into an energy, that, like a hurricane, swept before it men and parties....

Massachusetts singled out for punishment

"The ministers blundered, as usual, in meeting this issue. They proceeded as though they had to deal only with Boston and Massachusetts. It had long been a theory that the law of diversity was so deeply rooted and so paramount in its influence, that any thing like real political unity among the colonies would be impossible.... It was reasoned: The other colonies will not take fire at the proper punishment of those who have disobeyed the laws. They will leave them to suffer for their own offences; the shutting up of the port will be naturally a gratification to the neighboring towns; the other colonies will accept with pleasure any benefits they can

The above excerpts are from Richard Frothingham's "The Rise of the Republic", 1890

derive from the misfortunes of Massachusetts; the policy of singling out this colony will eventually prove a means of dissolving the bond of union....

Boston Port Bill passed

"The first of this series, the Boston Port Bill, was moved by Lord North on the 14th of March. It passed in about two weeks through the various stages, with very little debate....

Widespread indignation aroused

"This Act was received by separate arrivals at New York and Boston, and was circulated with wonderful rapidity from these centres through the colonies. It spoke for itself. It doomed a town to suffer for a deed which had been welcomed in every quarter with manifestations of joy. Pathetic appeal, or party manipulation, or personal influence, was not required to rouse a general indignation. This welled up instinctively from the American heart, and was expressed in every form. The Act was printed on paper with mourning lines; it was cried through the streets as barbarous murder; it was burnt by the common hangman on scaffolds forty-five feet high. The feeling that it was unjust and inhuman was expressed in passionate words. 'Join or die', a terse Rhode Island utterance reads: 'The insult to our virtuous brethren ought to be viewed in the same odious light as a direct hostile invasion of every province on the continent.' Thus the patriots gave themselves up to impulses that honor human nature. The Act was a failure from the moment of its promulgation.

Nine Committees of Correspondence meet in Boston

"The Boston committee of correspondence invited the committees of eight neighboring towns to meet for deliberation in Faneuil Hall. Men in that conference (May 12) took part in the counsels or the battles of the whole subsequent struggle. Samuel Adams presided, and Joseph Warren drew up its papers. The conference addressed a circular to the committees in all the colonies, recommending a suspension of trade with Great Britain, suggesting that the single question was whether the other colonies would consider Boston as suffering for the common cause, and resent the injury inflicted on her, and promising fidelity to the rights of America. On the next day a town meeting was held in Faneuil Hall, with Samuel Adams for the moderator. The inhabitants addressed (May 13) a circular 'to all the sister colonies, promising to suffer for America with fortitude, but confessing that singly they must find their trial too severe;' They entreated not to be left alone when the being of every colony as a free people depended on the event; and they also proposed, as the means to obtain redress, commercial non-intercourse.... Thus the patriots acted through their varied organizations in a spirit of order, and with promptness, dignity, and efficiency.

Boston circular appeals to all sister Colonies for support

The above excerpts are from Richard Frothingham's "The Rise of the Republic", 1890

All New England pledges aid

"The reception of these circulars was the occasion for memorable proceedings, which have often been related, but which ought not to be omitted in any narrative of these times. The inhabitants of Marblehead tendered the use of their wharves to the Bostonians, one of their number, Elbridge Gerry, the future Vice-President, saying that the resentment of an arbitrary ministry would prove a diadem of honor to the oppressed town. The merchants of Newburyport voted to break off trade with Great Britain, and lay up their ships until the port should be opened. Salem, in an address to Governor Gage, drawn up by Timothy Pickering, the future Secretary of State, averred that they must be lost to all feelings of humanity to raise their fortunes on the ruins of their neighbor. The same spirit was manifested in the other New-England colonies. The Connecticut assembly appointed a day for humiliation and prayer, and ordered an inventory to be taken of cannon and military stores. Providence, in Rhode Island, resolved that all the colonies were concerned in the Port Act, and recommended a congress. Portsmouth, in New Hampshire, declared that the administration were taking every method to disunite the colonies, but hoped their firm union would continue.

Effort to disunite Colonies pointed out

Virginia stirred

"The sentiment and determination of the patriots south of New England were represented in the proceedings of the Virginia House of Burgesses. On the reception of the news of the Port Act, all business gave way to the generous purpose to stand by Massachusetts. In resolves penned by Jefferson, they set apart the first day of June as a day of fasting and prayer, to invoke the divine interposition to give to the American people one heart and one mind to oppose by all just means every injury to American rights, and to inspire the minds of His Majesty and his parliament with wisdom, moderation, and justice. These resolves brought down a dissolution; and before others, proposing a congress, could be passed. The members then repaired to the Raleigh Tavern, where they declared that an attack made on one of the sister colonies was an attack on all British America, and threatened ruin to the rights of all, unless the united wisdom of the whole were applied; and they recommended the committee of correspondence to communicate with the other committees on the expediency of holding an annual congress. Two days later the circulars from the north were received, when the Burgesses who remained in Williamsburg - Washington was one - appointed a convention, consisting of representatives of all the counties, to meet on the first day of August.

House of Burgesses observes day of prayer

State-wide convention called

"This noble action, embodying the passion and humanity of a rich historic hour, was a fitting prelude to the spectacle which the

The above excerpts are from Richard Frothingham's "The Rise of the Republic", 1890

British men-of-war close Boston Harbor

colonies presented on the day (June 1) the Port Act went into effect. A cordon of British men-of-war was moored around the town of Boston. Not a keel nor a raft was permitted to approach the wharves. The wheels of commerce were stopped. The poor were deprived of employment. The rich were cut off from their usual resources. The town entered upon its period of suffering. The day was widely observed as a day of fasting and prayer. The manifestations of sympathy were general. Business was suspended. Bells were muffled, and tolled from morning till night; flags were kept at half-mast; streets were dressed in mourning; public buildings and shops were draped in black; large congregations filled the churches.

All Colonies deeply moved

"In Virginia the members of the House of Burgesses assembled at their place of meeting; went in procession, with the Speaker at their head, to the church and listened to a discourse. 'Never', a lady wrote, ' since my residence in Virginia have I seen so large a congregation as was this day assembled to hear divine service.' The preacher selected for his text the words: 'be strong and of good courage, fear not, nor be afraid of them; for the Lord thy God, he it is that doth go with thee. He will not fail thee nor forsake thee.' 'The people', Jefferson says, 'met generally, with anxiety and alarm in their countenances; and the effect of the day, through the whole colony, was like a shock of electricity, arousing every man and placing him erect and solidly on his centre.' These words describe the effect of the Port Act throughout the thirteen colonies.

Uncommon wisdom of the Whigs in the face of danger

"This train of events served to fix again all eyes on Boston. It was not required to be patient under suffering, to show forbearance under insult, and to be faithful to the cause in the face of danger. The feeling among its citizens was bitter, intense, and up to the verge of civil war. The Tories taunted the Whigs with following a set of reckless demagogues, who professed loyalty, but aimed at independence. They had brought down upon the town its calamity, and would be sent to England and expiate their crimes at Tyburn. The Whigs, as they directed public odium in every way on the Tories, averred that nothing was further from their hearts than a spirit of rebellion, and continued their confidence in a noble band of leaders. They were guiding a great movement with uncommon wisdom. The militia were not called out to resist the landing of the troops daily expected; the British fleet were not cannonaded from guns planted on the surrounding hills; the idea was not acted on, if it was suggested by the rash, of declaring independence, unfurling the

The above excerpts are from Richard Frothingham's "The Rise of the Republic", 1890

Pine Tree flag, and entering upon a Quixotic crusade against England.

English regiments occupy Boston - implant cannon

"The town bore its burden with dignity, and based its hope of deliverence on union. In a short time regiments from famous battlefields landed unmolested on its soil; hostile cannon were planted on its eminences and at the single outlet into the country; troops daily paraded its streets, and the place wore the aspect of a garrison. Details of the petty annoyance to which its citizens were subjected were printed from time to time in the journals. The strange spectacle touched the feelings of the patriots. Their admiration was raised by the genuine pluck evinced by the Bostonians in going on with their political action under the mouths of hostile cannon, and when this was in derogation of an act of parliament. The action had not been bolder when the town was free from troops. Thus the brave municipality stood manfully for the cause, exciting warm sympathy, intense interest, and the gravest apprehension.

Patriots continue their political activities

Generous gifts sent to sufferers in Boston

"The suggestion appeared in several quarters simultaneously that contributions should be tendered for the relief of such of the indigent as might be sufferers by the operation of the Port Act; it was approved and urged in the press, the pulpit, public meetings, and general assemblies; and was so promptly carried out that soon there was a flow from every quarter of cereals, live stock, provisions, wood, and money into Boston. The fraternal movement bore directly on the individual.

Contributors - by word and deed - in hundreds of localities

"The ardent and zealous workers in the cause in hundreds of localities, forming a circle more or less wide, went from door to door, from street to street, as they gathered the patriotic offerings; and the talk in the shop, on the farm, in the commercial mart, in the home, would naturally be of acts of power full of injustice, of violated liberty, of patriots suffering for the cause. The names of contributors in some places are still to be seen. The list in Fairfax County, Virginia, has at its head the name of George Washington for fifty pounds. The committees accompanied the gifts with letters laden with the deepest sympathy, and, as sterner events unfolded, - as will be seen in the next chapter, - with the most solemn pledges of support.....

"'Stand firm, and let your intrepid courage show to the world that you are Christians.' These words were born of generous impulses and a noble enthusiasm. They revealed the fact that, beneath the diversity that characterized the colonies, there was

The above excerpts are from Richard Frothingham's "The Rise of the Republic", 1890

Beneath diversity - American unity

American unity. The deeds they heralded were the blossoming of a rare public life, but the spirit was greater than the deeds. The blow dealt on Boston, like a wound on a single nerve, convulsed the whole body.

"The Boston Gazette of July 11, 1774, has the following, which illustrates the spirit of the times: -

"That unison of sentiment and action"

"'Messieurs Edes and Gill.
'Tis an old and just observation that professions cost nothing; 'tis equally true that when a man parts with his money in support of any cause, he evidences himself to be in earnest. I cannot but reverence my fellow-country-men, dispersed through this and the other governments, for their liberal and unsolicited contributions to support the poor and suffering people of Boston during the present conflict. What amiable charity! What glorious magnanimity is here displayed! Shall such a race of patriots, shall such a band of friends, be ever subdued? No, my persecuted brethren of this metropolis, you may rest assured that the guardian God of New England, who holds the hearts of his people in his hands, has influenced your distant brethren to this benevolence. 'Tis a glorious pledge of that harmony, that unison of sentiment and action, which shall connect such a band of heroes, as to make a world combined against them to tremble. Cultivate this rich, this fruitful blessing, - an extensive union: when once 'tis effected, it will intimidate your enemies, will animate your friends, will convince them both that you must be invincible, and thus you will obtain a bloodless victory.'"

"The popular party were now enabled to prepare for the work in store for them by extending their organization and interchanging sentiments....

August, 1774 to 1775.

The king was unwearied in efforts to give direction to the measures relating to America....

Regulatory Act voted

"The Regulating Act made elections of the council under the charter void, provided that the board should consist of not less than twelve

The above excerpts are from Richard Frothingham's "The Rise of the Republic", 1890

Local government shorn of power

members nor more than thirty-six, and vested their appointment in the crown. The Governor was clothed with power to appoint and remove judges of the inferior courts, justices of the peace, and other minor officers. The Governor and council were to appoint and remove sheriffs, who were authorized to select jurymen. Town meetings, except for the choice of officers, were forbidden, without permission of the Governor. The Act relating to the administration of justice provided for the transportation of offenders and witnesses to other colonies or to England for trial....

Offenders subject to deportation

Acts of English Parliament a threat to all

"In these Acts parliament assumed the power to alter the American Constitution at its will and pleasure. If it could deal in this way with Massachusetts, it could deal in a similar way with all the colonies. In fact, the laws were a complete embodiment of the principle of the obnoxious Declaratory Act.

Committee of Correspondence boldly circularizes Colonies

"These measures, on which hung great issues, were first made known to America through the drafts of the bills as moved in the House of Commons. They reached Boston on the second day of June, and were printed in the newspapers on the third. The action of the Boston committee was, as usual, prompt and decisive; and the committees throughout the province did not fall behind the Boston committee in boldness and zeal. 'We were chosen,' wrote Samuel Adams to Charles Thomson, of Philadelphia, 'to be as it were, outguards to watch the designs of our enemies; and have a correspondence with almost every town in the colony. By this means we have been able to circulate the most early intelligence of importance to our friends in the country, and to establish a union which is formidable to our adversaries.'

"The legislative committee immediately transmitted these bills to the other legislative committees, with a circular in which they say: 'These edicts, cruel and oppressive as they are, we consider but as bare specimens of what the continent are to expect from a parliament who claim a right to make laws binding us in all cases whatsoever.' The policy now marked out by the patriots of Boston is seen in the utterances of Samuel Adams, which continue to be calm and prophetic. 'Boston suffers with dignity: if Britain, by her multiplied oppressions, accelerates the independency of her colonies, whom will she have to blame but herself? It is a consolatory thought that an empire is rising in America.'...

"The popular party was then in the heat and glow of the noble enthusiasm inspired by the fact of union. It was natural that

The above excerpts are from Richard Frothingham's "The Rise of the Republic", 1890

Unanimous opposition to Acts of Parliament

measures, which struck at the ancient right of local self-government should rouse general alarm and indignation. Those who had been moderate and wavering became resolute and resentful. The condemnation of these bills was spontaneous and withering. They were doomed to annulment before intelligence was received of their passage into laws; and when Governor Gage received them officially, the public conviction of their enormity had become embodied in the sternest action....

Twelve Colonies enjoin Massachusetts to defy feudal England

"The newspapers were laden with political appeals and the proceedings of public bodies, enjoining unanimity and resolution. They showed that the popular party were arrayed in solid phalanx against the Regulating Acts.... Thus the will of the people, collected generally through the forms in which they were accustomed to proceed in political affairs, and expressed with as much regularity as circumstances would permit, was declared with respect to the two new Acts. It was, that they should share the fate of the Stamp Act and the Tea Act, even though the shedding of blood might be the consequence. And this verdict is found of record before the general congress met, or before the Acts were attempted to be put in force. In the natural course of events, a crisis was reached, involving ideas in deadly conflict with each other: for the public opinion of twelve colonies may be said to have enjoined the inhabitants of Massachusetts, for the sake of civil liberty, to refuse obedience to the two Acts, as imperatively as the king's instructions, in behalf of feudal England, enjoined General Gage to carry them into execution....

Patriots ignore ban on free speech and assembly

"The Governor now sent for the selectmen of Boston, and told them he should endeavor to put the Regulating Act into execution, especially the clause in relation to holding town meetings; and if any ill consequences followed, they only would be blamable. Town meetings, however, were held all over the province, and chose delegates to county conventions. The committees of correspondence were especially active, and held continual conferences. The words of a noble and brave man, who fell at Bunker Hill, will serve as a type of Massachusetts in this hour of trial: 'I consider the call of my country as the call of God, and desire to be all obedience to such a call. The committees of correspondence for the several towns in the county of Worcester have assembled, are in high spirits, and perfectly united. The committees of Cambridge and Charlestown are to have a conference tomorrow. I trust the whole county of Middlesex will soon be assembled by delegates. I have the greatest reason to believe will choose to fall gloriously in the cause of their country rather than meanly to submit to slavery.'

The above excerpts are from Richard Frothingham's "The Rise of the Republic", 1890

"Determined to die or to be free"

"A meeting of these committees from several counties, held in Faneuil Hall, matured measures for securing a thorough resistance to the two Acts, and for convening a Provincial Congress. The community was now thoroughly roused. It was said in the public prints: 'The spirit of the people was never known to be so great since the settlement, and they were determined to die or to be free.'

The farmers prevent court session

"A great uprising began on the 16th of August at Great Barrington. When the judges attempted to hold a court, the farmers thronged to the place, filled the building, and blocked up the avenue leading to it. The sheriff commanded them to make way for the court, but the answer was: 'No court will be submitted to but on the ancient laws and usages.' In Boston, the chief justice and associate justices and barristers, arrayed in their robes, went unmolested in procession from the town house in King, now State Street, to the court house in Queen Street, and took their accustomed places; but the jurors, both grand and petit, stood up and refused to be sworn. In Salem, the Governor issued a proclamation warning all persons against attending a town meeting, which was nullified within the sound of his drums. The mandamus councillors who accepted felt the storm of public indignation. As one, an honored citizen of Plymouth, and a Congregationalist, took his seat in the church on Sunday, a large number of persons rose and walked out of the house; when another in Bridgewater, a deacon, also a Congregationalist, read the psalm, the congregation refused to sing; and several councillors living in the country were compelled by gatherings of the people to resign. The county officers were similarly dealt with, and were universally compelled to decline their appointments. The patriots said that 'their souls were touched by a sense of the wrongs already offered them, as well as those which were threatened,' and that 'they would never rest, while one man who had accepted any office under the new Acts was possessed of any post of power or profit.' They averred that herein they acted in accordance with the Christian duty of each individual. They used no more force than was required to effect the object they had in view, - complete disobedience to the new Acts; and, expressing an abhorrence of mobs, they declared 'that, in a contest so solemn and a cause so great, their conduct should be such as to merit the approbation of the wise, and the admiration of the brave and free, of every age and country.' 'On experiment,' Dr. Ramsay remarks, 'it was found that to force on the inhabitants a form of government to which they were totally averse was not within the fancied omnipotence of parliament.'

Jurors refuse to be sworn

Appointments by king refused

"Abhorrence of mobs"

The above excerpts are from Richard Frothingham's "The Rise of the Republic", 1890

"The resistance to the two Acts was thorough....

Provincial Congress meets despite governor

"Governor Gage issued a precept for the choice of representatives to the General Court, and the towns elected them; but before the time for their meeting the Governor prorogued them. They met, however, at Salem, where they were summoned to meet, and resolved themselves into a provincial congress, chose John Hancock President, and Benjamin Lincoln Secretary, and then adjourned to Concord. The decisive business of this body may be said to have commenced with the creation (October 27) of 'The Committee of Safety'. On the next day this committee were directed 'to take care of the lodge in some safe place in the country warlike stores.' The congress dissolved on the 10th of December.

Committee of Safety formed

Massachusetts' militia equipped

"A second congress, chosen by those who elected the representatives, met at Cambridge on the 1st of February; and this body was in existence until the spring. These congresses chose a committee of supplies, provided for the organization of the militia, one quarter of whom were to meet at a moment's warning, and appointed general officers to command the militia. The committee of safety were empowered to summon this force to the field whenever General Gage should attempt to execute the Regulating Acts. This committee, on which were Hancock, Warren, and Samuel Adams, was virtually a directory appointed to see to the defence of the Commonwealth.

Pledge of the Minute-men

"Such was the local public authority recognized in this crisis. In obedience to its call, the towns, during the autumn and winter of 1774 and 1775, were fairly alive with military preparations. In many of them the minute-men signed an agreement pledging themselves to take the field at a minute's warning. On the days of drill the citizen soldiers some times went from the parade-ground to the church, where they listened to exhortation and prayer. The scene engrossed all minds, moved all hearts; ordinary business gave way to the demands of the hour. The newspapers are laden with political articles relating to the issue.... In some instances the cause was dishonored by personal violence, but in the main was kept remarkably true to social order. 'You,' say the provincial congress, 'are placed by Providence in the post of honor, because it is the post of danger. And while struggling for the noblest objects, - the liberites of your country, the happiness of posterity, and the rights of human nature, - the eyes not only of North America and the whole British Empire, but of all Europe, are upon you. Let us be, therefore, altogether solicitous that no disorderly behavior, nothing unbecoming our characters as Americans, as citizens and Christians, be justly chargeable to us.'...

The above excerpts are from Richard Frothingham's "The Rise of the Republic" - 1890

"At the dawn the British flag was displayed on the Tree of Liberty, and a discharge of fourteen cannon ranged under the venerable elm saluted the joyous day. At eleven o'clock a very large company of the principal gentlemen and respectable inhabitants of the town met at the Hall under the tree, while the streets were crowded with a concourse of people of all ranks, public notice having been given of the intended celebration. The music began at high noon, performed on various instruments, joined with voices, and concluding with the universally admired American Song of Liberty ..."
Boston Gazette, Aug. 22, 1768

"These annual celebrations were held at the suggestion principally of Otis and Samuel Adams, who, with the other leaders, were always personally present ...."
Wells, "Life of Samuel Adams"

January to November - 1775

Three million Americans in 1775

The United Colonies contained a population, according to the estimate of Congress, of three millions; other estimates placed it lower. Pioneers had penetrated the forests west of the Alleghanies, and begun settlements that grew into great States; but the body of the people lived on the belt of land stretching from the Atlantic coast to the Gulf of Mexico. The relative increase in twenty years, or since 1754, was as follows: New England had risen from 436,000 to 690,000; the Middle Colonies from 528,000 to 870,000; the Southern from 461,000 to 1,030,000. This people - a new race, moulding their institutions under Christian influences - were fixed in the traits that characterize Americans. Without the infection of wild political or social theories, they were animated by a love of liberty and a spirit of personal independence unknown to the great body of the people of Europe, while at the same time recognizing the law which united the individual to the family and to the society in which he is appointed to live, to the municipality and the commonwealth which gave him protection, and to a great nation which met and satisfied the natural sentiment of country. The colonies had reached their development as thirteen distinct communities, each of which though claiming a common property in certain fundamental ideas, had modes of life, likes and dislikes, aims and ambitions, and an internal polity in many respects local and peculiar. They had attained the condition, in Milton's words, long wished for and spoken of, but never yet obtained, in which the people had justice in their own hands, and law executed fully and finally in counties and precincts....

The Christian Idea moulding American institutions

Without the infection of European social theories

"The people waited, in keen anxiety, to learn the effect produced in England by the fact of union, and the measures of the congress... As the sword suspended by a thread was about to fall, Lord North caused it to be made known to Franklin that the administration, for the sake of peace, might repeal the tax on tea and the Port Act, but 'that the Massachusetts Acts, being real amendments of their Constitution, must, for that reason, be continued,

The above excerpts are from Richard Frothingham's "The Rise of the Republic" - 1890

as well as to be a standing example of the power of Parliament.' This involved the subjection of the free municipalities of America - indeed, its whole internal polity - to the caprice of majorities in a legislative body three thousand miles away, in which they were not represented, and consequently the establishment of centralization in its worst form. Opposed to this assumption was the principle of local self-government....

:aprice of foreign egislature

"The news of the reception of the petition to the king and of the address of both Houses of Parliament reached America when the popular party was in a state of great excitement. The numerous public meetings were demonstrations that one heart animated and one understanding governed this party. In Massachusetts, John Adams was urging in the public prints that all men were by nature equal, and that kings had but delegated authority, which the people might resume....

"The Massachusetts militia, as before related, were organized, and the committee of safety were empowered to call them into the field whenever the attempt should be made to execute by force the Regulating Acts; while General Gage was instructed to disarm the inhabitants. As the news from England became more warlike, the committee of safety authorized the purchase of military stores, a portion of which were carried to Concord, a rural town about eighteen miles from Boston; and they organized express riders to summon the militia, in case the king's troops should take the field. In this preparatory work Joseph Warren was particularly active.

/ilitary tores cached pon warlike ews from :ngland

"The military stores deposited in Concord General Gage resolved to destroy, and for this purpose planned an expedition which he intended should be a secret one. A detachment left Boston stealthily on the evening of the 18th of April, and continued their march during the night. Warren, however, obtained intelligence of the movement in season to despatch two expresses, by different route, into the country, with directions to call out the militia. The messengers mounted horses and spurred on from town to town on their eventful errand. 'The fate of a nation was riding that night'.

'ateful lecision of a royal governor

"At sunrise on the nineteenth of April, the detachment reached Lexington, a small town eleven miles from Boston, on the road to Concord. The militia of this place had promptly answered the summons to parade, and were fired upon by the troops, who killed some and wounded others. The detachment then moved on,

British troops on march to Concord

The above excerpts are from Richard Frothingham's "The Rise of the Republic", 1890

"The shot heard around the world"

reached Concord, about six miles from Lexington, at seven o'clock, and halted in the centre of the town, whence parties were sent in different directions to destroy the military stores. A guard of a hundred men was stationed at the old North Bridge. About ten o' clock, as a body of the militia were approaching this bridge, the guard fired upon them, when more citizens were killed and wounded. No mausoleum ever commanded such honor as Americans attach to the graves of these early martyrs to American liberty. This precious blood roused righteous indignation in the breasts of the yeomanry, who had been flocking in, and stood with their old firelocks in their hands on that village green. They resolved to avenge the death of their brethren. Two hours after the firing at the bridge the king's troops began their march for Boston, when the militia fell upon them in such fiery spirit, and with such deadly effect, that the march was soon turned into a run. The proud veterans were saved from total destruction by a reinforcement which left Boston in the morning and joined them at Lexington; and they found security only in the shelter of ships of war at night fall, when by the light of the flashing musketry they entered Charlestown and rested on Bunker Hill.

Early martyrs to American liberty

"Can a virtuous man hesitate in his choice?"

-Washington

"The news of this scene of blood roused the spirit of the patriots throughout the colonies.... The high resolve of that historic hour is embodied in the calm, sorrowful, determined words of Washington, penned in the quiet retreat of Mount Vernon. 'Unhappy,' he wrote, 'is it to reflect that a brother's sword has been sheathed in a brother's breast, and that the once happy and peaceful plains of America are to be either drenched with blood or inhabited by slaves. Sad alternative! But can a virtuous man hesitate in his choice?' - language in which the yearnings of the patriot give affecting solemnity to the implied resolve of the soldier. The use of force to repel force without a thought of consequences was instinctively and universally justified by the popular party, and the preparation for it which foresight had enjoined proved efficient at least for the crisis.

Patriots besiege British troops in Boston

"The bands appearing on the roads leading to Massachusetts had been organized and delegated by the public authorities to bear the sword for the common defence. They met in the towns around Boston, and here pitched their tents. They placed the British army in a state of siege, and thus rendered it useless for the purposes for which it was sent over. These events created the stage of armed resistance. Thus the ten years of discussion, formation of public opinion, political organization, and military preparation culminated in 'a Runnymede in America'....

Revolution inevitable

The above excerpts are from Richard Frothingham's "The Rise of the Republic", 1890

"..Such was the state of Virginia, when on the twentieth of March its second convention assembled at Richmond in the old church of Saint John, on the hill which overlooks the town...the Old Dominion renewed their assurances, 'that it was the most ardent wish of their colony and of the whole continent of North America, to see a speedy return to those halcyon days when they lived a free and happy people.' ...'What,' rejoined Henry, 'has there been in the conduct of the British ministry for the last ten years to justify hope? Are fleets and armies necessary to a work of love and reconciliation? These are the implements of subjugation, sent over to rivet upon us the chains which the British ministry have been so long forging. And what have we to oppose to them? Shall we try argument? We have been trying that for the last ten years; have we any thing new to offer?...In vain may we indulge the fond hope of reconciliation. There is no longer room for hope. If we wish to be free, we must fight! I repeat it sir, we must fight! An appeal to arms and to the God of Hosts is all that is left us! They tell me that we are weak; but shall we gather strength by irresolution? We are not weak. Three millions of people, armed in the holy cause of liberty, and in such a country, are invincible by any force which our enemy can send against us. We shall not fight alone. A just God presides over the destinies of nations... There is no retreat, but in submission and slavery...Is life so dear, or peace so sweet, as to be purchased at the price of chains and slavery? Forbid it, Almighty God! - I know not what course others may take; but as for me, give me liberty, or give me death.'"

- George Bancroft, "History of the United States", 1858
  Patrick Henry addresses the Virginia convention, Mar. 20, 1775

In CONGRESS, July 4, 1776.

A DECLARATION

By the REPRESENTATIVES of the

UNITED STATES OF AMERICA,

In GENERAL CONGRESS assembled.

WHEN in the Courſe of human Events, it becomes neceſſary for one People to diſſolve the Political Bands which have connected them with another, and to aſſume among the Powers of the Earth, the ſeparate and equal Station to which the Laws of Nature and of Nature's God entitle them, a decent Reſpect to the Opinions of Mankind requires that they ſhould declare the cauſes which impel them to the Separation.

We hold theſe Truths to be ſelf-evident, that all Men are created equal, that they are endowed by their Creator with certain unalienable Rights, that among theſe are Life, Liberty, and the Purſuit of Happineſs—That to ſecure theſe Rights, Governments are inſtituted among Men, deriving their juſt Powers from the Conſent of the Governed, that whenever any Form of Government becomes deſtructive of theſe Ends, it is the Right of the People to alter or to aboliſh it, and to inſtitute new Government, laying its Foundation on ſuch Principles, and organizing its Powers in ſuch Form, as to them ſhall ſeem moſt likely to effect their Safety and Happineſs. Prudence, indeed, will dictate that Governments long eſtabliſhed ſhould not be changed for light and tranſient Cauſes; and accordingly all Experience hath ſhewn, that Mankind are more diſpoſed to ſuffer, while Evils are ſufferable, than to right themſelves by aboliſhing the Forms to which they are accuſtomed. But when a long Train of Abuſes and Uſurpations, purſuing invariably the ſame Object, evinces a Deſign to reduce them under abſolute Deſpotiſm, it is their Right, it is their Duty, to throw off ſuch Government, and to provide new Guards for their future Security. Such has been the patient Sufferance of theſe Colonies; and ſuch is now the Neceſſity which conſtrains them to alter their former Syſtems of Government. The Hiſtory of the preſent King of Great-Britain is a Hiſtory of repeated Injuries and Uſurpations, all having in direct Object the Eſtabliſhment of an abſolute Tyranny over theſe States. To prove this, let Facts be ſubmitted to a candid World.

He has refuſed his Aſſent to Laws, the moſt wholeſome and neceſſary for the public Good.

He has forbidden his Governors to paſs Laws of immediate and preſſing Importance, unleſs ſuſpended in their Operation till his Aſſent ſhould be obtained; and when ſo ſuſpended, he has utterly neglected to attend to them.

He has refuſed to paſs other Laws for the Accommodation of large Diſtricts of People, unleſs thoſe People would relinquiſh the Right of Repreſentation in the Legiſlature, a Right ineſtimable to them, and formidable to Tyrants only.

He has called together Legiſlative Bodies at Places unuſual, uncomfortable, and diſtant from the Depoſitory of their public Records, for the ſole Purpoſe of fatiguing them into Compliance with his Meaſures.

He has diſſolved Repreſentative Houſes repeatedly, for oppoſing with manly Firmneſs his Invaſions on the Rights of the People.

He has refuſed for a long Time, after ſuch Diſſolutions, to cauſe others to be elected; whereby the Legiſlative Powers, incapable of Annihilation, have returned to the People at large for their exerciſe; the State remaining in the mean time expoſed to all the Dangers of Invaſion from without, and Convulſions within.

He has endeavoured to prevent the Population of theſe States; for that Purpoſe obſtructing the Laws for Naturalization of Foreigners; refuſing to paſs others to encourage their Migrations hither, and raiſing the Conditions of new Appropriations of Lands.

He has obſtructed the Adminiſtration of Juſtice, by refuſing his Aſſent to Laws for eſtabliſhing Judiciary Powers.

He has made Judges dependent on his Will alone, for the Tenure of their Offices, and the Amount and Payment of their Salaries.

He has erected a Multitude of new Offices, and ſent hither Swarms of Officers to harraſs our People, and eat out their Subſtance.

He has kept among us, in Times of Peace, Standing Armies, without the conſent of our Legiſlatures.

He has affected to render the Military independent of and ſuperior to the Civil Power.

He has combined with others to ſubject us to a Juriſdiction foreign to our Conſtitution, and unacknowledged by our Laws; giving his Aſſent to their Acts of pretended Legiſlation:

For quartering large Bodies of Armed Troops among us:

For protecting them, by a mock Trial, from Puniſhment for any Murders which they ſhould commit on the Inhabitants of theſe States:

For cutting off our Trade with all Parts of the World:

For impoſing Taxes on us without our Conſent:

For depriving us, in many Caſes, of the Benefits of Trial by Jury:

For tranſporting us beyond Seas to be tried for pretended Offences:

For aboliſhing the free Syſtem of Engliſh Laws in a neighbouring Province, eſtabliſhing therein an arbitrary Government, and enlarging its Boundaries, ſo as to render it at once an Example and fit Inſtrument for introducing the ſame abſolute Rule into theſe Colonies:

For taking away our Charters, aboliſhing our moſt valuable Laws, and altering fundamentally the Forms of our Governments:

For ſuſpending our own Legiſlatures, and declaring themſelves inveſted with Power to legiſlate for us in all Caſes whatſoever.

He has abdicated Government here, by declaring us out of his Protection and waging War againſt us.

He has plundered our Seas, ravaged our Coaſts, burnt our Towns, and deſtroyed the Lives of our People.

He is, at this Time, tranſporting large Armies of foreign Mercenaries to compleat the Works of Death, Deſolation, and Tyranny, already begun with circumſtances of Cruelty and Perfidy, ſcarcely paralleled in the moſt barbarous Ages, and totally unworthy the Head of a civilized Nation.

He has conſtrained our fellow Citizens taken Captive on the high Seas to bear Arms againſt their Country, to become the Executioners of their Friends and Brethren, or to fall themſelves by their Hands.

He has excited domeſtic Inſurrections amongſt us, and has endeavoured to bring on the Inhabitants of our Frontiers, the mercileſs Indian Savages, whoſe known Rule of Warfare, is an undiſtinguiſhed Deſtruction, of all Ages, Sexes and Conditions.

In every ſtage of theſe Oppreſſions we have Petitioned for Redreſs in the moſt humble Terms: Our repeated Petitions have been anſwered only by repeated Injury. A Prince, whoſe Character is thus marked by every act which may define a Tyrant, is unfit to be the Ruler of a free People.

Nor have we been wanting in Attentions to our Britiſh Brethren. We have warned them from Time to Time of Attempts by their Legiſlature to extend an unwarrantable Juriſdiction over us. We have reminded them of the Circumſtances of our Emigration and Settlement here. We have appealed to their native Juſtice and Magnanimity, and we have conjured them by the Ties of our common Kindred to diſavow theſe Uſurpations, which, would inevitably interrupt our Connections and Correſpondence. They too have been deaf to the Voice of Juſtice and of Conſanguinity. We muſt, therefore, acquieſce in the Neceſſity, which denounces our Separation, and hold them, as we hold the reſt of Mankind, Enemies in War, in Peace, Friends.

We, therefore, the Repreſentatives of the UNITED STATES OF AMERICA, in General Congress, Aſſembled, appealing to the Supreme Judge of the World for the Rectitude of our Intentions, do, in the Name, and by Authority of the good People of theſe Colonies, ſolemnly Publiſh and Declare, That theſe United Colonies are, and of Right ought to be, Free and Independent States; that they are abſolved from all Allegiance to the Britiſh Crown, and that all political Connection between them and the State of Great-Britain, is and ought to be totally diſſolved; and that as Free and Independent States, they have full Power to levy War, conclude Peace, contract Alliances, eſtabliſh Commerce, and to do all other Acts and Things which Independent States may of right do. And for the ſupport of this Declaration, with a firm Reliance on the Protection of divine Providence, we mutually pledge to each other our Lives, our Fortunes, and our ſacred Honor.

Signed by Order *and in* Behalf *of the* Congress,

JOHN HANCOCK, President.

Attest.
CHARLES THOMSON, Secretary.

Philadelphia: Printed by John Dunlap.

November and December, 1775,
and to July, 1776.

Sentiment of nationality

The course of events, after the popular leaders accepted the work of revolution, created a desire for independence and developed a sentiment of nationality. When the colonies had agreed to join in dissolving the connection with Great Britain, and had so instructed their representatives, they, in Congress assembled, voted that these colonies were free and independent States, and by the Declaration of Independence announced to the world that they had assumed a separate station among the powers of the earth; whereupon the people, in public meetings and by their general assemblies, ratified the Declaration, and pledged themselves to maintain it with their fortunes and their lives. Thus they decreed their existence as a nation.

King, Lords and Commons prepare to subdue America

"The king, in a speech from the throne (Oct. 26, 1775), declared that the war, on the part of the colonists, was 'manifestly carried on for the establishment of an American empire.' He stated, that, to put an end to the disorders in the colonies, he had increased the naval establishment and land forces, and was in treaty with foreign nations. He recommended the appointment of commissioners with large powers for the purpose of granting pardons to such of 'the unhappy and deluded multitude' as might be convinced of their error by the display of arms. The House of Lords, in their address in reply, heartily approved the decisive use of arms, yet could not sufficiently admire His Majesty's benevolent proposition relative to pardon. The House of Commons more than echoed the fierce words of the king in characterizing the colonial proceedings as the wicked pretences of ambitious and traitorous men, which had led unhappy fellow-subjects to set up the standard of rebellion; but they heard with gratitude 'the declaration of the father of his people' of his design to pardon.

"Important changes were made in the cabinet. Lord George Germain was appointed, in place of Lord Dartmouth, head of the American department.... In the picture of the times, these extreme measures do not stand out in connection with the progress of events in America, in the relation of proximate cause and effect, with the distinctness of prior measures of the ministry; yet

The above excerpts are from Richard Frothingham's "The Rise of the Republic", 1890

Americans informed of denunciations in England of their cause

the popular leaders could hardly have spared one of the terrible denunciations of King, Lords, and Commons, or the appointment of the violent Lord Germain. They were all needed, and did good service in the patriot cause, as accounts of them circulated in the newspapers. They found their way into the little towns in the forests beyond the Alleghanies, as well as into the flourishing municipalities along the Atlantic coast, - in which probably a far larger proportion of the people were taking an active part in politics than ever before, in any country, shared in the direction of public affairs. The key of their action was fidelity to the decisions of the General Congress. The work of this body may be summed up in a single sentence: while it accepted, after an American interpretation, the continuity of the body of English liberties, or of English constitutional law, it resisted the assimilation of American political life to the English model. In doing this, it said, 'Our cause is just'; and it was pronounced a Christian duty to defend it....

Decisions of the General Congress upheld

Independence from England urged -

1) To preserve American institutions

2) For expansion of American ideas over the continent

3) For spread of the Gospel "As the only escape from tyranny"

"While these scenes of war were occurring, and the highest hopes were followed by the keenest disappointments, the popular leaders of clear vision pressed independence as the next and only worthy step. The measure was urged as necessary to insure permanency to the civil and religious institutions of the colonies, - as essential to their material prosperity, in order to secure fair scope for the industrial energies of the land, - as vital to the expansion of American ideas over the continent, and to the creation of an opening for the spread of the Gospel, - as the only escape from tyranny, and the only guaranty of that government which is 'an ordinance of Heaven to restrain the usurpations of wicked men, to secure to all the enjoyment of their natural rights, and to promote the highest political interests and happiness of society.' It was urged that independence 'was the path of empire, glory, liberty, and peace,' and that labor in such a cause was labor on the side of Providence. 'The Almighty', said Chief Justice Drayton, of South Carolina, from the bench, 'created America to be independent of Great Britain: to refuse our labors in this divine work is to refuse to be a great, a free, a pious, and a happy people'....

"This sentiment was ministered to by the physical characteristics of the country: a vast, connected, and fertile land; the absence of impassable barriers between the several sections; a climate uniting the productions of the torrid and the temperate zones; majestic rivers inviting inland communication; an imperial line of coast, stimulating maritime enterprise. As the thoughtful reflected on the resources of this magnificent country, it seemed to them that

The above excerpts are from Richard Frothingham's "The Rise of the Republic", 1890

Colonists envision a country founded on "The Christian Idea of Man"

the Almighty had formed it for the abode of a people that should stand pre-eminent in the world. But their ideal of what should constitute a country was not simply hills and valleys, land and water, but spiritual things as well; and as they mused on the establishment upon a field like this of political liberty grounded in justice, - on the characteristics of the American race, - on the Christian idea of man that was moulding their institutions, - it seemed to them that human progress was about to receive a fresh impulse, 'as if the New World was to surpass the Old, and the glory of human nature was to receive the highest perfection near the setting sun.'

"Sentiment of nationality" welling up from the people

"In the inspiration of this thought of a glorious future, the popular leaders shaped and carried into effect measures having in view the founding of a republic. The ideal of the territory which the contemplated republic was to comprehend is seen in the common use of the term 'continental'; the ideal of the cause is seen in the common remark that it was the cause of human nature. By utterances and action in harmony with these views, the sentiment of nationality became the spring and passion of the popular party. To trace its development is to trace the steps of a free people, when, with minds exalted by such views, they assumed the dignity and responsibility of decreeing themselves a nation.

"A soldier writes: 'The whole series of divine dispensations, from the infant days of our fathers in America, are big with importance in her favor, and point to something great and good. If we look round the world, and view the nations with their various connections, interests, and dependencies, we shall see innumerable causes at work in favor of this growing country. Nature and Art seem to labor, and as it were travail, in birth to bring forth some glorious events that will astonish mankind and form a bright era in the annals of time.' - Independent Chronicle, Oct. 17, 1776.

Tories resist final separation from Great Britain

"It is not easy to select and compress into a small space such facts from the voluminous records of this period as will mark the stages of the growth of public opinion in favor of independence. The argument for it, viewed under the brilliant light of success, seems today to have been of commanding power; yet it was urged long before a majority would pronounce in its favor; and, even at the last, unanimity on it was far from having been obtained. A final separation from Great Britain was opposed by the Tories in solid phalanx, in the conviction that it was sure to be ruinous; and they were strong in talent, character, social and official influence, and numbers.

The above excerpts are from Richard Frothingham's "The Rise of the Republic", 1890

Some Whigs felt separation was premature

"A large party in the Whig ranks, in the fear that anarchy would result from a change, were in favor of preserving the connection with the mother country, and down to the last moment they urged that the door of reconciliation was still open; another portion had reached the conviction that a separation must take place, and were in favor of it, but held that the time for it had not come; and both classes comprehended characters held by that generation deservedly in respect, and by posterity in veneration.

New York and South lukewarm

"Then numbers, who took no decisive part in the struggle, were lukewarm; and this class are never to be overlooked in practical politics, for they are apt to veer to the side which they hope or expect will prove the strongest, and so turn the scale. Then there was the disposition, especially in New York and the Southern colonies, to trust time to bring about a redress of grievances.

Principles held to be republican in England - a travesty on true "Republicanism"

"It was much urged, also, that independence involved a landing in republicanism, as if to make this point clear were conclusive against the measure. Republican principles, since the Revolution, had been loaded with obloquy in England; and this feeling prevailed to no small extent in the colonies, particularly south of New England. It is scarcely just to state the position of a party in the language of its opponents; but a Whig appeal in favor of independence gives the gist of the matter with which the journals teemed, stating the points urged against it in these words: 'Intestine confusions, continual wars with each other, Republics, and Presbyterian governments compose the bugbear of the day; and the very name of them frightens people more than the whole force of Great Britain.'

Two ways of asserting independence

"As the popular leaders urged a dissolution of the bonds that connected the people with a monarchy, they sought not only to form local governments, but to establish a general government with a limited range of powers, to execute certain functions necessary to all, - or to form ties that would unite the people in a permanent political society, and combine the strength of the whole for the common defence. It was a grave question, whether the two objects of independence and a general government should be pressed at the same time. Some urged that, first, the colonies should abrogate royal authority, set up local governments, establish a constitution for the whole, form an alliance with France, and then they might safely venture to issue a declaration of independence. They held that the people should organize a general government before decreeing themselves a nation. Others, not less convinced of the necessity of a general government, bent their energies to the single work of bringing about an abrogation of royal authority

The above excerpts are from Richard Frothingham's "The Rise of the Republic", 1890

in the several colonies, and a joint declaration of independence, relying for success on the fact and the strength of union. They were in favor of decreeing themselves a nation, in the faith that a general government would follow in course.

"Among the latter was Samuel Adams....

Washington unfurls flag of United Colonies

"In the beginning of the memorable year seventeen hundred and seventy-six there was a public opinion in favor of independence in New England, and but little more than individual preferences for it in the Middle or Southern Colonies. On New Year's day Washington for the first time unfurled the Flag of the thirteen Stripes as the flag of the United Colonies. To array this flag, as the symbol of national power, against the far-famed banner of Saint George, involved great labor. It required time and patience to encourage the timid, to instruct the unenlightened, and above all, to surmount prejudice. So deeply seated was the affection for the mother country, that it required all the severe acts of war directed by an inexorable ministry and the fierce words from the throne to be made fully known throughout America, before the majority of the people could be persuaded to renounce their allegiance and assume the sovereignty.

Patience to instruct the unenlightened and prejudiced

Jefferson comments on Samuel Adams

"Jefferson says that Samuel Adams was constantly holding caucuses of distinguished men, in which the measures to be pursued were generally determined upon, and their several parts were assigned to the actors who afterwards appeared in them; but he does not give the dates of these consultations, or the names (with the exception of Richard Henry Lee,) of the persons who attended them, nor tell precisely what was done there. He ascribed great influence to Samuel Adams in promoting the Revolution. His labors in the cause had been for years so unremitting, that it may be justly said of him, 'His feet were ever in the stirrup, his lance ever in its rest.' A goodly band were not with him in urging the measure of independence. A contemporary happily remarks: 'For a nation to be born, it required all the mighty efforts of those bold, wise, and noble-minded statesmen who adorned this era in the annals of their country.'

Leaders for independence

"The popular leaders who are found earliest identified with independence are Samuel Adams, John Adams, Joseph Hawley, Elbridge Gerry, James Sullivan, and James Warren, of Massachusetts; Matthew Thornton of New Hampshire; Nathaniel Greene and Samuel Ward, of Rhode Island; Benjamin Rush and Benjamin Franklin, of Pennsylvania; Thomas McKean, of Delaware; Samuel

The above excerpts are from Richard Frothingham's "The Rise of the Republic", 1890

Rare public virtue attracted and held the confidence of the early American

Chase, of Maryland; Richard Henry Lee, George Wythe, Patrick Henry, Thomas Jefferson, and George Washington, of Virginia; Cornelius Harnett, of North Carolina; and Christopher Gadsden, of South Carolina. It is remarkable that the popular instinct kept so true to the cluster of Revolutionary statesmen. This remark is applicable not only to the band of patriots just enumerated, but to others also whose names are household words. Through the entire struggle, the people sought out, held fast to, and rallied around greatness and virtue, and made these qualities subserve the public good. No outpourings of obloquy, no thickening peril, shook this noble trust. No gusts of feeling from temporary reverses moved them to seek new guides; but as dangers multiplied, confidence strengthened. And so it was that out of rare public virtue grew our great republican government....

The Christian Idea

"The great question was now discussed at every fireside, and the favorite toast at every dinner-table was, 'May the independent principles of 'Common Sense' be confirmed throughout the United Colonies.'... It was said to a people trained under Christian influences, who habitually looked upward in every form of supplication, that the spirit which actuated the United Colonies 'was as much from God as the descent of the Holy Ghost on the day of Pentecost, and was introductory to something great and good to mankind.'

Unanimity not achieved

"The issue was of a nature to rouse passion, alarm wealth, and stir society to its depths. In each colony, the friends and opponents of independence, animated at times by intemperate as well as by judicious zeal, hurled against each other the usual weapons of partisan strife, poisoned by the hatred and revenge engendered by civil war. ...

"It happened that on the 15th of May a great popular movement also reached a decisive result. This bore directly on independence, demanded in November by a few, in January by only a small party, but in March by a public opinion becoming every day more importunate. This change was by no means unrepresented in Congress, which was paving the way to independence....

"While Congress was hesitating, 'A Lover of Order,' on the 9th of March, proposed through the newspapers that the constituents of each delegation should be invited to declare their sentiments on independence through their local organizations; remarking that in this manner the continent first declared their determination to resist by force the power of Great Britain, and in so important a question the Congress ought only to echo back the sentiments of the people, and their decision ought to determine the question....

The above excerpts are from Richard Frothingham's "The Rise of the Republic", 1890

"The following is the piece alluded to in the text. It is in the Boston newspapers of April 1. It is here copied from the Pennsylvania Evening Post of March 9, 1776:

Local assemblies should decide question of independence

"'Mr. Towne, - It is the opinion of many people among us that the Congress should not declare the colonies independent of Great Britain, without a previous recess to consult their constituents about that important question. But the complicated and increasing business of the Congress will not admit of such a recess. Would it not be proper, therefore, for their constituents to declare their sentiments upon that head as soon as possible? This may be done by the various committees and conventions on the continent. Their votes or resolves should determine the question in the Congress. It was in this manner the continent first declared their determination to resist by force the power of the British Parliament. The first Congress was nothing but the echo of committees and conventions. In the present important question concerning independence, the Congress should, as in the former case, only echo back the sentiments of the people. This can only be done through the medium of committees and conventions. The sooner, therefore, they are convened for that purpose the better.

A Lover of Order.'

Congress asks local assemblies to vote

"It corresponded with the work done; for, as no colony formed a local government until Congress recommended it to be done, so no delegation voted for a declaration of independence until authorized by its constituents.... Members of Congress soon after requested their Assemblies to express their sentiments on independence....

Confluence of the sentiment of independence

"The facts just stated may account for the movement respecting independence which, on the 15th of May, reached a result that gave a decisive turn to the course of events. The procedure in each colony is so important that it deserves to be given in full; but the narratives must necessarily be much abridged. They may, however, serve to show the source of the local streams, and how they came together, and formed a current wide, deep, and irresistible in its flow.

North Carolina and Rhode Island act on independence

"North Carolina was the first colony to act as a unit in favor of independence.... Rhode Island acted next on independence. Its people were satisfied with their charter. Under it they elected their rulers and made the laws. A portion, not inconsiderable in number, were adherents of the crown; and the measure of

The above excerpts are from Richard Frothingham's "The Rise of the Republic", 1890

independence had strong opponents.... Their venerable delegate in Congress, Stephen Hopkins, requested implicit instructions on this head....

Massachusetts votes for independence - British expelled from Boston

"Massachusetts was the next to act on independence. The popular party were in great exultation. The British army in March was driven from Boston, the government was in the hands of the people, and the Tories had emigrated or were powerless.... Virginia was profoundly agitated on the question of independence. The royal governor, Dunmore, had taken refuge with the British fleet. The House of Burgesses, summoned by him, held several sessions, and finally dissolved themselves. The political power resided in a convention consisting of delegates chosen by those qualified to elect Burgesses. The delegates were re-elected in pursuance of an ordinance of their own making.... On the 14th of May the convention went into a committee of the whole on the state of the colony, with Archibald Carey in the chair; when Colonel Nelson submitted a preamble and resolutions on independence, prepared by Pendleton.... The same paper also provided for a committee to form a plan of government for Virginia.... The convention agreed (June 12) upon the Famous Declaration of Rights declaring all men equally free and independent, all power vested in and derived from the people, and that government ought to be for the common benefit; also that all men are equally entitled to the free exercise of religion according to the dictates of conscience. It also complied with the recommendation of Congress, by forming a constitution and electing a governor and other officers. In this great procedure Virginia joined with North Carolina in confronting the instructions against independence of the Middle Colonies. Its action constitutes a brilliant link in the chain that marked the nation's birth.

Virginia - "Declaration of Rights"

"On the fifteenth day of May, only four of the colonies had acted definitely on the question of independence....

"The Virginia instructions were carried to Congress by their mover in the convention, Colonel Nelson. Three weeks elapsed before a motion on independence was submitted in this body....

Pennsylvania acts on independence in face of entrenched opposition

"Pennsylvania was fairly alive with the idea of independence. Nowhere had the question been more thoroughly discussed than in its press; and nowhere was the opposition to it more strongly intrenched, for it had on its side the proprietary government.... Personal preferences and political rivalries, however, gave way before the power of ideas.... On this well-prepared soil fell the Resolution of

The above excerpts are from Richard Frothingham's "The Rise of the Republic", 1890

the Fifteenth of May. The principle it embodied was accepted by the popular party as their rule of action, as they had accepted the Continental Association; and they determined that it should be respected as law throughout the province....

elaware
otes to
onfederate -
estriction
ecified

"In the three lower counties of New Castle, Kent, and Sussex, or Delaware, independence met with strong opposition. These counties were intimately connected with Pennsylvania, and shared largely its political feelings and agitations.... The Resolution of the Fifteenth of May brought on a crisis.... The popular party won a partial victory. The Assembly, on the 14th of June, authorized their delegates to concur with the other delegates 'in forming such further compacts between the United Colonies,' and 'adopting such other measures as shall be judged necessary' to promote the liberty of America, 'reserving to the people of this colony the sole and exclusive right of regulating the internal government and police of the same'....

New Jersey
conciliation
rty yields -
dependence
oted

"In New Jersey the struggle for independence was exciting and interesting. The opposing parties both in their elements and in their relation to the cause, were much like those of Pennsylvania. The Governor, William Franklin, continued to the last a zealous and dogged loyalist; and behind him was a strong party for reconciliation.... The Assembly yielded. It was soon prorogued, and did not reassemble. The political power was vested in a Provincial Congress; representing a constituency who had, in their municipalities, their party organizations, and their Assembly, agreed to abide by the decisions of Congress; and had approved of the Association.... The Provincial Congress voted (June 21) to form a government 'for regulating the internal police of the colony, pursuant to the recommendation' of Congress. On the next day a new set of delegates were chosen, who were empowered to join with the delegates of the other colonies in 'declaring the United Colonies independent of Great Britain,' and entering into a confederacy, 'always observing that, whatever plan of confederacy they entered into, the regulating the internal police of this province was to be reserved to the colony legislature.'

aryland
vote of
ounties
nctions
dependence

"In Maryland the party in favor of independence encountered peculiar obstacles. Under the proprietary rule the colony enjoyed a large measure of happiness and prosperity.... The political power was vested in a Convention which created the Council of Safety and provided for the common defence. This was, however, so much under the control of the proprietary party and timid Whigs that, on the 21st of May, it renewed its former instructions against independence; and, after considering the Resolution of Congress of the

The above excerpts are from Richard Frothingham's "The Rise of the Republic", 1890

Fifteenth of May, and providing for a suspension of the oaths of allegiance, it declared that it was not necessary to suppress every kind of authority under the crown, or to establish government on the power of the people. This action created the issue which stirred the neighboring colonies so profoundly, whether this decision or the recommendation of the United Colonies should stand. The popular leaders determined 'to take the sense of the people'.... Meetings were called in the counties, and the political sentiment embodied in their proceedings harmonized with that of the counties in Virginia and Pennsylvania, and of the towns in Massachusetts, in principle and object....

Maryland retains exclusive internal jurisdiction

"A convention assembled at Annapolis, on the 21st of June, in which were Chase, Carroll of Carrolton, Johnson, and Tilghman; and on the 28th it recalled the former instructions against independence, and authorized the delegates 'to concur with the delegates of the other colonies in declaring the United Colonies free and independent States,' and in forming a compact or confederation, 'provided the sole and exclusive right of regulating the internal government and police of this colony be reserved to the people thereof.' The result was hailed with the liveliest satisfaction by the popular leaders in Congress.

Georgia concurred - cause "not provincial but continental"

"In Georgia there was strong opposition to independence. The Provincial Congress chose a new set of delegates, and on the 5th of April authorized them to join in all measures which they might think calculated for the common good, - charging them 'always to keep in view the general utility, remembering that the great and righteous cause in which they were engaged was not provincial, but continental. It was circulated in the newspapers that the delegation were authorized to go to the full length of a separation from Great Britain.

South Carolina votes full concurrence

"In South Carolina independence was opposed by a large portion of the people. The new government, however, on the 23d of March, gave full authority to their delegates to agree to any measure judged necessary for the welfare of the colony or of America....

New York hesitant

"In New York there was great hesitancy in acting on the question of independence. The external danger was imminent; the internal strife, bitter. A party, which had in its ranks John Jay, Alexander Hamilton, Robert R. Livingston, and George Clinton, was certainly a power; but it had hard odds to contend against, and down to the date of the declaration it had failed to bring over a majority to decisive measures. The course of things here gave

The above excerpts are from Richard Frothingham's "The Rise of the Republic", 1890

New York requests advice from the Congress

the popular leaders in Congress great vexation. In vain did the New York delegates write letters soliciting instructions on the subject of independence. The Resolution of the Fifteenth of May elicited in the Provincial Congress - in which the political power resided - an elaborate report and, on the 31st of May, a measure designed to ascertain the sense of the electors on the propriety of instituting such government as Congress recommended. The final instruction to the delegates on independence was chilling.

Congress declines - deferring to "authority of the people"

"In reply to their pressing letter of the 8th of June, the Provincial Congress, on the 11th, advised them, that they were not authorized to vote for independence, that Congress declined to instruct them on that point, and that as measures had been taken to obtain the authority of the people to establish regular government, ' it would be imprudent to require the sentiments of the people relative to the question of independence, lest it should create division and have an unhappy influence on the other. ' However able and brilliant New York might have been in laying down the principles of the Revolution, it was the least unanimous in embodying them in the great measures of independence.

Connecticut and New Hampshire vote for Independence

"In New England the issues that stirred up the Middle Colonies were already virtually settled. The Governments were in the hands of a people who were longing for a declaration of independence. Only in Massachusetts, however, were the towns called upon to express their views; and the returns showed that a people could not be more united than this people were on the expediency of a declaration of independence. In Connecticut the king's name was disused in issuing writs and civil processes; the governor returned a cordial reply to the circular of Virginia on independence, expressing 'the most sensible satisfaction to see the ancient and patriotic Colony of Virginia had nobly advanced' to the point of instructing their delegates to propose independence; and the legislature, on the 14th of June, instructed their delegates to propose in Congress, 'to declare the United American Colonies free and independent States,' and to promote a permanent plan of union and confederation, - 'saving that the power for the regulation of the internal concerns and police of each colony' be left to the colonial legislature. The New-Hampshire legislature, on the 15th of June, instructed their delegates 'to join in declaring the Thirteen Colonies an independent State,... provided the regulation of their internal police be under the direction of their own assembly.'

"In the last days of June the agitation on the question of independence ceased in every colony except New York. Ten colonies -

The above excerpts are from Richard Frothingham's "The Rise of the Republic", 1890

12 Colonies subscribe to independence and confederation

North Carolina, Rhode Island, Massachusetts, Virginia, Pennsylvania, Delaware, New Jersey, Maryland, Connecticut, and New Hampshire - expressed their will in direct action upon it; while Georgia and South Carolina gave commissions to their delegates which covered the power to vote for it. Thus twelve of the United Colonies authorized their representatives to join in making a declaration of independence; and hence designated Congress to perform this high act of sovereignty.... The secret and providential influence which disposed the hearts and minds of the people to form a union, and to give the union the force of law, disposed them to go forward together and assume rank as a nation.

Each Colony held the right of self-government paramount

"All through this popular movement, the union is seen acting in obedience to the primal law of self-preservation, - clinging to life, and frowning on whatever tended to destroy life. Yet in all the enthusiasm roused by unfurling a national flag, and the prospect of attaining independence, there is manifested no desire for such consolidation as would weaken the old self-government. The intelligent grasp by the public mind of fundamentals in a republic is seen in the sagacious reservation by each colony of the right to regulate the internal police or to frame the local law. In this way the people, as they entered into the solemn covenant which recognized a common country, marked the outlines of the two spheres of political power - the two orders of trusts - which they intended to establish in a new American system, - local governments for the States, and a general government for the Union. Neither language nor acts could have been desired to show more conclusively that both political units - the State and the Nation - were designed to be paramount, each in its allotted sphere....

Two spheres - "The State and the Nation"

"The Declaration announced to the world the fact of The United States of America, and the justification of the fact. The existence of a new political sovereignty de facto among the nations is sufficient to establish it de jure. Sovereignty, as used in matters of international law, is classed as external and internal. To render external sovereignty perfect, it is necessary that the established powers should act; for it is by their recognition that a new power effects an entrance into the society of nations, and enjoys its advantages, - enters upon the rights to which nations are entitled, and the duties they are called upon reciprocally to fulfil. Hence the external sovereignty of the United States was imperfect until other nations recognized its independence. It was not so with its internal sovereignty. This was at once complete within the limits of its own territory, and in all action relating to its own citizens, - none the less complete for its not

The United States of America becomes a sovereign nation

The above excerpts are from Richard Frothingham's "The Rise of the Republic", 1890

American right of self-government free from a foreign influence

having been recognized by foreign powers. Nor were its people any the less a nation for their not having attained an adequate general government. They delegated the power to sever their relations with the monarchy, and to take steps to form a new government or confederation, and not only left the local law undisturbed, but stipulated that each community should retain full right over its domestic affairs; and this right was by the Declaration freed from the interference of a foreign power.

Allegiance of individual changed from monarchy

"The Declaration changed the allegiance of the individual from the monarchy to the new political unit of the United States. This power - in the language of Congress, in treaties, in official letters, in the thought of American statesmen, termed at once a nation - was in a state of war with Great Britain, and all persons residing in its jurisdiction were expected to govern themselves accordingly. The popular party accepted the declaration as though it were law; just as they accepted the Association and the Resolve on local government. It was the title-deed of the individual unit to his right in a common country. It was a test of loyalty. Whoever upheld it was counted as a friend; whoever spoke against it was an enemy; whoever took up arms against it was guilty of treason.

Principles of the Declaration of Independence

"The Declaration embodied the doctrine of the fundamental equality of the race, and thus clothed abstract truth with vitalizing power. Its mighty sentences aver as self-evident 'that all men are created equal: that they are endowed by their Creator with certain inalienable rights; that among these are life, liberty, and the pursuit of happiness; that to secure these rights governments are instituted among men, deriving their just powers from the consent of the governed; that whenever any form of government becomes destructive of these ends, it is the right of the people to alter or to abolish it and institute new government, laying its foundation on such principles and organizing its powers in such form, as shall to them seem most likely to effect their safety and happiness.'

Origin of American political institutions - "The Christian Idea of Man"

"This is the American theory, expressed 'in words the memory of which can never die.' It includes far more than it expresses; for by recognizing human equality and brotherhood, and the individual as the unit of society, it accepts the Christian idea of man as the basis of political institutions; and by proclaiming the right to alter them to meet the progress of society, it provided for the results of a tendency to look, not to the past, but to the future, for types of perfection that was brought into the world by Christianity. To maintain such a theory were fought the battles of the revolution. To build on it a worthy superstructure of government and law, was the work entered upon by heroes and sages, and bequeathed to posterity."

The above excerpts are from Richard Frothingham's "The Rise of the Republic" - 1890

Comment on Natural Rights of Colonists

Governor Hutchinson Dissolves Colonial Assembly

The meeting on Monday, the 2d of November, was at Faneuil Hall, and occupied nearly the entire day, - the inhabitants passing out and in during the proceedings. 'A very respectable number' was present throughout, and an increasing interest was shown. In the forenoon, Hutchinson's answer to the petition for a session of the Legislature was received. It briefly stated that the charter reserved to the Governor the full power from time to time to adjourn, prorogue, or dissolve the Assembly. In the exercise of that power, both as to time and place, he had always been governed by a regard to his Majesty's service and the interests of the Province. A compliance with the petition, he said, would be to yield to them the exercise of that part of the prerogative. There would be danger of encouraging the inhabitants of other towns in the Province to similar procedures, which the law had not made the business of a town meeting. This reply was read several times, and voted 'not satisfactory.' Its principles must have been received with mingled alarm and indignation, for they aimed a death blow at the immemorable right of the New England towns to discuss public affairs, upon which discussions depended the efficiency of their free elective representation.

Free Election Depends Upon Right of Public Assembly

"'I was aware,' said Mr. Adams, in a letter soon after, 'that his (the Governor's) answers would be in the same high tone in which we find them expressed; yet our requests have been so reasonable, that, in refusing to comply with them, he must have put himself in the wrong in the opinion of every honest and sensible man; the consequence of which will be that such measures as the people may determine upon to save themselves, if rational and manly, will be the more reconcilable even to cautious minds, and thus we may expect that unanimity which we wish for.'

Unreasonable Stand Taken by Governor Tends to Unite the People

"The meeting now numbering about three hundred, it was unanimously resolved as the opinion of the inhabitants, that 'they have ever had, and ought to have, a right to petition the King or his representative for a redress of such grievances as they feel, or for preventing of such as they have reason to apprehend, and to communicate their sentiments to other towns.'

Resolved: That the People's Grievances Shall be Heard

"It was now that Adams stood up and made his celebrated motion, which breathed life into the American Revolution, stamped with vitality all its subsequent measures, and arranged under the rules of perfect order and system what had, until then, been a series of inharmonious, desultory efforts, without concentration or method.

Samuel Adams Appears as Leader in Massachusetts

The above excerpts are from W. V. Wells' "Life of Samuel Adams" - 1865

Samuel Adams Proposes Establishment of a Committee of Correspondence

"'It was then moved by Mr. Samuel Adams, that a committee of correspondence be appointed, to consist of twenty-one persons, to state the rights of the Colonists and of this Province in particular, as men and Christians and as subjects; and to communicate and publish the same to the several towns and to the world as the sense of this town, with the infringements and violations thereof that have been, or from time to time may be, made.'

"It would seem, by the fragment of an account by a Loyalist writer, that the resolves were not adopted until night. He speaks of the vote, for sending the letter of correspondence, as having been passed about ten o'clock in the evening, and although the article in which this statement appeared contained erroneous assertions as to the number of persons present at the time, and was in that respect publicly contradicted by the selectmen, the fact of the night session is not denied. They also refer to the very respectable number who attended 'through the day' and to the 'three hundred or more,' who were present when the vote was taken, evidently at a late hour. That some debate succeeded Mr. Adams's motion is shown in this same statement of the selectmen, who speak of its having been 'twice read and amended.' It was carried at last by an almost unanimous vote. The system, however, was not launched upon its course without difficulty. Those who had questioned the wisdom of the scheme at first now failed to perceive its practicability or importance, and when the committee came to be appointed, it was found difficult to obtain members. Cushing, Hancock, and Phillips, three of the four Boston Representatives, pleaded private business and refused to serve; and Scollay and Austin, two of the selectmen, declined for a similar reason. The whole twenty-one, however, were raised; and James Otis, who had lately returned from Nantasket, whither he had been carried, was named chairman, as a tribute to his former services.

Selectmen Compose Committee of Correspondence

Difficulties Overcome

Attacks on Committee by Royal Governor

"Hutchinson described the Committee as in part composed of 'deacons,' 'atheists,' and 'black-hearted fellows, whom one would not choose to meet in the dark.' 'You may judge of this Committee,' said he, 'by their chairman, who is but just now discharged from his guardian, and is still once in a few days as mad as ever, - the effect of strong drink.' It has been said of Hutchinson, that 'he was considerate towards the orphan and the widow, and he heard private suits with unblemished integrity.' However much the praise may have been deserved, the unmasking of his true disposition, as betrayed in his private correspondence, reveals a malignity of heart and a cowardly desire to stab his enemies in

The above excerpts are from W. V. Wells' "Life of Samuel Adams" - 1865

the dark, which renders his character odious. The Committee was composed, for the most part, of plain democratic citizens, in moderate circumstances of life, and actuated beyond question by the loftiest patriotism. Their labors were to be arduous, without remuneration, and with no hope of reward beyond a sense of duty performed, and an approving conscience. But his Excellency could see no merit, except in an abject submission to a tyranny, which he, above all others, ought to have discountenanced, as a native of the Province, and one who had received innumerable marks of favor from his fellow-citizens.

System of Correspondence Reaches all the People of the Province

"The Committee held their first meeting at the Representatives Chamber on the 3d of November, and organized by electing William Cooper as their clerk, who was ordered to be present at all their meetings and to keep a fair record of their proceedings. How faithfully the service was rendered, is shown by the journals. They are entire and in perfect order, having passed into the family of Samuel Adams at the commencement of the war, and remained there for more than sixty years. The Loyalists had good reason to watch the growth of this novel power with deep misgivings of its effects. The comprehensiveness of the system, and the perfect harmony of its working, was soon apparent. Springing from the people, it was a compact little legislature of itself, entirely distinct from any other power, and its influence reached every part of the Province. The first act, after organizing, was to pass a vote: -

"'That every member be desired to declare to the chairman that he holds himself bound in honor not to divulge or make known any part of the conversation of this Committee at their meetings to any person whatsoever, excepting what the Committee shall judge proper to lay before the town, or to make known in their capacity of a committee.'

Intent of Committee

Method of Committee

"Mr. Adams's motion, creating the Committee, had specified three distinct duties to be performed, - to draw up a statement of the rights of the Colonists as men, as Christians, and as subjects; a declaration of the infringement and violation of those rights; and a letter to be sent to the several towns in the Province and to the world as the sense of the town. The drafting of the first was assigned to Samuel Adams, the second to Joseph Warren, and the last to Benjamin Church. In the mean time, while these papers were preparing, Adams wrote to other towns, urging their leading men to aid in forming the Confederation.

The above excerpts are from W. V. Wells' "Life of Samuel Adams" - 1865

"'Our timid sort of people, said he to Elbridge Gerry, 'are disconcerted when they are positively told that the sentiments of the country are different from those of the city. Therefore a free communication with each town will serve to ascertain this matter; and when once it appears beyond contradiction that we are united in sentiments, there will be a confidence in each other, and a plan of opposition will be easily formed and executed with spirit.... I earnestly wish that the inhabitants of Marblehead and other towns would severally meet, and if they see cause, among other measures, second this town, and appoint a committee to be ready to communicate with ours. This would at once discover a union of sentiments thus far, and have its influence on other towns.'

Emergence of a National Sentiment

Other Towns Invited into "Union of Sentiments"

"Gerry replied, with the assurance that the steps taken by the metropolis would succeed; but, said he, 'should they fail, the merit of those worthies who oppose the strides of tyranny will not be diminished; neither would their being overpowered by numbers alter the heroism of their conduct.' Adams again wrote, informing Gerry of the progress of the flame in Roxbury, Cambridge, and Plymouth.

"'May God grant,' he said, 'that the love of liberty, and a zeal to support it, may enkindle in every town. If our enemies should see the flame bursting in different parts of the country, and distant from each other, it might discourage their attempts to damp and quench it. I am well assured they are alarmed at the measure now taking, being greatly apprehensive of the same consequences from it which our good friend at Plymouth hopes and expects. This should animate us in carrying it into execution. I beg you would exert your utmost influence in your neighboring towns and elsewhere.'

"time to be rid of both tyrants and tyranny."

-Samuel Adams

"The good friend at Plymouth was James Warren, who had written to Samuel Adams that he believed there would be no difficulty in getting a meeting there, and seconding Boston. Adams replied to Warren that the time for 'complaining' had passed, and that it was 'more than time to be rid of both tyrants and tyranny.'

"When the reports of the several committees were prepared, they were presented on the 20th of November to a town meeting at Faneuil Hall by James Otis, who now, as chairman, made his final appearance in public, - the wreck of one of the most brilliant men of genius that America has produced, but yet sustained by the care and sympathy of some friends and the tender reverence of the people, whose cause he had ever ardently and sincerely supported.

The above excerpts are from W. V. Wells' "Life of Samuel Adams" - 1865

"'Samuel Adams,' says Hutchinson, writing to a friend, 'had prepared a long report, but he let Otis appear in it'; and again, in another letter: 'the Grand Incendiary of the Province prepared a long report for a committee appointed by the town, in which, after many principles inferring independence were laid down, many resolves followed, all of them tending to sedition and mutiny, and some of them expressly denying Parliamentary authority.' The report created a powerful sensation, both in America and in England, where it was for some time attributed to Franklin, by whom it was republished. It is divided into the three subjects specified in the original motion. The first, in three subdivisions, considering the rights of the Colonists as men, as Christians, and as subjects, was from the pen of Samuel Adams; his original draft, together with the preparatory rough notes or headings, being in perfect preservation. It is important, not only as a platform upon which were afterwards built many of the celebrated state papers of the Revolution, but as the first fruits of the Committee of Correspondence... There certainly is a similarity between the 'Rights of the Colonists' in 1772, and the 'Declaration of Rights' in 1774, and between them both and the Declaration of Independence; but as all are founded on the time-honored principles of Locke, Hooker, Sydney, and Harrington, some of whom are duly quoted by Samuel Adams in his treatise, the disputes as to the originality are needless..."

Samuel Adams the Leader

Authorship

The above excerpts are from W. V. Wells' "Life of Samuel Adams" - 1865

SAMUEL ADAMS READ JOHN LOCKE'S ESSAYS

MR. LOCKE, in his treatise on government, discovers the weakness of this position, that every man is born a subject to his prince, and therefore is under the perpetual tie of subjection and allegiance; and he shows that express consent alone makes any one a member of any commonwealth. He holds that submission to the laws of any country, and living quietly and enjoying privileges and protection under them, does not make a man a member of that society or a perpetual subject of that commonwealth, any more than it would make a man subject to another in whose family he found it convenient to abide for some time, though, while he continued under it, he was obliged to comply with the laws, and submit to the government he found there. Every man was born naturally free; nothing can make a man a subject of any commonwealth but his actually entering into it by positive engagement and express promise and compact..."

Samuel Adams
Boston Gazette, Oct. 28, 1771

Mr. SAMUEL ADAMS.

LIBERTY: NOT A STATE OF LICENCE

"To understand political Power, right, and derive it from its Original, we must consider, what State all Men are naturally in, and that is, a State of perfect Freedom to order their Actions, and dispose of their Possessions, and Persons as they think fit, within the bounds of the Law of Nature, ... But though this be a State of Liberty, yet it is not a State of Licence, ... The State of Nature has a Law of Nature to govern it, ... And Reason, which is that Law, teaches all Mankind, ... that being all equal and independent, no one ought to harm another in his Life, Health, Liberty, or Possessions. ..."

-John Locke, "Of the State of Nature" from "Of Civil-Government"

SAMUEL ADAMS WRITES ON LIBERTY: Year 1750 - Age 28

IN the state of nature, every man has a right to think and act according to the dictates of his own mind, which, in that state, are subject to no other control and can be commanded by no other power than the laws and ordinances of the great Creator of all things. The perfection of liberty therefore, in a state of nature, is for every man to be free from any external force, and to perform such actions as in his own mind and conscience he judges to be rightest; which liberty no man can truly possess whose mind is enthralled by irregular and inordinate passions; since it is no great privilege to be free from external violence if the dictates of the mind are controlled by a force within, which exerts itself above reason. This is liberty in a state of nature, which, as no man ought to be abridged of, so no man has a right to give up, or even part with any portion of it, but in order to secure the rest and place it upon a more solid foundation; it being equally with our lives the gift of the same bounteous Author of all things...we must distinguish and consider liberty as it respects the whole body and as it respects each individual. As it respects the whole body, it is then enjoyed when neither legislative nor executive powers (by which I mean those men with whom are intrusted the power of making laws and of executing them) are disturbed by any internal passion or hindered by any external force from making the wisest laws and executing them in the best manner; when the safety, the security, and the happiness of all is the real care and steady pursuit of those whose business it is to care for and pursue it; in one short word, where no laws are carried through humor or prejudice, nor controlled in their proper execution by lust of power in the great, nor wanton licentiousness in the vulgar. As it respects individuals, a man is then free when he freely enjoys the security of the laws and rights to which he is born; when he is hindered by no violence from claiming those rights and enjoying that security, but may at any time demand the protection of the laws under which he lives...He therefore is the truest friend to the liberty of his country who tries most to promote its virtue, and who, so far as his power and influence extend, will not suffer a man to be chosen into any office of power and trust who is not a wise and virtuous man. We must not conclude merely upon a man's haranguing upon liberty, and using the charming sound, that he is fit to be trusted with the liberties of his country...The sum of all is, if we would most truly enjoy this gift of Heaven, let us become a virtuous people..."

The above excerpts are from W. V. Wells' "Life of Samuel Adams" - 1865

SAMUEL ADAMS

"Rights Of The Colonists"

November, 1772

"Rights of the Colonists as Men

Life Liberty Property

Right of self-government

The social compact

Freedom of conscience

AMONG the natural rights of the Colonists are these: First, a right to life; Secondly, to liberty; Thirdly, to property; together with the right to support and defend them in the best manner they can. These are evident branches of, rather than deductions from, the duty of self-preservation, commonly called the first law of nature. All men have a right to remain in a state of nature as long as they please; and in case of intolerable oppression, civil or religious, to leave the society they belong to, and enter into another. When men enter into society, it is by voluntary consent; and they have a right to demand and insist upon the performance of such conditions and previous limitations as form an equitable original compact. Every natural right not expressly given up, or, from the nature of a social compact, necessarily ceded, remains. All positive and civil laws should conform, as far as possible, to the law of natural reason and equity. As neither reason requires nor religion permits the contrary, every man living in or out of a state of civil society has a right peaceably and quietly to worship God according to the dictates of his conscience.

Christian toleration in relation to "Subversive of society"

"'Just and true liberty, equal and impartial liberty', in matters spiritual and temporal, is a thing that all men are clearly entitled to by the eternal and immutable laws of God and nature, as well as by the law of nations and all well-grounded municipal laws, which must have their foundation in the former. In regard to religion, mutual toleration in the different professions thereof is what all good and candid minds in all ages have ever practised and, both by precept and example, inculcated on mankind. And it is now generally agreed among Christians that this spirit of toleration, in the fullest extent consistent with the being of civil society, is the chief characteristical mark of the true Church*. Insomuch that Mr. Locke has asserted and proved, beyond the possibility of contradiction on any solid ground, that such toleration ought to be extended to all whose doctrines are not subversive of society.

*See Locke's "Letters of Toleration"

The above excerpts are from W. V. Wells' "Life of Samuel Adams" - 1865

"A government within a government"

"The only sects which he thinks ought to be, and which by all wise laws are excluded from such toleration, are those who teach doctrines subversive of the civil government under which they live. The Roman Catholics or Papists are excluded by reason of such doctrines as these, that princes excommunicated may be deposed, and those that they call heretics may be destroyed without mercy; besides their recognizing the Pope in so absolute a manner, in subversion of government, by introducing, as far as possible into the states under whose protection they enjoy life, liberty, and property, that solecism in politics imperium in imperio,* leading directly to the worst anarchy and confusion, civil discord, war, and bloodshed.

"The natural liberty of man, by entering into society, is abridged or restrained, so far only as is necessary for the great end of society, the best good of the whole.

Original sovereignty of Individual never invalidated

"In the state of nature every man is, under God, judge and sole judge of his own rights and of the injuries done him. By entering into society he agrees to an arbiter or indifferent judge between him and his neighbors; but he no more renounces his original right than by taking a cause out of the ordinary course of law, and leaving the decision to referees or indifferent arbitrators. In the last case, he must pay the referees for time and trouble. He should also be willing to pay his just quota for the support of government, the law, and the constitution; the end of which is to furnish indifferent and impartial judges in all cases that may happen, whether civil, ecclesiastical, marine, or military.

"The natural liberty of man is to be free from any superior power on earth, and not to be under the will or legislative authority of man, but only to have the law of nature for his rule.**

"In the state of nature men may, as the patriarchs did, employ hired servants for the defence of their lives, liberties, and property; and they should pay them reasonable wages. Government was instituted for the purposes of common defence, and those who hold the reins of government have an equitable, natural right to an honorable support from the same principle that 'the laborer is worthy of his hire.' But then the same community which they serve ought to be the assessors of their pay. Governors have no right to seek and take what they please; by this, instead of being content with the station assigned them, that of honorable servants of the society, they would soon become absolute masters, despots, and tyrants. Hence, as a private man has a right to say what wages he will give in his private affairs, so has a community to

*A government within a government
** See Locke on government

The above excerpts are from W. V. Wells' "Life of Samuel Adams" - 1865

determine what they will give and grant of their substance for the administration of public affairs. And, in both cases, more are ready to offer their service at the proposed and stipulated price than are able and willing to perform their duty.

Liberty is a responsibility

"In short, it is the greatest absurdity to suppose it in the power of one, or any number of men, at the entering into society, to renounce their essential natural rights, or the means of preserving those rights; when the grand end of civil government, from the very nature of its institution, is for the support, protection, and defence of those very rights; the principal of which, as is before observed, are Life, Liberty, and Property. If men, through fear, fraud, or mistake, should in terms renounce or give up any essential natural right, the eternal law of reason and the grand end of society would absolutely vacate such renunciation. The right to freedom being the gift of God Almighty, it is not in the power of man to alienate this gift and voluntarily become a slave."

Man should not "voluntarily become a slave"

"Thus the Law of Nature stands as an Eternal Rule to all Men, Legislators as well as others. The Rules that they make for other Men's Actions, must, as well as their own, and other Men's Actions, be conformable to the Law of Nature, i.e. to the Will of God, of which that is a Declaration, and the fundamental Law of Nature being the preservation of Mankind, no Human Sanction can be good, or valid against it." Locke "Of Civil Government", Page 94

"The Rights of the Colonists as Christians

These may be best understood by reading and carefully studying the institutes of the great Law Giver and Head of the Christian Church, which are to be found clearly written and promulgated in the New Testament.

Magna Charta

"By the act of the British Parliament, commonly called the Toleration Act, every subject in England, except Papists, &c., was restored to, and re-established in, his natural right to worship God according to the dictates of his own conscience. And, by the charter of this Province, it is granted, ordained, and established (that is, declared as an original right) that there shall be liberty of conscience allowed in the worship of God to all Christians, except Papists, inhabiting, or which shall inhabit or be resident within, such Province or Territory. Magna Charta itself is in substance but a constrained declaration or proclamation and promulgation in the name of King, Lords, and Commons, of the sense the latter had of their original, inherent, indefeasible natural rights,* as also those of free citizens equally perdurable with the other. That great author, that great jurist, and even

Original inherent natural rights

*See Lord Coke's Inst., Blackstone's Commentaries, The Bill of Rights and the Acts of Settlement

The above excerpts are from W. V. Wells' "Life of Samuel Adams" - 1865

that court writer, Mr. Justice Blackstone, holds that this recognition was justly obtained of King John, sword in hand. And peradventure it must be one day, sword in hand, again rescued and preserved from total destruction and oblivion."

"The great end of Mens entring into Society, being the Enjoyment of their Properties in Peace and Safety, and the great instrument and means of that being the Laws establish'd in that Society; the first and fundamental positive Law of all Commonwealths, is the establishing of the Legislative Power; as the first and fundamental natural Law, which is to govern even the Legislative it self, is the preservation of the Society, and (as far as will consist with the publick good) of every person in it." See Locke "Of Civil Government", Page 93

"The Rights of the Colonists as Subjects

A body politic

A commonwealth or state is a body politic, or civil society of men, united together to promote their mutual safety and prosperity by means of their union.*

"The absolute rights of Englishmen and all freemen, in or out of civil society, are principally personal security, personal liberty, and private property.

"All persons born in the British American Colonies are, by the laws of God and nature and by the common law of England, exclusive of all charters from the Crown, well entitled, and by acts of the British Parliament are declared to be entitled to all the natural, essential, inherent, and inseparable rights, liberties, and privileges of subjects born in Great Britain or within the realm. Among those rights are the following, which no man, or body of men, consistently with their own rights as men and citizens, or members of society, can for themselves give up or take away from others.

Concerning legislative power

"First, 'The first fundamental, positive law of all commonwealths or states is the establishing the legislative power. As the first fundamental natural law, also, which is to govern even the legislative power itself, is the preservation of the society.' **

Legislative power has limit

"Secondly, The Legislative has no right to absolute, arbitrary power over the lives and fortunes of the people; nor can mortals assume a prerogative not only too high for men, but for angels, and therefore reserved for the exercise of the Deity alone.

"The Legislative cannot justly assume to itself a power to rule by extempore arbitrary decrees; but it is bound to see that justice

* See Locke and Vattel.
** Locke on government

The above excerpts are from W. V. Wells' "Life of Samuel Adams" - 1865

Known laws and independent judges

is dispensed, and that the rights of the subjects be decided by promulgated, standing, and known laws, and authorized 'independent judges'; that is, independent, as far as possible, of Prince and people. 'There should be one rule of justice for rich and poor, for the favorite at court, and the countryman at the plough.' *

Individual consent required

"Thirdly, The supreme power cannot justly take from any man any part of his property, without his consent in person or by his representative.

"These are some of the first principles of natural law and justice, and the great barriers of all free states and of the British Constitution in particular. It is utterly irreconcilable to these principles and to many other fundamental maxims of the common law, common sense, and reason, that a British House of Commons should have a right at pleasure to give and grant the property of the Colonists. (That the Colonists are well entitled to all the essential rights, liberties, and privileges of men and freemen born in Britain is manifest not only from the Colony charters in general, but acts of the British Parliament.) The statute of the 13th of Geo. 2, c. 7, naturalizes even foreigners after seven years' residence. The words of the Massachusetts charter are these: 'And further, our will and pleasure is, and we do hereby for us, our heirs, and successors, grant, establish, and ordain, that all and every of the subjects of us, our heirs, and successors, which shall go to, and inhabit within our said Province or Territory, and every of their children, which shall happen to be born there or on the seas in going thither or returning from thence, shall have and enjoy all liberties and immunities of free and natural subjects within any of the dominions of us, our heirs, and successors, to all intents, constructions, and purposes whatsoever, as if they and every one of them were born within this our realm of England.'

British Parliament's right of seizure challenged

"What liberty can there be where property is taken away without consent?"

"Now what liberty can there be where property is taken away without consent? Can it be said with any color of truth and justice, that this continent of three thousand miles in length, and of a breadth as yet unexplored, in which, however, it is supposed there are five millions of people, has the least voice, vote, or influence in the British Parliament? Have they all together any more weight or power to return a single member to that House of Commons who have not inadvertently, but deliberately, assumed a power to dispose of their lives, liberties, and properties, than to choose an Emperor of China? Had the Colonists a right to return members to the British Parliament, it would only be hurtful; as, from their local situation and circumstances, it is impossible they should ever

* Locke

The above excerpts are from W. V. Well's "Life of Samuel Adams" - 1865

Demand for local self-government

be truly and properly represented there. The inhabitants of this country, in all probability, in a few years, will be more numerous than those of Great Britain and Ireland together; yet it is absurdly expected by the promoters of the present measures that these, with their posterity to all generations, should be easy, while their property shall be disposed of by a House of Commons at three thousand miles' distance from them, and who cannot be supposed to have the least care or concern for their real interest; who have not only no natural care for their interest, but must be in effect bribed against it, as every burden they lay on the Colonists is so much saved or gained to themselves. Hitherto, many of the Colonists have been free from quit rents; but if the breath of a British House of Commons can originate an act for taking away all our money, our lands will go next, or be subject to rack rents from haughty and relentless landlords, who will ride at ease, while we are trodden in the dirt. The Colonists have been branded with the odious names of traitors and rebels only for complaining of their grievances. How long such treatment will or ought to be borne, is submitted."

Is complaining of grievances traitorous?

"Here is embodied the whole philosophy of human rights, condensed from the doctrines of all time, and applied to the immediate circumstances of America. Upon this paper was based all that was written or spoken on human liberty in the Congress which declared independence; and the immortal instrument itself is, in many features, but a repetition of the principles here enunciated, and of Joseph Warren's list of grievances, which followed the Rights of the Colonists in the report...."

The above excerpts are from W. V. Wells' "Life of Samuel Adams" - 1865

Reading of The Declaration of Independence

APPENDICES

THE AMERICAN FLAG

"Thou hast given a banner to them that fear thee, that it may be displayed because of the truth". - Psalm 60:4

As at the early dawn the stars shine forth even while it grows light, and then, as the sun advances, that light breaks into banks and streaming lines of color, the glowing red and intense white striving together and ribbing the horizon with bars effulgent. So on the American flag, stars and beams of many-colored light shine out together. And where this flag comes, and men behold it, they see in its sacred emblazonry no ramping lions and no fierce eagle, no embattled castles or insignia of imperial authority: they see symbols of light. It is the banner of dawn. It means Liberty; and the galley slave, the poor oppressed conscript, the downtrodden creature of foreign despotism, sees in the American flag that very promise and prediction of God: 'The people which sat in darkness saw a great light; and to them which sat in the region and shadow of death light is sprung up'. In 1777, within a few days of one year after the Declaration of Independence, the Congress of the Colonies in the Confederated States assembled and ordained this glorious national flag which we now hold and defend, and advanced it full high before God and all men as the flag of liberty. It was no holiday flag gorgeously emblazoned for gayety or vanity. It was a solemn national signal. When that banner first unrolled to the sun, it was the symbol of all those holy truths and purposes which brought together the Colonial American Congress...Our Flag carries American ideas, American history, and American feelings. Beginning with the Colonies, and coming down to our time, in its sacred heraldry, in its glorious insignia, it has gathered and stored chiefly this supreme idea: Divine right of liberty in man. Every color means liberty; every thread means liberty; every form of star and beam or stripe of light means liberty: not lawlessness, not license; but organized institutional liberty, - liberty through law, and laws for liberty. It is not a painted rag. It is a whole national history. It is the Constitution. It is the government. It is the free people that stand in the government of the Constitution".

- Henry Ward Beecher, 1861

PRINCIPLE OF CHRISTIANITY AND GOVERNMENT

"Religion in America takes no direct part in the government of society, but it must nevertheless be regarded as the foremost of the political institutions of that country; for if it does not impart a taste for freedom, it facilitates the use of free institutions. Indeed, it is in this same point of view that the inhabitants of the United States themselves look upon religious belief ... I am certain that they hold it to be indispensable to the maintenance of republican institutions. This opinion is not peculiar to a class of citizens or to a party, but it belongs to the whole of the nation ... " -De Tocqueville "Democracy in America"

"Political Sermons of the Period of 1776"

Preface to "The Pulpit of the American Revolution" by J. Wingate Thornton

This collection of Sermons presents examples of the politico-theological phase of the conflict for American Independence, - a phase not peculiar to that period... There is a natural and just union of religious and civil counsels, - not that external alliance of the crosier and sword called 'Church and State,' - but the philosophical and deeper union which recognizes God as Supreme Ruler, and which is illustrated in this volume of occasional Discourses and 'Election Sermons,' - a title equivalent, in the right intent of the term, to 'political preaching.' There is also a historical connection, which is to be found rather in the general current of history than in particular instances. In this we may trace the principle, or vital cord, which runs through our own separate annals since our fathers came to the New World, and also marks the progress of liberty and individual rights in England. 'New England has the proud distinction of tracing her origin to causes purely moral and intellectual, - a fact which fixes the character of her founders and planters as elevated and refined, - not the destroyers of cities, provinces, and empires, but the founders of civilization in America'... 'As near the law of God as they can' be, was the instruction of the General Court to their committee of laity and ministry, appointed to frame laws for the Commonwealth. Their first written code, under the charter of 1629, was drawn by a minister.... Thus the church polity of New England begat like principles in the state. The pew and the pulpit had been educated to self-government. They were accustomed 'to consider.' The highest glory of the American Revolution, said John Quincy Adams, was this: it connected, in one indissoluble bond, the principles of civil government with the principles of Christianity....

"The religious character and views of the founders of New England also appear in bold relief in the foundation of the venerable seat of learning at Cambridge. 'Christo et Ecclesle' heads the ancient seal of Harvard College, and the church was the colony. On the long roll of the benefactors of Harvard, the name of Hollis must ever stand preeminent in the regard of the whole country. In the

The above excerpts are from J. Wingate Thornton's "The Pulpit of the American Revolution" - 1860

year 1766, Thomas Hollis wrote to the Rev. Dr. Mayhew, 'More books, especially on government, are going for New England. Should those go safe, it is hoped that no principal books on that first subject will be wanting in Harvard College, from the days of Moses to these times. Men of New England, brethren, use them for yourselves, and for others; and God bless you!' And again: 'I confess to bear propensity, affection, towards the people of North America, those of Massachusetts and Boston in particular, believing them to be a good and brave people. Long may they continue such! and the spirit of luxury, now consuming us to the very marrow here at home, kept out from them! One likeliest means to that end will be, to watch well over their youth, by bestowing on them a reasonable, manly education; and selecting thereto the wisest, ablest, most accomplished of men that art or wealth can obtain; for nations rise and fall by individuals, not numbers, as I think all history proveth. With ideas of this kind have I worked for the public library at Cambridge, in New England.'...

"' Doubtless at the favored Seminary her sons drank deeply of the writings of Milton, Harrington, Sydney, Ludlow, Marvell, and Locke. These were there, by Mr. Hollis's exertions, political text-books. And the eminent men of that day were -

'By antient learning to the enlightened love
Of antient freedom warmed '...

"In Dr. Franklin's library were Locke, Hoadley, Sydney, Montesquieu, Priestley, Milton, Price, Gordon's Tacitus; and in a picture of John Hancock, published in 1780, are introduced portraits of Hampden, Cromwell, and Sydney. There are extant American reprints of these authors, or of portions of their works, issued prior to and during the Revolution, in a cheap form, for popular circulation, addressing, not passion, but reason, diffusing sound principles, and begetting right feeling. There could hardly be found a more impressive, though silent, proof of the exalted nature of the contest on the part of the Americans, than a complete collection of their publications of that period....

"Thus it is manifest, in the spirit of our history, in our annals, and by the general voice of the fathers of the republic, that, in a very great degree, -

"To the Pulpit, the PURITAN PULPIT, we owe the moral force which won our independence.

Boston, October, 1860." J. W. T.

The above excerpts are from J. Wingate Thornton's "The Pulpit of the American Revolution" - 1860

Thornton's biographical sketch of Mayhew

"(Dr. Mayhew was born, of an honorable family, at Martha's Vineyard, on the 8th of October, 1720. On the 17th of June, 1747, three years after his graduation at Harvard College with great reputation, he was ordained pastor of the West Church in Boston, of which the venerable Dr. Lowell is now pastor. The charge on the occasion came from the lips of his father, the Rev. Experience Mayhew, the distinguished missionary to the Indians. In his sermon on the repeal of the Stamp Act, 1766, there is this passage of autobiography: 'Having been initiated in youth in the doctrines of civil liberty, as they were taught by such men as Plato, Demosthenes, Cicero, and other renowned persons, among the ancients; and such as Sydney and Milton, Locke and Hoadley, among the moderns, I liked them; they seemed rational. And having learnt from the holy Scriptures that wise, brave, and virtuous men were always friends to liberty, - that God gave the Israelites a king in his anger, because they had not sense and virtue enough to like a free commonwealth, - and that where 'the Spirit of the Lord is, there is liberty', - this made me conclude that freedom was a great blessing'...)

Mayhew's preface to his discourse

"The ensuing Discourse is the last of three upon the same subject, with some little alterations and additions. It is hoped that but few will think the subject of it an improper one to be discoursed on in the pulpit, under a notion that this is preaching politics, instead of Christ. However, to remove all prejudices of this sort, I beg it may be remembered that 'all Scripture is profitable for doctrine, for reproof, for correction, for instruction in righteousness.' Why, then, should not those parts of Scripture which relate to civil government be examined and explained from the desk, as well as others?...Civil tyranny is usually small in its beginning, like 'the drop of a bucket,' till at length, like a mighty torrent, or the raging waves of the sea, it bears down all before it, and deluges whole countries and empires.... "

Title of discourse

"A Discourse Concerning Unlimited Submission
and Non-Resistance to the Higher Powers:

"The Substance of which was delivered in a Sermon preached in the West Meeting-House in Boston the Lord's-Day after the 30th of January, 1749/50.

"Published at the Request of the Hearers. By JONATHAN MAYHEW, A.M. Pastor of the West Church in Boston.

The above excerpts are from J. Wingate Thornton's "The Pulpit of the American Revolution" - 1860

Mayhew's discourse

It is evident that the affairs of civil government may properly fall under a moral and religious consideration, at least so far forth as it relates to the general nature and end of magistracy, and to the grounds and extent of that submission which persons of a private character ought to yield to those who are vested with authority. This must be allowed by all who acknowledge the divine original of Christianity. For, although there be a sense, and a very plain and important sense, in which Christ's kingdom is not of this world, his inspired apostles have, nevertheless, laid down some general principles concerning the office of civil rulers, and the duty of subjects, together with the reason and obligation of that duty. And from hence it follows, that it is proper for all who acknowledge the authority of Jesus Christ, and the inspiration of his apostles, to endeavor to understand what is in fact the doctrine which they have delivered concerning this matter. It is the duty of Christian magistrates to inform themselves what it is which their religion teaches concerning the nature and design of their office. And it is equally the duty of all Christian people to inform themselves what it is which their religion teaches concerning that subjection which they owe to the higher powers...."

"....On the 17th of October, 1777, at Saratoga, General Burgoyne surrendered his sword to General Gates....

Remarks by Thornton

"The glad news from Saratoga was like the noonday sun on the gloom and heaviness, engendered by continued reverses and suffering, pervading the colonies; it strengthened the heart of Washington, infused new life into the legislative councils, inspirited the people; and in the providential ordering of events, which human foresight or prudence could not have anticipated or prevented, and on which hinged the great issue, the faith of all was confirmed that God was with them, as he had been with their fathers. An incident, close in time with this auspicious and splendid achievement, illumines the record of our history, and by its light we may see the source of that marvellous strength in weakness, and endurance in trial, which George III., Lord North, and that 'right reverend bench' could never comprehend, nor their wit or power overcome. It was an order of Congress, directing the Committee of Commerce to import twenty thousand copies of the Bible, the great political text-book of the patriots....

"The preacher, Rev. Samuel Phillips Payson, son of Rev. Phillips Payson, of Walpole, Massachusetts, was born January 18, 1736,

The above excerpts are from J. Wingate Thornton's "The Pulpit of the American Revolution" - 1860

Payson

educated at Harvard College, 1754, ordained at Chelsea, October 26, 1757. . . . Mr. Payson was distinguished as a classical scholar, for his studies in natural philosophy and astronomy, and for his fidelity as a Christian pastor and teacher, but has, perhaps, a stronger claim to our grateful remembrance as a high-minded patriot in the days of his country's peril, difficulty, and darkness. . . . "

Title of sermon

"A Sermon Preached before the Honorable Council, and the Honorable House of Representatives, of the State of Massachusetts-Bay, in New-England, at Boston, May 27, 1778.

"Being the Anniversary for the Election of the Honorable Council. By PHILLIPS PAYSON, A. M. Pastor of a Church in Chelsea.

"Election Sermon."

But Jerusalem, which is above, is free, which is the mother of us all. So then, brethren, we are not children of the bond woman, but of the free. - Gal. iv. 26, 31.

Payson's Election Sermon

". . . . Next to the liberty of heaven is that which the sons of God, the heirs of glory, possess in this life, in which they are freed from the bondage of corruption, the tyranny of evil lusts and passions, described by the apostle 'by being made free from sin, and becoming the servants of God.' These kinds of liberty are so nearly related, that the latter is considered as a sure pledge of the former; and therefore all good men, all true believers, in a special sense are children of the free woman, heirs of the promise. This religious or spiritual liberty must be accounted the greatest happiness of man, considered in a private capacity. . . . Hence a people formed upon the morals and principles of the gospel are capacitated to enjoy the highest degree of civil liberty, and will really enjoy it, unless prevented by force or fraud. . . .

"The voice of reason and the voice of God both teach us that the great object or end of government is the public good. Nor is there less certainty in determining that a free and righteous government originates from the people, and is under their direction and control; and therefore a

The above excerpts are from J. Wingate Thornton's "The Pulpit of the American Revolution" - 1860

free, popular model of government - of the republican kind - may be judged the most friendly to the rights and liberties of the people, and the most conducive to the public welfare....

"In this view, it is obvious to observe that a spirit of liberty should in general prevail among a people; their minds should be possessed with a sense of its worth and nature. Facts and observation abundantly teach us that the minds of a community, as well as of individuals, are subject to different and various casts and impressions. The inhabitants of large and opulent empires and kingdoms are often entirely lost to a sense of liberty, in which case they become an easy prey to usurpers and tyrants. Where the spirit of liberty is found in its genuine vigor it produces its genuine effects; urging to the greatest vigilance and exertions, it will surmount great difficulties; (so) that it is no easy matter to deceive or conquer a people determined to be free. The exertions and effects of this great spirit in our land have already been such as may well astonish the world; and so long as it generally prevails it will be quiet with no species of government but what befriends and protects it....

"The baneful effects of exorbitant wealth, the lust of power, and other evil passions, are so inimical to a free, righteous government, and find such an easy access to the human mind, that it is difficult, if possible, to keep up the spirit of good government, unless the spirit of liberty prevails in the state. This spirit, like other generous growths of nature, flourishes best in its native soil. It has been engrafted, at one time and another, in various countries: in America it shoots up and grows as in its natural soil. Recollecting our pious ancestors, the first settlers of the country, - nor shall we look for ancestry beyond that period, - and we may say, in the most literal sense, we are children, not of the bond woman, but of the free. It may hence well be expected that the exertions and effects of American liberty should be more vigorous and complete....

"The slavery of a people is generally founded in ignorance of some kind or another; and there are not wanting such facts as abundantly prove the human mind may be so sunk and debased, through ignorance and its natural effects, as even to adore its enslaver, and kiss its chains. Hence knowledge and learning may well be considered as most essentially requisite to a free, righteous government.

The above excerpts are from J. Wingate Thornton's "The Pulpit of the American Revolution" - 1860

A republican government and science mutually promote and support each other. Great literary acquirements are indeed the lot of but few, because but few in a community have ability and opportunity to pursue the paths of science; but a certain degree of knowledge is absolutely necessary to be diffused through a state for the preservation of its liberties and the quiet of government.

"Every kind of useful knowledge will be carefully encouraged and promoted by the rulers of a free state, unless they should happen to be men of ignorance themselves; in which case they and the community will be in danger of sharing the fate of blind guides and their followers. The education of youth, by instructors properly qualified, the establishment of societies for useful arts and sciences, the encouragement of persons of superior abilities, will always command the attention of wise rulers....

"Despotism and tyranny want nothing but wealth and force, but liberty and order are supported by knowledge and virtue.

"I shall also mention the love of our country, or public virtue, as another essential support of good government and the public liberties. No model of government whatever can equal the importance of this principle, nor afford proper safety and security without it....

"Civil society cannot be maintained without justice, benevolence, and the social virtues. Even the government of the Jerusalem above could not render a vicious and abandoned people quiet and happy. The children of the bond woman, slaves to vice, can never be free. If the reason of the mind, man's immediate rule of conduct, is in bondage to corruption, he is verily the worst of slaves....

"I must not forget to mention religion, both in rulers and people, as of the highest importance to the public. This is the most sacred principle that can dwell in the human breast. It is of the highest importance to men, - the most perfective of the human soul. The truths of the gospel are the most pure, its motives the most noble and animating, and its comforts the most supporting to the mind. The importance of religion to civil society and government is

The above excerpts are from J. Wingate Thornton's "The Pulpit of the American Revolution" - 1860

great indeed, as it keeps alive the best sense of moral obligation, a matter of such extensive utility, especially in respect to an oath, which is one of the principal instruments of government....

"The qualities of a good ruler may be estimated from the nature of a free government. Power being a delegation, and all delegated power being in its nature subordinate and limited, hence rulers are but trustees, and government a trust; therefore fidelity is a prime qualification in a ruler; this, joined with good natural and acquired abilities, goes far to complete the character....

"A state and its inhabitants thus circumstanced in respect to government, principle, morals, capacity, union, and rulers, make up the most striking portrait, the liveliest emblem of the Jerusalem that is above, that this world can afford. That this may be the condition of these free, independent, and sovereign states of America, we have the wishes and prayers of all good men. Indulgent Heaven seems to invite and urge us to accept the blessing. A kind and wonderful Providence has conducted us, by astonishing steps, as it were, within sight of the promised land. We stand this day upon Pisgah's top, the children of the free woman, the decendants of a pious race, who, from the love of liberty and the fear of God, spent their treasure and spilt their blood. Animated by the same great spirit of liberty, and determined, under God, to be free, these states have made one of the noblest stands against despotism and tyranny that can be met with in the annals of history, either ancient or modern...."

Thornton's biographical sketch of Stiles

"(President Stiles was one of the most learned and high-minded men of his time. He was familiar with the lore of the Hebrew and Christian Church. He conversed and corresponded in Hebrew, Latin, and French, with facility, and was learned in the Oriental literature and antiquities connected with Biblical history. He taught in astronomy, chemistry, and philosophy. He and his friend Dr. Franklin were among the earliest statisticians in America, and his studies in this science exhibit the most comprehensive and enlightened views....

"Ezra Stiles, son of Rev. Isaac Stiles, was born in North Haven, Connecticut, December 10, 1727; graduated at Yale in 1747; delivered a Latin oration, in 1753, in memory of Dean Berkeley,

The above excerpts are from J. Wingate Thornton's "The Pulpit of the American Revolution" - 1860

and another at New Haven, in February, 1755, in honor of Dr. Franklin, with whom he had a life-long friendship. He was minister at Newport, Rhode Island, from 1755 to the beginning of the war of the Revolution, in 1777; became pastor of the North Church in Portsmouth, but was soon appointed President of Yale College, an office which he adorned; and died May 12th, 1795. The present edition of his Election Sermon is reprinted from the edition of 1783, at New Haven. It was reprinted in London, as a literary curiosity, in all the luxury and splendor of large paper and bold type. - Sparks's American Biography, xvi. 78; Sprague's Annals, i. 470, 479; Dr. Park's Life of Hopkins."

Title of sermon

"The United States elevated to Glory and Honor.

"A Sermon, Preached before His Excellency Jonathan Trumbull, Esq L. L. D. Governor and Commander in Chief, and the Honorable The General Assembly of The State of Connecticut, convened at Hartford, at the Anniversary Election, May 8th, 1783.
By Ezra Stiles, D. D. President of Yale-College.

"Election Sermon.

Stiles' Election Sermon

And to make thee high above all nations which he hath made, in praise, and in name, and in honor; and that thou mayest be an holy people unto the Lord thy God.'- Deut. xxvi. 19.

"...However it may be doubted whether political communities are rewarded and punished in this world only, and whether the prosperity and decline of other empires have corresponded with their moral state as to virtue and vice, yet the history of the Hebrew theocracy shows that the secular welfare of God's ancient people depended upon their virtue, their religion, their observance of that holy covenant which Israel entered into with God on the plains at the foot of Nebo, on the other side of Jordan. Here Moses, the man of God, assembled three million of people, - the number of the United States, - recapitulated and gave them a second publication of the sacred jural institute, delivered thirty-eight years before, with the most awful solemnity, at Mount Sinai. A law dictated with sovereign authority by the Most High to a people, to a world, a universe, becomes of invincible force and obligation without any reference to the consent of the governed....

The above excerpts are from J. Wingate Thornton's "The Pulpit of the American Revolution" - 1860

"But, as well to comfort and support the righteous in every age, and under every calamity, as to make his power known among all nations, God determined that a remnant should be saved. Whence Moses and the prophets, by divine direction, interspersed their writings with promises that when the ends of God's moral government should be answered in a series of national punishments, inflicted for a succession of ages, he would, by his irresistible power and sovereign grace, subdue the hearts of his people to a free, willing, joyful obedience; turn their captivity; recover and gather them 'from all the nations whither the Lord had scattered them in his fierce anger; bring them into the land which their fathers possessed; and multiply them above their fathers, and rejoice over them for good, as he rejoiced over their fathers. Then the words of Moses, hitherto accomplished but in part, will be literally fulfilled, when this branch of the posterity of Abraham shall be nationally collected, and become a very distinguished and glorious people, under the great Messiah, the Prince of Peace. He will then 'make them high above all nations which he hath made, in praise, and in name, and in honor, and they shall become a holy people unto the Lord their God.'

"I shall enlarge no further upon the primary sense and literal accomplishment of this and numerous other prophecies respecting both Jews and Gentiles in the latter-day glory of the church; for I have assumed the text only as introductory to a discourse upon the political welfare of God's American Israel, and as allusively prophetic of the future prosperity and splendor of the United States. We may, then, consider -

"I. What reason we have to expect that, by the blessing of God, these States may prosper and flourish into a great American Republic, and ascend into high and distinguished honor among the nations of the earth. 'To make thee high above all nations which he hath made, in praise, and in name, and in honor.'

"II. That our system of dominion and civil polity would be imperfect without the true religion; or that from the diffusion of virtue among the people of any community would arise their greatest secular happiness: which will terminate in this conclusion, that holiness ought to be the end of all civil government. 'That thou mayest be a holy people unto the Lord thy God.'...

The above excerpts are from J. Wingate Thornton's "The Pulpit of the American Revolution" - 1860

"Heaven hath provided this country, not indeed derelict, but only partially settled, and consequently open for the reception of a new enlargement of Japheth. Europe was settled by Japheth; America is settling from Europe: and perhaps this second enlargement bids fair to surpass the first; for we are to consider all the European settlements of America collectively as springing from and transfused with the blood of Japheth....

"How wonderful the accomplishments in distant and disconnected ages! While the principal increase was first in Europe, westward from Scythia, the residence of the family of Japheth, a branch of the original enlargement, extending eastward into Asia, and spreading round to the southward of the Caspian, became the ancient kingdoms of Media and Persia: and thus he dwelt in the tents of Shem. Hence the singular and almost identical affinity between the Persic and Teutonic languages, through all ages, to this day. And now the other part of the prophecy is fulfilling in a new enlargement, not in the tents of Shem, but in a country where Canaan shall be his servant, at least unto tribute....

"The population of this land will probably become very great, and Japheth become more numerous millions in America than in Europe and Asia;...

"All the forms of civil polity have been tried by mankind, except one, and that seems to have been reserved in Providence to be realized in America. Most of the states, of all ages, in their originals, both as to policy and property, have been founded in rapacity, usurpation, and injustice; so that in the contests recorded in history, the public right is a dubious question, - it being rather certain that it belongs to neither of the contending parties, - the military history of all nations being but a description of the wars and invasions of the mutual robbers and devastators of the human race....

"But a democratical polity for millions, standing upon the broad basis of the people at large, amply charged with property, has not hitherto been exhibited.

"Republics are democratical, aristocratical, or monarchical. Each of these forms admits of modifications, both as to hereditation and powers from absolute government up to perfect liberty....

The above excerpts are from J. Wingate Thornton's "The Pulpit of the American Revolution" - 1860

"But the abstract rationale of perfect civil government remains still hidden among the desiderata of politics, having hitherto baffled the investigation of the best writers on government, the ablest politicians, and the sagest civilians. A well-ordered democratical aristocracy, standing upon the annual elections of the people, and revocable at pleasure, is the polity which combines the United States; and, from the nature of man and the comparison of ages, I believe it will approve itself the most equitable, liberal and perfect....

"Our degree of population is such as to give us reason to expect that this will become a great people.... Should this prove a future fact, how applicable would be the text, when the Lord shall have made his American Israel high above all nations which he has made, in numbers, and in praise, and in name, and in honor!

"I am sensible some will consider these as visionary, utopian ideas; and so they would have judged had they lived in the apostolic age, and been told that by the time of Constantine the Empire would have become Christian. As visionary that the twenty thousand souls which first settled New England should be multiplied to near a million in a century and a half....

"As utopian would it have been to the loyalists, at the battle of Lexington, that in less than eight years the independence and sovereignty of the United States should be acknowledged by four European sovereignties, one of which should be Britain herself. How wonderful the revolutions, the events of Providence! We live in an age of wonders; we have lived an age in a few years; we have seen more wonders accomplished in eight years than are usually unfolded in a century....

"We have sustained a force brought against us which might have made any empire on earth to tremble; and yet our bow has abode in strength, and, having obtained help of God, we continue unto this day.... Every patriot trembled till we had proved our armour, till it could be seen whether this hasty concourse was susceptible of exercitual arrangement, and could face the enemy with firmness. They early gave us the decided proof of this in the memorable battle of Bunker Hill. We were satisfied.... Whereupon Congress put at the head of this spirited army the only

The above excerpts are from J. Wingate Thornton's "The Pulpit of the American Revolution" - 1860

man on whom the eyes of all Israel were placed. Posterity, I apprehend, and the world itself, inconsiderate and incredulous as they may be of the dominion of Heaven, will yet do so much justice to the divine moral government as to acknowledge that this American Joshua was raised up by God, and divinely formed, by a peculiar influence of the Sovereign of the universe, for the great work of leading the armies of this American Joseph (now separated from his brethren), and conducting this people through the severe, the arduous conflict, to liberty and independence. Surprising was it with what instant celerity men ascended and rose into generals, and officers of every subordination, formed chiefly by the preparatory discipline of only the preceding year 1774, when the ardor and spirit of military discipline was by Heaven, and without concert, sent through the continent like lightning. Surprising was it how soon the army was organized, took its formation, and rose into firm system and impregnable arrangement.

"To think of withstanding and encountering Britain by land was bold, and much more bold and daring by sea; yet we immediately began a navy, and built ships of war with an unexampled expedition. . . .

"A variety of success and defeat hath attended our warfare both by sea and land. In our lowest and most dangerous estate, in 1776 and 1777, we sustained ourselves against the British army of sixty thousand troops, commanded by Howe, Burgoyne, and Clinton, and other the ablest generals Britain could procure throughout Europe, with a naval force of twenty-two thousand seamen in above eighty British men-of-war. These generals we sent home, one after another, conquered, defeated, and convinced of the impossibility of subduing America. While oppressed by the heavy weight of this combined force, Heaven inspired us with resolution to cut the gordian knot, when the die was cast irrevocable in the glorious act of Independence. This was sealed and confirmed by God Almighty in the victory of General Washington at Trenton, and in the surprising movement and battle of Princeton, by which astonishing effort of generalship General Howe and the whole British army, in elated confidence and in open-mouthed march for Philadelphia, was instantly stopped, remanded back, and cooped up for a shivering winter in the little borough of Brunswick. Thus God 'turned the battle to the gate,' and this gave a finishing to the foundation of the American

The above excerpts are from J. Wingate Thornton's "The Pulpit of the American Revolution" - 1860

Republic.... And who does not see the indubitable interposition and energetic influence of Divine Providence in these great and illustrious events? Who but a Washington, inspired by Heaven, could have struck out the great movement and manoeuvre at Princeton? To whom but the Ruler of the winds shall we ascribe it that the British reinforcement, in the summer of 1777, was delayed on the ocean three months by contrary winds, until it was too late for the conflagrating General Clinton to raise the siege of Saratoga? What but a providential miracle detected the conspiracy of Arnold, even in the critical moment of the execution of that infernal plot, in which the body of the American army, then at West Point, with his Excellency General Washington himself, were to have been rendered into the hands of the enemy? Doubtless inspired by the Supreme Illuminator of great minds were the joint counsels of a Washington and a Rochambeau in that grand effort of generalship with which they deceived and astonished a Clinton, and eluded his vigilance, in their transit by New York and rapid marches for Virginia. Was it not of God that both the navy and army should enter the Chesapeake at the same time? Who but God could have ordained the critical arrival of the Gallic fleet, so as to prevent and defeat the British, and assist and cooperate with the combined armies in the siege and reduction of Yorktown? Should we not ever admire and ascribe to a Supreme Energy the wise and firm generalship displayed by General Greene when, leaving the active, roving Cornwallis to pursue his helter-skelter, ill-fated march into Virginia, he coolly and steadily went onwards, and deliberately, judiciously, and heroically recovered the Carolinas and the southern states?

"How rare have been the defections and apostasies of our capital characters, though tempted with all the charms of gold, titles, and nobility! Whence is it that so few of our army have deserted to the enemy? Whence that our brave sailors have chosen the horrors of prison-ships and death, rather than to fight against their country? Whence that men of every rank have so generally felt and spoken alike, as if the cords of life struck unison through the continent? What but a miracle has preserved the union of the States, the purity of Congress, and the unshaken patriotism of every General Assembly? It is God, who has raised up for us a great and powerful ally, - an ally which sent us a chosen army and a naval force; who sent us a Rochambeau and a Chastelleux, and other characters of the first military

The above excerpts are from J. Wingate Thornton's "The Pulpit of the American Revolution" - 1860

merit and eminence, to fight side by side with a Washington and a Lincoln, and the intrepid Americans, in the siege and battle of Yorktown. It is God who so ordered the balancing interests of nations as to produce an irresistible motive in the European maritime powers to take our part. . . .

"But the time would fail me to recount the wonder-working providence of God in the events of this war. Let these serve as a specimen, and lead us to hope that God will not forsake this people for whom he has done such marvellous things, - whereof we are glad, and rejoice this day, - having at length brought us to the dawn of peace. O Peace, thou welcome guest, all hail! Thou heavenly visitant, calm the tumult of nations, and wave thy balmy wing to perpetuity over this region of liberty! Let there be a tranquil period for the unmolested accomplishment of the Magnalia Dei - the great events in God's moral government designed from eternal ages to be displayed in these ends of the earth. . . .

"We shall have a communication with all nations in commerce, manners, and science, beyond anything heretofore known in the world. Manufacturers and artisans, and men of every description, may perhaps come and settle among us. They will be few indeed in comparison with the annual thousands of our natural increase, and will be incorporated with the prevailing hereditary complexion of the first settlers; - we shall not be assimilated to them, but they to us, especially in the second and third generations. This fermentation and communion of nations will doubtless produce something very new, singular, and glorious. Upon the conquest of Alexander the Great, statuary, painting, architecture, philosophy, and the fine arts were transplanted in perfection from Athens to Tarsus, from Greece to Syria, where they immediately flourished in even greater perfection, than in the parent state. Not in Greece herself are there to be found specimens of a sublimer or more magnificent architecture, even in the Grecian style, than in the ruins of Baalbec and Palmyra. So all the arts may be transplanted from Europe and Asia, and flourish in America with an augmented lustre, not to mention the augment of the sciences from American inventions and discoveries, of which there have been as capital ones here, the last half century, as in all Europe.

The above excerpts are from J. Wingate Thornton's "The Pulpit of the American Revolution" - 1860

"The rough, sonorous diction of the English language may here take its Athenian polish, and receive its attic urbanity, as it will probably become the vernacular tongue of more numerous millions than ever yet spake one language on earth. It may continue for ages to be the prevailing and general language of North America. The intercommunion of the United States with all the world in travels, trade, and politics, and the infusion of letters into our infancy, will probably preserve us from the provincial dialects risen into inexterminable habit before the invention of printing....

"The Saracenic conquests have already lost the pure and elegant Arabic of the Koreish tribe, or the family of Ishmael, in the corrupted dialects of Egypt, Syria, Persia, and Indostan. Different from these, the English language will grow up with the present American population into great purity and elegance, unmutilated by the foreign dialects of foreign conquests. And in this connection I may observe with pleasure how God, in his providence, has ordered that, at the Reformation, the English translation of the Bible should be made with very great accuracy - with greater accuracy, it is presumed, than any other translation.... It sustained a revision of numerous translators, from Tyndal to the last review by the bishops and other learned divines in the time of James I., one hundred and eighty years ago, and has never been altered since. It may have been designed by Providence for the future perusal of more millions of the human race than ever were able to read one book, and for their use to the millennial ages.

"This great American Revolution, this recent political phenomenon of a new sovereignty arising among the sovereign powers of the earth, will be attended to and contemplated by all nations. Navigation will carry the American flag around the globe itself, and display the thirteen stripes and new constellation at Bengal and Canton, on the Indus and Ganges, on the Whang-ho and the Yang-tse-kiang, and with commerce will import the wisdom and literature of the East. That prophecy of Daniel is now literally fulfilling - there shall be a universal travelling to and fro, and knowledge shall be increased. This knowledge will be brought home and treasured up in America, and, being here digested and carried to the

The aboveexcerpts are from J. Wingate Thornton's "The Pulpit of the American Revolution" - 1860

highest perfection, may reblaze back from America to Europe, Asia, and Africa, and illumine the world with truth and liberty....

"The United States will embosom all the religious sects or denominations in Christendom. Here they may all enjoy their whole respective systems of worship and church government complete....And who can tell how extensive a blessing this American Joseph may become to the whole human race, although once despised by his brethren, exiled, and sold into Egypt? How applicable that in Genesis xlix. 22,26: 'Joseph is a fruitful bough, even a fruitful bough by a well; whose branches run over the wall. The archers have sorely grieved him, and shot at him, and hated him. But his bow abode in strength; the arms of his hands were made strong by the arms of the mighty God of Jacob. The blessings of thy father have prevailed above the blessings of my progenitors, unto the utmost bound of the everlasting hill; they shall be on the head of Joseph, and on the crown of the head of him that was separated from his brethren.'

"Little would civilians have thought ages ago that the world should ever look to America for models of government and polity; little did they think of finding this most perfect polity among the poor outcasts, the contemptible people of New England, and particularly in the long despised civil polity of Connecticut, - a polity conceived by the sagacity and wisdom of a Winthrop, a Ludlow, Haynes, Hopkins, Hooker, and the other first settlers of Hartford, in 1636. And while Europe and Asia may hereafter learn that the most liberal principles of law and civil polity are to be found on this side of the Atlantic, they may also find the true religion here depurated from the rust and corruption of ages, and learn from us to reform and restore the church to its primitive purity....Religion may here receive its last, most liberal, and impartial examination. Religious liberty is peculiarly friendly to fair and generous disquisition. Here Deism will have its full chance; nor need libertines more to complain of being overcome by any weapons but the gentle, the powerful ones of argument and truth. Revelation will be found to stand the test to the ten thousandth examination....

"It was of the Lord to send Joseph into Egypt, to save much people, and to show forth his praise. It is of the Lord that

The above excerpts are from J. Wingate Thornton's "The Pulpit of the American Revolution" - 1860

'a woman clothed with the sun, and the moon under her feet', and upon 'her head a crown of twelve stars', should 'flee into the wilderness, where she hath a place prepared of God', and where she might be the repository of wisdom, and 'keep the commandments of God, and have the testimony of Jesus.' It may have been of the Lord that Christianity is to be found in such greater purity in this church exiled into the wildernesses of America, and that its purest body should be evidently advancing forward, by an augmented natural increase and spiritual edification, into a singular superiority, with the ultimate subserviency to the glory of God in converting the world....

"And thus the American Republic, by illuminating the world with truth and liberty, would be exalted and made high among the nations, in praise, and in name, and in honor. I doubt not this is the honor reserved for us; I had almost said, in the spirit of prophecy, the zeal of the Lord of Hosts will accomplish this....

"Having shown wherein consists the prosperity of a state, and what reason we have to anticipate the glory of the American empire, I proceed to show,

"That her system of dominion must receive its finishing from religion; or, that from the diffusion of virtue among the people of any community would arise their greatest secular happiness; all which will terminate in this conclusion: that holiness ought to be the end of all civil government - 'that thou mayest be an holy people unto the Lord thy God.'

"On the subject of religion we might be concise and transient, if indeed a subject of the highest moment ought to be treated with brevity.

"It is readily granted that a state may be very prosperous and flourishing without Christianity; - witness the Egyptian, Assyrian, Roman, and Chinese empires. But if there be a true religion, one would think that it might be at least some additional glory. We must become a holy people in reality, in order to exhibit the experiment, never yet fully made in this unhallowed part of the universe, whether such a people would be the happiest on earth....I wish we had not to fear that a neglect of religion was coming to be the road to preferment. It was not so here in our fathers' days.

The above excerpts are from J. Wingate Thornton's "The Pulpit of the American Revolution" - 1860

"Shall the Most High send down truth into this world from the world of light and truth, and shall the rulers of this world be afraid of it? Shall there be no intrepid Daniels, - great in magistracy, great in religion? How great was that holy man, that learned and pious civilian, when he shone in the supreme triumvirate at the head of an empire of one hundred and twenty provinces - venerable for political wisdom, venerable for religion!

"If men, not merely nominally Christians, but of real religion and sincere piety, joined with abilities, were advanced and called up to office in every civil department, how would it countenance and recommend virtue! But, alas! is there not too much Laodiceanism in this land? Is not Jesus in danger of being wounded in the house of his friends?....

"Whenever religion is erected on the ruins of civil government, and when civil government is built on the ruins of religion, both are so far essentially wrong....

'While we have to confess and lament the vice rampant in Christendom, we have reason to believe that the more Christianity prevails in a country, civil society will be more advanced. ferocious manners will give way to the more mild, liberal, just, and amiable manners of the gospel....

"But I must desist, with only observing that the United States are under peculiar obligations to become a holy people unto the Lord our God, on account of the late eminent deliverance, salvation, peace, and glory with which he hath now crowned our new sovereignty.... "

The above excerpts are from J. Wingate Thornton's "The Pulpit of the American Revolution" - 1860

"... Mr. Hooker, in his ecclesiastical polity, as quoted by Mr. Locke, affirms that 'laws they are not, which the public approbation hath not made so.' This seems to be the language of nature and common sense; for if the public are bound to yield obedience to laws to which they cannot give their approbation, they are slaves to those who make such laws and enforce them ..."

-Samuel Adams
Boston Gazette, Jan. 20, 1772

THE RECORDING OF NEW ENGLAND HISTORY

"The beginnings of New England were made in the full daylight of modern history. It was an age of town records, of registered deeds, of contemporary memoirs, of diplomatic correspondence, of controversial pamphlets, funeral sermons, political diatribes, specific instructions, official reports, and private letters...It was not a time in which mythical personages or incredible legends could flourish, and such things we do not find in the history of New England. There was nevertheless a romantic side to this history, enough to envelop some of its characters and incidents in a glamour that may mislead the modern reader. This wholesale migration from the smiling fields of merry England to an unexplored wilderness beyond a thousand leagues of sea was of itself a most romantic and thrilling event, and when viewed in the light of its historic results it becomes clothed with sublimity. The men who undertook this work were not at all free from selfconsciousness. They believed that they were doing a wonderful thing. They felt themselves to be instruments in accomplishing a kind of 'manifest destiny.' Their exodus was that of a chosen people who were at length to lay the everlasting foundations of God's kingdom upon earth. Such opinions, which took a strong colour from their assiduous study of the Old Testament, reacted and disposed them all the more to search its pages for illustrations and precedents, and to regard it as an oracle, almost as a talisman. In every propitious event they saw a special providence, an act of divine intervention to deliver them from the snares of an ever watchful Satan. This steadfast faith in an unseen ruler and guide was to them a pillar of cloud by day and of fire by night. It was of great moral value. It gave them clearness of purpose and concentration of strength, and contributed toward making them, like the children of Israel, a people of indestructible vitality and aggressive energy. At the same time, in the hands of the Puritan writers, this feeling was apt to warp their estimates of events and throw such a romantic haze about things as seriously to interfere with a true historical perspective.

Among such writings that which perhaps best epitomizes the Puritan philosophy is 'The Wonder-working Providence of Zion's Savior in New England', by Captain Edward Johnson, one of the principal founders of Woburn. It is an extremely valuable history of New England from 1628 to 1651...If we consider the Puritans in the light of their surroundings as Englishmen of the seventeenth century and inaugurators of a political movement that was gradually to change for the better the aspect of things all over the earth, we cannot fail to discern the value of that sacred enthusiasm which led them to regard themselves as chosen soldiers of Christ. It was the spirit of the 'Wonder-working Providence' that hurled the tyrant from his throne..."

The above excerpts are from John Fiske's "The Beginnings of New England"

GOVERNMENT BOTH CONGREGATIONAL AND CIVIL
"Johnson's Wonder-working Providence, 1647"

"A HISTORY OF NEW-ENGLAND

"From the English planting in the Yeere 1628 untill the Yeere 1652.

"Declaring the form of their Government, Civill, Military, and Ecclesiastique. Their Wars with the Indians, their Troubles with the Gortonists, and other Heretiques. Their manner of gathering of Churches, the commodities of the Country, and description of the principall Towns and Havens, with the great encouragements to increase Trade betwixt them and Old England. With the names of all their Governours, Magistrates, and Eminent Ministers.

Psal. 107.24. The righteous shall see it and rejoice, and all iniquity shall stop her mouth.

Psal. 111.2. The works of the Lord are great, and ought to be sought out of all that have pleasure in them.

London, Printed for Nath: Brooke at the Angel in Corn-hill. 1654."

"The Commission of the People of Christ shipped for New England, and first of their gathering into Churches."

Attend to your Commission, all you that are or shall hereafter be shipped for this service, yee are with all possible speed to imbarque your selves, and as for all such Worthies who are hunted after as David was by Saul and his Courtiers, you may change your habit and ship you with what secrecy you can, carrying all things most needfull for the Voyage and service you are to be imployed in after your landing. But as soone as you shall be exposed to danger of tempestious Seas, you shall forthwith shew whose servants you are by calling on the Name of your God, sometimes by extraordinary seeking his pleasing Face in times of deepe distresse, and publishing your Masters will, and pleasure to all that Voyage with you, and that is his minde to have purity in Religion preferred above all dignity in the world; your Christ hath commanded the Seas they shall not swallow you, not Pyrates imprison your persons, or possesse your goods. At your landing see you observe the Rule of his Word, for neither larger nor stricter Commission can hee give by any, and therefore at first filling the Land whither you are sent, with diligence, search out the mind of God both in planting and continuing Church and civill Government, but be sure they be distinct, yet agreeing and helping the one to the other; Let the matter and forme of your Churches be such as were in the Primitive Times (before Antichrists Kingdome prevailed) plainly poynted out by Christ and his Apostles, in most of their Epistles, to be neither Nationall nor Provinciall, but gathered together in Covenant of such a number as might ordinarily meete together in one place, and built of such living stones as outwardly appeare Saints by calling. . . .

The above excerpts are from Edward Johnson's "Wonder-Working Providence" - 1653
Marginal notes are by Edward Johnson

"What Civill Government the People of Christ ought to set up, and submit unto in New England"

"Fayle not in prosecution of the Worke, for your Lord Christ hath furnished you with able Pilots, to steere the Helme in a godly peaceable, Civill Government also, then see you make choyce of such as are sound both in Profession and Confession, men fearing God and hating bribes; whose Commission is not onely limitted with the commands of the second Table, but they are to looke to the Rules of the first also, and let them be sure to put on Joshuas resolution, and courage, never to make League with any of these seven Sectaries....

"Of the wonderfull Preparation the Lord Christ by his Providence, wrought for his peoples abode in this Western world."

"Now let all men know the admirable Acts of Christ for his Churches and chosen, are universally over the whole Earth at one and the same time, but sorry man cannot so discourse of them; And therefore let us leave our English Nation in way of preparation for this Voyage intended, and tell of the marvelous doings of Christ preparing for his peoples arrivall in the Western World, whereas the Indians report they beheld to their great wonderment that perspicuous bright blazing Comet (which was so famously noted in Europe; anon after Sun set it appeared as they say in the South-west, about three houres, continuing in their Horizon for the space of thirty sleepes....

"The Summer after the blazing Starre (whose motion in the Heavens was from East to West, poynting out to the sons of men the progresse of the glorious Gospell of Christ, the glorious King of his Churches) even about the yeare 1618, a little before the removeall of that Church of Christ from Holland to Plimouth in New England, as the ancient Indians report, there befell a great mortality among them, the greatest that ever the memory of Father to Sonne tooke notice of, chiefly desolating those places, where the English afterward planted."...

"Of the first Church of Christ, gathered at Salem in the Mattachusets Government"

"This year 1629, came over three godly Ministers of Christ Jesus, intending to shew his power in his peoples lowest condition as his manner is, thereby to strengthen their Faith in following difficulties, and now although the number of the faithful people of Christ were but few, yet their longing desires to gather into a Church was very great; And therefore addressed themselves to finde out the blessed Rules of Christ for preserving herein, who through the assistance of his Blessed Spirit, found that the Word of God, penned by the Apostles in many Epistles, written to particular Churches, consisting of such as are beloved Saints, by calling appearing so in the judgement of Charity, being tryed by the rule

The above excerpts are from Edward Johnson's "Wonder-Working Providence" - 1653
Marginal notes are by Edward Johnson

of the word, not scandalous in their Lives, for the society of such they sought, and in these beginnings found very few, seven being the lest (least) number a Church can be gathered, or conceived by just consequence from the Word of God....

"Of the second Church of Christ, gathered at Charles Towne in the Mattacusets Bay, 1631"

"And now the new-come Souldiers of Christ strengthen themselves in him, and gather a Church at Charles Towne, whose extent at present did reach to both sides of the River, and in very little time after was divided into two Churches.... This, as the other Churches of Christ, began with a small number in a desolate and barren Wildernesse, which the Lord in his wonderfull mercy hath turned to fruitfull Fields. Wherefore behold the present condition of these Churches compared with their beginnings; as they sowed in teares, so also have they Reaped in joy, and shall still so go on if plenty and liberty marre not their prosperity....

"Of the Third Church of Christ gathered at Dorchester, 1631."

"The third Church of Christ gathered under this Government was at Dorchester, a frontire Town scituated very pleasantly both for facing the Sea, and also its large extent into the main Land, well watered with two small Rivers; neere about this Towne inhabited some few ancient Traders, who were not of this select band, but came for other ends, as Morton of Merrymount, who would faine have resisted this worke, but the provident hand of Christ prevented....

"Of the Fourth Church of Christ gathered at Boston, 1631"

"After some little space of time the Church of Christ at Charles Town, having their Sabbath assemblies oftenest on the South side of the River, agreed to leave the people on that side to themselves, and to provide another Pastor for Charles Towne, which accordingly they did. So that the fourth Church of Christ issued out of Charles Towne, and was seated at Boston, being the Center of Towne and Metropolis of this Wildernesse worke (but you must not imagine it to be a Metropolitan Church)....

"Of the Fift Church of Christ, gathered at Roxbury, 1631"

"The fift Church of Christ was gathered at Roxbury scituated between Boston and Dorchester, being well watered with coole and pleasant Springs issuing forth the Rocky-hills, and with small Freshets, watering the Vallies of this fertill Towne, whose forme is somewhat like a wedge double pointed, entring betweene the two foure-named Townes, filled with a very laborious people, whose labours the Lord hath so blest, that in the roome of dismall Swampes and tearing Bushes, they have very goodly Fruit-

The above excerpts are from Edward Johnson's "Wonder-Working Providence" - 1653
Marginal notes are by Edward Johnson

trees, fruitfull Fields and Gardens, their Heard of Cowes, Oxen and other young Cattell of that kind about 350. and dwelling-houses neere upon 120....

"Of the Sixth Church of Christ, gathered at Linn. 1631"

"The Sixth Church of Christ was gathered at Linn, betweene Salem and Charles Towne, her scituation is neere to a River, whose strong freshet at breaking up of Winter filleth all her Bankes, and with a furious Torrent ventes it selfe into the Sea; This Towne is furnished with Mineralls of divers kinds, especially Iron and Lead. The forme of it is almost square, onely it takes two large a run into the Land-ward (as most Townes do). It is filled with about one hundred Houses for dwelling; Here is also an Iron Mill in constant use, but as for Lead they have tried but little yet....

"Of the seventh Church of Christ gathered at Water-Towne, 1631"

"The Seaventh Church of Christ gathered out of this wandering Race of Jaccobites was at Water-Towne, scituate upon one of the Branches of Charles River, a fruitfull plat, and of large extent, watered with many pleasant Springs, and small Rivulets, running like veines throughout her Body, which hath caused her inhabitants to scatter in such manner, that their Sabbath-Assemblies prove very thin if the season favour not, and hath made this great Towne (consisting of 160 Families)....

"The Congregationall Churches of Christ are neither favourers of sinfull opinions, nor the Lords over any, or many Churches, or mens Consciences."

"Now that I would they should take notice of is, that the Churches of Christ in New England, and their Officers have hitherto been so far from imbracing the erronious Doctrines of these times, that through the powers of Christ they have valiantly defended the truth, and cut down all deceivable Doctrine; the like hath not been done for many ages heretofore. Reverend and beloved in Christ, could your eyes but behold the efficacy of loving counsell in the Communion of congregationall Churches, and the reverend respect, honour and love, given to all Teaching Elders, charity commands me to thinke you would never stand for Classicall injunctions any more, neither Diocesan, nor Provinciall authority can possible reach so far as this royall Law of love in communion of Churches....

"Of the civill Government in N. England, and their nurture of the people upon their tender knees."

"The chiefe Court of supreame power of this little Commonwealth, consists of a mixt company, part Aristocracy, and part Democracy of Magistrates, that are yearly chosen by the major Vote of the whole body of the Free-men throughout the Country; and Deputies chosen by the severall Townes. They have hitherto had about 12 or 13 Magistrates in the Colony of the Mattacusets, the other Colonies have not above five or six...."

The above excerpts are from Edward Johnson's "Wonder-Working Providence" - 1653
Marginal notes are by Edward Johnson

CHRISTIAN MORALITY IN LEADERSHIP

"The Character of a Good Ruler - 1694"

Now that all these may be just, it is firstly required that they have a principle of moral honesty in them and swaying of them; that they 'love righteousness and hate iniquity'; that they be 'men of truth.' Exod. xviii., 21, for every man will act in his relation, according to the principle that rules in him: so that an unrighteous man will be an unrighteous ruler, so far as he hath an opportunity.

"They must also be acquainted with the rules of righteousness; they must know what is just and what is unjust, be 'able men,' Exod. xviii., 21. For, though men may know and not do, yet 'without knowledge the mind cannot be good.' Ignorance is a foundation for error, and will likely produce it, when the man applies himself to act; and if he do right at any time it is but by guess, which is a very poor commendation.

"Again, he must be one that respects the cause, and not the persons, in all his administrations, Deut. i., 17: 'Ye shall not respect persons in judgment,' etc. If his affections oversway his judgment at any time, they will be a crooked bias, that will turn him out of the way, and that shall be justice in one man's case, which will not be so in another.

"Farthermore, he must be one whom neither flattery nor bribery may be able to remove out of his way, Deut. xvi., 19: 'Thou shalt not wrest judgment, thou shalt not respect persons, neither take a gift;' and hence he must be one who hates both ambition and covetousness; Exod. xviii. 21, 'Hating covetousness,' which word signifies, a greedy desire, and is applicable to both the fore-cited vices; for if these rule him, he will never be a just ruler.

"Finally, he must be one who prefers the public benefit above all private and separate interests whatsoever. Every man in his place owes himself to the good of the whole, and if he doth not so devote himself, he is unjust; and he who either to advance himself, or to be revenged on another, will push on injurious laws, or pervert the true intention of such as are in force, is an unjust man; and he who is under the influence of a narrow spirit, will be ready to do so, as occasion offers.

"Nor is this justice to be looked upon as separate from the fear of God, but as influenced and maintained by it. He therefore that 'ruleth in the fear of God,' is one who acknowledgeth God to be

The above excerpt is from Samuel Willard, 1640-1707 as published in Library of American Literature by Stedman and Hutchinson, 1889 his sovereign, and carries in his heart an awful fear of him; who owns his commission to be from him, and expects ere long to be called to give in an account of his managing of it; which maketh him to study in all things to please him, and to be afraid of doing any thing that will provoke him.

"And accordingly he is a student in the Law of God, and 'meditates in it day and night;' making it the rule into which he ultimately resolves all that he doth in his place. We find that in the old law, the king was to write a copy of it with his own hand, and to make use of it at all times; Deut. xvii., 18, 19.

"If he hath any thing to do in the making of laws, he will consult a good conscience, and what may be pleasing to God, and will be far from 'framing mischief by a law.' And if he be to execute any laws of men, he will not dare to give a judgment for such an one as directly crosseth the command of God, but counts it ipso facto void, and his conscience acquitted of his oath.

"Yea, the fear of God will make him not to think himself lawless; nor dare to bear witness, by laws and penalties, against sins in others, which he countenanceth and encourageth by living in the practice of himself. But to use utmost endeavors that his own life may be an exemplification of obedience, and others may learn by him what a veneration he hath for the laws that are enacted for the good of mankind.

"In a word, he is one that will take care to promote piety, as well as honesty, among men; and do his utmost that the true religion may be countenanced and established and that all ungodliness, as well as unrighteousness, may have a due testimony borne against it at all times. So he resolves, Psal. lxxv., 10: 'All the horns of the wicked also will I cut off; but the horns of the righteous shall be exalted.'"

The above excerpt is by Samuel Willard 1640-1707 as published in Library of American Literature by Stedman and Hutchinson, 1889

JOHN LOCKE

"Some Thoughts Concerning Education - 1690"

A sound Mind in a sound Body, is a short, but full Description of a happy State in this World: He that has these Two, has little more to wish for; and he that wants either of them, will be but little the better for any thing else. Mens Happiness or Misery, is most part of their own making....

"As the Strength of the Body lies chiefly in being able to endure Hardships, so also does that of the Mind. And the great Principle and Foundation of all Vertue and Worth, is placed in this, That a Man is able to deny himself his own Desires, cross his own Inclinations, and purely follow what Reason directs as best, tho' the Appetite lean the other way.

Early

"The great Mistake I have observed in People's breeding their Children has been, that this has not been taken Care enough of in its due Season; That the Mind has not been made obedient to Discipline, and pliant to Reason, when at first it was most tender, most easy to be bowed. Parents, being wisely ordain'd by Nature to love their Children, are very apt, if Reason watch not that natural Affection very warily; are apt, I say, to let it run into Fondness. They love their little ones, and 'tis their Duty: But they often, with them, cherish their Faults too. They must not be crossed, forsooth; they must be permitted to have their Wills in all things; and, they being in their Infancies not capable of great Vices, their Parents think they may safely enough indulge their little Irregularities, and make themselves Sport with that pretty Perverseness, which they think well enough becomes that innocent Age. But to a fond Parent, that would not have his Child corrected for a perverse Trick, but excused it, saying it was a small Matter; Solon very well replied, 'Ay, but Custom is a great one.

"The Fondling must be taught to strike, and call Names; must have what he Cries for, and do what he pleases. Thus Parents, by humouring and cockering them when little, corrupt the Principles of Nature in their Children, and wonder afterwards to taste the bitter Waters, when they themselves have poisoned the Fountain. For when their Children are grown up, and these ill Habits with them; when they are now too big to be dandled, and their Parents can no longer make use of them as Playthings; then they complain, that the Brats are untoward and

The above excerpts are from John Locke's "Some Thoughts Concerning Education" - 1690. Marginal notes are by Locke.

perverse; then they are offended to see them wilful, and are troubled with those ill Humours, which they themselves infused and fomented in them; And then, perhaps too late, would be glad to get out those Weeds which their own hands have planted, and which now have taken too deep Root to be easily extirpated. For he that has been used to have his Will in every thing, as long as he was in Coats, why should we think it strange, that he should desire it, and contend for it still, when he is in Breeches? Indeed, as he grows more towards a Man, Age shews his Faults the more, so that there be few Parents then so blind, as not to see them; few so insensible as not to feel the ill Effects of their own Indulgence. He had the Will of his Maid before he could Speak or Go; he had the Mastery of his Parents ever since he could Prattle; and why, now he is grown up, is he Stronger and Wiser than he was then, why, now of a suddain must he be restrained and curbed? Why must he at seven, fourteen, or twenty Years old, lose the Privilege which the Parents Indulgence, till then, so largely allowed him? Try it in a Dog or an Horse, or any other Creature, and see whether the ill and resty Tricks, they have learn'd when young, are easily to be mended when they are knit: And yet none of those Creatures are half so wilful and proud, or half so desirous to be Masters of themselves and others, as Man.

Vice

...."Vice, if we may believe the general Complaint, ripens so fast now a days, and runs up to Seed so early in young People, that it is impossible to keep a Lad from the spreading Contagion, if you will venture him abroad in the Herd, and trust to Chance or his own Inclination for the choice of his Company at School. By what Fate Vice has so thriven amongst us these Years past; and by what Hands it has been nurs'd up into so uncontroul'd a Dominion, I shall leave to others to enquire. I wish, that those, who complain of the great Decay of Christian Piety and Vertue every where, and of Learning and acquired Improvements in the Gentry of this Generation, would consider how to retrieve them in the next. This I am sure, That if the Foundation of it be not laid in the Education and Principling of the Youth, all other Endeavours will be in vain. And if the Innocence, Sobriety, and Industry, of those who are coming up, be not taken care of and preserved, 'twill be ridiculous to expect, that those who are to succeed next on the Stage, should abound in that Vertue, Ability, and Learning, which has hitherto made England considerable in the World. I was going to add Courage too, though it has been looked on as the Natural Inheritance of Englishmen. What has been

The above excerpts are from John Locke's "Some Thoughts Concerning Education" - 1690. Marginal notes are by Locke.

talked of some late Actions at Sea, of a Kind unknown to our Ancestors, gives me occasion to say, that Debauchery sinks the Courage of Men: And when Dissoluteness has eaten out the Sense of true Honour, Bravery seldom stays long after it. And I think it impossible to find an instance of any Nation, however renowned for their Valour, who ever kept their Credit in Arms, or made themselves redoubtable amongst their Neighbours, after Corruption had once broke through, and dissolv'd the restraint of Discipline; and Vice was grown to such an head, that it durst shew it self barefaced, without being out of Countenance.

Vertue

"'Tis Vertue then, direct Vertue, which is the hard and valuable part to be aimed at in Education; And not a forward Pertness, or any little Arts of Shifting. All other Considerations and Accomplishments should give way and be postpon'd to this. This is the solid and substantial good, which Tutours should not only read Lectures, and talk of; but the Labour, and Art of Education should furnish the Mind with, and fasten there, and never cease till the young Man had a true Relish of it, and placed his Strength, his Glory and his Pleasure in it.

"The more this advances, the easier way will be made for other Accomplishments in their turns. For he that is brought to submit to Vertue, will not be refractory, or resty, in any thing that becomes him....

...."Fortitude is the Guard and Support of the other Vertues; and without Courage a Man will scarce keep steady to his Duty, and fill up the Character of a truly worthy Man.

Courage

"Courage, that makes us bear up against Dangers that we fear, and Evils that we feel, is of great use in an Estate, as ours is in this Life, exposed to Assaults on all hands: And therefore it is very adviseable to get Children into this Armour as early as we can. Natural Temper, I confess, does here a great deal: But even where that is defective, and the Heart is in it self weak and timorous, it may, by a right Management, be brought to a better Resolution. What is to be done to prevent breaking Childrens Spirits by frightful Apprehensions instill'd into them when young, or bemoaning themselves under every little Suffering, I have already taken notice. How to harden their Tempers, and raise their Courage, if we find them too much subject to Fear, is farther to be consider'd.

"True Fortitude, I take to be the quiet Possession of a Man's self, and an undisturb'd doing his Duty, whatever Evil besets,

The above excerpts are from John Locke's "Some Thoughts Concerning Education" - 1690. Marginal notes are by Locke.

or Danger lies in his way. This there are so few Men attain to, that we are not to expect it from Children. But yet something may be done: And a wise Conduct by insensible Degrees, may carry them farther than one expects.

...."That which every Gentleman (that takes any Care of his Education) desires for his Son, besides the Estate he leaves him, is contain'd (I suppose) in these Four Things, Vertue, Wisdom, Breeding, and Learning. I will not trouble my self whether these Names do not some of them sometimes stand for the same thing, or really include one another. It serves my Turn here to follow the popular Use of these Words; which I presume, is clear enough to make me be understood, and I hope there will be no Difficulty to comprehend my Meaning.

"I place Vertue as the first and most necessary of those Endowments, that belong to a Man or a Gentleman; as absolutely requisite to make him valued and beloved by others, acceptable or tolerable to himself. Without that, I think, he will be happy neither in this, nor the other World.

God

"As the Foundation of this, there ought very early to be imprinted on his Mind a true Notion of God, as of the independent Supreme Being, Author and Maker of all Things, from whom we receive all our Good, who loves us, and gives us all Things. And consequent to this, instill into him a Love and Reverence of this Supreme Being. This is enough to begin with, without going to explain this matter any farther; for fear, I lest by talking too early to him of Spirits, and being unseasonably forward to make him understand the incomprehensible Nature of that Infinite Being, his Head be either filled with false, or perplexed with unintelligible Notions of him. Let him only be told upon occasion, that God made and governs all things, hears and sees every thing, and does all manner of Good to those that love and obey him. You will find that being told of such a God, other Thoughts will be apt to rise up fast enough in his Mind about him; which, as you observe them to have any Mistakes, you must set right....And I am apt to think, the keeping Children constantly Morning and Evening to Acts of Devotion to God, as to their Maker, Preserver and Benefactor, in some plain and short Form of Prayer, suitable to their Age and Capacity, will be of much more use to them in Religion, Knowledge and Vertue, than to distract their Thoughts with curious Enquiries into his inscrutable Essence and Being.

The above excerpts are from John Locke's "Some Thoughts Concerning Education" - 1690. Marginal notes are by Locke.

Reading

...."When by these gentle Ways he begins to be able to read, some easy pleasant Book suited to his Capacity, should be put into his Hands, wherein the Entertainment that he finds might draw him on, and reward his Pains in reading, and yet not such as should fill his Head with perfectly useless Trumpery, or lay the Principles of Vice and Folly. To this Purpose, I think, Aesop's Fables the best, which being Stories apt to delight and entertain a Child, may yet afford useful Reflections to a grown Man; and if his Memory retain them all his Life after, he will not repent to find them there, amongst his manly Thoughts and serious Business....

"The Lord's Prayer, the Creeds, and Ten Commandments 'tis necessary he should learn perfectly by heart; but, I think, not by reading them himself in his Primer, but by Some-body's repeating them to him, even before he can read. But learning by heart, and learning to read, should not, I think, be mixed, and so one made to clog the other. But his learning to read, should be made as little Trouble or Business to him as might be.

...."As for the Bible, which Children are usually employ'd in to exercise and improve their Talent in reading, I think, the promiscuous reading of it, though by Chapters as they lie in Order, is so far from being of any Advantage to Children, either for the perfecting their Reading, or principling their Religion, that perhaps a worse could not be found. For what Pleasure or Incouragement can it be to a Child to exercise himself in reading those Parts of a Book where he understands nothing? And how little are the Law of Moses, the Song of Solomon, the Prophecies in the Old, and the Epistles and Apocalypse in the New Testament, suited to a Child's Capacity? And though the History of the Evangelists, and the Acts, have something easier, yet, taken all together, it is very disproportional to the Understanding of Childhood. I grant, that the Principles of Religion are to be drawn from thence, and in the Words of the Scripture; yet none should be propos'd to a Child, but such as are suited to a Child's Capacity and Notions. But 'tis far from this to read through the whole Bible, and that for reading's sake. And what an odd jumble of Thoughts must a Child have in his Head, if he have any at all, such as he should have concerning Religion, who in his tender Age reads all the Parts of the Bible indifferently as the Word of God, without any Distinction. I am apt to think, that this, in some Men, has been the very Reason why they never had clear and distinct Thoughts of it all their Life Time.

"And now I am by chance fallen on this Subject, give me leave to say, that there are some Parts of the Scripture which may be

The above excerpts are from John Locke's "Some Thoughts Concerning Education" - 1690 - Marginal notes are by Locke.

proper to be put into the Hands of a Child to engage him to read; such as are the Story of Joseph and his Brethren, of David and Goliah, of David and Jonathan, &c. and others, that he should be made to read for his Instruction, as that, What you would have others do unto you, do you the same unto them; and such other easy and plain moral Rules, which being fitly chosen, might often be made use of, both for Reading and Instruction together; and so often read till they are throughly fixed in the Memory; and then afterwards, as he grows ripe for them, may in their Turns, on fit Occasions, be inculcated as the standing and sacred Rules of his Life and Actions....

Law

...."It would be strange to suppose an English Gentleman should be ignorant of the Law of his Country. This, whatever Station he is in, is so requisite, that from a Justice of the Peace, to a Minister of State, I know no Place he can well fill without it. I do not mean the Chicane or wrangling and captious part of the Law: a Gentleman, whose Business is to seek the true Measures of Right and Wrong, and not the Arts how to avoid doing the one, and secure himself in doing the other, ought to be as far from such a Study of the Law, as he is concerned diligently to apply himself to that wherein he may be serviceable to his Country. And to that purpose, I think the right way for a Gentleman to study Our Law, which he does not design for his Calling, is to take a View of our English Constitution and Government, in the ancient Books of the Common Law; and some more modern Writers, who out of them have given an account of this Government. And having got a true Idea of that, then to read our History, and with it joyn in every King's Reign the Laws then made. This will give an insight into the reason of our Statutes, and shew the true ground upon which they came to be made, and what Weight they ought to have.

Method

...."Order and Constancy are said to make the great difference between one Man and another: This I am sure, nothing so much clears a Learner's Way, helps him so much on in it, and makes him go so easy and so far in any Enquiry, as a good Method. His Governour should take pains to make him sensible of this, accustom him to Order, and teach him Method in all the Applications of his Thoughts; shew him wherein it lies, and the Advantages of it; acquaint him with the several sorts of it, either from General to Particulars, or from Particulars to what is more General; exercise him in both of them; and make him see, in what Cases each different Method is most proper, and to what Ends it best serves.

The above excerpts are from John Locke's "Some Thoughts Concerning Education" - 1690. Marginal notes are by Locke.

...."The Great Men among the Ancients, understood very well how to reconcile manual Labour with Affairs of State, and thought it no lessening to their Dignity, to make the one the Recreation to the other. That indeed which seems most generally to have imploy'd and diverted their spare Hours was Agriculture. Gideon amongst the Jews was taken from Thrashing, as well as Cincinnetus amongst the Romans from the Plough, to Command the Armies of their Countries against their Enemies; and 'tis plain their dexterous handling of the Flayl or the Plough, and being good Workmen with these Tools, did not hinder their Skill in Arms, nor make them less able in the Arts of War or Government. They were great Captains and Statesmen as well as Husbandmen. Cato major, who had with great Reputation born all the great Offices of the Commonwealth, has left us an Evidence under his own Hand, how much he was versed in Country Affairs; and as I remember, Cyrus thought Gardening so little beneath the Dignity and Grandeur of a Throne, that he shew'd Xenophon a large Field of Fruit-Trees all of his own Planting. The Records of Antiquity both amongst Jews and Gentiles, are full of Instances of this kind, if it were necessary to recommend useful Recreations by Examples.

Conclusion

...."Though I am now come to a Conclusion of what obvious Remarks have suggested to me concerning Education, I would not have it thought, that I look on it as a just Treatise on this Subject. There are a thousand other things that may need consideration; especially if one should take in the various Tempers, different Inclinations, and particular Defaults, that are to be found in Children; and prescribe proper Remedies. The variety is so great, that it would require a Volume; nor would that reach it. Each Man's Mind has some peculiarity, as well as his Face, that distinguishes him from all others; and there are possibly scarce two Children, who can be conducted by exactly the same Method...."

The above excerpts are from John Locke's "Some Thoughts Concerning Education" - 1690. Marginal notes are by Locke.

STUDY OF AMERICAN HISTORY

Fundamentals in Education

The Declaration of Independence, Washington's Farewell Address, and the Constitution of the United States, should be studied by the youth of our country, as their political scriptures....

"The course pointed out must, it is apparent, make the pupil understand the study; but this may be, and the labour of the teacher not yet accomplished. The pupil must also be made to remember.... When the course of events is studied, for the purpose of gaining general information, the natural order of the thoughts must be regarded, if we expect that memory will treasure up the objects of attention. Each individual is to himself the centre of his own world; and the more intimately he connects his knowledge with himself, the better will it be remembered, and the more effectually can it be rendered in after life subservient to his purposes....

"These are reasons why our youth should be directed first to the study of our own history, keeping in view its connexion with our geography; but there are other reasons, why the study of American history is better not only for our own students, but for those of other countries, than that of any other nation, with which we are acquainted. History, it is said, is the school of politics. It is not, however, the mere knowledge of events, in which the student sees little connexion, which lays a foundation for his political knowledge. It is only when he is led to perceive how one state of things, operating on human passions, leads to another, that he is prepared when he comes into life, to look over the whole moving scene of the world - predict the changes which are to succeed - and should his be the hand of power, to put it forth, to accelerate or stop the springs of change, as he finds their tendency to be good or evil. There is no species of events like those related of America for producing this effect; and the young politician of other countries might begin with this, as the most easily comprehensible subject in the whole field of history. Here effects may be traced to their causes....

"As it respects the most important advantage in the study of history, which is improvement in individual and national virtue, we come boldly forward to advocate a preference for the history of the American Republic. Here are no tales of hereditary power and splendour to inflame the imaginations of youth with desires for adventitious distinction. Here are no examples of profligate females, where the trappings of royalty or nobility give to vice an elegant costume;

The above excerpts are from Emma Willard's "History of the United States, or Republic of America" - 1845 or, as with the celebrated Scot, where beauty and misfortune make sin commiserated, till it is half loved. Here are no demoralizing examples of bold and criminal ambition, which has 'waded through blood to empire'. The only desire of greatness which our children can draw from the history of their ancestors, is to be greatly good.

"It is not in the formal lesson of virtue, that her principles are most deeply imbibed. It is in moments when her approach is not suspected, that she is fixing her healing empire in the heart of youth. When his indignation rises against the oppressor--when his heart glows with the admiration of suffering virtue--it is then that he resolves never to be an oppressor himself; and he half wishes to suffer, that he too may be virtuous. No country, ancient or modern, affords examples more fitted to raise these ennobling emotions than of America, at the period of her revolution.

"And may not these generous feelings of virtue arise, respecting nations as well as individuals; and may not the resolution which the youth makes, with regard to himself individually, be made with regard to his country, as far as his future influence may extend? Would the teacher excite these feelings in his pupil, let him put into his hands the history of the struggle of America for her independence. Though doubtless there existed great personal turpitude in individuals in America, and great personal virtue in those of England, yet, as nations, how great is the disparity in the characters exhibited. England, seeking to make her filial child her slave, refuses to listen to her duteous pleadings, and applies the scourge. She deigns not to give even the privileges of civilized warfare, but sends forth the brand which lights the midnight fire over the heads of the sleeping family, and the tomahawk which cleaves the head of the infant in the presence of the mother. England also descends to base arts. She bribes, she flatters, she sows dissensions, she purchases treason, and she counterfeits money.

"In the conduct of France, too, though gratitude rises in our hearts for her actual services, yet history compelled, though sometimes sorrowfully, to follow truth, must pronounce that in her conduct as a nation, there is nothing virtuous or generous. Unlike her La Fayette, it was in success, not in misfortune, that she declared for America; and if at length she combatted with her, it was not that she loved her, or honoured her cause; it was that she feared and hated her enemy. If America had not taken care of herself, bitter to her would have been the care which France would have taken of her. Her embrace of friendship would have been found the pressure of death. How interesting in her youthful simplicity, in her maiden purity, does America appear, contrasted with these old and wily

The above excerpts are from Emma Willard's "History of the United States, or Republic of America" - 1845

nations. Who shall say, in reading the history of these transactions, that there is no such thing as national vice, or natural virtue?

"Will not acquaintance then with this tale, warm the young heart of the future statesman of America, to the detestation of national as of individual wickedness: and to the love of national as of personal virtue? He will say with exultation, my country was the most virtuous among the nations; this is her pride--not the extent of her dominion, nor the wealth of her revenue; this is the source of that greatness which it becomes her sons to preserve! And he will then resolve, that when manhood shall have placed him among her guardians, he will watch the purity of her character with jealous tenderness and sooner part with existence than be made the instrument of her degradation!"

The above excerpts are from Emma Willard's "History of the United States" - 1845

TO YOUNG WOMEN

On Education

The mind of the present age, acting on the mind of the next,' is an object of concern to every being endowed with intellect, or interested, through love or hope, in the welfare of the human race. Our age fully admits this sentiment; and we see not only the theorist and the practical man, but the divine, the philosopher, and the poet, devising modes of nurture for the unfolding mind, and striving to make useful knowledge the guest of the common people.... Is it not important that the sex to whom Nature has entrusted the moulding of the whole mass of mind in its first formation should be acquainted with the structure and developments of mind? that they who are to nurture the future rulers of a prosperous people should be able to demonstrate, from the broad annal of history, the value of just laws and the duty of subordination? the blessings which they inherit, and the danger of their abuse? Is it not requisite that they, on whose bosom the infant heart must be cherished, should be vigilant to watch its earliest pulsations for good or evil? that they who are commissioned to light the lamp of the soul should know how to feed it with pure oil? that they in whose hand is the welfare of beings never to die, should be fitted to perform the work and earn the plaudit of heaven?

"The natural vocation of females is to teach. In seminaries, academies, and schools they possess peculiar facilities for coming in contact with the unfolding and unformed mind. It is true, that only

The above excerpts are from Lydia H. Sigourney's "Letters to Young Ladies" - 1852

a small proportion are engaged in the departments of public and systematic instruction. Yet the hearing of recitations, and the routine of scholastic discipline, are but parts of education. It is in the domestic sphere, in her own native province, that woman is inevitably a teacher. There she modifies by her example, her dependants, her companions, every dweller under her own roof. Is not the infant in its cradle her pupil? Does not her smile give the earliest lesson to its soul? Is not her prayer for the first messenger for it in the court of Heaven? Does she not enshrine her own image in the sanctuary of the young child's mind so firmly that no revulsion can displace, no idolatry supplant it? Does she not guide the daughter, until, placing her hand in that of her husband, she reaches that pedestal, from whence, in her turn, she imparts to others the stamp and colouring which she has herself received? Might she not, even upon her sons, engrave what they shall take unchanged, through all the temptations of time, to the bar of the last judgment? Does not the influence of woman rest upon every member of her household, like the dew upon the tender herb, or the sunbeam silently educating the young flower? or as the shower and the sleepless stream, cheer and invigorate the proudest tree of the forest?

"Admitting, then, that whether she wills it or not, whether she even knows it or not, she is still a teacher, and perceiving that the mind in its most plastic state is yielded to her tutelage, it becomes a most momentous inquiry what she shall be qualified to teach. Will he not of necessity impart what she most prizes and best understands? Has she not power to impress her own lineaments on the next generation? If wisdom and utility have been the objects of her choice, society will surely reap the benefit. If folly and self-indulgence are her prevailing characteristics, posterity are in danger of inheriting the likeness.

"This influence is most visible and operative in a republic. The intelligence and virtue of its every citizen have a heightened relative value. Its safety may be interwoven with the destiny of those whose birthplace is in obscurity. The springs of its vitality are liable to be touched, or the chords of its harmony to be troubled, by the rudest hands.

"Teachers under such a form of government should be held in the highest honour. They are the allies of legislators. They have agency in the prevention of crime. They aid in regulating the atmosphere, whose incessant action and pressure causes the life blood to circulate, and return pure and healthful to the heart of the nation.

The above excerpts are from Lydia H. Sigourney's "Letters to Young Ladies" - 1852

"Of what unspeakable importance, then, is her education, who gives lessons before any other instructer; who preoccupies the unwritten page of being; who produces impressions which only death can obliterate; and mingles with the cradle-dream what shall be read in eternity. Well may statesmen and philosophers debate how she may be best educated who is to educate all mankind.

"The ancient republics overlooked the value of that sex whose strength is in the heart. Greece, so susceptible to the principle of beauty, so skilled in wielding all the elements of grace, failed in appreciating their excellence, whom these had most exquisitely adorned. If, in the brief season of youthful charm, she was constrained to admire woman as the acanthus-leaf of her own Corinthian capital, she did not discover how, like that very column, she was capable of adding stability to the proud temple of freedom. She would not be convinced that so feeble a hand might have aided to consolidate the fabric which philosophy embellished, and luxury overthrew.

"Rome, notwithstanding her primeval rudeness, seems more correctly than polished Greece to have estimated the 'weaker vessel.' Here and there, upon the storm-driven billows of her history, some solitary form towers upward in majesty, and the mother of the Gracchi still stands forth in strong relief amid imagery over which time has no power. But still, wherever the brute force of the warrior is counted godlike, woman is appreciated only as she approximates to sterner natures: as in that mysterious image which troubled the sleep of Assyria's king - the foot of clay derived consistence from the iron which held it in combination.

"In our own republic, man, invested by his Maker with the right to reign, has conceded to her, who was for ages in vassalage, equality of intercourse, participation in knowledge, dominion over his dearest and fondest hopes. He is content to 'bear the burden and heat of the day,' that she may dwell in ease and affluence. Yet, from the very felicity of her lot, dangers are generated. She is tempted to be satisfied with superficial attainments, or to indulge in that indolence which corrodes intellect, and merges the high sense of responsibility in its alluring and fatal slumbers.

"These tendencies should be neutralized by a thorough and laborious education. Sloth and luxury must have no place in her vocabulary. Her youth should be surrounded by every motive to

The above excerpts are from Lydia H. Sigourney's "Letters to Young Ladies" - 1852

application, and her maturity dignified by the hallowed office of rearing the immortal mind. While her partner toils for his stormy portion of that power or glory from which it is her privilege to be sheltered, let her feel that in the recesses of domestick privacy she still renders a noble service to the government that protects her, by sowing seeds of purity and peace in the hearts of those who shall hereafter claim its honours or control its destinies.

"Her place is amid the quiet shades, to watch the little fountain ere it has breathed a murmur. But the fountain will break forth into a rill, and the swollen rivulet rush towards the sea; and who can be so well able to guide them in right channels as she who heard their first ripple, and saw them emerge like timid strangers from their source, and had kingly power over those infant-waters, in the name of Him who caused them to flow?

"And now, Guardians of Education, whether parents, preceptors, or legislators - you who have so generously lavished on woman the means of knowledge - complete your bounty by urging her to gather its treasures with a tireless hand. Demand of her as a debt the highest excellence which she is capable of attaining. Summon her to abandon selfish motives and inglorious ease. Incite her to those virtues which promote the permanence and health of nations. Make her accountable for the character of the next generation. Give her solemn charge in the presence of men and of angels. Gird her with the whole armour of education and piety, and see if she be not faithful to her children, to her country, and to her God."

"... For the strength of a nation, especially of a republican nation, is in the intelligent and well-ordered homes of the people. And in proportion as the discipline of families is relaxed, will the happy organization of communities be affected, and national character become vagrant, turbulent, or ripe for revolution."...

The above excerpts are from Lydia H. Sigourney's "Letters to Young Ladies" - 1851

ABIGAIL ADAMS
TO
MERCY WARREN

Braintree, November, 1775.

"I am curious to know how you spend your time. 'Tis very saucy to make this demand upon you, but I know it must be usefully imployd and I am fearful if I do not question you I shall loose some improvement which I might otherways make. ... A patriot without religion in my estimation is as great a paradox as an honest Man without the fear of God. Is it possible that he whom no moral obligations bind can have any real Good Will towards Man, can he be a patriot who by an openly vicious conduct is undermineing the very bonds of Society, corrupting the Morals of Youth and by his bad example injuring the very Country he professes to patronize more than he can possibly compensate by his intrepidity, Generosity and honour? The Scriptures tell us righteousness exalteth a Nation."

The above excerpt is from "Warren-Adams Letters", Vol. I, 1743-1777, Massachusetts Historical Society Collections - 72

While the great public questions which agitated the continent engaged the earnest attention of Washington, he was active in every sphere of social duty, in his neighborhood. He was a communicant of the church of England, and took a lively interest in the affairs of Truro parish, in which Mount Vernon was situated. From his earliest years, his conduct had been subservient to a strong religious sentiment; and all through life it formed the basis of his majestic moral qualities. 'Neither in the parade of military life, nor in the cares of civil administration; neither in a state of depression, nor amidst the intoxicating sweets of power and adulation, did he forget to pay homage to the MOST HIGH, who doeth according to his will in the army of Heaven, and among the inhabitants of earth.'

"Religion and morality are indispensible supports"

"In that broader view of the influence of religion, which comprehends the public good as well as individual well-being, he seems to have been always impressed and controlled by the sentiments such as he expressed in after-years, when he wrote: 'Of all the dispositions and habits which lead to political prosperity, religion and morality are indispensable supports. In vain would that man claim the tribute of patriotism, who should labor to subvert these great pillars of human happiness, these firmest props of the duties of men and citizens. The mere politician, equally with the pious man, ought to respect and cherish them. A volume could not trace all their connections with private and public felicity. Let it simply be asked, 'Where is the security for property, for reputation, for life, if the sense of religious obligation desert our oaths, which are the instruments of investigation in courts of justice?'....Whatever may be conceded to the influence of refined education on minds of peculiar structure, reason and experience both forbid us to expect that national morality can prevail, in exclusion of religious principle.'

"National Morality"

"'Above all,' said a contemporary, 'he was influenced by the more permanent and operative principle of religion; by a firm and active persuasion of an all-seeing, all-powerful Deity; by the high consciousness of future accountability, and the assured hope and prospect of immortality.'

"Influenced by these sentiments and convictions, we see Washington piously reading the impressive funeral service of the church of England, at the evening funeral of Braddock; and acknowledging in a letter to his brother, the care of the kind

The above excerpts are from Benson J. Lossing's "Washington and the American Republic", 1870

Providence of God in preserving him from death on the field of Monongahela. We see him earnestly endeavoring to have chaplains in his little army on the Virginia frontier, and in his orders, rebuking the profanity of his troops; and in after-years, when leading the armies of the Revolution, he was ever solicitous to have the soldiers subjected to religious influences as often as possible. 'The general requires and expects of all officers and soldiers, not engaged in actual duty,' he said, in one of his earliest orders at Cambridge, in 1775, 'a punctual attendance on divine service, to implore the blessings of Heaven upon the means used for our safety and defence.' And his diary, kept for many years with great particularity, shows that he rarely omitted attendance upon divine service on Sunday, though the church nearest to Mount Vernon was seven miles distant.

"A punctual attendance on divine service"

"In 1765, Washington was vestryman of both Truro and Fairfax parishes. The place of worship in the former was at Pohick, and of the latter at Alexandria. His influence in their affairs was controlling and salutary. The reverend Mr. Massey, who was rector of Pohick church for many years, relates some circumstances respecting the location of that edifice, which illustrates Washington's address and sagacity. In the year 1764, the old church building, which stood in another part of the parish, had fallen into decay, and it was resolved to erect a new one. Its location became a matter of considerable excitement in the parish, some contending for the site of the old edifice, and others for one nearer the centre of the parish and more conveniently situated. Among the latter was Washington. A meeting was finally held to settle the question. Washington's neighbor and friend, George Mason, who led the party favorable to the old site, made an eloquent harangue, conjuring the people not to desert the sacred spot, consecrated by the bones of their ancestors. It had a powerful effect, and it was thought there would not be a voice in opposition to it. Washington then arose, and drew from his pocket an accurate survey which he had made of the whole parish, in which was marked the site of the old church, and the proposed locality of the new one, together with the place of residence of each parishioner. He spread this map before the audience, briefly explained it, expressed the hope that they would not allow their judgments to be guided by their feelings, and sat down. The silent argument of the map prevailed, a large majority voted in favor of the new site, and in 1765, Pohick church was erected. That venerated edifice was yet standing, in 1857, though in a state of great dilapidation. It is about seven miles southwest of Mount Vernon, upon an elevation on the borders of a forest, and surrounded by ancient oaks, chestnuts, and pines."

The above excerpts are from Benson J. Lossing's "Washington and the American Republic", 1870

AMERICAN SYSTEM OF GOVERNMENT

Elements of the New Political Institution

The mighty pyramid itself, half buried in the sands of Africa, has nothing to bring down and report to us, but the power of kings and the servitude of the people. If it had any purpose beyond that of a mausoleum, such purpose has perished from history and from tradition. If asked for its moral object, its admonition, its sentiment, its instruction to mankind, or any high end in its erection, it is silent; silent as the millions which lie in the dust at its base, and in the catacombs which surround it. Without a just moral object, therefore, made known to man, though raised against the skies, it excites only conviction of power, mixed with strange wonder. But if the civilization of the present race of men, founded, as it is, in solid science, the true knowledge of nature, and vast discoveries in art, and which is elevated and purified by moral sentiment and by the truths of Christianity, be not destined to destruction before the final termination of human existence on earth, the object and purpose of this edifice will be known till that hour shall come. And even if civilization should be subverted, and the truths of the Christian religion obscured by a new deluge of barbarism, the memory of Bunker Hill and the American Revolution will still be elements and parts of the knowledge which shall be possessed by the last man to whom the light of civilization and Christianity shall be extended."...

"What, then, is the true and peculiar principle of the American Revolution, and of the systems of government which it has confirmed and established? The truth is, that the American Revolution was not caused by the instantaneous discovery of principles of government before unheard of, or the practical adoption of political ideas such as had never before entered into the minds of men. It was but the full development of principles of government, forms of society, and political sentiments, the origin of all which lay back two centuries in English and American history....

"The English colonists in America, generally speaking, were men who were seeking new homes in a new world. They brought with them their families and all that was most dear to them. This was especially the case with the colonists of Plymouth and Massachusetts. Many of them were educated men, and all possessed their full share, according to their social condition, of the knowledge and attainments of that age. The distinctive characteristic

The above excerpts are from Daniel Webster's Address on the completion of the Bunker Hill Monument - 1843

of their settlement is the introduction of the civilization of Europe into a wilderness, without bringing with it the political institutions of Europe. The arts, sciences, and literature of England came over with the settlers.

That great portion of the common law which regulates the social and personal relations and conduct of men, came also. The jury came; the habeas corpus came; the testamentary power came; and the law of inheritance and descent came also, except that part of it which recognizes the rights of primogeniture, which either did not come at all, or soon gave way to the rule of equal partition of estates among children. But the monarchy did not come, nor the aristocracy, nor the church, as an estate of the realm. Political institutions were to be framed anew, such as should be adapted to the state of things. But it could not be doubtful what should be the nature and character of these institutions. A general social equality prevailed among the settlers, and an equality of political rights seemed the natural, if not the necessary consequence....

"What France has reached only by the expenditure of so much blood and treasure, and the perpetration of so much crime, the English colonists obtained by simply changing their place, carrying with them the intellectual and moral culture of Europe, and the personal and social relations to which they were accustomed, but leaving behind their political institutions. It has been said with much vivacity, that the felicity of the American colonists consisted in their excape from the past. This is true so far as respects political establishments, but no further.

"They brought with them a full portion of all the riches of the past, in science, in art, in morals, religion, and literature. The Bible came with them. And it is not to be doubted, that to the free and universal reading of the Bible, in that age, men were much indebted for right views of civil liberty. The Bible is a book of faith, and a book of doctrine, and a book of morals, and a book of religion, of especial revelation from God; but it is also a book which teaches man his own individual responsibility, his own dignity, and his equality with his fellow-man.

"Bacon and Locke, and Shakespeare and Milton, also came with the colonists. It was the object of the first settlers to form new political systems, but all that belonged to cultivated man, to family, to neighborhood, to social relations, accompanied them. In the Doric phrase of one of our own historians, 'They came to settle on bare creation'; but their

The above excerpts are from Daniel Webster's Address on the Completion of the Bunker Hill Monument - 1843

settlement in the wilderness, nevertheless, was not a lodgement of nomadic tribes, a mere resting-place of roaming savages. It was the beginning of a permanent community, the fixed residence of cultivated men. Not only was English literature read, but English, good English, was spoken and written, before the axe had made way to let in the sun upon the habitations and fields of Plymouth and Massachusetts. And whatever may be said to the contrary, a correct use of the English language is, at this day, more general throughout the United States, than it is throughout England herself....

"The great elements, then, of the American system of government, originally introduced by the colonists, and which were early in operation, and ready to be developed, more and more, as the progress of events should justify or demand, were, -

"Escape from the existing political systems of Europe, including its religious hierarchies, but the continued possession and enjoyment of its science and arts, its literature, and its manners;

"Home government, or the power of making in the colony the municipal laws which were to govern it;

"Equality of rights;

"Representative assemblies, or forms of government founded on popular elections.

"Few topics are more inviting, or more fit for philosophical discussion, than the effect on the happiness of mankind of institutions founded upon these principles; or, in other words, the influence of the New World upon the Old.

"Her obligations to Europe for science and art, laws, literature, and manners, America acknowledged as she ought, with respect and gratitude. The people of the United States, descendants of the English stock, grateful for the treasures of knowledge derived from their English ancestors, admit also, with thanks and filial regard, that among those ancestors, under the culture of Hampden and Sydney and other assiduous friends, that seed of popular liberty first germinated, which on our soil has shot up to its full height, until its branches overshadow all the land.

The above excerpts are from Daniel Webster's Address on the Completion of the Bunker Hill Monument - 1843

"But America has not failed to make returns....

...."America exercises influences, or holds out examples, for the consideration of the Old World, of a much higher, because they are of a moral and political character.

"America has furnished to Europe proof of the fact, that popular institutions, founded on equality and the principle of representation, are capable of maintaining governments, able to secure the rights of person, property, and reputation.

"America has proved that it is practicable to elevate the mass of mankind, - that portion which in Europe is called the laboring, or lower class, - to raise them to self-respect, to make them competent to act a part in the great right and great duty of self-government; and she has proved that this may be done by education and the diffusion of knowledge. She holds out an example, a thousand times more encouraging than ever was presented before, to those nine-tenths of the human race who are born without hereditary fortune or hereditary rank.

"America has furnished to the world the character of Washington! And if our American institutions had done nothing else, that alone would have entitled them to the respect of mankind.

"Washington! 'First in war, first in peace, and first in the hearts of his countrymen!' Washington is all our own!

"Born upon our soil, of parents also born upon it; never for a moment having had sight of the Old World; instructed according to the modes of his time, only in the spare, plain but wholesome elementary knowledge which our institutions provide for the children of the people; growing up beneath and penetrated by the genuine influences of American society; living from infancy to manhood and age amidst our expanding, but not luxurious civilization; partaking in our great destiny of labor, our long contest with unreclaimed nature and uncivilized man, our agony of glory, the war of Independence, our great victory of peace, the formation of the Union, and the establishment of the Constitution; he is all, all our own! Washington is ours....

"I claim him for America.... To him who denies or doubts whether our fervid liberty can be combined with law, with order, with the security of property, with the pursuits and advancement of happiness; to him who denies that our forms of

The above excerpts are from Daniel Webster's Address on the Completion of Bunker Hill Monument - 1843

government are capable of producing exaltation of soul, and the passion of true glory; to him who denies that we have contributed anything to the stock of great lessons and great examples; - to all these I reply by pointing to Washington!...

"But let us remember that we have duties and obligations to perform, corresponding to the blessings which we enjoy. Let us remember the trust, the sacred trust, attaching to the rich inheritance which we have received from our fathers. Let us feel our personal responsibility, to the full extent of our power and influence, for the preservation of the principles of civil and religious liberty. And let us remember that it is only religion, and morals, and knowledge, that can make men respectable and happy, under any form of government. Let us hold fast the great truth, that communities are responsible, as well as individuals; that no government is respectable, which is not just; that without unspotted purity of public faith, without sacred public principle, fidelity, and honor, no mere forms of government, no machinery of laws, can give dignity to political society.

"It is with indescribable regret, that I have seen the youth of the United States migrating to foreign countries, in order to acquire the higher branches of erudition ... Although it would be injustice to many to pronounce the certainty of their imbibing maxims not congenial with republicanism, it must nevertheless be admitted, that a serious danger is encountered by sending abroad among other political systems those, who have not well learned the value of their own."

-George Washington

"In our day and generation let us seek to raise and improve the moral sentiment, so that we may look, not for a degraded, but for an elevated and improved future. And when both we and our children shall have been consigned to the house appointed for all living, may love of country and pride of country glow with equal fervor among those to whom our names and our blood shall have descended! And then, when honored and decrepit age shall lean against the base of this monument, and troops of ingenuous youth shall be gathered round it, and when the one shall speak to the other of its objects, the purposes of its construction, and the great and glorious events with which it is connected, there shall rise from every youthful breast the ejaculation, 'Thank God, I - I also - AM AN AMERICAN!"

The above excerpts are from Daniel Webster's Address on the Completion of Bunker Hill Monument - 1843

APPENDIX

CHRONOLOGICAL TABLE

First Epocha
1578

First patent granted by an English sovereign, to lands in the territory of the United States, given by Queen Elizabeth to Sir Humphrey Gilbert.

ELIZABETH

Ineffectual attempts to settle the country

Year	Event
1583	Sir H. Gilbert takes possession of Newfoundland
1584	Sir W. Raleigh obtains a patent, and sends two vessels to the American coast, which receives the name of Virginia
1585	Raleigh sends Sir Richard Grenville, who leaves a colony on the island of Roanoke
1586	They are carried to England
1587	Raleigh sends a colony under Captain White, which is not afterwards found
1589	Raleigh sells his patent to the London company
1602	Bartholomew Gosnold sails in a direct course for America, and discovers Cape Cod
1603	Henry IV of France grants Acadia to De Monts
1604	He visits the country, discovers and explores the Bay of Fundy, and commences a settlement at Port Royal

JAMES I

Grants, settlements, governments organized, etc.

Year	Event
1606	King James divides Virginia between the London and Plymouth companies
1607	The Plymouth company makes an ineffectual attempt to plant a colony at the Kennebec The London company send a colony, who discover Chesapeake Bay, and establish THE FIRST EFFECTUAL SETTLEMENT AT JAMESTOWN Captain John Smith relieves the distress of the colony. He is taken prisoner by the Indians, but his life is saved by Pocahontas
1608	Quebec is founded by Champlain
1609	Hudson River and Lake Champlain are discovered A new charter is granted to the London company which effects a change in the government of Virginia. Lord De la War is appointed governor for life and the colony prospers
1611	George Percy and Sir Thomas Dale are governors of Virginia
1613	Pocahontas marries an Englishman, which leads to an alliance with the natives Private property in land established in Virginia The Dutch commence settlements on Hudson river The Virginians dispossess the French of their possession in Acadia The English take possession of Manhattan
1614	The navigation of the Hudson river granted to the Dutch West India company. The settlers at Manhattan resume their allegiance to Holland Capt. Smith explores the coast from Penobscot to Cape Cod, which is named New England
1619	The first general assembly is called in Virginia
1620	Young women sent to Virginia as wives for the planters and sold for tobacco; convicts are sent to the colony; negroes introduced, and slavery commenced.

The above excerpt is from Emma Willard's "History of the United States, or Republic of America" - 1835

CHRONOLOGICAL TABLE

Second Epocha
1620

Landing of the Pilgrims at Plymouth, after having framed on board the May Flower the first written political compact of America.

Grants, Settlements, Governments organized, etc.

JAMES I

1620	James I grants a charter to the grand council of Plymouth, for governing New England
1621	The colonists at New Plymouth, purchase of the grand council of Plymouth, a right to the soil James I grants Nova Scotia to William Alexander A district called mariana granted to John Mason Holland grants New Netherlands to the Dutch West India company Government of Virginia established
1622	The council of Plymouth grant to Gorges and Mason, a district called Laconia Indian conspiracy, which nearly proves fatal to the colony of Virginia
1623	Gorges and Mason send a colony to the river Piscataqua The Dutch erect fort Nassau on the Delaware
1624	London company dissolved and its rights return to the crown. A royal government established in Virginia
1627	Swedes and Fins settle on the Delaware
1628	Patent of MASSACHUSETTS obtained, and the first permanent settlement of that colony commenced at Salem
1629	The Massachusetts company receive a royal charter; its powers of government are transferred to New England NEW HAMPSHIRE granted to John Mason The Dutch purchase lands near Cape Henlopen
1630	Emigrants arrive in Massachusetts who settle at Boston and its vicinity CAROLINA granted to Sir Robert Heath First permanent settlement in MAINE

CHARLES II

1631	First general court held in Massachusetts Clayborne plants a colony in the Chesapeake Patent of CONNECTICUT granted to Lord Say and Seal, Lord Brook, and others
1632	MARYLAND granted to Lord Baltimore
1633	First house erected in Connecticut
1634	Settlement of Maryland commenced Government of Massachusetts changed from a simple to a representative democracy Commissioners appointed in England for governing the colonies
1635	Great accessions made to the New England colonies by emigrants from England Grand Council of Plymouth surrender their charter to the crown Fort Saybrook erected Windsor and Wethersfield settled
1636	Hartford settled Roger Williams commences the settlement of the state of RHODE ISLAND

The above excerpt is from Emma Willard's "History of the United States, or Republic of America" - 1835

APPENDIX

CHRONOLOGICAL TABLE

1637	Harvard College established at Cambridge Theological disturbances excited by Ann Hutchinson War with the Pequods
1638	New Haven settled by Eaton, Davenport, and others Mr. Coddington commences the settlement of the island of Rhode Island Exeter in New Hampshire founded
1639	The Virginians are again allowed to call a house of representatives Sir Ferdinando Gorges obtains a royal charter of the province of Maine Hartford, Windsor, and Wethersfield, form a constitution for the colony of Connecticut First house of representatives in the Plymouth colony called House of assembly established in Maryland First printing office in America established at Cambridge
1641	New Hampshire unites with Massachusetts
1642	Clayborne occasions an Indian war in Maryland

CHARLES I

Third Epocha
1643

Commencement of the confederacy, in the union of Massachusetts and Plymouth, with New Haven and Connecticut

1644	Roger Williams obtains a charter for the Rhode Island and Providence plantations Connecticut purchases the patent of the Plymouth company
1645	Clayborne again makes disturbances in Maryland
1646	Battle between the Dutch and Indians at Horseneck
1649	A part of Virginia is granted to Lord Culpepper and others
1650	First settlement in Carolina made around Albemarle Sound Dutch relinquish their claims to jurisdiction in Connecticut
1651	Swedish governor takes the Dutch fort on the Delaware Navigation act passed by the house of commons Civil War in Maryland, which ends in the submission of the proprietary government to parliament Virginia submits to parliament. New England is favoured by parliament
1653	Dispute between the United Colonies and the Dutch at New-York
1655	Dutch conquer the Swedes on the Delaware
1656	Fendal's insurrection in Maryland Quakers persecuted in Massachusetts
1660	Charles II restored to the throne of England Whalley and Goffe arrive at Boston
1661	Second settlement made in Carolina on Cape Fear river
1662	Maryland restored to its proprietor Charles II grants a charter to Connecticut, which includes New Haven Mint established at Boston

CHARLES I

GOVERNMENT UNDER CROMWELL

CHARLES II

Grants, Settlements, Governments organized, etc.

The above excerpt is from Emma Willard's "History of the United States, or Republic of America" - 1835

CHRONOLOGICAL TABLE

Grants, Settlements, Governments organized, etc.

CHARLES II

Year	Event
1663	Charles II grants a charter to Rhode Island Carolina granted to Lord Clarendon
1664	Patent granted to the Duke of York. New Netherlands submits to his authority Duke of York grants New Jersey to Berkley and Carteret Commissioners appointed to regulate the New England colonies
1669	Third settlement made in Carolina
1671	Charleston is founded; unites with the colony around Cape Fear. Carolina is called North and South Carolina. An attempt is made to introduce Locke's constitution
1672	Disputes between the settlers and proprietors of New Jersey
1673	WAR BETWEEN ENGLAND AND HOLLAND. The Dutch take New-York
1674	Peace is concluded, and New-York restored to the English. Andross appointed governor by the Duke of York
1675	Andross attempts to extend his jurisdiction over Connecticut
1675) 1676)	KING PHILIP'S WAR
1676	New Jersey divided into East and West Jersey Rebellion in Virginia excited by Nathaniel Bacon
1677	Virginia obtains a charter Massachusetts purchases Maine
1678	Andross usurps the government of the Jerseys
1679	New Hampshire becomes a separate royal government Randolph sent as inspector of customs in New-England
1680	New Jersey restored to its proprietors New Charleston founded. War with the Westoes
1681	First general assembly in New Jersey PENN RECEIVES FROM CHARLES II A GRANT OF PENNSYLVANIA
1682	Penn receives from the Duke of York a grant of the present state of Delaware East Jersey is transferred to Penn Penn, with 100 settlers, arrives in America, and founds Philadelphia
1683	Governor Dongan calls the first general assembly in New-York
1678- 1684	LaSalle, under the patronage of the king of France, discovers the country along the mississippi and the lakes, which is called Louisiana
1684	A treaty of peace is concluded with the Five Nations Unsuccessful expedition of the governor of Canada against the Five Nations Massachusetts is deprived of her charter

JAMES II

Year	Event
1686	James II appoints Sir Edmund Andross governor general of New England
1687	Andross attempts to take the charter of Connecticut; the government is surrendered to him
1688	New-York and New Jersey submit to his jurisdiction. General suppression of charter governments

The above excerpt is from Emma Willard's "History of the United States, or Republic of America" - 1835

APPENDIX

CHRONOLOGICAL TABLE

Grants, Settlements, Governments organized, etc. | King William's War

WILLIAM AND MARY

1689	Andross is imprisoned, and the government of Massachusetts in the hands of a committee of safety The government of New-York seized by Jacob Leisler Connecticut and Rhode Island resume their charters Montreal destroyed by the Five Nations
1689	Dover (N.H.) surprised by the Indians WAR BETWEEN ENGLAND AND FRANCE
1690	Governor of Canada sends three parties against the English settlements, which destroy Schenectady, (N.Y.) Casco, (Maine) and Salmon Falls (N.H.) Sir Wm. Phipps captures Port Royal, (Nova Scotia) and takes possession of the coast from thence to the New England settlements. Unsuccessful expedition against Canada French Protestants settle in Carolina and Virginia Sothel usurps the government of South Carolina
1691	French defeated at LaPrairie by Gen. Schuyler Samuel Allen purchases Mason's title to New Hampshire Stoughter governor of New-York. Leisler is condemned and executed

Fourth Epocha
1692

Massachusetts obtains a new charter, with extended territories but restricted privileges

King William's War

1692	Superstition respecting witchcraft prevails William Penn for two years deprived of the government of Pennsylvania
1693	Gov. Fletcher introduces Episcopacy into New-York Locke's constitution abrogated in Carolina
1694	Settlements on Oyster river destroyed
1695	Rice introduced into Carolina from Africa
1696	The French recover Port Royal and Pemaquid, and at length the whole of Acadia Gov. Archdale restores order in Carolina
1697	Unsuccessful attempt of the French to destroy the northern colonies Peace of Ryswic terminates King William's war
1698	Piracies of Capt. Kid
1699	Penn grants a third charter to Pennsylvania
1701	Unsuccessful attempt made in England to unite the charter governments to the crown

ANNE

1702	Government of West Jersey surrendered to the crown, and united with East Jersey Commencement of dispute in Massachusetts between the governors and the assembly GREAT BRITAIN AT WAR WITH FRANCE AND SPAIN Unsuccessful expedition from South Carolina against St. Augustine
1703	Appalachian Indians are subdued The territories separate from Pennsylvania The French and Indians devastate the country from Casco to Wells

The above excerpt is from Emma Willard's "History of the United States, or Republic of America" - 1835

CHRONOLOGICAL TABLE

Queen Anne's War

ANNE

1704 Deerfield destroyed
Church's expedition into the eastern part of New England

1706 Episcopacy introduced into Connecticut
French and Spaniards invade Carolina

1707 Unsuccessful expedition from New England against Port Royal

1708 Haverhill plundered and burned
Ecclesiastical constitution formed at Saybrook, called the Saybrook Platform

1709 Plan formed for the reduction of the French power in America

1710 Palatines settle in New-York, Pennsylvania, Virginia and Carolina
Col. Nicholson captures Port Royal

1711 Unfortunate expedition for the conquest of Canada

1712 Indian war in North Carolinañ the Tuscaroras are defeated, and unite with the Iroquois
South Carolina establishes a bank

1713 Treaty of Utrecht, which closes Queen Anne's war

GEORGE I

1715 Indian war in South Carolina. The Yamassees are expelled from the province, and settle in Florida

1716 The government of Maryland is restored to Lord Baltimore

1717 New Orleans is founded by the French

1719 Irish emigrants settle Londonderry, N.H.
Carolinians revolt against the proprietary government

1720 Royal government established in Carolina

1723 First settlement made in Vermont

1724 Indians instigated to hostilities by Father Ralle

1726 Two additional clauses, regulating the power of the governor, are annexed to the charter of Massachusetts

GEORGE II

1727 A fort is erected at Oswego, N.Y.

1729 North and South Carolina purchased by the crown, and erected into separate governments

1731 Crown Point built by the French

1732 Company formed in England for the settlement of Georgia

Fifth Epocha
1733

First settlement of Georgia made at Savannah, by Oglethorpe, and others

1736 Unsuccessful expedition of the French against the Chickasaws

1738 Insurrection of the blacks in Carolina
A College, (Nassau Hall(founded at Princeton, New Jersey, obtains a new charter

The above excerpt is from Emma Willard's "History of the United States, or Republic of America" - 1835

APPENDIX

CHRONOLOGICAL TABLE

	Year	Events	
	1739	WAR BETWEEN ENGLAND AND SPAIN	
	1740	Oglethorpe invades Florida, and makes an unsuccessful attempt on St. Augustine The French conclude a peace with the Chickasaws	
	1742	A Spanish fleet invades Georgia, but retires with loss	
Old French War	1744	War proclaimed between ENGLAND and FRANCE	
	1745	The colonists, under Col. Pepperell, take louisburg and Cape Breton from the French	
	1746	The French send a fleet to destroy the colonies	
	1748	Peace restored by the treaty of Aix la Chapelle	
	1750	The French make encroachments. A large tract of land, about Ohio river, is granted to the Ohio company, who erect trading houses, but are considered by the French as invading their territories	
	1752	Georgia becomes a royal province	
	1753	Washington sent from Virginia with a letter requiring the French to quit the English territories	
	1754	The French erect fort Du Quesne. Washington is sent to maintain the rights of the English; he is attacked at fort Necessity by a French force, and capitulates A CONGRESS OF DELEGATES, FROM SEVEN PROVINCES MEETS AT ALBANY. They propose a plan for the union of the colonies, which is rejected.	GEORGE II
French War	1755	June. Nova Scotia taken from the French July. Braddock leads an expedition against fort DuQuesne; falls into an ambuscade, and is totally defeated _____ Treaty with the Cherokees Sept. 8. The French are repulsed at lake George	
	1756	Formal declaration of war between England and France Aug. 14. Oswego surrendered to the French Fort Granby taken by the French and Indians	
	1757	An expedition is undertaken against Louisbourg, but abandoned Aug. 8. The French, under Montcalm, capture fort William Henry Dispute in Pennsylvania, between the proprietary governor and the people	
	1758	July 6. Louisbourg taken by the English, under Major-General Amherst July 8 Abercrombie repulsed at Ticonderoga Aug. 27. Fort Frontenac taken by Col. Bradstreet Nov. 25. The English take possession of fort Du Quesne Treaty with the Indians, between the Appalachian mountains and the lakes	
	1759	July 27. Gen. Amherst takes Ticonderoga Aug. 4. Crown Point surrenders to the English _____ Fort Niagara surrenders to the English Sept. 13. Battle on the heights of Abraham, in which the French are defeated, and General Wolfe killed Sept. 18. Quebec is surrendered to the English	
	1760	April 28. Battle near Quebec Sept. 8. Canada surrendered to Great Britain Massachusetts opposes the issuing of writs of assistance	

The above excerpt is from Emma Willard's "History of the United States, or Republic of America" - 1835

1761	Cherokees are subdued
1762	England at war with Spain Plans for changing the government of the colonies

Sixth Epocha
1763

Close of the French War, by the treaty of Paris

Causes of the Revolution, and Preparatory measures

1763	Detroit sustains a distressing siege from the Indians commanded by Pontiac
1764	Great Britain determines to tax the colonies, and accordingly lays additional duties on sugar, molasses, and other articles
1765	An act passed by the British parliament imposing stamp duties in America. Great opposition made to the stamp act in Virginia, Massachusetts, and the other colonies Oct. Congress meets at New-York
1766	Stamp act repealed; at the same time parliament declares her right to bind the colonies
1767	Parliament imposes new taxes
1768	Massachusetts requests the co-operation of the other colonies in resisting oppression, in consequence of which her assembly is dissolved Sept. 22. A convention is held at Boston Sept. 28. Troops are stationed at Boston
1769	Non-importation agreements, before partially entered into, are, in consequence of the oppressive measures of parliament, adopted by all the colonies
1770	March 5. Affray with the British troops at Boston Parliament removes the duties which had been imposed in the colonies, except those on tea
1772	Town meetings are held in Massachusetts
1773	A correspondence is established between the colonies Attempts made to import tea into the colonies; the cargoes of three ships are thrown overboard at Boston
1774	Parliament shuts the port of Boston, and otherwise invades the rights of the colonies Sept. 3. A continental congress assembles at Philadelphia; they declare their rights; adopt measures to procure a redress of grievances; petition the king; address the people of England, and prepare a memorial to their constituents Whigs and tories become the distinguishing names of the royalists and provincials The assembly of Massachusetts resolve themselves into a provincial congress, and prepare for defence
1775	Conciliatory measures are proposed by parliament, but rejected by the colonists Feb. 26. Attempt of the British to take field pieces at Salem April 19. WAR COMMENCES; the battle of Lexington May 10. Ticonderoga and Crown Point are taken by the Americans May 10. Congress again assembles at Philadelphia

GEORGE III

The above excerpt is from Emma Willard's "History of the United States, or Republic of America" - 1835

APPENDIX

CHRONOLOGICAL TABLE

1775 Royal governments laid aside in the southern colonies
May. British troops arrive at Boston
June 17. Battle of Bunker's Hill
June 15. GEORGE WASHINGTON elected commander-in-chief of the American forces
Georgia joins the confederacy

1775 The first of post-offices is established
Nov. 2. St. John's surrenders to the Americans
___ 12. Montreal is taken by the Americans
___ 13. Arnold appears before Quebec, but is compelled to retire
Dec. 7. Action between the royalists and provincials near Norfolk, Va.
____ Parliament refuses to hear the petition of the colonies; prohibits all trade and intercourse with them, and hires foreign mercenaries to send against them
Dec. 21. Americans are defeated at Quebec, and Montgomery killed
The British burn Bristol and Falmouth

1776 Jan. 1. Norfolk, Va. burned by the royalists
March 17. British evacuate Boston
April. Washington fixes his head quarters at New-York
June 15. Americans evacuate Canada
___ 28. British are defeated on Sullivan's island
Fruitless attempts at pacification

Seventh Epocha

1776

1776 July 4. THE DECLARATION OF AMERICAN INDEPENDENCE

Aug. 27. Battle on Long Island, in which the Americans are defeated
Sept. 15. The British enter New-York
Oct. 11. Americans defeated on Lake Champlain
___ 28. Battle of White Plains
Nov. 16. Fort Washington taken by the British
___ 18. Fort Lee evacuated by the Americans
____ Washington retreats across New Jersey
Dec. 26. Battle of Trenton

1777 Jan. 2. Battle of Princeton
March 23. British take the stores at Cortlandt Manor
April. Predatory excursion of the British to Danbury, Conn.
May 23. Exploit of Col. Meigs at Sag Harbour
May. LaFayette espouses the cause of American liberty
June 26. Cornwallis attempts to bring Washington to an engagement; defeats a party of Americans
July 5. Americans evacuate Ticonderoga
___ 7. Action at Hubbardton
Aug. 3. St. Leger invests fort Stanwix. -- 6. Gen. Herkimer is defeated
Aug. 16. Battle of Bennington
Sept. 11. Battle of Brandywine
___ 19. Battle of Stillwater
___ 20. Gen. Wayne surprised and defeated by the British
___ 26. British take possession of Philadelphia
Oct. 4. Battle of Germantown
___ 6. Forts Clinton and Montgomery taken by the British
Oct. 7. Battle near Saratoga
___ 15. Kingston, N.Y. burned
___ 17. Burgoyne surrenders his army to the Americans
___ 22. The British are repulsed at Red Bank

Nov. 15. Articles of confederation adopted by congress
___ 16. Americans abandon Mud island, and on the 18th, fort Mercer, on Red Bank
___ 11. Washington retires to winter quarters at Valley Forge
Intrigues against Washington

The above excerpt is from Emma Willard's "History of the United States, or Republic of America" - 1835

1778 Feb. 6 FRANCE CONCLUDES A TREATY OF ALLIANCE WITH AMERICA
England sends three commissioners to America who attempt to gain over the principal citizens by bribery
May. La Fayette defeats a detachment from the British army
June 18. The British evacuate Philadelphia
___ 28. Battle of Monmouth
A French fleet under D'Estaing arrives to aid America
July. The settlement of Wyoming destroyed by a band of tories and savages
Aug. Expedition against Rhode Island. __ 15. Sullivan besieges Newport.
__28. Raises the siege. __ 29. He defeats the British at Quaker Hill
Sept. 4. Gen. Gray's excursion to Buzzard's Bay
Dec. 29. Savannah taken by the British

1779 ____ Sunbury taken by the British, which completes the subjugation of Georgia
An unsuccessful attempt made by the British upon Port Royal
March 3. Gen. Prevost surprises the Americans at Briar Creek
May 12. Prevost attempts to take Charleston
May. The British make a descent upon Virginia, burn Norfolk and other towns
June 1. Clinton takes Stoney and Verplank's Points
___ 20. Indecisive engagement between the armies of Lincoln and Prevost at Stono ferry
July. The British make a descent upon Connecticut
___ 16. The Americans take Stoney Point
___ 19. The British, at Powles Hook, surprised by Major Lee
_____ Unsuccessful expedition against the British at Penobscot
Aug. 29. Sullivan defeats the Indians, and desolates their country
Sept. 23. Paul Jones' naval battle
Oct. 9. The French and Americans are repulsed from Savannah
Oct. 25. The British withdraw from Rhode Island
_____ Congress is beset by the intrigues of France and Spain
Armed neutrality

1780 May 12. Charleston is surrendered to the British
______ Clinton proceeds to establish royal government in South Carolina
June 23. Skirmish at Springfield, N. J.
______ Congress sanctions the depreciation of paper currency
July 10. A French squadron arrives at Rhode Island, with troops under Count de Rochambeau
Aug. 6. The British are defeated at Hanging Rock
Aug. 16. Battle near Camden, S. C.
Aug. 18. Tarleton surprises and defeats Sumpter
Sept. Arnold's treason at West Point discovered
Oct. 2. Major Andre executed as a spy
Oct. 7. Battle of King's Mountain

1781 Jan. 1. Revolt of the Pennsylvania troops
____ Arnold makes a descent upon Virginia, and ravages the country
Jan. 2. Great exertions made by the American government to raise money
Jan. 17. Battle of Cowpens, S.C.
____ Cornwallis pursues the Americans
March 15. Battle of Guilford, C. H.
March 16. Battle between the English and French fleets, off Cape Henry
April 25. Americans surprised and defeated at Hobkirk's Hill
April and May. Several British posts in S.C. taken by the Americans
June 5. Augusta capitulates to the Americans
June 18. Greene makes an unsuccessful attack upon Ninety-Six
Aug. 4. Execution of Col. Hayne
_____ La Fayette opposes the British in Virginia
Aug. 23. Cornwallis enters Yorktown
Sept. 5. Partial action between the English and French fleets, off the capes of the Chesapeake
Sept. 6. Forts Trumbull and Griswold taken by the British, and New London burned
Sept. 8. Battle of Eutaw Springs, S. C.
Sept. 29. Yorktown is invested by the American and French troops
Oct. 19. CORNWALLIS SURRENDERS TO THE ALLIES

The above excerpt is from Emma Willard's "History of the United States, or Republic of America" - 1835

APPENDIX

CHRONOLOGICAL TABLE

War of the Revolution

CONTINENTAL CONGRESS UNDER THE ARTICLES OF CONFEDERATION

1782	Oct. 8. Treaty with the states of Holland
1783	Feb. 20. Preliminary articles of peace signed at Versailles Sweden, Denmark, Spain, and Russia acknowledge the independence of the United States Sept. 3. DEFINITIVE TREATY OF PEACE SIGNED AT PARIS Nov. 3. American army disbanded Nov. 25. British evacuate New-York Dec. 23. Washington resigns his commission and retires to Mount Vernon
1784	The United States are encumbered with a heavy debt, which occasions great distress throughout the country
1785	Treaty concluded with Prussia
1786	Insurrection in Massachusetts and New Hampshire Delegates from five of the middle states meet at Annapolis, to concert measures for amending the government
1787	A general convention meets at Philadelphia, in which the constitution of the United States is framed
1788	Eleven states adopt the Federal Constitution

The above excerpt is fromEmma Willard's "History of the United States, or Republic of America" - 1835

LIST OF ILLUSTRATIONS

BIBLIOGRAPHY

BIOGRAPHIES OF HISTORIANS

BIBLIOGRAPHY

Adams, George Burton & H. M. Stephens: SELECT DOCUMENTS OF ENGLISH CONSTITUTIONAL HISTORY, Mac Millan Co., 1904.

Bacon, Leonard: THE GENESIS OF NEW ENGLAND CHURCHES, Harper & Brothers, 1874.

Bancroft, Charles: FOOTPRINTS OF TIME, R. T. Root Publishing Co., 1879.

Bancroft, George: HISTORY OF THE UNITED STATES, 10 vols., Little, Brown & Co., 1866.

Blackstone, Sir William: COMMENTARIES ON THE LAWS OF ENGLAND, Edited by William Carey Jones, Bancroft-Whitney, 1915.

Bradford, William: OF PLIMOTH PLANTATION, From the original manuscript, Wright & Potter Printing Co., Boston, 1901.

Burke, Edmund: WORKS, Little, Brown & Co., 1904.

Eggleston, Edward: THE BEGINNERS OF A NATION, D. Appleton and Co., 1896.

Fiske, John: AMERICAN REVOLUTION, 1896; THE BEGINNINGS OF NEW ENGLAND, 1898; CIVIL GOVERNMENT IN THE UNITED STATES, 1890; OLD VIRGINIA AND HER NEIGHBORS, 1897, Houghton, Mifflin and Co.

Frothingham, Richard: THE RISE OF THE REPUBLIC OF THE UNITED STATES, Little, Brown & Co., 1890.

Goodwin, John A.: THE PILGRIM REPUBLIC, Ticknor and Co., 1888.

Graham, James: THE HISTORY OF THE UNITED STATES OF NORTH AMERICA, Lee & Blanchard, 1846.

Green, John Richard: HISTORY OF THE ENGLISH PEOPLE, Harper & Bros., 1886.

Guyot, Arnold: PHYSICAL GEOGRAPHY, Ivison, Blakeman & Co., 1885.

Hall, Edwin: THE PURITANS AND THEIR PRINCIPLES, Baker & Scribner, 1846.

Hoare, W. H. : THE EVOLUTION OF THE ENGLISH BIBLE, J. Murray, 1901.

Johnson, Edward: WONDER-WORKING PROVIDENCE 1628 - 1651, Edited by J. Franklin Jameson, Barnes & Noble, 1952.

Locke, John: THE WORKS OF JOHN LOCKE ESQ., John Churchill, 3 vols., London, 1714.

AN ESSAY CONCERNING HUMAN UNDERSTANDING, 3 vols., Printed by William Fessenden, Brattleboro, Vt., 1806, Second American Ed.

Lodge, Henry Cabot: A SHORT HISTORY OF THE ENGLISH COLONIES IN AMERICA, Harper & Bros., 1881.

THE WORKS OF ALEXANDER HAMILTON, Edited by Henry Cabot Lodge, 12 vols., G. P. Putnam's Sons, New York & London, 1903.

BIBLIOGRAPHY

Lossing, Benson J. : WASHINGTON AND THE AMERICAN REPUBLIC, Virtue & Yorston, 1870.

Mackintosh, Sir James: MISCELLANEOUS WORKS, London, 1851, Longman, Brown, Green & Longmans.

Madison, James: THE PAPERS OF JAMES MADISON, 3 vols., Henry D. Gilpin, 1841.

LETTERS & OTHER WRITINGS OF JAMES MADISON, 4 vols., J. B. Lippincott and Co., 1865.

Merriam, C. Edward: A HISTORY OF AMERICAN POLITICAL THEORIES, Mac Millan Co., 1903.

Montesquieu (Charles de Secondat): THE SPIRIT OF LAWS, The Colonial Press, 1900.

Mosheim, Johann: ECCLESIASTICAL HISTORY, 2 vols., London, 1838 tr. by A. MacLaine, Tegg & Son.

Neal, Daniel: THE HISTORY OF THE PURITANS, 2 vols., Harper Bros., 1844.

Niles, Hezekiah: PRINCIPLES & ACTS OF THE AMERICAN REVOLUTION, A. S. Barnes & Co., 1876.

Palfrey, John Gorham: HISTORY OF NEW ENGLAND, Little, Brown & Co., 1859.

Robertson, William: THE HISTORY OF THE DISCOVERY AND THE SETTLEMENT OF AMERICA, 3 vols., Harper Bros., 1835.

Robinson, John: WORKS, Compiled by Robert Ashton, John Snow, London, 1851.

Sidney, Algernon: DISCOURSES ON GOVERNMENT, 3 vols., New York, 1805, Deare & Andrews.

Sigourney, Lydia H. : LETTERS TO YOUNG LADIES, Harper & Bros., 1852.

Sparks, Jared: THE WRITINGS OF GEORGE WASHINGTON, 12 vols., 1834-37, Boston, Hilliard, Gray & Co.

Thornton, John Wingate: THE PULPIT OF THE AMERICAN REVOLUTION, Gould & Lincoln, 1860.

Tocqueville, Alexis de: DEMOCRACY IN AMERICA, Scatcherd & Adams, New York, 1838.

Walker, George Leon: HISTORY OF THE CHURCH IN HARTFORD, Brown & Gross, 1884.

Webster, Daniel: THE WORKS OF DANIEL WEBSTER, Little, Brown & Co., 1851.

Wells, William V. : THE LIFE AND PUBLIC SERVICES OF SAMUEL ADAMS, 3 vols., Little, Brown & Co., 1865.

BIBLIOGRAPHY

Welsby, W. N. : LIVES OF EMINENT ENGLISH JUDGES, T. & J. W. Johnson, 1846.

Wilson, James: THE WORKS OF JAMES WILSON, Edited by J. De Witt Andrews, 2 vols., Chicago, 1896, Callaghan & Co.

Willard, Emma: HISTORY OF THE UNITED STATES, A. S. Barnes & Co., 1835.

Winsor, Justin: THE MEMORIAL HISTORY OF BOSTON 1630 - 1880, James R. Osgood & Co., 1881.

NARRATIVE AND CRITICAL HISTORY OF AMERICA, Houghton, Mifflin and Co., 1884.

Wellman, J. W. : THE CHURCH POLITY OF THE PILGRIMS, Congregational Board of Publication, Boston, 1857.

Wilberforce, Samuel: A HISTORY OF THE PROTESTANT EPISCOPAL CHURCH IN AMERICA, Rivingstons, London, 1856.

HISTORIC GALLERY AND BIOGRAPHICAL REVIEW, London, 1819, Vernor, Hood, and Sharpe.

LIBRARY OF AMERICAN LITERATURE, 11 vols., Edited by Stedman and Hutchinson, New York, 1889, Charles Webster and Co.

OLD SOUTH LEAFLETS, The Old South Association, Boston, Massachusetts.

BIOGRAPHIES OF THE HISTORIANS

by Mary Elaine Adams

BACON, Leonard
1802 - 1880

A Congregational clergyman and author, he was born in Detroit, Michigan. As a clergyman, he was known as a peacemaker, his wise counsels serving to resolve several bitter schisms within the Congregational Church. At the remarkably young age of twenty-three he was installed as pastor of First Church, New Haven, Connecticut. Bacon's most important literary work is "Genesis of the New England Churches" - 1874.

BANCROFT, George
1800 - 1891

Born at Worcester, Massachusetts, his father was a Uniterian clergyman, whose "Life of Washington" was highly praised. Bancroft entered Harvard College at the age of thirteen, and later pursued studies in Germany, taking a Doctor of Philosophy degree in 1820 at Gotingen. Originally, he intended to become a minister. But instead, he took up teaching and taught at Harvard College. He also was one of the founders of a school at Northampton. Soon he gave up teaching to devote himself to writing and to politics. He ran for Governor of Massachusetts, but though receiving a large vote, was not elected. During President Polk's administration, he was Secretary of the Navy. During his tenure of office, Bancroft founded the Naval School at Annapolis. It was also owing to his orders to the American Commander in the Pacific that California became a part of the United States. In 1846 Bancroft was appointed Minister to England. His talents as a diplomat were so marked that this appointment led to the post of Minister to Germany in 1867. President Grant re-confirmed Bancroft in this appointment until 1874. Despite his intense interest in writing a comprehensive history of the United States, his literary activities were amazingly versatile. He wrote on literature, politics, and current events. The efforts Bancroft put into his "History of the United States" were prodigious. His researches were indefatigable; he obtained pertinent documents or exact copies from public and private libraries in England, Spain, France, Germany, and Holland. He kept elaborate cross-reference notebooks and acquired a vast personal library to draw upon. In these volumes he also wrote cross-references on the fly-leaves so as to easily find any material he might need for his history. His early drafts of a work were spontaneous, enthusiastic - and extremely detailed. From these, he laboriously re-wrote and condensed, over and over. One volume was in its early draft some eight times longer than the final work. Bancroft's approach to the writing of history may be summed up best in his own words: "Each page of history may begin and end with Great is God and marvellous are his doings among the children of men; and I defy a man to penetrate the secrets and laws of events without something of faith. He may look on and see as it were the twinkling of stars and planets and measure their distance and motions; but the life of history will escape from him. He may pile a heap of stones, he will not get at the soul."

EGGLESTON, Edward
1837 - 1902

Born in 1837 at Vevay, Indiana, he was a Methodist preacher as well as an historian. It was after his retirement from the pastorate of the Church of the Christian Endeavor in Brooklyn, N. Y., in 1879, that he devoted himself entirely to writing. Among his works are: "A Household History of the United States" - 1888, and a "History of the United States"- 1888. He also wrote a "First Book of American History".

FISKE, John
1842 - 1901

"If the day should ever arrive (which God forbid) when the people of the different parts of our country shall allow their local affairs to be administered by prefects sent from Washington, and when the self-government of the states shall have been so far lost as that of the departments of France, or even so far as that of the counties of England, - on that day the progressive political career of the American people will have come to an end, and the hopes that have been built upon it for the future happiness and prosperity of mankind will be wrecked forever". So wrote John Fiske in 1888 in "The Critical Period of American History, 1783 - 1789". This eminent American historian was born in Hartford, Connecticut. From early boyhood he showed signs of exceptional talents. By the age of four he had taught himself to read haltingly. By the time he was six, he was able to read proficiently enough to dip into all the books in the family library, just "to see what they were like". At six he also began the study of Latin, followed later by French, Italian, German, Hebrew, and Sanscrit. He was graduated from Harvard in 1863 and from Harvard Law School in 1865. Although young Fiske was an outstanding student, he was severly criticized for his espousal of Herbert Spencer's doctrine of evolution. A sincere, though unorthodox Christian, Fiske was deeply shocked to learn that many people at Harvard considered him an atheist. Although he graduated from law school, Fiske never practiced law. His talents as a writer developed so rapidly that he was early able to support his wife and family by his pen alone. In spite of his controversial status, he lectured on philosophy at Harvard from 1869 to 1871. His best-known work during these early years as a writer was not in the historical field, but was on the philosophy of Spencer: "Outlines of Cosmic Philosophy". In the fundamental conclusions of both Christianity and cosmic philosophy, Fiske felt there was much in common and he closes this volume with the observation: "That harmony which we hope eventually to see established between our knowledge and our aspirations, is not to be realized by the timidity which shrinks from logically following out either of two apparently conflicting lines of thought - as in the question of matter and spirit - but by the fearlessness which pushes each to its inevitable conclusion. Only when this is recognized will the long and mistaken warfare between Science and Religion be exchanged for an intelligent and enduring alliance...".

Fiske was convinced that Christianity was the highest religious wisdom which the world had ever known and he felt that the doctrine of evolution would not only confirm the profound teachings of the Master, but would enlarge man's concepts of the nature of Christianity.

After the publication of Cosmic Philosophy, Fiske turned almost completely to writing and lecturing on American history. This came about unexpectedly, through an effort on the part of public-spirited citizens in Boston to save the Old South Meeting House. By 1879 people were at last beginning to realize that America's historic landmarks should not be torn down. To aid in the plan to save the Old South, Fiske was asked to give a series of lectures there on American political ideas. Through this series and others that followed throughout the country, Fiske became so popular as a lecturer on American history that he turned to the writing of full-scale histories - some of which had their beginnings in these lectures. Fiske's historical works were highly praised by the most influential periodicals of the day, by leading literary critics, fellow historians and by a large and enthusiastic reading public. Fiske's approach to history was, naturally, an evolutionary one in which he saw the emerging of America and its political principles as forming a vital link in the chain of history. The American concept of government he viewed as the most advanced in the world and as unique in nature, writing in "The Critical Period" of "the noble conception of two kinds of government operating at one and the same time upon the same individuals, harmonious with each other, but each supreme in its own sphere. Such is the fundamental conception of our partly federal, partly national, government...It was a political conception of a higher order than had ever before been entertained..."

FROTHINGHAM, Richard
1812 - 1880

Born in Charlestown, Massachusetts, he was a descendant of William Frothingham, who came from Yorkshire, England, with Winthrop's fleet. Not only an historian, he was also extremely active in Massachusetts politics for many years. He was a member of the State Legislature in 1839, 1840, 1842, 1849 and 1850. Well-known as a political writer, he ultimately became one of the proprietors of the Boston Post, where he was managing editor from 1852 to 1865. Frothingham was a prominent lay member of the Universalist Church. "The Rise of the Republic" - 1871, is regarded as his most important work, but he is also well known for other books dealing with various aspects of Massachusetts history.

GREEN, John Richard
1837 - 1883

This noted English historian was born at Oxford, England. He was an honor student at Oxford University. However, at one time his family was asked to withdraw him because of his independent views on monarchical rights as expressed in a paper on Charles I. By the time he returned to Oxford with a scholarship to Jesus College, he had developed a decided interest in history - the history of peoples and nations, rather than monarchs and states merely. With few friends and little encouragement, he set out on his own independent path of research and historical writing. He early learned "the intimate part religion plays in a nation's history, and how closely it joins itself to a people's life." In 1860 he left Oxford to become a curate in a poor East London parish. While he continued to write history, he was devoted to his duties as a minister and for some three years he spent nearly the whole of his income to help the poor and needy in his district. He supported himself by writing in the evenings for such magazines as Saturday Review. Becoming ill, he was told by his doctors that he had only six months to live. It was at this time that he began the work which was to earn him fame, "A Short History of the English People." Five years later he finished his book. It was welcomed by the public and by scholars and its sale soon reached 150,000. His other works published, include his more detailed "History of The English People" (1877-80) and his "Making of England" (1882), leaving his "Conquest of England" to be edited by his wife after his death in 1883.

GUYOT, Arnold
1807 - 1884

A well-known geographer and scientist, he was born near Neuchatel, Switzerland. He first planned to become a minister of the Gospel, but at last his increasing interest in the natural sciences resulted in his abandoning the idea of the ministry. His writings were devoted to glaciology, geography, and orography. Deeply religious, he wrote in 1884 a book entitled "Creation or the Biblical Cosmogony in the Light of Modern Science", in which he endeavored to reconcile science with the Bibical account of the Creation. He emigrated to America in 1848. From 1855 he was professor of geography and geology at Princeton. He published a series of school geographies called "Earth and Man" in 1849.

LODGE, Henry Cabot
1850 - 1924

Statesman and historian, he was born in Boston, Massachusetts, and was educated at Harvard University where he lectured on American history between 1876 and 1879. He was admitted to the bar in 1876 and subsequently served two terms in the Massachusetts legislature. He then became a Massachusetts representative in Congress in 1886. He wrote in the fields of economics, finance, and history, and was editor of the distinguished "North American Review" from 1873 to 1876. He is known particularly for his "Life and Letters of George Cabot"; "Short History of the English Colonies"; a life of "Hamilton"; "Webster"; "George Washington"; and "Studies in History."

MACKINTOSH, Sir James
1765 - 1832

This Scottish philosopher and historian was also active in affairs of government, becoming a member of Parliament in 1813. He was admitted to the bar at Lincoln's Inn in 1795. He held the chair of professor of law at Haileybury from 1818 to 1824. He is well known for his "Life of Sir Thomas More", "A Discourse on the Law of Nature and Nations", "On the Philosophical Genius of Lord Bacon and Mr. Locke", "Dissertation on the Progress of Ethical Philosophy, chiefly during the Seventeenth and Eighteenth Centuries" and "Review of Madame de Stael's 'De l'Allemagne'".

MOSHEIM, Johann Lorenz von
1694 - 1755

A distinguished German theologian and ecclesiastical historian. Edward Gibbon in his "History of the Decline and Fall of the Roman Empire", says of him, "In the history of the Christian hierarchy, I have, for the most part, followed the learned and candid Mosheim." He is best known for his "Institutes of Ecclesiastical History," published in 1726 and "De rebus Christianorum ante Constantinum commentarri" of 1753.

NEAL, Daniel
1678 - 1743

This historian who is best known for his history of non-conformity early showed his views by declining a scholarship to St. John's College, Oxford, in order to pursue his education in a seminary maintained by Protestant Dissenters. Later he studied for two years in Holland at Utrecht and Leyden. Returning to England in 1703, he became assistant pastor to a congregation of the Independents in London. He was appointed their pastor in 1706 and there he continued for thirty-six years. Although giving much time to the preparation of his sermons he also delved deeply into the study of history for which he had a natural bent. His first book was titled "The History of New-England: being an impartial account of the civil and ecclesiastical affairs of the country, with a new accurate map thereof: to which is added an appendix, containing their present charter, ecclesiastical discipline, and their municipal laws," which appeared in 1720. His greatest work "The History of the Puritans" appeared in 1732 with consecutive volumes appearing in 1733, 1736 and 1738. The final volume brought the history up to the Act of Toleration of 1689. Neal was an ardent advocate of religious liberty. "The Bible alone was his standard for religious truth, and he was willing and desirous that all others should be at perfect liberty to take and follow it as their own rule."

PALFREY, John Gorham
1796 - 1881

This American historian and theological writer was born at Boston. He was a Unitarian minister, and later a professor at Harvard. From 1847 to 1849 he was a member of Congress from Massachusetts and was an anti-slavery leader. His best known work is "A History of New England"(1858-64).

ROBERTSON, William
1721 - 1793

Scottish historian and clergyman, he was born in Borthwick, Mid Lothian, where his father, Rev. William Robertson, was the parish minister. In 1733, he entered the University of Edinburgh. After completing his education at the age of 20, the presbytery of Dalkeith gave him a licence to preach. Though very active in local and national church affairs, he somehow found time to write. For a time he contributed articles to literary reviews. His first work "The History of Scotland" was an instantaneous success. Fourteen editions were published in his lifetime. He was afterwards the author of other histories, including "The Age of Charles V" and "The History of the Discovery and Settlement of America". This latter work was not completed owing to the outbreak of the American Revolution. But in its incomplete form it was much admired by such fellow historians as Gibbon and Macauley, and the statesman, Burke.

WILLARD, Emma
1787 - 1870

"A nation cannot exist without religion. France tried that and failed. We were born a Protestant Christian nation, and, as such, baptized in blood. Our position ought to be considered as defined as that." So wrote Emma Willard, American pioneer in women's education. Born and brought up on a farm in Berlin, Connecticut, she opened her first school for girls in Middlebury, Vermont, in 1814. It was a genuine seat of learning, unlike the other young ladies' boarding schools of the period, which taught only such subjects as music, dancing, needlework, and deportment. From the field of women's education, she also branched out into general education, working with Henry Barnard in 1840 on the improvement of the common schools of Connecticut. Her histories, which came of her need for better textbooks, were highly praised by prominent men of the time, such as Daniel Webster and General Lafayette. New York became Emma Willard's permanent home where she spent most of her adult life. For in 1819 she moved her seminary to Waterford, N. Y., and later to Troy. It was New York's Governor De Witt Clinton who, greatly interested in her educational ideas for women, suggested the move. In 1821, after presenting her "Plan for Improving Female Education" to the Governor and the New York Legislature, the Legislature passed a measure granting a Charter to Waterford Academy for Young Ladies, which is believed to be the first such legislative decision giving recognition to women's rights to higher education. Mrs. Willard had many reasons for desiring improved education for women. As a deeply patriotic American, convinced of the superiority of the American Republic and its principles, as exemplifying the highest governmental concept the world had ever known, she believed that the preservation of the Republic depended on its women. For it was women who set the standards of a society, she felt, and would, therefore, save this Republic from the fate of previous republics. Right education would protect the country from debilitating forces, from softening up into love of luxury - followed by folly and vice. Women, with strengthened characters and trained intellects, would certainly raise up finer sons and hence better citizens of the Republic. "As an essential part of the body politic," she wrote, "women's corruption or improvement must affect the whole." Most important of all, Emma Willard discerned that Christian principles formed the foundation of all true education. "Moral improvement is the true end of the intellectual", she said, and when instructing young teachers, she admonished them to "bring God into all subjects", that their pupils might begin to see His wonderful government of the universe in all its aspects. By the time Emma Willard wrote "The Republic of America" in 1828, she was already well-known for her "Plan for Improving Female Education", for numerous poems, and for her book "Ancient Geography".

Because she felt that the Constitution of the United States, The Declaration of Independence, and Washington's Farewell Address were the "political Scriptures" of American youth which should be studied thoroughly, they were reprinted in full in the appendix of her history. In 1837, Emma Willard wrote her "Universal History", her motive being to show "the virtues which exalt nations and the vices which destroy them." Universal history she felt was an important subject to Americans, since the world was turning more and more to America for a solution to the problems of finding and founding sound and just governments. Whether or not a people could really be self-governing was the question Europeans were asking and they looked to America for the answer.

In this work Emma Willard asks: "Shall monarchy in its palaces and aristocracy in its lordly halls, then exult, as it is told that America is passing through anarchy to despotism - while mankind at large mourn, and reproach us that we have sealed their doom as well as our own, and that of posterity? Or shall we continue to be that people which of all others heretofore, or now existing, possess the most equitable government... ?"

WINSOR, Justin
1831 - 1897

A learned and distinguished American historian and librarian. He held the position of librarian of Harvard University and from 1868 to 1877 was superintendent to the Public Library of Boston. Among his numerous works are "Reader's Hand-Book of the American Revolution" (1880), "Bibliography of Orininal Quartos and Folios of Shakspere" (1880). He edited an 8 volume "Narrative and Critical History of America" (1884-89) and "Memorial History of Boston" (1880-82)

BIOGRAPHICAL SOURCE MATERIAL

Bacon, Leonard: "National Cyclopaedia of American Biography", 1901; "Century Dictionary and Cyclopedia", 1889.

Bancroft, George: "Library of the World's Best Literature", 1896; "Life and Letters of George Bancroft", 1908.

Eggleston, Edward: "Century Dictionary and Cyclopedia", 1889.

Fiske, John: "Werner's Library of the World's Best Literature", 1896; "John Fiske - Life and Letters", J. S. Clark, 1917.

Frothingham, Richard: "National Cyclopaedia of American Biography", 1901.

Green, John Richard: "Short History of The English People", 1898 edition by Alice S. Green; "Student's Cyclopaedia", 1899.

Guyot, Arnold: "National Cyclopaedia of American Biography", 1901; "Century Dictionary and Cyclopedia", 1889.

Lodge, Henry Cabot: "A Library of American Literature", Stedman and Hutchinson, 1889.

Mackintosh, Sir James: "Century Dictionary and Cyclopedia", 1889; "Miscellaneous Works of Sir J. Mackintosh", 1851.

Mosheim, Johann Lorenz von: "Century Dictionary and Cyclopedia", 1889; "History of the Decline and Fall of the Roman Empire", Edward Gibbon, 1906 Edition.

Neal, Daniel: "Memoir of the Life of Mr. Daniel Neal, A. M.", by Dr. Jennings and Nathaniel Neal Esq., 1743.

Palfrey, John Gorham: "Century Dictionary and Cyclopedia", 1889.

Robertson, William: Robertson's "History of America", 1835 edition.

Willard, Emma: "Emma Willard", Alma Lutz, 1929.

Winsor, Justin: "The Century Dictionary and Cyclopedia", 1889.

ILLUSTRATIONS

Page	Illustrations

INDICES

The short index, "Of Civil-Government" and the index to the marginal notes were prepared by William M. Hosmer and James B. Rose.

GENERAL INDEX

A SHORT INDEX TO JOHN LOCKE'S SECOND TREATISE "OF CIVIL-GOVERNMENT"

INDEX TO THE MARGINAL NOTES

Index to the Marginal Notes

Index to the Marginal Notes

Index to the Marginal Notes

Index to the Marginal Notes

Index to the Marginal Notes

Index to the Marginal Notes

Index to the Marginal Notes

Index to the Marginal Notes

Index to the Marginal Notes

Sermon, May 31, 1638, Text, 250
Settlement, Jamestown, 156
Weston's, again in want, 212
Settlers retaliate, 165
unruly, without good government, 211

Index to the Marginal Notes

Index to the Marginal Notes

Index to the Marginal Notes